THE DREAM OF THE
GREAT AMERICAN NOVEL

THE DREAM
OF THE
GREAT AMERICAN NOVEL

LAWRENCE BUELL

THE BELKNAP PRESS OF
HARVARD UNIVERSITY PRESS

Cambridge, Massachusetts
London, England
2014

Page 539 constitutes an extension of the copyright page.

Library of Congress Cataloging-in-Publication Data

Buell, Lawrence.
The dream of the great American novel / Lawrence Buell.
pages   cm
Includes bibliographical references and index.
ISBN 978-0-674-05115-7 (alk. paper)
1. American fiction—19th century—History and criticism.
2. American fiction—20th century—History and criticism.
3. National characteristics, American, in literature.
4. Literature and society—United States—History—19th century.
5. Literature and society—United States—History—20th century.
6. United States—In literature.   I. Title.
PS377.B84   2014
813.009—dc23   2013032745

*To my students at Harvard University and Oberlin College,
from whom I've learned at least as much as I've taught*

Contents

Abbreviations

AA   William Faulkner, *Absalom, Absalom! The Corrected Text.* New York: Vintage, 1990.

AAM   Saul Bellow, *The Adventures of Augie March.* New York: Viking, 1960.

AP   Philip Roth, *American Pastoral.* New York: Vintage, 1997.

AT   Theodore Dreiser, *An American Tragedy.* Ed. Thomas P. Riggio. New York: Library of America, 2003.

B   Toni Morrison, *Beloved: A Novel.* New York: New American Library, 1988.

CC   Edith Wharton, *The Custom of the Country.* In *Edith Wharton: Novels.* Ed. R. W. B. Lewis. New York: Library of America, 1985, pp. 621–1014.

CE   Ralph Ellison, *The Collected Essays of Ralph Ellison.* Ed. John F. Callahan. New York: Modern Library, 1995.

GG   F. Scott Fitzgerald, *The Great Gatsby.* Ed. Matthew J. Bruccoli. New York: Scribner, 1995.

GOW   John Steinbeck, *The Grapes of Wrath.* Ed. Robert DeMott. New York: Penguin, 2006.

GR   Thomas Pynchon, *Gravity's Rainbow.* New York: Viking, 1973.

GW   Margaret Mitchell, *Gone with the Wind.* New York: Warner, 1993.

HF   Mark Twain, *The Adventures of Huckleberry Finn*. Ed. Victor
        Fischer and Lin Salamo. Berkeley: University of California
        Press, 2003.

IM   Ralph Ellison, *Invisible Man: The Commemorative Edition*. New
        York: Modern Library, 1994.

MD   Herman Melville, *Moby-Dick*. 2nd ed. Ed. Hershel Parker and
        Harrison Hayford. New York: Norton, 2002.

SL   Nathaniel Hawthorne, *The Scarlet Letter*. In *"The Scarlet Letter"
        and Other Writings*. Ed. Leland S. Person. New York: Norton,
        2005, pp. 3–166.

USA   John Dos Passos, *U.S.A.: The 42nd Parallel, 1919, The Big Money*.
        Ed. Daniel Aaron and Townsend Ludington. New York:
        Library of America, 1996.

UTC   Harriet Beecher Stowe, *Uncle Tom's Cabin*. Ed. Elizabeth
        Ammons. New York: Norton, 2010.

THE DREAM OF THE
GREAT AMERICAN NOVEL

Introduction

> There is a moment in the life of concepts when they lose their
> immediate intelligibility and can then, like all empty terms, be
> overburdened with contradictory meanings.
>
> —GEORGIO AGAMBEN, *Homo Sacer* (1998)

> The novel has always been bound up with the idea of
> nationhood.
>
> —RALPH ELLISON, "The Novel as a Function of
> American Democracy" (1967)

> A true man will think rather, all literature is yet to be written.
>
> —RALPH WALDO EMERSON, "Literary Ethics" (1838)

THE DREAM of the Great American Novel (GAN) was born a century
and a half ago, in the wake of the Civil War. Although it soon degen-
erated into a media cliché that self-respecting literary critics at least pretended not to take seriously, it refused to die. Indeed, the "G. A. N."—as
Henry James of all people was the first to nickname it—still thrives.[1] The
contributors' columns of late Victorian magazines are echoed by turn-of-
the-twenty-first-century blogs and Internet message boards offering "top
ten" lists and forums for debating whether the GAN does or might exist,
which books come closest to the mark, and why. When I googled "Great
American Novel" while drafting this introduction, I came up with more
than seventy million hits, many redundant of course. This book tells the
story of that surprisingly resilient fascination, then uses it in Parts II–V as
a platform for exploring specific pathways that have helped certain novels
come to the fore as reference points for imagining U.S. national identity.*

---

* To avoid awkwardness I often resort below to the old-fashioned practice of using "U.S."
and "American" synonymously, notwithstanding that "America" often bears a very
different meaning outside the United States, for Latin Americans especially. I try to
make my intent clear enough to minimize unintended ambiguity.

This is a far more ambitious agenda than I originally intended. When I started planning this book some years ago, I had in mind a brisk, short narrative of the rise and fall of an amusing example of a national brag now long since obsolete and never amounting to much more than a parlor game. I was pretty much on the same mental wavelength as a cyber-manifesto a few years back that leads off with the rhetorical question, "Aside from pissing off the literati, does the Great American Novel, a monumentally nineteenth century concept, serve any higher purpose?"[2] For me too, the answer at first seemed: not much.

Indeed, we do well to approach the dream of the GAN warily. It is the brainchild of a bygone era, of anxious collective hand-wringing throughout the nineteenth century and beyond about what seemed to be the maddeningly slow emergence of a robust national literary voice—an anxiety that now seems all the more overblown for underestimating what had already been accomplished, such as Thoreau's *Walden*, Melville's *Moby-Dick*, and Whitman's *Leaves of Grass*, works now considered classic that didn't begin to get their just due until well into the twentieth century. By 1950, with growing confidence that U.S. literature no longer had anything to apologize for, insistence on the GAN as a priority for national arts and letters had subsided to a murmur. The rise of American literature studies as an academic specialization during the second quarter of the century codified and reinforced that confidence in U.S. fiction's cumulative accomplishment, as did increasing international recognition of the United States as a literary as well as techno-economic and military power. A string of critics from the 1930s through the 1960s dismissed the GAN as an anachronistic pipe dream, "faded into the limbo of lost literary causes."[3]

Within little more than a decade of its first launch in the late 1860s, in fact, we find the dream of the GAN getting bundled, as one observer dryly put it, into the same category as such "other great American things [as] the great American sewing-machine, the great American public school, [and] the great American sleeping-car."[4] The twentieth-century dismissal was not so much a new development as an intensification. Scrolling more slowly through the decades, we find an inverse, bad-tempered equivalent of the "escalator-effect" that Raymond Williams saw in the history of pastoral nostalgia—each generation fancying that the one before lived a life closer to nature.[5] The history of critical chatter about the Great American Novel often feels by contrast like a history of repeated disenchantment, each generation seeing the last as more gullible than itself.

Yet critical pissiness suggests the persistence of some sort of hydrant. "Simply because we no longer use the phrase, we should not assume that the notion itself no longer engages us," cautioned one critic during the 1960s, at one point when it looked as if the chimera had been killed off for good. Neither critical skepticism nor authorial diffidence ever kept scores of U.S. novelists from attempting big national fictions, then or now. Every American writer, Maxine Hong Kingston declared in the 1980s, "wants to write the Great American Novel."[6] Although Kingston's own thinking later shifted to the idea of "the global novel" instead, reflecting a broader seismic shift in turn-of-the-twenty-first-century thinking to which later chapters return, that didn't mean the permanent end of the GAN dream, but rather a more expansive sense of what it might be. Consider the spate of doorstop books of the late 1990s that tried to sum up the century, or at least the half-century, like David Foster Wallace's *Infinite Jest* (1996), John Updike's *The Beauty of the Lilies* (1997), Philip Roth's "American Trilogy" (*American Pastoral, I Married a Communist,* and *The Human Stain,* 1997–2000), Don DeLillo's *Underworld* (1999), and Neal Stephenson's *Cryptonomicon* (1999). In the last two especially, national history is made inseparable from world history.* September 11, 2001, triggered another round of novelistic inquests that is still playing itself out. Jonathan Franzen's *Freedom* (2010), for

---

* Compare Kingston's 2008 revision of her earlier statement: "If you [are] going to write a great American novel, then it is also the global novel" (Shirley Geok-Lin Lim, "Reading Back, Looking Forward: A Retrospective Interview with Maxine Hong Kingston," *MELUS: The Multi-Ethnic Literatures of the United States* 33 [Spring 2008]: 166). Kingston's *Tripmaster Monkey* (1989) seems to have been a personal turning point, as Kingston signaled in an essay of the same year that enlists *Tripmaster*'s multinational eclecticism to support the claim that "the global novel" that is to supersede "the dream of the great American novel" will be set "in the United States, destination of journeys from everywhere" (Kingston, "The Novel's Next Step," *Mother Jones* 14 [December 1989]: 39). Kingston's first two books (*Woman Warrior* and *China Men*) were already transnational in tracking diasporic memory among Chinese immigrant families; but *Tripmaster*'s Chinese American protagonist Wittman Ah-sing is cast as a more eclectic global hybrid: part post-Beat hippie, part Afro-badman, part Euro-decadent *poet maudit*, part Chinatown theater impresario, part the monkey trickster of the classic Chinese novel *Journey to the West* and multiple Afro-Asian folk sources, part Whitmanian bard, but also carrying the baggage of the first famous Anglo-American Chinaman stereotype, Ah Sin, from late nineteenth-century California writer Bret Harte's "The Heathen Chinee." The sum-of-the-parts instability of this compulsively performative figure is a bemused take on the slipperiness of "global identity" as a workable script, for both persons and novels.

example, so far the most widely acclaimed GAN contender among the growing number of post-9/11 fictions, imagines a middle America buffeted by crises both political and environmental of international scope that strain personal, family, and civic ties to the breaking point.

The persistent desire in the face of all skepticism and mockery for defining fictionalizations of national life implies a durable quasi-understanding among authors, publishing industry, and readers at large as to the legitimacy of reading "the national" through *N* number of putative touchstone narratives. This winking alliance gets reinforced whenever some random journalist compares Lyndon Johnson or George W. Bush to Captain Ahab stalking the whale—or when the political operative who used to be called "Bush's brain," Karl Rove, summed up his sense of being hounded by Democratic lawmakers: "I'm Moby Dick and they're after me."[7] Even the disaffected anti-GAN manifesto quoted a moment ago gets sucked into this vortex by going on to specify nine so-called parameters for GAN aspirants "that should go without saying," the last of which, incidentally, is that "it has to reference *Moby-Dick* as the Great American Novel."

Such sound bites suggest why GAN talk should neither be overweighted nor dismissed. Yes, a good deal of it must be taken with a grain of salt. A standing joke in the household of a former student of mine, as her novelist father later confirmed, was his standard exit from the dinner table: "Got to head back upstairs and write the great American novel." In this book, I've tried not to lose sight of his awareness that the GAN idea is absurdly oxymoronic if taken too solemnly, as meaning the one single once-and-for-all supernovel that even most of those attracted to the idea recognize will never be written. Nobody really wants that anyhow. What would writers do for an encore? Yet Thoreau's quip about "economy" holds also for Great American Novelism: it "admits of being treated with levity, but it cannot so be disposed of."[8] Something serious is also going on here. As a distinguished reviewer once remarked to me, although no serious critic today would claim this or that new book to be the Great American Novel, it's hard to think of a major American novelist who hasn't given it a shot.

Indeed it was an aspiring novelist who first put the mantra in circulation (see Chapter 1), and novelists have been crucial to keeping the idea alive. Upton Sinclair consciously set out to write the Great American Novel, hoping that *The Jungle* (1906) would be another *Uncle Tom's*

Cabin—which had been the first novel so acclaimed. Sinclair Lewis, later the first U.S. Nobel laureate in literature, told his publisher that he wanted *Babbitt* (1924) "to be the G.A.N. in so far as it crystallizes and makes real the Average Capable American." Edith Wharton called *The Custom of the Country* (1913) "my great American novel"; and though that may have been in jest, she went on to write a manifesto on the subject and lodge a claim for another novel with a like-spirited heroine by a younger contemporary.[9] In the mid-1990s the *New Yorker* ran an essay by British novelist-critic Martin Amis lauding Saul Bellow's *The Adventures of Augie March* (1953) as the GAN, in which he is not alone. In 2007, obituaries for Norman Mailer remembered him as the novelist who vainly pursued the dream of "the big one." The aging Mailer himself wistfully looked back upon John Dos Passos's *U.S.A.* trilogy (1929–1938) as the rightful GAN, if there was one.[10]

What do such claims really mean? When somebody insists that this or that novel is "the" or "a" GAN, what's being claimed other than that it's a book this one person really, really liked that supposedly contains some revelation about American life? It's easy to jump to the conclusion that the GAN has become one of those "empty terms" of the kind philosopher Georgio Agamben chastises, "overburdened with contradictory meanings," if it ever had substance to start with.[11] At first sight, GAN talk seems a mishmash of exclamations and pronouncements, with a few descriptive brushstrokes here and there. A certain ineffability seems as inherent to this dream as it is to the idea of the holy. Key to the *illusio,* as sociologist Pierre Bourdieu calls it, is "the informed player's investment in the game" arising from an attunement to the "artistic field" that in turn "reproduces endlessly the interest in the game and the belief in the value of its stakes."[12] For GAN talk has always been a markedly visionary affair—a straining to imagine a something as yet unrealized, a faith statement on behalf of a particular book. A critical account of it, then, requires a lot of connect-the-dots extrapolation.

The Plan of the Book

Chapters 1 and 2 tell the story of the unkillable dream in overview by charting the history of novelists' and critics' opinions and readers' responses from the mid-nineteenth century to the present. I then try to address the question of how GAN contenders emerge through a score of case studies from Nathaniel Hawthorne's *The Scarlet Letter* (1850), Herman Melville's *Moby-Dick* (1851), and Harriet Beecher Stowe's *Uncle Tom's Cabin* (1852) through Thomas Pynchon's *Gravity's Rainbow* (1973), Toni Morrison's *Beloved* (1987), and Philip Roth's *American Pastoral* (1997). Up to a point, then, *The Dream of the Great American Novel* unabashedly reinforces "the ideology of the singularity of the book"—the belief that individual literary works exhibit unique qualities of craft and vision that deserve closest attention.[13] My discussions of those I treat at length strive to identify what makes each one special. Feel free, then, to seize on those portions about the novels that interest you most, all of which have haunted me for many years and all of which I unpack in ways I hope will interest even comparative newcomers to literary criticism—for I strive to keep technical terminology to a minimum—yet at the same time provide surprises even for specialists.

The Dream of the Great American Novel is not just a series of freestanding essays about *N* number of books, however. Beyond that, it's about how to imagine those books as taking shape within broader contexts of shifting artistic practice and public priorities that they themselves sometimes influenced even as later generations redefined them quite differently: contexts without which their "unique" accomplishments wouldn't have been possible and can't be understood. This I do especially by organizing my chief exhibits in terms of four scenarios that have proven auspicious for generating GAN candidates—templates for storylines, recipes if you will—that have evolved and metamorphosed over time. Parts II–V take up four of these scripts in turn, as well as ways in which they tend to crisscross and fuse. Interwoven along the way are briefer discussions of hundreds of other novels, both American and otherwise, as well as a number of autobiographical and other nonfictional narrative works—recognizing how porous the boundary between "fiction" and "nonfiction" often is—in order to help define how the featured texts both sit within and press against the limits of their significant others.

Here, briefly, are the four scenarios. Perhaps the surest guarantee of GAN candidacy is to have been subjected again and again to a series of memorable imitations and reinventions in whatever genre or media, thereby giving the text a kind of master narrative status whether or not it set out to be one. The example on which Part II centers is Nathaniel

Hawthorne's *The Scarlet Letter* (1850). The fact that Hawthorne himself had no such aspirations, and for a long time *The Scarlet Letter* was rarely considered a plausible Great American Novel contender even by its admirers, and yet during the course of the book's 160-year history it clearly became such from continuous reinvention by artists and reinterpretation by critics, makes this case all the more arresting.

Script number two, highlighted in Chapters 4–6, centers on the life story of a socially representative figure (conventionally male, but not necessarily so), who strives whether successfully or not to transform himself or herself from obscurity to prominence. Novels of this kind, such as F. Scott Fitzgerald's *The Great Gatsby* (1925) and Ralph Ellison's *Invisible Man* (1952), unfold as inquests into the promise and pitfalls of that traditional American dream story for which Benjamin Franklin's *Autobiography* was the most influential homegrown prototype—or rather the formulaic version of Franklin as self-made man as it entered the bloodstream of nineteenth-century U.S. culture.

Script three, the subject of Chapters 7 through 9, I call the romance of the divide, or rather divides, plural—books from Harriet Beecher Stowe's *Uncle Tom's Cabin* to Toni Morrison's *Beloved* and beyond, whose plots turn on issues of sectional and/or ethnoracial division.* Often they dramatize those divisions through a multigenerational family history or a scene of cross-divide interpersonal intimacy. In order to keep discussion within manageable bounds, and in recognition of the significance for U.S. literary history as well as the nation at large of the North/South and white/black divides from the birth of the republic to the sesquicentennial of the Civil War now in progress, Part IV focuses almost wholly on those two divides almost until the very end. But in so doing it also takes notice of the fact that the defining regional and ethnoracial fault

---

* "Race" and "ethnicity" are closely related but nonidentical categories the precise relation between which has been and will continue to be much debated. Here and below, I generally follow social historian Joel Perlmann in taking ethnicity as the more inclusive category and treating "race as a subset of ethnicity," recognizing too that both terms refer to highly variegated socially constructed identities despite whatever genetic residues (Perlmann, "Reflecting the Changing Face of America: Multiracials, Racial Classification, and American Intermarriage" [1997], repr. in *Interracialism: Black-White Intermarriage in American History, Literature, and Law,* ed. Werner Sollors [New York: Oxford University Press, 2000], 513), sometimes using "ethnoracial" as a more indicative designation. What's most important, of course, is to try to register how the novelists themselves work through and against these categories.

lines in U.S. history and imagination have been multiple and overlapping in ways that have shifted over time such that this view from the 2010s will need revision as the century unfolds.

Script four is best showcased by compendious meganovels that assemble heterogeneous cross-sections of characters imagined as social microcosms or vanguards. These are networked loosely or tightly as the case may be, and portrayed as acting and interacting in relation to epoch-defining public events or crises, in such a way as to constitute an image of "democratic" promise or dysfunction. Melville's *Moby-Dick*, Dos Passos's *U.S.A.* trilogy, and Pynchon's *Gravity's Rainbow* are discussed at greatest length, but as before they are treated in the company of numerous others.

These scripts add up to a pluriverse in motion rather than a unitary conception of Americanness or the history of national fiction. The monolithic ring of "Great American Novel" is deceptive, on several counts. The different scripts complement each other but are also partly at odds, as with scenario two's focus on individual lifelines as against scenario three's on exemplars of disparate regions and groups. Then too, most of the novels discussed extensively are quicker to challenge national icons than defer to them. To some extent, that of course holds for serious fiction everywhere: to serve as an "archive of alternatives to the historically or sociologically 'real,'" as Americanist critic Christopher Castiglia puts it, or as a creative irritant in the spirit of Czech novelist Milan Kundera's declaration that "the stupidity of people comes from having an answer for everything. The wisdom of the novel comes from having a question for everything."[14] As already hinted, moreover, the expectation of something momentous perpetually waiting to be born is implicit in GAN thinking from the start: the assumption that the GAN is a plural disguised as a singular—a horizon to be grasped after, approximated, but never reached, a game that writers, readers, publishers all want to keep on playing.

So a book of this kind is necessarily an exploration of plural, shifting, and often dissonant pathways. Partly for that reason, *The Dream of the Great American Novel* is both less and more than a comprehensive history of U.S. fiction. For obvious reasons this book says almost nothing about the short story, even though it has often been claimed as a more distinctively national literary achievement than the novel—for reasons not always flattering, such as the supposedly short attention span of American audiences.[15] For economy and also for the sake of concentration on specific constellations of narrative practice, I treat no more than glancingly many works I admire, including some you may find in top-twenty lists of major American novels—Stephen Crane's *The Red Badge of Courage*, Ernest Hemingway's *The Sun Also Rises*, and Zora Neale Hurston's *Their Eyes Were Watching God*, to name just three. In treating certain novelists, I sometimes pass over works widely thought to be their best in favor of those that seem more clearly to bespeak a GAN aspiration. Henry James's *The Bostonians* looms larger here than his *Portrait of a Lady* or *The Ambassadors*. Even though I admire Edith Wharton's *The House of Mirth* even more than her *The Custom of the Country*, Toni Morrison's *Song of Solomon* even more than *Beloved*, and Philip Roth's *The Ghost Writer* even more than his *American Pastoral*, I single out the latter novels as being closer approximations of GAN scenarios. Indeed, no matter how well-crafted and esteemed a novel is, even its admirers might hesitate to propose it as a GAN. On this playing field, the middlebrow Harriet Beecher Stowe competes to greater advantage than otherwise with the much more aesthetically self-exacting Henry James (see Chapter 7). Conversely, some of the books featured below, Theodore Dreiser's *An American Tragedy* and John Dos Passos's *U.S.A.* trilogy in particular, are novels once believed to be surefire GAN contenders since fallen from favor.

By the same token, I pay what might seem disproportionate attention to certain mass-market best sellers. For even though the dream of the GAN has always presumed that such novels would be "serious" artistic efforts, the strategies of accredited masterworks can't be surgically separated from the formulas of popular writing. On the contrary, popular novels may embody the templates or recipes that make for Great American Novels as revealingly as the GAN aspirants or nominees themselves do. The accomplishment of William Faulkner's monumental *Absalom, Absalom!*, for instance, can't be understood apart from that of his best-selling contemporary Margaret Mitchell in *Gone with the Wind*, published the same year (see Chapter 9). In part, that's because the definition of the dream of the GAN is less in the hands of credentialed critics and scholars to determine than the result of a complex, messy interaction among them, readers at large, the literary entrepreneurialism of the writers themselves, the publishing and education industries, and self-accredited freelance journalists and bloggers.

In short, I don't offer the novels I discuss at length as a canon of mountain-peak achievements more deserving than all others to endure indefinitely, even though most if not all of them are considered canonical today.[16] My overriding interest is in unpacking them and the scripts that underlie them as keys to the DNA of the GAN, as variously understood and as evolving over time.

It will quickly become clear that this is not simply a made-in-America story. From the start, U.S. fiction has taken shape amid international force fields of diverse kinds; it has taken inspiration and found its significant others abroad as well as at home, and some of its most receptive readers and acutest critics too. None of the four scenarios is exclusive to the United States. All must be understood as variants of patterns widely diffused today throughout world literature. Script two, for instance, is a homegrown variation on the European bildungsroman (novel of formation) that has developed in cross-pollination with it, not just autonomously. At its outer edges, then, *The Dream of the Great American Novel* opens up into a meditation on the work of novels as carriers and definers of evolving "national imaginaries," not just from within but in conversation with others.[17]

Just How "American" Is the GAN Idea?

Anyone who cares about U.S. literature and culture has a natural interest in trying to understand what is distinctive about it. So is the dream of the GAN one of those marks of national distinctiveness? Can we find equivalents in other national literary histories? In a nutshell, the answers are "yes" and "only to a very limited extent."

To start with the common denominators that do exist, the "rise" of the novel in the early modern West was roughly concurrent and often interlocked with the rise of nationalism. The novel has been "bound up with the idea of nationhood," as Ralph Ellison claimed (*CE* 756). In recent critical theory, nation making itself has been metaphorically described as a kind of narrative creation; and in the literary histories of a fair number of countries as well as the United States, individual novels have been held up as nation-defining fictions. During the nineteenth and early twentieth centuries, half a dozen Latin American countries, Doris Sommer has shown, generated iconic "foundational" fictions that justified Creole dominance in the work of nation making: politico-amatory melodramas in which "civilization" is shown as rightfully triumphing over "barbarism." The Venezuelan novelist Rómulo Gallegos's *Doña Bárbera* (1929), in which the university graduate lawyer-hero spurns the advances of the volatile femme fatale title character for the sake of her immiserated daughter, was one such example.[18] Paraguayans have often taken Augusto Roa Bastos's dictator novel *I the Supreme* (1980) as their national novel, a surrealistic historical evocation of the country's nineteenth-century strongman that insinuates connections to the one then in power.[19] Alessandro Manzoni's *I Promessi Sposi* (1827–1840)—a Walter Scott–inspired historical romance written in the early years of the century-long struggle for political unification that features the trials of a seventeenth-century young couple whose marriage plans are almost wrecked by political and clerical machination, foreign invasion, and plague—is often thought to be Italy's national novel, perhaps even, some argue, an attempt to call the nation-state into being at last. Today it remains required reading at least once if not twice on Italian school syllabi.[20] José Rizal's *Noli Me Tangere* (1887), by all accounts the seminal Filipino national novel, is the bildungsroman of the political awakening of an idealistic youth who returns from education abroad to find the common people of his homeland preyed upon by corrupt clerics and grandees, including his own relatives, and himself a marked man forced to flee for his life when he tries to ameliorate their misery.

Even absent a coherent tradition of national fiction, we can occasionally find tours de force of individual entrepreneurship that seize upon the idea, such as Shashi Tharoor's *The Great Indian Novel* (1989), a compressed reinvention of the *Mahabharata*, the towering work of ancient Indian epic.

The only close approximation of the Great American Novel tradition per se, however, is Australia's. It too has a history, albeit less long-standing and less insistent, of GAN talk (using the same acronym) with a shifting set of nominees and definitional traits—also backhandedly underscored by occasional GAN parody—that seems to have developed autonomously if not wholly without regard to the American.[21] But in no other European or Eurocentric culture, the modern novel's original arena of incubation, have I found a counterpart. Russia, Germany, and France loom larger in the history of world fiction than the United States does even today; and Spain can claim Cervantes's *Don Quixote* as the modern Western novel's primal ancestor; but in none of those literary cultures will you find talk of "the Great Russian Novel" and so forth.

This spotty and uneven distribution of great novel–think over time begins to explain how better to understand outliers like the United States and Australia. In particular, one common trigger of talk about "great" or defining "national" novels has been cultural legitimation anxiety. This malaise seems to flourish best either in postcolonial situations where national identity remains contested, or where independence is desired but still unattained. "A national literature emerges," wrote Martinican man of letters Édouard Glissant, "when a community whose collective existence is called into question tries to put together the reasons for its existence."[22] The same holds for the vision of a defining national novel. The correlation is hardly universal—like Italy, Germany was self-consciously a "nation" long before it became a unified nation-state after a process almost as wrenching—but it's reasonably strong.

The critical scene today in Britain, the United States' "mother country," is also worth noting here. Until recently, British writers and critics generally either ignored GAN talk or ridiculed it as hyperinflated overcompensation. "American reviewers," sniffed one British critic of the late 1970s, "[seem to] have a stop marked 'Great American novel' which is pulled out at least once every twelve months."[23] But attitudes may be shifting. Since the early 1990s, observes critic Amanda Claybaugh, British literati have shown signs of hankering after the "Great British Novel" as anxiously as the Americans ever did. Why? Claybaugh suggests an underlying fear that "greatness lies firmly behind," that the future of the "English" novel lies in postcolonial work, including the American behemoth. The prospect of cultural and possibly also political devolution of Scotland and Wales may have compounded such worries. The recourses against them have been to rebrand past masters like Austen, Eliot, and Dickens as creators of the Great British Novel or to tout contemporary "state-of-the-nation" novels like John Lanchester's *Capital* (2012) as the "Great English Novel of the Millennium."[24] That the source of British concerns about novelistic greatness circa 2000 should be diametrically opposite that of Americans circa 1870—fears of a nation in decline versus the struggles of one on the rise—makes the shared syndrome of anxious hyperbole and uncertainty all the more provocative.

Anxieties about national cultural legitimacy cannot be the sole explanation, though, for why the dream of the GAN has stayed alive for a century and a half, well into the era of the national rise to the status of literary as well as politico-military world power. At least four other factors have likely contributed. I list them briskly as speculations to weigh as this book proceeds, since conclusive proof is impossible—and as an encouragement to interested readers to come up with others.

One may be sheer territorial bulk. The sense of national bigness has got to be part of the explanation for the serendipity of the two GANs. "To produce a mighty book you must choose a mighty theme" declares Melville's Ishmael in *Moby-Dick* (*MD* 349). The heady challenge of getting a whale-sized country between covers is almost certainly an incentive to dreaming about a possible great national novel even if not a guarantee.

Another may lie in the ambiguities inherent in the U.S. Constitution, reinforced by controversies from then to now, over the proper distribution of governmental authority among the federally related parts. The authority of the "sovereign" states in relation to the center has always been and will forever be debated. A similar contestedness has marked the long history of critical debate as to whether and how nationness can be robustly imagined by works of literature at other than a regional or sectional level, as well as disputes over the extent to which the experiences of minority groups can be generalized as part of a collective fabric.

The unusually strong valuation set by national ideology upon individualism, or more precisely individual fulfillment and self-realization, is still another likely suspect. It has given even greater impetus than the traditional European novel did to the view that the national story lies preeminently in the sagas of representative persons, in particular those who must struggle to make headway against social constraints. As we'll see especially in Part III, changes in sociocultural conditions, even when they call the viability or legitimacy of this individual-centric ethic into question, have generated revised versions of the storyline that show no sign of winding down.

A fourth likely factor is the future-oriented cast of thinking about U.S. nationness both at home and abroad that dates back to the American Revolution: The United States as an unprecedented experiment in republican democracy forever trying to make good on the promises of the Declaration. The United States as a culture of enterprise forever innovating and casting old technologies behind. Maybe it's too jaded, but it's not altogether offbase to consider the GAN a characteristic expression of the ethos of perpetual obsolescence inherent in capitalist democracy, U.S. style. Not that national history, culture, or narrative can be reduced to techno-economics or to any single driver. The broader point that needs stressing is the tradition of imagining the United States as more a country of the future than of the past. So long as that image persists, so too, most likely, will the GAN.

Why Now?

Now seems both an opportune time and a problematic one to be writing about this distinctive and durable preoccupation for U.S. literary and cultural history on which no book has yet been written.

On the upside, recent advances in critical thinking have made it more possible than ever before to think about national imaginaries in ways expansive enough to avoid parochialism. The understanding of U.S. literary history, as one leading Americanist puts it, has become more "deterritorialized" than at any time since "American literature" began as a field of study.[25] Scholars today are increasingly attentive to how "American literature comes into being through cross-pollination," more attuned than ever before to the multiple lines of connection that have embedded U.S. literature within larger Atlantic, hemispheric, and transpacific webs and have made for a complexly hybridized and increasingly diversified scene of creative production from the beginnings of settler-native contact on down.[26] Their accumulated findings have made it clear as never before that the histories of national literatures, U.S. and otherwise, can't be understood merely as autonomous processes taking shape from within. None of the novels discussed at length below came into being solely by contemplating the national scene or adapting homegrown artistic models. Their genesis and dissemination occurred via complex processes of migration of ideas, literary fashions, and cultural practices ultimately worldwide in scope.

To think in this way about national literary history can help one avoid the fallacy of consigning it to a separate box like an isolated, sealed-off laboratory experiment, as the great mid-twentieth-century Americanist Perry Miller once characterized the unfolding of Puritan thought during the century after first settlement. To think in this newer way also makes it more possible to conceive of U.S. literary history as a polylogue of often dissonant voices and perspectives and to guard against the temptation to overgeneralize on the basis of any one ethnic or regional subculture. As the editors of an important collection of recent critical essays on U.S./Latin American literary and cultural relations observe, "to attempt to move beyond the U.S. nation in American studies is not to abandon the concept of the nation but rather to adopt new perspectives that allow us to view the nation beyond the terms of its own exceptionalist self-imaginings," to appreciate "the unpredictability of national histories, and the protean character of the nation itself."[27] That goal I fully share.

The other side of this coin, however, is systemic distrust of the centripetal forces that give national imaginaries continuity and contour as ideological fictions. Such distrust isn't uniformly shared worldwide. China and a number of the nations of the European Union are becoming more nationalistic rather than less. But in the contemporary United States it runs strong, at least as strong as it ever has since the mid-1800s, when the dream of the Great American Novel began. Any newspaper-literate reader knows that the formerly boasted specialness of American institutions is looking a lot more tarnished these days, both worldwide and at home. Within the prevailing "field imaginary" of academic American studies, even more than among the general public, traditional "consensus" thinking that dwells upon the features making for a distinct, coherent, and purposeful sense of national identity worthy of respect if not celebration tends to be discounted as obsolete and self-serving if not bogus.[28] The historic feat of establishing the world's first postcolonial republic, the dream of a nonhierarchical society of democratic inclusion and equal opportunity, the comparatively open path to citizenship by naturalization, the frontier experience as a crucible of democracy, the entrepreneurial savvy and technological ingenuity that enabled transformation within a century of the largest hinterland ever colonized by a single nation from outback to global economic powerhouse— all these have been reassessed with increasing skepticism since the Vietnam era, a skepticism accelerated by U.S. emergence after 1990 as the unchallenged global superpower. This in turn has tended to put scholars who do American studies for a living on alert to challenge anything that smacks of exceptionalist thinking and, in the case of literary studies specifically, to direct critical thinking away from the "national" toward the subnational or the transnational. So fellow academics if not readers at large may well question the timeliness if not also the legitimacy of a book that looks to be devoted to tracking national aspiration to greatness in whatever form, literary or otherwise. Yet there are good reasons to forge ahead notwithstanding.

To start with the most obvious: the contribution of synthetic studies like this one potentially increases when the drift of critical practice happens to be running the other way, toward more dispersed and concentrated specialization. At such a time, studies that venture inclusive generalizations about continuities of critical thought and literary practice can have special value, provided they don't succumb to hardening of the critical arteries but recognize that they're describing formations in process, and provided they take due account—as I hope to do—of the centrifugal forces of dispersal, such as the series of ethnic literary "renaissances" that have played an increasingly major role in energizing "American" literature since the early 1900s.

Second is the elephant-in-the-room argument: nations are not going away any time soon. As the foremost German Americanist tersely puts it, "American national identity may be temporarily in crisis," but "the United States is a paradigmatic agenda-setting modern society, and no talk about the crisis of the nation-state can distract from the fact that there is enough nation-state left to affect all of us decisively."[29] Pressing a reciprocal line of thinking still more assertively, a leading Indian scholar of cultural nationalism lashes out against first-world fears since the devolution of the former Soviet republics that the greatest "danger to world peace is now posed by the resurgence of nationalism," seeing this mentality as a plot to keep the non-West in place, as if, "like drugs, terrorism, and illegal immigration," nationalism were "one more product of the Third World that the West dislikes but is powerless to prohibit."[30] In the understandable desire to avoid overgeneralization, especially of a gratuitously celebratory kind, it's confusing and obscurantist to operate as if there's no definable cultural "there" there. I recall an objection to an "American Literature Studies Now" lecture that I gave at a conference in China several years ago in which I stressed the importance of Atlantic world, American-hemispheric, and transpacific literary-cultural reciprocities and exchanges for today's American studies: "What ties U.S. literature together? Where's the coherence?" An old-fashioned complaint, but not unreasonable.

Indeed it seems axiomatic both that cultural insiders, be they flag wavers or not, are prone to exaggerate the alleged uniqueness of their national cultures, and that every nation's history, geography, culture is actually in identifiable ways distinct from every other. Thomas Bender's *A Nation among Nations* goes too far in its otherwise admirably insightful comparison of the histories of the United States and selected European nations in concluding that "on the spectrum of differences, the United States is one of many, and there is no single norm from which it deviates—or that it establishes."[31] That belies the numerous ways in which the United States really does stand out from other developed nations. Some of these seem incontestably bad, such as its refusal to endorse international accords that the rest of the world overwhelmingly supports and its percentage of incarcerated people, who also happen disproportionately to be minority males. Some seem good, such as the invention of the liberal arts college. Some seem either good or bad depending on how one views the matter, such as the percentage of residents who profess to believe in an afterlife. Some seem ethically neutral, such as the latitude across which U.S. national territory stretches. Similar lists could be drawn up for Japan, China, India, Indonesia, Germany, and Brazil. The takeaway point here is that there's no such thing as a generic national culture. To think or say anything substantive about any, you've got to grasp the exceptionalist nettle as it were, to unpack what looks distinctive. The relevant question is whether this or that point of evident distinctiveness looks to be benign, suspect, or neutral.

What then of the dream of the Great American Novel, which, as we've seen, is indeed a cast of thinking distinctive if not utterly unique to the United States? No small part of its fascination lies in the discrepancy between the fact that GAN-talk can't be exonerated from the charge of bad exceptionalism or national swagger and the fact that the novels held up as the likeliest candidates have been anything but patriotic. "One thing above all odd" about living in the United States, philosopher K. Anthony Appiah wryly remarks in the course of reflecting on his experience as a public lecturer, is "this country's imagination of itself as so new a creature on God's earth that it cannot learn from others."[32] Most of the writers featured in this book might have said the same. All perceived, and most were appalled by, the disparity between the traditional idealized image of the United States as a land of promise and its failure to make good on the Declaration of Independence's proclamations of liberty and equality as human rights. All were aware of the tradition of national brag that chronically irritated foreign travelers from the time of the early republic and continues to perturb even so urbanely even-handed an observer as Appiah. Their novels show it too, even though they all have their blind spots too, as we'll see below. So the dream of the GAN presents the arresting paradox of a cast of thinking that looks suspiciously chauvinistic at first sight but as you move down to the concrete level of the novels that have been at the center of its gaze seems much more like a custodian and carrier of the collective conscience and national self-criticism. Great American Novels are not expected to be rituals of self-congratulation like July 4 celebrations or Hollywood melodramas—although several of the prime candidates have been retrofitted to the latter. On the contrary, the historical record suggests that serious contenders are much more likely to insist that national greatness is unproven, that its pretensions are hollow, and that the ship of state is going down. This paradox in itself is reason enough to take the subject of Great American Novelism seriously.

Third and finally, to recognize the existence of distinctive influential national literary and intellectual traditions doesn't require settling the issue of whether national cultures, national literatures, are coherent. In fact, quite the opposite. Pascale Casanova's impressive *The World Republic of Letters* (1999), the most sweeping single-authored attempt yet to address the question of the place of national literature in an increasingly globalizing world, gives too foreclosing an answer. Since the Enlightenment, she argues, something like a loose "system" of publishing and other literary institutions has taken shape, organized on an increasingly global scale but with a built-in proviso of cultural specificity that she calls "the Herder effect," after the most influential theorist of early cultural nationalism, such that national literatures assume a Janus-faced character, both outward and inward looking. "Even the most international writers," she contends, "are first of all defined, in spite of their wishes to the contrary, by their native national and literary space"—thinking here of such figures as the Irish expatriates James Joyce and Samuel Beckett.[33] It comes as no surprise, given the critical trend lines I've been describing, to find Casanova's model faulted by Americanists for overreliance on nations as the key building blocks.

Today's "citizen of the World Pluribus of Letters," Mark McGurl replies, "disaffiliates from the empirical nation . . . in order to affiliate with a utopian sub-nation, whether that be African- or Asian- or Mexican-" or Native.[34] So far as the contemporary U.S. literary scene is concerned, he's certainly right. This judgment comes toward the end of a groundbreaking study of the prominent role of academic creative writing programs in shaping production of serious U.S. fiction from the mid-twentieth century onward, one major consequence of which, McGurl shows, has been to nurture and perpetuate the ethos of "high cultural pluralism."

McGurl ends his critique on a quizzical note, however, wondering about fiction of "the Program Era" whether "one can disaffiliate from the nation-state while still being affiliated with educational institutions located there."[35] This mood of skeptical wonderment just happens to be the mirror opposite of the mood of those who first articulated the dream of the Great American Novel 150 years ago, to which we're about to turn. Those critics of yore hankered for a novel that would deliver a representation of the American scene as solid as the nation-state that had just reconstituted itself after the Civil War seemed to be; but when they looked at what U.S. fiction had thus far delivered, what they especially saw was a scene of disparate provincialisms, a failure at the level of imagined nationhood, that they then offered prescriptions to remedy. In today's literary and critical scenes as McGurl astutely describes them, a version of what once would have been considered failure has become, for now at least, the preferred path. Yet the interplay between those mirror opposites—the tension between synthesis and particularism—has been crucial in perpetuating the dream of the Great American Novel from then to now, and it has been a central concern for many of the novels held up as the likeliest candidates. In short, the question of whether there's enough cultural glue conjoining the disparate parts of the U.S. nation-state to make for nationally coherent fictional traditions doesn't need to be answered in the affirmative in order to justify taking the GAN idea seriously. For the perceived (non)relation between fractious parts has itself been one of the drivers of GAN thinking from the start.

PART ONE

THE UNKILLABLE DREAM

1

Birth, Heyday, and Seeming Decline

He couldn't argue with America. It was one of those balloon names. It kept stretching as it filled up, getting bigger and bigger and thinner and thinner. What kind of gas it was, stretching the thing to its limits, who could say. Whatever we dreamed. And of course one day it would pop. But for now, it served its purpose. For now, it was holding together.

—COLSON WHITEHEAD, *Apex Hides the Hurt* (2006)

He was afraid the great American novel, if true, must be incredible.

—WILLIAM DEAN HOWELLS, *A Hazard of New Fortunes* (1890)

O FTEN WE CAN'T SPECIFY when a new idea gets put into circulation. In this case we can. It's one of the few things that's clear-cut about the history of the dream of the Great American Novel. The idea has a prehistory, as we'll soon see, but it was introduced as a critical concept in an essay of January 1868 by the novelist John W. De Forest. Today De Forest is remembered chiefly, if at all, for a book published the year before that anticipates his big idea, *Miss Ravenel's Conversion from Secession to Loyalty,* a landmark in its own right as the first significant Civil War novel, although fated to become one of those honorable subgalactic achievements that keep getting rediscovered and then falling off the critical radar screen (more on that in Chapter 7).

The phrase itself was already in the air, its odor already somewhat tainted. A few months before, the publisher of Rebecca Harding Davis's *Waiting for the Verdict* (1867), another Civil War fiction, today chiefly remembered for its gingerly engagement of the taboo subject of white-black miscegenation, had touted it as the Great American Novel. Even before that, we find the legendary showman P. T. Barnum spoofing such puffery as cliché lingo: "the land agent with his nice new maps and beautiful descriptions of distant scenery, the newspaper man with his 'immense circulation,' the publisher with his 'Great American Novel.'"[1] De Forest was the first to take the GAN idea seriously and to try to give it substance, although his essay too was part hype, ending with a plea for the international copyright protection that he and many other American writers believed was crucial for authorship to flourish in the United States.

The Birth of the Dream

De Forest envisaged a work that would capture "the American soul" by portraying "the ordinary emotions and manners of American existence" in a "tableau" that would grasp the full geographical and cultural range of national life, with the amplitude of a Thackeray, a Trollope, a Balzac. To date, he argued, American fiction had been overwhelmingly "local" or sectional; even its best fiction writer, Hawthorne, had captured "little but the subjective of humanity." The closest approximation so far had been Harriet Beecher Stowe's *Uncle Tom's Cabin* (1852), which, whatever its defects, did have "a national breadth to the picture, truthful outlining of character, natural speaking, . . . drawn with a few strong and passionate strokes, not filled in thoroughly, but still a portrait."[2]

De Forest risked self-contradiction in taking for granted that there must be such a thing as an "American soul" when the literary evidence to date, by his own say-so, argued the opposite. His assessment of American fiction was also doctrinaire, ruling out "romance" and positing that regional and national fiction were antagonistic. So too his judgments of particular books and authors. That he didn't even think to mention Melville reflects the then-prevailing view of him as a once-popular novelist who had long since lost his audience by perversely writing unreadable books. De Forest's praise of *Uncle Tom's Cabin* is also conventional in singling out the previous era's most famous fictional achievement in a distinctly postbellum and tribalist way, showing no interest at all in its passionate concern for the plight of African American slaves—an issue that northern whites preferred to believe war and constitutional reform had resolved—much less in the possibility that an African American writer might see things differently from a white one. Such limitations mark De Forest as the product of a specific background and time: a white Anglo-American Yankee working in the immediate aftermath of the war, with the vogue of fictional realism just coming into its ascendancy, long before the critical establishment began to take serious notice of the large and increasing body of literature by writers other than white Protestants.

Yet his manifesto was timely as well as time-bound. Calls for an autonomous national literature dated back to the Revolutionary era, but nothing like a consensus as to what might actually constitute national fiction had congealed. Why not? One key reason was the long-embedded provincialism that De Forest deplored. As the divisive impact of *Uncle Tom's Cabin* had proven, during the run-up to the Civil War, the imagined or "virtual" nation had ironically become more fragmented in inverse proportion to the early industrial era's strengthening of the very transportation and communications networks that enabled people, books, and other commodities to circulate faster and farther around the country.[3] Indeed, traveling north to south, east to west, or vice versa, still felt like traveling to a foreign place. Unlike Germany and Italy, the United States was a political unit before it was a nation, and not until after the war did it become common to speak of it in the singular. Before then, recalled the critic John Jay Chapman in the 1890s, "there was no nation," "only discordant provinces."[4] But now, with war behind and continental conquest and settlement in sight, the prospect of a pan-national fiction at last seemed feasible. Considered in the light of cultural politics, then, the dream of the GAN as first launched was at once the literary edge of what U.S. cultural historians have called the "romance of reunion" between northern and southern whites,[5] and part of a broad multifront push toward pan-national consolidation that also included a stronger hand for the federal government (especially through the Reconstruction years), the creation of public university systems, the completion of the transcontinental railroad, the subjugation of Native Americans in the trans-Mississippi west, and the advent of standard time zones. Not that De Forest would have endorsed this whole bill of particulars. He was neither a militant nationalist nor a devotee of the national penchant for brag from which his essay had rescued the GAN catchphrase. But his excitement at the idea of a pan-national novel marks it as a product of that expansionist moment.

The essay was timely in a more aesthetic sense too, as a barometer of prose fiction's rising critical prestige. Less than 5 percent of all works of American fiction before 1850 were marketed as "novels"; the preferred label was "tale,"[6] a term triply advantageous as a self-effacing disclaimer of pretense to strict accuracy, a gesture of solidarity to the lingering power of romanticism, and a gentle insinuation of a moral thrust. The closest student of antebellum fiction criticism persuasively suggests that by mid-century American reviewers had accepted the novel as the defining "literary art form of the nineteenth century," yet the emergence of the GAN idea required broader public acceptance of prose fiction as a high art form.[7] Sure enough, I have unearthed only a few scattered antebellum references to "the great American novel," the earliest an advertisement for an 1852 London penny edition reprint of (fortuitously) *Uncle Tom's Cabin*, a promotional hype that simply touts its status as runaway best seller—and an 1853 plea for financial assistance on behalf of an African American family at risk of being sold into slavery, published in the newspaper where *Uncle Tom's Cabin* was first serialized.[8] Stowe's publishers never used the term "novel" to market the book, promoting it rather as the "greatest of American tales," "the Greatest Book of the Age," or "the greatest book of its kind ever issued from the American Press."[9] This notwithstanding that reviewers on both sides of the Atlantic immediately classified *Uncle Tom's Cabin* as a novel in the Dickensian vein and that Stowe herself declared from the first her aim to achieve utmost mimetic accuracy, the very effect that came to be seen as the distinguishing mark of "novel" as opposed to "tale" or "romance": to portray slavery, as she put it, "in the most lifelike and graphic manner possible."[10] But after the Civil War, prose fiction established itself decisively as the literary form of preference, with "novel" as the paradigmatic form of prose fiction. At century's end, the novelist-critic William Dean Howells, then-esteemed dean of American letters, could insist with confidence that fiction had become "the chief intellectual stimulus of our time, whether we like the fact or not." "To-day is the day of the novel," Frank Norris agreed.[11] Posterity has confirmed the verdict. No span of U.S. literary history before or since the half-century between the Civil War and World War I defined itself and remains defined so predominantly in terms of its fictional output.*

---

* The novel's increasing prestige did not mean consensus as to what a "novel" was—far from it. As noted below, fiction remained undertheorized, and practice varied as fashions changed and the fiction market became more variegated. Mark McGurl, *The Novel Art: Elevations of American Fiction after Henry James* (Princeton, NJ: Princeton University Press, 2001), is a judicious analysis that stresses the increasing schism between middlebrow realism and emergent modernism. L. Buell, "Theories of the Novel in the Age of

De Forest's essay was also timely, whether or not he meant it to be, in its concurrence with a rising tide of cultural nationalist theory abroad. The conception of national literature as national expression in Hippolyte Taine's just-published *Histoire de la littérature anglaise* (1863) would strongly influence later formulations of American literary and cultural difference.[12] This too was the eve of Ernest Renan's seminal "What Is a Nation?" (1882), which defined "a nation" as "a soul, a spiritual principle," entailing "the possession in common of a rich legacy of memories" and "the will to perpetuate the value of the heritage that one has received in an undivided form." That personification is the remote origin of the most influential recent treatise on nationalism, anthropologist Benedict Anderson's *Imagined Communities* (1983, rev. 1991), which reconceives nationalist ideologies as collective fictions.[13]

Contrary to Renan and nineteenth-century nationalism theory generally, Anderson conceives nations as artifacts, as products of collective imagination, not as organic entities primordially present in embryo. By the same token, however, Anderson's model has energized critical thinking about the role of literature and the arts in the work of nation building; and it's instructive to apply it to the formative years of U.S. fiction theory. Although Anderson erred in holding that modern nationalism began with New World independence movements and that countrywide print networks were crucial to its emergence (the United States lacked anything like a national newspaper until long after the Revolution), still *Imagined Communities* and its sequel *The Spectre of Comparisons* (1998) did demonstrate the importance of print institutions generally and of narrative invention specifically to the construction of

---

Realism," in *Cambridge History of the American Novel*, ed. Leonard Cassuto, Clare Virginia Eby, and Benjamin Reiss (Cambridge: Cambridge University Press, 2011), 322–336, gives a concise overview of evolving novel theory in the United States at this time. For a classic critique of contemporary undertheorization, see Henry James, "The Art of Fiction," in *Literary Criticism*, vol. 1: *Essays on Literature, American Writers and English Writers*, ed. Leon Edel (New York: Library of America, 1984), 44–65. This much can be generalized, however, despite the lack of consensus: major U.S. novelists between the Civil War and the early twentieth century by and large strove like De Forest for greater verisimilitude than they saw in their predecessors—that is, a greater sociological probabilism in speech, character, description, and plot; but what they meant by that aspiration varied greatly. Some writers who might be thought of as "realists" rejected the rubric (Norris for one thought himself a romanticist), and, as modern critics regularly point out, "realism" is by definition oxymoronic: fiction's imagined worlds are never coextensive with the actual.

the sentiment of nationness. Through an Andersonian prism, one might even dare to contend that nations "depend for their existence on an apparatus of cultural fictions in which imaginative literature," and novels in particular, "plays a decisive role."[14] De Forest himself would never have made such a claim about the American novel, which for him barely existed. His view was closer to Renan's: that national fiction registered a national soul in the making, not that fiction was a nation-building force. He showed no interest whatever, for example, in *Uncle Tom's Cabin*'s nation-changing intent or its fabled influence in precipitating the Civil War, in which he himself had served with honor on the Union side. Nonetheless the GAN as he first framed it took the notion of fiction making and nation building as coordinate projects to a level of assertiveness that haunted later critical and novelistic practice. The very naïveté of Taine's, Renan's, and De Forest's hypostatizations relative to Anderson's demystification of nation as a produced effect abetted the mentality that a nation's artifacts might embody nationness even if they did not create it.

Defining the Terms, Somewhat

Despite the skepticism it predictably provoked, the dream of the Great American Novel soon entrenched itself as a staple of American literary journalism: as a mantra for publishers, reviewers, and critics. A mere three years after De Forest's essay, critics were speculating that the dream of the GAN must date back to the early national era, when "the absence of a fully developed literature" was first felt. Before long it was affirmed that "several generations . . . [had] died" waiting for the great national novel to appear.[15]

Unfortunately for clarity, although fortunately for opportunity, few who brandished the slogan, whether pro or con, tried to articulate more fully than De Forest had what a GAN might be. It was less "a theory" than "an obsession" or "mania."[16] At first sight, the plethora of critical assertions makes the GAN look rather like the allegorical figure of Giant Transcendentalist in Hawthorne's tale "The Celestial Railroad," whose chief trait is that nobody can distinguish his features, including himself. What Colson Whitehead's protagonist (an expert on brand naming) in *Apex Hides the Hurt* wittily thinks about "America" itself holds for the GAN with even greater force: it feels like "one of those balloon names," full of hot air, surely destined to pop some day, yet somehow miraculously "holding together."[17] But the vagueness with which it was bandied about during its early years at least should come as no surprise given that Anglo-American fiction criticism was still in its precritical infancy, "with no air of having a theory," as Henry James declared, as if "a novel is a novel, as a pudding is a pudding," and "our only business with it could be to swallow it."[18] What passed for "criticism" was as yet little more than impressionistic labeling. A census of GAN nominees yields only a scattergram. During the last fifteen years of the nineteenth century, when back-of-the-envelope nominations reached a peak, all of the following and more were proposed as having achieved the crown or as approaches thereto: Helen Hunt Jackson's *Ramona* (1884); Blanche Howard's *Guenn* (1884); F. J. Stimson's *King Noannett* (1896); Harold Frederic's *The Damnation of Theron Ware* (1896); *The Story of Margaret Kent* (1896), by "Henry Hayes" (pseud. Katherine Sherwood Bonner McDowell); *The Begum's Daughter* (1896), by Edwin Lassetter Bynner; *The Chosen Valley* (1892), by Mary Hallock Foote; Robert Grant's *Unleavened Bread* (1900); and Frank Norris's *McTeague* (1899). From a list of freelance verdicts, you can't say much more about a GAN nominee back then than that it was a book somebody liked a very great deal— and that the coinage was easy to debase. Of the books just listed, only Norris's and Jackson's are widely read today, Frederic's only by specialists, and the others are largely forgotten.

Yet from the impressionistic chatter some generalizations can be extracted about what commentators had in mind when they held forth on the subject of the GAN during the half century or so from the 1860s to the 1920s, when it was most extensively discussed. To begin with negatives, a GAN cannot be tiny. Fitzgerald's *The Great Gatsby* is the shortest work ever seriously proposed. It's always seemed permissible for the GAN to center on an individual figure, like *Huckleberry Finn*, but with the proviso that he or she should be in some sense socially representative. Relatedly, a GAN must not limit itself to rehearsing particular lives and events but provide at least implicitly some consequential reflection on U.S. history and culture and its defining institutions— democracy, individualism, capitalism, sectionalism, immigration, expansionism, signature landscapes, demographic mix. Not that the GAN has ever been expected to be a work of nationalist advocacy. On the contrary, from the start most who weighed in on the subject were quick to stress that "literature of the noblest sort . . . does not derive from brag."[19] It made sense from the start that the first nominee, *Uncle Tom's Cabin*—De Forest's verdict was seconded more enthusiastically by many others—should have denounced the social status quo.

GAN discussion from the 1870s through the 1920s tends to gravitate toward not only particular kinds of novels but also a handful of contested questions. Is the GAN to be conceived as a one-time event, or in the plural? May a book confine itself to a specific region or place and still qualify? Must it confine itself to American issues or the American scene? Must it be narrated in an objective-realist manner? May the author be expected to come from any particular background? How relevant are gender, ethnicity, even nationality?

On the first issue, the history of the GAN discourse mimics in reverse the history of the phrase "the United States." The GAN catchphrase starts as a singular, but increasingly with the assumption that a single novel-to-end-all-novels isn't to be expected. By World War I, if not before, the idea had firmly taken hold, and for good, that "the great American novel will be in the plural."[20] Over time, GAN rhetoric became a telegraphic way of proclaiming either the existence or the eminence of a selected group of novels and novelists of superior exemplarity and excellence that allowed both for the actual variegation of national life and for future additions that might surpass anything that came before. Although the notion of plural GANs seemed to some a confession of defeat or debasement of the coinage, to think in terms of an unfolding field of possibilities also followed from the futurological cast of thinking we already find in De Forest, and long before that in early national calls for a distinctively national literature as yet unborn and in the sense (dating from that same period) of the democratic experiment as itself a project still in the making.

Closely related to the pluralization of the GAN idea was the debate over whether regional fiction might qualify. More often than not, critics sided with De Forest's view that "the great American novel can never be a novel . . . wholly of provincial life, or of sectional life," but rather "of national life" and "based entirely or partly upon national ideas." Yet a sizeable contingent, particularly during the late nineteenth-century high tide of so-called local colorism, affirmed with Frank Norris that since the country "is a Union, but not a unit," a GAN must be sectional. The novelist Edward Eggleston likewise affirmed that "the 'great American novel'" was "appearing in sections"—pointing to his own

Hoosier Schoolmaster as one installment. One critic even went so far as to insist, "One little spot . . . one tiny round of human experience—no matter how narrow, so it be but deep enough—this is all the novelist needs." This was extreme, and others retorted that the "subdividing and minimizing process . . . of local tales" was in fact the prime impediment to the GAN. But it was agreed that the GAN might have a region-particular focus so long as its horizon of vision extended beyond that. "Lay the scene on the limitless prairie or on limited Fifth Avenue, but let the story rise above its geographical boundaries," as one consensus seeker summed up.[21]

It's notable that during the early heyday of GAN discourse far more critical energy was spent worrying about the place of regional cultures than about issues of gender and race.

The lingering prestige of *Uncle Tom's Cabin* throughout the nineteenth century, even as its antislavery activism seemed to white middle-class readers increasingly passé, was enough to make gender a virtual nonissue. The hypothetical great American novelist was generically referred to as a "he," but the GAN idea was seldom explicitly framed as a gendered concept. Never was it hinted that women were too frail, timid, or cloistered to be able to write the GAN. Male commentators did sometimes complain that the putatively female-weighted readership of novels made American writers pull their punches. (The "Iron Madonna," moaned novelist-critic H. H. Boyesen, "strangles in her fond embrace the American novelist.")[22] One rarely finds anticipations of late twentieth-century literary historians' diagnosis that women writers characteristically claimed the regional rather than the national as their special territory, whether in triumph or in retreat.[23] Although nobody nominated Sarah Orne Jewett or Kate Chopin, today the most-admired women regionalists, at the turn of the twentieth century regionalism and the question of whether nationness could be captured except through local particularity both loomed so large that most critics would have hesitated to deem such writers marginal. In this sense, turn-of-the-twenty-first-century critiques of regional realism that return Jewett et al. to the mainstream by rereading local colorism as vicarious exoticism marketed to privileged urbanites that was latently if not overtly classist, racist, even imperialist in character look like disillusioned counterparts of the broad late nineteenth-century acceptance of regional realism as central to the literary menu.[24] Only after about 1920 did premodern women regionalists begin to be marginalized in

American criticism, in synchrony with the rise of American literature studies as a male-dominated professional field.[25]

Race was a virtual nonissue for the opposite reason. Almost everybody who wrote about the GAN presumed it would be written by a white American. Hamlin Garland prophesied what had in fact already come to pass, that "the negro" would enter (southern) fiction "first as subject, second as artist in his own right," but almost nobody ventured to suggest, as one critic did, that "the coming novelist" might well be "of African origin," since undoubtedly "our great novel will not be written by the typical American."[26] Notable for the timing of its appearance (1886) amid sinking African American political prospects and cultural morale, this last was the lone assertion of the possibility of an African American–authored GAN to appear in the mainstream press before the mid-twentieth century; and even it is undermined by its rationale ("the African is . . . a natural story-teller"), the kind of stereotyping that made Uncle Remus a household name for fin de siècle audiences and tied the reputation of the era's foremost African American novelist, Charles Chesnutt, to his conjure tales (see Chapter 8). Respecting subject matter too, the prevailing assumption was that U.S. fiction would mainly be about white America, even if no one put it so baldly as the critic who insisted that among the mélange of "picturesque types" in national life, only the "cowboy and the mountaineer" were eligible subjects; that "Negroes, Indians, and Chinamen" might "stand decoratively about; but as real actors in the drama, they are not to be thought of," since "we" "cannot take any lively interest in a hero or heroine with whom we cannot to a certain extent identify," and "our imaginations can only with difficulty overleap the barriers of race."[27]

To apply cultural critic Michael Lind's handy three-stage mapping of the history of cultural inclusiveness in the precontemporary United States as seen from the top of the social heap down, even if 1865–1920 was no longer the epoch of "Anglo-America," it was still stuck in "Euro-America" a long distance from "Multi-America."[28] Few postbellum theorists of American nationality were able to get past Euro-ethnocentrism and even fewer among the first wave of historians of American literature, virtually all of whom down to 1900 and beyond defined it as "a subordinate . . . expression of the Anglo-Saxon spirit."* When GAN

---

* Howard Mumford Jones, *The Theory of American Literature,* rev. ed. (Ithaca, NY: Cornell University Press, 1965), 79–80. This whole chapter of Jones's pioneering (orig. 1948) ac-

pundits addressed the challenge of writing nonelite figures and subcultures into national fiction, then, they thought less about issues of race than of wealth and status, about incorporating such characters as "those who have lived all their lives in the treadmill of American industrialism," and they thought more about upcountry New England and Appalachia than about Native America or the Hispanic southwest.[29]

Related to debates about particularism of focus was a further concern about how directly a plausible GAN contender should address the American scene at all. Cosmopolitan critics insisted that consciousness and artistic excellence counted far more than locale, noting that other acknowledged national epics had taken place on foreign soil. *The Iliad,* Nathaniel Hawthorne's wayward writer-critic son Julian observed, "embodies, whether symbolically or literally matters not, the triumph of Greek ideas and civilization."[30] He might have said the same of *The Aeneid* or *Beowulf.* But those like Edith Wharton who opposed parochial restrictions on international settings did so aware of swimming against the tide. In one of the realist era's most thoughtful GAN vision statements (1927), Wharton defended expatriate fiction as a legitimate arena for GAN aspiration precisely because of its national exemplarity, contending that "the expatriate American" is "peculiarly typical of modern America—of its intense social acquisitiveness and insatiable appetite for new facts and new sights," a disposition, she added, also "disseminated among thousands who have never crossed the Atlantic." Here Wharton shrewdly linked the nation's rise to world-power status after World War I to the increase of residence and travel abroad during the first quarter of the century of which she herself was a part. But she leads up to this judgment tortuously and defensively, mindful of bucking a consensus that "the American novelist must submit to much

---

count of U.S. literary historiography, "'The Arms of the Anglo-Saxons'" (79–117) underscores the paradoxes of U.S. critical theory during the era. As assurance about the nation's future cultural prospects increased, literary-critical attitudes became more Anglophilic and Anglo-Saxonist rather than less, and the premise of an ethnoculturally incubated democratic and linguistic transit from Germany to Britain to the United States (with New England as the United States' defining element) ironically had the effect of marginalizing formal study of American literature in favor of English and especially Anglo-Saxon. This account is broadly sustained by Elizabeth Renker's history of the genesis of American literature as an academic field, *The Origins of American Literature Studies: An Institutional History* (Cambridge: Cambridge University Press, 2007). For the prior history of Anglophilia in U.S. literary culture, see especially Elisa Tamarkin, *Anglophilia: Deference, Devotion, and Antebellum America* (Chicago: University of Chicago Press, 2008).

narrower . . . limitations before he can pretend to have produced *the* (or *the greatest,* or even simply *an*) American novel": that is, "the great American novel must always be about Main Street, geographically, socially, and intellectually."[31] This amounted to a concession that she might have won the battle but not the critical war. A few years before, her *Age of Innocence* beat out Sinclair Lewis's *Main Street* for the Pulitzer Prize. But Lewis seemed closer to the broadly accepted prototype for American fiction. One recalls Fitzgerald's overheated fan letter to Lewis, praising *Main Street* as "the best American novel."[32]

Not that the prevailing views of what the GAN should be made such a fetish of adherence to the middle American average as Wharton claimed. True, Henry James, like Wharton herself, had regularly been typed even by sympathetic critics as an alien exotic on the score of his expatriation as well as his investment in the lives of the upper crust ("He never gets into the spirit of our American home-life"); and Frank Norris, contributing to a *San Francisco Examiner* forum on the GAN, was careful to distinguish between the greatest novel by an American (he nominated Lew Wallace's biblical epic *Ben-Hur*) and the best novel about the American scene (Howells's *A Modern Instance,* Norris thought).[33] True, Howells himself advocated an aesthetics of ordinary middle-class experience, for which he was honored in later years for having produced the Great American Novel, "if not in any one volume, still in the general mass of his work." One enthusiastic turn-of-the-century fan of his work commended to *The Literary World* a Buffalo bookseller's recipe for "the great American novel" in twenty-five chapters titled after books by Howells.[34] Yet Howells, like Lewis after him, also jostled the proprieties of the quotidian middle-class life that he commended as the American novelist's proper sphere, as in the book Norris praised (the first notable American novel to treat divorce head on and sympathetically), in his qualified defense of miscegenation in *An Imperative Duty* (1892), in his trilogy of utopian socialist romances, and in his anatomy of clashes between capital and labor in an increasingly multiethnic, polyglot urban America in *A Hazard of New Fortunes,* the most ambitious of all his novels. Ironically, Howells was chastised for timidity by younger-generation novelists who pushed his guarded critiques much further.

At all events, it was agreed that just as American authorship didn't guarantee the "Americanness" of the product, neither did self-conscious

Americanness of method or subject matter. Critics sometimes even warned against this as a clog or trap, admonishing that "the less self-conscious [an author] is of trying to be American, the more truly he will succeed in being so."[35] GAN commentators, then, were more sympathetic than not to Wharton's concern that novelists resist standardization, resist fetishizing the "dead level of prosperity and security" of middle America as the proper platform for a GAN. Lewis himself, her ostensible target, actually admired Wharton and shared her disdain for hinterland kitsch, though not her regret for the lack of "an old social organization which provided for nicely shaded degrees of culture and conduct," like the New York society of her late Victorian girlhood.[36]

Wharton's presumption of narrative realism was more squarely in line with prevalent GAN thinking. De Forest had been explicit on this point. So too the final manifesto of the realist-naturalist era by a leading practitioner, that of Theodore Dreiser in 1932, refers to the forever-awaited masterwork as "the great American realistic novel." This consensus did not pass unchallenged, being at cross-purposes with the near-universal verdict that Hawthorne was the nation's foremost classic writer of prose fiction. "What . . . is there against considering 'The Scarlet Letter' as a great American novel?" some retorted. But more often than not Hawthorne gets relegated in these discussions "to the wide realm of art rather than to our nationality." Henry James, who respected Hawthorne more than any other American precursor, nonetheless seemed to think of the hypothetical great American novelist as De Forest had, as "belonging to the family of Balzac & Thackeray."[37] Even as aesthetic modernism began to take hold, the impression persisted that the GAN should be a mimetic if not a documentary representation of national life.

The work of the 1930s hailed as the single most ambitious assault on the GAN to date, John Dos Passos's *U.S.A.* trilogy (1930–1938),[38] followed Joyce's *Ulysses* in employing stream-of-consciousness narration and mass media forms like newspaper and advertising lingo but counterbalanced this experimentalism with the detached reportorial objectivism with which the loosely intersecting lifelines of the twelve main fictive characters and their circles are narrated. Dos Passos himself claimed that the primary Anglophone model for his "chronicle novel" approach, as he called it, was Thackeray's *Vanity Fair,* a book he had read ten times, he said, "rather early in my life" before "I lost count."

Sure enough, when reissued in a deluxe illustrated edition a decade later, *U.S.A.* was hailed in critic Malcolm Cowley's review for the *New York Times* as "the most important and the best of the many American novels written in the naturalistic tradition"—the grand culmination of the legacy of Crane, Sinclair Lewis, Dreiser, Farrell, and Steinbeck.[39]

Monumentalism and Mockery: Dos Passos, Stein, and Others

Dos Passos's trilogy was a kind of ultimate embodiment of the old GAN dream of a comprehensive national fiction, but one that also turned De Forest's conception of the project on its head by exposing an irreparable rift in "the American soul." I reserve full discussion until Chapter 12 of *U.S.A.*'s remarkable effort to render a more multiperspectival account of national life in world-historical context than had ever yet been undertaken. The one point in need of stressing here is that *U.S.A.*'s achievement as a stylistic tour de force calls into question, if not undermines, the narrative realism to which it partially defers. Its stylistic heterogeneity registers a discontent with the sufficiency of traditional realism that had been brewing for a long time. By pitting a dehydrated version of it (twelve rather flat-character lifelines rendered in deadpan Hemingwayesque third-person) against thirty-odd stream-of-consciousness "Camera Eye" sections that dramatize the semiautobiographical persona's more vibrant subjectivity, *U.S.A.* presses 1920s-style satire à la Wharton, Lewis, and others toward a derealization of realist practice by exposing what its illusion of transparency tends to repress: the selectivity and superficiality of any "objective" narratorial gaze, the culpable impotence of the stance of narrative detachment, and the artificial character of the novelistic medium itself, especially as it becomes the conduit of mass media technologies, a rechanneling of the collective voices of yellow journalism, newsreels, and crowdspeak.

In all this *U.S.A.* seconds the two main charges against Howellsian realism laid down as early as the 1890s: blandness and pseudo-objectivism. These were the grounds on which naturalism pushed past realism's usual limits. ("Extreme realism," one of the first critical attempts to define "naturalism" tellingly called it.)[40] Thus Frank Norris allied himself with romanticism even though literary history now generally classes him, and most other naturalists too, among the realists. In his "Plea for Romantic Fiction," Norris denigrates realism as given over to "meticulous presentation of teacups, rag carpets, wall-paper and haircloth sofas," by contrast to "Romance" as a visionary, socially significant project that takes "the wide world for range" and "the un-plumbed depth of the human heart." The first part of this farrago leads straight to Lewis's putdown of Howells, in his 1931 Nobel Prize accep-tance speech, as a euphemizer with "the code of a pious old maid whose greatest delight was to have tea at the vicarage."[41] The second part reaches back to Norris's earlier praise of novels "with a purpose" like *Uncle Tom's Cabin* and forward to later-stage "realism"'s acknowledg-ment of the necessarily subjective character of narration, and still farther forward to mid-twentieth-century accounts of naturalism like Cowley's 1947 review of *U.S.A.* as a fusion of "realist" and "romance" elements, and to late twentieth-century criticism's more systematic dismantling of realism's pretensions to the objectivity it claimed for itself.[42]

Near the end of his life, the year after the three volumes of *U.S.A.* first appeared as a trilogy, Sherwood Anderson ventured a double-sided account of realism that anticipated this later critique by insisting both that imagination "feeds upon the life of reality" and that it nonetheless "will always remain separated" from it. "No man can quite make him-self a camera." Anderson professed shock that his *Winesburg, Ohio* had been taken "as an exact picture of Ohio village life" when in fact "the hint for almost every character was taken from my fellow lodgers" in a Chicago tenement, "many of whom had never lived in a village." With *Winesburg* in mind, fellow regionalist Mary Austin defended subjectifi-cation as a distinctively "American" practice. "The democratic novelist," she argues, must "be inside his novel rather than outside in the Victo-rian fashion of Thackeray," must abandon "the reference of personal conduct to an overhead Judgment which forced the earlier novelist to assume the god in the disposition of his characters . . . to a true demo-cratic desire of man to see himself as he is seen by the people with whom he does his business." Here and elsewhere, Austin anchors her credo in a view of democracy as originating in the will to "escape from social certitude," in a William Jamesean–pragmatist diagnosis of Amer-ican social life as a state of permanent impermanence, and in a vision of continental cultures and environments as too diverse to synthesize into a unitary panoramic vision.[43]

Austin operated from a conviction of American writers' necessary emplacement within distinct subcultures quite different from that of

most late twentieth-century revisionist critics of realism. Her argument
hinges on the belief in an intractable bioregional embeddedness to
which an "American" text a priori bears witness, whereas for the later
critics it was a matter of realist pretensions being compromised by or
serving as a protective cover for ideologies of class, gender, and race
from which not even the most far-sighted text was immune. But for our
purposes this broader two-part story line is what matters: the initial
canonization of panoramic verisimilitude after the Civil War as the
preferred vehicle for achieving the GAN, followed by successive waves
of discontent that started with the "extreme" realism of the naturalists.
By the 1920s, when the long hold of "realism'"s prestige as the preferred path for national fiction eroded further, realist practice had itself
morphed and hybridized—in the writing of Anderson, Austin, Jean
Toomer, F. Scott Fitzgerald, Nella Larsen, early William Faulkner, and
many others—to the point that the most ambitious assault on the GAN
of the "realist" era became a project that pressed traditional realist practices beyond their original limits into deliberately fissured, self-divided
bricolage. The political disenchantment that overtook Dos Passos in the
1920s undoubtedly added impetus to his quasi-Brechtian strategy of
alienated realism in *U.S.A.;* but his discontent with traditional realist
practice is visible from his earliest writing in the 1910s.

Considered, then, as a stab at the GAN along the lines of the Balzac-
Thackeray-style realism that the majority of commentators from De
Forest through Wharton during the heyday of GAN discourse from the
1860s through the 1930s supposed would be the form of that mythical
masterwork (or works), *U.S.A.* seems both a grand culmination and the
end of something, a deliberate train wreck. It turned realist aesthetics
against itself by exposing it both as artifice and as a technology whose
"overhead Judgment" was perpetually subject to ideological manipulation. In the process, *U.S.A.* redirected the original project of rendering
American social actualities first and foremost toward a more sweeping
indictment of American institutions than Crane, Norris, Lewis, Dreiser,
or even more avowedly radical writers like Sinclair and London had
attempted in a single project. In so doing, the trilogy exposed the fragmentation of unitary imagined nationality that De Forest had wishfully posited both by anatomizing the nation's widening economic and
ethnic divisions and by aggravating this diagnosis stylistically, through
its dispersion of focus and its mutually dissonant structural components.

Even before the rollout of volume one, however, a still more audacious challenge to the traditional realist template had already appeared,
by a writer whose metamorphosis from traditional realism to experimental modernism had been far more dramatic. This challenge was
Gertrude Stein's *The Making of Americans,* begun shortly after 1900,
completed by 1911, but published only in excerpts before 1925. When
Harcourt issued an abridgment in the 1930s, the prominent New York
publishing house took a gamble it came to regret that its success with
Stein's *Autobiography of Alice B. Toklas* (1933) might help create a market
for the masterpiece of one of the most celebrated and influential American literary modernists. (Harcourt had already snapped up the second
volume of Dos Passos's trilogy, which sold better, but not so well as
hoped.)[44] Stein started out intending to write a "history of a family's
progress"[45]—the subtitle of the final book—built around such familiar
motifs as the sagas of immigrant upward mobility and of marriage
across the east-west divide. The first draft shows a distant cousinship to
the likes of Thomas Mann's *Buddenbrooks* (1901) and John Galsworthy's
Forsyte Saga (1906–1921). The narrator even makes Howellsian noises
about rebutting conventional highbrow Euro-American disdain for
American "bourgeois life" as "sordid material uninspiring": "I am strong
to declare even here in the heart of individualistic America that a material middle class with its straightened [*sic*] bond of family is the one thing
always healthy, human, vital and from which has always sprung the best
the world can know."[46] But one immediately senses the mocking undertone of that "straightened" (whether or not Stein actually meant "strait-
ened" instead), senses the deliberately clichéd packaging of American
individualism and the iconic middle-class family saga.

Stein continued to build on this satirical view of the national generic,
but in a style increasingly at odds with the more conventional realism
that was to make Lewis the first U.S. Nobel laureate in literature. In *The
Making of Americans,* the original realist investment in tracking specific
persons, relations, events, and places in cultural context—ambivalent
from the start—gets displaced by the vision of a comprehensive typol-
ogy of human character that would deliver "sometime" "a complete
history of each one" via "descriptions of every kind of way every one
can be a kind of men and women." This grand design of an encyclopedic cartography of the possible forms of personhood is mainly played
out not at the level of representing nationally typic mores and mind-sets

as much as in narratorial generalizations about the social and inner life of the bourgeoisie. On the other hand, this aspiration, in turn, is shown as being retarded if not forever balked by U.S.-style standardization that de facto threatens to suppress individuation to the vanishing point: "vital singularity is as yet an unknown product with us"; "there is no place in an adolescent world for anything eccentric like us."[47] So in the long run, the aspiration to deliver a magisterial anatomy of American-ness and a transnational summa of middle-class social psychology re-main tied together, even as they pull against each other.

Stein registers the challenge of the deceptively transparent opacity of social surfaces as barriers to penetration to inner personhood in a linguistically sparse, abstrusely vatic, and endlessly self-adjusting nar-rative voice that becomes her characteristic mature style. Hence the logic of the present progressive *Making*. The quest for full disclosure of "bottom natures," whether of persons generally or of a single person's interiority (of David Hersland, who becomes the central figure),[48] is pursued through a rhetoric of semi-incremental repetition that stylisti-cally performs the sense of microdiscovery and perplexity such a quest inherently entails. ("Sometimes it takes many years of knowing some one before the repeating that is that one gets to be a steady sounding to the hearing of one who has it as a natural being to love repeating that slowly comes out from every one.")[49] The impossibility of holding 925 pages of such process writing in mind becomes clear after the first fifty. Critic Sianne Ngai astutely calls the effect produced by Steinian style "stuplimity": a "concatenation of boredom and astonishment"—also stressing, however, the impact of her avant-garde aesthetics of reitera-tion in poetry, prose, and visual media to this day, not least as a way of capturing the unfathomable multitudinousness of semi-interchangeable personhood in contemporary mass society, American or otherwise. For every critical dismissal, several have praised *Making* as a monumental linguistic and philosophic feat. What's unmistakably clear is *Making*'s explosion of realist narration from within, its "slow murder of the Vic-torian novel."[50]

Stein insisted that her novel was about "an essentially American thing," that it was "strictly American to conceive a space that is filled with moving."[51] Had she cared, she could have enlisted Walt Whitman's poetic catalogs as supporting evidence of the Americanness of her semi-reiterative process discourse and her "modular" construction of American humanity as unique yet interchangeable. But Stein's own thrust was clearly more satirical than celebratory. Critic George Knox considered *The Making of Americans* an ultimate dismantling of the whole GAN aspiration, a "caricature" of its hubris, "the effort to create a monumental national 'fiction' out of the prescriptive stuff of theory about a particular culture." Stein herself might have preferred Suzan Mizruchi's more empathetic summation, that the "national mind" in this novel "comes alive through cliché, parable, all the little stories that form the mental tissue of American life," which is to say American "ideology."[52] Whatever spin you give it, though, Stein's undoing of traditional realism, far more drastic than Dos Passos's, speaks for itself. Knox rightly linked *The Making of Americans* to the GAN parody literature that had begun to spring up in the 1920s, not to mention the insouciant self-parody of the physical fitness guru Bernarr Macfadden's short-lived *Great American Novel Magazine* (1929), which reprinted Rex Beach's Jack-Londonesque potboiler epic of Alaska, *The Silver Horde*, as its second issue.[53]

To spot a Great American Novel parody, look for the GAN mantra in the title. I've so far discovered six: *The Great American Novel* (1923), an antinovel by the poet William Carlos Williams, one of whose pseudo-protagonists is an automobile; *He Done Her Wrong: The Great American Novel and Not a Word in It—No Music Too* (1930), a cleverly drawn comic book novel by Milt Gross; Clyde Brion Davis's *"The Great American Novel—"* (1938), James Fritzhand's *Son of the Great American Novel* (1971), Philip Roth's *The Great American Novel* (1973), and Richard Clinton's *The Great American Novel* (1981). Williams's work has most significance for U.S. literary history overall, not just as a "first"—and by a leading American modernist to boot—but also because its self-consciously offbeat reflection on the challenge for U.S. settler culture of creating nationness in a world of words resonates with his *In the American Grain* (1925), next to D. H. Lawrence's *Studies in American Literature* (1923) the most seminal critical manifesto of the decade for later American studies. But Davis's *"The Great American Novel—"* gives a better flavor of the stereotypes that had accrued around the GAN idea by the 1920s and 1930s.

"The Great American Novel—" is the diary of a hapless imaginary journalist from Buffalo named Homer Zigler, who aspires to write the GAN but never gets it off the drawing board. But he does at least outline the magnum opus. The first sketch he calls "Restless Dynasty." The plot goes like this. A young farmer migrates with his bride after the

War of 1812 from the Adirondacks to Ohio. His oldest son moves further west to Missouri, producing one lococentric lad who becomes a small manufacturer and another who joins the California gold rush. Their progeny fight on opposite sides of the Civil War, and the next generation after that become adversaries in industrial warfare between capitalist titans in the late nineteenth century. The two subclan leaders, by now so dispersed that they've never met, get dramatically reconciled when the president of the United States arranges a summit meeting between them in order to save the national economy from being devastated by the feud. Fortunately they fall in love at first sight and get married instead of destroying the country. (Yes, the cousins conveniently happen to be of different sexes.)

Later on, Homer revises this scenario and retitles it "Brutal Dynasty," but I'll omit the details.

The scenario is a mélange of clichés. But that's precisely what makes it notable, so many stock ingredients thrown together: the great social upheavals of U.S. nineteenth-century history (westward expansion, North-South conflict, industrial emergence) told from the northern European settler perspective that still dominated public culture; local particularism, geographical mobility, and the image of family as national microcosm. Virtually all are foreshadowed in *Uncle Tom's Cabin*. It too builds its cultural geography around the history of the Yankee diaspora; it too constructs a multigenerational family history (that of the St. Clare family) as a kind of national microcosm, within which clashing attitudes toward slavery are played out; it too combines mobility with particularism; and even as it focuses chiefly on the second of the three great upheavals it draws on the other two in order to raise its social stakes.

By the time of *"The Great American Novel—,"* *Uncle Tom's Cabin* had long since fallen into the limbo where it languished from the 1910s through the 1970s, as a text belonging more to sociology than to literature, flawed by aesthetic crudity and racial caricature.[54] But as Davis would also have been well aware, the history of slavery, the Civil War, the North-South two-cultures clash, and its postbellum legacy remained hot literary topics—as indeed they still do. Two such literary blockbusters of very different kinds had appeared just two years before. Margaret Mitchell's *Gone with the Wind* was already on its way to outselling all previous American novels and William Faulkner's *Absalom, Absalom!*, never nearly so popular, is now critically acclaimed as one of the high points of American fiction. Their concurrence (see Chapter 9 for the many points of intersection between them) with Davis's sendup suggests a more complicated relation between GAN parody and aspiration than might be supposed. Far from a simple discreditation of serious attempts to chart major national conflicts and story lines, *"The Great American Novel—"* testifies to the durability of the aspiration to put national experience between fictional covers and to the durability of the story lines it parodies. It's additionally notable that the author's son, David Brion Davis, went on to become one of his generation's foremost historians of slavery and abolitionism.

The role of GAN parodies, then, has been symbiotic as well as dismissive. They presume enough continuing interest in the GAN game to command a readership for spoofing its chronic hazards—you bite off more than you can chew, you succumb to overblown stagy melodrama, and so forth.* As such, they have also helped to keep the game alive even as they caution against taking it too seriously.

Such was not, however, the view of the increasingly professionalized and sophisticated critical establishment of the interwar period, as "American literature" began to establish itself as a "field" within university English departments and as the "New Criticism"—intensive close reading of aesthetic texts—began to take hold among academic literature scholars and freelance critics. So far as the subject of the Great American Novel was concerned, the burgeoning tribes of professionals cast their lot with the parodists, not the aspirants. During the middle third of the twentieth century, the propensity of academic literary critics and historians to dismiss the GAN as the symptom of a quaint bygone episode of cultural history became pandemic. To them the GAN seemed always to have been "more nearly a shibboleth than a critical concept" and bracketed it as a late Victorian mannerism, running its course within "the two decades after the Civil War" or "the trying years

---

* The symbiosis between parodic and serious authorial engagement with the dream of the GAN still continues. Lynne Tillman's 1992 *Cast in Doubt* centers on a more sympathetically rendered Zigleresque figure who dreams of completing his unfinished *Household Gods,* the chief inspiration behind which is none other than Gertrude Stein's *Making of Americans.* Tillman's gentle satire seems an augury of her more intellectually ambitious *American Genius* (2005), rather as Roth's more bumptious satirical *Great American Novel* anticipates his much high higher-stakes American trilogy (see Chapter 6).

between 1870 and 1900."[55] It was an academic literary historian who first—in the late 1880s—had dismissed critical debate as to whether the GAN would be ever written as "an unimportant question," and another who published in 1935 the first and still-most-cited among various scholarly articles that followed over the next quarter century, declaring the GAN a "curious" long-dead phenomenon of "the last half of the nineteenth-century."[56]

Clearly this latter critic—better known for his compendious history of nineteenth-century American sentimental fiction no less dismissive of it as obsolescent kitsch[57]—was not thinking of Dos Passos's epic trilogy, whose final volume was yet to appear, or of the infinitely ambitious Thomas Wolfe, much less of the survival of the GAN aspiration in Theodore Dreiser's *American Tragedy* and F. Scott Fitzgerald's *The Great Gatsby* (on which more in Chapter 5). Still less would he have been prepared for the appearance a decade later of one of the best-documented cases of GAN aspiration on record, Ross Lockridge Jr.'s *Raintree County* (1948), a boundlessly ambitious but much more traditional novel than *The Making of Americans* and *U.S.A.*, that fused old-style realism, Joycean stream-of-consciousness, historico-cinematic panorama à la Dos Passos, and Wolfeian orotundity.*

Raintree uses a day in the life of a nineteenth-century Indiana schoolteacher that also happens to be the town's semicentennial to connect its protagonist's life history with U.S. social history at large during the epoch that Davis's Homer Zigler planned to cover in "Restless/Brutal Dynasty." The hero embarks on the eve of the Civil War on a disastrous marriage to a southern woman who destroys herself with guilt because she suspects she's part black, whereupon he enlists as a Union infantryman. A number of reviewers immediately recognized *Raintree* as a bid for the GAN, following—in more qualified tones—the publisher's claim that "this is the novel in which Americans will find themselves." Lockridge thought the same. Indeed his aspirations were truly monumental:

---

* Originally published by Houghton Mifflin, *Raintree* was reissued as a Penguin paperback in 1994, heralded as "the great American novel of Love, Tragedy, and Heroic Vision" (front cover), with the back cover displaying this 1992 pronouncement by Larry Swindell: "No myth is more imposing than the Great American Novel; but if it is truly unattainable, I believe that Ross Lockridge made a closer approach than any other writer has, before or since." For biographical background, see Larry Lockridge (Ross's son, himself a literature scholar), *Shade of the Raintree* (New York: Viking, 1994).

to "do for the American Culture" what "Plato's *Republic* did for . . . Greek Culture, [Thomas Mann's] *The Magic Mountain* for disintegrating and warring European cultures, [and] *Ulysses* for the modern obsession with supranational and subliminal areas of human behavior and culture."[58] Houghton Mifflin's promotional campaign helped place *Raintree* as a Book-of-the-Month Club main selection and win a six-figure contract from MGM for a film starring Montgomery Clift. In short, the publishers backed *Raintree* to the hilt as a GAN, despite the fact that they, the club, and MGM all believed the manuscript needed much pruning. This Lockridge grudgingly did, although it felt like amputation and may have contributed to his slide into depression and suicide soon after. What got trimmed most, significantly, was the novel's modernist side, its stream-of-consciousness interior monologues, resulting in a more traditionally "realist" product—and far larger sales, even at 1,066 pages, than *The Making of Americans* or *U.S.A.*

The *Raintree County* case demonstrates the persistence of the GAN as an aspiration for authors, publishers, and reviewers well beyond the point when the literary-critical and academic Americanist establishments pronounced its death. The boiling-down of the original *Raintree* further attests to the inertial force of panoramic-realist and U.S.-centric assumptions as to what a GAN should be and to the author's internalization of those norms to the point that his opus was amenable to reduction to several of the motifs Davis had parodied: for example, sectional and racial division in the Civil War era and beyond; chronicle as backdrop and backbone; personal odysseys as symptomatic of megatrends. These were conventions Dos Passos and Stein too had engaged but also bent or broken. For the GAN to regain credibility going forward, the stolidity of those default assumptions themselves would need to be questioned more aggressively. That indeed is what happened next. The surprising result was to revitalize the dream of the Great American Novel by redefining the standards for what deserved to count as "American fiction" in a way that the redefiners wrongly predicted would kill off the GAN for good.

2

Reborn from the Critical Ashes

There is an unthinkable gulf between us and America, and across the space we see, not our own folk signaling to us, but strangers, incomprehensible beings, simulacra perhaps of ourselves, but *other*, creatures of an other-world. . . . The present reality is a reality of untranslatable otherness, parallel to that which lay between St. Augustine and an orthodox senator in Rome of the same day. The oneness is historic only.

—D. H. LAWRENCE, "The Spirit of Place" (1918)

Actually, the novel might be having a great American moment. Right now.

—BRIAN STONEHILL, *Los Angeles Times* (1997)

D. H. LAWRENCE'S RIVETING HYPERBOLE was later dropped from the opening essay of his *Studies in Classic American Literature* (1923), the first modern manifesto of Anglo-American literary difference, which strongly influenced American literature studies as the field came into its own.[1] But that emergence happened only later. Lawrence's lingering condescension toward those post-Puritan saints in the outback of imperial culture mirrored the national intelligentsia's lingering self-doubts as to whether the United States had yet achieved a literary track record worthy of the name. As a summation of foreign consensus at that time, Pascale Casanova's claim that "American literary space" was still on "the far periphery" of the cultural map as late as the 1930s is amnesiac (What about Balzac's admiration for Cooper? Poe's impact on Baudelaire, Mallarmé, Valery? Hawthorne's on George Eliot?)—yet also revealing.[2] Although the United States was now a major player on the world stage, its literati were still seen, and saw themselves, as laggards. The dream of the GAN was still looking a lot like compensatory fantasy.

This situation was soon to change, however. Between the 1930s and the early 1960s, seven Americans won Nobel Prizes for literature as against zero through the 1920s, five of them novelists.* The surge of literary migrants to European cultural centers in the 1920s subsided with the Depression and was more than matched by the migration to the United States with the rise of the Third Reich of European artists and intellectuals, who helped strengthen New York's claim to have become the Western world's leading cultural center and helped transform the University of Chicago and other U.S. universities and colleges into world-class institutions.[3] One might suppose, and most reputable critics did, that American literature's coming of age both in the world's eyes and in its own ought to have spelled doom for the GAN, since American fiction no longer needed "to call attention to itself with nationalistic labels," as one critic put it.[4] But the long-run result was quite different.

Critical Professionalism and Paradigm Change

As the field of American literature professionalized during the second quarter of the twentieth century, the dream of the Great American Novel came under fire sooner than the realist aesthetics on which it was generally thought to depend. Following the lead of Vernon L. Parrington's monumental *Main Currents in American Life* (1926–1929), which saw the "spirit of sober realism" as the nation's proper intellectual future, surveys of U.S. fiction's history during the 1930s and 1940s tended to agree that realism was "the dominant line taken by American fiction in the twentieth century."[5] However defined, "realism" marked American fiction's coming of age. One 1930s textbook history rated Wharton "the foremost living American novelist." Another saw Dreiser as "the chief spokesman for the realistic novel" and *An American Tragedy* (1925) as "by any standard . . . the greatest and most powerful novel yet written by any American." Still another declared that "Dos Passos alone worked in a vast and various field—picturing a society in the whole, much as Balzac had done."[6]

By the 1950s, this consensus had evaporated. Even Dos Passos, who as we saw in Chapter 1 had already started to dismantle traditional realism, was now faulted for dramatizing "social symptoms rather than lives" and failing "to preserve the integrity of personal experience."[7]

* Sinclair Lewis (1930), Eugene O'Neill (1936), Pearl Buck (1938), T. S. Eliot (1948), William Faulkner (1949), Ernest Hemingway (1954), and John Steinbeck (1962).

The groundwork had been laid for the counterposition that prevailed for the next quarter century: that "romance," not "realism," was the mark of U.S. fictional distinctiveness—a view that Lawrence's brilliantly erratic reading of American literature as the half-disciplined expression of restive fugitives unleashed on the wilderness foresaw and helped bring about. Lawrence's leading American admirer, Leslie Fiedler, the new establishment's most flamboyant critic, looked about him and beheld a "depopulated pantheon." "Who can think of Dos Passos and Steinbeck without a twinge of shame for dead enthusiasms?" Dreiser's "merits seem irrelevant to our current situation." For "the contemporary American author no longer believes that a work of art can be judged primarily by its accuracy in reproducing ordinary speech or rendering literally the horrors of the Chicago slums; for us, the reality, the value, of a work of art lies in its symbolic depth and resonance, not in the exhaustiveness of its data."[8]

The history of "the American novel" through 1940 was accordingly winnowed down to selected masterworks by a few practitioners: Hawthorne, Melville, Twain, James, Hemingway, Fitzgerald, Faulkner, and a handful of others. It was the single most drastic realignment of U.S. fiction's historical landscape ever. By contrast, the next major shakeup was more gradual despite being more divisive: the "canon wars" of the 1970s and after, which ushered in today's unprecedented reexpansion of the scope of what was seen to count as significant American literature but left unresolved the question of whether the idea of "a" national canon still made sense for a literature increasingly seen as fissiparous, polyvocal, multiethnic, transnational. That shift unfolded, however, in a more gradual and incremental way, in waves of rediscovery of neglected works by women, African American, Native, Latino/a, and Asian American writers and, as these took form, with reference to an increasingly deterritorialized conception of "the American" itself in recognition of its broader transatlantic, transpacific, and hemispheric origins and cross-border affiliations.*

---

* Specialists will notice that this bare-bones account omits mention of the critical theory "revolution" of the 1960s and 1970s, of which structuralism and post-structuralism were the defining phases. Without doubt it has had a lasting impact on U.S. fiction studies. But until it montaged by turns with critical historicism and cultural studies in the 1980s and 1990s, to the extent that it engaged primary literature, such theory-oriented work

The midcentury American-fiction-as-romance paradigm was anticipated by F. O. Matthiessen's field-defining *American Renaissance* (1941), which credited U.S. literary emergence during the mid-nineteenth century to the work of five giants: Emerson, Thoreau, Hawthorne, Melville, and Whitman. The romance hypothesis was broached more directly in Lionel Trilling's *The Liberal Imagination* (1950), perhaps the all-time best-selling book of literary criticism by an American academic. It was spelled out over the next decade in a series of books more squarely devoted to American fiction than was Trilling's wide-ranging Arnoldian meditation on the interaction between art, culture, history, and ideas. Chief among them were Richard Chase's compact *The American Novel and Its Tradition* (1957), Fiedler's compendious *Love and Death in the American Novel* (1960), Daniel Hoffman's *Form and Fable in American Fiction* (1961), and Charles Feidelson's *Symbolism in American Literature* (1962). Specific emphases differed: Chase's was a genre study of what he took to be the characteristic Anglo-American difference in narrative form; Fiedler's was a sweeping psychohistorical interpretation that turned on American (male) writers' evasion of "mature" heteronormative sociality; Hoffman stressed American fiction's folkloric roots; Feidelson subtly unpacked the intricacies of literary craftsmanship and symbolic nuance. But they converged in their diagnosis of a distinctive continuity to American fiction centering on "adoption of techniques of planned derangement as a means of cracking open the certified structures of reality and turning loose its latent energies."[9]

The linkage of "Americanness" to "symbolic depth and resonance" could not have come at a more opportune moment for the coevolving fields of American literature and interdisciplinary American studies, both striving at this time to establish credibility, autonomy, and internal cohesion. The prestige of fictional modernism à la Joyce was at its height, with its subjective-experimental stylistic cast and aesthetics of difficulty, its predilection for the "mythical method," as T. S. Eliot called it in his 1923 review of *Ulysses*.[10] No longer did writers like Poe, Hawthorne,

---

tended more often than not to presuppose and reinforce the midcentury revisionists' conception of a highly selective canon. Obvious exemplars include the eminent Yale post-structuralists of the 1970s—Harold Bloom, Geoffrey Hartman, Paul de Man, and J. Hillis Miller—and Frankfurt School theorist Theodor Adorno.

and Melville, who seemed not to fit the template of Victorian realism from Austen through Hardy, need to be considered primitive. U.S. fiction now seemed ahead of the literary-historical curve rather than tied to a nineteenth-century model that European avant-gardes had long since left behind. "Classic" American fiction had anticipated the modernist revolution that expatriates like James, Stein, Pound, and Eliot had played a major part in achieving. All this corroborated what Stein never tired of saying, that the United States was the oldest nation because it was "the mother of the twentieth century," because of its antitraditional spirit of restless inchoate experimentalism. Stein also correlated American avant-gardism with its technomodernity, as Euro-modernist painters like Marcel Duchamp did as well, comparing the incantatory repetition of her prose to the Ford assembly line.[11] The realist-naturalist dispensation, then, had been a detour, except insofar as it could be redefined to suit the new template—as Twain, Crane, and Hemingway now were, and often Norris too and sometimes even Dreiser.

The heyday of the romance hypothesis was much shorter than that of the realist-naturalist dispensation. By the last quarter of the twentieth century the temptation to dismiss Trilling, Fiedler, and Chase had become as irresistible as Fiedler's dismissal of Dreiser and Dos Passos. The midcentury revisionists now stood indicted for having based their generalizations on what stood exposed by the 1980s if not before as a woefully inadequate slice of literary history through 1950: a handful of white male writers.[12] Frederick Douglass, Kate Chopin, Charles Chesnutt, W. E. B. Du Bois, Jean Toomer, Zora Neale Hurston, Richard Wright, Ralph Ellison, James Baldwin, and Toni Morrison had become standard American authors, soon to be joined by Catharine Maria Sedgwick, Harriet Jacobs, María Ruiz de Burton, Maxine Hong Kingston, N. Scott Momaday, Leslie Silko, Américo Paredes, Gloria Anzaldúa, and many others. Stowe, Jewett, and Willa Cather were recuperated after having been written off. The work of retrieval was accomplished by the convergence of an increasingly diverse literary marketplace in combination with an increasingly diverse cadre of leading-edge literary critics and academic specialists committed to a far more exhaustive re-reading of earlier literary history than had ever been undertaken. For academic critics, this process was intensified with the rise of 1960s feminism and civil rights agitation and by the felt need to deliver less dubiously selective versions of literary history to increasingly diverse student constituencies at a time of increasing challenge to white male Protestant cultural dominance at the national level.

The value set by the midcentury revisionists on exegesis of stylistic complexity and esoteric symbolism had a concentrated power, fascination, and teachability that continues to make "close reading" important to literary education to this day, and not just of accredited masterpieces. Yet overconcentration on the formal and thematic properties of the freestanding aesthetic text—the central project of what's still called the "New Criticism"—came to seem suspiciously cloistral, a retreat into academic glass bead games. That species of "professionalism" seemed in retrospect to correlate suspiciously with the downgrading of socially engaged realism and the political conservatism of many of the New Critics who advocated the rigorously intensive "close reading" that was their methodological hallmark. On the one hand, reenvisionment of the field of U.S. fiction as a cohort of masterfully intricate symbolic performances that could not be interpreted without initiation and hard work looked suspiciously like a defensive firewall designed to protect high culture against an emergent mass culture.[13] On the other hand, it created an "ideal order of eternal objects" that celebrated American art and civilization, consolidating the authority of American literature studies in the process,[14] and in a way conveniently marketable as an export commodity to showcase U.S. exceptionalism at the very moment when enthusiasm for American culture was starting to take off in a big way around the world in tandem with the nation's emergence from the ruins of the war as the leading superpower. From this standpoint, the momentum of U.S. literature studies of the period could be readily conceived in retrospect as part of the apparatus of postwar national aggrandizement, all the more so in light of government support from the 1940s onward for American studies initiatives at home and abroad.

Revisionists characteristically wind up oversimplifying their predecessors in order to make their case. So too with both the fomenters of the romance hypothesis and their later detractors. Trilling skewered the muddy cliché-ridden rhetoric of Dreiser's "realism," but by way of counterposition fell back on an equally nebulous conjuring term, "moral realism." Late twentieth-century critiques of "Cold War Criticism," in turn, rightly diagnosed the midcentury critical shift—and fiction's shift too—as tilting away from engagement with issues of social (in)justice toward a stylistic wavelength that was generally stand-offish if not downright hostile to political activism, even as its apotheosis of individualism as literary genius and as fictional theme seconded the era's penchant for moralizing about the virtues of American "freedom" as against socialist totalitarianism. Yet the earlier revisionists' actual political views were more heterogeneous than was often recognized.[15] The McCarthy era was also the dawn of the civil rights era; and the midcentury critics' commitment to freedom of individual expression was driven by politically conscious aversion to populist anti-Stalinism as well as to the socialist alternative. The 1950s can also be seen as a time when "the clogged arteries of official modern culture finally popped open,"[16] a time of unprecedented cross-pollination between "high," "folk," and "mass" culture of the kind displayed by Ellison's *Invisible Man* and Bellow's *Augie March,* and in the casting of the title figure of Nabokov's *Lolita,* once we extricate her from the prison house of narrator Humbert's urbanely defensive rhetorical cocoon. (*Lolita* was not just the romance with the English language that Nabokov called it, but also his handle-with-tweezers romance with American pop culture.) The enshrinement of late James and T. S. Eliot as high cultural icons overlapped with the rise of the Beats and with the turn of formerly high modernist/formalist poets like Robert Lowell to more open, accessible forms of expression. But this is not the place for extended rehashing of the degree to which midcentury American literature, Americanist criticism, and the revisionist romance hypothesis specifically can be explained as a byproduct of phobic aversion to mass culture and/or the pieties of Cold War liberalism. Our concern here is the bearing of the midcentury critical shakeup on the GAN as idea and aspiration.

The Dream of the Great American Novel Miraculously Survives Its Discreditation

Because the GAN was first framed as and continued long after to be deemed a realist project, it stood to reason that when realism became passé, "the perennially intriguing notion of the 'Great American Novel'" would be "replaced by interest in . . . the Romance Theory." And indeed its fomenters were convinced that the GAN was a misguided, amateurish notion that had long since outlived its usefulness if ever it had any.

For Trilling, it was "one of the dreams of a younger America" that demonstrated the impossible "burden of social requirement" traditionally placed on the novel, requiring it in effect "to give up, in the fulfillment of its assigned function, all that was unconscious and ambivalent and playful in itself." For Fiedler, it implied the meretricious "dream of an unlimited mass audience."[17]

Expatiating in 1972 in "Why They Aren't Writing the Great American Novel Anymore," Tom Wolfe cited Trilling's authority for pronouncing traditional social realism dead. "No novelist," Wolfe prophesied, "will be remembered as the novelist who captured the Sixties in America" à la Balzac or Thackeray because today "most serious American novelists would rather cut their wrists than be known as 'the secretary of American society' [Balzac's self-characterization], and not merely because of ideological considerations. With fable, myth and the sacred office to think about—who wants such a menial role?"[18]

Wolfe was being ironic here, of course. Far from wanting to dismiss Balzacian realism himself, his agenda was to demonstrate that "the new journalism"—a term he coined for an influential anthology of such work published soon after—was occupying the space the novelists had left vacant with their subjective, asocial turn. Journalism was destined to become the late twentieth century's cutting-edge narrative vanguard. It comes as no surprise to find Wolfe repeating pretty much the same charge against novelistic cloistralism in an unabashedly agenda-promoting manifesto of 1989 that proclaims his single-handed revival of documentary realism in his best-selling fast-paced novelistic anatomy of racial and especially class warfare in New York City, *The Bonfire of the Vanities* (1987).[19] He overshot the mark on both occasions. Traditional realism never did die out, not by a long shot, although the tide of modernist and postmodernist fashion put it on the defensive. That it thrives to this day is clear, to take just one case in point, from the career of Jonathan Franzen, whose two meticulously crafted novels of the present century, *The Corrections* (2001) and *Freedom* (2010), both family sagas aspiring to broader national stakes that center on paradigmatic midwestern middle-class couples and their progeny, were widely seen as GAN aspirants or contenders. *Freedom* put Franzen on the cover of *Time* on 23 August 2010, with the caption "Great American Novelist." Even more telling has been the post-postmodern turn by a number of consequential turn-of-the-twenty-first-century novelists toward fusion of experimental narrative techniques with recognizably traditional realist practice: Don DeLillo, Richard Powers, David Foster Wallace, William Vollmann, Ana Castillo, Colson Whitehead, and many others. So late twentieth-century fiction became considerably more complicated than the story of the rise to dominance of the antirealist experimentalism of John Hawkes, John Barth, Donald Barthelme, and Robert Coover. Indeed traditional realism even generated at least one serious candidate for the GAN during its supposed 1960s-through-1980s disappearance, John Updike's *Rabbit Angstrom* (1960–1990), on which more below.

In the long run, the short-lived romance hypothesis, as Wolfe's flourish about the "sacred office" backhandedly suggests, probably served more as a reanimator than a depressant for the GAN dream by hyperfocusing attention on select monumental works. The midcentury apostles of "symbolic depth and resonance" were dead-serious counterparts of the GAN parodists in their strenuous attempts to distinguish art fiction as intricate imaginative constructs from schlock tied to old-style chronicle narration. However much they disdained the seeming amateurishness of the GAN mantras of yore and their tainted association with middlebrow realism and middlebrow culture, their efforts to identify an elite canon of supernovelists and supertexts did not extinguish the dream but revived it under another name. The veteran man of letters Malcolm Cowley, a shrewd observer of the changing literary scene from the 1930s through the 1960s, tellingly claimed that the new establishment's masterpiece-intensive rehabilitation of classic American literature made it possible for the first time in history to believe that "the great American novel had indeed been written." Moreover he was certain which book had come out on top, going so far as to suggest that the "principal creative work of the last three decades in this country" wasn't any new artistic breakthrough but "the critical rediscovery and reinterpretation of Melville's *Moby-Dick* and its promotion, step by step, to the position of national epic."[20]

Not everyone, then or now, would go all the way with Cowley on this. But the three novels Leslie Fiedler placed at the top of the American fictional chain of being in *Love and Death in the American Novel*— Hawthorne's *The Scarlet Letter,* Melville's *Moby-Dick,* and Twain's *Huckleberry Finn*—which happened to be three of the four pre-1900 novels most admired by high school and college teachers in the most extensive poll of the mid-1920s[21]—have remained among the most often named pre-1920s fictions in turn-of-the-twenty-first-century polls, both by middlebrow/high middlebrow literary establishment groups like the American Booksellers Association and National Books Circle, whose members were canvassed for a 2007 WNET (PBS) survey (*Huckleberry Finn, Moby-Dick,* and *The Scarlet Letter* rank 1, 3, and 4, with *The Great Gatsby* and *Invisible Man* 2 and 5), and by such freelance bloggers as Christopher Schmitz of Rocky River, Ohio, whose top twenty "Contenders for Great American Novel" (with *Huckleberry Finn, Moby-Dick,* and *The Scarlet Letter* ranked 1, 2, 3) were posted at Amazon.com from November 2003 through this writing (2013).[22]

Such continuities extend only so far, and they are far from self-interpreting. The teachers of 1925 and the Ohio blogger both put Cooper's *The Last of the Mohicans* and Stowe's *Uncle Tom's Cabin* in fourth and fifth place among most plausible pre-1900 contenders, whereas the most Fiedler would concede in 1960 was that *Uncle Tom's Cabin* was "the greatest of all novels of sentimental protest" and that Cooper's frontier romances made him the first "truly American writer" as the pioneer author of "boys' books"—ammunition for Fiedler's broader claim that classic American fiction was essentially boys' fiction. He shuddered to think that *The Last of the Mohicans* might be "the most widely read of American novels" worldwide.[23] He later granted that *Uncle Tom's Cabin* had inaugurated the middlebrow tradition of blockbuster "inadvertent epic," which he proceeded to trace with reluctant wonder through D. W. Griffiths's *Birth of a Nation* and the racist fiction of Thomas Dixon on which it was based to *Gone with the Wind* and (in a final post-1960s turn of the screw) the best-selling multigenerational Afro-diasporic chronicle and TV series *Roots* (1976), by the African American journalist Alex Haley. But Fiedler never got past the sense that the emotionally overheated Stowe was a "problematical" figure as "a contender for inclusion in [the] misogynist canon" of American fictional masters from Washington Irving to Saul Bellow.[24] Of all the midcentury revisionists he took by far the greatest interest in popular culture, but even he felt impelled to draw a bright line between the rightful canon and the popular substrate. No such scruples restrained the Ohio blogger, who praised *Uncle Tom's Cabin* as a "novel that wrung tears and actually made a difference," and appealed to mass culture retakes for his endorsement of *Mohicans* ("Remade decades later as 'Dances with Wolves.' M*A*S*H also tipped its hat.")[25]

How then to evaluate the net effect on later musings about the GAN that resulted from the midcentury push for a more intellectually high-powered account of U.S. fictional distinctiveness centered on select masterpieces of "romance"? Perhaps its most relevant long-run influence was to remove the greatest stumbling block in the way of taking the idea of the Great American Novel seriously after the tastemakers had pronounced realism obsolete and with it the widespread presumption— reinforced by Dos Passos's *U.S.A.*, Lockridge's *Raintree County,* Stein's *The Making of Americans,* and Homer Zigler's script for "Restless/Brutal Dynasty" in their very different ways—that the narrative form of the GAN must replicate the nation's vast, sprawling, semichaotic social textures and landscapes from the macro to the minute. As the critic Alfred Kazin mused in a dismissive review of an overstuffed chronicle of the 1950s, the GAN had "never in itself been a bad tradition." The problem was that obsession with "documentation for its own sake" had "turned the 'great American novel' into the great American bore."[26] Midcentury revisionism set forth an alternative model of "greatness" that despite its own fall from favor a few decades later helped ensure, long after the romance hypothesis was discredited as vehemently as its fomenters had discredited the dream of the GAN, that the field of eligibles would permanently be opened to a wider range of stylistic registers than De Forest, James, and Howells had envisaged. Not that caveats like Kazin's ever put a serious brake on authorial hankering to create sprawling megafictions, as Chapter 13 will show. Nor, for that matter, did the mid-twentieth-century revisionists, either. The book held up by Malcolm Cowley as the Great American Novel they rediscovered is a prime example: *Moby-Dick.*

Relatedly, the aesthetics of difficulty didn't fade away any more than fictional realism did. What did erode, much more as a result of broad cultural history trend lines than of the pronouncements of literary critics and theorists, was the firmness of the high culture versus mass culture distinction among critics, creative writers, and a sizeable though indeterminate number of literature consumers alike. Modernism had established its avant-garde status on the basis of delivering "smart" serious fiction as against "stupid" middlebrow.[27] But U.S. novelists of the second half of the twentieth century acclaimed as possible GAN candidates often seem to have had it both ways, achieving both idiosyncratic complexity of style and architecture and robust market appeal. Ellison, Bellow, and Morrison are cases in point. Neither extreme length nor extreme pursuit of the aesthetics of difficulty has been a bar to consideration, either. For an appreciable number of turn-of-the-twenty-first-century readers, Thomas Pynchon's *Gravity's Rainbow* (1973) or David Foster Wallace's *Infinite Jest* (1996) are the GANs of our day, both of them far longer and more intricately arcane than anything by Melville or James or Faulkner at their most ambitious.

Midcentury revisionism did also help effect durable changes in reputation, both up and down. Two striking cases of the first were the Faulkner and Fitzgerald revivals. By the third quarter of the century Faulkner was enthroned as the preeminent U.S. fictional modernist and *The Great Gatsby* had become a curricular staple for colleges and high schools, a byword in American pop lore, and a perennial GAN nominee. It made the American Booksellers/National Book Circle's top five and was ranked number two next to Joyce's *Ulysses* in the Modern Library Board's 1998 designation of the top twentieth-century novels. Conversely, the only novels in the realist-naturalist tradition to make it into the top twenty—Steinbeck's *Grapes of Wrath*, Dreiser's *American Tragedy*, and Richard Wright's *Native Son*—trailed *Lolita*, Faulkner's *The Sound and the Fury*, and Joseph Heller's *Catch-22*. Here too the midcentury shakeout had long-term results.[28]

But top-down critical authority extended only so far. In the Modern Library Board rankings, Henry James, the American novelist the revisionists tried hardest to promote—and for literature specialists succeeded—fared less well than Dreiser and Dos Passos, at twenty-sixth (for *The Wings of the Dove*). So the inertial force of cultural capital and sanctioned critical authority often but by no means always influenced public taste. Pretty much the same can be said of the freelance turn-of-the-twenty-first-century blogosphere, as for the dozens who contributed to the 1897 *San Francisco Examiner* forum on the GAN. The first two (of six) criteria for the GAN that kicked off a 2006 post by one Tyler Cowen offers a rough-and-ready snapshot of this paradoxical situation: "1. It must reward successive rereadings and get better each time. 2. It must be canonical and grip the imagination."[29] His choice of *Moby-Dick* set the tone for a number of others to weigh in with similar classics (e.g., *Huckleberry Finn*, *The Great Gatsby*, Faulkner's *The Sound and the Fury* and *As I Lay Dying*), as well as more recent novels presumed canonical: Salinger's *Catcher in the Rye* (also number 12 for Schmitz and among the WNET survey's top ten), Harper Lee's *To Kill a Mockingbird* and Joseph Heller's *Catch-22* (both also in WNET's top ten), and Cormac McCarthy's *Blood Meridian* (number 17 for Schmitz). Yet that didn't stop respondents from dismissing just about every "approved" choice as dull or overblown, complaining about having been assigned them in school, and suggesting unlikely alternatives like Orson Scott Card's sci-fi melodrama *Ender's Game*.

Turn-of-the-twenty-first-century bloggers who have weighed in about the GAN on Amazon.com and scores of other websites probably number in the low ten thousands at most and surely don't comprise a random slice of humanity. The party is wide open, but in order to join it you need technological literacy and access, a secondary if not a college education, considerable spontaneous literary interest, and enough free time. No doubt freelance journalists, critics, and practicing or aspirant creative writers make up a disproportionate percentage of the voices you're hearing in this section. My guess is that the group as a whole is younger and more intellectually venturesome and hip than the average book club subscriber, but more or less in the same socioeconomic bracket or at least headed that way.

Their collective testimony seems partly, but not altogether, to bear out David Shumway's prediction toward the end of his 1994 history of American literature as an academic discipline, that despite multiple challenges to the pre-1970s map of U.S. literary history as biased against writing by women and nonwhite writers, and despite increasing critical insistence that U.S. literary culture could only be understood transnationally—through its interdependencies with other American hemispheric, "Atlantic world" and "Pacific" cultures—nonetheless "there will remain a core canon that will include most of the authors who were the focus of the discipline of the 1950s and 1960s."[30] Shumway was right that academic American literature studies has developed itself during the past half-century so as to underestimate, indeed almost deliberately to refuse to grant, its status as a self-perpetuating industry of knowledge production with a strong investment in canonical authors. Since its inception in 1965, *American Literary Scholarship*, the annual review of notable scholarship in the field (sponsored by the American

Literature Group of the Modern Language Association of America), has always allocated a large fraction of space (about 35 percent) to a dozen or so major mid-nineteenth- to mid-twentieth-century great white writers, with Hawthorne, Melville, Twain, and Faulkner the only novelists granted whole chapters during the entire run.[31] Yet from the standpoint of reader reception outside the professoriate, the situation looks rather different.

Neither in late nineteenth-century contributor's columns nor in contemporary blogs do GAN postings—fortunately—make for self-perpetuating institutionalization. Yes, they revolve to a considerable extent around familiar, approved masters and masterworks, but the ground rules are open, with no finite number of pieces or players. They allow for unpredictable and spontaneous movements, with complete freedom to topple icons if you wish. Except for certain online e-journals, they aren't patrolled as academic criticism is. You don't need a PhD; there's little peer review. In academic work "critical originality" is required, but regulated. In the GAN blogosphere it's equally OK to write unoriginally, to second others' opinions, or to be fractiously irreverent, especially when it comes to some book you were taught to admire but don't. To some extent, grassroots GAN cyber-commentary feels like a discourse of semiliberation from one's former teachers, although today this distinction looks less firm than it did at the start of the millennium because the professors themselves are increasingly going online and e-journals that feature literary criticism by academics have been burgeoning.

The freedom and elasticity of the cyber-marketplace of ideas and pontifications about the GAN don't necessarily make it interesting—a little surfing goes a long way—but it does guarantee a certain kind of openness. It encourages receptiveness to the possibility of some recent or future work of surprising power, to the lure of a book that specialists tend either to ignore or bracket as second rank, like Jack Kerouac's *On the Road* or Harper Lee's *To Kill a Mockingbird,* or to some heterodox notion of what Americanness is or ought to be. Are you a skeptic who doubts if the GAN has been written, or, if it has or nearly has, whether there's likely to be a rival? Do you believe it's not a mere myth, but it just hasn't happened yet? Are you one of those who's convinced that Michael Chabon's *The Amazing Adventures of Kavalier and Clay* (2000) or Joy Williams's *The Quick and the Dead* (2000) or Junot Diaz's *The Brief*

Wondrous Life of Oscar Wao (2007) is a strong contender for the GAN of the new century? Or Abraham Verghese's *Cutting for Stone* (2009)? Among oldies, do you favor Salinger's *Catcher in the Rye* or even *Raintree County* to *Gatsby*? Does Lynne Tillman's *American Genius* fashion a slyly ironized GAN around "the national disease" of "sensitivity"? You can find all this and much, much more online; and the best of it, like British cultural critic Kasia Boddy's astute analysis of Tillman, is very good indeed.[32]

Chaos Configured? Morrison and Updike as Great American Novelists

The lively cyber-dialogue attests that the dream of the Great American Novel remains an ongoing keen interest for twenty-first-century readers and writers—and perhaps also, as literary and media critic Brian Stonehill suggested, that "the novel might be having a great American moment. Right now." But so what? That doesn't in itself prove the underlying idea of the GAN is worth serious attention. It remains to be seen what GAN-oriented thinking can tell us about how the novels in question work, about national culture generally, about novels as carriers or definers of cultural nationality, and about what value to set on all that—whether it's cultural asset or cultural baggage. It will take the rest of this book to address these matters fully, and I'll undertake only a preliminary mini-reconnaissance here, via the unlikely dyad of John Updike and Toni Morrison.

At first sight, they make a very odd couple, apart from both having middle-states small-industrial-city roots, Ivy League degrees, and high profiles both as novelists and as critics. Updike was the late twentieth century's most prominent voice and exemplar on behalf of the Howellsian tradition of descriptivist middle-class realism, to which, unlike such earlier limit-bumping Howellsians as Sinclair Lewis, he declared loyal allegiance. ("It is, after all, the triumph of American life that so much of it should be middling. Howells' agenda remains our agenda—for the American writer to live in America and to mirror it in writing.")[33] Morrison, arguably the most illustrious U.S. novelist at the turn of the twenty-first century, would seem to stand squarely against Updike as the leading laureate of African American experience, no less committed to a "black" perspective ("When I say 'people,' that's what I mean").[34] Stylistically, Morrison breaks from realism, preferring to write about "people who aren't representative" and suffusing her imagined worlds with a sense of the uncanny, the supernatural, the mythic in ways that have prompted Morrison-Faulkner comparisons that type her as the great late twentieth-century American novelist as Faulkner was for high modernism.[35] Yet both Morrison's *Beloved* (1987) and John Updike's *Rabbit Angstrom*—the tetralogy of *Rabbit, Run* (1960), *Rabbit Redux* (1971), *Rabbit Is Rich* (1981), and *Rabbit at Rest* (1990)[36]—have been urged as candidates for the GAN.

Updike's death in 2009 elicited a spate of obituaries with testimonials to that effect by fellow writers—a marked contrast to those a few years before for Norman Mailer ("Updike's remote Jewish other," the British novelist Ian McEwan called him).[37] The third and fourth Rabbit novels won Pulitzer prizes. For its part, *Beloved* was the first novel by an African American to win a Pulitzer and crucial to Morrison's Nobel Prize award a half-dozen years later. The Pulitzer was controverted by an unprecedented lobbying effort led by African American writers and critics that was denounced in turn by the "organized cultural right";[38] but the novel's staying power has validated the choice. No U.S. novel of the last quarter of the twentieth century has been more extensively taught and critically discussed. It came as no surprise that *Beloved* was rated by a comfortable margin the best work of American fiction of the previous twenty-five years in a 2006 *New York Times* poll of sixty-one "prominent writers, critics and editors" (*Rabbit Angstrom* was one of four runners-up along with DeLillo's *Underworld,* Cormac McCarthy's *Blood Meridian,* and Philip Roth's *American Pastoral*),[39] although the poll predictably touched off another media dispute—high-profile polls always do—including insinuations that *Beloved* was merely an affirmative action choice. *Beloved* does seem to polarize readers more than *Rabbit Angstrom.* As of June 2013, *Rabbit Angstrom* was getting a 4.7-star rating from 40 Amazon.com respondents as against 3.8 stars from the 742 reviews for *Beloved.* But the two sets of posts reveal that the difference largely if not entirely reflects the captive audience factor—readers assigned *Beloved* in school.[40]

That despite sharply discrepant styles, imagined countries, and self-defined relation to middle American culture Morrison and Updike could both be cast as GAN contenders is one among many signs of the heterogeneity that the GAN idea has accrued over time. This is not to

say that the GAN is an infinitely stretchable concept. Some noteworthy parallels underlying the obvious contrasts between their work will
begin to explain. One has to do with career trajectory. Both writers
won critical acclaim quickly, but their rise to galactic status involved
gradual ascent from relatively modest-scale early projects to much more
ambitious ones, reminiscent of the Virgilian tradition of aspiring poets
working their way up from pastoral to epic.

Morrison's pilgrimage from her first novel, *The Bluest Eye* (1970),
through *Beloved,* her fifth, shows a strong preoccupation from the start
with the family as a central but deeply problematic unit and more specifically with how the injury parents inflict on children gets internalized by both. That pilgrimage also involved a reconception of those
issues over time so as to translate them into a more broad-reaching saga
of national proportions. In *Beloved,* the saga is positioned within the
same epoch of inter-American—and also transatlantic—anguish that
produced the first GAN contender, *Uncle Tom's Cabin,* in which dismem-
berment of the family is also the microcosmic arena in which the pathology of institutionalized slavery is most viciously played out, with
one of its two plotlines also featuring the escape of a desperate slave
mother northward across the river from Kentucky to Ohio.* What's
most obviously distinctive about *Beloved,* relative to *Uncle Tom's Cabin,* is
of course that American slavery, Civil War, and aftermath are retold
by a novelist who, herself the descendant of slaves, re-creates history
wholly through the eyes of the protagonist Sethe and her family. Most
nineteenth-century narratives by ex-slaves were as-told-to accounts
recorded by white scribes, and virtually all were published under white
surveillance with significant portions of their life experiences censored
out. But by the time *Beloved* appeared, the way had been prepared by
two decades of "neo-slave" fiction by African American authors—on

---

* Morrison's four previous novels could be read in retrospect as preparations for *Beloved.*
The backstory of African American migration from southern to northern cities and
towns is key to the Ohio-set *Bluest Eye* and *Sula. Song of Solomon* takes the narrative in
reverse, from Detroit back to Virginia (with a hint at African origins). *Tar Baby,* whose
base of operations is a Philadelphia grandee's estate on a small French Caribbean island,
explores the (im)possibility of its gentrified female African American protagonist's return to Afro-diasporic populist roots. A case could be made for any of Morrison's first
three novels as fictional achievements at least as distinguished as *Beloved* on their own
terms. But of all Morrison's ten novels to date, *Beloved* announces itself, as it were, as the
likeliest GAN candidate.

which more in Chapters 6 and 10—not to mention the intensive post–civil rights era recuperation of the history of American slavery and racism of which neo-slave narrative was a part. By the end of the twentieth century, the cultural margin had started to become the center for cutting-edge writers and critics far more dramatically even than during the run-up to the Civil War when *Uncle Tom's Cabin* appeared.

Yet early discussions of the Great American Novel idea, beginning with De Forest's commendation of Stowe, anticipate the possibility of work like *Beloved* even if they can't bring it into focus, in the sense that they recognize that the most crucial issue that needs to be faced in order for national fiction to come into being is the "margin" versus "center" problem. If the early versions of this conundrum were framed mainly as a question of region versus nation, during the past century it has been framed increasingly as a question of "minority" versus "mainstream" or "white middle class"—not that the territorial and ethnoracial domains can be surgically separated. Indeed, one of the principal story lines in the evolution of the dream of the GAN generally from inception to the present, as Parts III and IV confirm, has been the ethnicization or minoritization of the original GAN templates. The remarkable combination of force and subtlety with which *Beloved* negotiates that critical engagement with its significant white literary predecessors will be discussed in detail in Chapter 10.

Updike, to turn now to him, won early acclaim for his short stories, still often considered his strong suit. The first, and shortest, of the quartet that became *Rabbit Angstrom* was a one-shot project to which he returned fortuitously, by his own sayso, in order to provide his publisher with a promised new novel in lieu of another project he found himself unable to continue at the time. He had envisaged *Rabbit, Run* in relatively modest terms, as "a realistic demonstration of what happens when a young American family man goes on the road—the people left behind get hurt"—provoked partly by Kerouac's *On the Road.* The protagonist, Harry Angstrom, is a narcissistic oversexed former high school basketball player in his late twenties from a place modeled on Updike's southeastern Pennsylvania hometown who never lives up to—or lives down—his teenage stardom but repeatedly causes trouble and anguish for himself and everyone close to him by impulsively succumbing to hyperactive fantasies, vacillating between grudging domesticity and abortive breakout. It was sometime between the second and third Rabbit books, Updike recalled, he got the idea for "a single coherent volume, a mega-novel" that would correlate Rabbit's essentially redundant post-adolescent saga with the vicissitudes of American life from the 1950s through the 1980s.[41] Yet already in novel two, *Rabbit Redux,* he had got into the chronicle-novel groove he would sustain for the duration, tracing Angstrom family life through the generations, and elaborating *Rabbit, Run*'s occasional device of linking the protagonist's motions to the current of national and world events, using a Dos Passos-like leitmotif of newspaper and TV reportage as a recurrent undertone, with Rabbit listening off and on, now and again really trying to get his head around it all, and in the long run living out his life in a state of mental semi-awareness, defensively buffered from but also buffeted by perturbations in the social macrocosm.

At heart a patriotic, God-fearing conservative Republican, sexist and ethnocentric, Rabbit grows up in the Eisenhower era and goes out with Reagan and the Cold War. But he can jump the rails spectacularly when "reality" intrudes. The most dramatic instance, in *Rabbit Redux*—by far the strangest of the quartet, in line with the volatility of the 1960s itself—comes when he gets involved with a damaged-goods, lost-soul hippie half his age who invites an almost equally troubled parole-skipping African American Vietnam vet to bunk with Rabbit and his son for an extended stay when his wife is consorting with Rabbit's fellow salesman from the Toyota dealership her family owns and where he now works. Rabbit by turns denounces and joins the vortex of sex, drugs, and radical polemics that follows. Finally, outraged neighbors torch the house, missing Skeeter but incinerating Jill in a semireprise (first time water, fire next time) of *Rabbit, Run*'s most traumatic event, Janice Angstrom's accidental drowning of their infant daughter.

To dwell on this episode misrepresents what *Rabbit Angstrom* does best, however. Jill and Skeeter are creatures from another planet, although Skeeter is literally a local. Nuanced description of the workaday angst of making it solidly into middle-class white America and struggling to stay there is Updike's forte—ethnography of the precise social niches, the minute but galling frustrations, the tangled interactions of his middling muddlers. Of Howells it's been rightly said that "he understood that the tipping of a hat brim might betray an entire system of power." The same holds for Updike's rendition of Rabbit's world, where the photograph of the dead patriarch overlooks the family dinner table, "in a gold frame broader than his daughter and grandson got." The oscillating social capital of product brands, the nuances of locker room lingo, the bathroom decor of a "garrison colonial,"[42] the look of downscale houses where the tacky plaster birdbath in the yard balances off center, the self-destructive pleasure of binging on junk food (all itemized) despite your angina (minute warning signs also itemized), the embarrassments of middle-aging sexual underperformance—on these subjects Updike is commanding—to the point of surfeit, some have thought. In any case, descriptive plenitude, as in Howells and Sinclair Lewis, becomes a means of satirizing nondismissively Rabbit's enmeshment within middle-class commodity culture and local reverberations of national and world events. Presumably that's what Updike had in mind when he called Rabbit "a ticket to the America all around me."[43] That *Rabbit Angstrom* sometimes seems awash in inert data reflects Rabbit's inability to make sense of it. However hard he presses against his provincial limits, in the long run they contain and fashion him.

Viewed this way, Updike's project begins to look less like an antithesis to Morrison's and more like a reciprocal. The intractable mediocrity and impotence of Rabbit and his compeers register among other things the late twentieth-century decline of white Protestant middle America into just another ethnic group,[44] as Rabbit and his cronies grouse about blacks, immigrants, and other upstarts. Skeeter's intrusion, contrived as it is, is a barometer of this. When Skeeter bullies Rabbit into reading *The Life and Times of Frederick Douglass* out loud (the slave narrative part), in a transparently symbolic reversal of the master-slave relation, Rabbit really gets into it. "'Oh, you do make one lovely nigger,'" Skeeter "sings" back—which in fact is the role to which Rabbit is getting reduced in "real life" as his father-in-law's hireling, not just as Skeeter's pro tem sidekick in his own home.[45] This episode is also the most salient of the many scenes in which the tetralogy bears out Morrison's later insistence, and Ellison's before her, that white American literature has been profoundly influenced by the copresence of African Americans— usually banished to the subtexts, she stresses. That Rabbit would prefer not to have to deal with Skeeter in the first place, doesn't really want him around, is relieved to get rid of him, and fears his return makes him a textbook example of Morrison's reading of the white canon.

The subject of evasion/repression has been no less crucial to Morrison's fictional projects, and to none more so than *Beloved. Rabbit Angstrom* and *Beloved* also resonate here to the extent that both are narratives about coping strategies for managing traumatic pasts and threatening present realities. Rabbit's penchant for not facing past misdemeanors squarely is a kind of white middle-class equivalent of Sethe's survivalist struggle of "work[ing] hard to remember as close to nothing as was safe" (*B* 6). Again and again, Morrison described the writing of this novel as a process of overcoming resistance, not just of white deniers but also her own, to facing slavery's horrors. *Beloved* "is about something that the characters don't want to remember, I don't want to remember, black people don't want to remember, white people won't want to remember."[46] In both Morrison and Updike, family becomes the locus for dramatizing the enactment and the warping effects of the dynamic of repression versus the return of the repressed, and in both the example par excellence becomes a haunting of the narrative by the memory of the tiny daughter destroyed by the mother's filicide.

The analogy has its limits, of course. A drunken mother's negligence hardly equates to a desperate slave mother's infanticide. The death of baby Rebecca June Angstrom is an isolated casualty of domestic dysfunction that doesn't begin to assume the national, indeed world-historical, proportions of the lost Beloved as a symbol of African American victimization that stretches back across the Middle Passage. That is surely a key reason why Morrison's Great American Novel has attracted greater critical and public attention. Another might be the intensity factor itself. Perhaps Updike was every bit as committed as Morrison to making the horizon of his novelistic world stretch beyond what is comfortable for his characters to acknowledge, but the genial effortlessness by which he seems to do this makes for a considerably lower narrative temperature ("Angstrom" itself suggests the inconspicuous: an angstrom is .1 nanometer), whereas *Beloved* supercharges even its tiniest capillaries of detail, as when Sethe's daughter Denver, approaching Lady Jones's house for the first time in a dozen years, "was shocked to see how small the big things were"—"letters cut into beeches and oaks by giants were eye level now" (*B* 245). Once readers fall even halfway under Morrison's spell, they aren't nearly so likely to wonder down the line, "Are these details really worth attending to?" Morrison's challenge is on the opposite side: Can the weird intensity sustain itself as a credibly integral expression of social derangement under racism without falling into manneristic excrescence?

But I threaten to stray from the main point of pairing *Rabbit Ang-strom* and *Beloved* in the first place, which was not to judge relative merit but to offer a preliminary demonstration of what putting such disparate works in conversation can disclose about the kinds of fictional accomplishment that might be expected of a GAN prospect. I've begun to suggest some of the constituent genres and other traditions of narrative practice that stand behind each book. Admittedly any such dyadic comparison risks oversimplifying the menu of eligible strategies, but the risk is lessened when one bears in mind that to envisage novels as potential GANs is necessarily to conceive them as belonging to more extensive domains of narrative practice that draw on repertoires of tropes and recipes for encapsulating nationness of the kinds sketched briefly in the Introduction—such that you can't fully grasp what's at stake in any one possible GAN without imagining the individual work in multiple conversations with many others, and not just U.S. literature either. It's through its interdependencies as well as through its particularities that an individual novel becomes seen as a possible GAN. That's why I'm not overly worried about letting two late twentieth-century fictions, for the moment, stand for all. Take this short Morrison-Updike comparison as a kind of warm-up exercise for the more expansive treatment of the various informing scripts to follow, Part IV's being, as we'll see, especially relevant to the cases of *Rabbit* and *Beloved*. But the surest of all recipes is to become a household word by having your story retold down through the generations and spread across the popular media to boot. That's the story Chapter 3 will tell.

PART TWO

SCRIPT ONE: MADE CLASSIC BY RETELLING

3

The Reluctant Master Text

The Making and Remakings of Hawthorne's
The Scarlet Letter

The transparency and simplicity of a text bears no direct relation to its capacity to enter tradition. It may be its very impenetrability, demanding constantly renewed interpretation, that
confers on a sentence or a work the authority which dedicates
it to posterity.

—THEODOR ADORNO, *Minima Moralia* (1951)

I love Hawthorne, I admire him; but I do not know him. He
lives in a mysterious world of thought and imagination which
he never permits me to enter.

—JONATHAN CILLEY (1802–1838), Bowdoin classmate,
U.S. congressman

THE CASE FOR HAWTHORNE'S importance to the DNA of American
fiction is open and shut. Hawthorne is "the only major author
never to have been underestimated," the only one "never to have lived
in the limbo of the non-elect," as critic Richard Brodhead has observed.
That declaration came in the mid-1980s, during the still-early stages of
an intense controversy over the U.S. literary canon—what should be in
or out, whether there should be one at all—that has resulted in a far
more heterogeneous and more open-bordered conception of what
counts as "American" literature. Yet Hawthorne's position as a like-it-
or-not landmark remains.[1] This is especially true of his first major long
fiction, *The Scarlet Letter* (1850). It holds a unique place in U.S. literary
history. This was the work that made Hawthorne famous overnight and
for good, the work that established him securely in the judgment of the
Euro-American critical intelligentsia of the next hundred years as the
most consummate artist in U.S. fiction before Henry James. As James

himself summed up in his book on Hawthorne, the first extensive critical study of any national creative writer (1879), "Something might at last be sent to Europe as exquisite in quality as anything that had been received."[2]

Hawthorne was the first fiction writer in U.S. literary history to win broad international acclaim for superior artistry and the first to become widely required schoolroom reading. Today *The Scarlet Letter* remains the most-often-taught long work of premodern American literature in secondary and college courses. Generations of students may—and do—complain about its having been inflicted upon them prematurely.[3] Yet it seems certain to remain a key reference point for U.S. literary history. As the best-known literary attempt during the era of U.S. literary emergence to articulate something like a myth of colonial origins, it invites remembrance as "the inaugural text of the indigenous canon," even though the first national novels of quality date from the late 1700s and *The Scarlet Letter* was a late entry into a populous field, as one of the last of several dozen novels about the Puritan era dating back to the 1820s.[4] Were a vote taken among critics of American literature as to the first indisputably classic U.S. long fiction, *The Scarlet Letter* would almost surely win.

No less important a measure of durability than the critical verdict is the verdict of the culture—not that the two can be pried apart. *The Scarlet Letter* has catalyzed writers and artists in every generation since, most but by no means all American. George Eliot's first novel, *Adam Bede* (1869), rewrote Hawthorne's tale of the consequences of the illicit affair between Reverend Arthur Dimmesdale and Mistress Hester Prynne as a young nobleman's seduction of a local maid. Harold Frederic's *The Damnation of Theron Ware* rewrote it as the story of a naive Methodist minister driven awry by the mystique of a local Catholic charmer. In *Washington Square* (1880) and *The Portrait of a Lady* (1882), Henry James drew on *The Scarlet Letter*'s scenario of a penned-in heroine quietly resisting patriarchy by strategies of indirection; and Brodhead plausibly claims that the title image of James's late masterpiece *The Golden Bowl* (1904) takes to a still greater pitch of refinement the "warping" effect of Hawthorne's symbolic scarlet *A* that "makes one object in a field of objects" assume an obsessively "gigantic prominence."[5] In Faulkner's *As I Lay Dying* (1930) the clandestine amour between ex-schoolteacher Addie Bundren and Reverend Whitfield that birthed her fractious son Jewel reprises Hawthorne's triangle of Hester-Dimmesdale-Pearl. John Updike's three neo–*Scarlet Letter* novels conjure up contemporary avatars of Dimmesdale, Hester, and Hester's spiteful husband Chillingworth: *A Month of Sundays* (1975), *S.* (1988), and *Roger's Version* (1986). Bharati Mukherjee's *The Holder of the World* (1993) bends *The Scarlet Letter* into a picaresque, time-traveling plot that takes Hester around the world to find true love at last (briefly) with an Indian prince, Pearl's "real" father. In *In the Blood* (1999) and *Fucking A* (2000), African American dramatist Suzan-Lori Parks reinvents Hester as a feisty back-to-the-wall welfare mother and abortionist with multiple kids and no dads in sight.

Since 1985 alone, *The Scarlet Letter* has generated across three continents at least four novels, four plays, three operas, two musicals, three films (one in Korean), and two dance creations.[6] The scarlet *A*, its defining symbol, continues to serve as a touchstone motif for mass culture down to this day, as the stuff of screaming print and cyber-headlines about the stigmatization of sex workers and sex offenders, right-wing reaction to contraception, the sins of sitting U.S. presidents (remember the Bill Clinton–Monica Lewinsky affair?), down to the presidential campaign of 2012, when journalists opined that Republican candidate Mitt Romney's "scarlet letter" might be the health care legislation that he championed as governor of Massachusetts on which were based the federal "Obamacare" reforms he opposed. These cases are all ephemeral, but the percolation effect of *The Scarlet Letter* as mantra endures.

Perpetuation doesn't mean unqualified homage, of course. Many of the letter-slinging pundits may not even have read the book. Even its serious readers have taken potshots. James thought it lacked passion. In recent times, it's been taken to task for evading the burning moral-political issue of its day, slavery. Mukherjee's generally affirmative *Scarlet Letter* entry for the *New History of American Literature* also voices some strong reservations about its unwillingness to challenge Puritanism more pointedly.[7] But as Parks commonsensically declares, the use value of the "Great Tradition" is to provoke its potentially daunted successors to extract from it the seeds of the "Next New Thing."[8] Here she names the single most important recipe for ensuring Great American Novel candidacy: continuous generativity as provocation and reference point.

Hawthorne as a Nonnational Writer

How to explain that generativity? "Cultural capital"—prestige conferred by the accumulated verdicts of respected critics, teachers, and literati—is part of the story, but it takes us only a certain distance. The question is all the more tantalizing since *The Scarlet Letter*'s durability as a national literary icon was such an unlikely upshot. It was almost certainly never meant as a key to national identity or to tell the story of a national crisis such as Stowe would attempt a few years later in *Uncle Tom's Cabin*. Both authors were birthright New Englanders self-conscious of their regional roots, but the vista of *The Scarlet Letter* is resolutely provincial by comparison. When Hawthorne spoke of "my native land" he almost always meant New England, not the United States as a whole. When the Civil War broke out, he hoped that "New England might be a nation by itself." As early as the Mexican War of 1846–1848, he welcomed the prospect of the separation of the South from the North. New England, he famously remarked, was "as large a lump of earth as my heart can really take in."[9] Partly on that account, the first framer of the Great American Novel idea, J. W. De Forest, a fellow New Englander who had also written a novel during the 1850s about the Puritan era, found no place for Hawthorne despite esteeming him "the greatest of American imaginations." Hawthorne's penchant for romance was another disqualifying factor. His "personages" seemed to "belong to the wide realm of art rather than to our nationality," to be "as probably natives of the furthest mountains of Cathay or of the moon as of the United States of America."[10]

Nor would Hawthorne have disagreed. On the contrary, De Forest's verdict did little more than recycle the language of the well-known preface to Hawthorne's second major long fiction, *The House of the Seven Gables* (1851), in which he distinguishes his brand of narrative from novelistic realism. Although "the personages of the Tale," Hawthorne declares, "give themselves out to be of ancient stability and considerable prominence," they "are really of the Author's own making, or, at all events, of his own mixing. . . . He would be glad, therefore, if . . . the book may be read strictly as a Romance, having a great deal more to do with the clouds overhead, than with any portion of the actual soil of the County of Essex." Such protestations can't be taken at face value. Hawthorne overstates the distinction between "romance" and "novel,"* in this case partly from wanting to ward off local charges, including a possible lawsuit, of slanderous misrepresentation. But it wasn't merely a dodge for him to claim that *Seven Gables* came from cloudland nor, despite the extensive historical research that went into his fictions of the New England past, that in telling the story he had allowed himself "nearly or altogether as much license as if the facts had been entirely of my own invention" (*SL* 33). In Hawthorne's longer works, "Romance" is best understood as a name for the penchant for turning known, named places—often including meticulous descriptive renderings of manners and landscapes—into fable-like thought experiments that behold them askance, whether in satire or wonder, to belie the appearance of factual solidity and narrative closure by conjuring up an aura of the mysterious. Whether or not the biographical Hawthorne was as elusive a creature as his college roommate Jonathan Cilley took him to be, his fiction certainly strove for the kind of impenetrability effect that Theodor Adorno was to hold up as the hallmark of fiction that endures. So it was that both of De Forest's grounds of disqualification turned out in the long run more to fortify than compromise *The Scarlet Letter*'s candidacy as a possible Great American Novel.

* Quotation from Nathaniel Hawthorne, *The House of the Seven Gables,* ed. William Charvat et al. (Columbus: Ohio State University Press, 1965), 3. The degree to which "novel" and "romance" were distinguishable in Hawthorne's day has been a matter of long debate complicated by disputes about the adequacy of the thesis (see Chapter 2), first broached during the Victorian era but crystallized into short-lived orthodoxy in mid-twentieth-century Americanist criticism, that classic U.S. fiction characteristically differs from British in its predilection for romance. For refutation of that argument, see Nina Baym, "Concepts of the Romance in Hawthorne's America," *Nineteenth-Century Fiction* 37 (March 1984): 426–443; and John P. McWilliams Jr., "The Rationale for American Romance," *boundary 2* 17 (Spring 1990): 71–82. For a detailed rejoinder that rehabilitates the thesis at least in part, see G. R. Thompson and Eric Carl Link, *Neutral Ground: New Traditionalism and the American Romance Controversy* (Baton Rouge: Louisiana State University Press, 1999). Emily Miller Budick, *Engendering Romance: Women Writers and the Hawthorne Tradition* (New Haven, CT: Yale University Press, 1994), demonstrates Hawthorne's continuing importance for women practitioners of romance modes down to the near present. Marc McGurl, *The Novel Art: Elevations of American Fiction after Henry James* (Princeton, NJ: Princeton University Press, 2001), insightfully assesses the "militant probabalism" that prompted post–Civil War writers like De Forest to press the distinction between novel and romance, concluding that despite appearances to the contrary, (postbellum) novelistic practice and criticism were "confident and broad enough" to perceive romance "as a minority position" within "the discourse of the novel itself" (46). To avoid partisanship, however, this chapter avoids both terms in favor of quasi-synonyms like "long fiction," "narrative," "story," and "tale."

Provincial Discontent: Hawthorne's Arts of Entrapment

Precisely because *The Scarlet Letter* is one of those books you think you know even if you've forgot or never read it, a refresher may be in order. The narrative proper unfolds in and around mid-seventeenth-century Boston during the first generation of Puritan settlement. It foregrounds a quartet of characters bound together by the symbolic *A*, a legally imposed stigma that becomes a multivalent symbol: the beautiful, embattled Hester Prynne; Arthur Dimmesdale, the charismatic but delicate junior pastor; Pearl, the precocious child of their secret affair; and Hester's elderly physician-husband, who assumes the alias of Roger Chillingworth after belatedly arriving during the opening crowd scene to witness Hester, already sentenced to wear the scarlet *A* on her chest forever as convicted adulterers sometimes were in those days, refusing the importunities of her interrogators (including Dimmesdale) to name her partner. The plot oscillates between Hester and Dimmesdale over the seven-year period of their inner sufferings—him literally flagellating himself for his reluctance to confess his fatherhood, she with quiet persistence making her lonely way as a seamstress on the margins of the community. Chillingworth quickly intuits the father's identity and insinuates himself as the minister's housemate to ferret out proof positive and torture him further. Pearl grows up indulged and hoydenish, in dress and deed a walking scarlet letter, a juvenile embodiment of the limit-bumping passion Hester has superficially repressed except for her ornate embroidery of the stigmatizing *A* ("greatly beyond what was allowed by the sumptuary regulations of the colony") (*SL* 40). As such Pearl becomes both consolation and trial. Her volatility rouses fears of demonic possession, and her irrepressible fascination with the letter unnerves Hester. Shocked even more by Dimmesdale's decline, she retracts her earlier promise to Chillingworth to keep his identity secret too and contrives to meet Dimmesdale in the forest—the first and only time we see them alone together. They renew their pledges and resolve to flee to Europe after she reveals that his supposed friend is his worst enemy. But to her chagrin, Dimmesdale, sensing himself a dying man, decides at the last minute to confess in public. In a provocatively magical ending that dares you to write it off as contrived, Dimmesdale dies immediately after and the prey-deprived Chillingworth quickly follows suit. Pearl is liberated from elfin purgatory by her father's public recognition of her to grow up a normal human child and, thanks to Chillingworth's bequest, "the richest heiress" of the New World to boot (164). Pearl and Hester soon decamp for the Old, but after a time Hester returns to her solitary cottage wearing the scarlet letter, to live out her life as confidante and counselor to the community's younger women.

The narrative proper is framed by a semiautobiographical preface set in the present. "The Custom-House" doubles as a satirical account of the author's stint as Surveyor of Customs for the port of Salem, from which he had recently been fired for reasons he partly conceals,[11] and, in a seriocomic nod to a shopworn gothic motif, as a fictitious tale of discovering in the attic of the Custom House the "authentic" manuscript of Hester's story supposedly recorded by a late-colonial predecessor, one Surveyor Pue. Most first-time readers find this preface tedious and prolix—I always advise students to read it last. But the split-consciousness effect of a sharp then/now break coexisting with multiple insinuations of links across the centuries is crucial to what *The Scarlet Letter* is all about. The author's recent misadventures as an official dismissed amid furor, rumor, and scandal align him both with Hester's ordeal of public exposure and with Dimmesdale's reluctance to make a clean breast of it until the end.[12]

More like Homeric epic or Shakespearean tragedy than a standard nineteenth-century novel, the narrative proper starts in medias res, and for similar reasons. The plot-instigating events have already happened—the mismarriage, the migration, the affair, the pregnancy, the arrest, the birth, the sentence—as if to conjure up a sense of fatality, or original sin. The opening sketch of the Puritan community reinforces the impression of an already fallen world. This utopian venture is almost new, but already it has a cemetery, a jail, a crime problem.

The sense of options prematurely foreclosed, if ever open to start with, is reinforced by the intensely patterned narrative structure. The plot turns on three scenes of public exposure spaced evenly apart, on the "scaffold" fronting the church where the town pillory also stands, the Puritan equivalent to the guillotine, as the narrator notes in wry allusion both to the officially sanctioned violence of French revolutions after 1789 and 1848 and to the Puritan beheading of King Charles soon to come.[13] In the first scene, Hester suffers public shaming. In scene two, exactly at midpoint, Dimmesdale halfway suffers with her, when he chances a nocturnal penance there and calls her and Pearl to join him as they pass by; but wily Chillingworth lures him away before anyone notices, his reputation still intact. In scene three, at the end, Dimmesdale confesses and the nuclear family reunites, briefly. At the first and third scenes, virtually all named townspeople are present or mentioned. Each half of the main narrative that the three scenes anchor focuses first on Hester, then on Dimmesdale, with the crossover exactly at midpoint when they meet: first at the governor's mansion, when she badgers him into persuading Governor Bellingham to let her keep the wayward Pearl, and later in the forest. Hester and Dimmesdale, in turn, are flanked, shadowed, haunted by the two main supporting characters, Pearl and Chillingworth, who despite obvious contrasts play symmetric roles. Both are figures (even more) uncanny than the protagonists,[14] with overtones of the demonic, who both soothe and torture, embodying as they do the secret links that bind the quartet.

This intensely schematic patterning, almost surgically precise in its staging-out and distribution of attention, is both an aesthetic tour de force in itself and a mirror of the suffocating constraints on thought and action within *The Scarlet Letter*'s imagined world. It's further reinforced by the book's long silences. Rarely was there a work of long fiction so sparse in dialogue. Its trifold strategy of containment—by self, community, and narrative overvoice—registers the communal restraints on conduct either under Puritan or under Victorian American mores, depending on how you read it.[15] The detailed rendering of village and natural landscapes, exquisitely wrought but bordering on the excessive, strengthens the impression of enchainment in place.

In its framing of the rival claims of individual self-realization and communal stability, *The Scarlet Letter* views a paradigmatic seventeenth-century crisis through a nineteenth-century lens. The Puritan-era crisis was the so-called antinomian controversy provoked by Hester's quasi-prototype Anne Hutchinson, who claimed, to the scandal of the oligarchs, that the rightful guide to action was the immediate dictate of the Holy Spirit within. Hutchinson's later Puritan detractors likened such heresy to bastardy—one way of reading Pearl. The equivalent nineteenth-century issue was broadly the question of how far morality should be privatized and more especially, for this book, whether the claims of love might override societal canons that limit-bumping liberals widely saw as especially onerous for women. That the antebellum era was a time of greater grassroots challenge to monogamous marriage than any later period of U.S. history until the present *The Scarlet Letter* also recognizes when it has Hester insist to her lover, "What we did had a consecration of its own" (*SL* 126). Her justification—"We felt it so! We said so to each other"—wasn't far different from the "sacred inwardness," the "self-consecrating interior glow," with which Nathaniel and Sophia Hawthorne viewed their own intimacy during their long engagement: as substantially married, wedded or no.[16] The scenario of an embattled female lover disputing the terms of institutionalized patriarchy that define her in terms of a sexuality presumed wayward and vulnerable is the scarlet thread that connects the bygone with the mid-nineteenth-century present—the "sex-freedom link," Michael Colacurcio aptly terms it.[17] The refractory Puritan daughter had been a familiar motif in New England historical romance well before *The Scarlet Letter*, pioneered a generation before by the feminist writers who inaugurated the genre, Lydia Maria Child (*Hobomok*, 1824) and Catharine Maria Sedgwick (*Hope Leslie*, 1827); but Hawthorne took the theme to a further degree of aesthetic finesse and ethical complexity.

The Scarlet Letter passes judgment on the issues at stake without putting them to rest. Key to that ambiguation is the remarkable elasticity of the narrative voice. For the most part the narrator is guardedly controlled to the point of pedantic fussiness ("By degrees, nor very slowly, her handiwork became what would now be termed the fashion") (*SL* 57), yet with outbursts that resonate with the characters' bottled-up agitation ("Such was the ruin to which she had brought the man, once—nay, why should we not speak it?—still so passionately loved!") (124). He is also strikingly at odds with himself in how much he presumes to know about what's going on at any moment. Sometimes he seems an ignorant time traveler from another epoch, perplexed at why the quaintly attired crowd in the opening scene has gathered with all eyes on the prison door: it might be this, it might be that. From this perspective he shoots an alienated glance at the senior minister, John Wilson, in the first scaffold scene, looking "like the darkly engraved portraits which we see prefixed to old volumes of sermons," with "no more right than one of those portraits would have, to step forth" and "meddle with a question of human guilt, passion, and anguish" (47–48). Yet elsewhere the narrator shows X-ray vision into the hearts of the main characters—except for Pearl, who's always seen from the outside, in keeping with the mystique that invests her until the end. Then too he may sound definitive but proceed to contradict himself, as when he ventriloquizes first a Puritan perspective and then a modern perspective on Puritanism on the same page, exaggerating both times: first calling Pearl "an imp of evil, emblem and product of sin" with "no right among christened infants," yet a few lines later calling the Puritan children who teased her "the most intolerant brood that ever lived" (64). Such instability starts before the narrative does. Upon perusing the "original manuscript," the narrator's peremptory judgment is that Hester's late-life do-gooding activities after returning to Boston must have made her seem like "an intruder and a nuisance" (27), as if to disavow the earnestness of the tale that follows.

The most arresting switch comes shortly after midpoint. Until now, Hester has on the whole been portrayed empathetically, almost as a model of heroic womanhood under duress. But as we approach the pivotal forest scene, where she literally lets her hair down, the narrator seems to disown her. Ostracism "had made her strong, but taught her much amiss" (128). Hester becomes recast as the temptress responsible for the couple's second fall by persuading Dimmesdale to elope. Her alienation now seems dangerously anarchic.[18] The last scaffold scene comes as another humiliation for her. As Dimmesdale rejoices that he's saved at last, Hester feels bereft and despairing. And the narrator sides with Dimmesdale, at least backhandedly, drawing the preachy moral ("among many," he hedges, "which press upon us from the poor minister's miserable experience"): "Be true! Be true! Be true—Show freely to the world, if not your worst, yet some trait whereby the worst may be inferred!" (163). As if that weren't enough, the epilogue pictures Hester returning to Boston with her mountain of guilt still not atoned: "Here was yet to be her penitence," as if those years of silent pain counted for nothing. That the tale is so orchestrated that the spells afflicting Chillingworth and Pearl are broken only when the nuclear family is reunited in public, yet the lovers are then immediately separated forever, suggests that some moralistic compulsion has driven the narrator to override his own narrative logic.

What to make of such self-division? Was Hawthorne, as the romantics read Milton's *Paradise Lost,* of the devil's party without knowing it? Readers differ and always will. There is much to commend the centrist view of a decidedly nonschismatic Hawthorne. That accords with the persona Hawthorne displayed in public life. Despite strong antisocial and reclusive tendencies, despite tastes that drew him to reside in a hotbed of intellectual and reform ferment (the transcendental Concord of Emerson, Thoreau, and Bronson Alcott), Hawthorne's correspondence transmits an urbane man-of-the-world persona that helps explain why he was the only important creative writer in U.S. history ever to be the intimate friend of an American president. One critical path, accordingly, has been to take *The Scarlet Letter*'s denouement as acquiescing to the necessity of a restraining social order as a brake on runaway individualism. A prominent early reviewer surmised, for example, that the author "made his guilty parties end, not as his own fancy or his own benevolent sympathies might dictate, but as the spiritual laws, lying in back of all persons, dictated to him."[19] In recent times, the most cogent elaborations of this general line of thinking have been Larry Reynolds's scrupulous study of Hawthorne's politics and Sacvan Bercovitch's elegantly argued interpretation of Hester's saga as encapsulating the compromise inherent in American liberalism between the claims of individual and society. Bercovitch reads *The Scarlet Letter* "as the story of a stranger who rejoins the community by compromising 'for principle.'" Hester's return makes ideological sense as a reenactment of the social covenant or compact the individual citizen freely makes under liberal democracy. Her return is an act of free choice continuous with but not identical to her earlier individualism in acknowledging the symbiosis of collective consensus and individual dissent at the heart of the American way.[20]

Other readers, however, starting with some of *The Scarlet Letter*'s early feminist admirers,[21] have stressed that even though the narrator may grant that "the world's law validly exists to restrain our disruptive social excesses," the novel's critique of the "outrage to human privacy and human consciousness" by the patriarchy is far stronger than any critique of the unreconstructed Hester. Conversely, Hester is shown to have changed "the Puritans more than they have changed her." "No amount of penitence on Hester's part," Myra Jehlen shrewdly remarks, "can undo [Hawthorne's] act in having invented her." Well before the end, observes Lauren Berlant in a searching exegesis of *The Scarlet Letter* as "a counter-National Symbolic," the state has "lost control over the A's and Hester's meanings, and therefore over collective memory and identity" as the people re-embrace her as "the town's own Hester" and redefine the meaning of the letter from "adulteress" to "able" (*SL* 106).[22]

After her death, she's laid to rest next to Dimmesdale under a single gravestone. And who knows what might really have gone on in those group meetings with younger women after Hester's return?[23]

The case for *The Scarlet Letter* as a narrative that destabilizes more than it forecloses is reinforced by its disruptions of the Richardsonian or "sentimental" plotline, the template for the untold prehistory of the Hester-Dimmesdale affair. Such novels traditionally turned on the sexual temptation of a young woman by an ardent male, ending, if she succumbed, in disgrace, poverty, and death, with pregnancy, childbirth, and infant mortality often thrown in for good measure. Such had been the tenor of the first popular American novels, William Hill Brown's *The Power of Sympathy* (1789), Susanna Rowson's *Charlotte Temple* (1791), and Hannah Foster's *The Coquette* (1796). These early American texts mattered far less to Hawthorne, however, than Jean-Jacques Rousseau's *Julie, or The New Héloïse* (1761)—"perhaps the biggest bestseller of the century," according to historian Robert Darnton.[24] Hawthorne read it "with great sympathy" in youth, dipped into it again sometime before writing *The Scarlet Letter*, and when traveling through Switzerland in the late 1850s found himself greatly "affected by" the scene of "the loves of St. Preux and Julia," convinced that their story "still retains its hold upon my imagination." The parallels between the two fictions, rarely since discussed, prompted Leslie Fiedler to declare a half century ago that "the basic pattern of the *Nouvelle Héloïse* is repeated in *The Scarlet Letter:* a second temptation after a first fall, ending in an unnatural triangle perpetuated under strange circumstances."[25]

Julie—itself a reworking of the storied twelfth-century history of the seduction of precocious Eloise by scholar Peter Abelard, leading to his castration by her outraged relatives and monastic immurement for both—does indeed anticipate *The Scarlet Letter*'s adult ménage à trois. The outwardly dutiful and dignified but inwardly passionate heroine and the ardent but self-chastising and finally ascetic tutor-seducer, conjoined by a secret liaison that both see as consecrated, both yoked to the upright but cerebral older husband that Julie's status-conscious father forced on her who puts the ex-lovers to the outrageous test of inviting St. Preux into the household to tutor Julie's children in full knowledge of that old amour—all these reappear transmogrified in the Hester-Dimmesdale-Chillingworth triangle. Both *Julie* and *The Scarlet Letter* dramatize the agonizing disparity between their lovers' desires and the sublimated, underactualized lives into which the milieux of Rousseau's Swiss Alpine village and Hawthorne's Boston contort them.

Julie's metamorphosis from mistress to dutiful wife to the astonishing deathbed confession of longing to die so as to keep from succumbing again to fleshly temptation and thus allow eternal reunion with St. Preux, who seems to have brought his own passion under strict control, sheds suggestive light on Hester's dismay at Dimmesdale's pious deathbed dismissal of their possible heavenly reunion and her own later return to Boston, brandishing that communally redefined *A* to the last. Fiedler—like Henry James before him—finds Hawthorne prudish by contrast ("passion is rendered . . . not as lived, but as remembered or proposed"), but the reverse is more true. Although the measured reserve of Hawthorne's narrator pales by comparison to Rousseau's steamy epistolary eroticism, Julie and St. Preux achieve a degree of dutiful repression that *The Scarlet Letter* shows Dimmesdale hard put to maintain and Hester refusing to accept. Instead of killing off his heroine as Rousseau did, and as Anglo-American sentimental novelists did with more moralistic dispatch, Hawthorne lets his fallen woman live on unwed, her integrity and worldly passion intact, and lets their bastard daughter flourish.

To imagine a dotted line from Rousseau to Hawthorne is to raise further questions about the adequacy of conceiving *The Scarlet Letter* as an "American" tale. Traditionally, Hawthornians have tended to take this more or less for granted, whether they read *The Scarlet Letter* as a seventeenth-century-focused or a nineteenth-century-focused text, whether they read it as a narrative of containment or of resistance. Lately, though, a more quizzical view of *The Scarlet Letter*'s investment in the national has emerged. "Underlying the primary attention given to New England history in the novel" has been descried "a subsurface of English history . . . carefully structured in order to examine American Puritans within a framework larger than the provincial boundaries of New England." Again and again "residual attachments to Old World culture and theology" seem to "permeate the consciousness of these emigrant characters," as when Hester in the first scaffold scene maintains her strength and sanity by mentally harking back to her earlier life in the Old World; or when, reunited with Dimmesdale in the forest, she beholds Pearl advancing on them "as if one of the fairies, whom we left in our dear old England, had decked her out to meet us" (*SL* 132).

At such moments, *The Scarlet Letter* seems more a text about migration and diaspora, a work of "Anglo-Atlantic poetics," than a text about the consolidation of the Puritan origins of national culture.[26]

Imagining Euro-Atlantic Diaspora: New England Derealized

The Scarlet Letter confirms its skepticism about the possibility of America as new departure by ending with a glimpse of where Hester Prynne is buried, next to the "old and sunken grave" of Arthur Dimmesdale, with a space between but a single tombstone marking both, worn by the weathering of 200 years. On that "simple slab of slate," the tale concludes,

> as the curious investigator may still discern, and perplex himself with the purport[,] there appeared the semblance of an engraved escutcheon. It bore a device, a herald's wording of which might serve for a motto and brief description of our now concluded legend; so sombre is it, and relieved only by one ever-glowing point of light gloomier than the shadow:
>
> —"ON A FIELD SABLE, THE LETTER **A,** GULES" (166)

Well indeed might "the curious investigator" be perplexed, so encrypted is this passage. Its return-to-starting-point fitness is obvious enough: Chapter 1 mentions the cemetery in the same breath as the prison, as among a colonial government's first allotments of space for public uses. But so cryptic a return! What calls itself a "description" actually "describes nothing."[27] The basic idea is clear enough: some kind of symbolic red-on-black design. But the design is rendered neither quite as language nor as picture but hieroglyphically via the arcane semiotics of heraldry.

To be sure, it's typical of Hawthorne's colonial tales to proliferate emblematic schema and instill a sense of remoteness of past from present. They squint back at quaint old tombstones, houses, furniture, and other colonial artifacts from an immense aesthetic distance, like Thoreau prompted by an old painting of seventeenth-century Concord to wonder whether real people could truly have existed back then. In this both were engaging in a familiar ritual of romantic gothicization of the antique that revealed them—more than they let on—to be children of the early industrial era, the first to undergo what the next century would call future shock. Yet *The Scarlet Letter*'s closing scene is an out-lier even by that standard. Though explicitly identified as the colo-ny's first burying ground, it feels more like an English graveyard than a New England one, whose old slabs generally sported no such adorn-ments.[28] Presumably it was commissioned by the grown-up, Europe-anized Pearl. The passage may also intend a glancing blow at the rising interest in pedigree among the northeastern elite as the nineteenth cen-tury unfolded. (The nation's first such organization had been founded in Boston shortly before the novel appeared.) In any case, the inscription is atypical of standard colonial and antebellum funerary design.[29]

More to the purpose, though, is what's encrypted there—a palimp-sestic overlay of two sable/gules allusions in provocative passages from classic English writers. One is the conclusion to the English Puritan poet Andrew Marvell's "The Unfortunate Lover," a strangely contorted metaphysical lyric. The other is from Walter Scott's introduction to *Wa-verley* (1814), the first in his multivolume fictional epic of Scottish his-tory from the mid-1600s to the mid-1700s that secured his reputation as the father of the historical romance, Hawthorne's own self-designated genre. Neither is unknown to Hawthorne criticism, but neither have they been much discussed.[30]

> This is the only *Banneret*
> That ever Love created yet:
> Who though, by the Malignant Starrs,
> Forced to live in Storms and Warrs;
> Yet dying leave a Perfume here,
> And Musick within every Ear:
> And he in Story only rules
> In a Field *Sable* a Lover *Gules*.[31]

[My story will emphasize] those passions common to men in all stages of society, and which have alike agitated the human heart, whether it throbbed under the steel corslet of the fifteenth century, the brocaded coat of the eighteenth, or the blue frock and white dimity waistcoat of the present day. Upon these passions it is no doubt true that the state of manners and laws casts a necessary colouring; but the bearings, to use the language of heraldry, remain the same. . . . The wrath of our ances-tors, for example, was colored *gules;* it broke forth in acts of open and sanguinary violence against the objects of its fury. Our malignant feel-ings, which must seek gratification through more indirect channels, and undermine the obstacles which they cannot openly bear down,

> may be rather said to be tinctured *sable*. But the deep-ruling impulse is the same in both cases; and the proud peer, who can now only ruin his neighbor according to law, by protracted suits, is the genuine descendant of the baron, who wrapped the castle of his competitor in flames, and knocked him on the head as he endeavoured to escape from the conflagration. It is from the great book of Nature, the same through a thousand editions, whether of black-letter, or wire-wove and hot-pressed, that I have venturously essayed to read a chapter to the public.[32]

Whether Hawthorne wrote with either passage in mind is unknown, but almost surely he knew both. He was an attentive reader of Renaissance emblem poetry, and he read and reread Scott, "his boyhood favorite among novelists," from youth through late life.[33] In any case, the passages seize upon the primary passions at play in *The Scarlet Letter:* love and vengeance. *The Scarlet Letter* recognizes both Marvell's insight that love-longing is fulfilled vicariously, not in life, and Scott's that the bloodless procedural vengeance of the early modern and contemporary eras—be it the judicial repression of the Puritan state or Chillingworth's freelance machinations or the decapitation of Surveyor Hawthorne—is as sanguinary in its own way as the medieval baron's. Hawthorne's bourgeois-era retelling of the love/repression/separation tale of his forever passionate Eloise and her self-castrating Abelard is as poignant as the original. His romance fuses the two sable-gules polarities, drawing like his predecessors on the idiom of heraldry to achieve a semblance of aesthetic control of the uncontrollable through schematic abstraction.

The power of *The Scarlet Letter* doesn't hinge on catching those esoteric allusions. The scheme of symbolic color opposition throughout the narrative—starting with the bicolor typography of the red-on-black title page, a first for U.S. publishing history—speaks for itself. As in Hawthorne's retelling of Greek legends in the children's book he was soon to write, you can sense the story of Hester and Dimmesdale being cast into "legend," however scanty your knowledge of those antecedent realms of legend.[34] What counts most is the sense of something timeless or perennial about the story hinted in "The Custom-House's" seriocomic passages on ancestral memory and mental time travel from nineteenth century back to seventeenth, sustained by the stately formality of the narrative voice, and capped by the gravity of the closing scene. Costumes differ across centuries; emotions remain the same. Marvell's hapless wight is a perennial lover-loser. The grand narrative of the Waverley novels of transition from feudal to bourgeois isn't a one-way movement but the birth of a new avatar. *The Scarlet Letter*'s quiet affiliation with these texts helps establish its story not as a Yankee either/ or—not just as a Puritan tale *or* a fable of modern New England in Puritan drag—but as part and parcel of Eurodiasporic collective memory stretching back to the Middle Ages. In this sense, *The Scarlet Letter* seems no more time- or nation-bound than Akira Kurosawa's cinematic rendition of Shakespeare's *King Lear* in his *Ran* seems uniquely Japanese. This may help account for the proclivity of later creative artists to retell and update the story again and again.

The more we think of *The Scarlet Letter* vis-à-vis Scott, Marvell, or Rousseau, the less inevitable it seems to conceive it as embedded within an American line of descent. The more it makes sense that the precursor to which Henry James and some of its early British reviewers likened it was John Gibson Lockhart's *Adam Blair* (1822), a novel of ministerial adultery in post-Puritan Scotland. The more it begins to make sense that the first major rewriting of *The Scarlet Letter* should have been George Eliot's *Adam Bede* (1859). It too is a historical fiction incorporating a pair of illicit lovers named Hester and Arthur who come to grief in a provincial social context that intensifies guilt, suffering, and repression. Why should not an English country town of the turn of the nineteenth century be as promising a venue for a Hester-Arthur story as seventeenth-century New England when the story's remote origins lie somewhere back in the Middle Ages?

With one side of his mind, Hawthorne was certainly attracted to the idea of writing "tales of my native land"—his working title for an uncompleted early book project. Indeed his was one of the most prolific of all responses to lawyer-orator Rufus Choate's call for fictions of New England history that would rival Scott's Waverley novels, in a lecture given in Hawthorne's native Salem, Massachusetts.[35] Historically ordered, Hawthorne's colonial tales together with his first three book-length romances—*The Scarlet Letter, The House of the Seven Gables,* and *The Blithedale Romance*—form an episodic historical romance of New England history that extends from the first generation of settlement to the transcendentalist commune at Brook Farm. Along the way, Hawthorne also ground out a three-volume history of colonial New England for children, *Grandfather's Chair*. Yet with another side of his mind, he clearly distrusted the standard settlement-to-nationhood story line. Much of his late writing was devoted to the Anglo-American connection and unfinished romances of ancestral linkage or inheritance. His "American" masterpiece bespeaks much the same hesitancy as his last short historical tale, "Main-Street" (1849), in which an amateur showman attempts to stage a series of tableaux of local history to a marginally invested local audience only to break down during the Great Snow of 1717 when his crude mechanical contrivance fails. So much for the patriotic boosterism of Rufus Choate.

In *The Scarlet Letter*, too, the story of Hester and Arthur is not shown to have any lasting American issue. The mother country is wistfully pictured as a place of robust vitality and healthy merriment, the new world of Puritan Boston as a diminished shadowland. "We have yet to learn again the forgotten art of gaiety," the narrator sighs (*SL* 147) during the one festive scene. "The Custom-House" portrays a nineteenth-century America already moribund. That the mid-nineteenth-century United States was in the midst of an unprecedented spurt of territorial expansion and economic growth one could never tell from this sketch. The author's hometown is in decay. The country doesn't seem to be going anywhere. That is the most strikingly idiosyncratic aspect of *The Scarlet Letter*'s vision of history: not its representation of Puritan nostalgia for the mother country (for many did return home, as Hawthorne knew); not the contrast between Puritan austerity and latter-day liberalization (already a cliché); but the sense that the whole New World experiment might be fizzling out. Two centuries of New England history end in the anticlimax of the Custom House.

This was by no means the flesh-and-blood Hawthorne's whole view of the matter. "In other moods," George Dekker points out, "Hawthorne could argue earnestly that the sadly imperfect liberal democracy nurtured in the United States, and especially in New England, was the best hope of mankind." Such may also have been his prevailing view as a citizen. But it was not a view in which he could rest content. New England also meant for Hawthorne, as Robert Milder writes, "the starvation of the senses, the imagination, the feelings, and the erotic nature consequent on living in a post-Puritan world."[36] So neither his fictions of the New England past nor *Grandfather's Chair* are willing to draw the line connecting colonial New England to present-day national efflorescence that was axiomatic to the likes of Choate and Daniel Webster, not to mention the New England–dominated schoolbook industry of Hawthorne's day. In *The Scarlet Letter,* in the one moment during either the introduction or the story proper when the grand narrative is told with any enthusiasm, it remains inaudible and suspect—Dimmesdale's sermon, said to foretell the colony's "high and glorious destiny" (*SL* 157)—a standard ministerial theme on certain ceremonial occasions, then and (even more) in Hawthorne's day. *The Scarlet Letter* makes sure to keep the reader at a great distance from this performance—outside the church with Hester, who doesn't catch a word of it, except for its undertone of "plaintiveness" and "anguish" despite the "majestic"-sounding voice (154). All we know for sure is that Dimmesdale composed it in an abnormal and agitated state. The rapturous prophecy is not to be believed.

The Old World past cannot be disowned in this romance because its New World sequel is so diminished. The reduction of the protagonists to ghosts of their former selves shows this plainly enough. Dimmesdale "had come from one of the great English universities, bringing all the learning of the new age into our wild forest-land" (*SL* 48). It's all downhill from there. Internalization of the provincial thought police socializes him into such timidity that Hester's challenge in the forest ("be a scholar and a sage among the wisest and the most renowned of the cultivated world. Preach! Write! Act!") sickens rather than invigorates him (127). Hester's mind, by contrast, expands to the point that she assumes "a freedom of speculation, then common enough on the other side of the Atlantic," but by colonial Puritan standards "a deadlier crime than that stigmatized by the scarlet letter" (107). In this brave new world, what Hester has become cannot socially exist. Despite *The Scarlet Letter*'s detailed ethnography of early colonial culture and institutions, its imagination of place remains more diasporic than nativized. The standard of cultural vitality remains transatlantic and colonial life and culture underactualized and without issue—characters, narrator, author all disaffiliated from the New World settlement that's supposed to be their habitat. Hester's return to Boston to her old role as letter wearer must be understood not just in a forward-looking fashion—whether as template for the republican covenant of consent or as augury of some counterorthodox utopia eventually to come—but also as confirmation of the scanty options to which the narrative has shown that the decision to emigrate condemns one.

Seen in this light, *The Scarlet Letter* begins to seem less about colony consolidation or nation building than about the ordeals of immigrant transplantation, a dislocating experience whose investment in issues of independent nationhood, or even of autonomous region, is tentative at best. So seen, its closest affiliations seem to be with narratives of rebuffed or imperfect adaptation to a place conceived through half-assimilated eyes as alien ground, from the captivity narrative of Mary Rowlandson to James's *The Europeans* (1878) to Flannery O'Connor's "The Displaced Person" (1955) to Chang Rae Lee's *A Gesture Life* (1999). *The Scarlet Letter* does not so much insinuate "Here is national fiction" as pose the question: "Can there be such a thing?" or "Why should there be?" And beyond that: "Is it true that the nation should be the fundamental reference point of collective political identity, fantasy, and practice?" "How permanent is the nation as an associative form?"[37] That *The Scarlet Letter* raises such fundamental questions surely also helps explain its fertility as a national master text. What De Forest saw as disqualifying it from GAN contention—that Hawthorne's imagination was insufficiently moored to American soil—turned out to be a preeminent reason for *The Scarlet Letter's* staying power. It seizes on the liminal point when settlement culture has just begun to take precarious root, so that the disposition of one adultery case involving a single refractory woman could seem of utmost urgency from the top down for the preservation of public order;* and the community's adults live their lives in the double consciousness of expatriation from a still-beckoning otherworld to which they might well return—a world that would call the direction, the solidity, and the viability of the New World experiment into question.

The Scarlet Letter's extended spatial horizon, glimpsed fitfully at intervals, resonates with "The Custom-House" narrator's ambivalent verdict on his ties to Salem, his home base in the enclave the Puritans started. He acknowledges a certain "feeling for old Salem, which for lack of a better phrase, I must be content to call affection"; but he pro-

* As Hester approaches Bellingham's mansion to resist the move afoot to transfer Pearl to "wiser and better guardianship," the narrator observes that this was the same moment "when a dispute concerning the right of property in a pig" caused "an important modification of the framework itself of the legislature" (see *SL* 68 and its explanatory footnote). As Colacurcio dryly notes, "a world where a pig can alter a legislature is a world in flux" (*Doctrine and Difference,* 207).

ceeds to write it off as "the mere sensuous sympathy of dust for dust," an inertial residue, asphyxiating to the creative spirit. In his famous parting shot he insists, "Henceforth, it ceases to be a reality of my life. I am a citizen of somewhere else." To resort to seventeenth-century Puritan romance as the main narrative is in keeping with the distance he now covets: to see his ancestral home "through the haze of memory" (*SL* 11, 35).

Great American Novel Despite Itself: The Retellings

A crucial factor behind the Hawthorne "tradition," claims Brodhead, the closest student of its nineteenth-century American phases, is that Hawthorne "seems only very partially to have realized the potentials he senses, in the writing of his work," so that "other writers undertake to produce the powerful forms they see only half-achieved in him."[38] "Gives the impression of seeming" would be closer to the mark; but the observation points to a key trait of Hawthornian style implicit in what we've just been witnessing. "Most persons of ability," Emerson wrote, "meet in society with a kind of tacit appeal," as if to imply, "I am not all here."[39] *The Scarlet Letter* gives off a similar impression of suppressed potential through its overdetermined structure, its carefully measured narrative voice that only now and then seems to drop the mask, its self-conflicted judgmentalism, its continual intimations that the story told here delivers less than full disclosure, its hints of latent intuitions that it will not even "acknowledge or define," as with Hester and Dimmesdale in the forest scene, even after they have renewed their vows (*SL* 132). That is why it is not utterly outrageous for Roland Jaffe's 1990s Hollywood adaptation of *The Scarlet Letter* to end with the Indians rescuing Hester, Dimmesdale, and Pearl and burning down Boston. Or why the much more faithful PBS miniseries of the 1970s shouldn't be faulted overmuch for jumping the rails in the forest scene by representing Hester and Dimmesdale as actually having sex. For the narrator repeatedly emits signals to the effect that he might wish things could work out differently even though he knows they can't and increasingly agrees they shouldn't.

Take Hawthorne's tantalizing but cursory evocations of the Atlantic world of which 1640s Boston was part. These have been of mounting interest, for literary critics and creative writers alike, as the "American imaginary" has been increasingly reconceived in transnational terms during the past quarter century. By contrast to what Hawthorne well knew was the colony's heteroglot demographic, *The Scarlet Letter* relegates Native Americans to bit parts around the margins of the first and last crowd scenes even while evoking them as offstage presences: Chillingworth's captors and instructors in herbalism and the exurban enclave of Christian converts visited by Dimmesdale. Africans are invisible, barely even hinted at. Except for the last scaffold scene's cameo of the swashbuckling sea captain and his crew from the Spanish Main, *The Scarlet Letter,* as Laura Doyle observes, "occludes the active world of transatlantic trade, interloping, and political maneuvering."[40] Transatlantic consciousness is otherwise registered at the level of the privileged orders: Bellingham's attempt to replicate an English garden; Hester recalling girlhood residence; allusions to Dimmesdale's Cambridge education; Chillingworth's belatedly revealed fortune; Pearl's marriage into a family whose escutcheon has "bearings unknown to English heraldry" (*SL* 165). In one particularly extravagant burst of Anglophilic nostalgia, the narrator idealizes "the sunny richness of the Elizabethan epoch" as "a time when the life of England, viewed as one great mass, would appear to have been as stately, magnificent, and joyous, as the world has ever witnessed" (146).

Among recent attempts to see this horizon extended, none does so with more panache than Bharati Mukherjee's *The Holder of the World* (1993), whose metahistorical agility compensates for its elements of fluorescent zaniness. *Holder* features a contemporary female narrator, Beigh Masters, who, like Hawthorne, is a skilled historian conscious of her family's New England antecedence and is nominally employed—reminiscently of Surveyor Hawthorne—in "asset management." Even more than the "Custom-House" narrator confesses himself to have been, Beigh is transfixed by the novel's Hester figure, Hannah. (*Holder* also features two other characters provocatively named Hester.) Hannah is not an immigrant but a Massachusetts frontier child whose widowed mother deserts her during King Philip's War for the sake of an Indian lover. Thus starts a picaresque plot that takes Hannah through Puritan girlhood in Salem, brief residence in London, then to the original India—the reverse transit from the Bengali-born author's. Replicating her mother's interracialism, she becomes mistress of the ruler of a Hindu state, fleeing it after he is killed by the conquering Moghul emperor to return to New England with her unborn child, predictably named Pearl. Gabriel Legge, the shady merchant-pirate who whisked Hannah from Salem to England to India, is a blow-up of Hawthorne's dodgy captain who contracts to take Hester, Dimmesdale, and Pearl back to England.

Hannah's extrication from her monitorial Puritan foster-parents does not save her from irksome domestic reconfinement. Gabriel turns sour, jealous, and patriarchal, prompting her flight inland from the Indian port colony of multinational traders where he's virtually imprisoned her. Still, her globe-circling odyssey is the antithesis to *The Scarlet Letter*'s centripetalism: Hawthorne multiculturalized, Hawthorne transnationalized, Hawthorne in living color, *The Scarlet Letter* Bollywoodized. *Holder* unpacks the geopolitics barely hinted at in Hawthorne's text, connecting the remotest ends of empire, dramatizing the hyperactive, raffish fortuity of colonial enterprise. Two of the clues from which the narrator reconstructs Hannah's lifeline are her sampler of "the uttermost shore"—Hannah too is deft with the needle—and an Indian artist's renditions of "the Salem Bibi": mirror images of the termini of the Anglophone world.

Mukherjee ingeniously updates the judgment passed on *The Scarlet Letter* in a noted article of the 1940s, "Scarlet A Minus": that Hawthorne lacked the courage of his novel's best convictions.[41] For *Holder* too, Hawthorne "sh[ied] away from the real story of the brave Salem mother and her illegitimate daughter" even though it was Hannah's "stories of the China and India trade" that induced Hawthorne's great-grandfather to become the first of the clan to go to sea. *Holder*'s corrective one-ups "The Custom-House's" whimsical anecdote of imagined reconnection to the past, when the narrator puts the moth-eaten letter to his chest and feels the strange pulsation of heat. With the aid of virtual reality software designed by her Indian boyfriend, an MIT researcher, Beigh is transported back to the moment when Hannah and her servant-companion Bhagmati (whom she renames Hester after a childhood friend) steal "the world's most perfect diamond" from the Moghul emperor. Beigh feels the diamond as it is handed off by faltering Hannah to the fleeing Bhagmati/Hester, feels herself mowed down by the sharpshooter's bullets that mortally wound Bhagmati, then feels herself wield Bhagmati's knife and "plunge the diamond into the deepest part of me." Beigh's software doesn't get her quite where she'd hoped—into Hannah's mind/body—but they do meet, virtually, face to face.[42]

Given *Holder*'s insistence on deterritorializing *The Scarlet Letter* as the way to seize hold of its "true" story, its Americanization of the denouement is especially provocative. Mukherjee's Hester and Pearl return to New England to stay. What's more, they return as proto-republican libertarians. "'We are Americans to freedom born!' White Pearl and Black Pearl [their local nicknames] were heard to mutter, the latter even in school." *Holder* sets itself against Hawthorne's "morbid introspection into guilt and repression that many call our greatest work." Hawthorne wrote, she adds, against "the distant memory of a shameful, heroic time," whereas this novel seeks to "bring alive the first letter of an alphabet of hope and of horror stretching out, and back to the uttermost shores."[43] So *Holder* declares itself a truer and more wholehearted tale of national origins than the backward-looking, downbeat one Hawthorne himself was able to tell.

This self-positioning of *Holder* as the more rightful story makes sense in light of Mukherjee's insistence, "I am an American writer, in the American mainstream, trying to extend it. . . . I am not an Indian writer, not an exile, not an expatriate. I am an immigrant." Contra the investment of Christopher Bigsby's *Hester* in the Anglo-European prehistory of the Hester-Chillingworth-Dimmesdale story and Paula Reed's exploration of the Old-World adventures of mother and daughter after they expatriate, *Holder* seeks a next-stage, deparochialized Americanization.[44] So too the counter-Americanization of the motifs of pariah-mother, elf-child, and diaspora in Toni Morrison's *Beloved*.

To place such emphasis on *Holder* is to risk understating the range of uses to which *The Scarlet Letter* has been put and overstating the degree to which it figures for later adapters as a central premise versus subsidiary motif. Some of the best *Letter*-inflected novels, like *Beloved*, enlist it much more tangentially. In Faulkner's *As I Lay Dying*, a mordant mock-epic of a poor white farming family's accident-ridden quest to fulfill the matriarch's wish to be buried in her family's plot in town, *The Scarlet Letter* makes a veiled cameo appearance in two chapters that recall the dead Addie's clandestine affair with the pastor who conducts her funeral service and in the figure of her truculent but loyal illegitimate son Jewel, Addie's trial but also her favorite among the five siblings, whose brute strength saves her coffin from flood waters and a barn fire along the way. How might the scandal of adultery between local minister and headstrong matron play itself out in this even more benightedly super-stitious backwater? (Answer: it wouldn't be as hard as one might think to stay below the radar of neighborly surveillance, and it mightn't have been so inwardly corrosive for the adulterers either.) What about the fate of the illegitimate child? (Answer: in hardscrabble Yoknapatawpha outback real-time, neither fatherly recognition nor fortune await, but alienation confers survival skills as well as scars.) Faulkner's engage-ment with *The Scarlet Letter* is done so unobtrusively, however, that read-ers don't need to catch the allusions any more than appreciation of *The Scarlet Letter* hinges on thinking "Marvell," "Scott," and "Rousseau"—or even "Anne Hutchinson" for that matter. But perceiving them makes the dead-end grimness of Addie's scanty life choices more resonant, as well as her bond to the child who gives her the most grief, Jewel's bond to her, and the oiliness of this preacher's hypocrisy—confident that God has forgiven his slip.

Similarly, both Henry James's *The Portrait of a Lady* and William Dean Howells's *A Modern Instance,* the first significant U.S. divorce novel, quietly update *The Scarlet Letter* by building plots around the question of how, with the bad old order of parentally arranged marriages like Hes-ter's supposedly displaced by the better new order of love marriage by consent and parenting indulgent to the point of laissez-faire, a free-spirited young woman like James's Isabel or Howells's Marcia with suitors aplenty could opt for such disastrous mismatches as the coldly imperious aesthete Osmond (Isabel) and on-the-make wastrel Bartley Hubbard (Marcia). Yet you might read through the better part of each book before suspecting that either was written with *The Scarlet Letter* in mind. Only then come hints like Isabel's embracement of Osmond's il-legitimate child Pansy as consolation when her marriage sours and Osmond's Chillingworth-like antipathy to Isabel's sensitive invalid cousin Ralph, whom Osmond knows she loves much more dearly than himself or any other man. Or Howells's belated development of Bartley's one-time chum Ben Halleck, whose outsized conscience torments him through and beyond his Dimmesdale-ish decision to enter the ministry with the scruple that even after the faithless husband is dead and gone it might be wrong to marry the widow—the girl of his youthful dreams even before Bartley set eyes on her—because he hankered for Marcia while Bartley was still alive.[45]

Reciprocally, close adherence to the Hawthornian original hardly guarantees success. The film that sticks most closely to the original text, the PBS version, got bogged down in striving for historically precise rendition of the descriptive tableaux—one of countless cautionary tales of American cinematic flattening of great novels by prioritizing objective realism at the expense of subjectified narration. A century before, George Eliot's *Adam Bede,* a novel in the style of Victorian realism centered like Hawthorne's on a four-sided entanglement in a bygone provincial setting, also sacrificed much of *The Scarlet Letter'*s narrative interiority, but to better effect by daring to reconceive it tragicomically. On the one hand, *Adam Bede* splits the Hester figure between pretty but wayward Hetty, who is tried and nearly executed for the panicky infanticide of the baby she has by squire Arthur—handsome, kind, well-meaning at heart but no less susceptible than she—and the Methodist exhorter Dinah, her cousin and friend who becomes her chief consoler in prison, an episode that recalls Hester's last vocation as prophetess turned counselor to younger women. On the other hand, the novel reproduces Hawthorne's male dyad in the estrangement between the squire and noble Adam, a skilled carpenter and model workman, Arthur's friend in youth and then trusted retainer until they come to blows over the disgrace of Hetty, for whom Adam had also pined. But the remorseful seducer makes amends by getting Hetty's death sentence commuted to banishment, by banishing himself to an army life, and by humbling himself to a forgiving Adam, who is then freed up to recognize what others close to them have long known, that worthy Dinah is his proper mate.

This makes for an unusually tidy and upbeat closure for a post–*Scarlet Letter* novel—as if Eliot had opted to make *Adam Bede'*s central premise the strange hopeful aside in Hawthorne's epilogue that the aversion between Chillingworth and Dimmesdale might be transformed into "golden love" in the hereafter (*SL* 164). But then again, few reinventions are as unrelievedly somber as Hawthorne's, Suzan-Lori Parks's red-letter plays excepted. *Holder of the World* foresees the dawn of American freedom. Christopher Bigsby pictures a returned Hester who "never let regret become her life." Faulkner lets the family succeed in getting Addie buried, although the chief beneficiary is the shiftless widower who gets the false teeth he wants and a replacement wife as well. Updike's rompish satire *S.* liberates the ironically named Sarah Worth from a bad marriage to a hotshot Boston surgeon, then from a sexually overcharged pseudo-utopia presided over by an "Indian" guru later unmasked as one Art Steinmetz of Watertown, Massachusetts, to wind up contentedly solo on a Bahamian island, bankrolled by funds partly seized with rough justice from her marital assets and embezzled from the ashram during her stint as pro tem financial officer. Even *Roger's Version*, far the best of Updike's otherwise underwhelming *Scarlet Letter* trilogy, imagines the Dimmesdale figure finally decamped and "Esther" at least nominally back together with the husband she'd earlier chastised as a "cold, play-it-safe bastard," both of them minding for the nonce this book's Pearl surrogate, the illegitimate biracial daughter of Roger's niece.[46]

Maybe such swerves go to show the contagion of the supposedly chronic American disrelish for the tragic. But there's no iron law here. Few generalizations about the scattergram of *The Scarlet Letter*'s aftereffects can be made to stick except that the Pearl figure usually gets reduced to a comparative bit part (Hetty's murdered baby is an extreme case, but predictive too); and that transpositions of *The Scarlet Letter*'s plot always swerve from Hawthorne's equal-time nominal allocation of space between their protagonists in favor of emphasizing either a reinvented Hester or a reinvented Dimmesdale.

If it is Dimmesdale, an American adaptation will tend to make this figure some kind of cleric who implodes: Frederic's Theron Ware, Updike's Tom Marshfield in *A Month of Sundays*, the protagonist's divinity student adversary in *Roger's Version*. The durability of the religion frame bespeaks not so much deference to Hawthorne as the remarkable persistence of religion—and with it fears of religious hypocrisy and predation—as a force within national culture to an extent that has made the contemporary United States an outlier among the world's economically advanced nations. Literary historian David Reynolds plausibly suggests that the stereotypical "lip-smacking reverend rake" of popular nineteenth-century sensational literature provided fodder for Hawthorne's imagination of Dimmesdale, as it did with even greater vehemence in the earliest known reinvention of *The Scarlet Letter* plot, Alice Cary's *Hagar* (1852), which turns on a hypocritical minister's desertion of the worthy young woman he has seduced and impregnated, absconding with their infant child to boot.[47] In twenty-first-century U.S. culture, that stereotype thrives as vigorously as ever.

But more often, understandably, the preferred figure is Hester, who radiates far greater energy. Dimmesdale is shadowy, Hester dynamic. He's timid; she's bold. He can't think outside the box; she can and has, too long ever to fit neatly back. Dimmesdale is atavistic, with his monkish penances. Hester is by contrast "modern"—as "liberated," Nina Baym observes, "as woman can hope to be liberated" in such a time and place.[48] Hawthorne's "sex-freedom link," we've seen, followed earlier antebellum romancers of seventeenth-century New England in centering the critique of social hierarchicalism in the figure of a rebellious daughter, more independent minded than her Puritan sisters would have been, confronting an establishment more monolithic than seventeenth-century Puritanism actually was. Later Hester-centric books elaborate that confrontation and abet, even when they don't gratify, the desire to see her emancipated from the constraints Hawthorne's version of the tale imposes on her. James's Isabel defying Osmond's prohibitions against visiting Pansy and Ralph, Updike's satiric emancipation of S, and Mukherjee's and Reed's rewritings of Hester's post–New England adventures abroad are cases in point.

Such novels have a further interest for our purposes, as bending *The Scarlet Letter* in the direction of the kind of protagonist-centered plotline discussed in Part III, narratives involving transformation from obscurity to prominence. In James, it's Isabel's metamorphosis from innocent girl of slender means stuck in upstate New York to heiress and cynosure of the Anglo-European elite; in Mukherjee, the transit from frontier outback to power behind an Indian throne; in Reed, from Boston pariah to Oliver Cromwell's inner circle. Even though *The Scarlet Letter* was not the up-from bildungsroman that Catharine Maria Sedgwick's *Hope Leslie* came much closer to being, it gave aid and comfort to that kind of story line by plotting Hester's trajectory as inverse to Dimmesdale's decay. Never mind that pushing this line of interpretation very far runs afoul of the narrator's disapproval of Hester's insurgent antinomianism. Never mind that Hester's success in winning back community respect belies her mounting alienation from it. Not only does *The Scarlet Letter* cater more than the narrator lets on to the desire to see this young woman flourish as her courage and determination deserve, the finale unleashes it in the next generation through Pearl's rags-to-riches transformation from ragamuffin to aristocrat.

Speaking of Pearl's marriage to that continental grandee, *The Scarlet Letter* also leans toward the romances of the divide, discussed in Part IV.

As a provincial tale written against the limits of provincialism so as to commingle the exoticism of its strangeness and the toxic claustrophobia of its confines, it anticipates Twain's *Huckleberry Finn* in a minor key, not to mention the more God-haunted southern gothic of Faulkner, Flannery O'Connor, and many others. The specific fault lines of North/South and black/white foregrounded in Chapters 7–10 pass largely unnoticed in *The Scarlet Letter;** but its broaching of the Euro-Atlantic divide(s)—explored more intensively in Hawthorne's late work inspired by sojourns in Britain and Italy *(Our Old Home, The Marble Faun)*—prefigures the centrality accorded that international theme by James, Wharton, and a number of the American modernists, not to mention its passage to India in Mukherjee's *Holder.*

The Scarlet Letter also provided a platform for next-generation writers for whom sectarian divides seemed more important cultural fault lines than for most Hawthorne readers today. Harold Frederic's best-selling *The Damnation of Theron Ware,* itself once thought by some to be the mythical Great American Novel,[49] is one of the strongest of a spate of late-century Anglo-American novels about ministers losing their faith. Frederic draws ingeniously on *The Scarlet Letter* in framing small-town upstate New York as a battleground between an internally divided Methodism, other Protestant sects, and the specter of an insurgent, racialized Irish Catholicism. Theron's hard-shell Methodist parish is a shriveled comedown from Boston's First Church in the 1640s, evangelical fervor having been so trumped by self-serving formalism that even his silver-tongued oratory can't unbend it. Theron himself is a tinpot Dimmesdale, intellectually shallow and insouciantly hedonistic underneath his nice-boy proprieties. The novel unfolds a quasi-naturalistic plot of his undoing through which Hawthornian allusions reverberate (the opening gambit of the guessing game outside the town church, the tryst in the forest, etc.). Theron becomes fascinated by the town's exotic-seeming knot of much better-educated and more worldly Catholics: his counterpart Father Forbes; Forbes's strange physician-scientist

---

* Some critics, however, have argued for the importance of African American subtexts to *The Scarlet Letter,* such as Jay Grossman (focusing on the symbolic black man) and Michael Newberry (the thematics and ideology of public exposure for Hester/Dimmesdale vis-à-vis such antebellum slaves and slave narrators as Harriet Jacobs) (Jay Grossman, "'A Is for Abolition?' Race, Authorship, *The Scarlet Letter,*" *Textual Practice* 7 [Spring 1993]: 13–30; Michael Newberry, *Figuring Authorship in Antebellum America* [Stanford, CA: Stanford University Press, 1997], 97–118).

friend Dr. Ledsmar, a morphed Chillingworth; and above all the gorgeous Celia Madden, daughter of the town's wealthiest Catholic family and the church organist. (The frontispiece of the first edition sports a Beardsleyesque image meant to double as Celia's portrait and a stained glass image that reminds Theron of her.)[50] At first these urbane Catholics patronize the young minister for his ingenuous charm. But as he becomes smitten by Celia, negligent as a pastor, alienated from his blameless wife Alice, and goaded to oafish behavior by groundless jealousy of Celia's closeness to Forbes and of Alice's one supporter among his parish elders, his new friends reject him as a nuisance and leave him to a self-destructive drunken bender, to be rescued deus ex machina fashion by a Methodist worker who helps him patch it up with Alice and sends them west to Seattle to give Theron a fresh start—as a real estate agent. All this does nothing to dispel Forbes's prediction—upending the supposed message of Dimmesdale's last sermon—that Irish Catholicism will become America's faith: "it will embrace them all, and in turn influence their development, till you have a new nation, and a new national church, each representative of the other."[51] A generation later, *Theron Ware* helped inspire Sinclair Lewis's much bigger-selling ministerial exposé *Elmer Gantry*—whose title character stood for the next half-century as a byword for clerical hypocrisy and salaciousness.

The Scarlet Letter even anticipates, though more dimly, the novels taken up in Part V, which turn in varying degrees on images of groups that model different forms of "democratic" collectivity in the making or under duress. This the book mostly does negatively, through the crowd scenes that make visible the demands of society on the individual as a regulating force. As Bercovitch shows, Hawthorne well knew that a direct line between the Puritan primordium that *The Scarlet Letter* images so grimly and the republican fruits of the American Revolution had been drawn by the founding fathers of New England heritage and again by such leading nineteenth-century American historians as George Bancroft—also the Democratic Party boss who secured him his Custom House job.[52] That Hawthorne refuses more than perfunctory satirical gestures at anything like a full-fledged social novel opens him up to the charge of falling on the delinquent side of the demarcation line between "national" (engaged) and "literary" (socially evasive) fiction.[53] Still, *The Scarlet Letter*'s spectral, two-dimensionalized rendition of colonial beginnings foreshadows more sustained fictions of democratic social order, albeit mostly by the negative route of countering the tendency to idealize its alleged inception point in the colonization of New England. What anthropologist Kai Erikson called Puritanism's sociology of deviance, its intense policing of infractions minor as well as major,[54] reflected an anxiety about the fragile nascence of the social system that seems at first belied, yet on second thought confirmed, by the massing of the whole community to witness Hester's initial shame and again for the Election Day ceremonies of which Dimmesdale's sermon and self-exposure are the climaxes. A kind of anxious survivalism drives such assemblages. As Hawthorne readers well know, his fiction is full of ensemble scenes, ranging from the ominous (the jeering crowd in "My Kinsman, Major Molineux") to benignly relaxed contemplation of the variegated human scene ("The Toll-Gatherer's Day," "Sights from a Steeple," "The Hall of Fantasy"). Taken together, they show a marked if guarded partiality for imagining forms of inclusive sociality freed from the coercive herd-think that made the Puritan version of it so invasive.

The affinities between *The Scarlet Letter,* its successors, and the formations in terms of which the rest of this book is organized doubtless help explain its durability as a master-text, although of course they hardly exhaust that explanation. A singular text constitutes its own force field, casts its own shadow. That is the single most important conclusion to be drawn from the multiple latter-day permutations of the *Scarlet Letter* story. But since the shadows cast do partly converge into constellations, and since "the" Great American Novel has for more than a century been thought of in the plural, with certain specific templates at least implicitly in mind, we do well to give more emphasis to them from here on, starting with the one most closely tied to American cultural history's single most iconic story line.

PART THREE

SCRIPT TWO:
ASPIRATION IN AMERICA

Introduction

American Dreamers in Context

SINCE COLONIAL TIMES, American audiences have been attracted to coming-of-age stories featuring the extraordinary adventures of ordinary persons. In a way, there's nothing new or distinctively "American" about this. On the contrary, it's key to what originally made novels seem novel compared to ancient epic and medieval romance—the shift from tales of legendary heroism to stories about more recognizably familiar persons. The coevolution of liberal individualism and "democratic" institutions intensified the focus on the lifelines of more ordinary people, and has made individual flourishing or the lack thereof a common litmus test of cultural vitality even as the individual is imagined as operating within and/or against a cultural collectivity that in some sense also defines him or her.

The American contribution to the history of such stories is both peripheral and central. The novel was a European invention, a product of the Renaissance that started to take off in the late 1600s. The seminal statement of the theory that the measure of a robustly mature culture should be the fully realized individual life came with Friedrich Schiller's *Letters on the Aesthetic Education of Man* (1794). That in turn became the premise of the bildungsroman, the novel of "development" or "formation" that charts the protagonist's growth from childhood to social maturity, the genre-defining example of which Schiller's friend Wolfgang von Goethe was even then composing: *Wilhelm Meisters Lehrjahre* (Wilhelm Meister's apprenticeship,

1796).* At that point, U.S. fiction was in its infancy. Not until the second quarter of the century did Weimar thinking start to take hold in the United States, chiefly through British middlemen like Goethe's translator Thomas Carlyle. Yet well before Schiller and Goethe sat down to write, British America had generated its own paradigmatic narrative of individual formation, more egalitarian and also more utilitarian than Schiller's, for whom personal flourishing implied the highest pitch of intellectual refinement and sociality. This homegrown variant was the story of remarkable rise from humble origins. It became this nation's single most defining mythic narrative both at home and abroad.

How American writers seized upon, ramified, and quarreled with this script, yet remained bonded to it regardless of the empirical facts, is the story that the next three chapters tell. The centerpiece will be a half-dozen twentieth-century novels from F. Scott Fitzgerald's *The Great Gatsby* and Theodore Dreiser's *An American Tragedy* to Ralph Ellison's *Invisible Man* and Philip Roth's *American Pastoral* that have been held up either in their time or after as GANs. All of them focus on protagonists imagined as national exemplars who attempt for better and for worse to act out versions of the traditional American dream script.

In correlating the travails of their protagonists' history with national history and values, such novels belie the exceptionalism they seem to assert, since the correlation itself is broadly typical. The "up-from" plots by U.S. writers do indeed stand out for their engagement of the stereo-

---

* The German professor of aesthetics Karl Morgenstern coined "bildungsroman" in its modern sense in 1819, with special reference to *Wilhelm Meisters Lehrjahre,* but the term was rarely used as a genre designation until the twentieth century. Ever since, critical discussion has been bedeviled by controversy between loose and strict constructionists. Some of the latter narrow down the set of the eligible to the vanishing point. Yet as Marc Redfield remarks, the "more the genre is cast into question the more it flourishes," and the term itself seems "ineradicable" (Marc Redfield, *Phantom Formations: Aesthetic Ideology and the Bildungsroman* [Ithaca, NY: Cornell University Press, 1996], 42, 43). I favor a loose definition in the spirit of Douglas Mao's perception that any "definition" of this moving target is at best a "rough and ready" approximation that shimmers somewhere in between two of his summations: "a long narrative concerned with a fictional individual's maturation" (a bit too sweeping?) and "the story of a young person achieving, for better or for worse, some rapprochement with a social reality that had at first seemed hostile" (a bit too constraining to accommodate modernist swerves and disruptions?) (Douglas Mao, *Fateful Beauty: Aesthetic Environments, Juvenile Development, and Literature 1860–1960* [Princeton, NJ: Princeton University Press, 2008], 6, 93). While "bildungsroman" is accepted as an English term, I italicize *Bildung* to recognize that there is no English equivalent to the German term, which implies both aspiration and process and the connotations both of "image" and "formation."

typical image of a country especially hospitable to upward mobility. But beyond a point they are variations of the bildungsroman template, originally a Eurocentric form but now diffused worldwide. Narrative theorist M. M. Bakhtin famously defined the bildungsroman as presenting "an image of *man growing* in *national-historical time.*" Literature scholars rightly continue to stress the importance of its "soul-nation allegory," as Jed Esty terms it.[1]

Once it was thought that the bildungsroman was a distinctively nineteenth-century European form designed to model some kind of postfeudal, nonrevolutionary compromise between "the ideal of *self-determination*" and "the equally imperious demands of *socialization*," and that it collapsed in modernity as the social world "solidified into impersonal institutions" and "the new psychology started to dismantle the unified image of the individual." So affirmed Franco Moretti in an influential 1987 study, and with some reason.[2] The dissolution of the last chapter of James Joyce's *Portrait of the Artist as a Young Man* (1916) into disjointed subjective fragments is a far cry from the tidy denouements of Charlotte Brontë's *Jane Eyre* (1847) and Charles Dickens's *David Copperfield* (1850). Yet despite literary modernism's disruptions of the traditional bildungsroman by accentuating the questions that such "classic" cases as George Eliot's *The Mill on the Floss* (1860) and Flaubert's *Sentimental Education* (1869) had already begun to raise about the progressivity of personal development, societal coherence, and the fit between the two, the genre persists to this day, not least in the literatures of the developing world, although critics differ as to precisely how. For Joseph Slaughter, postcolonial bildungsroman, like its nineteenth-century predecessors, goes hand in hand with human rights law to "project individuated narratives of self-determination as cultural alternatives to the eruptive political act of mass revolt." Critical theorist Pheng Cheah, by contrast, follows nationalism theorist Benedict Anderson in claiming *Bildung* and bildungsroman as conduits for emergent postcolonial aspiration.[3] You need not strain to choose between Cheah's "liberationist" or Slaughter's "regulationist" reading in order to be convinced, as another postcolonial critic shrewdly puts it, that bildungsroman's reputation in some quarters for being "a bad traveler" beyond its time and place of origin is overblown.[4]

The pervasiveness of novels of intertwined personal and social or national formation, first in the Western world and then worldwide, creates more problems than solutions, however, when it comes to trying to bring U.S. literature of this kind into focus. Because the United States instigated the world's first successful bourgeois revolution against a monarchical power, and because it generated a homegrown mythic narrative of bootstrapping self-improvement even before the Germans first started theorizing about *Bildung* and bildungsroman, it might seem that the heyday of American novels built on the up-from script would have coincided with if not anticipated the heyday of the European bildungsroman during the first two-thirds of the nineteenth century. But in fact they did not come into vogue until the Anglo-European bildungsroman was on the verge of metamorphosing from its "classic" expression in Goethe, Walter Scott, Jane Austen, and Charlotte Brontë and becoming overtaken with the perplexities we find in Joyce's *Portrait* and Kipling's and Conrad's images of "frozen youth" on the imperial periphery.[5] Indeed the GAN candidates that most squarely engage the culturally sanctioned up-from mythic narrative date only from the second quarter of the twentieth century, following scenarios in which the traditional plot of identity formation unfolds in symbiotic tension with the imperatives of social adjustment and collides with the modernist emphasis on imperfect, failed, or arrested development. Probably by no coincidence, this was also a time when the credibility of the up-from culture myth itself had come under increasing pressure. Yet neither the myth nor the story line that embodied it withered away. On the contrary, both have persisted into the twenty-first century in mutated forms, in a striking mixture of recognition, critique, revision, and defiance of the diminished probability of actually living out the traditional dream script.

4

"Success" Stories from Franklin
to the Dawn of Modernism

They went on to other secrets. How a self-made man should
always say he was born in something like a log cabin, prefera-
bly with no running water.

—GISH JEN, *Typical American* (1991)

He's the best physician that knows the worthlessness of the
most medicines.

—BENJAMIN FRANKLIN, *Poor Richard's Almanac* (1733)

THE PREHISTORY OF NARRATIVES of transformation from humble beginnings stretches back long before the invention of the modern
novel. Versions pervade world folklore, as in the tales of Aladdin and
Cinderella. It's at the core of many conversion narratives, saints' lives,
and canonical stories of charismatic prophets from Moses to Jesus to
Mohammed. Some of the earliest English fictional classics told stories
of transformation of otherwise unremarkable people, such as John
Bunyan's *Pilgrim's Progress* (1678), an allegorical narrative of an ordinary
man's progress from sin to salvation, and Samuel Richardson's *Pamela*
(1740), whose virtuous servant-girl heroine resists her employer's attempts at seduction until he relents and proposes marriage instead.

Such stories left an indelible mark on U.S. national thought and
writing. In the best-known among the many hundreds of antebellum
slave narratives, Frederick Douglass describes the "turning-point" of
his life in bondage—his decision to fight back against Covey the slave-
breaker—as a conversion experience whereby he was born anew, as the
"resurrection" of his manhood from the "tomb of slavery" to the "heaven
of freedom."[1] The first widely popular American fictional genre, the
"sentimental" novel, characteristically features a *Pamela*-like ordeal in
which the virtuous resolve of a heroine of precarious social status is

tested by a predatory male. (The last section of this chapter examines one of *Pamela's* best-selling American daughters, Maria Cummins's *The Lamplighter*.)² More distinctive to the imagination of U.S. national experience, however, was the image promoted in colonial times of a comparatively open and classless society and bountiful resources offering better prospects of advancement for the average person than Old World hierarchicalism did.

This image was predictably deployed as hype by overzealous, often sleazy promoters of colonization, to the ruin of the unwary. It was narrowly targeted, too: first and foremost to white Protestant males of northern European origin. But the promise of advancement seemed borne out often enough to take permanent hold, reinforced as well by the Declaration of Independence's proclamation of "all men"'s right to life, liberty, and the pursuit of happiness. That hopeful image made this country synonymous with "opportunity" and, in time, with a particular kind of life narrative: "the American dream" of the "self-made man" who from modest or even severely disadvantaged beginnings can improve his position in life dramatically by dint of hard work, self-discipline, and good fortune. Both at home and abroad, there still seems something characteristically "American" about the life stories of Abraham Lincoln, Harry Truman, Bill Clinton, and Barack Obama.

Such stories obviously do not "reflect statistical realities as much as they tell of possibilities," wisely cautions an early twenty-first-century sociological study of "new elites" of non-European immigrant background, the chief beneficiaries of the abolition of country quotas in 1965.³ Today the United States ranks near the *bottom* among developed countries in respect to actual upward mobility; inflation-adjusted income for the top decile of Americans has risen dramatically since the 1970s while remaining flat or declining for the rest.⁴ But even from the time American up-from stories began, those who circulated them often only half believed. Take for example Hector St. Jean de Crèvecoeur's classic definition of the prototypical American as a thrifty, industrious, productive "new man" derived from the common peoples of all Europe in his *Letters from an American Farmer* (1782).⁵ His poster-boy example, the penniless Scots immigrant Andrew the Hebridean, who became a prosperous middle-states farmer, is effectively neutralized during the later stages of the book when attention gets directed elsewhere, first to the horrors of plantation slavery and then to the chaos of the Revolution, which drives the narrator to take refuge with a tribe of hospitable savages. *American Farmer* undermines its early claims even more than the author probably intended by its admixture of empathy and disrelish for the two largest outcast groups on whose subjugation the fulfillment of its pan-European vision depends. So as U.S. fiction develops over the next two centuries, it should come as no surprise to find serious novels centering on transformational life sagas—including all those discussed in detail in Part III—disputing conventional valuations of success, satirizing the self-made man myth as chimerical or deformative, and casting themselves more as cautionary tales of failure or overreach than as tales of triumph.

This history of skeptical fascination synchronizes uneasily with the history of the American dream as a conjuring phrase. The myth wasn't even given its now-familiar name until the twentieth century. It was put into circulation during the depths of the Great Depression by historian James Truslow Adams, in the epilogue to his best-selling *Epic of America*. Adams seizes upon the phrase in order to dramatize what he takes to be an ethos vital to traditional American culture now threatened with extinction by modern bureaucracy and conformity that he sees as the baleful aftermath of the closing of the frontier a generation before. Adams labors to combat the stereotypical equation of success with material prosperity, "a dream of motor cars and high wages merely." On the contrary, he insists, it's rightfully "a dream of a social order in which each man and woman shall be able to attain to the fullest stature of which they are innately capable, and be recognized for what they are, regardless of the fortuitous circumstances of birth or position."[6] In effect Adams confesses that the American dream is actually plural and contestable. There's the pesky reductive stereotype, American Dream$_1$ so to speak, and then there's the proper ideal, American Dream$_2$, the dream of "the Great Society" as he calls it—the very phrase Lyndon Johnson later used to characterize his sweeping reform program of the 1960s—in which every person's *Bildung* might be fully realized. Adams writes from an unstable and idiosyncratic mixture of allegiances: part nostalgic libertarianism and part progressive, loyal yet also hostile to the upward mobility drive. What especially deserves stressing is his awareness that the dissonance between the dream's two versions had long bedeviled and would forever haunt thinkers, writers, and citizens at large from Crèvecoeur to Wuthnow's new elites, as would

the fear of the evaporation or betrayal of what had once seemed a crucial definer of the achievement possible for an ordinary American.

American Dilemma: Uneven Development of Early Fictions of Development

Persistent conviction that individual self-realization, however defined,
is key to the health of the national body politic undoubtedly goes a long
way toward explaining the long-standing popularity of real-life stories
of remarkable transformation of unlikely youths. But the history of U.S.
fiction's engagement with that mythic narrative is far from straightforward. That is why this chapter will unfold differently from the others
that follow—not centered for the most part on one or a small number
of featured novels but on the uneasy flirtation between the national
myth of individual opportunity and American coming-of-age fiction
over the course of a century, until memorable fusions finally begin to
appear in novels of the late 1800s and after.

In particular, we need to confront a curious and striking mismatch
between the stereotypical American dream narrative and the course of
national fiction. The standard version of the success myth pictures the
hero as a young man. But in the era's memorable up-from fictions,
women protagonists figure a good deal more prominently than men.
Indeed, so far as male youth-to-maturity plots are concerned, before
the twentieth century U.S. literature offers few close equivalents to the
Anglo-European bildungsroman, which typically follows the protagonist from early childhood to young adulthood through the negotiation
of the sexual, social, and mental trials of growing up in and against his
or her social context. Walter Scott's *Waverley* (1814), William Make-
peace Thackeray's *Pendennis* (1850), Charles Dickens's *David Copperfield*
(1850) and *Great Expectations* (1861), George Meredith's *The Ordeal of
Richard Feverel* (1859), Samuel Butler's *The Way of All Flesh* (1903), D. H.
Lawrence's *Sons and Lovers* (1913), James Joyce's *Portrait of the Artist as a
Young Man* (1916)—such novels as these are one of British literature's
signature genres throughout the long nineteenth century. Never mind
for the moment that the novels toward the later end of the spectrum, as
recent critics have pointed out, tend to undo the genre's original premise by presenting male development as arrested or failed, with the protagonist and society left at odds.[7] The key point for now is that in U.S.

fiction the male bildungsroman established itself much more tardily than in Anglo-European literary history.

Among memorable early republican and antebellum novels in particular, few closely fit this mold. Charles Brockden Brown's *Arthur Mervyn; or, Memoirs of the Year 1793* (1799) is a notable quasi-exception, featuring a mentally hyperactive country youth's tortuous quest for recognition, place, and standing in the early republic's metropolis. But the novel oscillates between Arthur's adventures and the paroxysms of epidemic-ridden Philadelphia, which his puzzlingly impulsive and erratic behavior is used to register and focalize. Melville's first eight books are all more or less male initiation stories, but either told as delimited episodes in lives scarcely otherwise developed or as downright repudiations of the youth's progress plot that equate initiation with victimization. In the novels that won James Fenimore Cooper greatest fame, featuring antebellum fiction's single most original and influential male character, he could not bring himself to tell the story of frontiersman hero Natty Bumppo's coming of age until *The Deerslayer* (1842), the fifth and last of the Leatherstocking series, and then only as an afterthought—so he claimed—in response to public demand. It's often said that the "wavering heroes" of Walter Scott's adaptation of bildungsroman to Anglo-Scottish border romance are insipid by contrast to the idiosyncratic, colorful Highland and Lowland types that surround them. Indeed Scott said so himself.[8] In effect Cooper's democratizing transposition of that model accentuated the bias by subjugating Scott's genteel protagonist to the American counterpart of his vernacular provincial retainer-companion, who figures in the Waverley novels as a kind of latter-day Sancho Panza, Don Quixote's colorful and hyperactive but distinctly subaltern and comic servant.

Even in later nineteenth-century U.S. fiction, this same trend line persists. The most supremely gifted novelist of the period, Henry James, shows considerably greater interest in the awakening of young women like Isabel Archer in *Portrait of a Lady* (1881) and Maggie Verver in *The Golden Bowl* (1904) than in adolescent males. Altogether, among fictions before the 1920s that have emerged as plausible Great American Novel candidates, only Mark Twain's *Huckleberry Finn* (1885) and Stephen Crane's *The Red Badge of Courage* (1895) come remotely close to enacting boyhood-to-maturity plots centered on obscure but socially typic young men.

The archive of young women's up-from transformation narratives for the same period is much richer, with numerous stateside equivalents to Richardson's *Pamela,* Austen's *Pride and Prejudice* (1813), Charlotte Brontë's *Jane Eyre* (1847), and Eliot's *The Mill on the Floss* (1860). For much of the nineteenth century, the principal defining template for U.S. women novelists was an updated adaptation of the Richardsonian female bildungsroman, featuring an isolated, impecunious, undersocialized girl, either orphaned or bereft, whose education with the aid of kindly mentors in self-discipline, refinement, and poised resistance of unwarranted patriarchal (and/or matriarchal) manipulation eventually confers maturity and the socioeconomic security of a companionate marriage.[9] The three best-selling antebellum novels next to *Uncle Tom's Cabin* are all variants on this pattern: Susan Warner's *The Wide, Wide World* (1850), Maria Cummins's *The Lamplighter* (1854), and E. D. E. N. Southworth's *The Hidden Hand* (1859), as is the recently discovered early African American novel, Hannah Crafts's *Bondwoman's Narrative* (ca. 1853–1861). From the 1860s to the dawn of modernism, U.S. female up-from novels continued to run strong.

Here then is a bemusing paradox. Premodern American men were given license to grow in ways denied even most well-born white women of the aspiring middle classes, not to mention African and Native Americans. Men rather than women in the early industrial United States oversaw the emergent culture of capitalism according to whose canons, as critic Philip Fisher sums up, "creative destruction rules," "the future, not the past, is the reference point for present thought and action," and "the free individual, not the community or group" becomes "the heart of the matter of representation."[10] Yet the female leads of premodern American fiction tend to become, whereas the memorable males tend to remain pretty much their core selves: Cooper's Leatherstocking; Melville's Tommo, Ishmael, and Ahab; Hawthorne's Dimmesdale (the contrast between Hester's inner growth and his reversion to type is striking, as we saw in Chapter 3). The same more or less holds for Henry James's Christopher Newman and Basil Ransom, and for the impressionable Lambert Strether in *The Ambassadors,* whose midlife swerve away from his patron Mrs. Newsome's marching orders in France is less a growth spurt than a release of pent-up juvenescent enthusiasms. As Chapters 6 and 8 explain further, it holds too for Twain's unwillingness to let Huck Finn enter puberty; and it arguably even holds for Stephen Crane's treatment of Henry Fleming's development in *Red Badge,* whose ending leaves unresolved whether his seeming break-through from greenhorn cowardice to battle-tested manhood is but another in a series of impulsive actions. But debatable cases aside, why the general proclivity for givenness over growth in the casting of male protagonists?

Traditional Americanist criticism found a ready answer in the supposed preference of "classic" (i.e., major male) American writers for "romance" over "novel," for narratives featuring symbolic figures like Cooper's Natty Bumppo and Melville's Ahab and Poe's Arthur Gordon Pym enacting their dramas outside the pale of mundane society on the frontier, the high seas, the recesses of the past, the phantasmagoria of the mind. Following D. H. Lawrence's 1923 psychohistorical diagnosis of the nation's "classic" male writers as witnessing to the condition of Americans as masterless escapees from the confines of Euroculture, Leslie Fiedler's *Love and Death in the American Novel* (1960) defined the paradigmatic (male) plot running through such canonical works as Cooper's *Last of the Mohicans,* Melville's *Moby-Dick,* and Twain's *Huckleberry Finn* as a plot of evasion of adult social and (hetero)sexual responsibility by escape to the frontier from female-dominated settlement culture. In these terms, it made perfect sense for the first male protagonist of the first canonical tale, Irving's "Rip Van Winkle," to be the town deadbeat who sleeps through the Revolution and for the classic American hero, whatever his age, to be a symbolic youth who refuses to grow up.

According to this line of thinking, the wayward disposition of "classic" U.S. fiction's male protagonist followed from the defining conditions of premodern national society, conditions that several of the writers themselves—Cooper, Hawthorne, and James especially—identified as impediments for would-be social novelists. Chief among these were the dearth of established cultural institutions and centers, the vertiginous pace of social change and mobility, the as-yet unsettled state of the vast hinterland and the lure of westwarding and wilderness. Such charges understated the degree of social crystallization already achieved, especially in the northeastern region where most of the leading authors dwelled. But for Lawrence and Fiedler actualities were less consequential than what they took to be the prevailing national imaginary, meaning for them the ideology of a wide-open America as against a closed-up

Europe, both for better and for worse. Their interest was in how this semifictional schema, which foreign observers helped shape and perpetuate, affected novelistic practice, such that Cooper's frontier romances became translated and imitated throughout Europe, and Anglo-European writers from Goethe to Balzac, Stendhal, and Flaubert kept conjuring up the image of America as a place of new beginnings that offered escape from conventional regimes of growing up. Lawrence's own neoprimitivist fascination with the North American southwest was a conspicuous instance. Although neither discuss the book, he and Fiedler would have found it telling that the closest approximation to conventional male bildungsroman by a major U.S. author during the early nineteenth century was Cooper's *Satanstoe* (1845), a historical novel set in highly stratified, deference-oriented late colonial Anglo-Dutch New York, whose protagonist must laboriously master and negotiate the minute social gradations and touchy relations among British, British-American-New Yorker, British-American-Yankee, and Dutch American subcultures on his way to successful resolution of the marriage plot, here as always "the narrative and social convention par excellence for embedding subjects into the fixed state of adulthood."[11]

The view of classic American fiction as preeminently defined by "melodramas of beset manhood" that feature outdoor life away from female-coded settlement culture has since been exposed as an androcentric reduction simplistic even for males.[12] That in itself by no means completely robs the original thesis of all explanatory power. Historically, the hinterland expansionism on an unprecedented territorial scale that gave rise to frontier iconography was indeed disproportionately a male-instigated affair, although women writers contributed as much as men did to Western literature—no less than 343 authors by the mid-1920s according to the most authoritative count.[13] By the same token it makes historical sense that the masculine fantasy of perilous sorties into "virgin land" by typic frontiersmen would have persistent aftereffects, such as promotion of space as "the new frontier" in the 1960s or the mystification of American wars against non-Western peoples in Vietnam and elsewhere as the conquest of savagery all over again. That in turn made it predictable that at the level of cultural stereotype U.S.-ness would continue to be defined internationally in terms of such male-tilted images as wild west, wide open spaces, cowboy culture, and the like; and that "the Western" remains not only the stuff of popular media but even—albeit in increasingly self-critical ways—of such avant-garde contemporary American novels as Cormac McCarthy's *Blood Meridian* (1985), with its surrealistic *danse macabre* between the eternal "kid" and the murderous judge, in which scores of disposable Indians and Mexicans get slaughtered by the gangs of irregulars with whom they hook up. All this begins to suggest, but without explaining fully, why one of nineteenth-century liberal individualism's signature genres should have been so scantly practiced by the premodern male writers of the nation that pulled off the Enlightenment era's most successful bourgeois revolution.

Bildungsroman tradition itself offers further clues. First, many if not most of the touchstone examples build in a countercurrent of resistance to maturity or "proper" socialization by no means wholly overcome. *Wilhelm Meister's Apprenticeship* itself shows inklings of this, in Wilhelm's reflexive distaste for his father and his friend Werner's mercantilism; his attraction to the theater; the creepily invasive undertones of the mysterious Society of the Tower's surveillance of him; and the testimony of the journal of "the Beautiful Soul" that sits alongside Wilhelm's narrative as a never-quite-refuted alternative of autonomous, free-standing development. As the nineteenth century unfolds, the countercurrents increase. Meredith's *Richard Feverel* becomes a tragic battleground between the authoritarian father—a one-man Society of the Tower with a prescribed script—and the ardent son caught between headstrong resistance and internalized dutifulness. In Rainer Maria Rilke's *Notebooks of Malte Laurids Brigge* (1910), disaffection shields the protagonist against socialization so that he remains, in his inner life and idiolect at least, resolutely aloof. Altogether, picaresque wandering and antiauthoritarian pushback often prove to be incompletely digested bildungsroman motifs, and resistance to "maturity" on the part of the male protagonist is more to be expected than otherwise. From this standpoint, Melville's Tommo in *Typee* and Ishmael in *Moby-Dick*, even Twain's Huck, begin to look more like variations on a norm than outright aberrancies.

The hypothesis that the conjoined rise of industrial capitalism and colonization makes for narratives of uneven and arrested development in Anglo-European fictions of development is additionally helpful here. In Conrad's *Lord Jim*, Jed Esty points out, the hero's perpetual adolescence seems "a version of the natives' backwardness," each romanticized and frozen in time-space so as to create an impression of relative "historylessness" even as Patusan is destroyed by "the brutal externalization of change" personified by the nefarious Gentleman Brown.[14] Essential Englishness and nativeness get reassuringly idealized, with the stratifying lines between them also reassuringly (from a European perspective) reinforced, but at the cost of being exposed as anachronistic, inoperative, and co-opted by empire's relentless advance. Rather the same could be said of Cooper's portrayal of the intimacy between Natty and Chingachgook, from their debut as battered septuagenarians in *The Pioneers* (1823), but far more so in the later novels' greater idealization of them, as the Leatherstocking series ranges back through the last half of the eighteenth century from the Louisiana Purchase to the French and Indian War, at increasing distance from the forward momentum of nineteenth-century continental conquest during the Jacksonian era, whose abuses the author perceived but opted to treat elegiacally rather than frontally by concentrating on their prehistory. Twain's decision to keep Huck in perpetual boyishness, and in patronizing intimacy with his black companion, is likewise integral to the decision to fix the novelistic present in the antebellum past and confront only by insinuation the unfinished business of emancipation. In both the Leatherstocking saga and *Huckleberry Finn*, to resist linear biography of the male leads helps immunize them from complicity as agents of the forces of expansionism and racial subjugation beyond their power to control.

In order to come more fully to terms with the gender gap specifically in nineteenth-century U.S. fictions of development, however, we must consider still another line of thinking suggested by Moretti's contentious assessment of traditional bildungsroman's country-by-country track record. Stable moral and societal norms, he argues, correlate inversely with novelistic vitality. The English bildungsroman was more insipid than the Continental because "there is really not much left for the protagonist of the English *Bildungsroman* to do." She or he is born into "a moral universe that already exists, external and unchangeable."[15] Early British bildungsroman in particular he classifies as fairy-tale melodrama that dispenses justice in predictable ways—little more than exercises in cultural self-satisfaction. Behind this slash-and-burn deprecation of Austen, Dickens, and Charlotte Brontë is the provocative double-sided notion that the genre flourishes most inventively where rule of law and cultural legitimation of human rights are most precarious, producing such fascinating deviants as the disaffected, Napoleon-worshiping petit-bourgeois Julien Sorel in Stendahl's *The Red and the Black* (1830) (Moretti's favorite) but dwindling into formula as the social friction diminishes. Might the paucity of classic U.S. male bildungsromans have something to do with the fact that a culture of individual rights seemed more solidly in place for middle-class white American males sooner even than for British?

More recent studies provide some supporting evidence. Building on Moretti's correlation of genre and ideology while rejecting the judgment that bildungsroman died out in the nineteenth century, Joseph Slaughter views it as "the novelistic genre that most fully corresponds to . . . the norms and narrative assumptions that underwrite the vision of free and full human personality development projected in international human rights law," which can thus serve as a "cultural surrogate" for a human rights regime not yet in place.[16] Slaughter extends to the postcolonial world Marianne Hirsch's claim for bildungsroman as "the most salient [twentieth-century] genre for the literature of social outsiders, particularly women or minority groups," finding in novels like the Kenyan Marjorie Oludhe Macgoye's *Coming to Birth* (1986) challenges to "the historical gender and racial exclusions of the state" that attempt to inscribe "universal democratic forms" in advance of their institutionalization. The crucial work of postcolonial bildungsroman, then, is to allegorize the orderly advance of human rights, both being regimes that "construct the individual as a social creature and the process of individuation as an incorporative process of socialization."[17]

Whether you stress bildungsroman's potential for enablement or constraint will likely depend on the value you set on individual autonomy as the confirmation of a viable liberal social order. Sifting upward mobility narratives from a social democratic perspective, Bruce Robbins finds heartening signs of caregiving, mutuality, and institutionalized welfare (even in sites like prisons and the FBI) that suggest that even this liberal signature genre doesn't model unmitigated capitalism. Nancy Armstrong, by contrast, stresses how British bildungsroman and nineteenth-century British mainstream fiction generally works toward the production of a certain kind of subject, who "adapts to a position more limited than its [actual] subjectivity," whereby individuals are seen as becoming "fully themselves" only in relation to the social

collectivity, "the imaginary nation."[18] These opposing valuations con-
cur with Slaughter's, though, in diagnosing bildungsroman as a re-
flector and promoter of the smooth operation of individuation within
representative governmental regimes. This prospect seems likely to
appeal most to those who prize social recognition as key to personal
flourishing and least to those inclined to suspect social acceptance as
compromising to personal integrity. This may take us further toward
understanding why leading premodern American writers tended to favor female up-from narratives over male. The next stage must be a
closer look at the homegrown ideological underpinnings of the Americanization of the (male) up-from story that had begun to take form
before the bildungsroman was invented, even before the nation itself
officially began.

(Mis)Making Men: The Franklin Legend as Model and as Target

For ambitious young men of the early republic, the most celebrated
real-life embodiment of successful aspiration was Benjamin Franklin.
Indeed to this day Franklin still probably feels more familiar than the
other figures of the American Revolution owing to the percolation effects of the work now considered one of the first American literary classics, Franklin's unfinished memoir now known as his *Autobiography,*
although the term wasn't coined until after his death. It was issued in a
series of incomplete versions starting a few years after he died in 1790
(first French, then English) but, oddly, not in toto until the Civil War
era. In four installments written over a decade and a half, Franklin
recalls with ingratiating archness his rise to transatlantic fame as the
story of a runaway printer's apprentice who rose by dint of wit, energy,
wile, and charm to affluent businessman, polymath, politician, and
fomenter of numerous public improvements in the two leading me-
tropolises of the Anglo-American world.

This story line—legendary well before the memoir was fully
published—of outstanding achievement "by thrift and diligence, and
by constant application to the work of self-perfection" (or the appearance of such) expressed and reinforced the young nation's self-
conception "as a place where anything was possible if you tried hard
enough."[19] Yet it also proved a divisive prototype. To readers so diverse
as abolitionist Frederick Douglass, lawyer Abraham Lincoln, home-

steading experimenter/transcendentalist Henry David Thoreau, novelist Herman Melville, showman P. T. Barnum, and banking magnate Thomas Mellon, Franklinism might seem either an inspiring pathway (Douglass, Lincoln, Barnum, Mellon) or an apotheosis of worldly calculation (Thoreau, Melville). Furthermore, though confessedly often opinionated and mischievously heterodox, the Franklin persona attaches no intrinsic importance to precedent breaking or to originality as such. To that end, he stresses the virtues of hard work, perseverance, and mastery of approved models—in his case, *Pilgrim's Progress,* Cotton Mather's moral essays, and the neoclassical journalism of Addison and Steele. This too appealed more to the likes of Douglass and Lincoln, who started life at the bottom of the social ladder and had to pick up literacy and learning on the fly, than to Thoreau, who was culturally advantaged enough to afford the luxury of denying that he had ever heard a syllable of good advice from his seniors.

By the second quarter of the nineteenth century if not before, republican imagination had set in place the image of the new nation itself as a culture of individual opportunity for the determined, energetic (white male) person, of which the Franklin figure—a cropped and retrofitted simplification of the original—was the canonical embodiment.* After emancipation, African Americans like Frederick Douglass, whose 1845 *Narrative* had "established the tradition of the self-made African

* Nian-Sheng Huang, *Benjamin Franklin in American Thought and Culture 1790–1860* (Philadelphia: American Philosophical Society, 1994), 35–107, charts the growth of the Franklin legend in the nineteenth century. The biographical Franklin, who practiced self-cultivation of mind as well as manners and became a patron of learning and the arts after he made his fortune, must be distinguished from the reductive stereotypes. Predictably, anti-Franklinism has usually been directed more at the dream linked to his name than to the actual life record (Nian-Sheng Huang and Carla Mulford, "Benjamin Franklin and the American Dream," in *The Cambridge Companion to Benjamin Franklin,* ed. Carla Mulford [Cambridge: Cambridge University Press, 2008], 156). As critic Martha Banta points out, "the dream that starts out in the Franklinian mode" is inherently liable to deteriorate into "a demeaning search after wealth and respectability" (*Failure and Success in America: A Literary Debate* [Princeton, NJ: Princeton University Press, 1978], 269). Franklin himself was at least partly protected against the bondage to the work ethic that *Poor Richard's Almanac* seems to celebrate by the British-colonial master class aspiration to become a gentleman. He confesses as much in his memoirs by framing them as a message of advice to his son in the tradition of Lord Chesterfield's letters. Indeed historian Gordon Wood demonstrates that Franklin's attraction to the life of an expatriate British gentleman after his retirement from business in Philadelphia almost caused him to miss out on the Revolution; see Wood's *The Americanization of Benjamin Franklin* (New York: Penguin, 2004).

American," was prepared to declare that except for the former slave
states the nation deserved its reputation as "preeminently the home
and patron of self-made men."[20] The short-form version of the Franklin
prescription for achieving personal fulfillment and social prestige was
on the way to becoming standard wisdom: disciplined hard work, "not
transient and fitful effort," as Douglass expressed it, "but patient, enduring, unremitting and indefatigable work, into which the whole heart
is put." By the same token, the legendary Franklin figure looked as much
like the story of the merchant Werner as the story of the intellectually
and aesthetically aspiring Wilhelm—likely one reason why Douglass's
famous set-piece oration on self-made men, delivered "more than fifty
times" between the late 1850s and the 1890s, holds up Lincoln and not
Franklin as "the King of American self-made men."[21]

The model of working your way to leadership by the tireless pursuit of success in business while dedicating your spare hours to self-
improvement offered itself as either a template or a target. If you took
free-standing individuality or creative expression as the rightful payoff
of a society so open in principle, you might consider small-minded and
restrictive an up-from script that held up business savvy as the crucial
passport to personal fulfillment and social recognition. You might refuse that version of "maturity"; you might find that story line as boring
and regressive as Moretti finds most British bildungsromans, especially
if you were aware that "Americans" were becoming proverbial for their
materialism and workaholism. You might hold it responsible for helping perpetuate the bad tradition of utilitarian condescension toward
the arts.

If you were a novelist, you might favor accentuating the countercurrents that the bildungsroman recognized but tended to suppress,
such as quest narratives of figures striving perpetually for self-renewal
and against quotidian confines even at the cost of isolation or annihila-
tion. Or narratives that indicted the nation's failure to make good on
the liberties proclaimed by the Declaration or such endemic downsides
of republican democracy as the "tyranny of the majority" Alexis de
Tocqueville observed that overrode principled dissent.[22] Such were the
paths followed by Thoreau, Melville, and Twain. In *Israel Potter* (1855),
Melville goes so far as to reinvent Benjamin Franklin sardonically as a
shady spymaster and con man who barrages the embattled antihero
with self-help slogans and then leaves him in the lurch.

If, on the other hand, you evaluated social recognition not from the standpoint of an Emerson feeling hamstrung by groupthink and a pedigree of six ministerial ancestors but as one forced to experience the injuries of class and race wallpapered over by equal-opportunity double-talk, then you might feel much more attracted to the up-from script, which took seriously, even when it did not guarantee the payoff, the importance of self-fashioning as a pathway to social recognition. That helps explain the salience of female bildungsromans in premodern American literature as well as why in the 1900s the tribulations of "growing up ethnic" became the modern American bildungsroman's single most remarkable literary success story.

Up-from fictions, and the canonization of the idea of the self-made man itself as national self-definer and mantra, were nineteenth-century upshots of tendencies that were anticipated by Franklin's career but took longer to evolve. Among these were the increased mobility of the early industrial era with accelerated immigration, urbanization, and geographic expansion; the romantic valuation of interiority (provoking, for instance, more scenes of solitary pondering in nineteenth-century autobiography than Franklin gives us); the dignification of the ordinary citizen as republican-democratic theory evolved during the Jacksonian era and voting rights were extended to all white male citizens; and the campaigns for women's rights and the freedom of African American slaves. None of these guaranteed an increase in the actual percentage of up-from lifelines, only that the antebellum era, more than any before it, would become "the age of the self-made man."[23] We owe the phrase itself to Senator Henry Clay's 1830s epithet for his region's merchants. In the same decade began the unstoppable vogue of presidential candidates supposedly born in log cabins or the like, to which novelist Gish Jen drolly alludes in this chapter's first epigraph. It started with the 1840 campaign for William Henry Harrison (who was actually of privileged background). What set William Dean Howells on the way to becoming "the Dean of American Letters" in the late nineteenth century was an 1860 up-from campaign biography of the first genuine article, Abraham Lincoln. (Howells's fictional debut in the *Ashtabula Sentinel* had featured a virtuous orphan boy who marries his boss's daughter after rescuing her from drowning.)[24] A lesser classic in a related genre was Horatio Alger Jr.'s boy's life of the just-assassinated James A. Garfield, *From Canal Boy to President* (1881). Alger was the

right man for the job, already famous for a series of dime novels starting with *Ragged Dick* (1867) that featured street urchins who remake
themselves into successful businessmen through self-starting initiative,
thrift, sound morals, persistence, and luck.

The usual catchphrase for the Alger formula, "rags to riches," gives a
rearview-mirror misrepresentation of how his fiction actually works.
Alger defined success not as extraordinary affluence but as a respectable job with a decent income; and his heroes attain it not merely by
seizing the main chance but through self-discipline, honesty, and also
generosity. (Alger heroes often have single mothers to whom they are
devoted.) "To be self-made" in Alger's terms, historian Daniel Walker
Howe points out, "was to have made, not money, but a self"—and furthermore his understanding of what counted as self-making expressed
the broader antebellum view that "the self-made man" was one "who
has successfully pursued self-improvement and had attained an appro-
priate balance of character."[25] In that same spirit, Harriet Beecher
Stowe's 1872 *Lives and Deeds of Our Self-Made Men* concentrated on reformers and Civil War heroes to the complete exclusion of businessmen. Nor was the self-improvement ethic, as Alger renders it and as
midcentury American culture understood it, inconsistent with altru-
ism. Ragged Dick's readiness to go against "obvious self-interest" and
support even less fortunate waifs points away from rugged individualism toward a "postindividualist future" of which new charitable institutions like the Children's Aid Society, which Alger supported, are
an early chapter in U.S. history.[26] The Horatio Alger Association of Distinguished Americans (founded 1947) seems to have got the Alger ethic
nominally right but substantively wrong. According to its website, www
.horatioalger.com, members are supposed to exemplify philanthropy,
"honesty, hard work, self-reliance, and perseverance over adversity";
but the typical honoree is a CEO, whereas the typical Alger hero felt
lucky to become a merchant's clerk.

Alger's restrained definition of legitimate success comports with
more prominent nineteenth-century novelists' skittishness about cases
of spectacular ascent to riches. At the close of Hawthorne's *The Scarlet
Letter,* Pearl becomes the richest heiress of the New World offstage as a
fortuitous byproduct of the mutual destruction of Chillingworth and
Dimmesdale. In Stowe's *Uncle Tom's Cabin,* Augustine St. Clare's affluence is a curse, reinforcing lazy acquiescence to a social system he

abhors. For Henry James, the first major U.S. novelist to take the orbits of the ultra-rich as his special province, the interest is not in the acquisition of wealth but the next-stage dilemmas wealth confers: the quest for aesthetic and moral refinement, the perils of predation. The one protagonist-centered American novel of the nineteenth century still widely read today that takes in anything like the whole transit of the making (and breaking) of a self-made millionaire, Howells's *The Rise of Silas Lapham* (1885), telescopes the story of Lapham's business ascent into a tidbit of retrospective exposition in order to use it as the springboard for a morality play. Howells telegraphs awareness of the already shopworn rags-to-riches part of the story in Chapter 1 by shrink-wrapping it into the journeyman reporter Bartley Hubbard's write-up of his interview of Latham, a mélange of "perfunctory clichés of self-making"—the "regulation thing," as Bartley dryly remarks and Silas agrees.[27] Howells's variation on the theme is to turn the arrogant paint baron's saga into a "failure" story in which business collapse means moral rise. Lapham redeems himself by resisting the temptation to swindle his way out of bankruptcy and by returning to the spartan up-country self-sufficiency where he started. Robert Herrick engineers an opposite outcome in his *Memoirs of an American Citizen* (1905), a sardonic tale of another poor country lad turned Gilded Age magnate whose super success hardens him into a ruthless moral monster who alienates all his old intimates.

The swiftness with which Herrick's searching but schematic anti-Franklin novel slipped into oblivion might have given extra bite to his testy appraisal a half-dozen years later of what American fiction had so far failed to address. One of its glaring omissions, he maintained, was "the great American fact for the past generation," the saga of the captain of industry—a story, Herrick feared, that was no longer possible, since the next generation must be an age of inheritors, of "trusteeship" rather than "the pioneer days of capitalism."[28] Ironically, even as he wrote this, at least two now-classic up-from narratives of obscure young men who made it big were nearing closure: Theodore Dreiser's *The Financier* (1912), the first in a fictional trilogy based on the career of the streetcar entrepreneur and robber baron Charles Yerkes, and Andrew Carnegie's never-quite-completed *Autobiography* (set aside for the sake of the war effort). Herrick rightly wondered at the belatedness of up-from novels that accorded any real sympathy to the "gospel of wealth," in Carnegie's resonant phrase, or to the aura of making it to the top of the socioeconomic heap. But Herrick might have looked to his own novelistic instincts for the explanation why. For writers like him and Howells—and James, Hawthorne, and Cooper too—nobility of self-restraint always trumps self-servingness. Fables of self-made men seemed tolerable only in proportion to the protagonists' acuteness of conscience. That of course was Alger's agenda too.

So too with postbellum literature's greatest box-office success, Lew Wallace's *Ben-Hur: A Tale of the Christ* (1880), the biggest-selling American novel between *Uncle Tom's Cabin* and *Gone with the Wind*.[29] *Ben-Hur* is, in the most literal sense imaginable, the rags-to-riches story of a young Jewish aristocrat wrongfully arrested at the start for attempted murder of the Roman procurator and sent to the galleys for life. The hero is freed and made fabulously rich when he saves his commander from drowning in a naval battle and is rewarded by adoption as his son and heir. Ben-Hur's wealth, intelligence, charisma, and athletic prowess—the latter clearly a mark of the rise of organized sports and "muscular Christianity" in the late-century United States—aided by the Jewish-sympathizing underground, including an old family retainer, enable him to defeat his enemies and rescue his long-imprisoned mother and sister, both wasted by leprosy. But the novel's crucial last turn is the completion of his spiritual *Bildung* in the form of his conversion to the Jesus cult, as a result of which he foregoes his long-standing ambition to foment rebellion against Rome and redirects his enormous wealth and the influence that goes with it away from revolutionary nationalism to the building of the catacombs.

Ben-Hur illustrates more dramatically than all the Alger books put together both the potential vitality of the masculine version of the American up-from-poverty dream script and the challenges of converting it into bildungsroman without tailoring it to the procrustean formula of moralistic fable—as did Carnegie's *Autobiography* to a considerable extent. The novel values wealth's power for good but takes no interest in moneymaking. Slave labor is Ben-Hur's only work, and even though his discipline and determination are admirable, Wallace contrives it so that his megamillions get showered on him by inheritance, twice over, not by entrepreneurialism. The novel rejoices in his restoration to the status of Judean grandee, but only when spiritual purification has raised him above wrongful use of his fortune.

That the spiritual crisis of the Gilded Age should have seemed to Wallace and to Alger before him the most promising angle from which to fictionalize male lifelines was a predictable result of the imperfect fit within the concept of self-making per se between the post-Protestant idealization of forging virtuous character and the conception of social prominence as its rightful payoff. The historical Franklin's *Autobiography* resolved this contradiction by its genial, man-of-the-world acquiescence to virtuous seeming as a proxy for virtuous being, and by stressing his decision to retire from business early so as to focus more wholly on the public good. But nineteenth-century theorists of self-transformation like Emerson, Thoreau, and Alger himself took a more assertive integrity-first approach that held up intrinsic character and not just the appearance of such as the crucial requisite, even to the point of entertaining—as did Emerson's "Self-Reliance" and Thoreau's *Walden*—alternative, antisocial conceptions of transformational success involving separation from society rather than fusion. Weimar *Bildung* was recycled into canonical U.S. literature through Emerson's schismatic warnings in "The American Scholar" and "Self-Reliance" against letting mass opinion compromise integrity. Although Emerson also sometimes played apologist for American enterprise and manifest destiny,[30] never for him did the activation of self-culture seem so dependent upon the state of national culture as it did for, say, Schiller in Germany or for Matthew Arnold in mid-Victorian Britain. Likewise, Alger's moralistic fables of enterprise, Wallace's recourse to conversion to forestall Ben-Hur's militant anti-imperial nationalism, and Howells's and Herrick's more direct critiques of unscrupulous business tactics all imagine proper self-making as a matter of resistance to corrupting social influence.

Anti-aristocratic suspicion of leisure-class decadence complicated the challenge of devising republican fables of virtuous self-making by reconceiving Franklinesque polymathy in more narrowly work-focused terms. That the antebellum self-made man was conceived along the lines of Henry Clay's merchants rather than the multifaceted philosophe that Benjamin Franklin became helps account for Thoreau's oscillation between thumbing his nose at the work ethic and offering his homesteading experiment and the creative breakthrough it enabled as alternative forms of work,[31] and for the fact that the fictional classic of the era most exhaustively given over to detailing a workplace's regimes—*Moby-Dick*—treats the business end of the operation as a second-order pursuit. The spokesman for good business sense, Starbuck the first mate, is reduced to whimpering subalternity. Nineteenth-century novels that featured as the main event the story to which *Moby-Dick* gives briefest possible mention, Captain Ahab working his way up from cabin boy, risked self-parody. A case in point is the last notable fiction to follow Franklin's advice-to-junior formula, *Letters from a Self-Made Merchant to His Son* (1901), by George Lorimer, long-term editor of the *Saturday Evening Post*. The merchant, a Chicago tycoon from small-town Missouri, initiates his errant but basically tractable heir into the intricacies of the meatpacking business with a combination of anecdotal reminiscence and droll-imperious Poor Richard–style maxims that the book seems to want the reader to accept as earthy wisdom even while seeing the father (who halfway realizes this himself) as the rough-and-ready product of a former era, a bit fussily small-bore in his work-obsessiveness ("You've got to eat hog, dream hog—in short, go the whole hog if you're going to win out in the pork-packing business").[32]

Only with turn-of-the-twentieth-century naturalist fiction's receptivity to the social Darwinist claim that individual life is determined by biological drives and socioenvironmental forces and with the resultant challenge to the assumption of moral agency from modern theories of mental development that grounded aesthetic experience and desire in the material world itself—only then does U.S. fiction seriously entertain the possibility that the drive for material success might be a legitimate expression of human needs and aesthetic desire. Only then appear robust fictionalizations of up-from masculine self-making without moralistic strings tightly attached and rendered in anything like a comprehensive ethnographic way, in the work of Frank Norris, Jack London, and Theodore Dreiser.[33] Strange though it might seem given the long-standingness of poor-boy, up-from autobiographies from Franklin to Douglass to Barnum to Carnegie, the first canonical American novel to follow this script to the letter—and even then, to cast the plot aside in disgust—dates only from 1909.

Fittingly, this was a semiautobiographical novel by "America's first millionaire novelist,"[34] whose life itself was a rags-to-riches story: Jack London's *Martin Eden*. It chronicles the amazing transformation of the uncouth but generous-spirited title character from semiliterate seaman to best-selling author by prodigious feats of self-improvement and marathon writing. What opens the way for Martin's eventual marketplace breakthrough is the ignition of his formidable energy and willpower by a serious-minded bookish young woman whose genteel family takes him in by happenstance (an Algeresque reward for rescuing her brother from ferryboat bullies), with whom, of course, he falls in love. London's relentless documentation of the tacky minutiae and violent mood swings of Martin's struggle up from ignorant Grub Street tyro makes this novel a more searching rendition of the blow-by-blow tribulations of professional self-making than anything before it in U.S. fiction. But it is entirely traditional in ironizing success as the world measures it. Martin's growing sophistication opens his eyes to the meretriciousness of the mass market and to the timidly conventional character and taste of his adored Ruth. So the comeuppance of his earnest, increasingly high-minded drive for self-betterment is contempt for his own hard-won success and for those who admire it, followed by an emotional breakdown that drives him to suicide, after a parting gesture of working-class solidarity poignantly at odds with his new cynicism: he distributes much of his new wealth among needy relatives and acquaintances who had befriended him in the past. As an odyssey of awakening to entrapment in the bourgeois success machine, *Martin Eden* twists upward mobility narrative sharply in the direction of the lower-depths factory fiction of his friend Upton Sinclair, whose novel *The Jungle* (1906) was also influenced by the author's ordeals as an impoverished young author. For Martin too, the world of literary professionalism as experienced from the bottom up proves nothing better than a sweatshop at last.

Women's Up-From Stories: Antebellum to Wharton

So much for the inhibitions besetting early U.S. writers' up-from fictions of male self-fashioning. Let's now turn to the more copious archive of women's fictions in a similar vein.

Maria Cummins's *The Lamplighter* (1854) makes a good starting point, as the best-selling female bildungsroman of its day. Issued the year after *Uncle Tom's Cabin* by the same publisher, John P. Jewett, the novel was promoted as "the great American romance," "superior to all other emanations of the American and European Press."[35] *The Lamplighter* follows heroine Gertrude from abused, emotionally volatile child in a mid-nineteenth-century Boston slum to triumphant closure, reconciled with her long-lost father and wed to her dearest childhood friend who, after years of mercantile outposting to India, returns to assume a place of honor and affluence among Boston's business elite. The juvenile Gertrude is a waif with an edge, who lashes out against her tormentors like the young Jane Eyre. Like Jane and most other antebellum heroines of the genre, Gerty is tamed by a series of compassionate protectors who impose what critic Richard Brodhead calls sentimental fiction's "disciplinary intimacy,"[36] a lovingly coercive education in patience, self-command, and considerateness, including sincerely principled willingness to put another's well-being ahead of her own, to the point of yielding her best chance to escape a shipwreck to the selfish belle she (wrongly) believes has beguiled her beloved William. Health, beauty, mind, and multitalented accomplishment blossom in tandem with emotional, social, moral, and religious maturity. Too good to be true? Of course. After all, this is basically formula-driven fiction. Plenty of melodrama and tears along the way. It's easy enough to understand why Joyce satirized Cummins's heroine in gushy Gerty McDowell of *Ulysses*'s "Nausicaa" chapter. But it's also easy to understand why the book would have interested him enough to use it as a lever for discomposing his generally male-centered plotline.[37] For one thing, even more than in most women's fiction Gertrude is disciplined not so much into submission as into autonomy, and with it a perceptive acuity that makes her the book's most respected figure, even to elders and social betters. The grown-up Gertrude has "an honorable pride which would not endure to be trifled with."[38] Internalization of right instincts earns her right of resistance, at least within limits. When her foster father self-interestedly balks at her inconvenient departure to nurse a sick poor woman who had been a mother to her, she opposes his ostentatiously hurt feelings with her virtuous ones, thinking, "I will never be such a traitor to my own heart, and my own sense of right."[39]

Gertrude's advancement becomes more piquant by contrast to the vicissitudes of her mentor, the angelic Emily Graham. The gentle, refined, affluent Emily commits herself "to cure that child of her dark infirmity";[40] but Gertrude's role switches over time from ward to caregiver. Indeed she becomes the only person who can shield Emily, blinded in youth in a tragic accident, from circumambient domestic nastiness and alleviate her mysterious bouts of debilitating headache and other such prostrations. Except that Emily somehow outlasts her valetudinarianism to enjoy a parallel storybook marriage, she too is another genre stereotype, the preternaturally "good" girl who doubles as model and antimodel. Like Jane Eyre's schoolmate Helen Burns or Alice Humphreys in Warner's *Wide Wide World,* Emily's fragility underscores Gertrude's gumption. However much Gertrude internalizes Emily's ethics of loving Christian submissiveness, "the model of sympathy she advances," critic Cindy Weinstein observes, "is not one of self-abnegation but rather self-possession." Here we see *The Lamplighter* push back against what Lauren Berlant calls the "sentimental bargain" of substituting "sublime self-overcoming" for more contrarian alternatives these characters "ought to be able to imagine themselves" pursuing.[41]

Another reason for enlisting this novel here is how it relates Gertrude to sundry cases of male self-making both successful and not. Her playmate and future husband William is a proto-Algerish lad who is given the stereotypical big break by a rich merchant disposed to be sympathetic as a one-time poor boy himself. Gertrude's first protector, the eponymous lamplighter Trueman Flint, is a case of frustrated bootstrapping: a conscientious orphan from Vermont condemned to a menial job by a crippling accident. The heroine's long-lost father, improbably revealed as also Emily's long-lost love, was forced into self-making by youthful indiscretion and cruel connivance. These ancillary odysseys inject a clear-sighted awareness of the instabilities in early industrial capitalism that the myth of self-making is designed to acknowledge, buffer, regulate, and celebrate at the same time. No less important, they include Gertrude. Though she lacks much formal education, merit and luck land her a job as assistant schoolmistress that we're given to understand might have been a pathway to self-sufficient professionalism had she not felt that caregiving and then marriage should take precedence. So her story ultimately reaffirms conventional middle-class gender divisions but it also goes to show how a gravely disadvantaged girl—given intrinsic ability and lucky breaks—might set herself on a track to achieve middle-class professional success and blossom into a hero as well as a heroine. The novel ventures this not as covert protest against the ideological correctness of the prevailing domestic ideal but as an affirmation of the urgency of middle-class *Bildung* for both men and women, reinforced by the demonstration that the economically unstable, increasingly stratified urban United States offers no social safety net for the disadvantaged, no sources of security beyond boot-strapping and ad hoc mutual support.

During the next three-quarters of a century, U.S. novels of women's maturation complicate the *Lamplighter* template in a number of ways, two of which deserve special mention. One is to sabotage the marriage plot itself. The protagonist-narrator Cassandra in Elizabeth Stoddard's *The Morgesons* (1862) fights free of small-town provincialism, takes con-trol of the family estate, and marries the man of her choice on her own terms over the protests of the fiancé's family. Yet the novel holds out no future for the happy couple. After knocking off their two-year Euro-pean honeymoon in less than a sentence, *The Morgesons* abruptly ends with the unresolved question: After marriage, what? The elliptical last scene flicks through glimpses of Cassandra's sister's strangely catatonic baby, her alcoholic brother-in-law's death, and the married couple "clung together" over his corpse "mutely question[ing] each other." Stoddard seems to have anticipated Moretti's charge against *Jane Eyre*: "Any *Bil-dungsroman* worthy of the name would have had Jane remain among the needles of Thornfield" after discovering that Rochester's mad first wife still lived.[42] Reflecting back on the novel years later, Stoddard chided Cassandra and her Byronic Cousin Charles—the married man who had awakened her sexually and who continued to haunt her dreams—for not having the guts to defy convention and create a "new world" of their own—a self-criticism too, of course.[43] Henry James's *Portrait of a Lady* (1881) divides the marriage plot against itself with ut-most subtlety, first by showing Isabel Archer under pressure not to re-ject eminently eligible suitors she doesn't want, then by showing her maneuvered into choosing the nefarious Osmond, then by having her slowly awaken to the disastrous mistake of that choice, and finally by leaving her—and the reader—in a state of anguished irresolution as to what she will do about it. For the novel doesn't so much end as break off, with Isabel heading home to Florence, perhaps—but who can say?—to requite her husband by devoting herself to furthering the love match he opposes between his daughter Pansy and Ned Rosier, whose characters look suspiciously papier-mâché compared to Isabel's. What-ever slender basis for hope that hypothetical next-generation union holds out, *Portrait* leaves the impression, as Susan Fraiman remarks of

Pride and Prejudice's Elizabeth Bennet, that it might better have been titled "The Humiliation of Isabel Archer."[44]

Other female bildungsromans offer professionalism more pointedly than *The Lamplighter* does as an alternative to marriage. In Fanny Fern's *Ruth Hall* (1855), the semiautobiographical heroine turns in desperation to literary journalism after her husband's death impoverishes her, whereupon she both makes it big and marries the publisher who most respects her, so that she can thumb her nose at the mean-spirited well-heeled relatives who left her in the lurch. The aspiring artist-heroine of Elizabeth Stuart Phelps's *The Story of Avis* (1877) sacrifices herself on the altar of domesticity, whereas the protagonists of Sarah Orne Jewett's *The Country Doctor* (1884) and Willa Cather's *The Song of the Lark* (1915) avoid marriage in favor of medical and performance careers, the first completely and the second until her career is fully launched.

Lark is a particularly revealing example of an up-from narrative from infancy of a smart, energetic, but callow small-town Colorado girl from a large family of Scandinavian immigrants as she feels her way unsteadily toward the operatic big time, aided at the outset by a number of kindly locals who recognize that there is something special about her but lack the sophistication to do more than fumblingly cheer her on. As the book shifts back and forth among narrative voice, multiple observer perspectives, and Thea's mind stream, one of its best effects is its rendering of the earnest provincial insouciance of her Colorado friends, and especially of Thea herself: how she remains a mystery to herself. She knows she's different from her sister Anna, who reads watered-down "sentimental religious story-books" and copycats "the spiritual struggles and magnanimous behavior of their persecuted heroines,"[45] whereas Thea feels most herself in the Woolfian room of her own that her vaguely prescient mother grants her. But until she goes to Chicago to study with teachers trained in Europe, she doesn't begin to foresee the singer she might become, and even then she alternates for a long time between unfocused longing and apathy.

Song of the Lark and *Portrait of a Lady* are two of the strongest nineteenth-century bildungsromans built around the plot of an American girl maturing from provincial juvenescence into a cosmopolitan refinement then obtainable only by removal to some European cultural center—Germany for Thea, Italy for Isabel. In each, sophistication comes at a cost. In James—the far more innovative artist but also more the old-fashioned moralist here—Isabel's comeuppance is her disastrous attraction to Osmond as a personification of consummate taste. In his perceptive study of the novel as the crucial point when James's mature style began fully to emerge, critic Michael Gorra rightly contends for *Portrait*'s accomplishment as an exceptional achievement both as a breakthrough in the direction of protomodernist style—its rendering of the motions of consciousness experienced from the inside—and in the judgment it passes upon Isabel's quixotic American-girl insistence on pursuing an Emersonian American-exceptionalist ethos of free-standing individual self-sufficiency.[46] (Gorra further notes that Isabel's strange readiness to enter into the mismatch with standoffish, fastidious Osmond is quickened by her sense of him as a soulmate in this regard.) In this latter respect, *Portrait* looks like a subtler variant on male up-from narratives like *Silas Lapham* and *Martin Eden*, which highlight forms of moral imperilment that go with material success and sophistication rather than a young woman's uphill battle for recognition like *The Lamplighter*, *Ruth Hall*, and *Song of the Lark*. For Cather's Thea, by contrast, the transit to Europe is a career opportunity rather than a moral test; and *Lark* imagines its sturdy nonintrospective heroine pretty much taking the leap in stride, as a next-stage adjustment in a series of necessary outplacements that began long before. The setbacks she absorbs are the inevitable trade-offs of diva professionalism. Painful though it is, you've got to put your lover on hold when he becomes a drag. (No need to invent an Osmond-like serpent for Thea's garden because she wouldn't have been much tempted by him anyway.) Even though you don't feel happy about it, you resist the call to forego the big engagement in order to return home on the chance— true, alas—that your mother might be dying. "It takes a great many people to make one—*Brünhilde*," the lover ruefully remarks.[47]

Lark's greater investment in the saga of youthful ambition realizing itself, relative to the moral bookkeeping aspect, is partly generational: a mark of the thirty-year gap between it and *Portrait*. Though not ranked among naturalists like London or Dreiser, Cather shares their fascination with assertive characters driven by a combination of internal energies and larger socioenvironmental forces. *Lark* also makes motions of seconding their understandings of materialistic and aesthetic motives as interlinked drivers of upward mobility by counterpointing Thea's saga with the subplot of her Moonstone patron Dr. Archie, who at midlife escapes the frustrations of his piddling small-town medical practice and a mean-spirited wife when his long-time dabbling in mining investment pays off and the wife's demise permits him to escape to Denver—and to lend Thea the money to study in Germany. Yet a wall of ideological as well as geographical separation divides his up-from story from that of Thea's artistic aspirations.

The first really sustained and systematic up-from novel of female development to treat the quests for *Bildung* and for wealth as inextricably codependent is Edith Wharton's *The Custom of the Country* (1913)—which also happens to be the only bildungsroman before the 1920s, male or female, to be named by its author as a possible Great American Novel.[48]

Custom follows the progress of the stunningly beautiful parvenu Undine Spragg from the midwestern metropolis of Apex City (which might have suggested the Zenith of Sinclair Lewis's *Babbitt*) on a take-no-prisoners assault first upon New York, then French society, through three increasingly scandalous divorces to a rapprochement with husband number one. That old flame, Elmer Moffatt, an Apex hanger-on who mesmerized her as a teenager but was bought off and sent packing by her father after their elopement, is now a railroad billionaire, thanks to an alliance with Mr. Spragg's high-rolling former business crony. Along the way, spendthrift Undine drives her indulgent parents into genteel poverty; drains the family resources of her pedigreed but hapless second husband Ralph Marvell, who kills himself in chagrin; fights her third, a more stubborn Burgundian aristocrat, to a standstill; and treats her young son, whom she never wanted in the first place, as a spoil of marital wars. Add to this that Undine's halfhearted stabs at improving her mind leave her incurably disinterested in art, books, and ideas except for their performance or cash value, and you have a far less appetizing portrait than Dreiser's Carrie Meeber in *Sister Carrie* (1900) or Wharton's own Lily Bart in *The House of Mirth* (1905). Lily too is condescending and snobbish, but appealing for her sense of taste, the pathos of her fall, and her capacity for generous-spiritedness, especially near the end, when she rejects the dishonorable path to recouping her finances. Undine can't be so pitied or admired. Like her namesake of German legend, she seems a sprite without soul: "a cool spirit within her seemed to watch over and regulate her sensations, and leave her incapable of measuring the intensity of those she provoked" (*CC* 816). If ever Undine underwent an endearing, wide-eyed girl-from-the-provinces stage like Isabel, Thea, or the young Carrie, we never see it.

But neither is Undine merely a cautionary example of self-interested calculation. Passages like the one just quoted interlink her closely with the ironic coolness of the narrative voice itself, refracting the recently divorced socialite author's own struggles between propriety and transgression, between mortification and rage at being made a spectacle. Undine is a gage thrown down, a weapon for skewering high-toned Knickerbocker and Gallic patriarchies in two fell swoops. She's proof that however much both deplore what she stands for socially, they depend upon the wealth of the new-moneyed "Invaders." Then too, her brassy verve puts social betters in the shade. When she shocks the Marvell clan by offhandedly defending divorce as a legitimate recourse for the social climber and, "flushed and sparkling," declares that she expects *"everything"* of life, the patriarch suavely replies "'My child, if you look like that you'll get it'" (685).

The novel thereby deploys Undine's crasser version of the youthful Isabel Archer's cosmopolitan longings to question James's hallmark international theme. Unlike James, for whom Parisian society represented a pitch of mystified refinement he found alluring but impenetrable and somewhat alien,[49] the Wharton of *Custom* admits little difference between American polite society and French as regards morality, cupidity, even taste. Yes, customs differ, but the underlying ethos is pretty much the same. For Undine, the transit from New World back to Old, a crucial rite of passage in the fiction of James and Cather, is incremental rather than epiphanic. Her imperviousness to the finer points of politesse on both sides of the water is mirrored by the novel's irony toward both. But *Bildung* of a sort does happen. Undine is a quick study; she cleans up her vocabulary (pruning slangy midwesternisms like "I don't care if I do"); she picks up new fashions; she becomes increasingly adept at reading unfamiliar social types, including foreigners whose inner lives remain opaque to her. She never learns to tell one Old Master from another, but she does learn how to bring off an elegant dinner party. In short, she's a survivor. She's more a latter-day Becky Sharp in Thackeray's *Vanity Fair* than a Daisy Miller, whom James feels compelled to make a tragic victim both in judgment on her rashness and as vindication of her virginal integrity.

Speaking of *Vanity Fair,* Wharton's account of why James didn't "get" *Custom* and erupted in disapproval after gamely trying to say nice things about it was that "he had long since ceased to be interested in the chronicle novel" and favored something tightly constructed around a finite international incident, like his own late fiction presumably.[50] But Wharton needed a "chronicle" approach to follow Undine's incremental geographic and social progress step by step.

And all the more so because of Elmer Moffatt, whose transformation saga is even more spectacular than Undine's. Elmer is Wharton's megascale version of the Gilded Age rags-to-riches metamorphosis, of Vanderbilt proportions as against Alger's clerks. Though he stays mainly in the shadows until the later chapters, Elmer's lifeline is even more deeply interwoven with the heroine's than William's in *The Lamplighter* and Archie's in *Song of the Lark.* Hermione Lee rightly notes that Wharton could easily have made *Custom* a novel about American business culture if she'd wished, by giving a bit more play to Elmer's intricate machinations, which counterpoint Undine's.[51] Not only do they directly affect the fortunes of Undine and those around her; more important, they go to show that financial and social success are two sides of the same coin. Although Wall Street is present only by allusion and Undine understands none of the technicalities when Elmer tells her the history of it all, she nonetheless hangs like "a new Desdemona on his conflict with the new anthrophagi," understanding him perfectly at the level that counts, because "Every Wall Street term had its equivalent in the language of Fifth Avenue" (*CC* 976). That's satirical, of course—the novel makes Undine's discarded husbands more attractive than she—but the satire also cuts in the opposite direction as the wealth and social capital of the ex-husbands crumble before the joint efforts of Elmer and Undine and the exes stand exposed as anachronisms, destined "to go down in any conflict with the rising forces," as the most worldly of Ralph's circle sizes up his predicament (807). After his first close encounter with Elmer, Ralph tellingly fantasizes about putting "the thundering brute" in a book: "There's something epic about him—a kind of epic effrontery" (790). That's pretty much what Wharton did with Undine, but with the additional strokes of making Elmer-Undine a matched pair and relishing as well as satirizing their colossal effronteries.

To picture Undine triumphant but still restless is a logical conclusion to the novel's double vision of her. Elmer is starting to grate. "His loudness and redness, his misplaced joviality" make him suffer by comparison to "his two predecessors," triggering "perceptions that had developed in her unawares." Yes, she has everything she always wanted, including the only man who ever swept her off her feet; but "she still felt, at times, that there were other things she might want if she knew about them" (*CC* 1012). This is *Custom*'s equivalent to Dreiser's closing glimpse of successful but unsatisfied Carrie in her rocking chair. To adapt critic Jennifer Fleissner's diagnosis of such female "drifting" in naturalist fiction, a moment like this shouldn't be taken just "as the mere desiccated fruit of a heartless capitalist system" that insists on devouring more even after it has consumed everything in sight but also "as a serious form of seeking," to which the customary social options "no longer offer an adequate response."[52]

Something quite like this critique-from-within scenario of the interdependence of up-from materialism and idealistic drift lies at the center of the novels of the 1920s and after to which we turn in Chapters 5 and 6. *The Custom of the Country* itself isn't likely to win acclaim as the Great American Novel it perhaps aspired to be, the acclaim that Dreiser's *An American Tragedy* did in its time and that Fitzgerald's *The Great Gatsby* still does. Wharton's heroine is too repellent and *House of Mirth*'s wonderfully concise power will always rivet more readers than *Custom*'s more ambitiously far-reaching but also rather diffuse and redundant satire. But at the very least, *Custom* was a near miss, a remarkable achievement whose sophisticated recasting of the American dream script anticipates more closely than any predecessor, male or female, the terms with which Dreiser, Fitzgerald, William Faulkner, Saul Bellow, Ralph Ellison, and Philp Roth conceived their own discrepant versions of up-from narrative.

Belated Ascendancy

Fitzgerald to Faulkner, Dreiser to Wright and Bellow

> Show me a hero and I will write you a tragedy.
>
> —F. SCOTT FITZGERALD, *The Crack-Up* (1945)

> "All my decay has taken place upon a child."
>
> —EUGENE HENDERSON, in Saul Bellow,
> *Henderson the Rain King* (1959)

L ITERARY HISTORIAN GORDON HUTNER calls 1925 the year the modern American novel "surely might be said to have ascended," and with good reason.[1] This was the year of Willa Cather's *The Professor's House,* the high point of her long career; of Dos Passos's *Manhattan Transfer,* a breakthrough for U.S. fictional modernism; of *Arrowsmith,* the third of Sinclair Lewis's five 1920s best sellers that were to make him the nation's first Nobel literature laureate; of Hemingway's first major book, *In Our Time;* of Anzia Yezierska's *Bread Givers,* a noteworthy advance for Jewish American and American immigrant fiction; of Gertrude Stein's monumental *The Making of Americans,* finished a dozen years before but published only now; and, at year's end, the biggest seller of them all, Anita Loos's *Gentlemen Prefer Blondes,* a pert chronicle of the triumphs of play-dumb but conniving upstart Lorelei Lei that Edith Wharton (recalling her own Undine Spragg) went so far as to hail as the long-awaited GAN.[2] But the two novels of 1925 that came nearest the mark were Dreiser's *An American Tragedy* and Fitzgerald's *The Great Gatsby.* In them the "American dream" story of a young man's longed-for transformation from obscurity to social pinnacle, the dream that was yet to be given the name we now know it by, at last received canonical embodiment—and critique—in landmark novels.

Why then, after so long a wait? It's tempting to look to World War I for the explanation. Wars can be cultural catalysts. The Civil War, we saw in Chapter 1, gave rise to the dream of the GAN and quickened the ascent of the realist aesthetic that the GAN's first framers presupposed. World War I made the United States "the most powerful nation in the world" economically. The country's late entry into the war had cost it little, and its allies' need and postwar Europe's disarray had made the United States "the world's greatest financial and creditor nation" and reconfirmed its standing as the leading powerhouse of manufacturing and food production. Europe's increasingly fragile hold over its far-flung colonies was starting to make America's foreign policy seem prescient, of acquiring power "less by outright territorial expansion than by colonizing the future," by marketing "the modernization process itself."[3] Might not a burst of cultural energy be expected from all this?

Sure enough, the 1920s saw the concurrent rise of New York as a cosmopolitan multiethnic cultural center; the rise of American modernism at home and abroad; the first major movement in African American literature, music, and art; and the inception of the Southern Renaissance, soon to become the most potent of the many literary regional efflorescences since the Civil War. But it took all this and more to begin to efface lingering doubts about national literary backwardness. The coexistence of runaway materialism with the runaway moralism exemplified by Prohibition became convenient symbols of that belatedness, as the decade's most outspoken cultural critic, H. L. Mencken, repeatedly insisted. That postwar U.S. foreign policy retrogressed into anti-immigrationist Anglo-Protestant isolationism intensified his scorn.

Discontent always generates better art than chauvinism, however. In the second quarter of the nineteenth century, it had helped energize the first emergence of world-class literature that F. O. Matthiessen would call "the American Renaissance." The energy that drove *The Scarlet Letter* and *The House of the Seven Gables* arose largely from their aversion to the dead hand of Puritan tradition, and that of *Uncle Tom's Cabin* from its commitment to reanimate that tradition in the cause of social justice. So it may be more predictable than surprising that the two novels to confront the traditional up-from story more searchingly than any predecessor should have appeared at a particularly charged moment in the long history of lamentation about the perceived discrepancy between U.S. techno-economic might and its comparatively underwhelming impact—or so it seemed—upon Western arts and letters.

Nor should it seem strange that both these novels do so critically and disaffectedly, even as they give full play to the up-from narrative's cultural force and psychological allure. To have done otherwise would have been to ignore history. Throughout Western literature, bildungsroman had been recoiling against its founding premises. "In the modernist Bildungsroman," as critic Gregory Castle observes, "normative modes of socialization and social mobility" came to "serve as the starting point for an immanent critique of socially pragmatic Bildung, of upward mobility."[4] The novelistic paper trail had become unmistakable: Flaubert's Frédéric Moreau, George Eliot's Maggie, Hardy's Jude the Obscure, Conrad's Jim, Rilke's Malte, Joyce's Stephen Dedalus, and just yesterday as it were Thomas Mann's Hans Castorp of *The Magic Mountain* (1924). Then too, the myth underlying the distinctive American variant of the genre, embodied by the Franklin legend, was looking ever more elusive. The statistical chances of attaining big-time success from the bottom up in 1920s America had markedly lessened. To the extent that the dream was seen as a lost illusion of yesteryear, adherence to it was apt to seem regressive, and those still fixated on it, like the protagonists of *Gatsby* and *American Tragedy,* suspiciously like Oscar Wilde's Dorian Gray, bonded to obsolete self-idealizations that destroy them. So it was that the American male bildungsroman's coming of age—its full-on engagement of the culture's most distinctive youth-to-maturity script—ironically threatened to leave U.S. literature without a compelling alternative: to reproduce on a more psychologically and sociologically sophisticated level the gestures of moral recoil we saw in Howells's *The Rise of Silas Lapham* and London's *Martin Eden.* The accomplishments first of that undoing and then of its refashioning under reconceived auspices are the central concerns of this chapter and the next.

Double Helix: An American Tragedy *and* The Great Gatsby

At first sight, Dreiser and Fitzgerald make an unlikely couple: the gruff, grizzled veteran who had worked his way laboriously up from the ranks of newspaper journalism versus the precociously dazzling sophisticate. The impression of *An American Tragedy* as the product of an older generation is heightened by Dreiser's imperfect updating of the 1908 case on which the novel is loosely based. Although the novel supposedly happens in the present, one could never know from reading it that the war in which Gatsby won his medal had just taken place.[5] Still more telling are the differences in narrative rhetoric: Dreiser's ponderously Olympian chronicle versus Fitzgerald's concise impressionism. *An American Tragedy*'s descriptive prolixity puts it on the paleolithic side of the divide between documentary naturalism and *Gatsby*'s taut, subjectified, telegraphically symbolic modernism. Dreiser seems driven by "an unshakeable determination to tell it all,"[6] whereas for Fitzgerald the measure of accomplishment seems rather to be—as Hemingway declared—how much you can leave out, how much you can pack into a quick glimpse of cuff links made from the "finest specimens of human molars" or Gatsby's "gorgeous pink rag of a suit" (*GG* 77, 162). Both novels invest their protagonists with a certain ineffability, but Fitzgerald through omission, Dreiser by straining after what can never be pinned down. Gatsby is featureless except for his radiant smile (the author confessed that he never "saw him clear myself").[7] Dreiser's Clyde Griffiths is imaged at full length again and again: by the narrator, by dozens of other characters, by himself mirror gazing, and as mirrored again in his arrogant look-alike cousin Gilbert. The circuit of his hapless striving from waif to upstart to loser is traced three times over: in his early misadventures as a Kansas City bellhop; then more exhaustively in the upstate New York ordeals that constitute the main action; and then again during the trial scenes of Part III, which replay the entire sequence from his salad days to his employment in his rich uncle's factory to his affair with the supervisee and poor-aspiring-girl counterpart whom he later tries to ditch for an alluring socialite, leading to a feckless, panicky series of failed attempts to secure an abortion and then to get rid of her under cover of a pretended wedding journey.

These contrasts are in keeping with the facing-both-ways eclecticism of the notable fictions of the 1920s—realism in decline but still running strong, modernism insurgent but not dominant. The ratio shifted decisively in the 1940s, when Dreiser's star fell as Fitzgerald's rose, as New Critical methods of close textual reading came into fashion. It may forever remain a mystery why *Gatsby* got lukewarm reviews and sold poorly despite Fitzgerald's accrued glitter as the laureate of the Jazz Age, whereas Dreiser's thousand-page whopper, which even his friend and admirer Mencken considered a "botch" until the trial scenes, became far and away his biggest seller, widely praised as "the greatest American novel of our generation."[8] Two points seem certain, however. First, the seriousness with which each novelist took his project. *An American Tragedy,* two decades of intermittent work in the making, was Dreiser's most concerted assault on the GAN, even more so than the unfinished Cowperwood trilogy, based on the rise and collapse of streetcar magnate Charles Yerkes (1837–1905), for the last volume of which he seems to have lost enthusiasm. *Gatsby* wasn't Fitzgerald's most elaborate novelistic project either, but he insisted that he had never striven so hard "to keep his artistic conscience as pure as during the ten months put into doing it."[9] Second, the two projects are intrinsically more alike than first appears. Look closely, and you begin to make sense of Fitzgerald's admiration for Dreiser during the 1920s as his "measuring stick of greatness" and for *An American Tragedy* as "without doubt the greatest American book that has appeared in years."[10] Fitzgerald's other major fiction, especially *The Beautiful and Damned* (1922) and *Tender Is the Night* (1934), shows a neonaturalist penchant for scripting the rise and degeneration of culturally symptomatic protagonists who become complicit victims of the circumstances that made them.

So *An American Tragedy* and *The Great Gatsby* offer complementary strategies for dramatizing the desire to leap from nowhere to somewhere while exposing it as poignantly delusive—the maxiform and miniform. Against the background of a century of fictional adaptations of the Franklinesque narrative of worldly success from humble beginnings—whether in affirmation like Lorimer's *Letters of a Self-Made Merchant,* in critique like Howells's *Silas Lapham,* or in ambivalence like London's *Martin Eden—An American Tragedy* and *The Great Gatsby* were quantum leaps forward in the intricacy, acuity, and multiperspectivalism of their conjurations of the dream script's hazards and allure. That both authors were self-conceived outsiders from midwestern Catholic backgrounds and Dreiser's was dirt poor to boot would have added edge to their renditions of the old story.

Both plots feature undereducated poor midwestern white boys aspiring to the leisured life of the eastern upper crust by whatever shortcuts possible. Those aspirations come to center on beautiful, rich, unobtainable young women whose shallowness they absurdly misperceive: the rich girl with the voice "full of money" as Gatsby says of

Daisy (*GG* 127). What hooks both men is more a dream of total aesthetic gratification than of wealth per se. In keeping, the romance of life at the top is what motivates them, rather than the labor of the climb. To be sure, *An American Tragedy* details its minutiae as *Gatsby* does not. Dreiser gives as much play to Clyde's delight in his first tips as a juvenile bellhop as Andrew Carnegie did at earning his first nickel and negotiating his first business loan. The novel meticulously anatomizes hotel concierge sociology, the brothel where Clyde gets initiated into sex, the layered echelons and work routines of the employees in Uncle Samuel's collar factory, the decorums of boardinghouse life. But for Clyde, as for Gatsby, all that seems trivial compared to the goal of acceptance by the smart set.

Gatsby seems the much more hard-headed operator, juggling between debonair party host and round-the-clock boss of his racketeering empire. But we never see him in a workplace. His business acumen remains as mysterious as that of Henry James's millionaires. By contrast, *An American Tragedy* puts work front and center for long stretches, at least as much as in any other prospective GAN. To expose Clyde as a misfit too moonstruck to stay on task exposes the defects of the work regime itself. As cultural critic Martha Banta points out, Clyde's failure as bottom-rung manager underscores the fallacies of the so-called scientific modern management methods advocated by Frederick Winslow Taylor, based on a wishful model of top-down management-labor cooperation that was supposed to make American industrial efficiency the envy of the world. "The disjunctions among the work ethic touted by the owners, the work procedures laid down by the managers, the machine technology installed in the factory, and the human element introduced by the employees' desires" in the overheated close quarters where Clyde is assigned to oversee a bevy of young women predictably make his job unmanageable. After flouting the factory's rule against boss-worker fraternization, Clyde flunks "his first, and most crucial, task of scientific management" then thrust on him, of figuring out how Roberta "can efficiently abort."[11] He desires not so much to take command as to be uplifted; to relish life's higher pleasures without having to work too hard for them, like the shiftless Aladdin of Arab legend—a telltale motif throughout. He personifies the dysfunctional ethos of "drift" that cultural critic Walter Lippmann had identified as the great enemy of the proper "discipline of democracy."[12]

Gatsby is far more purposeful in pursuit of his dream girl—not one to get distracted by a Roberta Alden on his way to a Sondra Finchley. But the novel puts him on a continuum with dreamy Clyde: gripped by the desire to become "his Platonic conception of himself"; by an "appalling sentimentality" that leads to his addiction to the gilded memory of "the first 'nice' girl he had ever known," "bright with the bought luxury of star-shine"; to his nighttime gazing at the green light on Daisy's dock; to postadolescent panic at the threshold of their reunion that balloons into exuberance only to collapse when Daisy can't match the ferocity of his obsession by denying she ever loved Tom (*GG* 104, 118, 155, 157).

Both novels imagine social worlds where "selfhood is conferred by the public" gaze rather than tangible accomplishment.[13] Gatsby and Clyde form their personae from the mass media. Listening to Gatsby's social talk is "like skimming hastily through a dozen magazines" (*GG* 71). Clyde can't imagine how to rid himself of Roberta until he's inspired by a newspaper article (*AT* 505–506). This is the postheroic world of what Robert Herrick had characterized as the inheritor generation, the one after the Vanderbilts and the Carnegies.[14] *An American Tragedy*'s Samuel Griffiths has created the family wealth and in business matters remains in charge, ordaining that nephew Clyde be given a fair chance to make his way, though according to his cohort's social Darwinist ethic only by starting at the bottom and at the lowest wage consistent with minimal respectability. Gilbert and especially Clyde are oriented more toward status, image, and play than toward the work ethic, although Gilbert's super-serious workplace persona bespeaks another sort of typic generational succession, from the age of the inventor-entrepreneur to that of the manager-engineer. All this makes for an environment in which Gilbert can resent Clyde both because he lacks proper training and because he is more handsome, while Clyde's good looks and presumptive standing as a Griffiths win him admission to the chic younger set. In Fitzgerald, likewise, although the offstage Gatsby may be a modern-style robber baron cut from the same cloth as his high-rolling patron Dan Cody, in the social world to which he aspires, the idle rich Buchanans call the tune. At the climax, Tom shuts Gatsby down as abruptly as Daisy then snuffs out Tom's mistress Myrtle Wilson, Gatsby's conventionally vulgar parvenu counterpart.

Up to a point the lines of social division seem permeable, allowing Clyde and Roberta their parallel fantasies of escape from poverty, and provoking Tom, the embattled master class figure, to decry Gatsby's invasion of his domestic patriarchate as a slippery slope to the "'intermarriage between black and white'" (*GG* 17, 137). Here and elsewhere *Gatsby* is better attuned than *An American Tragedy* to the momentum of the 1920s by recognizing the interrelated trend lines of postwar anti-immigrationist white solidarity and the increasing visibility of ethnic others as cultural agents, of which the Harlem Renaissance was the most significant example.[15]

Dreiser and Fitzgerald knew how long the odds against a Gatsby-type metamorphosis had become. In 1925, the chances of young men with parental backgrounds like Gatsby or Clyde making it into *Who's Who in America* were less than one-hundredth of a percent, whereas almost half of the future top businessmen who reached adulthood in 1870 had, like Thomas Mellon and Andrew Carnegie, "originated in the lower classes."[16] American millionaires living in 1925 were only half as likely to have started life poor (20 percent) than those deceased. "The wealthy class of the United States," declared the leading student of social mobility in 1925, was "becoming less and less open" and transforming "into a caste-like group."[17]

Higher education had also become more important for the younger generation (nearly half of the mid-1920s *Who's Who* roster had some college experience), making the market for college graduates more competitive. So Gatsby as an "Oggsford" man is value added for Meyer Wolfsheim, while Yale graduate Nick Carroway, *Gatsby*'s narrator, works as a low-paid bond salesman and Gilbert Griffiths the Princetonian owes his position as his father's right-hand man to family no less than Clyde and plays a distinctly subordinate role in setting company policy. The mismatch between the growing complexities of the workplace in a maturing industrial order versus the aura of the 1920s as an everything-goes boom time—an aura Fitzgerald helped perpetuate—may have added bite to both narrators' mixture of scorn and sensitivity toward minute social distinctions. Nick professes to find the worlds of fashion as hollow as Gatsby's extravaganzas; but he remains acutely aware of the differences between tasteful Buchanan opulence and the "caravansary" of "roughneck" Gatsby, rather as Gilbert holds it against Clyde that he shows up for work wearing "'one of those bright pink striped shirts like they used to wear three or four years ago'" (*GG* 53, 120; *AT* 219).*

The difference between Clyde's mass-produced garb and Gatsby's cornucopia of tailored shirts that makes Daisy weep is a tiny indicator of a much bigger difference in social typicality. As this chapter's first epigraph hints, Gatsby's trajectory follows that of the Aristotelian tragic hero as then understood: the exceptional figure, larger than life, who comes to grief by a hubristic overreach that marks him as fated even as his charisma endows him with a special grandeur and ultimately even a sort of moral authority. Clyde's story is the tragedy of common parlance: one of those tabloid disasters that sometimes overtake the unremarkable, "the lowest common denominator of tragic effect," as Robert Penn Warren put it. For Clyde is "less a 'self' than a composite of previously written texts, less individual voice than voiced by mass culture."[18] Dreiser himself stressed that Clyde was "not unique" but a "prototype," adapted from the actual instance that seemed best to typify the chronic American "disease" of "fortune-hunting": a "young ambitious lover of some poorer girl" who tried to ditch her when "a more attractive girl with money or position appeared."[19] This case involved another C. G., one Chester Gillette, also a child of pious religionists taken into his rich uncle's upstate New York factory, executed in 1906 on circumstantial evidence for murdering his pregnant girlfriend and supervisee in a lonely Adirondack lake.[20] Unlike Gatsby, who awes the moralistic Nick with the purity of his grand obsession ("you're worth the whole damn bunch put together," *GG* 162), Chester/Clyde was the dupe of his, "the

---

* It was a stroke of genius to have the Griffiths Company manufacture collars rather than skirts as in the original murder case. For "collars" implied all this in the 1920s: high fashion (as in the snappy "Arrow Collar Man" advertisement that flourished 1905–1930); a means to give "polish and manner to people who wouldn't otherwise have them, if it weren't for cheap collars," as one of Gilbert's college classmates dryly parrots his professional credo (*AT* 370); and a technology on the wane, about to be superseded by Arrow's new line of shirts equipped with soft collars, soon to be followed by the invention of Sanforization, which enabled ready-made preshrunk shirts with firm collars. Collar manufacture, then, encapsulated the interdependence between the histories of mass production and of fashion and underscored the irony of the tie between the affluent Griffiths and their poor relation, to whom such items of male haberdashery are as crucial as his surname to elevating him above the lower orders in the eyes of the Lycurgus, New York, citizenry. Even Uncle Samuel thinks better of Clyde when he sees him decked out, Arrow Man–like, in a tuxedo "with a smart pleated shirt" (*AT* 247). However old-fashioned his literary style, middle-aged Dreiser sometimes showed as keen an eye for fashion as debonair young Fitzgerald.

asinine notion in America that everyone has an equal opportunity to become a money master," as Dreiser put it in another context. Hence the old debate over whether his novel should count as a "true" tragedy.[21]

But to call one case tragic and the other not is to risk the false dichotomy that cultural critic Raymond Williams chastises in those who complain about the "loose and vulgar uses of 'tragedy' in ordinary speech and in the newspapers." Williams saw midcentury tragedy theory trending toward "an increasingly isolated interpretation of the character as the hero" that was both nonclassical (for Aristotle, individual character was subsidiary to plot, social standing, decrees of fate, etc.) and blind to humanity's social being, conducing to a retrograde ennoblement of autonomous personhood even as tragedy was supposedly being democratized away from its ancient emphasis on privileged elites. Such compartmentalization of "human agency" from "social and political life" lies behind the perverse "separation of tragedy from 'mere suffering.'"[22] Williams probably would have judged both *Gatsby* and *An American Tragedy* to be testaments to dead-end liberalism, as he did Arthur Miller's *Death of a Salesman*; but he would have recognized both as tragedies, and *American Tragedy* as the more "modern." Whereas Miller's own theory of the tragedy of "the common man" went along Aristotelian lines (built upon a figure, whether high or low, "ready to lay down his life . . . to secure . . . his sense of personal dignity"), Williams viewed Miller's Willy Loman in Dreiserian terms as "the conformist, the type of society itself," who "brings tragedy down on himself, not by opposing the lie, but by living it." That squares perfectly with Dreiser's view of Chester Gillette's case, "the real American tragedy." His was "not an anti-social dream as Americans should see it, but rather a pro-social dream. He was really doing the kind of thing which Americans" would have considered "the wise and moral thing for him to do" had it not led to murder.[23]

Dreiser was a philosophic fatalist as Fitzgerald was not. He professed to believe in survival of the fittest and to conceive human thought, life, and behavior as driven by "chemic" mechanisms ("Man . . . is a chemical compound, bottled and sealed in realms outside his ken"; "we are all harnessed and driven, as much as any ox").[24] But Fitzgerald creates a formidable doom machine of his own, starting with Nick's upfront disclosure that his tale is an elegy for a dead man. The tale itself concentrates on Gatsby's last days; and the passages into which his prehistory gets condensed stress that his emotional life had been arrested five years before, at that magic prewar moment when he was smitten by Daisy. In her innovative study of literary naturalism, Jennifer Fleissner remarks on the peculiar quality of compulsive repetition or "stuckness" that its characters display, such as the narrator's self-entrapment in the room with the yellow wallpaper in Charlotte Perkins Gilman's story or Trina's compulsion to hoard money in Frank Norris's *McTeague*.[25] But nothing in the naturalist canon surpasses the stuckness of Gatsby's fixation (which Nick underscores and prolongs by his own fixation on Gatsby's). For Gatsby to insist that the past can be revoked and relived is to become the instrument of his own undoing. The fatalism culminates in *Gatsby*'s famous parting shot of Nick at night on the shore gazing out over Long Island Sound and likening Gatsby's first glimpse of the green light at the end of Daisy's dock to the "Dutch sailors'" sighting of the "fresh, green breast of the new world": "the last time in history" that "man" was brought face to face "with something commensurate to his capacity for wonder." Alas for Gatsby, he didn't grasp that "his dream" "was already behind him, somewhere back in that vast obscurity beyond the city, where the dark field of the republic rolled on under the night" (*GG* 189).

To read Gatsby as a symbol of the great American dreamer, then, is to read the dream itself as already sealed and gone, locked somewhere in the remote inaccessible past. The disclosure has been well prepared by previous links between Gatsby and the relics of a former time—Dan Cody, "the pioneer debauchee," and Ben Franklin himself, whose moral perfection scheme in part two of the *Autobiography* is reprised in the "schedule" of duties and resolves young Jimmy Gatz scrawled in the inside back cover of his copy of *Hopalong Cassidy* (*GG* 106, 181). The myths of frontier and mercantile individualism as repackaged for mass consumption get neatly compacted into one image here.

At times the two doom machines become quite preachy, despite Dreiser's philosophic amoralism and Nick's insistence that he's "inclined to reserve all judgments" (*GG* 5). In fact Nick seizes upon the smallest gaucheries and moral lapses. He claims to exempt Gatsby from his recoil against the decadent spectacles he's witnessed but insists in the next breath that Gatsby "represented everything for which I have an unaffected scorn" (6). The narrator of *An American Tragedy* caustically sizes up Clyde's veniality, "this sly and yet muddy tergiversation"

(*AT* 446)—and everyone else's too. Yet both narrators also empathize with what they expose as specious. As with Clyde's rapture at the sight of the imposing faux-English front yard of his rich uncle's Lycurgus mansion, with its "lone cast iron stag pursued by some cast iron dogs": "The beauty! The ease! What member of his own immediate family had ever dreamed that his uncle had lived thus!" (215). And the young Gatsby, just before kissing Daisy, imagining "out of the corner of his eye" how "the blocks of the sidewalk really formed a ladder and mounted to a secret place above the trees" (*GG* 117). In *Gatsby*, this effect is magnified by Nick's position as country cousin awed despite himself by the scale at which both old-money Buchanans and parvenu Gatsby live, and by the audacity of Gatsby's dream. So Gatsby's aura is built up at least as much as it is torn down. The "deathless song" of Daisy's voice captivates Nick almost as much as it does Gatsby (101). However appalled their narrators seem about the ultimate consequences, both novelistic worlds, as Douglas Mao writes of Dreiser, seem to postulate, and sympathetically, "that responsiveness to beauty is hard-wired in the human organism."[26]

That ethico-aesthetic ambivalence may help explain the misty elusiveness that surrounds both figures, especially Gatsby. Fitzgerald ensures this from the start by never allowing Gatsby to be seen from the inside. In reconstructing his last hours, Nick can suppose, but he can't know, that as Gatsby floated on his pool he would have beheld "a new world, material without being real," as phantasmagoric as the spectral assassin "gliding toward him through the amorphous trees" (*GG* 169). As for *American Tragedy*, even as it seems to record Clyde's every palpitation it exploits the unacknowledged oxymoron inherent in the very concept of narrative "omniscience,"[27] by pitting the seeming commitment to full disclosure against the intimation that people in general, Clyde included, are muddles ("Clyde growing more and more moody [in jail] and deciding, maybe, that there was no real hope for him after all" *AT* 720). The arresting inward turn of the narration as Clyde grows more panicky clinches this—Dreiser's "naturalistic drama of consciousness," as critic Donald Pizer calls it—that presses past the boundary between Howellsian verisimilitude and narrative modernism. The narrative voice ventriloquizes Clyde's turmoil: "the horror of this business and the danger, now that it was so close at hand—the danger of making a mistake of some kind—if nothing more, of not upsetting the boat right—of not being able to—" (*AT* 558).[28] The novel leaves hanging the question of what judgment to make of Clyde's precise degree of responsibility for Roberta's death. No trial could establish it definitively. He himself never resolves the question. Clearly he plotted murder, but clearly he's not a hard-boiled criminal type.[29] He vacillates at the critical moment, and the boat capsizes by accident although he refrains from trying to save Roberta from drowning. So he goes to his execution wondering "'Had he?'" (930), and Dreiser's publisher got good publicity mileage by offering a prize for the best essay on the subject. Both novels, then, invite judgment on cases symbolic of the American success drive gone awry only to complicate the issues to the point of ensuring they would be wrangled about forevermore.

Fitzgerald, Faulkner, and Beyond: Americanization of Observer-Hero Narrative

Dreiser may have been the American novelist whom Fitzgerald most admired in the mid-1920s, but the novel he praised most highly was Conrad's *Nostromo* (1904). In 1923, Fitzgerald claimed that he would "rather have written" it "than any other novel"—"chiefly because 'Nostromo,' the man, intrigues me so much." What gave Nostromo his "haunting and irresistible appeal" was his combination of symbolic representativeness and personal charisma: *Nostromo*'s recognition that this "man of the people" (here Fitzgerald recycles Conrad's own epithet) is "one of the most important types in our civilization," "one of the most powerful props of the capitalistic system."[30]

No less compelling to Fitzgerald than Nostromo as socially symbolic figure would have been Conrad's stylistic architecture.* Like many of Conrad's famous focal figures—James Wait in *Nigger of the Narcissus*, Jim in *Lord Jim*, Kurtz in *Heart of Darkness*—Nostromo is fashioned

---

* That Fitzgerald's enthusiasm for Conrad was widely shared by American readers is convincingly shown by Peter Lancelot Mallios, who reconstructs the remarkable stateside vogue Conrad enjoyed in the 1910s and 1920s across disparate readerships, according for instance to whether they preferred to trace his brooding genius to his Slavic roots, as Mencken did to fortify his attack on the fetishization of Anglo-Saxonism among the WASP intelligentsia, or to stress Conrad's embrace of his adopted Englishness, as did many of those WASP literati, including the fomenters of the southern literary renaissance (Peter Lancelot Mallios, *Our Conrad: Constituting American Modernity* [Stanford, CA: Stanford University Press, 2010], 41–217).

mainly as a projection of others' images of him and how he knows himself to be seen by others in turn directs his own self-conception and performative orchestration of his charisma. Among such Conrad creations, Nostromo might have seemed especially pertinent to Gatsby. Despite his humble peasant-seafarer origins, Nostromo's charisma makes him an indispensable henchman for the dominant Euro-American-run silver-mining concern in the novel's imaginary Latin American banana republic and finally the pivotal, storied figure in the breakaway region's independence story. Like Gatsby, too, Nostromo proves an unstable compound of idealism and greed, proud of his reputation for incorruptibility yet eventually corrupted by the silver entrusted to him, and undone by an erotic entanglement.

The contrasts in scale make the affinities all the more striking. *Gatsby* is little more than a novella compared to *Nostromo*'s profuse anatomy of Costaguana: its factions jockeying for power; its copious dramatis personae of Creoles, immigrants, and foreigners in their different social niches; its successive political upheavals. It is as if Fitzgerald had undertaken a panoramic history of the United States from the war years through prohibition as orchestrated by Meyer Wolfsheim and other underground kingpins with Gatsby reduced to a kind of glittering front-man role—which is how Wolfsheim seems to think of him.

Not that *Nostromo* is *Gatsby*'s only possible Conradian prototype. A case can also be made for the significance of the affinities between Gatsby and Jim as one who also "embodies the youthful imagination" and insists on reliving the past and between *Gatsby* and *Heart of Darkness* as texts that dramatize the narrator's need "to disencumber himself of the memory of his hero and its influence on his present life by telling the story."[31] What especially binds *Gatsby* to all three Conradian texts is a shared structure: an externally viewed magnetic figure who strives to embody some societal ideal that the novel exposes as alluring but dangerous. Peter Lancelot Mallios perceptively calls this way of framing focal characters "metanational." It's a means, that is, "of approaching nationhood as not an objective fact but an imaginative social construct" by "constellating a novel of intense perception and socially conjunctive will around an *absent* character center" that puts the emphasis on the chaotic, uncongealed, inevitably fractured and never-to-be-seamlessly-completed process of the nation-making imagination.[32] So Jim exemplifies the dysfunctionality of ruling-class decencies; and

Kurtz in *Heart of Darkness,* to whose making "all Europe contributed,"[33] fashions himself, as narrator Marlow sees it, into a Jekyll/Hyde symbol of Euro-imperialism's toxic brew of idealism and rapacity. But *Nostromo* is the one Conrad novel to apply this design to the process of nation making per se—and furthermore a nation in the Americas that high-octane Anglo-capitalism made possible—and the title figure becomes a kind of dream screen onto which the cross-currents of idealism, vanity, self-servingness, and greed the success of the enterprise unleashes play through to his eventual destruction.

Neither *Gatsby* nor *Nostromo* can be reduced to a fable of capitalism's seductions, as if *Gatsby* were on the same page as Nathanael West's caustic satire of American dreamism in *A Cool Million* (1934) or as if Conrad were H. G. Wells. As Conrad critic Geoffrey Harpham proposes, the device of the luminous free-standing figure who becomes the mirror of the collective gaze may imply not so much a settled critique of the work of nation making as desire to avoid having to rest in any fixed doctrinal or ideological position on the matter.[34]

Perhaps this flexibility helps explain the long attraction of American fiction—starting well before Fitzgerald and even Conrad—to the kind of split-focused narrative structure in which a symbolically charged actor gets viewed largely from the perspective of more quotidian dramatized observers. In broadest terms, this narrative turn, which comes into fashion about the turn of the nineteenth century, seems an offshoot of what Harold Bloom has called "the internalization of quest-romance,"[35] that is, the shift under romanticism from defining heroism in terms of external acts (Achilles, Odysseus, Beowulf, Gawain, Milton's Satan) to interior odysseys, theaters of mind. The mental odysseys of Byron's heroes and Wordsworth's semiautobiographical personae become more consequential than their deeds. In fiction, observer-hero narrative, as I like to call it,[36] has been particularly amenable to registering conditions of social and ideological instability in its casting of the relation between focal figure and narrator/observer(s) as a symbiotic tension between a rigid, obsolescent order of values and a more "modern," disenchanted, pragmatic, and intellectually mobile emergent one exemplified by the observer(s). The observer(s) get drawn to the purposeful single-mindedness of the hero figure and up to a point mesmerized but sooner or later recoil against his rigidity, obstinacy, and hubris so as to reassert distance even if not break the spell entirely.

So it was with the earliest canonical British example, William God-win's *Caleb Williams* (1794), a novelistic reflection on the tenacious hold of a doomed aristocracy on the emergent underclasses via the tortured bond between Caleb the servant-narrator and his benevolent-seeming master Falkland, to whom he is admiringly deferential, to the sacrifice of his personal safety even as he exposes Falkland as a murderer, lead-ing to a breathless sequence of flight, capture, and (depending on which of the two endings you favor) Caleb's acquittal or his incarceration and descent into madness. So too, with qualifications discussed in Chapter 11, in *Moby-Dick*'s juxtaposition of the mental worlds of relentless Ahab and the skeptical, relativistic Ishmael, whose meandering ruminations and egalitarian geniality stand at odds with the captain's monomania-cal conviction that he is "the Fates' lieutenant" charged to hunt down the white whale (*MD* 418), an obsession as atavistic as the neofeudal shipboard hierarchy that he personifies and oversees. So too the an-tithesis drawn in Hawthorne's *Blithedale Romance* between the domi-neering Hollingsworth and narrator Miles Coverdale, self-admittedly a trivial creature by comparison but protected by dilettantish urbanity against getting too far into the post-Puritan reformist zealotry that Hollingsworth personifies. Likewise, in a mellower turn of the device, Owen Wister's *The Virginian* (1902), the seminal literary Western, views the omnicompetent factotum range hand through the admiring eyes of a genteel visitor whom he befriends and initiates, but who personifies the postfrontier era into which the Virginian himself gets pulled when he marries the local schoolteacher from Vermont. Willa Cather's *My Ántonia* (1918) dramatizes more nostalgically the passing of the frontier by having the successful but dissatisfied businessman-narrator revisit his Nebraska boyhood haunts on a journey home after long absence only to find that the Bohemian immigrant girl who made it seem lumi-nous is now a wife and mother—still vigorous, but more earthbound and ordinary than the figure of memory.

The U.S. national imaginary's long-standing conception of the coun-try as defined by a future continuously in process has surely reinforced the penchant for depicting metasocial figures who embody defining stages of social crystallization but also their evanescence, as conjured up, mystified, and bracketed by narrators who represent more "mod-ern," quotidian conditions and whose ambivalent bonding to the hero (or heroine) confirms both the hold of the obsolescent formation and its transience.[37] Among these metasocial observer-hero narratives, *Gatsby* stands out as the first notable novel built squarely upon the "meta" of the up-from legend-building process.

It's hard to know whether to be more bemused by how long it took for a *Gatsby* to materialize, seeing that the shifty but urbanely charming Franklin persona had pointed the way for its appearance so long before, or by its swift replication in at least two memorable works of like kind thereafter, Faulkner's *Absalom, Absalom!* (1936), with the fabulous Thomas Sutpen as absent center, and Robert Penn Warren's quasi-Faulknerian *All the King's Men* (1947), in which the rise and fall of populist potentate Willie Stark, a stylized reinvention of the populist Louisiana politician "Kingfish" Huey Long, is seen through the eyes of a glumly self-focused but grudgingly admiring staffer. Neither book owed anything to Fitzgerald, who during these years chiefly interested younger satirists of upper-middlebrow pathology like John O'Hara and J. D. Salinger. But Faulkner if not also Warren shared Fitzgerald's admiration for the same Conradian scenario, an admiration that for Faulkner would have been heightened by *Moby-Dick,* which he devoured as a teenager, before the Melville revival of the 1920s. Indeed Faulkner and the poet Hart Crane were the first major American writers for whom Melville truly mattered, whereas for Fitzgerald and Dreiser he didn't even exist. In the mid-1920s Faulkner declared that he wished he'd written *Moby-Dick* and later that it was one of the few novels to which he often returned.

Unsurprisingly, the Conrad novel that meant most to Faulkner, more even than *Moby-Dick,* was *The Nigger of the Narcissus,* a book with a very different cynosure from Nostromo, the prickly tubercular black seaman James Wait, who exerts an uncanny influence over the rest of the crew through his manipulative mood swings between denial and flaunting of his imminent death. More than Nostromo, Jim, Kurtz, even Gatsby, Wait is almost a complete cipher. Conrad rightly stated that even though Wait was based on an actual person whom he believed he partially understood, the novel itself shows him as "nothing" in himself, but "the centre of the ship's collective psychology and the pivot of the action."[38] That squares with Faulkner's own guardedness as a novelist of the color line operating in the Jim Crow South, hesitant to portray African Americans from the inside, even while supercharging his fiction with white fantasies about blacks and generating a series of black characters—as symbolic sites and mirrors of white admiration, longing, perplexity, outrage: Dilsey in *The Sound and the Fury;* Joe Christmas of *Light in August;* Lucas Beauchamp of *Go Down, Moses* and *Intruder in the Dust;* Charles Bon of *Absalom.*[39] But Faulkner's investment in focal characters who mirror the conflicting desires of those around them wasn't limited to nonwhites. It starts with the horribly injured dying veteran Charles Mahon, in his first novel *Soldiers' Pay;* it continues with the figures of Caddie Compson and Addie Bundren in *The Sound and the Fury* and *As I Lay Dying*—absent sister and deceased matriarch, without whom their families disintegrate—and culminates with *Absalom*'s Sutpen, a metanationally symbolic figure in whom the figures of Captain Ahab and Jay Gatsby seem to fuse into one.

Conrad might have percolated through to *Absalom* in more ways than one. Here as in other ways only starting to receive full attention, Faulkner's life as a literary immortal might have bled into his (much better-paid) work as a writer of so-so Hollywood film scripts and vice versa. Shortly before starting work on the novel, he had dashed off a script rejected by MGM, provisionally titled *Mythical Latin-American Kingdom Story* with suggestive echoes of *Nostromo* including a quasi-equivalent of the title figure in the person of a pilot for an American gold-mining baron also intrigue-entrapped despite his man-of-action swagger and fixation on matters of honor.[40] Especially given the interest soon to be taken in Faulkner by Carlos Fuentes, Gabriel Garcia Márquez, Mario Vargas Llosa, and other superheroes of the midcentury Latin American boom in magical realist fiction and their conception of his genius as incipiently hemispheric in reach, it's tempting to imagine the Latin American Conrad standing behind the Faulknerian masterpiece that gestures most extravagantly toward the Caribbean. Whereas *Gatsby* threatens to shrink into a regional fable with Nick's downbeat parting shot that he and all the other major characters were displaced midwesterners who never quite adjusted, *Absalom* metamorphoses from a nominally southern deconstruction of Lost Cause legend into a transnational epic.

In the process, among all possible Great American Novels, *Absalom* takes the parsing of its version of the remarkable transformation tale at the heart of the American dream idea to the furthest limit, glimpsing the saga of Thomas Sutpen through the overheated, incantatory rhetoric of not one but four obsessively recursive narrators, plus an anonymous overvoice. I reserve until Chapter 9 full unpacking of the brew of rant, innuendo, rhapsodics, irony, and judgmentalism with which these narrators supercharge the narrative, in order to concentrate here on Sutpen's transit itself, the volcanic core.

In the slyly understated fashion Faulkner often used with editors and undergraduates, he liked to describe his project as "the story of a man who wanted a son and got too many" and so they destroyed him: a man who obstinately persisted in "trying to establish a dynasty" even after the Civil War had wrecked the plantation system, "still trying to get even with that man who in his youth" as an illiterate redneck kid had ordered him, "Go to the back door."[41] That pretty well sums up the bare bones of Sutpen's life: the dust-to-dust circle of a semiliterate lad from nowhere in the hills of what later split off as West Virginia who ruthlessly bootstraps his way to short-lived grandeur as a Mississippi planter in compensatory reaction to a boyhood rebuff from the black butler of the Tidewater aristocrat to whom his father had ordered him to deliver a message.

Sutpen's transformation from flummoxed waif to grandee begins in the West Indies, to which the lad decamps from the upper South because he's heard you can get rich quick there. As the overseer of a French Creole's sugar cane plantation, he somehow manages to "subdue" a slave uprising—a perplexing anachronism, since Afro-Haitians overthrew their masters fifteen years before Sutpen was born, perhaps explicable only as foreshadowing what will later overtake him by tying his star to a doomed plantocracy. For Sutpen is defeated not so much by the Civil War per se as by the curse of slavery, and more precisely not by the curse of slavery as economic system but by the master-class racism that underlies the curse whose aftereffects, the novel testifies, persist long after Sutpen's downfall. Sutpen had married the Creole planter's daughter after she nursed him back to health following the slave revolt. But when he finds she is mulatto, he tries to buy her off by establishing her and their son Charles in New Orleans and starting over in the Mississippi outback. Almost-white isn't good enough for his purist version of gentrification. By unstinting effort with the band of Haitian slaves he brought with him, despite local hostility toward his secretive ways and unknown past Sutpen prospers magnificently, boasting the grandest mansion for miles around and a second family. On the eve of the Civil War, all this starts to crumble. Perhaps by the discarded first wife's machinations, son one winds up as the University of Mississippi class-mate and friend of son two, who invites him home for vacation. Son one becomes engaged to son two's sister. Because the all-white son has internalized tribal taboo, and because the near-white son presses his suit, the former is driven to fratricide despite their long-term intimacy after Sutpen tells him—or so the narrators surmise—the secret of son one's identity, symbolically in the war's waning moments. The tortured surviving brother then flees, never to return until old age, wasted, to die. Long before that, though, Sutpen himself is literally mown down by the scythe of his handyman Wash Jones, also of white-trash origins, after a last-ditch third attempt to continue the male line by seducing Wash's teenage granddaughter.

The sense in which this hero figure's story unpacked by the book's four primary observers spanning three generations might be conceived as "metanational" may not be altogether obvious. The more common practice has been to read *Absalom* more as an allegory of the fall of the old South than as a national one. The most influential reading of the latter kind, Eric Sundquist's, likens Sutpen's trajectory to Abraham Lincoln's. Sundquist especially has in mind Faulkner's highlighting of what one of the narrators terms, in a devastatingly ironic understate-ment, the "trouble" of Sutpen's "innocence"—his dogged adherence to his juvenescent dream of greatness without facing the fatal flaw destined to bring down the house. "Sutpen's crisis of innocence, as well as the flaw that engenders it," Sundquist infers, "is the nation's," personified by Lincoln himself.[42] Both personal and national grand designs pre-sumed a denial of white-black inextricability exemplified by Lincoln's expressed opposition to miscegenation, by persisting as long as possible in maintaining and then seeking to restore the political house divided, by prioritizing union over abolition. All this helps explain the logic of *Absalom*'s point-by-point correlation between the onset, course, and termination of national and familial fratricide. But a more fundamen-tal likeness between Sutpen and Lincoln is their consanguinity as in-carnations of the myth of the self-made man, and more specifically of poor white Appalachian autodidacts rising to commanding albeit short-lived prominence within their spheres.

To press the Sutpen-Lincoln parallels very far, however, is to under-state the immensely greater monstrousness of Sutpen's "innocence." Lincoln showed himself capable of growing beyond and acting against his residual racism even if not breaking altogether from it, of greater flexibility on the question of white and black coexistence within the republic of the future than he first showed. But Sutpen remains fixated on that boyhood moment of humiliated subalternity. In all of U.S. literary history, it would be hard to find a more chilling instance of the trope of arrested development used to dramatize the hazards of the up-from dream script. Here Faulkner moves significantly beyond Dreiser's and Fitzgerald's exposure of the regressive character of the up-from aspiration when they cast their protagonists as starstruck, star-stuck lads in the bodies of adults by driving home the for-white-men-only rider still prevailingly attached to the dream script that ironically defined it as product, perpetuator, and aggravator of drastic social as well as economic inequalities.*

Might Sutpen's ghostliness insinuate not only the pathology of persistent Lost Cause nostalgia but also the coming eclipse of the poor white as the paradigmatic hero of the obscurity-to-prominence saga? In retrospect, it's clear that Sutpen represented a losing cause in more ways than one. A saga built around the upward mobility of an ignorant but tenacious hillbilly lad might have seemed au courant circa 1900, as in John Fox Jr.'s best-selling *Little Shepherd of Kingdom Come* (1903); but by the 1930s, the poor white odyssey was coming into greater competition with stories of up-from struggle focused on (even) more socially marginal protagonists, as we'll soon see. Richard Wright's would be remembered, Studs Lonigan's largely forgotten. Did Faulkner sense this with anything like the clarity with which he recognized the regressive fixation of the plantation myth? Maybe not. That Warren's *All the King's Men*—centered on a poor southern white country boy's rise to political mogul—won the Pulitzer Prize a decade later lends force to the dictum

---

* Even more than Gatsby's and Clyde's, Sutpen's regressive "innocence" and the racial and economic equalities that produce and result from it recall the "antidevelopmental" figurations of "frozen" youth in British bildungsromans of the late nineteenth- and early twentieth-century provincial and imperial outbacks that Jed Esty ascribes to a combination of uneven development both at home and on the imperial peripheries ensuing from the interlinked advances of industrial capitalism and empire (*Unseasonable Youth* [New York: Oxford University Press, 2012], 7–160). The affinity might help explain Conrad's appeal to Faulkner. In any case, Sutpen fuses, or rather wavers between, subaltern and master-class frozenness. The benighted southern cracker provenance that drives his obsession with that adolescent moment when he resolved to become the grandee also ensures that after he has gratified that mimetic desire his conception of himself will oscillate forever between those two poles.

of Faulkner's Gavin Stevens in *Requiem for a Nun*, "the past is never dead. It's not even past."[43] But that Faulkner might at least have dimly foreseen is suggested by *Absalom*'s decision to let the imagined quest for paternal recognition by the fractionally nonwhite first son Charles Bon become for the novel's younger-generation narrators Quentin and Shreve an obsession even more compelling than Sutpen's own story. As *Absalom*'s multiple narrators' fascination for revisiting the Sutpen case suggests, he is by no means the only figure in the novel who's pictured as stuck in adolescent innocence. The same holds for the narrators themselves, especially Miss Rosa, whose life is said to have ended forty-five years before with Sutpen's offensive proposal that their marriage should hinge on her bearing him an heir, but also the mentally hyper-active roommates, who get so sucked back into the deep past as they strain to piece together the whole Sutpen story that Quentin feels like a ghost himself. All this raises a question insinuated in *Gatsby*, and before that in the partiality of Conrad's narrator Marlow for dwelling on by-gone episodes (in "Youth," *Lord Jim*, and *Heart of Darkness*). Is the pivotal instance of undevelopment necessarily the apparent one, the hero fig-ure, or may it not also be—and occasionally to an ever greater degree—the fantasizing narrator? The most impressive mid-twentieth-century American novel to follow the scenario of the transformation of an or-dinary white kid into extraordinary charismatic figure using the observer-hero structure suggests precisely that, and in the process ren-ders judgment on the kind of monstrous "innocence" Thomas Sutpen embodies: Vladimir Nabokov's *Lolita* (1955). Here the trope of undevel-opment becomes a fantasy that the narrator's own confessed arrested development impels him to inflict on his object of desire. Nabokov mischievously reinvents the narrator as an urbane pedophile, hooked on preadolescent "nymphets" ever since an unconsummated affair in his early teens, who gorges himself upon a girl who seems the reincar-nation of his long-dead Annabel Lee.

Nabokov would have shrunk from the comparison to Faulkner, whose "stale romanticism" he disliked.[44] To link *Lolita* to *Absalom* as just suggested may indeed seem off the wall both from the standpoint of old-style misogynistic readings of the novel as an attack on the pious simplism of the stereotypically chaste American girl—"Annabel Lee as nymphomaniac"—or feminist-responsive readings of its psychody-namics of child molestation.[45] Although Nabokov makes *Lolita* an intertextual echo chamber, within which Poe figures most saliently on the American side, it doesn't seem at first that the novel is much interested in either bildungsroman generally or the homegrown up-from script specifically. Yet the novel offers trenchant reflection on both in effect if not intent. *Lolita*'s claim to tell an American story, of sorts, hinges for one thing on its apotheosis of the ordinary—the banally vulgar, some would say—through Humbert Humbert's mystification of his love object. The subtlety with which *Lolita* updates for the pop culture era the old Jamesian motif of making American girls from Daisy Miller to Isabel Archer and Maggie Verver objects of perplexed fascination by European(ized) male sophisticates shouldn't keep one from noticing how this also reflects back upon the American bildungsroman through the gazer's determination that the beloved youth stay put in the nymphet state. Youth must forever remain immature, Humbert himself being forever so.

Here *Lolita* seems to be subtly positioning itself both within and against midcentury fiction's tendency to resist entering adulthood, as in the work of Salinger, McCullers, Capote, Roth, Kerouac, Updike, and many others. This too was the moment of the Fitzgerald revival; of Saul Bellow's invention of the self-pitying fifty-six-year-old perpetual adolescent Eugene Henderson who sounds off in this chapter's second epigraph; of Fiedler's overheated critique of premodern American literature as addicted to stories of girls and boys regardless of chronological age, with the American heroine typically pre- or desexualized. *Lolita*'s contributions here, in addition to acknowledging obliquely through the device of the émigré narrator the European role in abetting that fantasy of eternal American juvenescence, were to insist on the sexual energies that Lawrence and later Fiedler claimed that American writers chronically buried deep within their subtexts and to make maturity happen in the face of overwhelming narratorial desire that it not. What's more, *Lolita* makes it happen for Humbert in the most humiliating way. Even though he hates it, Lolita will grow up and he himself will be forced to see her as a hugely pregnant, cigarette-smoking, redneck housewife. That doesn't keep him from clinging to the shreds of his grand illusion, but it makes the work of sustaining it a lot harder.

One way of understanding Nabokov's disturbing masterpiece, then, is as a kind of wake-up call that the up-from emergence narrative as

Fitzgerald and Faulkner had framed it needed an upgrade, badly. But who would listen remained to be seen.

Dreiser, Wright, Bellow, and the Ethnic Turn in Up-From Narrative

By the time American publishers dared to take on *Lolita*, three years after its debut in France, *Gatsby* had bested *An American Tragedy* as a plausible GAN candidate for both critical and popular audiences. By the 1960s, veteran critic Irving Howe reckoned that Dreiser had "dropped out of the awareness of cultivated Americans," although he himself thought the novel "a masterpiece, nothing less."[46] Doubtless *Gatsby's* staying power owes something to its brevity and zippy pace, which has lent itself to adoption as a school text since the 1950s, when annual sales rocketed from a few thousand to more than 300,000.[47] But the textbook boom would never have started without a tailwind of critical consensus in favor of *Gatsby's* concisely wrought intricacy as against Dreiserian sprawl. "The most perfectly crafted work of fiction to have come out of America," the eminent British Americanist Tony Tanner called *Gatsby* at century's end.[48]

Yet Dreiser seemed the far more imposing figure for the generation of writers that followed him, especially for "ethnic modernism," as Werner Sollors terms the variegated fusions of narrative experimentalism and older-style realism among the burgeoning hyphenated-American literatures we now belatedly recognize as having changed the acknowledged face of U.S. fiction during the middle half of the twentieth century.[49] Two cases in point are Richard Wright, widely acclaimed at midcentury as the foremost African American novelist, and Saul Bellow, the nation's second non-WASP novelist (after John Steinbeck) to win the Nobel Prize (1976). Wright's *Native Son* (1941), the first Book-of-the-Month Club main selection by an African American writer, virtually rewrites *An American Tragedy's* plot.[50] Bellow's *The Adventures of Augie March* (1953) became his breakthrough book owing to its surge of Whitmanian, Twainian, and Dreiserian energy in exfoliating Augie's wanderings and musings as a prototypical hyphenated American in and around Chicago.

Like *An American Tragedy*, *Native Son* is a protagonist-centered third-person narrative that follows, and ambiguates at every turn, a crime-manhunt-trial-aftermath sequence loosely based on a specific highly publicized murder case but mindful of many similar ones. For both writers, these prototypes reflected the long-embedded hunger, frustration, and sense of outcasting they themselves had known in early childhood as migrants from rural hinterlands first to Chicago, then to New York. *Native Son* even follows Dreiser's tripartite short/long/long plot sequence. Its section titles—"Fear," "Flight," "Fate"—would have served perfectly well for *An American Tragedy.* Like Clyde, Wright's Bigger Thomas is convicted on circumstantial evidence for first-degree murder of a pretty young (white) woman amid public hysteria. (His deliberate second homicide, of his black girl friend, is ironically reduced to a side issue.) Like Clyde's, Bigger's case becomes a political football and the stuff of lurid newspaper headlines. His attorney, Boris Max, also refuses to enter the temporary insanity plea that might have been his best option in favor of a losing strategy reminiscent of Clyde's lawyer Belknap's "defense" of Clyde as a "mental and moral coward," painting Bigger as a monster created by capitalist culture. In both books, this strategy has the rhetorical advantage of putting society on trial. The parallels extend to secondary motifs like the embattled but controlling mother, the importunate preacher who strives to bring (and in *An American Tragedy* almost succeeds in bringing) the condemned hero to the Lord, and the histrionic reenactment by the prosecution of the violence done to the victim's body.

Clyde and Bigger are both shown from the start as callow and fragile youths, driven by impulse and dream fantasies prompted by media stereotypes. Anxious for peer approval, each also "look[s] upon himself as a thing apart" (*AT* 16), treats others instrumentally, and creates a wall of reserve to protect himself as best he can against the confusion and vulnerability that threaten to undo him. Both novels dramatize this inner chaos through interior monologue, especially during their frantic attempts to escape eventual entrapment and their attempts at self-understanding in prison facing trial and death.

Wright intensifies the concentration on Bigger's mind stream, cutting Dreiserian editorializing to a minimum and crediting Bigger with self-generating a firmer sense of identity in the aftermath of the two killings. ("He had committed murder twice and had created a new world for himself.") His insistence at the end, "'What I killed for must've been good'" because "'I didn't know I was really alive in this world until I felt things hard enough to kill for 'em,'" is Bigger's takeaway and not the novel's exoneration of his crime.[51] It's probably meant to horrify the reader as much as it horrifies Max, underscoring as it does the defensive psychic reaction to having been stigmatized as an antisocial monster—including, ironically, by Max in his "defense." But to make Bigger's story a narrative of awakening of sorts is to make *Native Son* a far more powerful self-creation narrative than *American Tragedy,* far more than the sociological case study that both novelists described their books as mainly being.

In his autobiography *Black Boy,* Wright paid tribute to Dreiser's *Sister Carrie* and *Jennie Gerhardt*—two of the books to which he was steered by his boyhood discovery of Mencken's *Prejudices*—as reviving "in me a vivid sense of my mother's suffering," and awakening for the first time "a sense of life itself," including the intolerable gap between his condition as a southern Negro and the writerly aspirations such books reinforced.[52] Wright would also have been conscious of Dreiser's masterpiece as a benchmark for his own, if not when composing it, at least from the time his agent praised the manuscript's portrayal of Bigger as "superior to the protagonist in Theodore Dreiser's *American Tragedy.*"[53] And certainly Wright wanted Bigger's story to be seen not merely as race fiction but as an "American" story. Bigger was a native son, he explained, both as an American and as "a Negro nationalist in a vague sense because he was not allowed to live as an American." Here Wright synthesized W. E. B. Du Bois's theory of African American consciousness as double consciousness—the unresolvable sense of being both black and American, "two warring ideals in one dark body"—and Dreiser's conception of the "real" American tragedy as the monstrous result of an "unfit" youth taking the "right" Algeresque step of accepting a leg up from a rich patron.[54] Wright was also tapping into an insurgent omni-ethnic consciousness, arising from the twist given by the Depression years to the vertiginous growth and diversification of the great American cities. "All of America," as critic Marcus Klein writes, "could now be seen in terms of the ghetto, as a broad land populated everywhere by discrete clusters of the despised aliens."[55]

Unlike Dreiser, Wright didn't stop at framing *Native Son* in Americanist terms. He saw resonances between Bigger-style disaffection and violent militancy worldwide both left and right: Japan in China, Hitler in Europe, Communism in Russia. The anger Lenin shared with Gorky as they strolled around London ("There is *their* Big Ben," "*their* Westminster Abbey") Wright saw as "'the Bigger Thomas reaction.'"[56] Whereas Dreiser, when lionized in Russia after *An American Tragedy,* repaid his hosts by praising American entrepreneurial individualism, Wright as a frustrated black intellectual in the Jim Crow era was already headed toward permanent exile. Yet the difference between them was also one between older- and newer-style cosmopolitanisms, and it narrowed with Dreiser's shift toward socialism in the 1930s. Wright had more than Dreiser's Americanness in mind when he saluted him as the nation's "greatest living humanist" at an American Communist Party–sponsored luncheon in Dreiser's honor. Dreiser had refused to endorse 1920s literary expatriatism, claiming—equivocally—to find "America as satisfactory to me, as stimulating, I am sure, as Russia ever was to Tolstoi or Dostoevski." But Wright saw Dreiser, not without justice, as an honorary alien, "derived from Spencer and Marx."[57]

Wright's critical and popular success on the basis of *Native Son* and *Black Boy* (1945) established him as a unique figure among African American writers on the transcontinental literary scene. On the one hand, his protagonists could be seen in transracial terms, as when Simone de Beauvoir praised *Black Boy* as an exemplary and transposable struggle of individual consciousness "against the resistances of the world."[58] On the other hand, both books tapped into a long-standing tradition of protagonist-centric ethnic representation, from the slave narratives of Equiano, Douglass, and others to more recent life narratives (both fiction and nonfiction) that invited mainstream readers to see the protagonist as a heroic representative of minority struggle for recognition. *Black Boy* gives a far more somber spin to that generally can-do tradition, and sharply at odds with the thrust of such immigration narratives as Mary Antin's upbeat Plotsk-to-Boston *Promised Land* (1912), cited in J. T. Adams's 1931 *Epic of America* as decisive proof that the now-embattled "American dream" of the "common man" rising "to full stature" has long "held of hope and promise for mankind."[59]

If *Black Boy's* front-and-center anguish—still greater in Wright's original *American Hunger,* whose bitter up-north section he was forced to cut in order to get mainstream publisher backing—called the American dream into question, *Native Son,* like *An American Tragedy,* threatened to discredit it completely—as in fact Antin herself had done.[60] But the point that especially deserves stressing here is the "fit" between the template of the narrative of up-from struggle and the sense of exemplary minority experience. That Wright found *An American Tragedy*'s scripting of its lily-white Protestant world a plausible model for *Native Son* is strong evidence of this. But still stronger evidence is the copious archive of stories, both novelistic and autobiographical, of young minority protagonists struggling to make headway against social inequality that gathered increasing momentum from the 1920s onward.

By the same token, the sheer familiarity of the up-from story posed challenges as well as opportunities for ethnic/minority authors. Especially if the protagonist were cast as a sympathetic figure, the hyperconcentrated intimacy of the form might induce a just-like-me, this-is-my-dream-too response to the disregard of the particularities of either the person or her embattled cohort, as when historian Adams thrilled to Antin's "I am the youngest of America's children, and into my hands is given all her priceless heritage."[61] Alternatively, attempts to put the struggle in ethnographic context threatened to cater to the vicarious relish for tales of exotic others. But to intensify its bitterness beyond a limited degree could scare off mainstream readers, as Wright's handlers forewarned.

Writers strove to guard against these hazards in various ways. *The Autobiography of Malcolm X* (1965) executes its bildungsroman plot as a two-stage conversion narrative that indulges but also sets limits on the voyeuristic sensationalism with which its protagonist's criminal past is portrayed and then neutralizes potential readerly aversion to his career as a black Muslim firebrand by stressing how pilgrimage to Mecca impressed him with Islam's actual multiracialism.[62] Américo Paredes's *George Washington Gómez*, a landmark for Chicano fiction written around 1940 though published only in 1990, focuses on the early years of a bright orphaned protagonist whose hardscrabble community rallies the moral and financial support to get him the education and professional credentials that enable him to become a community leader, only to upset what promises to be a joyful homecoming when the fatally assimilated young Gomez betrays the community's trust by siding with the forces of Anglo-Texan development. But Paredes's sympathetic portrayal of the community's position is likely to convince even readers predisposed to believe that a top-flight education must be the best gift a barrio boy could possibly receive to think again: to realize the potentially deformative effects of even the most benign-seeming forms of upward mobility. Carlos Bulosan's autobiographical bildungsroman *America Is in the Heart* (1946), a key work of the same period both for Asian American and for Filipino Anglophone literatures, reruns the Antinesque immigrant saga in a more plangent key. The protagonist Allos/Carlos must contend again and again with poverty, racism, and illness to gain a modest toehold in America, with the safety nets of family, clan, and benevolent patronage that support him along the way much more fragile and tattered than for Antin and Gomez. As its title implies, this crafty narrative makes room for both a radical reading as a testimony to continually broken promises and a melodramatic reading as a plea for identification with the protagonist's earnest striving.

Another hazard of protagonist-centered ethnic narratives focused on the struggle for recognition is their susceptibility to tokenism. Before a minority literary culture has achieved more than modest visibility on the mainstream literary scene, it is liable to be reduced in the public eye, in syllabi, and in literary history too, to one or two instances. So, for example, at the start of the Native American and Asian American "renaissances" of the late twentieth century, Scott Momaday's *House Made of Dawn* (1968) and Maxine Hong Kingston's *Woman Warrior* (1975) each seemed for a time the representative conduit of an entire group's literary voice.

Readerly hankering for narratives of representative minority figures' struggles for voice, advancement, and recognition surely doesn't just have to do with vicarious identification with ethnic others or desire for the advancement of the disprivileged. It also resonates with the "mainstream" liberal ideology of individual fulfillment that underwrites American dream scripts whether defined materially or in psychological-spiritual terms. By no means does that necessarily imply desire for an assimilationist plot, however, any more than narratives of struggle by ethnically representative protagonists necessarily equate to embracement of ethnic solidarity.[63] Wright's early reception is an instructive case. *Native Son*'s acclaim by reviewers as "the finest novel as yet written by an American Negro" was driven to a large extent by its perceived dramatization of "the essential Negro-in-America" that left "one with the feeling that never before, in fiction, has anything honest or important been written about the American Negro."[64] That Wright refashioned the ethnic life-narrative template with such stark and lurid vehemence reinforced the "never before" impression made by the

Book-of-the-Month Club's promotion of *Native Son* as the first work of African American literature picked as a main selection. On the other hand, the frisson of authenticity was inseparable from the image of solitary struggling genius—an image encouraged by Wright himself. Even though the first full flowering of African American literary modernism had already occurred, and though Wright's career could not have taken off as it did when it did without the assistance of Harlem Renaissance veterans like Langston Hughes in forging literary networks and providing timely mentorship, neither *Black Boy* nor the original *American Hunger* give more than the faintest signs of social or intellectual indebtedness to fellow African Americans.

For the next dozen years, *Native Son* held its place as the great African American novel, even if not the Great American Novel that some considered *An American Tragedy* to be; and the Black Arts movement of the 1960s sustained that reputation for a time among left-leaning intellectuals both black and white. But literary fashions were changing in ways that were starting to make Wright's work look obsolescent. This story can be told as an interethnic tale of disaffected younger mentees, especially James Baldwin and Ralph Ellison, who admired Wright's devotion to craft but turned it against him by critiquing his brand of social protest fiction as catering, so Baldwin charged, to "the notorious national taste for the sensational" and caricaturing African American culture. Bigger Thomas, Ellison declared, had been "brutalized by Wright," who "could never bring himself to conceive a character as complicated as himself."[65] There is something weirdly oedipal about the discrepancy between Baldwin's recollection of his starstruck first meeting with his "idol since high school" and his kill-the-king dismissal of *Native Son* a few years later. The same goes for Ellison's denial that Wright's novella "The Man Who Lived Underground" had any influence on his own writing,[66] despite the fact that its story of a traumatized black man subsisting in a literal urban underground anticipated *Invisible Man* more closely than the eminent precursor both authors claimed, Dostoyevsky's *Notes from the Underground*. Wright's friendship, assistance, and writing enabled Ellison's literary emergence to a much greater extent than the latter implied in his fastidious distinction between (ethnic) "relatives" like Wright and (literary) "ancestors" like Dostoyevsky, Twain, Faulkner, and even Hemingway (*CE* 185). Ironically, not the least of the affinities between those two "relatives," and Baldwin too, was reluctance to grant much merit to African American literary forebears.

Mainly, though, Ellison and Baldwin were reacting against being judged by what they considered the dated procrusteanism of Wright's protest aesthetic. Ellison especially was galled when the model was revived in the 1960s and *Native Son* held up against *Invisible Man* by radical critics both black and white as "the genuine article" (*CE* 165). Yet *Invisible Man* did eventually displace *Native Son* as the greater fictional classic. The quarrel Ellison and Baldwin picked with Wright was symptomatic of broader discontent with neonaturalist realism among younger-generation writers of the 1940s and 1950s generally, of the broader shift in critical taste that made "Dreiserian" synonymous with klunkiness and canonized Fitzgerald as the impresario of nuanced intricacy and distilled symbolic resonance. J. D. Salinger's gesture toward the end of *Catcher in the Rye* (1951) was symptomatic: to have his antihero Holden Caulfield despair of being able to repeat Nick Carroway's gesture of wiping the "obscene word" from the front steps of Gatsby's mansion pays homage to *Gatsby*'s rising prestige. A quarter century later, the writer-critic George Garrett could insist that he had "never known, or indeed known of, a contemporary American writer who did not admire *The Great Gatsby*."[67]

Ironically, he overlooked the nation's most recent Nobel literature laureate: Saul Bellow, who thought that Fitzgerald "couldn't distinguish between innocence and social climbing."[68] Bellow disliked the "extreme concern for expression," the fetishization of "neatness and correctness" that he saw behind the newer American writing and the praise then being lavished on Hemingway and Fitzgerald. This he wrote with special reference to *Gatsby*'s surrealistic cameo of the blighted urban landscape presided over by the billboard of T. J. Eckleberg's vacant spectacles—an obvious allusion to Anglo-American modernism's most iconic poem, T. S. Eliot's *The Waste Land* (1923). (Eliot returned the compliment by praising *Gatsby* as the first advance for national fiction since Henry James).[69] Bellow's put-down comes in a 1951 review essay, "Dreiser and the Triumph of Art," praising Dreiser not despite but because of the disorderly vagueness and stiltedness increasingly held against him. Yes, he "was a great novelist who wrote badly," but "there are few modern writers whose passion for the subject is so steady," especially his rendering of inchoate desire amidst fascinating urban squalor. Critical finickiness toward Dreiser, Bellow charges, may imply "resistance to the feelings he causes readers to suffer."[70]

Bellow was playing through a quarrel with himself here. After two tautly compact novels about different kinds of Jewish protagonists under duress, he was testing out a much more unbuttoned literary voice. *Dangling Man* (1944) was the fictional diary of an alienated Kafkaesque "Joseph," unemployed and immobilized, waiting to be drafted; *The Victim* (1947) was a grimmer prerun of the Jew-shadowed-and-doubled-by-needy-and-troubled-Gentile plot that Bernard Malamud would later take up in *The Assistant* (1957). Both those early books were distilled, polished, Euromodernist performances that ensured Bellow would become the first eminent American novelist to inhabit academia for the rest of his working life. They seemed to take Jewish American fiction to a new level of aesthetic sophistication. *The Adventures of Augie March,* by contrast, was a sprawling, risk-taking novel that extravagantly hybridized the ethnic bildungsroman template. To some extent, it recalled the up-from plots of *Promised Land,* Abraham Cahan's *The Rise of David Levinsky* (1917), and Yezierska's *Bread Givers,* all of which feature restless, inquisitive protagonists who press beyond conventional tribal limits. In addition Bellow transfuses *Augie* with large doses of Whitmanian expansiveness, Twainian picaresque, and Dreiserian *flânerie.* He yokes Augie to Walt right off the bat ("I am an American, Chicago born"); and Augie's droll-tricky-aimless wanderlust throughout the book makes him a Jewish Huck Finn. Later Bellow also compared him to the wide-eyed experience-and-novelty-hungry "young Theodore [Dreiser] of *Dawn,*" "just arrived in Chicago."[71]

If Bellow's first two books had made him a leading Jewish American novelist, *Augie,* as Leslie Fiedler had prophesied, made him "the first Jewish-American novelist to stand at the center of American literature."[72] The one-two feat of his friend Ralph Ellison and then himself winning National Book Awards in successive years is a symbolic marker of the coming of age for U.S. ethnic fiction more generally. Controversy would long continue—it still does—as to whether such books are more fruitfully read through an "ethnic" or "minority" lens or as "American" writing; and, relatedly, as to whether U.S. "multiculturalism" broadly is better conceived as leaning toward disjunctive particularisms or toward commonality within variegation.* But however one comes down on such issues, the mid-twentieth century marks the moment for national fiction when it became impossible for anybody who wanted to be thought of as really on the cutting edge of the literary scene to overlook that writers of non-northern-European Christian extraction were publishing some of the most important new novels.

Today it is the belatedness of that awakening that seems strange. After all, the literary aspiration—and at best also the result—had long been there. But it was easy enough in the late 1700s to write off Phillis Wheatley as aberrant, or coached. It was still quite possible in 1900 to ignore Charles Chesnutt, the first African American writer to harbor the GAN aspiration, even though in retrospect it is clear that the U.S. literary scene had become much more heterogeneous than a half-century before.[73] Even in the mid-twentieth century it was possible to write off the Harlem Renaissance as a flash in the pan. But not much longer.

Because *Augie March* was Bellow's breakthrough book, and because it accomplished the particular kind of liberation it did by rechanneling the voices of so many great precursors, it has been held up as a likelier Great American Novel candidate in preference to his later novels, even if in hindsight it also seemed, as one critic put it, more "a declaration of insight and intention" "than a record of achievement." Bellow agreed

---

* The archive of critical commentary on how to understand "multiculturalism," especially the questions of the extent to which it can be understood as a semi-united front versus a congeries of disparate trajectories and whether multiculturalism is or is not a good thing, is enormous and dissonant. It is tempting to throw up one's hands and conclude with novelist Ishmael Reed that "a precise definition seems to have been lost in the din of sound bites of performance intellectuals" ("Introduction," in *MultiAmerica: Essays on Cultural Wars and Cultural Peace,* ed. Ishmael Reed [New York: Viking, 1997], xxi). To hold up two contrasting efforts in definition and analytical registers, both of which I respect: Gregory Jay offers a helpful introduction from a pro-multiculturalism standpoint especially directed toward teachers (*American Literature and the Culture Wars* [Ithaca, NY: Cornell University Press, 1997]); Christopher Douglas provides a critical "genealogy" of multiculturalism since the mid-twentieth century from a more skeptical standpoint (*A Genealogy of Literary Multiculturalism* [Ithaca, NY: Cornell University Press, 2009]). Over the years, *MELUS, Modern Fiction Studies,* and many other journals have published insightful articles on literary multiculturalism and particular strands thereof. Two takeaway points, at all events, are the manifestly increasing presence during the past century or more, not only in the United States but also in other Europhone countries, of multiple minoritarian literary movements yielding artistic work of high importance; and the impossibility of mapping this expanding field without recognizing the presence of both distinctive and interlinking literary and cultural threads.

that the book "ran away with me," that "I had just increased my free-dom, and like any emancipated plebeian I abused it at once."[74] Indeed *Augie*'s first half is far the more fresh and exciting, as it follows the good-looking, genial, venial, erratic, irrepressible proletarian antihero on his irregular course of half-education, family dramas, and other entanglements, by turns obliging and evading the clutches of sundry folk who want to adopt or mold him, negotiating a picaresque assort-ment of jobs along the way: store clerk, burglar's assistant, rich wom-an's escort, dog schlepper, book thief, labor organizer, and much else. The novel starts to spin out of control at midpoint, in a long sequence when femme fatale Thea Fenchel reappears to whisk Augie off to vari-ous ill-fated adventures in Mexico, eventually ditching him. His mar-riage to Stella, whom he meets there, and his intermittently traumatic seasoning in the Merchant Marine provide extra topical ballast—for among its other agendas the novel attempts a kind of rompish ethnog-raphy of the Depression and war years—and they also pseudo-fulfill some Copperfieldian stereotypes, such as the brace of dark lady/light lady love affairs with proper marriage after amorous fling and social maturation of a sort. By the end, Augie's "illicit dealing" in postwar Europe has made him a much bigger fish than his querulous older brother Simon (*AAM* 529)—but without lessening his wide-eyed ebul-lience. To the end, he remains—so he says—a "sort of Columbus of those near at hand," fascinated by "this immediate *terra incognita* that spreads out in every gaze." If he should turn out "a flop at this line of endeavor," well, "Columbus too thought he was a flop, probably, when they sent him back in chains. Which didn't prove there was no America" (536).

An older, more sober Bellow recoiled against his own creation. Au-gie was "*such* a blue-eyed *ingenu* and [led] *such* a charmed life"; "he didn't want to acknowledge the worst"; he "wanted to play the Ameri-can naïf." Indeed, Bellow went still further and confessed to willful blindness. Writing his novel in postwar Paris like Augie himself, he knew perfectly well, "when I took a deep breath I was inhaling the cre-matorium gases still circulating in the air" yet nonetheless "I enjoyed a nostalgic Chicago holiday."[75] The novel's sole Holocaust allusion is a vague aside about "perhaps" having met "a person who used to be in Dachau" and doing "some business with him in dental supplies from Germany" (*AAM* 522). But though he came to accept Augie's insouci-ant coyness as his own evasion, Bellow continued, rightly, to see the novel as a stylistic breakthrough from "straight mandarin" to a "new sort of sentence" that would be "something like a fusion of colloquialism and elegance . . . street language combined with a high style."[76]

Bellow worked from multiple models and came up with an idiolect of his own. The Dreiserian strain isn't so visible as in *Native Son*'s reinvention of *An American Tragedy*. But Augie's rite of passage in the whorehouse, his frantic fumbling attempts to secure an abortion for his friend Mimi, his resistance to staying on task for very long, the characterological type of the unaggressive and moony but inwardly restless naïf whose good looks and edge of shyness make him erotically interesting to possessive upscale women—all these recall Dreiser's Clyde. A deeper, stylistic affinity is *Augie*'s verbose and tangled rhetoric, one that registered in Bellow's more cerebral and drolly offbeat narrative voice the effort of a hedonistic, overeager autodidact of sensitive but unrefined tastes mentally to come to terms with yet keep from being overwhelmed by the fascinating welter of circumambient people and things. Consider the seriocomic gaucherie of Clyde's first sight of Sondra Finchley ("as smart and vain and sweet a girl as Clyde had ever laid his eyes upon—so different to any he had ever known and so superior . . . the most adorable feminine thing he had seen in all his days," "arousing in him a curiously stinging sense of what it was to want and not to have," *AT* 251); then flash forward to soulful Augie pining after Esther Fenchel, "eaten with hankering and thinking futilely what brilliant thing to do" to land her, but realizing "that she knew she had great value, and that she was not subject to urgent-heartedness" (*AAM* 139). Here Bellow seems to be striving for an equivalent of the anti-eloquence he praised in Dreiser, including infusions of earnest cliché language and overstuffed broken-backed clauses. To be sure, there are other pre-texts for this voice, Yiddish as well as American. It isn't just Dreiser that's going on here. The point is simply that Dreiser played a significant part in helping nudge Bellow toward a kind of literary voice that would register the ethos Augie sums up in one of his characteristic seat-of-the-pants aperçus: "imperfection is always the condition as found; all great beauty too, my scratched eyeballs will always see scratched" (*AAM* 260).

Wright gave naturalist realism in *Native Son* a more caustic 1930s edge by intensifying the satirical irony and the psychological intensity of *An American Tragedy* in its relentless ethnography of socioenvironmental entrapment. *Augie March* reinvented 1930s naturalism also by recourse to a character who according to standard naturalist practice should be the object of the ethnographic gaze, but by both making him his own narrator and granting him the zestful inquisitiveness that erupts throughout Dreiser's unbuttoned memoir, even its recollections of hapless immiserated poverty. The result was a carnivalesque hybrid that improbably welded protagonist-narrator as autonomous neo-Whitmanian self with protagonist–social actor as creature of circumstance more sordid and compromising than he ever allows. Perhaps too improbably. That *Invisible Man,* an analogous hybrid, seems to have made (as of the 2010s, anyhow) a stronger imprint on literary and cultural history surely has something to do with its more persuasive fusions of rhetorical hijinks with high seriousness, of documentary diffuseness and the controlled symbolic intricacy of high modernism. But both *Augie* and *Invisible Man,* to which we now turn, witness to the midcentury investment in a subjectified reinvention of the social novel "without entirely exploding the form of the social novel itself."[77]

6

Up-From Narrative in Hyphenated America

Ellison, Roth, and Beyond

> I think that what we really have to do is to create a country in
> which there are no minorities—for the first time in the history
> of the world.
>
> —JAMES BALDWIN, "In Search of a Majority" (1961)

> America's dilemma has been our resistance to ourselves—our
> denial of our immensely varied selves. But we have nothing to
> fear but our own fear of our own diversity.
>
> —RONALD TAKAKI, *A Different Mirror:*
> *A History of Multicultural America* (1995)

B ALDWIN'S WORDS REFLECT the spirit of 1950s integrationism reinforced by the expatriate experience of being typed by Europeans
as "American" despite his personal sense of marginalized disaffiliation.
During the 1960s, his writing took a more schismatic turn toward the
obverse position historian Ronald Takaki summed up shortly before
the millennium. The contrast between those two affirmations registers
how national narrative was propelled in the interim by a series of ethnic literary and critical insurgencies—African American, Asian American, Latino/a, and Native American especially—toward what now looks
to some an unprecedentedly fissured literary scene of multiple dispersed
camps. The sense of the unprecedented is understandable but also simplistic insofar as it relates to the long-standing fascination with the lives
of socially representative aspiring young protagonists. As we saw in
Chapter 5, these had already long since been a crucial form for immigrant and ethnic writing. But what then of the up-from plotline? What
of immigrant and ethnic narrative's ongoing engagement with the
"American dream" story?

One might expect such work to be less concerned with generalizing about the national than Dreiser, Fitzgerald, and Bellow were, and for it to treat the stereotypical dream (even) more caustically as delusive glitter. To some extent the literary record bears this out. But a more complicated picture emerges from the most notable Great American Novel projects by hyphenated American writers during these years that revisit and reframe the up-from script, a picture reinforced by a broader scan of the novelistic scene during these same years. The differences between Baldwin's and Takaki's credos begin to seem as much a matter of degree as of kind.

Ellison's Invisible Man *as Literary Event*

Richard Wright's *Native Son* was taken more as a "blueprint for Negro writing," to borrow the title of his programmatic essay of 1937, than as a bid for the GAN, however much it stressed the national significance of the Bigger Thomas case. *Invisible Man*, by contrast, seems to have been a direct assault on the Great American Novel.[1] Indeed no previous American novelist, black or white, so insisted on being understood as building upon the accrued achievement of his or her great American literary precursors. None would have gone so far as to maintain that "the writer, *any* American writer, becomes basically responsible for the health of American literature the moment he starts writing seriously."[2]

Such self-consciousness would not have been possible without broader rising confidence about the stature of national literature within the literary world at large as the fields of American Literature and American Studies congealed, as U.S. literature gained international prestige, and as the country emerged from a second world war that crippled European and Japanese infrastructures and doomed their empires to extinction as the strongest economic and military power on the planet but also as a major cultural force. For the rest of the century, American English, American film, American music, and American (fast) food as well as American books became increasingly pervasive worldwide. This sense of incremental global impact was quickened by Cold War rivalry between Soviet communism and Western democracy, of which the United States was seen as the leading bastion.

For Ellison himself, the sense of high calling qua American writer was strengthened by the instant fame of *Invisible Man* as a breakthrough for Negro fiction at the most opportune of moments, just as the civil rights era was dawning with Supreme Court–mandated school desegregation in 1954. He worried at the outset that *Brown v. Board of Education* might bracket him as the memorializer of a bygone era.[3] Precisely the opposite happened. *Invisible Man* opened up a never-ending series of opportunities for high-profile interviews and conferences, critical essays and position papers, fellowships, and visiting professorships. Ellison played the genius-of-the-integration-era role to the hilt, starting with his National Book Award acceptance speech. There he identified his novel's "significance" with its "experimental attitude and its attempt to return to the mood of personal responsibility for democracy which typified the best of our nineteenth-century fiction" and as such a response to the "growing crisis" in American fiction, which, except for Faulkner, had been prevented from representing the "diversity" and "extreme fluidity" of American life by the dual constraints of Hemingwayesque "hard-boiled" fiction and "the tight, well-made Jamesian novel" (*CE* 151–152). Thus Ellison grandly dismissed almost a century of national fiction from Howells through Wright. It was an astounding compound of deference and disdain. Of poetic influence, critic Harold Bloom has claimed that the strong British writers "swerve from their precursors," whereas the Americans seek to "complete" theirs.[4] Ellison did both.

Later he qualified this sketch of American fiction's needful redemption. Sometimes he would put James on the side of the angels. He would praise *Native Son* as "one of the major events in the history of American literature" and Hemingway for a jazz artist–like austerity of devotion to craft despite fixation on "elaborating his personal myth." He would make amends for writing off Fitzgerald by working up a lesson plan for *Gatsby* as an incipiently multiracial text whose plot turns on the identification of the "death car" by an elegantly dressed black man.[5] Indeed, Ellison became one of the keenest literary critics of any American novelist.

By "experimental attitude" he meant the postrealist form of subjectified narrative voice that he saw as corresponding to the fluidity and strangeness of national experience, "a realism dilated to deal with the almost surreal state of our everyday American life."[6] In *Invisible Man*, this "dilated realism," as Ellison scholar Adam Bradley calls it, proves especially potent in rendering at ground level "the theme of a young Negro's quest for identity" during the 1920s and 1930s (*IM* xxiv). As

Ellison elsewhere put it, "What is called surrealism in one place might be seen as mundane reality in another." It was "true to reality" that the misadventures of a black naïf muddling through the ordeal of the African American Great Migration from southern rural slow time to northern urban fast time during the interwar years should get dramatized in a hallucinatory fashion, and that his first near-death experience up North, the bizarre operation he undergoes in the factory hospital, should be read not as a medical procedure but symbolically as "a metaphor for a new birth."[7]

The novel itself as a freestanding achievement together with the dozens of autocritiques and reassessments that Ellison made of it during the rest of his working life gave *Invisible Man,* even more than Bellow's *Augie,*[8] the look of a stylistically hip modernist reframing of the traditional up-from narrative with a distinctively ethnic valence also designed to reorient, replenish, redirect national fiction. As such it offered itself as both model and target.

The plot of *Invisible Man* unfolds as a story of up-from striving repeatedly balked. In a series of picaresque misadventures, the anonymous protagonist-narrator—his namelessness mirrors both his excessive pliability and his invisibility or nonrecognition by others except as stereotype—gets tested again and again by such obstacles and temptations as an intelligent, ambitious, but too obliging black youth might encounter during the late Jim Crow era. At each stage he struggles mightily for recognition but meets with humiliating, sometimes life-threatening setbacks that force him to flee or abruptly change course. Slowly he becomes more streetwise, but he never manages to get ahead of the curve; and at the end he is driven to the underground lair where we saw him at the start.

In the plot proper, we first see Invisible—to call him that for short—as the valedictorian of a segregated high school in the deep South. The town's white oligarchy rewards his deference with a nice briefcase and a college scholarship, but only after subjecting him and his classmates to a humiliating "Battle Royal" in which the youths are forced to fight each other and pick up coins from an electrified mat, and subjected to sexy taunts by a white stripper. At college, Invisible allows the visiting white trustee-benefactor, Mr. Norton, to whom he's assigned as chauffeur, to inveigle him into meeting the loquacious black farmer Jim Trueblood, who transfixes the Brahmin with the tale of unwittingly impregnating his own daughter. When Invisible unwisely takes Norton for refreshment to a local hangout, a gang of inmates from the local black insane asylum promptly arrive, riot, and trash the place. The college's Machiavellian president, Dr. Bledsoe, expels Invisible forthwith and duplicitously sends him north for his next ordeal with three sealed "recommendations" that actually warn, "Keep this nigger boy running." Eventually the disaffected gay son of another rich blue-blood trustee, scandalized by this trickery, secures him a blue-collar job in his father's paint factory, where a crusty (black) foreman who resents the overschooled, underskilled kid sees to it that he gets dispatched in a near-fatal boiler explosion. Cushioned by the insurance payoff and a kindly down-home boarding house matron, Invisible wanders around Harlem, where his spontaneous intervention on behalf of an old couple being evicted from their apartment catches the notice of a local (white) organizer for "the Brotherhood" (transparently the communists, though Ellison denied it), which recruits him as an orator. For a while his eloquence at rallies wins him prestige in the community and entry into the inner circle; but he runs afoul of the black nationalist agitator Ras the Exhorter and then with the Brotherhood itself, when its abrupt decision to deprioritize black outreach threatens to brand him a race traitor among his constituency. Resorting to hipster disguise to evade Ras's men, he finds himself mistaken for the slippery Rinehart—preacher, gambler, con man—a symbol of ghetto-style protean opportunism, "the personification of chaos," as Ellison later called him.[9] Invisible then tries a deception of his own, suggested by his grandfather's enigmatic deathbed exhortation to "overcome 'em with yeses, undermine 'em with grins, agree 'em to death and destruction" (*IM* 16). He pretends to the Brotherhood that its Harlem recruitment operation is thriving rather than going sour. This proves another doomed attempt to follow too literal-mindedly scripts ranging from the conventional to the radical that he borrows from somebody else. It implodes when Ras incites riot, in the midst of which Invisible is attacked by gangs both black and white, chased down a manhole, and symbolically castrated. The framing narrative of the prologue/epilogue shows him hiding out, processing his traumas, and planning his next move.

This itinerary of explosive encounters in the style of "dilated realism" establishes Invisible as individuated yet exemplary. By ushering him through a series of paradigmatic coming-of-age ordeals like the "Battle

Royal"—a segregationist "ritual in the preservation of caste lines"—
Ellison sought to fashion a plotline both "Negro" and "American"—
inseparable domains for him.[10] This symbolically charged cultural
hybridity he claimed, with reason, as itself a distinctively "modern"
literary practice. Joyce's fiction and Eliot's *The Waste Land,* he declared,
had first awakened him to "the literary value of my folk inheritance"
(*CE* 112).[11]

Invisible Man's first-person subjectification, though, was its key
resource for differentiating itself from "the sociological approach" that
seemed a chronic limitation of earlier African American fiction (*CE* 75).
It enabled the disciplined improvisation Ellison associated both with
jazz performance and with the mutually discrepant Euromodernist
voices of Eliot and Hemingway.[12] As with Bellow's *Augie,* it also allowed
for fuller voicing of thought, emotions, and language from formal to
colloquial and back again than the forms of narrative containment
practiced by Wright and Fitzgerald.

"Who knows but that, on the lower frequencies, I speak for you?"
the novel's 600-page monologue teasingly ends, as Invisible prepares to
leave his underworld and rejoin society (*IM* 572). The insinuation that
one solitary black man's jazz might somehow be the voice of America
seems even more consequential in retrospect than its ambitious author
could have foreseen. Ellison had no way of knowing how fashionable
this narrative angle was in the process of becoming: the alienated,
wounded first-person's quasi-confessional, quasi-evasive headlong monologue, often in a distinctive subcultural idiom (ethnic or otherwise), its
tonalities a rich admixture ranging from comedic-playful to meditative-
philosophical to manic-impassioned. "Within the postwar discourse of
'mass society,' 'conformity,' and 'totalitarianism,'" critic Thomas Schaub
dryly remarks, "the first person voice of the alienated hero" became au
courant, invested with a piquantly "subversive aura."[13] All novels ranked
highest in the *New York Herald Tribune Book Week's* 26 September 1965
poll, which named *Invisible Man* the best American novel since World
War II, were of this kind. Nabokov's *Lolita* (1955) was the runner-up
and Salinger's *Catcher in the Rye* (1954) placed third, with Robert Penn
Warren's *All the King's Men* (1947) and Bellow's *Augie* (the National
Book Award winner after *Invisible Man*) just a little further down. Add
to this Kerouac's *On the Road* (1957), Bellow's *Henderson the Rain King*

(1959), Kurt Vonnegut's *Cat's Cradle* (1963), Norman Mailer's *Why Are We in Vietnam?* (1967), and Philip Roth's *Portnoy's Complaint* (1969), together with the "confessional" turn in mid-twentieth-century U.S. poetry (Robert Lowell, Sylvia Plath, Anne Sexton, James Wright), and the feature story of midcentury U.S. literary history starts to look like a story of the liberation of the histrionic-confessional theater of the self-consciously isolated and marginalized first-person voice.

None of these writers were on Ellison's radar screen during the run-up to *Invisible Man,* although after Bellow's admiring review the two became lifelong friends. Ellison's working models for ironized-evasive, inflected, errant first-person narrative were more classic than contemporary: Dostoyevsky's underground man, Melville's Ishmael, Twain's Huck Finn. But he was acutely aware of living at a moment when European existentialism and such literary conduits as Camus's *The Stranger* (1942), another offbeat confessional narrative, were conspiring with the American critical turn exemplified by Lionel Trilling's *The Liberal Imagination* (1950) to devalue 1930s-style realist protest fiction in favor of the interiority of individual personhood as a free-world answer to socialism and as pushback against the threat of conformist standardization that critics on the left saw mass culture as posing. *Invisible Man* delivered handsomely on both counts. As a novel intent on redeeming representation of African American life from mainstream stereotypes as well as from the internalized constraints of his peers through an up-from narrative of aspiration derailed by susceptibility to groupthink, it became the first broadly compelling candidate for Great American Novel from a nonwhite standpoint—all the more so because of the self-consciousness with which its author, in a lifetime of autocommentaries, positioned himself in relation to his eminent precursors.[14] "First broadly compelling," but hardly first. Though Ellison himself conceded no indebtedness, the scenario of a protagonist's attempted escape from stultifying confinement had been crucial to African American literary history from the start, from the earliest slave narratives to James Weldon Johnson's *Autobiography of an Ex-Colored Man* (1912), Zora Neale Hurston's *Their Eyes Were Watching God* (1937), and Richard Wright's "Big Boy Leaves Home" (1938) and *Black Boy.* But not until *Invisible Man* did such a tale garner so swift and lasting acclaim among the umpires of the literary world as a novelistic accomplishment of the highest order.

In time, success became a burden as Ellison sought vainly for the next four decades to complete his even more ambitious second opus, posthumously published as *Three Days before the Shooting* (2011), which Bradley may be right in claiming as "this century's first candidate for the Great American Novel" because "it reflects the complexities of American life in a way that a finished novel could not."[15] Ellison's life-long labor on that second project reinforces the suspicion that the GAN must either be a premature crystallization or a never-ending work in progress. But rather than moralize further, let's return to the second of his acceptance-speech claims for *Invisible Man*'s significance, its attempted revival of the social vision of the classic American novel that except for Faulkner he believed had languished since Twain.

Up to a point, Ellison's position reflects the new midcentury critical orthodoxy: the ascendancy of realism in late nineteenth-century U.S. literature marked not a maturation but a swerve, for national fiction's distinctiveness relative to the British lay in romance rather than novel. To the extent that he favored a subjectified "realism" transfused by ritual and symbol over "objective" narration, Ellison's fiction and critical theory can be fitted to that template. But his view of what made important fiction important was neither antirealist nor antipolitical. The crucial value he set on classic American literature was the seriousness with which it recognized—albeit dimly, through the veil of whiteness—the gap between democratic promise and actuality, and in particular the status of "the Negro" as a symbol of "human and social possibility" whose actual "institutionalized dehumanization" exposed the flaw in "the democratic master plan." Ellison's position, which foreshadowed Toni Morrison's invention of literary-critical "whiteness" studies,[16] defined African American experience as the historic pivot of American life, which Ellison tersely summed up as "a drama acted out upon the body of a Negro giant" (*CE* 85); yet at the same time it allowed for a generous glass-half-full approach to the Euro-American novelists he admired.

Surpassing a Classic Benchmark: Invisible Man *versus* Huckleberry Finn

Especially instructive as a window onto Ellison's positioning of *Invisible Man* within the history of U.S. fiction was his preoccupation with Mark Twain's *Huckleberry Finn*, whose own claims to Great American Novel status Ellison in fact helped to define. Ellison played an intriguingly ambiguous role in what Jonathan Arac has called *Huckleberry Finn*'s "hypercanonization" as a kind of abolitionist conversion narrative. This view of *Huck*'s importance as one of American fiction's crowning achievements became standard in the 1950s thanks to a group of influential American critics who more or less followed Trilling's lead in reconceiving a book originally read as picaresque satire as a work of high moral and political seriousness starring a hero who revolts against the regime of plantation slavery that had conditioned him (a regime these critics implicitly likened to the communist menace), when he resolves in the memorable thirty-first chapter to "go to hell" rather than betray Jim by alerting his owner to his whereabouts. Though not the first dissenter from this reading, Arac argues with unequaled thoroughness against the problematic "mythicization of history" wrought by *Huckleberry Finn*'s displacement of *Uncle Tom's Cabin* as *the* classic national antislavery novel, "despite its having been written at a time when slavery did not exist and was defended by no one."[17]

Although that understates the prior degree of readerly admiration for *Huckleberry Finn* as well as some of the novel's complexities, as we'll see in Chapter 8, Arac is right that its apotheosis as Huck's conversion narrative dates only from this point. The critical retrofitting may help explain why the first GAN contenders to bear distinct marks of *Huckleberry Finn*'s influence date from then on: *Invisible Man*, Bellow's *Augie*, Kerouac's *On the Road*—all first-person tales of attempted youthful breakouts that refuse to imagine their protagonists as headed for extinction like London's Martin Eden, Fitzgerald's Gatsby, Dreiser's Clyde, Wright's Bigger, and Faulkner's Sutpen. In any case, postwar critical and novelistic establishments certainly did, as noted before, show a marked tendency to privilege the "imaginative space of psychological interiority" as against the imbrication of the personal within the social that reinforced, intentionally or not, the importance then attached within national culture at large to freestanding individuality as the perceived mark of American or "free world" distinctiveness.[18]

Ellison's interest in *Huckleberry Finn* dated back long before the Cold War, however. No American novel so fascinated him from boyhood on. He recalled himself and his childhood buddies identifying with Huck's irreverence toward the "blindness of 'civilization'" ("We were 'boys,' members of a wild, free, outlaw tribe which transcended the category of race") (*CE* 52). He even nicknamed his own brother Huck Finn (112). Hopping freights to college at Tuskegee was "the next best thing to floating down the Mississippi on a raft" (769). The African American migration westward as well as north, into the "territory" where Ellison's family settled, was like what "Huckleberry Finn decided to do."[19] His early fiction includes a series of Twainish pieces about two boys, Riley and Buster, who idle about and spin tall tales in innocuous defiance of Riley's Aunt Polly–like mother. Small wonder, then, that Ellison should have drawn upon *Huckleberry Finn* in his retrospective 1981 introduction to a new edition of *Invisible Man* to describe the kind of cultural work he saw his and other serious American novels as having aspired to deliver: "a raft of hope, perception and entertainment that might help keep us afloat as we tried to negotiate the snags and whirlpools that mark our nation's course toward and away from the democratic ideal" (*IM* xxxi). Here and elsewhere Ellison predictably singled out Twain's "compelling image of black and white fraternity." In particular, his early "Twentieth-Century Fiction and the Black Mask of Humanity" (drafted 1946) pictures Jim "not simply [as] a slave" but as "a rounded human being" and "symbol of humanity," describes Huck's attempt to free him "a bid to free himself of the conventionalized evil taken for civilization" and Huck's struggle with his conscience as grandly emblematic of the adolescent nation torn "between accepting and rejecting the responsibilities of adulthood" (*CE* 88–89).

Ellison also cautions, though, that "the artist is no freer than the society in which he lives," meaning that on both sides of the color line artists must "start with the stereotype . . . then seek out the human truth which it hides" (*CE* 98–99). Including Twain. Jim is a white writer's inadequate portrait of a slave contorted to fit "the outlines of the minstrel tradition." Only "from behind this stereotype" do "we see his dignity and human capacity—and Twain's complexity—emerge" (104), and even then not completely. This points to Ellison's most distinctive claim about *Huckleberry Finn:* his dissent from the usual denigration of its last third, which turns on Tom Sawyer's rigamarole plot to liberate Jim (who Tom knows has already been freed), in line with Hemingway's dictum that "'All modern American literature comes from . . . *Huckleberry Finn*'" but after Jim is stolen from Huck the rest of the book is "just cheating."[20] Ellison too prized *Huck* as the first canonical American novel in a colloquial voice. What angered him was the dismissal of

the very "part of the action which represents the formal externalization of Huck-Twain's moral position"—Huck's realization that he must
"'steal' [Jim] free" (*CE* 719).

Not everyone would buy this assessment, not by a long shot. Isn't it
downright sadistic to let Tom hijack the novel and torment Jim day after day with his brainless shenanigans? Maybe so, but Ellison makes
some telling rebuttals. First, Twain knew that slavery didn't end when
it ended. Southern "conscience" remained intact, and the North kow-
towed. The fake re-liberation bit was Twain's mordant diagnosis of Reconstruction's fate. Here Ellison anticipates the best modern critics of
Twain's humor, who have also written the most astutely about the
novel's "unforgivable" ending. "Jim's situation at the end of *Huckleberry
Finn*," Neil Schmitz sums up, reflects the Negro's in Reconstruction,
"free at last and thoroughly impotent, the object of devious schemes
and a hapless victim of constant brutality." Since Huck himself gets reduced to the status of "nigger," so "the full paradox of Reconstruction"
gets exposed twice over."[21] "This is the 'joke' of the book," agrees James
Cox—"the moment when, in outrageous burlesque, it attacks the sentiment" which it triggered in its previous orchestration of Huck's bonding to Jim, evoking for latter-day readers "so much indulgence and
moral approval that the censor is put to sleep."[22]

These pronouncements actually sound too cynical for Ellison, who
liked to think of Twain as a "great moralist" (*CE* 761) and of Huck as a
candidate for moral redemption. But he was even more disposed than
most Twain scholars to conceive of the United States, categorically, as
"a land of masking jokers" (CE 109) and to put all of American expression under the sign of joke. He looked to black and white humor, minstrel show and trickster tales, as a would-be democratic society's recourse
for carnivalesque disruption of social hierarchies and racial taboos. Ellison's obiter dicta do this more pointedly than his formal essays. In
one interview about *Invisible Man*, he bursts out, "Look, didn't you find
the book at all *funny?*"[23] Rereading *Moby-Dick*, he writes friend and fellow writer Albert Murray, he's tickled to find it so "pervaded by the
spirit of play. . . . The thing's full of riffs, man; no wonder the book
wasn't understood in its own time, not enough moses [black people]
were able to read it!"[24] One of Ellison's shrewdest appraisals of the state
of American fiction criticism ("Society, Morality, and the Novel," 1957)
pounces upon Henry James's catalog in his 1879 book on Hawthorne of

the alleged dearth of materials that confronts the American novelist (no court, no country squires, no ivied ruins, no great museums, etc.) and mocks Trilling's influential reading of the passage (as proof that social fiction is impossible in America) for overlooking James's parting shot: "The American knows that a good deal remains; what it is that remains— that is his secret, his joke, as one may say. It would be cruel, in this terrible denudation, to deny him the consolation of his natural gift, that 'American humor' of which [in] late years we have heard so much."[25] Trilling, retorts Ellison, would have done better to turn "his critical talent to an examination of the American joke," for "perhaps *this* has been the objective of the American novel all along, even the Jamesian novel, and perhaps this is its road to health even today" (*CE* 718).

Just what James had in mind will remain forever mysterious. Was it an equivocal nod to the slew of mostly forgotten but then transatlantically popular humorists (Artemus Ward, Petroleum V. Nasby, Mark Twain, and others) whom James suspected, with reason, that Anglo-American readers might consider more authentic renditions of American literary difference than Hawthorne—or himself?—given how seriously such Victorian luminaries as Virginia Woolf's father Leslie Stephen had been taking these humorists as the *vox Americana*?[26] Might Ellison have been thinking of how James's own *The Bostonians* (1886) turns the stereotypical North-meets-South marriage plot (see Chapter 7) into a post-Reconstruction satire in which doggedly reactionary southerner confronts New England reform gone decadent? The best scholarly guess is likely how Ellison saw the matter: that for James "the humor arises out of the gap between the cultural ideal and the everyday fact, with the ideal shown to be somewhat hollow and hypocritical, and the fact crude and disgusting."[27] Growing up black between the wars, he reminisced, "we learned quite early that laughter made the difficulties of our condition a bit more bearable." Though "we hadn't read Henry James, . . . we realized . . . that American society contained a built-in joke, . . . centered in our condition," and "welcomed any play on words or nuance of gesture which gave expression to our secret sense of the way things really were" as against how they were supposed to be (*CE* 607). That's a good gloss on his summation of Twain's accomplishment: he "demonstrated that the novel *could* serve as a comic antidote to the ailments of politics" (*CE* 483).

So even as Ellison furthered *Huckleberry Finn*'s canonization as a serious work of social reflection whose "moral core" was "race" (*CE* 779), he admired Huck's moral performance less than Twain's comic one. Ellison's "comic antidote" reading fused the older satiric-picaresque take on the novel with newer-style concentration on *Huckleberry Finn* as a moral reflection on race. The images converged in the theory of Twain's satire as triggered by disgust at Reconstruction's failure. That accomplishment bookended Ellison's hoped-for intervention as comic anatomist at what he could not yet be sure was the end of the Jim Crow era.

Invisible Man makes for a far different reading experience from *Huckleberry Finn*, however. For one thing, the narrative voice is much more polyvocal. At one extreme, Invisible's reflective musings lean toward the hyperliterate, cerebral polish of Ellison's essays. At times the narrator's idiolect becomes sculpted to the point of Victorian orotundity, as in: "Somewhere beneath the load of the emotion-freezing ice which my life had conditioned my brain to produce, a spot of black anger glowed and threw off a hot red light of such intensity that had Lord Kelvin known of its existence, he would have had to revise his measurements" (*IM* 254). Yet that stiltedness gets repeatedly broken up by lyrical riffs and collages of cultural bits, high and low, often run together. Sometimes Invisible breaks through the veneer of his own polite-speak, playfully recycling Jahweh's words to Moses in the book of Exodus in giddy delight at his first taste of yummy soul food on a Harlem winter day: "'I yam what I am!'" (260). More often, folkspeech and rhythms well up from the cornucopia of circumambient voices, or from within Invisible's mind stream, especially at moments of stress or excitement. So Larry Neal, after belittling Ellison in the 1960s as a Black Arts movement critical standard-bearer,[28] despite lingering distaste for his politics, has only to quote one of Invisible's stretches of excited monologue (*"Ha! Susie Gresham, Mother Gresham, guardian of the hot young women on the puritan benches who couldn't see your Jordan's water for their private steam . . ."*) [*IM* 112] in order to insist, "Dig. Here is your black aesthetic at its best."[29] Harlem street vendor, sharecropper, peckerwood darky piggy bank, Sambo doll, Afrocentric street harangue, stuffed-shirt Booker T. Washington speeches, the literary undergrounds of Dostoyevsky and Wright, T. S. Eliot's "East Coker," updates of Faulknerian typecasting (surly Lucius Brockway as a more trenchant version of

Lucas Beauchamp of "The Fire and the Hearth" and *Intruder in the Dust*), the magnate Mr. Emerson and the historic Emerson's sometime disciple Charles Eliot Norton as plutocratic trustees of Invisible's alma mater—all these get tumbled together.

Sometimes the allusiveness becomes pedantically recherché. As Ellisonians have shown, the site of the early tavern brawl is The Golden Day, the title of the 1925 book by Lewis Mumford that first mapped the contours of F. O. Matthiessen's "American Renaissance" around the same five great figures but passed over the abolitionist insurgency that this chapter bumptiously resupplies.[30] Twain's novel gets referenced via young Emerson's proposition to Invisible to enter into a "Jim and Huck" relationship, starting with a party at the "Club Calamus" and continuing with Invisible as his valet (*IM* 182–189). All this, perhaps even the gay subtext, goes over the narrator's head; but the academically literate reader will connect the montage of *Huckleberry Finn* and Whitman's poems of "manly comradeship" to critic Leslie Fiedler's "Come Back to the Raft Ag'in, Huck Honey," a provocative interpretation of cross-racial male friendship in classic wilderness romance as "innocent homosexuality" that Ellison disliked for trivializing Twain's honorable if failed attempt to envision cross-racial egalitarianism.[31]

The links between *Invisible Man* and *Huckleberry Finn* run much deeper than the arcane skirmish with Fiedler. Invisible too is a mentally hyperactive youth struggling against the deforming—and often physically threatening—effects of toxic "sivilisation." To be sure, Huck is a bad-boy rebel to Invisible's dutifulness, as well as being cagey where Invisible is clueless. And of course Invisible's Algeresque success drive is antithetical to Huck's partiality for drift and laze. But both get subjected to analogous hazing experiences involving successive near-deaths and rebirths, at each stage of which both are more cat's-paws than free agents. Both must wing it through emergencies with improvised strategies that tend to misfire. The offside of Huck's resilience is Invisible's prime weakness too: readiness to accommodate. Huck adapts himself not just to raft life with Jim, where he's happiest, but also—with amazing good cheer—to a stint of incarceration by Pap, to the Grangerfords' regime, to the exploitative King and Duke, and above all to Tom. The common denominator here is entrapment within your authorities even after they start to feel irksome or ludicrous.

At book's end Huck is back exactly where he started, about to be sivilized by another Sawyer family aunt. ("I been there before" is the last sentence.) *Invisible Man* performs an analogous circling from underground to underground, but that's clearly not to be the end of his story. If *Huckleberry Finn* is "anything but a bildungsroman,"[32] Ellison's is anything but a boy's book. *Invisible Man*'s epilogue tries to think its way toward a next stage of social maturity. One of the novel's "last substantive additions,"[33] it has its problems, as novelistic endings often do. Invisible's superconscientiousness becomes tortuous and murky as he puzzles over how to convert ancestral memory into something productive by fashioning the grandfatherly deathbed pronouncement that's haunted him from the start—"I have been a traitor all my born days, a spy in the enemy's country" (*IM* 15)—into a game plan for negotiating life above ground more workable than his disastrous last experiment was. How can the old man's "life is war" summation of his seemingly acquiescent life help Invisible deal with his own violently mixed impulses, "to throw my anger into the world's face," yet somehow rejoin it (570)? He hopes, though the prospect scares him too, "that even an invisible man has a socially responsible role to play" (572), presumably by thrusting his voice before a public that's refused to see him. Such is his takeaway from his whole anguished history of striving, misdirected aspiration, and disillusionment. As Robert O'Meally sums up: from his starting point "as a kind of Afro-American Jonathan, a 'green' yokel pushed into the clownhouse of American society," he comes to accept "his southern black folk past and sees that ordinary blacks like his grandfather, Trueblood, Mary, Tarp, Dupre" are "of ultimate value, no matter what the Bledsoes and the Jacks say."[34]

Invisible's inconclusive but persistent attempt to rechannel family memory has even bigger social stakes than this. Subsumed in the epilogue, as Bradley and Foley both point out, are excerpts from the journal of a "potential double," deleted from the final text, that entertains the vision of a pan-Africanist vision of black people as "the rightful heirs of its humanist tradition" because their history of brutalization points them toward "a way of life more universal, more human and more free than any to be found in the world today." The published epilogue doesn't so much suppress this smoldering resentment as subtilize it by infusing vehemence with irony and broadening it into a "call to account not simply for the fate of black people in America but the fate of the nation as a whole."[35]

Ellison doesn't strain plausibility by letting Invisible congeal a specific plan. That would be too sharp a break from the satirical casting of him, not to mention a denial of the bald fact that "the ideal of achieving a true political equality eludes us in reality," as Ellison continued to insist for the rest of his life (*IM* xxx). Still, Invisible moves from juvenile innocence toward maturity of aspiration as Twain's eternal boy does not—and as Fitzgerald's Jay Gatsby, Dreiser's Clyde Griffiths, and Faulkner's Thomas Sutpen do not, caught as they all are in dream worlds of regressive fantasy. More specifically *Invisible Man* follows a "negative Bildungsroman" trajectory,[36] of growth by rejection of alternatives found unviable that we find in such modernist bildungsromans as Joyce's *Portrait of the Artist as a Young Man* and Thomas Mann's *Magic Mountain* and before that in Henry James's *Portrait of a Lady* and Willa Cather's *Song of the Lark*. It makes sense that Ellison's friend and mentor Kenneth Burke should have read *Invisible Man* as an African American reinvention of Goethe's *Wilhelm Meister*, each putting its protagonist through the transformations needed to present the entire inventory of "'ambiguities'" he needed "to confront in the process of growing up."[37] Burke might have gone a step or two further and brought in young Wilhelm's fascinated-embarrassed susceptibility to puppetry, theater, and offbeat wandering performers vis-à-vis *Invisible Man*'s deployment of folk songs like "Run, Nigger Run" as another kind of backdrop for Ellison's coming-of-age project. Just as in the "slavery-born folk rhyme blacks could laugh both at themselves and at the dread patrollers," O'Meally observes, so Ellison "elaborates on the running motif ['Keep this nigger boy running'] by making a joke of the Invisible's Man's flight as he is pursued by 'patter-rollers' of a different sort: by Bledsoe, Norton, Brockway, Wrestum, and Jack," who "threaten his freedom at every turn."[38] Where Wilhelm casts behind his folk/bohemian "underground" existence and soberly enters the elite, *Invisible Man* refuses to let Invisible settle into a unitary perspective or voice, ensures that he does *not* disown the subculture in which he was incubated.

All this helps explain why *Invisible Man* now stands as the first novel of an up-from saga centered on a representative minority protagonist to become—so it now seems—a sure-fire GAN prospect. It wasn't an easy passage. Despite the National Book Award, first-year sales were respectable but unspectacular—around 20,000 copies by the end of the first year.[39] Until the 1970s, *Invisible Man* was read far more enthusiastically by white mainstream literati than by African American critics, its top spot in the 1965 *Herald Tribune* poll countered by a 1968 *Negro Digest* survey proclaiming Richard Wright "the most important Black writer of all time."[40] One contributor to a special 1970 issue of *Black World*, playing the Uncle Tom card with a vengeance, denounced Ellison as a "denigrator of the great tradition of Black protest writing."[41] For decades the question was debated as to whether to categorize *Invisible Man* as an "Afro-American" novel or an "American novel," period, as if it couldn't be both at the same time. Since the early 1990s, however, the category dispute has subsided as the firmness of the dividing lines between "minority" and "mainstream" literature have themselves come under question and the view that the latter cannot be understood without the former as well as vice versa has become well-nigh axiomatic. In the early twenty-first century *Invisible Man*'s critical monumentalization on all sides seems increasingly secure, with two major Ellison biographies, a book-length "political companion" as well as a "reference guide" to *Invisible Man*, two critical studies focused in whole or part on the novel's composition, and many other significant books and articles.* Among audiences at large, *Invisible Man* remains widely and enthusiastically read, with a 4.3 rating from Amazon.com's 393 reviewers (1996–June 2013). Few of the many readers who first encountered it as required reading complain about its being foisted on them, sometimes as early as middle school—in contrast to (say) Amazon.com reviewers of *The Scarlet Letter* and even *The Great Gatsby*. A number of respondents propose *Invisible Man* as "a" or even "the" Great American Novel. Most who trouble to explain their reaction connect their sense of its power

---

* The biographies are Jackson, *Ralph Ellison;* and Rampersad, *Ralph Ellison;* the companions mentioned are Michael D. Hill and Lena M. Hill, *Ralph Ellison's "Invisible Man": A Reference Guide* (Westport, CT: Greenwood, 2008); and Lucas Morel, ed., *Ralph Ellison and the Raft of Hope: A Political Guide to "Invisible Man"* (Lexington: University Press of Kentucky, 2004); the critical books on the genesis of *IM* are Bradley, *Ralph Ellison in Progress;* and Foley, *Wrestling with the Left.* The contemporary growth spurt in Ellison studies might be seen as bookmarked by the partial publication of Ellison's unfinished second magnum opus as *Juneteenth* (New York: Random House, 1999), ed. John Callahan, and the complete manuscripts as *Three Days before the Shooting* (New York: Modern Library, 2011), ed. John Callahan and Adam Bradley; and it also includes intensified attention to the significance of Ellison's criticism (see especially Kenneth W. Warren, *So Black and Blue*).

with its exploration of hyphenated Americanness, of how to negotiate between being black and being American.

Ellison to Neo-slave Narrative and Beyond

Despite Ellison's reluctance to grant it, *Invisible Man*'s genesis, critical ascendancy, and enduring prestige was inseparable from the broader advance of ethnic bildungsroman and life writing that had been gaining momentum throughout the first half of the twentieth century, in such works as Antin's *Promised Land* (1912), Johnson's *Autobiography of an Ex-Colored Man* (1912), Cahan's *The Rise of David Levinsky* (1917), Mourning Dove's *Cogewea* (1927), Paredes's *George Washington Gómez* (1935–1940, 1990), Bulosan's *America Is in the Heart* (1945), and Jade Snow Wong's *Fifth Chinese Daughter* (1945). Indeed so great was the outpouring throughout the last century of significant novels focused on the lifelines of paradigmatic young hyphenated American protagonists by Bellow, John Okada, Philip Roth, N. Scott Momaday, Leslie Silko, Rudolfo Anaya, Maxine Hong Kingston, Toni Morrison, Alice Walker, Bharati Mukherjee, Gish Jen, Junot Díaz, and many others as to make it seem in retrospect very strange indeed that fictions of white Protestant experience dominated the mainstream fictional marketplace well into the twentieth century. From a presentist perspective it seems almost perverse that before the 1930s no U.S. novelists of other than white Christian background won anything like widespread critical acclaim as first-rate literary talents.

Not that growing-up fiction about "nonethnic" youth dried up or ceased to be read, of course. Salinger's Holden Caulfield of *Catcher in the Rye* still remains very much alive (3,333 Amazon.com reviews, 4-star rating as of June 2013), as does Scout Finch of Harper Lee's *To Kill a Mockingbird* (2,480 reviews, 4.6 stars), sometimes assigned alongside *Invisible Man*. Don DeLillo's *Libra* (1988), an adroit speculative reconstruction of the life of Kennedy assassin Lee Harvey Oswald through the fog of conspiracy theory left unresolved by the Warren Commission report, stands as a Cold War classic. These are just a few examples. The broader point, though, is that in today's climate of markedly "diminished Anglo-Protestant conformity,"[42] not just in avant-garde university and cultural circles but also for novel readers at large if not for all sectors of the national public, WASPness is well on the way to becoming just another marked ethnicity. The national imaginary that has coevolved among American creative writers and their audiences already points toward the certain future a few decades hence when the majority of residents in the United States will be "majority minority," as the percentage of its newborns already are.

Up to a point, the prominence of ethnic narratives of aspiration—novels, autobiographies, memoirs—in the late twentieth-century U.S. literary marketplace seems a logical extension of a long-standing interest on the part of reading communities at large in the struggles of lives led or thrust beyond the pale that is by no means limited to the national literary scene or to the lifelines of ethnic minorities. Familiar cases in point from earlier American literary history include narratives of Indian captivity, of soldiers, of shipwrecked sailors, of perilous travel to remote spots, of scouts and trappers and homesteaders, of relatively unmarked immigrants like Andrew the Hebridean. As Ann Fabian shows in her valuable study of nineteenth-century U.S. writing of and by largely unlettered folk, the market for narratives about white "beggars," "convicts," and "prisoners of war" wasn't cleanly distinguishable from that for slave narratives.[43] But the minoritarian turn in protagonist-centric narrative from the mid-twentieth century onward was more than an incremental uptick. It has also changed how American novels are written and read and how its history is written.

To return once more to *Huckleberry Finn* as a benchmark, the ethnic turn has influenced critical thinking about that text not only by intensifying controversy over its depiction of blacks, but by altering its place in a reconceived national literary history to which African American writing has come to be seen as much more crucial than in the 1950s, when the *Huck*-as-abolitionist-conversion-narrative thesis was set in place. The African American original(s) behind Huck's character and language have been excavated. The complications of Twain's fascination with blackface minstrelsy have been explored, one critic claiming minstrel show as the model for the novel's three-stage plot.[44] Jim's unobtrusive influence and his cannily strategic adaptations have been scrutinized as never before, taking Jim as the novel's moral center, sometimes invoking Ellison as precedent.[45] Nancy Rawles's novel *My Jim* (2005) rewrites *Huckleberry Finn* from the standpoint of Jim's wife, on the premise that Twain "wanted to make his story primarily about Jim, but didn't feel he could get away with it."[46] Among the most intriguing hypotheses advanced in this newer work is that Twain was significantly influenced by slave narrative. It's been a matter of lively speculation if he might have got the idea for Huck's ruse of pretending his raft mate had smallpox from J. W. C. Pennington's *The Fugitive Blacksmith*, if William Wells Brown's more riverine and trickstery narrative might have been a closer model, or if Twain's acquaintance with Frederick Douglass might have extended to a careful enough reading of his *Narrative* to make the occasional correspondences in name and figuration more than coincidental.[47]

This last interest followed from the still-recent rediscovery of slave narrative as a major literary accomplishment in its own right, a model for later African American narrative, and an impetus for one of late twentieth-century African American literature's signature genres, neo-slave narrative: novelized renditions of life under slavery and its aftermath written since the death of the last surviving slaves.[48] Although the first of these dates from the 1930s, it took almost three more decades for neo-slave fiction to take off—the upshot of the civil rights movement and its more militant sequels together with the unprecedented scrutiny of the archives of African American history and art those movements prompted. But after Margaret Walker's *Jubilee* (1966), based on the life of the author's great-grandmother, the proliferation was dramatic.

Ellison, whose formative years came well before the boom, seems to have been taken aback by it almost as much as one can imagine Twain feeling if told that *Huckleberry Finn* was a slave narrative in whiteface. Ellison groused that he "wouldn't have had to read a single slave narrative" to create *Invisible Man*'s northward quest for freedom plot. Yet his rejoinder supports the now-accepted contention of Henry Louis Gates Jr. and Charles T. Davis that "the Afro-American literary tradition, and especially its canonical texts, rests on the framework built, by fits and starts and for essentially polemical intentions, by the first-person narratives of black ex-slaves."[49] *Invisible Man* bears this out. Its first-person-told tale of its antihero's transit confirms the fit between latter-day African American literary practice, cultural memory, and slave narrative plot, of which the Great Migration North story that underwrites Invisible's itinerary was the defining early twentieth-century avatar. *Invisible Man* exemplified the unleashing of recuperative historical energy that enabled the boom the author could not foresee, through its emphasis on the hazards of suppressing or misconstruing the importance of slavery's past and aftermaths for survival in the present. Indeed "Ellison's broad move to reconnect the contemporary black generation to its slave-born grandparents," as literary historian Lawrence Jackson observes, "was a reclamation of the first order, a profound spiritual rescue."[50]

One indication of the rapid burgeoning of neo-slave narrative was the appearance of three major discrepant projects keyed to 1976, the nation's bicentennial. Alex Haley's Africa-to-America multigenerational family chronicle *Roots* was a hugely popular book and TV miniseries by the coauthor of *The Autobiography of Malcolm X* (1965). Ishmael Reed's experimental-surrealistic *Flight to Canada* was a rompish sendup of Stowe's *Uncle Tom's Cabin*. Scenes of modern technoculture montage with the antebellum stage sets; the Underground Railroad goes aerial; and "Uncle Robin" takes over the old plantation at the end, dispossessing the master class. Octavia Butler's *Kindred* was a somber speculative fiction focused on a young African American writer newly married to another aspiring (white) writer who gets repeatedly, traumatically yanked back from the bicentennial present to the Maryland plantation where her maternal great-great-grandmother was born in order to protect but finally murder the messed-up white scion who fathers her ancestress. Time-collapsing texts like *Flight to Canada* and *Kindred* witness both to slavery's pastness as legalized institution—to how "a full century and a half 'after the fact,' 'slavery' is *primarily* discursive" as Hortense Spillers writes—and also (as her scare quotes suggest) to how it continues to haunt the present. "Antebellum slavery didn't leave people quite whole," as Butler laconically explains her decision to return Dana to the present for good minus her left arm.[51]

A number of neo-slave novels from David Bradley's *The Chaneysville Incident* (1981) to Edward Jones's *The Known World* (2003) have since won major prizes. The likeliest Great American Novel candidate among them, Toni Morrison's *Beloved* (see Chapter 9), was not orchestrated along Ellisonian lines, being less centered on its protagonist per se than on her in relation to family, place, and past. Yet the genre seems as hospitable to plotlines of an up-from kind as Frederick Douglass's *Narrative* was, and the same holds for the post-neo-slave fictions of turn-of-the-twenty-first-century African American writers just now becoming prominent.

Of the former, there's no more striking example than Ellison's most loyal acolyte, Charles Johnson, who honored him as "an elder who forged a place in American culture for the possibility of the fiction I dreamed of writing."[52] Johnson's *Oxherding Tale* (1982) and *Middle Passage* (1990) are fabulistic rites of passage of naive but quick-witted narrators, mischievous by contrast to Invisible, who get subjected to symbolic ordeals involving a series of typic authority figures both white and black. *Middle Passage*'s Rutherford Calhoun, a thieving scapegrace freed at his Illinois master's death, stows away on what he belatedly discovers is a slaver owned by the very man he sought to flee: a black New Orleans underworld kingpin who tried to force him into marriage to discharge a debt. Rutherford then gets caught in a triangular struggle between a superintelligent tyrannical Ahabian captain, a mutinous crew, and their insurgent cargo of slaves, who take over the ship à la Melville's "Benito Cereno." Each faction tries to manipulate him, but wily Rutherford comes out on top. By taking over the ship's logbook—a seriocomic replay of the symbolic importance traditional slave narrative attaches to literacy as a master-class tool—Rutherford neutralizes his nemesis Papi Zeringue by exposing him as the slave ship's principal owner and stealing back from him the once-rejected fiancée for whom he now longs. For *Oxherding Tale*'s Andrew Hawkins, the half-white product of a bizarre wife-switching caper engineered by his drunken master, the ordeals end by passing into the master class and include along the way a pedantic hypereducation by an eccentric transcendentalist tutor who happens also to be a disciple of Karl Marx, a stint as sex slave to the mistress to whom he's hired out, and escape from the clutches of a never-miss slave catcher who recognizes him through his mask of whiteness. The two novels' discrepant outcomes, maturity as middle-class black versus white gentleman "householder,"[53] are enabled by regimes of education both hands-on and esoteric, involving a syncretic mix of Eurocentric and non-Western archives, tropes, worldviews.

Johnson's recherché thought experiments aren't likely to gain the traction of an *Invisible Man* or a *Beloved*.[54] No less brainy and well crafted but more accessible are Colson Whitehead's turn-of-the-twenty-first-century fictions of wonky aspiring young black professionals who rethink if not abandon their fast-track ambitions when some job-related crisis forces them to confront episodes from the racial past they'd either suppressed or never knew: *The Intuitionist* (1997), *John Henry Days* (2001), and *Apex Hides the Hurt* (2006). *The Intuitionist*, for instance, charts the rise, chastening, and triumph-of-sorts of the nation's first black female elevator inspector. Elevator verticality makes a nifty metaphor for upward mobility in a metropolitan world personified by this janitor's daughter with "a thing for geometric forms" and star graduate of the mythical Institute for Vertical Transport.[55] As an intuitionist, Lila Mae Johnson inspects not by examining the mechanism as the rival "empiricists" do but by sensing whether it's in order. At this she is "never wrong," the narrator reiterates; but her ineptness at reading people gets exposed when an elevator crash in a building that just passed her inspection sets the detective story in motion. It's a case of industrial sabotage, as she immediately suspects but is slow to unravel. Several major errors have to do with color: the baseless suspicion that her sole black colleague had been manipulated into plotting against her; her failure to spot the supposed soul brother to whom she turns for help as a white industrial spy in disguise; and her belated discovery that the master theorist of intuitionism, James Fulton, was a black man passing for white whose pronouncements she'd never rightly understood, like *"horizontal thinking in a vertical world is the race's curse,"* and whose tomes—so his African American housekeeper/mistress tells Lila Mae— were published more as a "joke" on the great white empiricist establishment than as settled doctrine. The last scene pictures a newly confident Lila Mae, now working freelance but more zealously than ever, "filling in the interstitial parts" of Fulton's unfinished third volume, believing herself his heir apparent and sure she can "make the necessary adjustments" to arrive at the "perfect elevator." Is this justified? Well, "She is never wrong. It's her intuition."[56] So the text coyly ends.

Whitehead's and Johnson's novels confirm the persistence of racially coded up-from plotlines, but under conditions different from those of *Invisible Man*. The encumbrances to self-advancement here have less to do with institutionalized discrimination than with negotiation of social identities. And social identity turns more on deciding what kind of black person (or not) one will be than on reframing the relation between race and nation, a concern engaged obliquely but not frontally. For Ellison, the promise of ethnic bildungsroman is to generate a voice with the power to alter the national imaginary by making it realize and attend to what had always been a crucial though invisible constituent. Johnson and Whitehead both answer Ellison's rhetorical question "What would America do without blacks?" the same way he did. They too delight in calling attention to the presence of blacks in unexpected places: Andrew Hawkins as southern gentleman, Rutherford as shipmaster pro tem, Fulton the black inventor, the Midwestern town with the Brahmin name of Winthrop (in Whitehead's *Apex*) revealed as a one-time black settlement whose origins the narrator ensures will get brought to the fore. But *Bildung* in these novels has less to do with nationness than with raceness, whether at the subnational level of professional or regional niche as in Whitehead or at the transnational ethno-cosmological level of Johnson's imagined Afro-diasporic contingent of Allmuseri.

It might seem that the increased preoccupation with ethnic identity in these recent fictions might portend the final unraveling of the GAN dream. And all the more so given that academic U.S. literature studies as well as the scene of national fiction production itself has been devoting an increasing fraction of its energies to specialized examination of the cultural particularities of African American, Latino/a American, Asian American, and Native American literatures. But Johnson's and Whitehead's novels also suggest an undiminished, although reconceived, interest in revisiting the upward mobility script that we've been tracing in the last several chapters from Franklin and Crèvecoeur. In that sense, the dream of the GAN—at least this version of it—clearly remains very much alive. The assumption of permanently irreversible fragmentation of the national imaginary during the present era presumes too much. The narrative of up-from aspiration is likely not only to survive but to thrive in the age of the hyphen, if only as an adversary to take issue with and dismantle over and over again. We see further evidence in the culminating achievement of one of the leading U.S. novelists of the generation after Ellison, and—more complexly—in the work of younger and midcareer writers at work today across the ethnic spectrum.

Roth's American Trilogy: American Pastoral *as Success Story "Undone"*

Among late twentieth-century U.S. writing's big-scale fictional undertakings that seemed to anticipate the approaching millennium—David

Foster Wallace's *Infinite Jest,* John Updike's *The Beauty of the Lilies,* Don DeLillo's *Underworld,* Neal Stephenson's *Cryptonomicon*—none was more ambitious than the one most closely tied to the ethnic up-from script: Philip Roth's "American trilogy": *American Pastoral* (1997), *I Married a Communist* (1998), and *The Human Stain* (2000). Roth had satirized the pretentiousness of the dream of the GAN in a rollicking mock epic of that title (1973) about the lost history of an imaginary baseball league, told by a senescent narrator with the garrulity of an Ishmael and the paranoia of an Ahab. Later, though, his investment in the correlation between lifeline and nationness took a more serious turn, culminating in a "thematic trilogy," as he called it, built around "the historical moments in postwar American life that have had the greatest impact on my generation": the McCarthy era (novel two), the civil rights and antiwar militancy of the 1960s (novel one), and Clinton's impeachment (novel three).[57] As with Henry James and William Faulkner, there's something captious about singling out as the closest GAN approximation one or even a cluster of novels by a writer so prolific whose talent has spread out over so many phases. But a *Guardian* reporter's judgment on the occasion of Roth's 2011 receipt of the Man Booker International Prize seems on target: it was "the magisterial trio" that decisively "secured his reputation as one of his country's greatest living writers."[58]

American Pastoral, I Married a Communist, and *The Human Stain* are more a series of stand-alone ventures than Dos Passos's *U.S.A.* or Updike's Rabbit tetralogy. But the family resemblances are considerable. Each is an observer-hero narrative that centers on a hard-driving larger-than-life character originally from the social margins. Each is observed by the same first-person narrator, Roth's old alter ego Nathan Zuckerman, familiar from a half-dozen novels of the 1970s and 1980s but here reborn after a decade's hiatus as the antithesis of the brash twenty-something who began his career in *The Ghost Writer* (1979) by seducing "Anne Frank" away from his own literary idol. The 1990s Zuckerman is an aging sexagenarian, left impotent and incontinent by prostate surgery, who has withdrawn to a cottage in western Massachusetts for reasons never fully explained ("I don't want a story any longer. I've had my story").[59]

In *American Pastoral* the featured character is Seymour ("Swede") Levov, the miraculously blond elder son of a hard-driving Jewish father who built a thriving high-end ladies' glove manufactory in Newark,

New Jersey, from scratch. The Swede is a star athlete idolized by younger neighborhood boys including Nathan. He becomes a "very adroit businessman" in his own right (*AP* 67), marries the Irish Catholic Miss New Jersey of 1949 over paternal objection, takes over as company president, and settles in the affluent gentile exurb of Old Rimrock, in a 170-year-old stone farmhouse on a hundred acres that he's coveted since youth. All this seems a triumphant realization of the shtetl-to-suburbia dream that thrived after World War II—until his teenage daughter, radicalized by the Vietnam War, bombs the local post office/general store, kills the village doctor, and disappears. In *I Married a Communist* the focal figure, Ira Ringold, is a roughneck labor agitator turned public spokesman-advocate for the disempowered little guy, briefly famous as a radio personality and admired by the young Nathan for his Progressive idealism and man-of-the-world charisma—until his mismatched marriage unravels to the point that his wife exposes him in a revengeful autobiography after which the novel is titled. In *The Human Stain* he is Coleman Silk, a classics professor and hard-nosed reformist dean at the college near Zuckerman's retreat, recently forced into retirement as the result of a campaign instigated by his (female) department chair for an unintentionally racist slur directed at two student no-shows. ("Spooks" to the old-fashioned Silk meant "ghosts," not "blacks," and he didn't realize the students were African American.) Ironically, we discover—though among the locals only Zuckerman discovers the secret—that Silk is himself a light-skinned African American who's been passing as Jewish his whole adult life. In each novel, Roth's variant of observer-hero narrative registers, more or less, a sense of being privy to history in the making that is voiced most extravagantly at the point in *I Married a Communist* when young Nathan gets caught up in "Iron Rinn" Ira's socialist advocacy on behalf of the little guy: "I had never before known anyone whose life was so intimately circumscribed by so much American history . . . so immersed in his moment or defined by it."[60]

Other threads bind the trilogy besides Zuckerman and the rise and fall of the epoch-defining figure. All three novels link that figure to "charismatic American presidents":[61] Seymour Levov is "our Kennedy" (*AP* 83); Ira self-consciously impersonates Lincoln and even looks a bit like him; Silk's postretirement amour with a college custodian half his age draws snickering comparisons to the Monica Lewinksy scandal that nearly brought down Clinton's presidency. In each novel, a sibling informant belatedly provides Zuckerman with the inside scoop on the protagonist: the Swede's truculent younger brother Jerry, Nathan's high school classmate; Ira's steadier older brother Murray; and Silk's younger sister, who reveals how Coleman came to pass for Jewish. In each, much younger women become weapons of destruction that catalyze the hero's undoing: in *American Pastoral,* the Swede's daughter Merry and her mysterious self-styled comrade-surrogate who calls herself Rita Cohen; in *I Married a Communist,* Eva's daughter Sylphid and her friend Pamela, with whom Ira has an affair; in *The Human Stain,* Silk's lover Faunia and his feminist colleague-turned-nemesis Delphine Le Roux. All three novels are cast as tragedies whose project is "to embrace your hero in his destruction," as Zuckerman describes his intent as Levov's biographer (*AP* 88), most explicitly *The Human Stain,* where Silk's hubris as a specialist in classical tragedy disdainful of packaging the subject for women students so as to defer to contemporary political correctness triggers Delphine's vendetta, and he and Zuckerman become friends as a result of literally dancing together. All three protagonists and Zuckerman himself hail from north Jersey urban Jewish neighborhoods, Roth's own Newark being the launching pad for novels one and two.

All three novels, then, unfold assimilation stories of upward mobility from ethnic enclave to different kinds of transethnic prominence: Levov into the exurban squirearchy, Ira into spokesman for the revolutionary-progressive anti-McCarthyite left, Silk into leadership at his provincial but aspiring liberal arts college. *The Human Stain* updates the first two by highlighting in retrospect "the comparative ease with which Jews might pass,"[62] even in the 1940s when Silk opted to reinvent himself as Jewish, let alone at century's end, by which time Jewish leadership in most walks of life—especially the intelligentsia—was long since a given.

Readerly preferences will differ. *I Married a Communist* comes closest to engaging national politics head on and develops the youthful Zuckerman most fully. *The Human Stain* provides the most complex meditation on ethnicity and the most intimate portrait of the older Zuckerman; and its out-there premise of a black man posing as Jewish and then busted as a racist is Roth at his most daring. For the present chapter it might seem to have a special claim as a possible homage to

Ralph Ellison, whom Roth admired both as craftsman and as model, as an older-generation genius unafraid to take issue with his tribe and ready to defend Roth's right to do so. It's been suggested that Coleman Silk might be a quasi-reinvention of Invisible, perhaps of Ellison himself.[63] Yet I favor *American Pastoral* instead, both on its own terms and for present purposes, despite Ross Posnock's thoughtful caveat that the novel's commitment to densely mimetic reconstruction of his subject's life "creates remarkable realist power but also militates against the imaginative audacity that marks Roth's finest work."[64] True up to a point, but to saturate the reader in the minute details of Newark Maid's glove making over two generations spanning four decades from startup to globalization and to devote the last and longest of its four parts to microscopic unpacking of the macabre twists and turns of one grueling dinner party at the junior Levovs' require their own kind of audacity. The "excessive" piling up of material and procedural detail not only makes for a scrutiny of its dramatis personae by contrast to which the two later novels seem sketchy but also creates the extra twist of belying the perplexity and agnosticism the narrator confesses upfront by tempting you to forget about them amid the pseudo-documentary exfoliation that follows. Far from being the work of straight-up realism it seems, *American Pastoral* transmits a now-you-see-it, now-you-don't effect that flickers suggestively between facticity and phantasmagoria.

At the end of *I Married a Communist* and *The Human Stain* only second-order questions remain, such as what comeuppance if any might overtake Delphine or whether Zuckerman will really be forced to relocate for fear of reprisal from Coleman's probable murderer. The stories of Ira's and Coleman's rise and fall are for all practical purposes complete. *American Pastoral,* by contrast, makes a point of insisting from the start that the Swede's opacity can't be penetrated even as it gives the appearance of proceeding to do just that. The question Zuckerman starts with, what did the unflappable Swede "do for subjectivity?" (*AP* 20), never gets more than a hypothetical answer. He grants that he has "dreamed" his "realistic chronicle" (89). He mentions just two brief meetings with the Swede during their adult lives. At the second (Zuckerman age sixty-five, Levov seventy), he senses something amiss. Yet at his high school reunion a few months later, he's stunned by Jerry's news that Seymour has just died from the metastasized cancer he had told the envious Zuckerman he'd beat, and what's more that the Swede was an "unsatisfiable father" with "unsatisfiable wives" and a "monster" daughter who blew her family's life apart then went underground for the remaining thirty-five years of her life ("Good-bye, Americana; hello, real time") (*AP* 67, 69). Zuckerman doesn't fully trust Jerry either; he's as pushy, irascible, self-important, and hyperbolic as Ira Ringold will be. Yet his testimony becomes the platform and springboard for Zuckerman's whole "speculative fiction" about Seymour's life as a grownup.[65]

Zuckerman's relegation to a bit part in *American Pastoral* relative to *Communist* and *Human Stain* might be discounted as evidence that Roth hadn't yet figured out what to do with him. (The early drafts, dating back to the early 1970s, start with Seymour narrating in the first person, then shift to third.)[66] But however that may be, during the first eighty-nine pages before the narrator disappears into his chronicle, the novel makes a point of stressing how the narrator's frustration at not being able to penetrate the icon's facade grates against the lingering aura of this "household Apollo of the Weequahic Jews" and the assimilationist dream he represents for the community, Zuckerman included (*AP* 4). Their second encounter provokes a self-disgusted rant about the impossibility of not misreading other people. "You fight your superficiality, your shallowness, so as to try to come at people without unreal expectations," but "you get them wrong before you meet them," "while you're with them," and again when you try to "tell somebody else about them," so that "the whole thing" is nothing more than "an astonishing farce of misperception" that drives you to conclude that what living's all about is getting people wrong "and then, on careful reconsideration, getting them wrong again. That's how we know we're alive: we're wrong" (*AP* 35).

So when the novel then casts the Swede as a blinkered misperceiver of those nearest him—baffled that his adored daughter could have gone so awry, oblivious to wife Dawn's amour with a neighbor of impeccable WASP pedigree—it's only in a sense replaying the terms of Zuckerman's self-critique. "How to penetrate to the interior of people was some skill or capacity he did not possess" (*AP* 409)—Zuckerman's judgment seems more than a little ironic given what he's said about himself. Nor can his irritated attempts to "roil the innocence of this regal Swede" at their last meeting (34) be separated from the rhetorical animus behind his later images of Merry driving the Swede to his knees with her accusations of his filthy capitalism. Or behind unleashing the despicable "Rita Cohen" to play on the Swede's desire to talk shop, as Zuckerman himself earlier did, as a setup for then excoriating him, blackmailing him, and trying to lure him into sex. Or behind Jerry's overreaction, when the Swede telephones him for support, lashing out in a resentment at times positively Zuckerman-like: "You don't reveal yourself to people, Seymour. You keep yourself a secret. Nobody knows what you are. You certainly never let *her* [Merry] know who you are. That's what she's been blasting away at—that façade" (275).

The harrowing one-day sequence from the autumn of 1973 that consumes the last three-fifths of the book seems to be asking throughout: "How many blows can this guy absorb without getting utterly destroyed?" First, Rita Cohen's mind-bending letter directing him to Merry. Then finding her only ten minutes away from his office living in a squalid slum, grotesquely transformed (as the city of Newark had been) from bomber to malnourished ascetic Jain. Then being horrified by her tale of hand-to-mouth life on the run, twice raped but killing twice more. Then completely losing it when she rebuffs his fumbling attempts to rescue her. Then getting yelled at by Jerry when he phones him for advice. Then, returning home, reducing wife, parents, himself to tears by accidentally blurting out Merry's name just before the big dinner party. Then discovering toward the start of it the affair between wife and neighbor that's been unfolding under his nose for months. Then dealing with an accusatory telephone call from Rita, right after which comes an explosive scene with another guest, his daughter's ex-counselor (briefly his own ex-lover) who he's just learned had sheltered Merry when she disappeared but never let on. Then a long guilty flashback of the premarital inquisition to which father Lou had insisted on subjecting wife Dawn. Then the whole party imploding when the drunken wife of Dawn's lover stabs Lou with a fork. And much more in between, as the tension-fraught party conversation weirdly yaws from Lou's unstoppable laments about the death of Newark and lapsed standards of glove making to what to make of porn star Linda Lovelace—protracted rigamaroles that weirdly mirror back the contrast between traditional work eth(n)ics that really delivered and a younger generation seemingly broken beyond repair. During all of which, Seymour never stops obsessing about Merry, to the point that he misguesses Lou's sudden howl of pain as a fatal heart attack caused by her sudden reappearance.

The cumulative effect eerily recalls the boyhood scene mentioned several times in which the Swede first gives awestruck ten-year-old Nathan his nickname after painfully extricating himself from a pile of tacklers: "Basketball was never like this, Skip" (*AP* 70). How much can the golden boy take? What gives Zuckerman's "chronicle" its edge is the mix of wonder and vengeance with which it builds the Swede up and knocks him down again and again and again.

But to think of *American Pastoral*'s "realism" as nothing more than a cover for a narratorial hatchet job goes too far in the opposite direction. Yes, there is something more than a little sadistic about the extremes to which it takes the hesitant cosseted daughter turned incendiary turned ascetic, not to mention her even more surrealistic maenad-like inter-mediary Rita (whose existence Merry denies). But beyond that, *American Pastoral* seems given over to dramatizing two incompatible life worlds or *epistèmes*, each impenetrable from the other side. No more do these bizarre young women inhabit "real time" than the dream of "quaint Americana" does. It's Roth's version of Virginia Woolf or Willa Cather positing that around 1908, or 1922, the world broke in two.

The asymmetry between the two worlds, post-1945-style assimila-tionist dreamtime versus 1960s recoil, that makes the one seem like the everyday imperfect and the other off the charts lies of course in the decision to behold the divide from the standpoint of the elders. As the embodiment of a generation's dreams, the Swede evokes both the lure of that never-to-return age of postwar innocence and the mix of stupefaction and remorseful guilt at the converging upheavals of the 1960s: Cold War containment culture appalled by the horrors of Viet-nam, liberal individualism morphing into revolutionary countercul-ture, the slow incrementalisms of the integrationist era buckling in the face of urban riot and arson, with Newark the paradigm case.

It's tempting to read *American Pastoral*'s pattern of movement and countermovement—Seymour's American pastoral disrupted by the "counterpastoral" of the "indigenous American berserk" (*AP* 86)—as a one-way dismantling of all the Swede stands for. Consider the sequence on his secret fantasy of himself as a latter-day Johnny Appleseed, a fan-tasy oblivious to the dodgy backstory behind the dumbed-down chil-dren's-book version he goes by: Johnny Appleseed as Swedenborgian mystic with a strange hankering for young girls, as agent of westward expansion, as promoter of a Yankee signature crop then cultivated not as health food but for its alcoholic properties, as man of property who died owning a tract of real estate ten times the size of Seymour's. Critic Aimee Pozorski takes the Swede's naïveté as culpable blindness to the seamy side of the nation's past.[67] And why not?—Except that Zuckerman himself is so steeped in the sunny memories of postwar pastoral innocence, glowingly summed up in his high school reunion speech ("Let's remember the energy," 40–44). Lingering nostalgic flashbacks surge throughout the book, such as how Coach Ward gave teenage Swede his nickname, which he then carried "like an invisible passport, all the while wandering deeper and deeper into an American's life, forthrightly evolving into a large, smooth, optimistic American" such as his ethnically marked forebears could never claim. Passages like these are all compensatory efforts "to reconstitute the undivided oneness of existence" before Merry exploded (207, 206). That isn't the Swede's yearning so much as the novel's project. We can't know for sure the extent to which the Swede is party to all this. We can't know if Johnny Appleseed ever crossed his mind. These are Zuckerman's implants, his vicarity. The talismanic nickname bit goes back to a shared youthful zest for mainstream sports that resurfaces again at their chance 1985 meeting at a Mets game, and back from there to the author who once reminisced, "the solace that my Orthodox grandfather doubtless took in the familiar leathery odor of the flesh-worn straps of the old phylacteries in which he had wrapped himself each morning, I derived from the smell of my mitt"—not because of wanting to be a major leaguer, but the sense of "membership in a great secular nationalistic church from which nobody had ever seemed to suggest that Jews should be excluded."[68]

Altogether, *American Pastoral* dismantles the Swede, postwar innocence, and the assimilationist dream without really undoing the figure that is made to embody them. It breaks off in domestic chaos, but not before conjuring a saga of up-from Levov family self-making over three decades and two generations never erased, however defaced. Only nominally does the cynical dinner guest get the book's last laugh. The Swede is still standing. As we've been told, even though he will grieve lifelong for Merry and even though Jerry will continue to jeer, he'll recompose himself, start a new family, and father three sturdy sons. His greatest business success still lies ahead: taking Newark Maid completely global, detaching it for good from blighted Newark, amazingly "more or less unharmed by the city's collapse" (*AP* 24). The novel leaves it open, masterfully, as to whether the removal's 1973 timing was related to his meeting with Merry, who until then is said to have kept him Newark bound as a gesture of solidarity with African American have-nots against father Lou's urging to relocate. And whether the Swede's Lou-like bitterness about Newark's ruination in his last meeting with Zuckerman does or does not mean he's cast liberal do-gooderism behind him for profit's sake. Be that as it may, *American Pastoral* avoids subjecting its American dreamer to the abjection of a Clyde Griffiths or the violent death of a Gatsby or a Sutpen; nor does it leave him in the limbo of an Invisible Man or Augie March. Death from prostate cancer is obviously wretched, but not that, not anything, undercuts the tribute Jerry pays, for all his bad-mouthing: "My brother was the best you're going to get in this country, by a long shot" (66).

In a "self-interview" about *The Great American Novel* (1973) about the time he began drafting *American Pastoral,* Roth described the former as "discovering in baseball" a means of comic rendition of "the *struggle* between the benign national myth of itself that a great power prefers to perpetuate, and the relentlessly insidious, very nearly demonic reality (like the kind we had known in the sixties) that will not give an inch in behalf of that idealized mythology."[69] *American Pastoral* undertook that more wholeheartedly from the same baseline of sport mania. By no coincidence is baseball, the so-called national pastime, the Swede's best sport. In that same 1973 essay, Roth professed not "to know what America is 'really like'" and distinguished his narrator's attempt "to imagine a myth of an ailing America" from his own "attempt to imagine a book about imagining that American myth" during "this last demythologizing decade of disorder, upheaval, assassination, and war."[70] In *American Pastoral* he found a way to evoke that sense of confusion about national destiny in the form of a paradigmatic up-from ethnic protagonist's lifeline that granted but also pushed back against the opposite seductions of dismissal and nostalgia.

Overall, *American Pastoral* achieved almost as memorable a fusion of the personal and the paradigmatic as *Invisible Man.* Its reassessment of up-from ethnic aspiration and Ellison's sit at opposite ends of a corridor—or escalator. *Invisible Man* stands as a call to Americans at large to recognize the suppressed minority presence that has been a crucial but unacknowledged shaping force. As such it is a fable of rightful entry so far denied. In *American Pastoral* that entry is pretty much completed, for Jews at least. Zuckerman and Levov and Jerry rise from lower-middle-class Newark Jewish enclave to become tops in their fields. But the novel becomes a fable of the costs that such success extracts. Such projects witness to the durability of ethnic marking, however. Once an ethnic, always an ethnic in some sense. In ethnic up-from fiction of the late twentieth century and beyond, even in the age of more "equal opportunity" for formerly stigmatized groups—those with the right skill sets, that is—to make it big is not to leave the ancestors behind. Conversely, the upward mobility drive in *Invisible Man* and *American Pastoral* has been thoroughly internalized within ethnic communities themselves—sometimes more tenaciously than among Brahmin scions like young Emerson and Dawn's neighbor-lover. So the turn to ethnic protagonists' growing-up narratives in late twentieth-century U.S. literature and beyond doesn't in itself mean pitching the old American dream out the window. On the contrary, it's likely to remain alive as a topic and nexus if not as mantra. But no less likely to be reconceived in fresh and—perhaps—more penetrating ways.

The Way We Live Now?

In the 2010s, U.S. national destiny seems more iffy than when Roth wrote *American Pastoral,* let alone 1990, when the Soviet Union was in collapse and fears of Japanese economic preeminence on the wane. This century's nation to watch seems more likely to be China than the United States. The widening gap since the 1970s between the ever-rising incomes of the highest U.S. wage earners and the bottom 90 percent is increasingly notorious. Today the statistical chance of an American rising from the bottom quintile to the top is lower than for most nations in the developed world. The American dream has taken a beating for this, blamed as a major roadblock to public awakening to the enormity of the "Great Divergence."[71] Clearly the hoary exceptionalist stereotype of the United States as a classless society, always a stretch, is long since anachronistic.

The thought experiments of contemporary ethnic and immigrant writers offer some illuminating ways of dealing with this paradox. One is to credit the enablers. Barack Obama's memoir *Dreams of My Father*

(1995), published to little fanfare at the outset of his political career but a best seller when reissued after his landslide senatorial victory, makes a good starting point. This book could easily have been written as the only-in-America success story of individual smarts and determination beating the odds that President Obama's career is often, and with considerable justice, seen as being. Obama the autobiographer, though, stresses his dependence at every stage on elders, relatives, friends, spouse who corrected naïveté and called him out for obstinate self-focus; and stresses furthermore that his was not just an American odyssey but an eclectic journey ranging from Java to Kenya with a geographic center in the nation's newest, most peripheral, least demographically typical state. All this makes for a story of self-fashioning as a collaborative and migratory process across cultures in which moving forward means again and again looping back to the familial. Julia Alvarez's *How the Garcia Girls Lost Their Accents* (1991) achieves semi-analogous results within a Latina-diasporic matrix by situating its chief protagonist in family/clan contexts throughout and by reversing chronology. It opens with grown-up Yolanda back in the Dominican Republic looking for an eligible mate, then traces her elite family's history backward through the stages of its arduous but materially successful immigrant odyssey to recoup itself, back to the point just before they fled their homeland to escape then-dictator Trujillo when Yolanda was a small child. Here too bonds of family that include a strong sense of ethnic identity seem vital to formation of adult personhood. Yet a rift opens up both between her and her family as a bookish scribbling outlier, and between her Americanized self and her no-longer-familiar homeland and its stifling decorums. Contra young Obama's sometimes disorienting but wholly grateful reconnection with his relatives in Kenya, Yolanda's return, the novel implies, will widen the distance from her culture of origin.

Here, then, is a second resource for contemporary and ethnic narrative that unfolds along up-from lines: to stress the balance sheet between the bond to home culture or homeland and an attenuation if not outright break that feels scary but also compelling. Bharati Mukherjee's *Jasmine* (1989) and Ha Jin's *A Free Life* (2008), for instance, center on immigrant protagonists painfully making their way after hasty departure from their homelands: Jin's Nan impelled by the political crackdown after the 1989 Tiananmen Square Massacre, Mukherjee's Jyoti (later Jasmine, then Jane, then Jasmine again) as a terrified teenage refugee suddenly widowed by a Sikh extremist's bomb intended for her. In style and texture, Mukherjee's jumpy, shock-ridden plot (on her first night in the U.S. as a below-the-radar illegal, Jyoti is raped, then knifes her assailant to death) could not differ more dramatically from Jin's slow-ruminating chronicle of Nan, his wife Pingping, and son Taotao. Nan laboriously puzzles through how to get by/get on in the United States without abandoning his desire to write poetry, first as disaffected graduate student, then as restaurant owner, finally as night watchman. Jasmine, as Manhattan nanny, as Iowa banker's wife, and as mistress of the divorced employer who later seeks her out, is virtually isolated from compatriots, whereas Nan stays in contact with the fractious communities of overseas Chinese and with relatives back in China, and his own wife and son turn out to be a crucial steadying force despite years of friction. Both protagonists mentally inhabit two worlds throughout. Memories of the forsaken homeland haunt them and probably always will. But they're not about to repatriate. For her it might be literally suicidal, for him spiritually so. Despite never expecting to feel at home in the United States, they'd rather be there than "home."

Fictions of second- or third-generation hyphenated American youths often use comparable balancing strategies. Junot Díaz's geeky Dominican American antihero Oscar Wao can find sexual and spiritual fulfillment only by returning to the Dominican Republic, but as the narrator foresees he goes to his death, a macabre literalization of what might face Alvarez's Yolanda were she to stay. In Sandra Cisneros's more upbeat *Caramello* (2002), growing up requires family trips back to Mexico and immersion in the collective memory of which the elders who remained there are the guardians; but life starts and maturity completes itself for the title character in Hispanic Chicago. In Helena María Viramontes's *Under the Feet of Jesus,* young Estrella and her family of Chicano migrant farm workers suffer horribly, and she sees her boyfriend shrivel away after being sprayed with toxic insecticides by a crop-dusting plane. But knowing that her morose stepfather intends to return to Mexico only fortifies Estrella's gritty resolve, quixotic as it may be. Perhaps she will become—though the novel leaves it open—the custodian of the documentary proof of the family's rightful status as U.S. residents that her flagging mother hides under the feet of their Christ statue, though the icon itself is broken.

Never does this novel come remotely close to mentioning the sub-ject of "the American dream." Yet clearly a sort of up-from aspiration underwrites the mother's vigilant guardianship of the legitimating pa-pers and even more so, in a more spiritualized register, the final glimpse of Estrella's mysterious experience of spiritual uplift from her elevated perch in the attic of their ramshackle sharecropper barn. This brings us to still another resource that contemporary ethnic and immigrant fic-tions sometimes bring to aspiration-in-America themes. Stereotypical American dream-think is undercut as delusive snake oil you need to protect yourself against even as the force of the up-from drive itself is acknowledged as motive and certain forms of it are granted a certain qualified legitimacy. For Mukherjee's Jasmine, the dream is a dubious proposition to start with that's permanently discredited when she finds its chief advocate, her late husband's old teacher who had emigrated to the States and urged him to follow, stuck in a much humbler niche than the "professorji" he pretended to be. Still, her scrappiness, perse-verance, and capacity for deferred gratification mark her as a more savvy pursuer of life, liberty, and happiness. The antihero Ralph Cheng of Gish Jen's *Typical American* (1991) starts as a clueless immigrant graduate student who doesn't know what the American dream is even as he starts to act out a Chinese counterpart of the upward mobility push that hinges more on family interdependence and well-being than on individualistic go-ahead. Ralph then gets derailed by the stereo-typical brand embodied by his sleazy compatriot Grover Zing, who embroils him in get-rich-quick schemes that nearly destroy the family, until he wakes up at the eleventh hour to the superiority of the im-ported version he'd been muddling through before.

Ha Jin's Nan is more immunized than Ralph against the stereotype by a principled resistance to letting his life be ruled by the success drive; but it plays through *A Free Life* as a (to him) enigmatic lure for a number of those around him with which Nan makes peace at the end by redefining it on his own terms, as "something to be pursued only," and at the risk—willingly taken as the price of the freedom—of "wast-ing his life without getting anywhere."[72] By contrast, in Brian Ascalon Roley's *American Son* (2001), in which an overworked Filipino immi-grant mother and her two sons struggle to keep the collective head above water, the dream is both completely discredited in principle even as it is acknowledged as an inexorable force. The genteel stateside aunts who parrot it are caricatured; but the drive for a more respectable and sanitary lifestyle and better education for her kids that drove the embattled mother from dirty Manila to dangerous L.A. into an exhausting regime of multiple marginal jobs is only too real. A bitterly ironic version of it is sustained in the next generation by the cynical, sadistic, but family-loyal older son Tomas's petty-gangster entrepreneurialism that illegally furnishes Mom with comforts of home she couldn't otherwise afford but distresses her no end, all the more so as the more good-boy younger son falls under his brother's influence.

More complex, though more decisive, in its engagement with up-from-ism is Chang Rae Lee's *Native Speaker* (1997), which unfolds a two-stage struggle through and beyond the model minority trap. Here maturity hinges on achieving safe distance from two ethnic up-from scripts—one traditional, one cosmopolitan—so as to equate ethnic affiliation with the downside of American dreamism but recognize both as intertwined and characteristic phases of self-fashioning for an aspiring youth in the turn-of-the-twenty-first-century U.S. conscious of starting from a position of cultural outsidership. Lee's college-educated Korean American protagonist first struggles to fulfill the conventional expectations of the autocratic immigrant grocer father who pushes him to assimilate while never letting him forget his heritage. This lands Henry a job as a surveillance agency sleuth on the strength of his second-generation adeptness at making himself transparent. Despite growing self-contempt at having to betray the people into whose confidence he insinuates himself, he forsakes his well-compensated position for good only after his last assignment, a high-flying immigrant Korean city counselor. He feels drawn to this John Kang as a more worldly and charismatic father than his biological one. But when he discovers that this seemingly idealistic public servant, masterful in his rapport with his global village of Queens constituents, is a two-timing husband, gambler, and on-the-make racketeer, Henry snaps his ties with both Kang and workplace—after dutifully submitting his report to the firm—for an undefined future that promises less economic advancement but more inner peace and mutuality, reconciled both to his father's memory and to his estranged American wife. Henry's conscienceful retreat from the fast track makes for a latter day model-minority quasi-equivalent of Howells's Silas Lapham's retreat from entrepreneurial overreach a century before.

Contemporary novels of immigrants and hyphenated Americans like those just surveyed, and Obama's memoir too, both sustain and qualify the claim of cultural critic Ali Behdad's *A Forgetful Nation*, that in defiance of the experiential facts the official "myth of immigrant America is itself a forgetful narrative," oblivious in its celebrations of immigrants as "adventurous heroes" when the great majority were "economic refugees" or "indentured laborers for whom immigration meant servitude," and foreclosing in the assumption that immigration must mean leaving one's country of origin decisively behind.[73] Behdad anchors his historical argument in Crèvecoeur's famous dictum in *Letters from an American Farmer* (1782): "*He* is an American, who, leaving behind him all his ancient prejudices and manners, receives new ones from the new mode of life he has embraced."[74] Recent archival work, including publication of the letters excluded from that colonial classic, paints a more tangled picture of the historical author's situation.[75] We now recognize him as "an international wanderer" with "personal affiliations in many nations," well aware of the interdependencies among the economies of the northern U.S. regions that he treats as virtuously self-sufficient and the slave-based Euro-Caribbean that he later treats with a glancing shudder.[76] The ethnic markers and transnational affiliations of the "American" Crèvecoeur have been resupplied, so as to enable a more calibrated, qualified, and mature assessment of Andrew's upbeat success story as an idealized counterpoint to actual lifelines that, like the author's own, were more precarious, fraught, and self-divided and whose cultural variegation seldom fit comfortably into a totalizing rubric like "American," with its implication of unitary culture and tidy borders. The narratives of aspiring minority immigrants and American ethnics that have loomed so large in U.S. literature from the early twentieth century onward serve, and will continue to serve as long as the United States continues to be thought of with whatever basis to nurture a culture of aspiration, not only as works of high artistic excellence at best but also as a resource for enabling a more fine-grained, hardheaded understanding of what aspiration in the United States has actually meant, does mean, and should.

These last reflections are not likely to satisfy those who believe that fictions of aspiration centering on ethnoracial outsiders have been overplayed in recent U.S. literature and in school curricula or, worse, that such plots of aspiration are mere apologies for capitalist individualism, a more fundamental root cause of social inequality than racism.[77] In response to this line of argument, here are a few parting shots. For the paradigmatic poor aspiring youth in serious U.S. fiction to switch within less than a century from a white kid from a slum or hardscrabble farm to a ghetto or barrio youth of color is admittedly a problematic distortion of the demographic facts—but at both ends. Conceivably the pendulum will swing back at least partway as the United States becomes majority minority. But whether or not it does, the ethnic turn in American up-from stories of aspirant youth, far from giving acquisitive individualism a free pass, has tended—with exceptions of course—to bring issues of social justice more robustly to the fore than in earlier novels of aspiration. At least in part, that's because the condition of marked ethnicity conduces to even greater like-it-or-not self-consciousness of the (un)fairness of social arrangements across the board. If American literature's future plots of aspiration continue to do as self-exacting a job of scrutinizing the ethics of the up-from aspirations that they dramatize as Ellison, Roth, and most of the writers briefly mentioned in this closing section have done, literature and public culture and maybe even society at large will be the gainers.

PART FOUR

SCRIPT THREE: ROMANCING THE DIVIDES

Introduction

Shifting Ratios, Dangerous Proximities

Y OU ALREADY KNOW this story too—some version of it at least. Two
young people from very different contexts meet, become mutually
attracted, and despite the barriers between them, pair up. The traditional novel favors a marriage plot; but the bond might be friendship
rather than love and need not be heteronormative. The social divisions might have to do with class, religion, region, nationality, race, or
ethnicity—often several. In Jane Austen's *Pride and Prejudice,* it's class
difference that aggravates tension between the equally strong-minded
Miss Bennet and Mr. Darcy. In Walter Scott's *Waverley,* multiple impediments keep the titular hero from his proper soulmate: the romance
of the Highlands personified by fiery chieftain Fergus Mac-Ivor, the
charms of his no less fiery sister, and the lure of the Jacobite insurgency.
If, as here, the novel has to do with nation making, the complications
of the relationship register national fault lines that must be overcome.
Both the internal divisions between Scottish regional cultures and the
strains of Scotland's absorption into Great Britain get symbolized by
Edward's flirtation with the romance of Highland feudalism before he
settles into the snug harbor of marriage with Lowland heiress Rose
Bradwardine.

The intimate and the sociohistorical domains are also potentially
in conflict. Novels in which the interpersonal story dominates risk
short-circuiting the social complexities. Personal relationships are only
one constituent of a sociopolitical order. At worst, "history is evacuated
of its content, and violence [of conquest] is aestheticized as sentiment,"

as one critic tartly sums up turn-of-the-twentieth-century California writer Gertrude Atherton's novels of Hispanic women snapped up by gringos.[1] Novels given over to meditation on characteristic divisions inhibiting nationhood that have come closest to fulfilling the dream of the GAN are more guarded and complex in relying on personal intimacies as proxies for negotiating social divisions, attracted though they also are to scenes of interpersonal rapport as a means of dramatizing the theme.

The cultural divides that have weighed most heavily for the U.S. national imaginary have to do with region and with race or ethnicity:* Old World/New World, East/West, North/South; white/red, white/black, white/nonwhite, to name some of the most obvious and long-standing. As Chapters 5 and 6 begin to suggest, even more pervasive among Great American Novel candidates than engagement with the Franklinesque up-from script or coming-of-age stories generally has been the work of imagining across or from within both of these two kinds of divides. This is the overriding concern of the novels discussed in Part IV.

Territorial and racial otherness posed almost equally formidable challenges for underprepared Euro-American settlers from the start. But through a combination of fortuity and Eurocentric cultural logic, for the U.S. critical establishment from the early national era through the end of the nineteenth century "region"—sectionalism—by and large seemed more important as a literary issue than did ethnicity or race. Whereas Eurosettler Australian literary nationalists, once continental conquest got under way, tended to think holistically of country as continent and did not begin developing robust regionalist traditions until the mid-1900s,[2] American settler literati presumed almost from the start that the route to imagining the national lay through evocation of specific regional cultures—Irving's Dutch New Yorkers versus in-migrating Yankees; the New Englands of Sedgwick, Hawthorne, and

---

* On the relation between "race" and "ethnicity" and my use of those and related terms here and elsewhere, see Introduction, footnote, page 7. As for the significance of gender considerations here: in most though not all the works featured in Part IV, as we'll quickly see in Chapter 7, issues of gender do indeed loom large, both for their own sake and as symbolic reinforcers of regional and ethnic divides. But because more often than not gender figures as symbolic reinforcer in fairly predictable ways (e.g., by coding the dominant as "male"), I discuss it selectively below, concentrating for the most part on unusual variations.

Thoreau; the South Carolinian Lowland/Piedmont patchworks of William Gilmore Simms; the frontier life, talk, and storytelling relayed by Cooper, James Kirke Paulding, Caroline Kirkland, and many others. Of course these writers were also very well aware that Indians and Africans were ingredients in the demographic mix of potential interest to audiences abroad as well as at home. But when it came to lit-talk as opposed to talk about social concerns, these and other minorities tended to get treated as part of some territorial district, as with Indians in romances of the forest or frontier, slaves in antebellum plantation fiction, and Irving's New York Dutch.

In part, this penchant for thinking regionally reflected the concurrence of the national literary takeoff with the localist emphases of Anglo-European romanticism: border balladry, emerging Irish and Scots fiction, Wordsworth's celebration of the English Lake Country, the Alpine poetics of Byron and the Shelleys, the gothic novel's invention of medievalized Mediterranean outbacks. Even more decisively, however, the first wave of U.S. regionalism reflected the hasty assemblage of the republic itself from colonial building blocks of discrepant origin, and the challenge and excitement of coming to terms with the diverse environments and cultures mutually unfamiliar to each other that the nation gobbled up during the nineteenth century faster than the national imaginary could digest them.

A third notable factor became still more important later on, during the second and much larger wave of U.S. regionalisms between the Civil War and World War II, the specific era to which "regionalism" as a literary-critical term is most often although somewhat reductively applied: New England local colorism; the midwestern farm novel; the literary discoveries of Appalachia, cowboy culture, and Hispanic California; and the Southern Renaissance of the interwar era. As critic Hsuan Hsu writes of the lure for both writers and readers of this later regional dispensation, "Affect does not expand from the hearth outward into the nation and then the world" but the reverse. To some degree, that had been true all along. Washington Irving, James Fenimore Cooper, Nathaniel Hawthorne, Caroline Kirkland, and Harriet Beecher Stowe also wrote from the aesthetic distance of metropolitan expatriation with benefit of "prior, present, or imagined transnational contact," as Hsu observes of Frank Norris's California, Booker T. Washington's New South, and Sarah Orne Jewett's Dunnet Landing.[3] But as urbanization and industrialization advanced the middle-class tendency to imagine regions as backwaters intensified.*

When evoking bygone times, regionalism tended to take on a "'fly-in-amber quality,'" as Raymond Williams perceived and as Hsu seconds—a hankering to preserve "local cultures that seemed to be vanishing" before "capitalist consolidation."[4] "Pre-railroad times" was Stowe's wistful rubric for the bygone early national New England of her regional imagination.[5] One baleful consequence of this was a nostalgically racialist reduction of upcountry and backcountry as all-white enclaves, such as the imagined Appalachias of the late nineteenth century, or of regionalism itself as an all-white project, as with the aesthetic "agrarianism" of the so-called Fugitive group during the Southern Renaissance.[6] On the other hand, as Carrie Tirado Bramen points out, some writers of the postbellum era and early twentieth century, both white and nonwhite—María Amparo Ruiz de Burton, Hamlin Garland, and W. E. B. Du Bois are the cases she cites—"configured the region as a contemporary place of struggle rather than a nostalgic projection of a past community."[7] Regionalism could be a launching pad for those "darkies" that the Fugitives sought to keep in their place, as in Chesnutt's conjure tales written against Joel Chandler Harris and in Jean Toomer's *Cane;* or in the work of John Joseph Mathews, Darcy McNickle, and other Native American literary "subregionalists" of the 1930s, as cultural historian Robert Dorman calls them;[8] or for white writers like Mari Sandoz and Mary Austin, who insisted on the multiethnicity of the Midwest and the Southwest.

Regional and ethnic identification are obviously very different ways of marking off "part" from "dominant" to a considerable extent at odds with each other. In part, the disparities are a matter of historical contingency. Turn-of-the-twentieth-century regionalists and ethnic pluralists,

---

* Rightly understood, as Stephanie Foote has argued and is now more widely recognized, "region" should be conceived as urban as well as rural, especially as immigrant ethnic neighborhoods became an increasingly visible part of burgeoning U.S. cities (Stephanie Foote, *Regional Fictions: Culture and Identity in Nineteenth-Century American Literature* [Madison: University of Wisconsin Press, 2001], 124–153). Carrie Tirado Bramen's subtle and astute assessments of regionalism vis-à-vis cultural production and of "urban picturesque" are additionally helpful in assessing the intersections and tensions between imaging of urban and rural districts during this period (Carrie Tirado Bramen, *The Uses of Variety: Modern Americanism and the Quest for National Distinctiveness* [Cambridge, MA: Harvard University Press, 2000], 115–198).

for example, adopted "a common strategy of unity-in-distinctiveness" though by and large they "targeted different subcultures."[9] But they are also intrinsic to the difference between land and people. Territory stays put; *Homo sapiens* is a "natural alien," as the environmental theorist Neil Evernden puts it, the one animal with no fixed habitat.[10]

Now and then, territory and *ethnos* have seemed nearly coextensive, as with Alta California before 1848 and Indian reservations today, but rarely to the extent of, say, Slovenia in the former Yugoslavia or the Albanian-dominated Kosovo province that later broke away from Serbia. For the most part, not only have U.S. regional demographics at any point in time been ethnically pluralistic, they have tended to become more so; and ethnic identification always has been at least incipiently transregional if not also transnational or diasporic. The idea floated in the 1960s to form a separate homeland somewhere in the deep South for African Americans didn't meet with much more enthusiasm than the conspiracy in Sutton Griggs's somber fable *Imperium in Imperio* (1899) to make Texas a black republic. In any case, for a dominant culture to conceive minorities, nonwhite or white, as embedded within specific places is to start down the slippery slope of stereotyping them as subhuman: Indians as creatures of the forest, blacks as creatures of the jungle, Appalachian whites as hillbillies. Such is the malodorous history of what Jeff Karem calls "the romance of authenticity," as with the editorially coerced amputation of the up-north chapters of Richard Wright's autobiography in order to ensure placement of the Negro life in "proper" southern context.[11]

Yet the two fields interpenetrate, for better as well as for worse. Bond to region (Yankee, Southern, Texan) can plausibly be conceived as a species of ethnicity insofar as both imply a felt particularity of inheritance and cultural solidarity. Similar stereotypes, both positive and negative, attach to both regional and ethnic identification: negatively, parochialism, tribalism, xenophobia, substandard patois; but positively, cultural solidarity, pungent speech, local knowledge denser and deeper than book learning, the sense of bioregional belonging that potentially incentivizes civic participation and practices of environmental sustainability. In relation to dominant cultures, ethnically coded and region-emplaced peoples—and many groups qualify as both—face analogous prospects of colonization, assimilation, extinction. Throughout the rise of industrialization that roughly coincides with the ascendency of the modern novel and crystallization of modern nation-states, forms of regional and ethnic particularity associated whether stigmatically or wishfully with the bygone or atavistic have been seen by turns as inexorably doomed and as surprisingly resilient.

On the one hand, as the editors of an early twenty-first-century symposium of historians on U.S. regionalisms put it, they can be seen as "holdovers, cultural lags waiting for the homogenizing effects of mass media and transportation to erase them."[12] One U.S. literary scholar, extending this line of thinking to ethnicity, characterizes region and race as analogously unstable marginal positions that the dominant national culture of capitalism can be counted upon to absorb again and again.[13] On the other hand, both have repeatedly outlived prophesies of their demise and surely will continue to do so. "Regionalism and localism are every where in the world today like a grass fire, apparently extinguished but alive at the roots," one economic historian writes.[14] The point applies with even greater force to ethnic consciousness. Neither in fact nor controversy are ethnic and regional particularisms likely to go away anytime soon.* Indeed the reverse may prove truer, as seen in the strengthened cultural and political clout of the "Celtic fringe" in contemporary Britain and the regional and ethnic "renaissances" that have powered much of the creative energies in U.S. literature for the past century.

---

* That regional and ethnic designations are akin in being porous, contested, and shifting might tempt one to question this prediction. As to ethnicity in U.S. history, certainly some ethnics have become dramatically less otherized over time, especially such once-thought-unassimilable Euros as Irish, Poles, and Italians, but more recently East Asians, as compared to the dreadful days of Chinese exclusion and Japanese internment only a few generations ago. Conversely, as critic Betsy Erkkila has argued in the case of Jefferson's *Notes on the State of Virginia*, even the work of (some of) the major figures most closely associated with white dominance on closer inspection can be seen as surprisingly invested in interracialism (Betsy Erkkila, *Mixed Bloods and Other Crosses: Rethinking Literature from the Revolution to the Culture Wars* [Philadelphia: University of Pennsylvania Press, 2005], 37–61). "Region" is no less unstable a category. How many U.S. regions are there? Five? Nine? Eleven? Geographers disagree. The South, often considered the most distinctive of all U.S. regions, was scrupulously parsed by its leading mid-twentieth-century cultural geographer, Eugene Odum, as a congeries of eight subregions. (This book, lumpingly and more conventionally, uses "South" to refer to the states south of the Mason-Dixon line and stretching west across the junction of the Ohio and Mississippi rivers from Missouri south to Texas.) Be that as it may, "ethnicity" and "region" remain wired into the U.S. national imaginary to this day notwithstanding disputes about definition and boundaries.

Romances of the divide in what later became the United States date back almost to first contact, the earliest canonical instance being the tale of Pocahontas: her rescue of Captain John Smith followed by her marriage to an Englishman. It's been plausibly claimed that the tropes of Eurosettler imagination of white-red relations stand behind later images of white-black relations, considering for example the captivity narrative tradition as a constituent of slave narrative, the stark Manichean contrasts drawn in early settler literatures between "good" and "bad" Indians, the exoticization of the racial other, and the record of liberal sympathy for Indian suffering in the context of presuming their inevitable disappearance from or subjugation to the dominant white society.[15] But early frontier writing, voluminous and consequential though it is, belongs rather to the prehistory of the GAN than to its story proper. From the ascendancy of the novel in the mid-nineteenth-century United States until the late twentieth, the most crucial divides for the national imaginary have been the color line between white and black and the line of regional division between North and South.

Fifty years from now, this will seem much less self-evident than it did for the first two centuries after U.S. independence. Since the 1950s, the demise of legal segregation, patterns of immigration, southern urbanization, and sunbelt migration from the northern states have eroded traditional regional differences between North and South. The evolving national demographics and diversifying scene of literary production that have made Hispanic Americans the nation's largest minority and have made both American-hemispheric and transpacific writing an increasingly major presence in national letters during the last several decades have started to generate new cartographies of "American" literary history. In 2050 the history of what counts as defining fictions of the divide is certain to look different from the way it does at this moment of the sesquicentennial of the American Civil War, when the political map of blue state–red state division east of the Mississippi still roughly approximates the old North/South division, when the great twentieth-century migration of African Americans northward has only started significantly to reverse itself, and when the spirit of secessionism in the South still survives.

Hence the concentration in Chapters 7–10 on Harriet Beecher Stowe's *Uncle Tom's Cabin* (1852), Mark Twain's *Huckleberry Finn* (1884), William Faulkner's *Absalom, Absalom!* (1936), Toni Morrison's *Beloved* (1987), and a host of constellated texts mostly focused on the same divides, the evolving sense of their relative importance, and the changing assessments of the possibility and the desirability of bridging them. Taken in sequence, these novels and their various companion texts showcase the defining permutations of U.S. "divide" romance from its crystallization to its fissioning, reinvention, and renewal in recent times.

It will immediately become clear that fictional negotiations of regional and ethnic divides almost inevitably get written from one side or another, though with some notable offsetting complications. Stowe wrote as a vehement northern critic of the pathology of the antebellum South's peculiar institution, however much she tried to qualify along the way her indictment of southern white people and culture; and her concerted attempt to portray African Americans sympathetically was compromised by the insular parochialism and lingering prejudices about race that beclouded the thinking even of most well-meaning northern white abolitionists of her day. Faulkner wrote self-consciously as a white southerner, Twain as a semi-deracinated white ex-southerner, both striving for some admixture of disownment from and acknowledgment of the lure of regional memory, but presuming quite different degrees of understanding across the color line. Morrison came to *Beloved* as an African American northerner, casting herself as an outsider to the still-dominant white culture, both North and South, that she must have known would be her primary domestic audience.

Especially when an author is writing from the perspective of strongly normative value commitments, as with Stowe, neutrality is not to be expected even when striven for. Up to a point E. M. Forster tried to give Muslim and Hindu culture a fair shake in *Passage to India* (1924), but his novel remains solidly committed throughout to the view that India— climate, geography, architecture, people—is geographically and culturally a very strange place compared to Europe, and that Indian Moslems are much easier to fathom and deal with than Hindus because they seem more Europeanized. Bengali intellectual Nirad Chaudhuri returned the compliment in his travel narrative *Passage to England* (1959), emphasizing the strangeness of the country's manners, its character, even its atmosphere (the curiously oblique light of the higher latitudes).

Narratives of the divide rarely posit schism, period, and leave matters there. Divides are conjured up in order to become bridges of some kind. So divide narratives typically at least flirt with themes of reciprocity, intimacy, mutual enlightenment even when, as with Forster's Fielding and Aziz, not only cultural misunderstanding but even the very earth seems to drive their horses apart. But "flirtation" does not equate to assurance that durable solidarity is in the offing. The self-exacting novels that stand up as GAN candidates do not force closure of that sort, do not try to ordain a unified national imaginary by fiat, but rather take the form of inquests into the impediments the divides create to satisfying the desire for such.

Partly for this reason, a certain aesthetics of secrecy, or at least covertness, percolates increasingly throughout fictions of the divide, an ethos of confessedly imperfect understanding, arising from various sources: mutual distrust or information withheld, concession of unrecoverable heritages or histories, intuitions ingrained from inhabiting one side of a divide that can't be fully articulated even if you wished, as maybe you don't. Even an author like Stowe whose narrative voice often seems omniscient and confident in passing judgment will sometimes acknowledge implicitly if not confess openly that authoritative mediation of the divides is impossible. "You cant understand it. You would have to be born there"—so Faulkner's Quentin, in *Absalom, Absalom!* rebuffs his Canadian roommate's inexhaustible curiosity as to why southerners endlessly relive the Civil War. "Do you understand it?" the roommate asks. "I dont know" Quentin replies. Then he takes it back, then repeats that he doesn't know (*AA* 189). The insiders themselves may not fathom what they need to know. Even if Stamp Paid, the black community's Mercury in *Beloved,* could actually hear the "thoughts of the women of 124," Sethe and Denver and Beloved, they'd be "recognizable but indecipherable" (*B* 199). That's surely one reason why this particular vein of national fiction, however dramatic its metamorphoses over time, continues to seem inexhaustible. By the terms of its project, it is committed to outreach, but with wildly differing degrees of confidence in the possibility of free unprejudiced reciprocity across the divides. Perhaps even more fundamental an ongoing energizer of this script for U.S. fiction is the uncertainty at the core of the national imaginary itself from the start as to the prospect of fusing its disparate territorial and demographic constituents together without sacrifice to the integrity of some, if not all.

7

Uncle Tom's Cabin *and Its Aftermaths*

The Greatest Book of the Age

—1852 bookseller advertisement for *Uncle Tom's Cabin*

The Most Popular of Stories

—Publisher's advertisement for late nineteenth-century
illustrated edition

G REAT AMERICAN NOVEL CANDIDATES lean toward moral seriousness
more often than not, but Harriet Beecher Stowe's *Uncle Tom's Cabin*
stands alone in its enlistment of art in the service of activism. In that
sense it is the least "novelistic" of all possible GANs. Its particular kind
of didacticism, resting on impassioned appeals to conscience, is itself
risk taking. In presuming that all readers would share its own core values at heart however reluctant they might be to grant it, *Uncle Tom's
Cabin* risks alienating readers to whom those values seem less than self-
evident. In trusting to the irresistible force of sympathetic appeal to
one's uncorrupted inner child, it risks annoying more sophisticated
readers by catering to what cultural critic Lauren Berlant calls "infan-
tile citizenship," the tradition of conceiving the American public as a
virtual child.[1] Even so, no American novel has come close to matching *Uncle Tom's Cabin*'s impact. Melville, Twain, Faulkner, and Morrison have been read worldwide. *Uncle Tom's Cabin* changed the world. Of
what other novel could the same be said?

Its impact was immediate. In old age, Henry James recalled that
Uncle Tom's Cabin seemed "less a book than a state of vision, of feeling
and of consciousness" in which people "walked and talked and laughed
and cried." It galvanized mounting antislavery sentiment in the North
and provoked a barrage of refutations both South and North, including
some thirty anti-*Tom* proslavery novels.[2] Though evidence is scant for

Stowe family legend that Abraham Lincoln greeted Stowe as the little woman who made the great war, the novel surely played a role in catalyzing it. A number of veteran politicians on opposite sides were convinced it did. Chief Justice Roger Taney, who presided over the landmark *Dred Scott* decision (1857) that voided the Missouri Compromise and denied legal standing to African Americans throughout the North, blamed *Uncle Tom's Cabin* for fomenting the "political hate" that ensured the constitutional crisis of 1861.[3] Abroad, *Uncle Tom's Cabin*'s impact was no less sensational than at home. The British edition outsold the American by three to one, and the book was quickly translated, often several times over, across Europe and beyond, into Flemish, Welsh, Slovenian, Wallachian, and Armenian as well as all major languages. Stowe's framing of slavery as *the* burning national issue resonated with foreign as well as domestic dismay at the scandal of slavery persisting in the country that first proclaimed individual liberty as universal human right. Beyond that, *Uncle Tom's Cabin* was seen by readers worldwide as speaking to the plight of the downtrodden in all its forms: industrial workers, Russian serfs, women of the royal Siamese harem, and—as with the first Chinese translation and its theatrical adaptation, at the turn of the twentieth century—the imperial subjugation of non-Western peoples by the great powers, including the United States. Lenin called it his favorite book of childhood—"a charge to last a lifetime."[4]

The first call for "the great American novel," by novelist John W. De Forest in 1868, understandably named *Uncle Tom's Cabin* as the closest approximation yet. This judgment was based not on its abolitionism, however, so much as "the national breadth to the picture," the panoramic reach that combined the geographical scope of a Whitman with the sociological comprehensiveness of a Dickens (who recognized his imprint but judiciously refrained from calling *Uncle Tom's Cabin* a derivative in public).[5] Despite his record as Unionist, antislavery man, and Civil War veteran, De Forest typified postbellum northern white opinion in hoping that because the country had put an end to armed conflict and slavery it was on track to achieving a bona fide unity of vision. Much more than Cooper's frontier romances and Hawthorne's provincial gothic, *Uncle Tom's Cabin* seemed inclusively pan-national.

Actually it was far from that. It was a northern white Christian woman's antislavery polemic. Yet De Forest's judgment also made sense. Not only does the novel squarely confront the burning moral and political dilemma of its day, it takes in more of the fast-expanding republic's territory than any significant precursor, ranging through all major regions of the country east of the Great Plains: Northeast, Midwest, South, Southwestern frontier. Along the way it unpacks the workings of their characteristic institutions: the rival economic orders and ideologies of slavery versus free labor; legal and (Protestant) religious establishments; a wide range of family structures—middle-class nuclear, multigenerational-communitarian, southern-patriarchal—including denial of family privileges to the enslaved; and the unprecedented social mobility of the early industrial era as differently experienced by white and black Americans.

In so doing, *Uncle Tom's Cabin* taps into the richest single vein of New World writing during the colonial and early national prehistory of the novel's emergence as an autonomous genre, travel narrative. This and the deployment of narrative as a theater of moral ideas mark *Uncle Tom's Cabin* a product of the era when literary professionalism was starting to become a live option and national fiction had begun to gain attention abroad, but art was still seen as needing to be justified by some instrumental purpose, meaning moral improvement and/or useful information. Most other antebellum narrative classics—Cooper's Leatherstocking saga, Richard Henry Dana Jr.'s *Two Years Before the Mast*, Frederick Douglass's *Narrative*, Thoreau's *Walden*, Hawthorne's *Scarlet Letter*, Melville's *Moby-Dick*, Harriet Jacobs's *Incidents in the Life of a Slave Girl*—share Stowe's hybrid investment in aesthetic invention cum commitment to documentary elaboration and moral or spiritual inquest.

"The Greatest Book of Its Kind"

The main plot of *Uncle Tom's Cabin* opens and closes in the upper South, on the Shelby family's Kentucky plantation. Here slavery is said to take its mildest form: caring masters, contented slaves. But no sooner is this happy paternalism mentioned than Chapter 1 announces the traumatic disruption to come. Debt-ridden Mr. Shelby reluctantly sells to the repellent trader Haley two favorite slaves, faithful Tom and the young son of Mrs. Shelby's maid Eliza. A melodramatic flight-and-pursuit subplot ensues when Eliza overhears the deal, flees north with little Harry in a desperate scamper across the late-February Ohio River ice floes, reunites with husband George—himself a fugitive from a sadistic master—to escape together to Canada through the kindness of strangers and the good fortune of all three being light-skinned enough to pass for white. Tom is torn from his sorrowing family and taken to New Orleans by riverboat, never to return.

At first he is lucky enough to be bought by the wealthy Augustine St. Clare, whose saintly daughter Eva—an avatar of the "sinless" prepubescent Romantic child—Tom has saved from drowning. His steady integrity wins him trusted retainer status, all the more quickly because the indulgently lackadaisical master and his hypochondriacal self-focused wife run such a slack ménage. Even St. Clare's prim Vermont cousin Ophelia, enlisted as a combination nanny and steward, can't neaten up the place. For a while Tom prospers, despite longing both for home and for freedom. But Eva succumbs to tuberculosis and St. Clare soon dies in a chance mishap before fulfilling his promise to emancipate Tom, a telling case of right-thinking but self-disenabling liberalism. St. Clare is the book's most brilliant and trenchant critic of slavery, but all talk and no action, whereas the no-nonsense Ophelia sees to it that he deeds her ownership of Topsy, who becomes transformed by Eva's kindness from impish rogue to dutiful child. To the consternation of the rest of the household, St. Clare's widow, Marie, "principled against emancipating" (*UTC* 296), sells his slaves at auction, whereupon Tom plunges into the vortex of traditional gothic and late nineteenth-century naturalist fiction like Upton Sinclair's *The Jungle* (1906), which in fact was hailed as "The *Uncle Tom's Cabin* of wage slavery."[6]

Tom is bought by a worst-case master, renegade Vermonter Simon Legree, whose policy is to drive his slaves relentlessly for the largest cotton crop possible. Legree dislikes Tom from the start for his piety, his imperviousness to intimidation, and his refusal to engage in the brutality Legree expects from the overseer he wants Tom to be. Tom almost despairs, but visions of Eva and Christ—the two merge for him—inspire him to resume the role of the informal pastor to fellow slaves that he had been at the Shelbys'. Urged to flee with Cassy and Emmeline, Legree's former and intended future mistresses, Tom stays put. Infuriated by his refusal to disclose their escape plan, Legree has him beaten to death by his two black henchmen. But Tom lingers long enough to convert Sambo and Quimbo, who are conscience-struck by his fortitude and Christian forgiveness, and to say farewell to his would-be rescuer young George Shelby, now the family head. George at least has the consolation of freeing his own slaves upon returning home and helping ensure that his fellow passenger Cassy on the river journey back—none other than Eliza's long-lost mother—eventually rejoins her extended family in Canada, with Emmeline in tow as well as another woman who turns out to be George Harris's long-lost sister.

Unlike Hawthorne and Melville, Stowe never thought of herself as a romancer or novelist by vocation while writing *Uncle Tom's Cabin,* even though it made her one. Those rubrics were still too laden with the taint of frivolity for this daughter of a family of post-Puritan ministers, or for a large fraction of her primary target audience of believing Protestant Christians. The promotional catchphrases used by *Uncle Tom's Cabin*'s first publisher were simply "the greatest book of its kind" or "the greatest of all American tales."[7] This proved a very smart move. As critic Barbara Hochman points out, because it "straddled the divide that separated morally and spiritually serious works of literature from works that were frowned upon as foolish," *Uncle Tom's Cabin* was read by many readers who otherwise spurned the suspect genre.[8] Stowe's decision to issue *A Key to "Uncle Tom's Cabin"* aimed at defending its factual accuracy was in keeping with the strategy of framing her book as something other and better than a conventional novel. She confronts charges of misrepresentation head on by agreeing at the outset that the book should be "sifted, tried, and tested, as a reality" and defending it as such with an arsenal of empirical evidence.[9] Factual plausibility was the premodern American novelist's other main recourse, besides moral uplift, for persuading audiences of fiction's intrinsic worth. Melville had taken a similar tack in protesting the authenticity of his first book, *Typee,* a romanticized account of his brief captivity in Polynesia after jumping ship. The slave narratives that formed a key part of Stowe's data base took far greater pains to stress that their own stories of captivity, however improbable-seeming, were no fictions.

Uncle Tom's travelogue aspect, as literary historian Trish Loughran observes, made for a "spatial primer" reminiscent of the *Primary Geography for Children* Stowe once wrote for her sister Catherine's textbook series. As such it registers both the nation's marked advance toward consolidation (in transport, publishing, economic interdependence) from its "disintegrated origin" as an assemblage of colonial enclaves, and the intensified divisiveness that followed from the very ability to engage a "nationally dispersed reading constituency from a centralized location," by underscoring the fearful prospect of a bad nationalism pressing northward via the new, stiffer Fugitive Slave Law, outrage against which had transformed Stowe from journeyman cobbler of short sketches into celebrity author.[10] This strikes at the first of the two self-divisions that have most perplexed, troubled, outraged the novel's readers ever since—around region and around race.

As to region, *Uncle Tom's Cabin*'s agenda is both inclusively "national" by design and schismatically provincial in thrust. Toward the South, it is both irenic and judgmental. There's no reason to doubt Stowe's claim of trying to bend over backward to avoid giving offense to white southerners. She makes her arch villain a New Englander. She makes her most brainy and articulate white character a slaveholder. She decries northern complicity in abetting slavery. She dramatizes the hypocrisy of northern abolitionists' aversion to personal contact with blacks, as when Ophelia at first recoils from Topsy as if she were a noxious insect. She portrays southern whites as mostly kind and decent. She minimizes the bloody scenes of whipping and other torture standard in such antislavery tracts as Theodore Dwight Weld's *American Slavery as It Is* (1839), later denouncing a British reprint that put a whipping scene on the cover. Yet slavery is unambiguously branded a social evil. More than that, it is a sin—a sin furthermore, as critic Ann Douglas observes, analogous "to original sin, as the Calvinists defined it . . . inherited from and transmitted by the founding fathers," through the Constitution's strategic silence.[11] In an era when Christian theology was far more influential than now among the nation's intelligentsia both North and South, *Uncle Tom's Cabin* indicts slavery as unchristian. The proslavery argument from Scripture, more formidable then than one might now suppose, gets dismissed out of hand. A Christian slaveholder is an existential possibility but a moral self-contradiction. Slavery corrupts even the most admirable masters. It tears apart black families. No slave dares feel secure. No black character finds lasting happiness while enslaved. Nor does the novel permit the victim to be blamed. No slaves in this book are malign or imbruted except by the system that malforms them. However sympathetically *Uncle Tom's Cabin* portrays southerners, its bottom line is that the South's "peculiar institution" makes it a sick society—or, more precisely, insane. Stowe's exposé foreshadows modern autopsies of Third Reich sociopathology, from Erich Fromm's *Escape from Freedom* to Daniel Goldhagen's *Hitler's Willing Executioners*. And it radiates an even greater fear of contagion from the long arm of slavery reaching throughout the North.

One telltale way *Uncle Tom's Cabin* by turns euphemizes and indicts the South is to orientialize and/or gothicize it—a staple of travel writing since Herodotus. The deeper south we go, the stranger it gets.[12] The domestic life of the white Shelbys of Kentucky doesn't greatly differ from that of their Ohio counterparts, except of course for slaveholding. The St. Clare manse feels far more exotic, seductively magnificent and pleasing to the senses, but the household arrangements chaotic— "shiftless," in Ophelia's favorite epithet. The moral rot gets completely exposed with its collapse after St. Clare's death and the abrupt switch of scenes to the fearsome slave warehouse, now revealed as the city's defining economic institution, where Tom and his companions in misery get auctioned off like animals. Legree's once-elegant plantation house in a lonely upriver outback has gone to rack and ruin. It's hell on earth not only for his slaves but for him as well, especially after Cassy starts haunting his attic and his conscience as part of her escape plot, in a reprise of the superseded Bertha Rochester in Charlotte Brontë's *Jane Eyre* and a prequel to Linda Brent's long self-confinement in Harriet Jacobs's *Incidents in the Life of a Slave Girl* (1861), the last of the great antebellum slave narratives. It comes as no surprise, then, to find southerners still fuming about the novel a century later, as when Margaret Mitchell expressed her great satisfaction to—irony of ironies—a German fan right before World War II that *Gone with the Wind* was "helping refute the impression of the South which people abroad gained from Mrs. S's book."[13]

Today Stowe's regional distortions, such as they were, seem more pardonable than they once did. Not so her treatment of race. Nineteenth-century African American as well as liberal northern responses to *Uncle Tom's Cabin* were laudatory by contrast to white southern reviewers' fury at Stowe's critique of the South. Frederick Douglass promoted the book in his *Paper*. Paul Laurence Dunbar and Frances Harper wrote two of the many poetic tributes by African American writers. Throughout the nineteenth century, ex-fugitives tied themselves to Stowe's star by claiming, whether from pride or pragmatism, to be the real Uncle Tom or the real George Harris. At the 1893 Columbian Exposition Douglass, then in his mid-seventies, volunteered to pose as a photographic model of Uncle Tom. Younger African American intellectuals who had never known slavery at first hand sometimes turned to *Uncle Tom's Cabin* as a historical sourcebook; Mary Church Terrell wrote a pamphlet *Appreciation* of its account of slavery's abuses (1911). From a present-day perspective, though, those early accolades seem remarkably forbearing. Surely, one suspects, they must have been written less from unalloyed enthusiasm than from pragmatic recognition that the enemy of my enemy is my friend, considering the novel's dependence on viewing African Americans through the stereotypical lens of nineteenth century "romantic racialism":[14] its essentializing of Africans as inherently childlike, affectionate, emotional, pious, cheerful. George Harris's mechanical aptitude, self-discipline, purposefulness, and audacity get ascribed to his admixture of Anglo-Saxon blood. Contemporary critics point out that *Uncle Tom's Cabin* and blackface minstrelsy were "conjoined cultural twins" twice over,[15] through the cultural context upon which Stowe drew and the novel's subsequent absorption by the popular media (plays, minstrel shows, films, cartoons, even ads for commodities like "Uncle Tom" or "Topsy" tobacco). The novel itself includes comic Jim Crow performances by two black children, Eliza's son Harry at Mr. Shelby's command for the amusement of the slave trader, and later on (more than once) by the irrepressible Topsy.

Uncle Tom's Cabin's multiple popularizations further threatened to blunt its activist thrust, neutering its hero, reducing its saga to comic hijinks, pious drivel, and nostalgic local colorism indistinguishable from the plantation romance it tried to skewer. Stowe's image of Tom as a forthright man in his prime was displaced by theatrical, artistic, and eventually cinematic images of an aged Uncle Remus type. Postbellum publishers abetted this reframing of the novel, as did the author herself to some extent. A blurb for an 1877 reprint tellingly characterized her as "a writer of romances . . . so humorous, so exceedingly ingenious in depicting the ludicrous side of things, that they rank with the most charming stories in English literature." A deluxe edition of the early 1890s, one of many issued just before expiration of copyright that made *Uncle Tom's Cabin* a fin de siècle as well as antebellum best seller, recruited as illustrator Edward Windsor Kemble, whose commissions for *Huckleberry Finn* and the fiction of Joel Chandler Harris and Thomas Nelson Page had established him as the premier genius "for depicting the Southern negro in the old slave days."[16] Whereas earlier editions featured illustrations of black and white characters interacting, often around scenes of reading that dramatized the importance attached to literacy both by slaves themselves and by their antislavery advocates, late-century illustrators tended to depict white and black as separate from one another, with slaves for the most part as uncouth field hands. Such slanted recastings as much as the novel itself stand behind such astringent latter-day pronouncements by scholars of Afro-Atlantic culture as: "*Uncle Tom's Cabin* is best approached as a . . . culture in which the bacteria of nineteenth-century racism flourished"; and that it helped establish "a range of character types that served to bind and restrict black authors for decades."[17]

To what extent should the book itself be held accountable, rather than the cultural miasma upon which it could not have avoided drawing even if it wanted to, and which threatened to engulf it thereafter? To distance the original artifact from its debased adaptations, as I've just been doing, is one standard line of defense. Edmund Wilson set the tone for this in a groundbreaking survey of Civil War writing that anticipated the late twentieth-century Stowe revival, when he stressed how "startling" he had found the "eruptive force" of the original text after coming to it via blackface travesties that had reduced it to "half a minstrel show and half a circus."[18] Yet attempted surgical separation of text from context isn't any more persuasive than conflation of the novel with its redactions. A more plausible glass-half-full approach to understanding literature from this—or any other—bygone era must balance due recognition of breakthrough accomplishments against the limits of their horizons of perception. Perhaps *Uncle Tom's Cabin*'s accomplishment is best summed up as a brave if flawed attempt to think beyond one's sociohistorical limits according to two opposing logics I'll unpack momentarily. It's a northerner's attempt to think strenuously across a hardening regional divide. It's a white person's attempt to comprehend nonwhites sympathetically at a moment when even most white northerners considered them less than fully human, and as such a groundbreaking work of moral extensionism.[19] It's a woman's attempt in an age of increasing separation of home place from workplace to comprehend the male world of affairs. It's a middle-class author's attempt to comprehend the extremes at both ends of the social ladder. It's an evangelical Protestant believer's attempt to speak also to people of other faiths including even agnostics and atheists. For degree of difficulty attempted, the novel deserves at least a 9.5 out of 10, even if for execution less.

Stowe is by turns an invoker of stereotypical binaries (men are like this, women are like that; whites are like this, blacks like that) and a collapser of them when they threaten to bind her. The book's most revelatory moments come when these two logics get pitted against each other.

All readers quickly notice *Uncle Tom's Cabin*'s curious economy of names, especially duplications across the color line. Senator and Mrs. Bird give their dear dead son Henry's clothes to Eliza's son Harry. George Harris, likened at one point to a Hungarian freedom fighter, has the same name as the Shelby heir who strikes down Legree over Tom's dead body and returns home to become "the liberator." Mrs. Shelby and George Harris's sister are both named Emily. Such duplications quietly reinforce more assertively universalizing moves, such as the narrator's exhortation: "If it were *your* Harry, mother, or your Willie, that were going to be torn from you by a brutal trader . . . how fast could *you* walk?" (*UTC* 46). This device of "reflective naming," one critic argues, is "a rhetoric of equality," designed to make us "see whites and blacks as equal."[20] Yet at other times naming seems to drive a wedge between the races, as in Cassy, Chloe, Cudjoe, and Topsy versus Arthur, Augustine, Evangeline, Ophelia. Can one imagine such monikers transposed to the other side?

Yes one can. The most telling example occurs during a sequence shortly after Tom's arrival at the St. Clares' that begins by noting his innocent pleasure in the gorgeousness of this "Aladdin's palace" of an establishment. At first sight, the novel seems to get swept up by the romantic racialism Stowe had imbibed from such sources as Alexander Kinmont's *Twelve Lectures on the Natural History of Man* (1839), which argued that blacks make better Christians than whites because they are more submissive, that the essentially childlike nature of Africans predestines Africa to become the seat of the first truly Christian race.[21] The narrator pauses to sketch Tom's portrait. Decked out in his new livery, "his well-brushed broadcloth suit, smooth beaver, glossy boots, faultless wristbands and collar," Tom "looked respectable enough to be a Bishop of Carthage, as men of his color were, in other ages" (*UTC* 163). This sounds jocose, but it's a bombshell in disguise. To whom does it refer? To several figures, the plural suggests, but among them surely

St. Augustine, widely believed by African American writers then and now, and by Stowe herself, to have been nonwhite.* If you're looking for a true patriarch, hints the text, here's your man. Here is the true Augustine, not the papier-mâché Augustine who happens to be the legal master. Stowe could hardly have enlisted a more prestigious image of spiritual authority from among the early church fathers than "that great poet of theology," as *The Minister's Wooing* (1859) calls him.[22] Catch the allusion, and it disrupts the ostensibly dominant symbolism of naming the St. Clare brothers after opposite giants of the "Dark Ages": Augustine (the spiritual hero) and Alfred (the kingly hero). That in turn snaps into place a skein of other metaphorizations of Tom starting with the first glimpse of him in his cabin at the Shelby place as "a sort of patriarch in religious matters" (*UTC* 27). It's one of those incipiently epiphanic passages that seem to override any countersuggestions about black inferiority implied by Tom's phenomenal forbearance and the fantasy of "poor Africa" humbly and belatedly emerging from "the furnace of affliction" to its rightful place as "the highest and noblest in that kingdom which [God] will set up" (164).

If you catch the allusion. Few do, and no wonder. No less provocative than the hint that the true Augustine was/is a man of color is its relegation to a cursory aside. Did Stowe wish to avoid offending white readers? Did she lack the courage to believe that a barely literate slave could bear comparison to the foremost early Christian patriarch?

Probably yes and no. *Uncle Tom's Cabin* was written within and against what antislavery advocates saw as an increasing conspiracy by the mainstream white opinion, North as well as South, not to rock the

---

* Augustine (354–430) was actually bishop of Hippo, farther west on the African coast, although his formative years were spent in Carthage. Stowe would have known both this and that the famous bishop of Carthage was the martyr Cyprian (200–258), cited as an authority in her *Key* (456). Nineteenth-century African American intellectuals like Frederick Douglass, William Wells Brown, and Alexander Crummell were convinced that Augustine, Cyprian, and other African church fathers were black (William Wells Brown, *The Black Man* [Boston: Redpath, 1863], 63; Frederick Douglass, *Selected Speeches and Writings*, ed. Philip S. Foner and Yuval Taylor [Chicago: Lawrence Hill, 1999], 99–100; Alexander Crummell, *The Future of Africa* [New York: Scribner, 1862], 311–312), as were nineteenth-century black American Catholics generally (Cyprian Davis, *History of Black Catholics in the United States* [New York: Crossroad, 1990], 12). So were a number of liberal and evangelical white Christians of the era, including Stowe. Her later encomium to Sojourner Truth compared her eloquence to that of "the African Saint Augustine or Tertullian" (Harriet Beecher Stowe, "Sojourner Truth: The Libyan Sibyl," *Atlantic Monthly* 11 [April 1863]: 480).

boat.[23] Against this, Stowe adopted a dual strategy of conciliation and pushback. The passage in question shows that the author possessed more ammunition than she chose to use, that she picked her battles carefully. She seems to have anticipated that even receptive readers would think she had tried to prove too much as it was in "making out the African race to be a great race," as Charles Dickens wrote in an otherwise appreciative tribute that Stowe tucked into her preface to the 1879 reprint edition.[24] But to dwell on Tom's likeness to the historical Augustine would in any case have run counter to the novel's prevailing skepticism toward book learning and officially sanctioned authority as encumbrances to facing the plain truth of things. The affinity of spirit that develops between St. Clare and Tom after Eva's death, with master turning to slave for guidance but unable to take the leap of faith, establishes Tom as superior to any Augustine, not the hero as Christian thinker but as the reenactment of Christ. That was the crucial point of Stowe's romantic-racialist idealization of Africanity: not that some church fathers were black, but that Africans make better Christians than Euros do. Here the pivotal cross-color affinity is of course between Tom and Eva. Both their deaths are crucifixions, literally from illness and beating but symbolically—and more substantively—voluntary sacrifices designed, by themselves and their author, to move and transform a fallen world.

This aspect of *Uncle Tom's Cabin* has not worn well. Its supernaturalism, its idealization of Eva and Tom and their rapport, its reliance on the "sentimental power" of readerly identification with sympathetic, suffering victims seem repellently anachronistic to many modern readers, especially "critical" readers trained to value irony over affect. Trusting to the affective power of her faithful "pictures" to induce moral awakening, Stowe did not foresee how they might be dismissed as ideological artifacts or, worse, read pornographically as a "carnal fantasy of erotic desire." Conceiving the Eva-Tom intimacy as a union of kindred believing souls, Stowe never anticipated that Eva's "'I want him'" might be taken as obliquely channeling white female desire for the black male body.[25] Conceiving Tom's conduct on Legree's plantation as "a state of insurrection for conscience's sake," she could not have anticipated that his nonresistance might provoke James Baldwin to charge that he has been "robbed of his humanity and divested of his sex," as "the price for that darkness with which he has been branded."[26] Hoping that the deaths and apotheoses of Eva and Tom would impress her Christian readership as irresistibly charismatic, Stowe could not have anticipated that they might be dismissed as mawkishly fluorescent.

On the other hand, if *Uncle Tom's Cabin* is judged by its own avowed objective, to dramatize the moral claims of African Americans by the criteria that most mattered to her—family, affection, duty, integrity, piety—it's hard to imagine a more powerful performance, considering the pressures both external and internal that any author faced in those days when taking up so radioactive a subject. At her best, Stowe manages to revivify the most shopworn of clichés. A case in point is the keepsake that becomes a totem object conjoining recipient and giver: portraits, letters, rings, coins, autographs, shells, bouquets. In *Uncle Tom's Cabin*, the keepsake par excellence is the locket of hair, in the first instance the curls Eva has snipped off and distributed to the household to remember her by: "'when you look at it, think that I loved you and am gone to heaven, and that I want to see you all there'" (*UTC* 264). A predictable tear fest ensues, but the afterlife of the locket proves wonderfully luminous and intricate. On the Legree plantation, Tom is stripped of his talisman by Sambo and Quimbo, who misrecognize it as "'a witch thing . . . something that niggers gets from witches.'" Legree recoils in horror, for the lock reminds him of the mother he had brutally spurned, who blessed him on her deathbed nonetheless, sending him "a lock of long, curling hair." Legree burned it, just as he now orders Tom's to be thrown in the fire, but the "necromancy of evil" that "turns things sweetest and holiest to phantoms of horror and affright" returns with double force so that from here on he feels bewitched—aka damned (338–339). So in Stowe's fictional world, critic Lynn Wardley sums up, "blacks and whites are bound equally by the spell of stories or charms that conjure a spectral presence or compel an involuntary response." Sentimental and Afrocentric ritual practice interpenetrate; "precious memento, sacred relic, and African fetish may be indistinguishable."[27] Well, not quite "indistinguishable." To equate the white witchery of Christian love with voodoo, the novel makes clear, is superstition. But sensitivity to the spiritual aura of material objects is a ground of affinity between black and white that sometimes works unambiguously in favor of the former, as with St. Clare's defensive opposition to Eva's deathbed haircut ("'Eva's curls are my pride,'" *UTC* 262) versus the slaves' gratitude for her gift lockets.

The intertwinement of Eva and Tom as intimates in life and exemplary spiritual kindred in death is not of course *Uncle Tom's Cabin*'s sole epicenter. Its significance can't be understood without reckoning how it is offset by the subplot that centers on Eliza and George, the "secondary hero" as Robert Stepto calls him.[28] The downside of Stowe's audacious "first" of making a black man the first modern flesh-and-blood Christ figure in the history of the novel was that it threatened to blunt the reform agenda's secular thrust. Uncle Tom is a devoted family man who, however, forsakes his family and ensures its permanent breakup when he opts for missionary work rather than the chance to escape. Is the text at odds with itself, then? Hardly. Tom is the voluntary scapegoat who draws the book's violence upon himself so others can be saved, and as such is set forth not as model for emulation so much as proof that under slavery the just are always crucified. He himself urges first Eliza and then Cassy not to imitate him but to follow "natur." He blesses their disobedience. The double plot dramatizes complementary but discrepant paths: the martyr's way (conferring freedom and equality through heavenly salvation) and the drive for freedom and emancipation in the here and now. Neither means to undercut the other but to fuse in one configuration. The Eliza/George subplot, with its Cassy/Emmeline sidebar, not only reaffirms mainstream sentimental values by dramatizing that the preservation of the family is as sacred a value and as strong a motivational force for African Americans as for middle-class whites, but also throws its moral authority on the side of (selective) lawbreaking, violent resistance (if only in a pinch), even, albeit in muffled form, miscegenation (Emily Harris de Thoux's apparently happy marriage to a French Creole).

To be sure, Stowe was no John Brown. She was not even Lydia Maria Child, who almost alone among prominent mid-nineteenth-century white women activists contended for miscegenation as remedy for racism, first white-red, then white-black. Especially irksome, to African American readers then and to most critics today, is the novel's decision to end its subplot by packing George, Eliza, and even Topsy off to Africa as missionaries to Liberia. Here, as critic Lori Merish delicately puts it, Stowe "fails to imagine African Americans as full participant citizens in an American democracy."[29] George Harris's grand design to Christianize Africa looks suspiciously imperialistic to boot, veering Stowe's antislavery critique in the direction of what Amy Kaplan trenchantly calls "manifest domesticity,"[30] such that the denouement of *Uncle Tom's Cabin* begins to montage with the likes of *Northwood* and *Liberia* by Stowe's literary acquaintance Sarah Josepha Hale, on whom more below. Stung by the complaints of Frederick Douglass among others ("madame, we are *here*, and here we are likely to remain"),[31] Stowe expressed regret at this denouement but she let the text stand.

Less often noted, though, is that *Uncle Tom's Cabin* actually has two discrepant endings. The other is its very last chapter ("Concluding Thoughts"), which anticipates *A Key to "Uncle Tom's Cabin"* by switching from narrative to exhortation (to the "men and women of America") and insisting on the truth-to-life of her account. Although this chapter also nods approvingly to the idea of an ultimate Liberian solution, it stresses as a precondition the imperativeness of according ex-slaves open-hearted welcome and education in the northern states; and it goes on to praise the success stories of those among them who had achieved "comparative wealth and social position, in the face of every disadvantage and discouragement," including some who had "risen to highly respectable stations in society"—naming Douglass, J. W. C. Pennington, and Samuel Ringgold Ward (*UTC* 407). This culminating touch recognizes the fact and implies the desirability of a biracial nation; and so too, more emphatically, does the final chapter of *A Key*, which reiterates this same passage, embraces the policy of "some" northern states to "accord to the coloured freeman full political equality and privileges," and omits any mention of African return.[32]

Self-Revision: Stowe's Dred

The discrepancies between the closing chapters of *Uncle Tom's Cabin* and *A Key* demonstrate that Stowe continued to wrestle with the core issues in light of further thoughts and changing circumstances. As sectional animosity intensified, she seems to have recognized the inadequacy of either charismatic martyrdom or thrilling flight as sufficient to address the national curse. "How the blood & insults of [Senator Charles] Sumner and the sack of Lawrence [Kansas] burn within us I hope to make a voice to say," she wrote one British correspondent.[33] Her much more militant next novel, *Dred: A Tale of the Dismal Swamp* (1856), bears this out. Far more than *Uncle Tom's Cabin*, *Dred* is imbued with righteous wrath. It pushes into territory *Uncle Tom* had relegated to shuddering side glimpses. It conjures up a far more imposing title figure—a maroon chief of titanic strength, formidable intelligence, and irresistible eloquence who can bring a whole community (white as well as black) to its knees as an unseen voice prophesying divine judgment from the treetops at the height of a revival meeting. As a Mandingo shaman's grandson gifted with second sight, as Denmark Vesey's lost son and spiritual kin to Nat Turner, Dred is a southern white's nightmare embodiment of black insurgency. Conversely, the novel's model instance of a white southerner's gradual emancipation program—treat slaves respectfully, instill literacy and efficient work habits—gets wiped off the map when the arch villain incites mob violence against the genteel reformers. Their retreat to Canada spells the demise of southern liberalism à la George Shelby Jr.

Dred also delivers a more searching anatomy of judicial and religious establishments' complicity in maintaining slavery against internal dissent and the triumph of lust and greed over benevolent generosity. The scandal of forced miscegenation is foregrounded by the novel's leading planter family, the Gordons. Its dissolute but wily and vengeful scion Tom is even more toxic than Simon Legree for being within the family's fold. Tom Gordon's even more intelligent and far more admirable quadroon elder brother Harry is driven to greater extremes than George Harris. After Tom tries to steal Harry's wife and does re-enslave and dispossess his legally emancipated half-sister, Harry flees to join Dred. Although it oversimplifies the complex balancing of values, characters, and incidents to read this novel as flatly disowning "sentimentalism disconnected from specific political activism,"[34] *Dred*'s proliferation of heat-of-the-moment conversions giving way to apathy or recidivism is indeed a far cry from *Uncle Tom's Cabin*'s highlighting of Senator Bird's about-face from his encounter with Eliza and the conversions of Sambo and Quimbo. *Dred* makes clear that Clayton the idealistic reformer is nobler than his chum Russel, a genial, venial chameleon angling for a political career—but also that Russel is dead right in insisting, "your plans for gradual emancipation . . . are utterly hopeless" because the South is obdurate and "the mouth of the north is stuffed with cotton."[35]

Russel's realism is obviously calculated to enrage the reader against the restraints of "realism" as such. This is perhaps the most crucial difference between the two novels. Both alternate between sociological realism and visionary melodrama, but *Dred* is more intensely self-divided. It is both more cognizant of the practical obstacles to social change and more insistent on thrusting forward countermodels that seem strangely aberrant if not impossible for the South of the mid-1850s: a local minister who is a vehemently outspoken abolitionist, a filial son of a pillar of the judiciary who knowingly breaks the law against teaching slaves to read, and above all Dred, who is even more a "moral miracle" than Tom, without such probabilistic grounding as Tom's history as Shelby's longtime trusty retainer. Whereas Tom's language and manners remain tied to Stowe's conception of how an earnest untutored slave would behave and talk, Dred speaks in a pastiche of the Hebrew prophets and erupts onto the scene at crucial moments like a deus ex machina—"part Spartacus and part Hawkeye."[36] These improbabilities seem less a problem of control than a design to pit "realistic" and "utopian" elements against each other (even) more starkly than in *Uncle Tom's Cabin.*

Dred's "anti-sentimental" cast has found more favor with contemporary readers than in Stowe's own day,[37] some even arguing for its superiority to *Uncle Tom's Cabin.* But it makes sense that *Uncle Tom's Cabin,* not *Dred,* became the book read round the world, and that even today it continues to be *Uncle Tom* that gets proclaimed "the great American novel," as on the cover of the 2006 *Annotated Uncle Tom's Cabin.* That earnest concern generally appeals to a wider readership than wrathful disgust is surely part of the explanation why. Beyond that, *Dred*'s many semi-reprises of its predecessor's dramatis personae rarely succeed so well as their prototypes. George Harris's counterpart Harry is torn by self-division and largely eclipsed. His wife, Lisette, is a superficial version of Eliza consigned to a bit part. Eva's adolescent quasi-analogue Nina Gordon remains so long a frivolous belle that her transfiguration into serious-minded plantation head seems unconvincing; and her abrupt offstage death as nurse-in-chief during a cholera epidemic seems a perfunctory happenstance martyrdom. Nina's wobbliness, in turn, compromises her lover, Clayton, whose moral superiority to St. Clare as the superintelligent slaveholding liberal who actually acts on his principles gets further neutralized by impracticality and quixoticism. Among the many secondary black characters, none have Topsy's vitality. Stowe does endow *Dred*'s equivalent to the black matriarch, the

Gordons' longtime retainer, Milly, with a complex and striking back-story of outrage at her owner for selling her children, but that only makes her postconversion containment of her smoldering resentment seem more forced. Rather the same holds also for Dred: the novel hobbles its seeming resolve to make him more a black messiah than an Uncle Tom by having him prophesy throughout that the time for insurgency is not yet. It was not wholly a post-Reconstruction betrayal for the frontispiece illustration in the *Dred* volume of Stowe's 1896 collected works to picture a Tom-like figure praying piously in the swamp. *Dred's* two clearest advances over *Uncle Tom's Cabin* in character refiguration are its domestication of the Legree figure as Gordon family monster and local agitator, and its infinitely more sophisticated handling of its exemplary man of law: Clayton's father as against *Uncle Tom's* Senator Bird. Mindful though he is that existing statute protects bad masters, Judge Clayton flintily invokes precedent to reverse the verdict his son's eloquence has won in a lower court. Otherwise, despite its intensified sense of urgency and shrewder analytic penetration at a number of points, *Dred* seems destined for less success as an act of fictional outreach.

Perhaps some such realization that she was not likely to be able to repeat her first success contributed to Stowe's decision, even before the Civil War, to shift away from slavery and back toward the New England regionalism that had been her first fictional subject and was to become her last. For this, she has been periodically chastised, with some justice, as a retreatist, starting as early as De Forest: "Stricken with timidity, the author shrank into her native shell of New England."[38] From *The Minister's Wooing* to her last novel, *Poganuc People* (1876), the primary place-time of Stowe's imagination was indeed the early national New England past. After the first of these later novels, the issue of slavery fades from view. But the charge underestimates both Stowe's importance as a pioneer of American regional realism and the significance of the regional within the national for *Uncle Tom's Cabin* itself, given over as it is to parsing nationness through the prisms of regional consciousness, difference, and collision. *Uncle Tom's Cabin's* innovativeness and cogency seem all the greater when set next to previous North-South romances of which it was a deviant offshoot and the later novels that it helped engender.

North-South Divide Romances before and against Stowe

Uncle Tom's Cabin became the first enduringly prominent of a long series of novels, tales, and narrative poems from the early nineteenth century to the late twentieth that negotiate the North-South divide. The genre dates from the 1820s, soon after the Missouri Compromise had ushered in the antebellum era by formalizing slavery's northern boundary west of the Mississippi and initiating the practice of admitting equal numbers of new free and slave states, and as the final end of slavery in the North coincided with intensified repression of antislavery sentiment in the South. The first fictions of the divide adapted patterns previously used both to contrast and to bind together British culture regions by Walter Scott (Scotland/England) and Maria Edgeworth (Ireland/ England).

The earliest notable U.S. example is *Redwood* (1824) by Catharine Maria Sedgwick, the nation's leading woman novelist before 1850, which turns on the regeneration of a Virginia gentleman and his flighty daughter when they become reunited with the previously unknown saintly elder daughter of Mr. Redwood's long-dead first wife, whom they meet by happenstance amid a household of improbably virtuous Vermont Yankees with whom they stay for an extended period when the father is injured in a carriage accident. Sarah Josepha Hale, later to become one of the nation's most influential women of letters as editor of *Godey's Lady's Book,* built her first novel, *Northwood* (1827), on a more elaborate cross-sectional comparison, following the life of young Sidney Romilly as he is adopted in boyhood by a childless uncle and aunt and taken from his New Hampshire home to South Carolina, thence to return as a young man in order to become morally solidified, intellectually awakened, and properly married to a Yankee girl, after which the couple return south, where Sidney becomes a truly enlightened planter.

Each book is unabashedly *A Tale of New-England* (Hale's subtitle) that offers up "typical" New England village life as moral norm, as corrective both to southern indiscipline and to British hauteur, complete with Currier-and-Ives-style cameos of such social rituals as Hale's long Thanksgiving scene—a first for U.S. literary history that foreshadows her long lobbying effort with a succession of presidents from the 1840s on to get Thanksgiving recognized as a national holiday. Each novel unfolds a pro-union storyline on Yankee terms whereby the improvidence of southern parenting is atoned through an ideal marriage involving a lineal or adopted child of the South purified by Yankee influence.

Northwood is especially germane here for its second life as an anti-*Tom* novel. Hale published a revised version in 1852 with a new subtitle, *Life North and South*, adding a long conclusion on Sidney's plans, together with his Yankee bride Anne, to educate his slaves for eventual freedom—in Liberia—guided by the journal of his late father, a New Hampshire squire whose middle-ground views from the 1827 edition are now extended more pointedly. Yes, slavery is "no doubt a great evil," Mr. Romilly writes, but an evil for which Britain and not the South is responsible. "Tearing up of the whole system" at this point would be worse, as imperiling to the union; and at all events both the Bible and the Constitution would "regulate" slavery, not abolish it. To all this and more the 1852 *Northwood* affixes the authorial seal of approval in a preface deploring that abolitionists "forget the *master* is their brother, as well as the *servant*" and a peroration announcing that "the mission of American slavery is to Christianize Africa."[39]

In negotiating the differences North and South, *Redwood* and *Northwood* give full recognition of "the lurking fear" that Jennifer Rae Greeson traces back to early republican writing "that a Plantation South rife with tropical deviance could contaminate or overcome U.S. nationality."[40] Not so *The Planter's Northern Bride* (1854), by transplanted northerner Caroline Lee Hentz, Stowe's onetime friend during their years in Cincinnati. This novel administers a much more emphatically pro-southern retort to *Uncle Tom's Cabin* in the form of an intersectional marriage plot in which the noble South Carolinian Russel Moreland, divorcé though he is, manages on a visit North to win both the affections of Eulalia, the angel daughter of the leading local abolitionist, and the father's reluctant consent to boot. Before their marriage, the bride's saintly, politically middle-of-the-road minister prophesies, "Providence has a mission for you to perform," to "be a golden link of union between the divided interests of humanity."[41] That is precisely what happens—not that she ever has much influence on her husband's ideas, although he worships the ground she walks on. Rather her gradual conversion to his benign patriarchy becomes crucial to the novel's legitimation of it. *The Planter's Northern Bride* shrewdly inverts a number of key Stovian devices in addition to the tropes of enlightenment and conversion. It casts Moreland as a self-styled "missionary" to the North, flanked by an outspokenly loyal slave who underscores the novel's many contrasts between the plight of so-called free labor with the happy plantation life to which he incessantly longs to return. It reprises the device of the New England renegade as arch villain in the form of a sleazy abolitionist who betrays Moreland's hospitality by inciting rebellion among his slaves. It reinvents the Tom-Eva, Ophelia-Topsy relations via Moreland's "sprite"-like daughter Effie, a "tricksy, wayward fascinating little creature" whom the gentle Eula (shades of Poe's "Eulalie"?) succeeds in completely winning over.[42] Shrewdest of all is Hentz's deployment of the divorced first wife to give an appearance of evenhanded judgment by partway acquiescing to the standard Yankee critique of southern male impetuousness—southerners were proverbially violence-prone then and through most of the twentieth century—and by granting Eula a missionary role as palliater of Moreland's smoldering resentment against his ex and his coldness toward Effie, whom he has seen as her effigy.[43]

But this same resourcefulness, which helped make *The Planter's Northern Bride* the best selling of all anti–*Uncle Tom* novels, goes to show the importance and the innovativeness of Stowe's deformation of the conventional marriage plot device in terms of which Hentz, Hale, and Sedgwick contain and resolve their romances of the North-South divide. Not that *Uncle Tom's Cabin* devalues marriage by any means. On the contrary, heterosexual union as moral norm and social glue looms much larger in *Uncle Tom's Cabin* than, say, *Redwood*, which shows a guarded fascination with the allure of Shaker communitarian celibacy and great sympathy for freely chosen singleness as an honorable alternative, a point of more explicit advocacy for Sedgwick—herself a spinster—in some of her later work. Henry Louis Gates Jr. and Hollis Robbins rightly stress that *Uncle Tom's Cabin* is "preoccupied with marriages" throughout: "broken-up marriages, failed marriages, fatalistic and tired marriages, bittersweet, evergreen, surprisingly emotional marriages; hasty, postponed, 'if-only' marriages; in name-only, bitter, clinging, and doomed marriages."[44] This is mostly a catalog of disasters, however, demonstrating how slavery destroys family life for masters as well as slaves.

In *Uncle Tom's Cabin*'s long central section, the backstories of two failed North-South romances across two generations of the St. Clare family emerge as crucial to *Uncle Tom's Cabin*'s southern strategy. The first are Augustine's parents. His father, the book's earliest case of New England migration southward, a man of ramrod "iron will" like the brother who stayed behind, is offered as proof that post-Puritan and planter patriarchies are identical under the skin. Augustine St. Clare's gentle pious Franco-Creole mother, who pleads in vain for humane treatment of the field hands, despondingly retreats to domestic solitude and early death, consoled only by her devotions and her rapport with her sensitive son, the antipode of brother Alfred, who takes over the plantation. Augustine, for his part, replicates the failed cross-sectional marriage plot another way when his engagement with "a high-minded and beautiful woman" during a trip north is broken off by the interference of relatives who want her to marry in the fold (*UTC* 139)—as he learns only after casting his lot with the stereotypically spoiled southern heiress Marie Benoir, an egregious mismatch.

Uncle Tom's Cabin's ultimate disownment of the standard plot device for negotiating the North-South divide romance is to relegate it to cursory retrospective, barely allowing it to figure in the story proper. That, the book implies, is what the state of social emergency produced by institutionalized slavery requires. To take that emergency seriously means banishing "normal" love to the Eliza-George subplot, which pops up only at intervals after the early chapters. In this respect if not others, *Uncle Tom's Cabin* unfolds less like the domestic novel it is generally thought to be than the slave narratives on which Stowe also drew—Douglass's and Josiah Henson's, among others—where the loves of the protagonists are ancillary or elided, partly of course as a distraction from the narrative's core agenda but also as a reflection of how slavery systemically works to contort, deny, or extinguish the bonds of affection among slaves.

Uncle Tom's Cabin's strategy of dividing romance by relegating the love-romance to the subplot differentiates it from virtually all its nineteenth-century successors. These post-Stowe novels tend either to play up love-romance at the expense of purposeful social critique or teeter uneasily between them. The most searching books give fullest recognition to the potential for the claims of cultural context and interpersonal desire to pull against each other, with the first serving as potential impediment to the second to the end of questioning the claims and the legitimacy of each in relation to the other. That is what *Uncle Tom's Cabin* does more resolutely, and so too in different ways, as we shall see, do Mark Twain's *Huckleberry Finn*, Faulkner's *Absalom, Absalom!*, and Morrison's *Beloved*. But it's not an easy combination to bring off. More often than not, the pathos of the interpersonal saga trumps the social anatomy agenda or dwindles into claptrap irrelevance. This holds even for most of the significant reform-oriented fictions of North-South divide written in *Uncle Tom's Cabin*'s wake. All qualify as "novels with a purpose" in the broadest sense but more often than not they mirror the tendency for the reform agendas of such Anglo-American fictional hybrids of "verisimilitude" and "purposefulness" after Dickens and Stowe to become, as Amanda Claybaugh contends, more "strategic" than squarely "committed."[45]

What Can Reform Fiction Do as Encore? Nineteenth-Century Novels after Stowe

Elizabeth Gaskell's *North and South* (1855) is the earliest and one of the most adroit reinventions of U.S. antebellum fiction's North-South schema, one that testifies to the portability of Stowe's geography of cultural and economic difference across national lines. But it also becomes a cautionary tale of sorts for the reason just noted. Gaskell transposes the schema to mid-Victorian Britain for a critical reconnaissance of the hard-driving, social-Darwinist mill culture of the industrial Midlands as seen through the eyes of a disoriented daughter of a comparatively leisurely, bucolic, Anglican South. Desirous as it clearly is of spotlighting the plight of immiserated workers, *North and South* gets increasingly absorbed by the saga of protagonist Margaret Hale's maturation from reflexive dismissal to respect and then love for strongman mill owner John Thornton, who turns out to be deeply principled, sensitive, and also filial—a far cry from the ruthless autocrat she initially takes him for. As the marriage plot thickens, with its various setbacks and surmountings peaking in the counterpointed reversals of Thornton's bankruptcy and Margaret's unexpected inheritance, the project of comparative scrutiny of clashing regional cultures and ethics tends to get co-opted by its investment in engineering happy closure for the featured pair.

Lydia Child's *Romance of the Republic* (1867) is no less foreshortened by propitiation of its unionist marriage plot despite its greater political audacity. Child's boldly contrarian scripting of amalgamation as the solution to racial—and regional—division threatens to be trivialized by the poignant melodramas of the orphaned quadroon sisters from New Orleans, Rosa and Floracita, who, after many ordeals, find happiness in storybook marriages to well-heeled northern white protectors, and by the percolation effects of a baby-switching imbroglio involving the two infants fathered by the man who spirited them away to his Georgia island hideaway under pretense of rescuing them from slavery, seduced Rosa, then married a white heiress for her money. The case for miscegenation is adeptly unfolded in a series of spirited debates. But the novel attempts nothing like Stowe's and Gaskell's reconnaissance of social niches from lofty to low. The scores of places through which the plot whirls, up and down the states and across the Atlantic several times over, are little more than cardboard stage sets, strongly weighted toward the upper crust, especially when Rosa's suitably named husband, the munificent Boston merchant Mr. King, emerges by midpoint as infallible sleuth, problem solver, and dispenser of distributive justice.

Helen Hunt Jackson's *Ramona* (1884), which redirects divide romance toward the Southwest, better manages to take in the whole social gamut from affluence to poverty; the complex tensions between Hispanic, Anglo, and Indian as Anglo squatters and profiteers tighten their hold on postbellum Alta California; and an impressive array of characteristic place-scapes from hacienda to mission to coastal city to outback native and squatter enclaves to remote canyonland and mountain refuges where the remnant Indian bands get driven. Jackson hoped *Ramona* might "do for the Indian a thousandth part of what *Uncle Tom's Cabin* did for the Negro";[46] and indeed the two books were often compared. José Martí took the trouble to translate *Ramona*, which he understandably preferred to *Uncle Tom's Cabin* for its denunciation of Anglo incursion ("taking possession of California was not only a conquering of Mexico but a conquering of California as well," declares the narrator), for its sympathetic portrait of the heroine he praised as "la mestiza arrogante," and for what he took to be its sympathy for interracialism generally—which indeed was more progressive than Stowe's.[47] The novel finds no fault whatever with Ramona's having been the child of an Indian mother and Scots father, her elopement with her Indian lover Allesandro and later marriage to her Mexican cousin Felipe; and it excoriates the turfy Castilian hauteur of Ramona's aunt, who deems Ramona indelibly tainted by her mixed blood yet forbids her to consort even with the noblest of all possible Indians. "The race was never meant for anything but servants," scoffs the aunt.[48]

Yet *Ramona* fell short of "The Great American Novel" its publishers claimed, given over to the degree it was to the ordeals of Ramona and the men who love her. Imagine an adolescent girl as lovely, pure, and sensitive as Eva St. Clare, raised in baffled ignorance of why her aunt-matriarch disdains her, awakened to love by a Native American prince charming, with whom she flees from the virtual captivity of the señora's ranch. Their cruel subjection to increasing harassment as Allesandro's people get snuffed out—episodes that dramatize the bare-knuckled racist land grabs Jackson had exposed in her *A Century of Dishonor* (1881), the era's leading work of pro-Native advocacy—are unfolded as a chronicle of domestic disasters: the death of one infant and nearly another; Allesandro's descent into defeatism, madness, and death; followed by Ramona's own further suffering until near-miraculous rescue by a poor white woman with a heart of gold. Finally her rich cousin Felipe, now liberated from matriarchal thrall, whisks her off to old Mexico with baby Ramona where they live happily ever after.[49] As with Child's brief for miscegenation, what might have been the bold political move of recentering California in Mexico gets blunted by the domestic melodrama, with *amor vincit omnia* replayed twice over, the book's Uncle Tom counterpart reduced to a symbolic vanishing Indian and the novel's most immediate legacy the ecotouristical allure of its portrayal of "hacienda culture."[50]

That Allesandro doesn't turn out to be the moral miracle he initially seems and that his death accomplishes precisely nothing are nonetheless significant hardheaded realistic touches that reflect the movement of postbellum fiction toward more open-eyed confrontation with the underlying social issues of intranational division than *Uncle Tom's Cabin*'s religiocentrism permits. The realist pushback brought problems of its own, however, as postbellum literature's first important fictionalization of Civil War combat and Reconstruction suggests. J. W. De Forest's

Miss Ravenel's Conversion from Secession to Loyalty (1867) draws heavily on the author's gritty recollections of service on both fronts. His fiction and his dispatches both treat obsolete romantic tropes with a satiric eye. One battle memoir wryly recalls escaping enemy fire by slithering snakelike through the tall grass as Cooper's Indians did. ("If the last of the Mohicans had been present, he would have paid me his most emphatic compliments.")[51] *Miss Ravenel* sometimes talks directly back to *Uncle Tom's Cabin*, as in its mock lament that Dr. Ravenel's "tolerably exemplary" factotum on the Reconstructed plantation he manages for a while was not the hoped-for "actual Uncle Tom" but "like some white Christians . . . had not yet arrived at the ability to keep the whole Decalogue."* What qualifies *Miss Ravenel's Conversion* as a realist breakthrough is its systematic deflation of idealized views of war, romance, and for that matter humanity at large. Of the two Union soldiers smitten by the unionist Louisiana doctor's rebel-sympathizing daughter outposted to a New England town until New Orleans falls, the charismatic Colonel Carter who snags her first is a brash and venial windbag despite his courage and military acumen, and the protagonist Private/Lieutenant Colburne is a naively high-minded but colorlessly self-effacing soul whose efficient service goes largely unrewarded by the corrupt politico-military establishment and unnoticed by Lily, until Carter's death in a quixotic Pickett-like charge widows her and Colburne's reduction to near invalidism finally awakens her to the fact that she cares about him.

De Forest's satirical edge, however, drives a wedge between intersectional romance and intersectional analysis that disenables both. *Miss*

---

* J. W. De Forest, *Miss Ravenel's Conversion from Secession to Loyalty,* ed. Gordon Haight (New York: Harper, 1939), 236. Leaving aside anti-*Tom* fictions' pretensions to greater accuracy, this tradition of talkback based on actual experience starts with Solomon Northup's *Twelve Years a Slave* (1853), a powerfully searching account of a kidnapped free black from upstate New York who was trapped for more than a decade in Simon Legree country that has never received its due as one of the great slave narratives, doubtless because it was assisted by a white collaborator, David Wilson, and the evidence for Northup's control of the text is less conclusive than for, say, the Harriet Jacobs–Lydia Child collaboration in *Incidents in the Life of a Slave Girl. Twelve Years* was dedicated to Stowe and regularly advertised together with *Uncle Tom's Cabin,* but Northup does not hesitate to take issue with Stowe at certain points, stressing for example that when reluctantly forced to serve as overseer he would wield the whip when his master was present, "not having the Christian fortitude of a certain well-known Uncle Tom" (Solomon Northup, *Twelve Years a Slave,* ed. Sue L. Eakin and Joseph Logsdon [Baton Rouge: Louisiana University Press, 1968], 172).

Ravenel's Conversion condescendingly infantilizes Lily and treats romance as child's play compared to the national emergency at hand. The
"male lead," one critic quips, "has to risk his life in battle merely to become a man," whereas "the female lead gets to remain a girl even after
marrying twice."[52] Lily is ironized to the point that both the love triangle and her two-step conversion (first to unionism, then to abolition,
mirroring the evolution of northern opinion) seem incidental to the
proper business of the plot. But just what is that proper business? Ostensibly the messy invasion of Louisiana and the attempted rehabilitation of the South, centering on Ravenel's and Lily's short-lived attempts
to educate ex-slaves into capable workers. But with the final return
North of the surviving characters the novel seems to wash its hands of
all that. So the first major novel of the Reconstruction era ironically
turns out to be the first post-Reconstruction novel. As critic Kenneth
Warren points out, overall it seems less invested in war and reconstruction as such than in the work ethic, and what's more a work ethic
coded white, preeminently concerned that "whites in leisure pursuits
recognize the need to work."[53]

As such, *Miss Ravenel's Conversion* anticipates the diminishing
chances for enlisting North-meets-South romance in social critique of
unreconstructed southern culture as postbellum cascaded into the
1870s and beyond, given the widening historical distance from the abolitionist heyday combined with the bias of realist aesthetics toward
critical detachment if not downright irony. The odds became even
greater after Reconstruction ended and as Lost Cause mythology replaced romantic racialism as the preferred mainstream script for intersectional romance, such that the closest lineal descendant of *Uncle Tom's
Cabin*'s politicized sentimentalism in the Jim Crow era was its ideological opposite: Thomas Dixon's "Reconstruction trilogy" (1902–1907), the
first of whose embattled white-power melodramas "refuted" *Uncle Tom's
Cabin* (*The Leopard's Spots*, 1902), and the second of which (*The Klansman*,
1905) inspired D. W. Griffith's classic film *Birth of a Nation* (1915). The
work of the foremost northern novelist to take Reconstruction as his
central theme confirms this.

Lawyer, man of letters, and lifelong advocate for African Americans' civil rights Albion W. Tourgée had not only been a Union officer
but had also served for an extended period as a Reconstruction judge,
on the strength of which experience he wrote several novels and other

books. His most successful, *A Fool's Errand* (1879), sold 100,000 copies and was likened to *Uncle Tom's Cabin* by both reviewers and the author himself. Indeed its interspersal of realist narration with "documents" both actual and fictitious (epistles, newspaper articles, and the like) give it the look of *Uncle Tom's Cabin* and *A Key* rolled into one. In hope of recouping both his health and his fortune, after returning home from war the protagonist, Comfort Servosse, invests in a North Carolina plantation, where his white neighbors' welcome turns to skittishness, then animosity, as he advocates equal rights for African Americans and decries the insurgent Ku Klux Klan. The fecklessness and poltroonery of federal officials, white antipathy to black aspiration, clandestine lynchings and other harassment of African Americans and liberal whites, and the final defeat of the "fool" Servosse's reform initiatives get dramatized with relentless irony. Eventually, he himself is forced to admit, in a passage that might have suggested the title of Dixon's first volume, that "he had expected too much, that he had been simple enough to believe that the leopard *might* change his spots, while yet the Ethiopian retained his dusky skin."[54] Indeed, the narrator's Swiftian ironizing of Servosse's naïveté creates a greater counterforce to the author's actual political convictions than any of the potshots of his unreconstructed ex-Confederates during their heated debates with Servosse. Long before the end, it becomes clear that not their obstinacy but his quixoticism has become U.S. history's lost cause.

Although Tourgée continued to resist this in life—he was the plaintiff's lawyer on the losing side of *Plessy v. Ferguson* (1896), the Supreme Court case which affirmed the "separate but equal" segregation regime that lasted more than half a century thereafter—the denouement of *A Fool's Errand* reads as if this outcome were already a foregone conclusion. The final softening of local opinion toward the honest but obnoxious Yankee, only after it becomes obvious that Reconstruction is dead in the water, compounds the irony, as does the love match between Servosse's spunky daughter and the son of one of her father's adversaries. Tourgée reprises Stowe's device of undoing the unionist ploy of wallpapering over cross-sectional animosities via the marriage plot to the opposite effect. In Stowe, the pathologies wrought by slavery irreparably disrupt "normal" family life, among whites as well as blacks. In Tourgée, "normal" family life (for whites) becomes possible only after you stop gritting your teeth over white racism.

As a work of confessedly outraged impotence, *A Fool's Errand* was postbellum literature's ne plus ultra for the reformist impetus that *Uncle Tom's Cabin* more memorably embodied. It and its companion novel, *Bricks without Straw*, stood as proof that future novelistic treatments of the North-South divide would need to build differently upon the irony of slavery and racism continuing to thrive long after having been thought dead. Tourgée's formula of shock and outrage—the fool belatedly awakened in horror to the counterproductiveness of his obstinate do-gooderism—threatened to become tiresomely predictable to the increasingly distracted target audience: the "truth" few wanted to hear any more even if it were true.*

What then? One recourse was to redirect progressive reform energies elsewhere, as Helen Hunt Jackson did for the plight of Native Americans in the West, and as the first important Mexican American Anglophone writer, María Ruiz de Burton, did in *The Squatter and the Don* (1884), protesting Anglo domination of the Spanish inhabitants of Southern California by arrogant cliques of Anglo homesteaders and railroad magnates. Another was to update North-South divide fiction by fusing memory of the abolitionist era with more current hot-button issues, as in Henry James's *The Bostonians* (1886).

The James-Howells correspondence of the early 1880s suggests that if there ever was a moment when James contemplated taking a shot at the Great American Novel, this was it. James was explicit about wanting *The Bostonians* to show "I *can* write an American story," in which reform would be at the core. When some Bostonians cried slander, James gamely insisted that the novel was "the best fiction I have written."[55] But it was predictable that his engagement with reform issues should run contrary to Stowe's and afoul of the dwindling contingent of New England activists. Even as James planned *The Bostonians*, his constitutional reluctance to harness art to activism was being reinforced by his reaction to his fellow novelist-critic Walter Besant's *The Art of Fiction* (1884). James's counterthrust of the same title, as Claybaugh sums up, "repeatedly challenges what Besant takes entirely for

* Including even Stowe, who, as Greeson points out, had moved in a "frankly regressive direction" in an *Atlantic Monthly* sketch, "Our Florida Plantation," published the same year as *A Fool's Errand*, in which she portrays her black retainers with condescending drollery and the venture itself as a failed investment, leaving the impression that the plantation system itself remained "firmly in place" (Greeson, *Our South*, 257, 256).

granted, the purposefulness of the novel."[56] The spirit in which *The Bostonians* unpacks its chosen reform themes was in keeping.

To have seized upon "the situation of women" and "the agitation on their behalf" as a postbellum sequel and equivalent to antislavery made good historical sense.[57] Women's rights and African American emancipation had been interlinked by many advocates of both since the early antebellum era; and their decoupling in the Fifteenth Amendment (1870), which enfranchised African American males at the cost of postponing women's suffrage for another half century, incensed progressives and touched off a new wave of feminism. *The Bostonians*'s rendition of those reform energies, though, shares Tourgée's diagnosis of the postbellum era as a postheroic age without the same ring of conviction that the issues at stake were worth agitating in the first place. The battle between feminist reform and patriarchal reaction is unfolded with coolly detached ironic ambivalence. The result is the postbellum era's most brainy, subtle demolition of the terms of the traditional North-South divide romance both micro and macro: both the intimate level of cross-sectional union and the symbolic work of the marriage plot as unionist mediation of underlying cultural and ideological divides.

In *The Bostonians,* the glory days of New England reform ferment are long gone, their sole vestige the moribund Miss Birdseye, a "frumpy little missionary" at whose decease the age "of moral passion and noble experiment would effectually be closed." She is in fact the only major character to die, shortly before the finale. Feminism's public face nets out as a series of theatrical performances starring the radiant ingénue Verena Tarrant, the offspring of bohemian parentage who has somehow "kept the consummate innocence of the American girl." The magical immunity of her inner self from tarnished context puts her in a long line of suchlike Jamesian heroines from Daisy Miller to Milly Theale. But the novel also ironizes Verena's naive desire to please those attracted to her that makes her first susceptible to appropriation by feminist handlers and then by the vehemently antifeminist suitor who sweeps her away just as she is to appear on the stage for what has been billed as her greatest oratorical performance yet. Verena's "treason" seemingly goes to show what the narrator has hinted and the bullheaded bridegroom believes all along, that her feminism is merely theatricalized and that like other girls she really cares "far more for Charlie than the ballot."[58] But in skewering feminism as movement, the novel also backhandedly sustains the feminist indictment of traditional heteronormativity by showing Verena hauled away by brute force into what it predicts will be an unhappy marriage.[59]

The chief plot device for scripting the competition for Verena's allegiance between the force fields of feminism and patriarchy is the doomed "reunion" of distant cousins, the painfully refined bluestocking Olive Chancellor, who becomes Verena's sponsor, mentor, and perhaps also lover, and the doggedly conservative Mississippi ex-Confederate officer and planter Basil Ransom, who steals Verena away. Ransom is transparently a figure of the unreconstructed rebel who invades the North, one whose misogyny confirms his atavism, albeit with a few offsetting complexities. Yes, he hankers "to reform the reformers"; he deems "women essentially inferior to men"; he yearns to save American manhood from "damnable feminization." On the other hand, Ransom considers the Civil War a "national fiasco" and slavery an "imbecility"; and he lays siege to the citadel of Yankee feminism only at Olive's invitation, a gesture of kindness toward her impoverished southern relatives that she quickly rues.[60] Still, *The Bostonians* is fairly seen as a subtler rerun of Caroline Hentz's deployment of myth against myth: chivalrous southern manhood versus the Yankee stereotype of a masculine North confronting a feminized South played out in Stowe's juxtaposition of the brothers St. Clare, in Oliver Wendell Holmes's 1861 antisecessionist "Lament of Brother Jonathan for Sister Caroline," and in De Forest's tale of Lily's reclamation. By contrast to Russel Moreland's urbane charm offensive, however, Ransom's chivalrics are exposed as paleolithic, making for a flatter character than his adversary Olive, who emerges for all her finicky self-deluding defensiveness as far more resonantly intricate and poignant.

Not that the novel forces a choice. Some critics have astutely contended for a concession to resurgent southernism here;[61] but to my eye *The Bostonians*'s version of North meets South stages a deliberate impasse. Ransom's triumph is quixotically hollow, Olive's seriocomically humiliating. A cartoon-like version of the South's post-Reconstruction resurgence is set against a satiric rendition of northern reform energies dwindling into petty squabbles and publicity mongering. That *The Bostonians* narrows down at the close to a melodramatic rescue scene (and in a theater to boot) involving the three central characters, all reduced to contorted versions of themselves, suggests that the gravity of this novel's social critique is less than it might seem.

That is not to say that the novel is simply at odds with itself, tempted though one might be to think so from the narrator's Hawthornian vacillation between purporting to know his characters' most secret thoughts and disclaiming ability even to guess them. On the contrary, *The Bostonians* seems pretty sure of its ground in having discovered that at this late date urbane irony, rather than heavy sarcasm à la Tourgée, would be needed in order to engage, for the white intelligentsia anyhow, the national compulsion to revisit the Civil War. James would have known that *Uncle Tom's Cabin* was now being marketed more as "entertainment" and iconic memory than for any continuing traction in addressing burning injustices of the here and now. James's late-life recollection of it as the first for-adults book he read shows that his image of it as an adult was filtered through popular drama and minstrelsy. He had been groomed to novelize reform in the idiom of *The Bostonians* by other life experiences too, such as his bullheaded father's fascination for Swedenborgianism, transcendentalism, and other fringy isms of the day. (The James children had been the Emerson children's playmates during Henry Sr.'s visits to Concord.) What James was less prepared for, less even than Stowe, not to mention De Forest or Tourgée, was to write about the South and southern memory. Ransom was a poor proxy for convincing dramatization of the predicaments of uneven North-South development and the melodrama of neo-Confederate resurgents beset by carpetbaggers and uppity oversexed freedmen that Thomas Dixon was on the verge of cooking up. Only a cultural insider of genius with a disposition for casting progressive social anatomy into a narrative that was plausible, compelling, nuanced, and not too preachy could hope to neutralize that, and maybe not even then.

8

The Adventures of Huckleberry Finn
and Its Others

No Huck and Jim, no American novel as we know it.

—RALPH ELLISON, "What America Would Be
without Blacks" (1970)

I know I am on the weaker side in point of popular sympathy,
but I am on the stronger side in point of justice and morality.

—CHARLES CHESNUTT to Booker T. Washington (1901)

B Y THE TURN of the twentieth century, *Huckleberry Finn* (1884) had
begun to eclipse *Uncle Tom's Cabin* as the Great American Novel
about slavery and southern culture. Despite the late twentieth-century
revival of *Uncle Tom's Cabin*, *Huckleberry Finn* remains by far more widely
read and by far the more frequent GAN nominee. Since the 1940s, it
has been "a universally assigned college text," and the Library of Congress website goes so far as to endorse it as the genuine article, as "really" "the 'great American novel'" that "in every generation writers joke
about writing."[1]

Moving from the one to the other, it's easy to understand why *Huck*
has kept its place. It is much more racily idiomatic and fast-paced, freed
of Victorian rhetoric and theological supernaturalism, packed with a
mixture of the hilarious and the bizarre involving an even greater
range of unforgettable characters, and interspersed with richer evocations of landscape and community—the mark of a one-time cultural
insider and former steamboat pilot who knew the Mississippi basin and
its river towns like the back of his hand. All this makes it one of the
most striking cases in world literature of a sequel surpassing a highly
successful predecessor, *The Adventures of Tom Sawyer* (1876). Where *Tom
Sawyer* stays comfortably within boy's-book limits and basically

remains a good-boy book too despite mischievous swipes, *Huckleberry Finn* is provocatively orchestrated as a bad boy's book that only adults can fully understand. Again and again, comic lightheartedness threatens to metamorphose into a chamber of horrors to which the "innocent" Huck gets subjected as victim or witness or reluctant accomplice: child abuse, adult hypocrisy, theft, gratuitous cruelty, callous racism, murder in cold blood. This makes for a much more mind-bending performance than *Tom Sawyer*. What to make of such a mixture of hilarity and dread? The author made a point of putting readers on "'NOTICE'" not to look for a "Motive" or "a Moral," much less "a Plot" (*HF* xxxi). Professional critics, approaching the novel for the umpteenth time, usually ignore that disclaimer as an irrelevant piece of authorial grandstanding. Should they? Might Twain have been insinuating that *Huckleberry Finn* had unleashed some chaotic forces for which he didn't want to be held responsible? How you answer that question has a lot to do with the conclusions you draw about whether *Huckleberry Finn* qualifies as a possible GAN and, if so, of what kind.

Comedy as a Substitute for Politics

The Adventures of Huckleberry Finn: Tom Sawyer's Comrade features one of U.S. literature's most memorable narrators. We first see Huck where *Tom Sawyer* left him, in the seemingly secure but restive condition of being "sivilized" into gentility as the ward of the good widow Douglas and her prissy sister Miss Watson. But Pap, presumed dead, soon reappears and hauls Huck off to a remote cabin, locking him up by day and whipping him whenever drink or sullenness gives him a mind to. Huck welcomes the return to idleness but hates the confinement and the beatings, so he figures out a way to fake his own murder and decamp with everything of value to nearby Jackson Island. After playing Robinson Crusoe for a while, he's relieved to hook up with a fellow fugitive, Miss Watson's slave Jim, who's been on the run since learning she plans to sell him. The two head downriver on a salvaged raft aiming to turn up the Ohio River at Cairo, Illinois, and freedom for Jim. Here Huck first confronts and suppresses his doubts about the rightness of abetting a runaway slave. But the flight-to-freedom plan fizzles when they float past the junction in a fog and get separated, and nearly killed, when a steamboat runs them down.

Scrambling ashore on the Kentucky side of the river, Huck is be-friended by the proud Grangerfords, at war with the neighboring Shep-herdson clan in an ancient feud whose origins no one can remember. No sooner does Huck make friends with his new buddy Buck Grangerford than he and all the men in the family are wiped out in a failed attempt at revenging the elopement of a Grangerford sister with a Shepherdson son that Huck had unwittingly assisted. The shaken Huck rejoins Jim, hiding out with the recovered raft, and a happy interlude follows. But soon they make the near-fatal mistake of rescuing two seedy con men fleeing a local mob. Claiming to be royalty in disguise, the "King" and "Duke" lord it over Huck and Jim and dragoon Huck as accomplice in a series of abortive scams at hick river towns that culminates in an elabo-rate ruse to pose as the British relatives of the wealthy late Peter Wilks. After their plot is foiled by a remorseful Huck, fake royalty's luck runs out and they resort to selling Jim.

By sheer chance, Jim winds up incarcerated at the farm of Tom Sawyer's Aunt Sally Phelps, at the very time the family is expecting Tom himself, whom they don't know by sight. Huck proceeds to imper-sonate Tom, who, when he arrives, pretends to be his own brother Sid. Tom then enlists a flummoxed and reluctant Huck in a wildly elaborate "evasion" plan to free and flee with Jim. A series of weirdly farcical es-capades end in Jim's post-escape recapture when he refuses to desert Tom, who's been wounded by pursuing vigilantes. Tom then reveals that Jim was already free by the terms of the penitent and now-deceased Miss Watson's will, and Jim reveals that the dead body upriver he had shielded Huck from seeing was Pap. So both Jim and Huck are freed at last, although Huck frets at having come full circle, with Aunt Sally threatening to "sivilize" him anew. He resolves to "light out for the Ter-ritory" (*HF* 362), though whether he actually does is left unresolved.

Huckleberry Finn's satire of human nature's least appetizing sides seems at first thought the antithesis of *Uncle Tom's Cabin*'s call to bring human behavior into line with its highest ideals. Nothing would be more predictable than to launch the main part of this chapter by contrasting Stowe's impassioned indictment of slavery with Twain's comic one, which oscillates between slapstick and cynicism. Yet Twain and Stowe shared more than just the upscale Hartford, Connecticut, neighborhood where they lived after they became noted authors and, before long, also friends. Sense of humor was one such bond. When Mrs. Clemens scolded her husband for visiting Stowe without a coat and tie and he apologized by having his butler deliver them to Stowe on a tray, she chuckled that he had "discovered a *principle* . . . that a man may call by installments."[2] We overlook the affinity when we cast Twain as the frontier humorist, period, and Stowe as the genteel crusader, period.

To be sure, the contrast does hold up to a point. Recognition of Twain's achievement in raising backcountry yarn-spinning from minor genre to high art lies behind his fellow satirist H. L. Mencken's praise of *Huckleberry Finn* as "the greatest work of imagination that These States have yet seen" and Ernest Hemingway's pronouncement that "All modern American literature comes from . . . *Huckleberry Finn.*"[3] *Huck Finn* realized at last the promise of U.S. fiction's long quest for a distinctively "native" voice after a century of guarded experiments in proffering low-life characters as authentic American (stereo)types. Whereas Irving, Cooper, and Stowe used superintending genteel narrators to keep Rip Van Winkle, Natty Bumppo, and Uncle Tom in place, Twain accomplished U.S. fictional realism's greatest linguistic breakthrough by letting the slipshod son of the local bum tell his own tale in his own words. Yet Stowe herself was a raconteur of droll regional tales and lore, as in her *Oldtown Folks* (1869) and *Sam Lawson's Oldtown Fireside Stories* (1872). Never would she have been remotely tempted to declare, as Twain did, "if I could have the nigger show [i.e., the blackface performances of T. B. Rice] back again in its pristine purity and perfection I should have but little further use for opera."[4] Yet *Uncle Tom's Cabin* too, as we've seen, shows how easily Stowe could also be drawn over the same line into racial slapstick.

Conversely, Twain's bumptious irreverence belied a strong attachment to sentimental moralizing. Why had all his fellow-humorists been forgotten? his *Autobiography* elsewhere muses. "Because they were merely humorists. Humorists of the 'mere' sort cannot survive. . . . Humor must not professedly teach and it must not professedly preach, but it must do both if it would live forever."[5] Indeed such lesser lights as Artemus Ward and Petroleum V. Nasby *had* been forgotten. The legacies of antebellum preachment and sentimental moralism pervade *Huckleberry Finn* to the core, even as both are ridiculed as the stuff of scam and narcissistic self-deception. The novel contains as many weeping scenes as *Uncle Tom's Cabin*. True, many of them get ridiculed as "tears and flapdoodle" (*HF* 213), like the King's fake-unctuous effusiveness with the Wilks girls. But Twain's plot no less than Stowe's hinges on contrasting goodness of heart with corruption of mind as dramatized preeminently through the intimacy between a white child and a child-like black man of sterling worth. If *Huckleberry Finn* meant to satirize the likes of Eva St. Clare in the person of the late much-lamented Emmeline Grangerford, whose pious elegiac artistry gives Huck the "fantods" (138), it also pays fervent tribute to spontaneous heart wisdom in its more backhanded way. Mary Jane Wilks, whose loving, trusting, earnest, generous-spirited disposition compels Huck to rat on the con men, is straight out of sentimental fiction. Though Twain scholars cringe to recall it, this was the writer who insisted that "the best" book he ever wrote, the one he personally loved best, was his tedious syrupy historical romance of the virgin martyr Joan of Arc seen through the eyes of her admiring secretary and page.[6]

The dotted lines of affinity begin to explain why *Huckleberry Finn* has been defined by critics as a distinctive American performance in (at least) two sharply discrepant ways, each polarized by extremes of praise and blame.

The path first preferred, Mencken's, was to read the novel as a modern *Don Quixote* with a frontier-regionalist twang, as American literature's defining work of backcountry humor. Honorifically so regarded, *Huckleberry Finn* looks like a "vivid and original picture of life," blessedly "unstrained" in its comic spirit, and "more valuable" than *Uncle Tom's Cabin* precisely for being "written without partisanship, and without 'a purpose.'" Such was the view of late Victorian fairy-tale collector and man of letters Andrew Lang, the first to propose *Huck* as "the great American novel" in 1891. Similarly, a century later, novelist Kenzaburo Oe, in his Nobel Prize acceptance speech, recalled how his fascinated reading of *Huckleberry Finn* as a child in a remote Japanese valley seemed to "justify my act of going into the mountain forest at night and sleeping among the trees."[7] Skeptically regarded the same way, however, this tale told by a wisecracking young slacker looks raffish, scabrous, and unfit for kids (contra the promotion of the novel as a book for all ages). That was the impetus behind Louisa May Alcott's successful effort to ban *Huckleberry Finn* from the Concord Library, and by campaigns in recent years by parent and community groups to remove it from school curricula for its incessant repetition of the N-word.

The second path has been to read *Huckleberry Finn* as an assault on slavery and racism amid all its tomfoolery. Honorifically so regarded, the key to the novel seems the moral heroism of Huck's twice-over decision to ignore the conscience that nags him to turn in Miss Watson's runaway slave as the institutionalized morality of the slavery era inculcates. That was the view of the mid-twentieth-century canonizers discussed in Chapter 6, who saw Chapter 31 as the novel's turning point: Huck's second and more desperate wrestling with the fear of public shame and divine judgment that would fall on a white boy who "helped a nigger to get his freedom" that prompts him first to write a whistle-blowing letter to Miss Watson, then tear it up as he grits his teeth and says to himself, "All right, then I'll go to hell" (*HF* 268, 271). Skeptically so regarded, though, the novel tries to seize this moral high ground but botches the job, whether because Twain intermittently "loses sight of Huck's moral sensitivity," or, as novelist E. L. Doctorow puts it in an astute and otherwise appreciative estimate, because the author wholly "lost his resolve or his way" in the last section featuring Tom Sawyer's "nonsensical, overcomplicated, boy's book fantasy escape plan."[8]

Obviously these disparate readings often blend together in practice. And they should. T. S. Eliot, for one, found a way to reconcile his pleasure in Huck's vagabondage and Twain's mesmerizing evocation of the river (of Eliot's own Missouri boyhood) with a defense of the novel's moral seriousness. "The *style* of the book, which is the style of Huck," he argues, delivers "a far more convincing indictment of slavery than the sensationalist propaganda of *Uncle Tom's Cabin*" precisely because Huck's "passive and impassive" "acceptance of his world" makes him "more powerful than his world, because he is more *aware* than any other person in it."[9] Eliot's attempt to dignify (im)passivity as moral insight was myopic, but he did well to try to coordinate somehow the contrary elements of wanderlust and satire.

Twain himself pointed toward a more promising synthesis when summing up the novel's purport a decade later in notes for his 1895–1896 Australian lecture tour, which included a performance of "Smallpox & Lie," the earlier episode in which Huck resists his ingrained conviction that runaway slaves should be returned to their masters and protects Jim from recapture by persuading two bounty hunters that the hooded man on the raft has the dread disease. Here, Twain writes, "a sound heart & a deformed conscience come into collision & conscience suffers defeat." The "middle-aged slave" and the "son of the town drunkard" are "bosom friends, drawn together by community of misfortune" (*HF* 619). The contrast between Twain's relative matter-of-factness and Trilling's soupy description of the Huck-Jim friendship as a "community of saints" is telling.[10] Huck's dilemma, continues Twain, exposes what seemed "natural enough to me then," but "seems now absurd": that not only southern slaveholders with a vested interest in maintaining the system but even "the paupers, the loafers the tag-rag & bobtail" of the white community like "Huck & his father the worthless loafer should feel it & approve it." Which goes to show "that that strange thing, the conscience—that unerring monitor—can be trained to approve any wild thing you *want* it to approve if you begin its education early & stick to it" (*HF* 619).

In other words, Huck's predicament dramatizes the pervasiveness of slavery's corrupting influence throughout the white South and the ability—of those on the social margins at least—to resist it in a pinch when the heart is good; yet the novel must treat this comically in acknowledgment of the distance between the benighted past and the more enlightened present.

Twain's autoanalysis goes a considerable way toward explaining the co-presence of racist and antiracist thinking in Huck and in *Huck* generally. What it stops short of doing, and what confirms why the book will forever remain controversial, is directly to address the novel's wistfully nostalgic immersion in that supposedly discredited bygone era— the pleasures of laziness, slanguage games, remembered riverscapes. These testify to the continuing allure of those olden days, from which neither novel nor author were so deconditioned as Twain's Australian notes suggest. Long residence up north, including the internalization of liberal northern values that drove *Huckleberry Finn*'s satire of the regional backwater of Twain's boyhood, never effaced his fondness for recollecting it. Twainians must forever reconcile themselves to the fact that Samuel Clemens never lost his partiality for southern gentlemanly attire and creature comforts, never stopped referring casually to "niggers," and profited from minstrelish imitations, sometimes in quite dubious taste, like his performance of *Huckleberry Finn*'s "King Sollermun" episode before a racially mixed audience at Oberlin College, a bastion of progressive evangelical reform and onetime hotbed of antislavery activism and the country's first college to admit African Americans on an equal basis with whites.[11] But whatever Twain's residue of unreconstructed southernness, however problematic his mutual admiration society with Joel Chandler Harris of Uncle Remus fame (one of *Huckleberry Finn's* most ardent early admirers), it would be even more perverse to cast the novel as a cookie-cutter example of late-century local colorist euphemizations, as critic Nancy Glazener describes them: "in place of the sectional opposition between North and South, they offered a peaceable array of regions whose distinctive histories and ways of life could be sampled without controversy."[12] In any case, to draw a moralistic line in the sand and insist that *Huckleberry Finn* should have striven for nothing less than 100 percent disengagement from the contaminations of the era it portrays would be like insisting that Stowe should have edited out all of Topsy's pranks and concentrated only on the shame and outrage of her early abuse.

Yes, Twain was willfully blind in claiming that the "passionate & uncompromising" support for the subjection of slaves to masters on the part of antebellum white trash "is not in our remote day realizable." Albion Tourgée would have corrected him in an instant. But then again Twain wrote that passage specifically from the perspective of a regional expatriate attesting to the hindsight wisdom of a quarter century's remove from the scene, and his specific point was that fetishization of "the awful sacredness of slave property" was dead, not racism generally (*HF* 619). Beyond that, though, *Huckleberry Finn* not only beats the dead horse of antebellum chattel slavery, but also delivers an oblique if not a frontal post-Reconstruction satire of the new South, both by direct allusions like Chapter 22's to the Ku Klux Klan (191), by Pap's rant against uppity free blacks claiming the right to vote (another of Twain's favorite performance pieces), and by insinuation throughout that de facto slavery continued after emancipation. That is the serious point behind the farcical denouement, when Tom goes to the most convoluted lengths possible to free an already liberated slave. "The shadow of the so-called New South was on Twain" when he wrote that ending, observes the leading student of the mordant complexities of Twainian humor. Tom's hankering "to lengthen the process of emancipation indefinitely," another critic suggests, "foreshadows critiques of 'gradualism' by black leaders from W. E. B. Du Bois to Martin Luther King, Jr."*

Significantly, Huck's intimacy with Jim and his two put-downs of his "conscience" never negate the master-class colonization of his mind. Both at start and close his favored companion is, hands down, Tom Sawyer, "a younger version of the Southern gentleman," as critic D. L. Smith observes.[13] Along the way, Huck repeatedly invokes Tom as a model—thinking how he might have helped Huck fake his death, inspired by his memory of Tom's daring to board the wrecked *Walter Scott,* thinking of his scheme to help out the Wilks sisters how Tom himself "couldn't a done it no neater" (*HF* 248). By no coincidence is Huck's final alias "Tom Sawyer." That he puts up with "royalty" for as long he does, to Jim's imperilment, despite knowing the King and Duke are frauds, foreshadows his decision to go along with Tom's "evasion" plot despite knowing how loony it is. Huck's shrewd irreverence makes him stand out as the book's smartest character, and winningly good-hearted too—he can even pity the duo that bullied and bilked him when he sees them tarred and feathered. But socially he is the perennial subaltern kid, accommodating to the adult world despite his noises about breaking away. His ductility together with the belated revelation that his soul struggles over whether to turn Jim in were utterly irrelevant to Jim's liberation pit *Huckleberry Finn* against the ethos of *Uncle Tom's Cabin* by exposing "the poverty of treating racial justice as a question of sentiment (requiring a 'change' of heart) instead of as a question of structure (requiring new political policies)."[14] This shift away from trusting to individual conversion to catalyze social change is symptomatic of broader shifts toward pragmatism during the postbellum era in

---

* Neil Schmitz, "Twain, *Huckleberry Finn,* and the Reconstruction," *American Studies* 12 (Spring 1971): 65; Harold K. Bush, *Mark Twain and the Spiritual Crisis of His Age* (Tuscaloosa: University of Alabama Press, 2007), 193–194. Brook Thomas helpfully points out that "political and civil rights" for African Americans were still at least nominally "in force" when Twain was writing *HF* and that anti-Reconstruction reaction among southern whites had not gathered full momentum. In the early 1880s, "the problem was not unfair laws; it was the failure to obey and to enforce fair ones" (Brook Thomas, *Civic Myths: A Law-and-Literature Approach to Citizenship* [Chapel Hill: University of North Carolina Press, 2007], 140). Twain's unfinished novella *Tom Sawyer's Conspiracy,* on which he worked in the late 1890s, is more explicit than *HF* on the subject of southern white communities' hostility toward free blacks. But then so too was the abortive "Tom Sawyer among the Indians," written immediately after *HF.*

religion, philosophy, law, and the culture of professionalism generally that go far beyond issues of slavery and racism.

None of the above is meant to suggest that the personal camaraderie Huck forms with Jim is other than genuine, other than a sign of his ability to press at least fitfully beyond his social conditioning, and other than crucial to the novel. But the strength of that tie is easy to overestimate. The best-known pre-contemporary affirmation of its centrality—Leslie Fiedler's controversial reading of Huck-Jim as an "innocent homosexual" bond—overstates the significance that either Huck or the novel attaches to it. Fiedler did well to seize upon and question the peculiar fascination Euro-American white romances of the divide display again and again for scenes of cross-racial intimacy as fragile utopian counterspaces.[15] But the conception of an intimate eroticized tie doesn't wash, for this novel at any rate. Huck's first reaction to discovering Jim on Jackson's Island, a boy's-story version of Crusoe discovering Friday, tells the whole story from his side: "I warn't lonesome now" (*HF* 51). Jim solaces Huck's need for company as a backup substitute for the likes of Tom. The tie will never be as close as even Huck's brief friendship with Buck Grangerford, a same-age white boy. Toni Morrison rightly declares that Huck needs Jim to relieve the "terror" and "melancholy" of wrecks, blood feuds, corpses, and near-death experiences that litter their downriver course yet that "no enduring adult fraternity" can emerge.[16] That isn't to dismiss the author's characterization of Huck and Jim as "bosom friends drawn together by community of misfortune," only to put that friendship in a perspective that respects the novel's actual savviness. Unlike the unqualified mutual affection of Eva and Tom or Eva and Topsy, in the solidarity of bottom dogs Jim and Huck, empathy and self-interest pull against each other, and neither probably fathoms the other beyond a point, certainly not Huck.

As Neil Schmitz writes, Jim "remains apart from Huck's conception of raft life."[17] His quest for freedom is at cross-purposes with Huck's desire for carefree and comforting companionship. Nowhere does this emerge more pointedly than when Jim withholds until the very end of the book his knowledge that the corpse in the floating house they encountered upriver early on, the body whose face Huck didn't want to see and Jim didn't want him to, was Pap. Although why Jim kept mum so long is never explained, the insinuation seems clear enough. His secret is the obverse of Tom's. Tom's disclosure of Jim's freedom would deprive him of his pretext for keeping Jim entrapped in his evasion scheme; Jim's disclosure of Pap's death would alleviate the fear that drove Huck to join forces with Jim. However much he may play along with Huck and Tom, however much he may actually care for them, Jim doesn't fully confide in either because it's not in his interest to do so. So at least it seems. That *Huckleberry Finn* keeps Jim's thinking largely opaque rather than pretending to full knowledge of it is a tribute to the novel's tact, however offensive its language to a modern liberal ear.

What I am calling novelistic tact here is obviously in a sense nothing more than a byproduct of first-person dramatized narration, which keeps the reader from knowing the interior of any character's mind except for Huck's. But by making Huck privy to Jim's occasional displays of what seem spontaneous feeling below the accommodating surface (chewing Huck out for tricking him, confessing remorse at striking his "disobedient" little daughter after realizing she was deaf and dumb), and by having the white characters at large keep up their barrage of pop-offish and generally demeaning remarks about blacks while the blacks themselves remain guardedly in the shadows, *Huckleberry Finn* establishes itself as more scrupulously aware than *Uncle Tom's Cabin* of the challenges of thinking across the color line from one's own side of the divide.

So the novel inevitably delivers a more diminished vision of universal human nature than Stowe's, for whom it follows from the fact that black souls and white share the same spiritual and moral equipment and have the capacity to understand each other intuitively, however different their emotional circuitry. *Huckleberry Finn* does not abandon this framework wholly, but it operates from a more skeptical sense of how racism forces efforts at cross-racial thinking into speculation, caricature, and fantasy. In this Twain anticipates his great modern successors, Faulkner and Morrison.

It is quite otherwise with the novel's evocation of place. Its reminiscences of the long-forsaken regions of youth differ markedly both from Stowe's cartoon versions of southern manners and from *Absalom, Absalom!*'s conjuration of the antebellum South as a mythic locus of haunted memory. In Twain, no matter how far Huck ranges, no matter how anxious and disoriented he gets, he can recall and relay the grainiest details of scenes never seen before or again—the Grangerfords' furniture; the slatternly appearance of the first Arkansas river town, right down to the fences "made of different kinds of boards, nailed on at different times," leaning "every-which way," with "gates that didn't generly have but one hinge—a leather one" (*HF* 181). Or the Phelps farm further downriver: "A rail fence round a two-acre yard, a stile, made out of logs sawed off and up-ended, in steps, like barrels of a different length, to climb over the fence with" and so on (276). Did I call *Uncle Tom's Cabin* a species of documentary travelogue? I take it all back. *Here* is the true "reality effect,"[18] much closer to total immersion in palpable facticity than *Uncle Tom's Cabin*'s genre paintings of the Bird parlor or the Kentucky tavern where the elegantly disguised George Harris confronts his former boss. Like Solomon Northup correcting *Uncle Tom's Cabin*'s phantasmagoric rendering of Legree's plantation with a detailed account of how slaves actually picked cotton thereabouts, *Huckleberry Finn* displays an intimately knowledgeable command of socioenvironmental materiality wherever the narrator casts his eye.

Descriptive exfoliation far beyond what the plot requires had been a hallmark of fictions of the divide from the start, as with Cooper's prolixity in detailing the layout of Templeton village in *The Pioneers* (1823), the fugitives' cave hideout at Glens Falls and Tanemund's camp in *The Last of the Mohicans* (1826), the buffalo stampede and the prairie fire in *The Prairie* (1827) and the shores of Glimmerglass and Tom Hutter's floating island in *The Deerslayer* (1841). These cannot be written off as imperfect control over the medium. They were indispensable for putting readers in touch with previously undiscovered country—as Cooper's foreign admirers from Balzac to D. H. Lawrence were keen to point out. The ridicule Twain famously heaped on Cooper for violating nineteen of the twenty-two cardinal rules of romance was a lover's quarrel over rhetorical strategies—Cooper's ponderous formality and romantic heightening being Twain's special aversions—not about the importance of thick description in transmitting the feel of unfamiliar territory.

Twain's greater verisimilitude—more like early Winslow Homer than the romantic landscapes of Thomas Cole or Frederick Church— put him in the forefront of the new surge of regional realism then gaining momentum throughout the entire Anglophone world from Scotland to Australia. Infusions of local speech, folklore, customary rhythms of work and play as well as landscape particularity were all part of this reality effect in Twain, in fellow American regionalists Sarah Orne Jewett and Mary Noales Murfee, in Thomas Hardy's Dorset novels, in the Australian novelist Joseph Furphy, in the Scots novelist George Douglas Brown. As with the first wave of Anglophone regional tales from early nineteenth-century Ireland and Scotland, regions "whose culture was being threatened with erasure" by a dominant imperial/metropolitan power,[19] these later regionalisms reflected a broader socioeconomic shift toward industrial modernization and urban centralization that stimulated demand on the part of increasingly metropolitan reading publics for reconnection of some sort with worlds they no longer knew well, or perhaps never knew at all except from elders or from media distillations. Authors responding to this demand, whether cosmopolitanized out-migrants like Twain and Willa Cather or stay-putters like Hardy and Jewett, helped shape such expectations through a mixture of vicarious identification and standoffishness toward those regional otherworlds they conjured up. Sarah Orne Jewett's *Country of the Pointed Firs* (1896), which records an urbanite's impressions of a summer's sojourn in a small coastal Maine village that time has passed by, can plausibly be read either as ecotouristical packaging of quaint rustics as collectible miniatures for genteel consumption or as expressing unfulfilled yearning to be accepted into a community of which the genteel narrator can never be fully part.

In postbellum fictions of the North-South divide, these effects were exacerbated by the widening disparity between the North's industrial takeoff and the South's comparative backwardness. Even before the Civil War, the South's unevenness of economic development, its slowness to industrialize, the comforts enjoyed by northerners of moderate means compared to even many of the southern gentry—all these were commonly remarked upon by northern or northern-identifying reformers, as in *The Narrative of Frederick Douglass* and Frederick Law Olmsted's *The Cotton Kingdom*. (One sign of *Uncle Tom's Cabin*'s attempted forbearance toward the South is that it is less categorical about southern backwardness as such—the roads of southern Indiana are as bad as those of the Dixie outback.) With the ruin wrought by Civil War on the South's economy and infrastructure, the visible North-South difference became more drastic. Northern travelers in the South during the early postbellum years like John Muir and John Townsend Trowbridge beheld a devastated landscape. Northern and southern pundits both spoke of the "Africanization" of the South, meaning not just its high percentage of blacks but also the fear that the region as a whole was slipping into a third-worldish condition.[20] The muddled and foreshortened Reconstruction years left a backwash of confusion, misunderstanding, and mutual resentment that made North-South difference seem at least as great as before the war despite slavery's demise and political reunification.

Huckleberry Finn dramatizes that cultural situation masterfully by portraying a South that seems materially, palpably, intimately, at times even cozily present yet is also intractably, uncannily, repellently strange. Huck's long description of the Phelps Farm exemplifies this. The solidity of that passage—chock full of such tacky but down-home sights as faded whitewashed buildings and dozing hounds strewn about—sits in symbiotic tension with Huck's emotional disorientation at this point in the story. Foraging through a sparsely populated place he's never been in search of Jim, desperate to recover him but uncertain how to bring it off, he's overtaken by an almost suicidal despondency as the farm comes into view. The hot stagnant silence makes him feel "like everybody's dead and gone," "makes a body wish *he* was dead, too, and done with it all" (*HF* 276). This panicky spasm then gives way before the catalog of farmscape minutiae, as if Huck's dry rendering of it as a variation on countless other "one horse-cotton plantations" were a way of steadying himself for the effort he knows he'll have to make when he meets the people. Then anxiety flares up again as he hears the spinning wheel inside the house: "then I knowed for certain I wished I was dead—for that *is* the lonesomest sound in the whole world" (277). Of course it's not the wheel or the spinner that's lonesome and afraid but Huck himself. When you're as disoriented as he is for most of the novel, even the most pedestrian details can turn creepy.

In this case everything turns out fine and dandy—much too fine to suit most readers. But that same readerly recoil goes to show that the novel's typical approach is not to allow mundane descriptivism to stand for long without contorting it into some sort of menace. That first Arkansas river town cameo starts on a note of mundane drollery with a wry scan of muddy streets, hogs wallowing freely about, and idlers goading the town dogs to attack the pigs for sport; but then it takes a grisly sardonic twist, imagining that the loafers' supreme pleasure "might be putting turpentine on a stray dog and setting fire to him, or tying a tin pan to his tail and seeing himself run himself to death" (*HF* 183). Controlled satire morphs into unmitigated disgust at this barbarous place.

To understand the larger stakes here, it may help to think of *Huckleberry Finn* as one of a series of Twainian experiments in imagined time travel: to sixteenth-century England in *The Prince and the Pauper* (1881), the *Tom Sawyer*-ish book he wrote in between the two main stages of composing *Huckleberry Finn* (boy-prince Edward switches identities with a commoner lad, to the confusion and imperilment of both); *A Connecticut Yankee in King Arthur's Court* (1890; factory foreman transported to medieval Camelot wins knighthood by impressing the court with his industrial-era "magic" and attempts modernization of Arthurian England with disastrous results); and *Pudd'nhead Wilson* (1894), which spans from antebellum to the present (the protagonist, deemed a crank since arriving in sleepy Dawson's Landing, Missouri, uses his hobby of modern fingerprint technology to uncover a long-ago black/white baby-switching event and identify the right [white] criminal). Each novel differs from the others and from *Huckleberry Finn* in ways too complex to detail here, but they all share the device of satirizing from a generally democratic-progressive standpoint the undue importance accorded race and class distinctions by a woefully ignorant and pliable public in a former time so as to register both the absurdly paleolithic nature of the prejudices satirized and the threats posed to those who resist them.

Yankee is Twain's most far-reaching effort in this vein, implying at least four possible allegorical interpretations of the Yankee-Camelot juxtaposition: northern industrial democracy versus a medievalized Old South; upstart American democracy and practical know-how powering eclipse of the retrograde neofeudal mother country; top-down expertise bringing a "new deal" (the Yankee actually uses this phrase) to the impoverished but unruly masses; and first-world militarized capitalism's attempted dominance of the colonial periphery—in each case with something like equal-time, cut-two-ways exposure of the hubris of the forces of "enlightenment" and old-order backwardness.[21] But *Huckleberry Finn* is Twain's subtlest rendering of how it feels to navigate bygone time-space where society as usual seems alternatively inviting and systemically deranged. Its boy-narrator from the social fringes, forced again and again to improvise in order to prevent being trapped or crushed by the adult world, maintaining composure as best he can but unable to avoid getting discomposed by fear or pity or disgust, simulates but also complicates the time-traveling reader-outsider's engagement with that far-off, wacked-out milieu of planet Southland in the way it positions Huck as both insider and outsider to that scene.

Huck's banter and good-heartedness make that world seem more inviting to the reader than it is to him, indulging a measure of the old-times nostalgia Twain had allowed himself in the book that immediately preceded it, *Life on the Mississippi* (1883), from which standpoint the technological advances in steamboat navigation that made hard-won mastery of every mile of river course obsolete is seen more as a loss of masterful intuitive savvy than as a triumph of industrial know-how. The riverine landscapes of *Huckleberry Finn*, by contrast, feel unmastered, unmasterable, raw, barbaric. The only signs of economic progress are the steamboats that threaten to destroy the raft. Drifting on the raft, as critic Stephanie LeMenager shrewdly puts it, is a kind of "parody of Manifest Destiny in which Providential protection is denied."[22] Enlightened adult leadership is fitful at best. Widow Douglas and Judge Thatcher are impotent; the new judge is too pliable to keep Pap behind bars; the Phelpses are dense; the Grangerford and Shepherdson patriarchs are locked in their insane feud; Colonel Sherburn murders in cold blood.

Huck's role as satirist masks how he himself exemplifies the cultural benightedness to which he bears witness. As an undereducated semiliterate averse to work, school, respectable dress, and proper speech, for all his wit and charm this backwater gamin personifies southern unsivilization at a time when the gap between northern progress and southern stagnation had never seemed greater to Twain's primary target audience. In short, Huck's a trickster figure not only as witty narrator and artful dodger but also as authorial device. Through him the novel unfolds the spectacle of a regional culture stuck in an immature state of development with nothing better in sight even as it tempts the reader to abet the desire of the figure who gives expression to that culture to avoid the responsibility of ever having to grow up. Cultural critic Tom Lutz calls "the slacker" the "necessary twin" of the model American workaholic.[23] By that logic Huck's vicarious appeal then and now as counterforce, as the most ingratiating slacker in national literature, seems all the more irresistible.

Altogether, then, picaresque time travel with Huck as one's Virgil was calculated to deliver a far more thorough proxy immersion in the particularities of its southern bailiwicks than *Uncle Tom's Cabin* had done while avoiding Stowe's forthrightness of judgment on the issues at stake, meaning both slavery's baleful aftereffects specifically and southern stuck-in-timeness more generally. In contrast to standard practice in North-South divide romance from Sedgwick and Hale through De Forest, Child, and James, Twain leaves *Huckleberry Finn* without a superintending narrative consciousness, even one so vacillating as James's. The result is a maximal authenticity effect with a minimum of adjudication. The biographical Twain's considered views about slavery, racism, and the state of the South in the 1880s may well have been at least as progressive as the biographical Stowe's; but for whatever reason Twain the author opted, as Amanda Claybaugh puts it, for "a novel that is divided by the very question of purposefulness."[24] A much more direct descendant of *Uncle Tom's Cabin* among late nineteenth-century time-traveling American fictions was the best-selling novel two years year later that its author saw, and reviewers recognized, as Stowe's direct successor in the social activist vein, Edward Bellamy's *Looking Backward: 2000–1887.* In this novel of looming industrial-era apocalypse, an effete Brahmin falls asleep in his fancy mansion to awake to a turn-of-the-twenty-first-century democratic-socialist utopia where the burning issues of the Progressive Era, the struggles between capital and labor and the gap between poverty and affluence, have been miraculously resolved by peaceful evolution. The balance of the book is taken up with an unpacking of this new and better order of things in a series of one-sided dialogues between the astonished time traveler and an intergenerational duo, the kindly doctor who attends him and the doctor's daughter, whom the protagonist finally marries.

Such doctrinal clarity was the antithesis of Twain's recourse to comedy as "an antidote to the ailments of politics," in Ellison's memorable phrase (*CE* 483). *Huckleberry Finn*'s racially progressive aspect remains by contrast studiously "tacit," as Michael T. Gilmore observes, "rather like Twain's unpublicized acts of support for blacks or Booker T. Washington's backstage lobbying against legal discrimination." Why? Gilmore suspects strategic self-censorship ("an overt attack on white supremacy would have destroyed Twain's reputation as America's humorist"). Claybaugh proposes that Twain was suspicious of reform tactics as such.[25] Those guesses may be as good as any we're ever likely to have.

At all events, as the nineteenth century drew toward its close, if you wanted to write reform fiction, you were more likely to gain a wide sympathetic hearing as a pro-labor novelist, even if you came out as a utopian socialist like Bellamy and Twain's friend William Dean Howells, than as an advocate for the rights of African Americans or as the critic of an increasingly defensive white South. This is further confirmed by the failure of the other two ablest late nineteenth-century U.S. novelists who addressed the "Negro" and "Southern" problems to gain anything like *Huckleberry Finn*'s readership, to gain anything like the hearing their artistic accomplishments deserved. These were the Louisiana-born Confederate ex-officer George Washington Cable and North Carolina–born Charles W. Chesnutt, the foremost African American novelist before Zora Neale Hurston and Richard Wright.

Unperceived Rivals: Cable's The Grandissimes, *Chesnutt's* The Marrow of Tradition

Cable was a sometime mentor to Chesnutt, whom he once sought to recruit as a literary assistant, and also a personal friend of Twain. Billed as "the twins of genius," Twain and Cable teamed up for a tour of the northern lecture circuit as reader-performers during the same winter season (1884–1885) in which *Huckleberry Finn* was published and Cable's polemic essays "The Freedman's Case in Equity" and "The Silent South" established him as the white South's most trenchant critic of racism and segregation. David Blight, a leading historian of Civil War memory, calls Cable "the model dissenter in Southern literature."[26] In addition to taking on race issues, he also wrote against asylum and prison abuse. As a performer, however, Cable tended to draw on his repertoire of Creole sketches and songs and follow a chaster version of Twain's appeal to regional and ethnoracial exoticism.[27] Whereas Twain's migration northeast in the 1860s was basically a lifestyle choice, Cable's relocation in the 1880s was driven at least partly by conscience, by the conviction that he could address the social problems of the South more openly from a northern base.[28]

Cable's fictional masterpiece, *The Grandissimes* (1880), predated his move. Perhaps partly for that reason, the novel approaches its critique of southern pathology even more obliquely than Twain did. Set in a historical era even more remote than *Huckleberry Finn*'s, turn-of-the-nineteenth-century New Orleans at the time of the Louisiana Purchase, *The Grandissimes* gives itself over in even greater degree to a richly sensuous, calibrated evocation of the particularities of life in place, at the center of which is the most self-exacting extended effort to render the quiddities of dialect speech and song undertaken by any work of American fictional realism. This extraordinarily rich particularism of language, custom, and gesture comes at the cost of a certain ethnographic pedantry and involution that suggests why the novel never took hold as Twain's did, or as Cable's own short tales did. It wasn't *Huckleberry Finn*'s already classic standing so much as its earthiness of voice that led Hemingway to praise it as a breakthrough achievement. Hemingway would have had scant patience with *The Grandissimes*'s " 'ow you lag doze climade?'" (How do you like this [those?] climate?), not to mention its teasingly untranslated/untranslatable snatches of Franco-Creole song.

But as with the convolutions of Henry James's late work, or—better—Chesnutt's conjure tales, *The Grandissimes*'s rhetorical impenetrability is more than a tour de force demonstration of the asymptotic limit of precise rendering of expressive nuance, though that is indeed one of its great accomplishments, as cultural critic Brian Hochman points out in a searching analysis of the novel in light of Cable's interest in then-new phonograph technology.[29] To begin with, the choice of historical moment is itself crucial—one of many ways *The Grandissimes* signposts itself as a postcataclysmic national fable, rather than a charming evocation of the aura of a unique region, period. The plot traces through the messy perturbations within "the little Creole capital" as inhabitants both white and nonwhite adjust to Louisiana's absorption into the union—laying out thereby a kind of retro-anticipatory vision of what should and/or might befall the postbellum South.[30]

In this *The Grandissimes* achieves an artistic triumph that undermines its prospects of gaining a wide hearing for its heterodox social vision. It starts with a festive but enigmatic masked ball scene in which the guests struggle to recognize each other's identities—a miniform allegory of this closed but multiply divided community's state of guarded confusion about issues of history, politics, and race. Only by slow degrees and in discontinuous impressionistic glimpses does the anonymous narrator, who assumes the guise of a coy insider, usher the reader into the intricacies of local custom, history, family feuds and skeletons, and ethnoracial fault lines. Like Twain, Cable relies on an intermediary consciousness as proxy, also an innocent of sorts but not a cultural insider: the intelligently principled but initially clueless newly arrived apothecary, Joseph Frowenfeld, literally a German immigrant but a kind of proxy Yankee given his liberal values. Immediately prostrated by the malarial climate about which he's slyly queried in the snatch of dialogue quoted above, Frowenfeld is again and again befuddled by such Franco-Creole conundrums as the coexistence of not one but two Honoré Grandissimes—the charismatic clan leader with whom he forms an intimacy that enlightens both, and his no less cultivated elder quadroon half-brother, a wealthy landlord forever balked by the color line, who attracts Frowenfeld's sympathy and support.

As the apothecary settles in, aided by the white Honoré's attentiveness, immigrant though he is he also becomes the book's medium for propagating egalitarian "northern" values at the moment of Louisiana's annexation. Gradually *The Grandissimes* becomes a more agenda-driven novel than it first seemed, but always reserving the right to derail that momentum by plunging its moralist into confusion. Despite being a target of pranks, resentment, even physical attack, Frowenfeld winds up becoming an agent of top-down reform through his influence on the white Honoré, who switches roles from condescendingly gracious initiator to receptive initiate, trying as best he can to redress his clan's bad legacy of obstinate pride and racism. In this way, and through Frowenfeld's eventual marriage to a Creole woman from the rival De Grampion clan, whose ancient feud with the Grandissimes Honoré ends by fiat, the divides of regional difference get successfully romanced—for the whites at least—in something like a model transition from a patronage-based feudal hierarchy toward a more democratic, mercantile order based on contract.

Not so the divide of race. The Grandissime brothers can become business partners, albeit to the scandal of their white kin, but they can never restore the intimacy of their school days in Paris. The beautiful quadroon Palmyre, smitten by the white Honoré, is forcibly paired off with his namesake the "f.m.c." (free man of color). The novel is haunted throughout—as were white southerners at large both before and after the Civil War—by the specter of black insurgency: in particular, by the memory of the tellingly named Bras-Coupé ("arm cut off"), whose tragic story is placed at the very center of the novel. A Jaloff prince of titanic strength and volcanic will, Bras-Coupé refused to submit to servitude and was maimed in his prime according to the *code noir* for striking his master twice, by order of the Grandissime magistrate-patriarch who had purchased him, Agricola Fusilier. This haughty, truculent, unreconstructed old racist who insists that the American dispensation must soon pass ironically takes pride in his own mixed-race descent, from Native American royalty as well as pedigreed French ancestry.[31] Near the end, the chronically depressive Honoré f.m.c. becomes Bras-Coupé's unlikely revenger when he repels a savage attack from the irascible Agricola by knifing him to death. For this he is exiled to France, where he soon commits suicide. Such is the sad upshot of an earlier scene when Frowenfeld tries to exhort the f.m.c. to exert himself on behalf of fellow nonwhites ("free in form but slaves in spirit") only to be told, to his consternation, that "Hiv I trah, I h-only s'all soogceed to be one Bras-Coupé" and that there can be no solution for his people until Agricola "ees keel." As regards a major renegotiation of color lines in postannexation New Orleans, and by extension the post-Reconstruction South, this novel's spirit of reform yields little more than the suboptimal consolation of enlightened impotence: the heightened awareness, as Honoré puts it, of being "a spectacle to civilization, sitting in a horrible darkness."[32]

This impasse underscores the self-dividedness of Cable's position as a racial progressive. Like most other liberals of his day both white and black, including Twain, he distinguished equality of civil rights from "social equality," meaning ultimately racial amalgamation. Certainly on principle, probably also from prudence, he took pains to insist that both black and white prefer mingling with their own kind, pointing as proof to what he took to be complete absence of interracial sex and marriage at the nation's only two integrated student bodies, Oberlin and Berea.[33] *The Grandissimes* did a far better job than *Huckleberry Finn* in its calibrated rendering of a great range of nonwhite figures as well as in dramatizing through the pride, rage, and despair of both Bras-Coupé and Honoré f.m.c. the claims of black rights denied. But no less was the novel committed to keeping relations across the color line in the desired new world order civil (as between the brothers Grandissime) rather than intimate (Palmyre's hopeless love for the white Honoré). Had *The Grandissimes* made a concerted attempt to dramatize the "safer" intimacy of fraternal companionship between the two Honorés during their European salad days, perhaps it might have bested as a defining image of camaraderie across the color line Twain's treatment of the Huck-Jim relation that Ellison summed up in the shrewd combination of tribute and equivocation that leads off this chapter: "No Huck and Jim, no American novel as we know it" (*CE* 581).

Quite apart from this guardedness on the subject of cross-racial fraternization, Cable's commitment to rendering the fraught tangle of Franco-Creole society and its near impenetrability to outsiders made it inevitable that *The Grandissimes*'s oblique engagement of the issues of race and Reconstruction would have no "discernible, practical influence on his readers or his era" apart from irritating the self-appointed custodians of New Orleans Franco-Creole memory.[34] It's not surprising that the novel should have enjoyed nothing better than a very modest success d'estime,[35] until literary modernism made the aesthetics of difficulty fashionable and the twentieth-century southern literary renaissance began to attract enough interest in the southern literary past to grant *The Grandissimes* a place on the map of literary history as a worthy precursor of the likes of Faulkner's *Absalom, Absalom!,* the centerpiece of Chapter 9. By contrast, the failure of Charles Chesnutt's *The Marrow of Tradition* (1901) to gain the widespread attention its author hoped takes a bit more explaining.

Marrow was a no less ambitiously far-reaching socioanalysis than *The Grandissimes* of racial and class fault lines in a southern city over several generations, in this case from the late antebellum era to the present. Chesnutt was a no less seasoned writer than Cable; he was backed by an even more prestigious literary publisher (Houghton Mifflin); and *Marrow* was written in a more accessible stylistic register. The first African American novelist to be published by major white publishing houses, Chesnutt had attracted notice as a rising talent for his conjure tales, designed along the lines of Joel Chandler Harris's Uncle Remus dialect stories but as a corrective to their plantation-era nostalgia. But Chesnutt's literary ambitions were always higher than that. White enough to pass but always black-identified even after migrating North, Chesnutt harbored from youth onward the dream that a black writer who knew the South far better than Stowe or Tourgée might write a book more authoritative and attention getting than theirs. In *Marrow,* Chesnutt thought at first that he might have pulled it off. He wrote Booker T. Washington that it was "by far the best thing I have done"—"a comprehensive study of racial conditions in the South" that "my publishers boldly compare with *Uncle Tom's Cabin* for its 'great dramatic intensity and its powerful appeal to popular sympathies.'"[36]

Marrow reprises, closely enough to have been read as a roman à clef, the course of a notorious 1898 North Carolina episode that had enraged Chesnutt. What became known as the Wilmington riot was the product of a combination of legal chicanery and rabble-rousing more accurately described as a white "revolution" or "pogrom," fomented by racist Democrats to undermine the alliance of Republicans and populists that had briefly restored a measure of African American political representation to state and local government.[37] Chesnutt denounced the "riot" to fellow (white) North Carolinian Walter Hines Page as "an outbreak of pure, malignant and altogether indefensible race prejudice" that left him "personally humiliated, and ashamed for the country and the State." *Marrow* details an unmistakably similar putsch in the fictional Wellington from the conspiracy of a local trio to the outbreak of promiscuous violence it instigated as a sign of what Chesnutt (wishfully) characterized as a "temporarily successful movement for the disenfranchisement of the colored race in the South."[38]

Marrow coordinates synthetic reflection on history, politics, and culture with a concentrated portrayal of its implications for two families genealogically interlinked across the color line, the black-bourgeois Millers and the white blue-blood Carterets. Janet Miller, wife of a gifted and altruistic local stevedore's son who has returned after first-class medical training in the North and Europe to head a new hospital that specializes in training nurses, is the black half-sister of Olivia Carteret, whose unreconstructed husband is the conspiracy's original organizer and spokesman as editor of the town's leading white paper. To boil Chesnutt's complex analysis down to barest essentials, the European-educated Dr. Miller becomes the novel's chief exemplar of such northern-coded traits as the culture of professionalism, egalitarian liberalism, and rule of law, as against Major Carteret the white-tribalist hierarch who values honor above law and order. The wives focus the romance of the divide at the familial level. Janet longs for some sign of recognition by Olivia, who reacts phobically, her generic racism aggravated by their looking so alike as to be mistaken for each other and by the Millers having presumed to buy up the Carteret mansion after the war bankrupted the family.

The anonymous narrator, studiously urbane and ostensibly non-judgmental for the most part, gives neither side a free pass but makes his underlying sympathies clear. The cross-section of white southerners from beneficent patriarchs to roughneck thugs are made understandable on their own terms, but in order to expose the lengths to which they are prepared to go to keep the black community in subjection using wealth and social connection for legal chicanery, political rigging, and control of the mass media.

Predictably, the Millers and their black compeers suffer far worse than the Carterets and other whites, but win a moral victory of sorts. Many African Americans are killed or run out of town, as against a single named white fatality. Miller's hospital is burned to the ground, and his only son is slain by a stray bullet. But the residually decent Carteret is aghast to see the violence spiral out of control and humbled when Miller angrily refuses his plea to leave his grieving wife to operate on Carteret's gravely ill son Dodie. This is the symbolic comeuppance of an early scene when Carteret refused Miller admission to his home on a similar errand over the objection of a white specialist summoned from Philadelphia who explicitly requested Miller's help. More crucial to interfamily dynamics per se, the wall of separation gets breached between Janet and Olivia, who has been inwardly troubled since her discovery—and destruction—of the proof that her widowed father had legally married and provided a handsome legacy for his ex-slave housekeeper after his first white wife's death during the brief postwar period when miscegenation was legal in North Carolina. When Miller rebuffs Carteret, Olivia rushes to beseech Janet, embracing her as a sister and promising restitution. The grieving mother replies in scorn ("I throw you back your father's name, your father's wealth . . . they are bought too dear") but relents and orders her husband to attend Dodie, "that you may know that a woman may be foully wronged, and yet have a heart to feel."[39]

Does the tracheotomy succeed? Do the sisters reconcile? Will Carteret change his stripes? Will the hospital get rebuilt? Will the black community recover? All this is left hanging. Chesnutt publicly insisted that *Marrow* was "a study in pessimism" precisely because he believed "that the forces of progress will in the end prevail." The novel itself is not so sure, nor was Chesnutt in fact. As he wrote Washington shortly after, "I have no confidence in that friendship of the whites which is to take the place of rights, and no expectation of justice at their hands unless it is founded on law."[40] *Marrow*'s final chapter—Olivia Carteret's desperate plea—is a grim inversion of Eliza to Mrs. Bird, "Ma'am, have you ever lost a child?" (*UTC* 76). Although Chesnutt had little interest in childhood as a fictional subject, he knew that the vulnerable child was a potent symbol of the state, or fate, of the body politic. But he placed no such confidence as Stowe did in "sentimental power" to trump racism.[41]

Chesnutt's optimism, such as it was, rested not on isolated expressions of affect but on social change over the long haul. In several striking essays shortly before *Marrow,* Chesnutt sought to counter the "dream of a pure white race, of the Anglo-Saxon type," by stressing the demographic fact that the category of "white man" had already become as incoherent as the patchwork of state-by-state definitions of whiteness and miscegenation, and declaring it a "foregone conclusion" that from this crucible would evolve a "future American race" marked by "complete racial fusion." He did well to caution that this process was "likely to be extremely slow"; for only in the early twenty-first century, a generation after the last state anti-miscegenation laws had been repealed and a half-century after they had been ruled unconstitutional, did biracial marriage began to climb markedly in the deep South (though still a miniscule percentage and still opposed by nearly 50 percent) and polyracial self-identification become widespread enough to make what Chesnutt foresaw seem anything like a viable future possibility.[42]

It took nearly the same length of time for *Marrow* to be recognized as a major novel. Despite Houghton Mifflin's promotion of it as the *Uncle Tom's Cabin* of its day, sales were mediocre, fewer than 4,000 copies after three years as against Chesnutt's idea of 20,000 to 30,000 as the benchmark of "popular success";[43] and reviews were distinctly mixed. Turn-of-the-century American readers at large preferred Winston Churchill's *The Crisis* (1901), a straight-up divide romance of the Civil War era (white Missouri girl wooed by Union and Confederate swains), and even more so Thomas Dixon's toxically racist *The Leopard's Spots* (1902), whose sales topped 100,000. *The Leopard's Spots* skewers *Uncle Tom's Cabin* (e.g., Simon Legree resurfaces first as Scalawag, then wizard of Wall Street; George Harris's son's suit for the daughter of Brahmin New England's leading champion of black rights gets vindictively rebuffed), moving in the finale to a replay of the white triumphalist version of the

Wilmington outbreak, with hero Charlie Gaston winning the governorship—thanks to suppression of the black vote and inflammatory appeals to Anglo-Saxon unity, "the manhood of the Aryan race," and the Negro's appalling insolence—by "the largest majority ever given a candidate for that office in the history of North Carolina." Along the way, Dixon throws in for good measure a chapter, "The New America," that celebrates the Spanish-American War as a triumph of ex-Confederate military genius that "reunited the Anglo-Saxon race."[44]

Dixon's handlers were under no illusion that he was a more talented writer than Chesnutt. His publisher, none other than Chesnutt's former editor and confidant Page, now relocated from the *Atlantic* to Doubleday, Page, and Company, accepted his former Carolina clubmate's manuscript on the recommendation of Frank Norris (*The Octopus* was another of the firm's best sellers) as well as the rest of Dixon's "Reconstruction trilogy"—*The Klansman* (1905) and *The Traitor* (1907)—despite his "low opinion of Dixon's talents as a writer." What's more, the firm had the bad taste to promote *Leopard's Spots* together with Booker T. Washington's *Up from Slavery*, to Washington's distress. The liberal Page's weak excuse was that "giving exposure to Dixon's racism was the most effective way to combat such prejudices."[45]

Dixon's box office success, and the even greater success of D. W. Griffith's film *Birth of a Nation* (1915), based on *The Klansman*, attest to the strength and durability of ideological appeals to white solidarity and white power abroad from the late nineteenth century into the 1920s. That the Anglo-Saxon or (more broadly) the Anglophone race was destined to dominate the world, with the United States taking the lead from the British Empire, became a journalistic commonplace. The advance of this mentality among white northerners more concerned with the challenge of absorbing hordes of immigrants from eastern and southern Europe, and East Asia too, into an economy growing as fast as China's in the early 2000s was both a cause and an effect of the success of the South-led campaign during the half century after Appomattox to refight—and largely win—the war over Civil War memory as a contest between white heroes that eventuated in a reunion of the Blue and the Gray with blacks largely left out. After Reconstruction ended in 1877, even liberal northern journalists expressed relief that "the negro will disappear from the field of national politics," that "the nation as a nation, will have nothing more to do with him."[46] Until well after large-scale black migration northward had begun, the "Negro Question" remained seen as a problem best left to the South to resolve.

It was predictable, then, that *Huckleberry Finn's* no less searching but much more equivocal satire of southern backwardness would prove far more compelling to a national audience than *Marrow's* did, and that *Marrow* would be eclipsed during Chesnutt's lifetime by the likes of Dixon's trilogy, notwithstanding Chesnutt's infinitely greater mastery of his medium. As the scholar who has studied *Marrow's* reception most closely points out, northern readers did not relate to it as a book directed to them, while southern readers excoriated it even when they respected its craftsmanship.[47] "How difficult it is to write race problem books so that white people will read them," Chesnutt lamented.[48] His earlier autoanalysis to Booker T. Washington had proven all too prophetic: precisely because *Marrow* was "on the stronger side in point of justice and morality," Chesnutt found himself decidedly "on the weaker side in point of popular sympathy." Even William Dean Howells, hitherto an influential supporter on the strength of Chesnutt's conjure tales, was repelled by *Marrow's* "bitterness." Up to a point, Howells's reaction typified his general aversion to what he considered the gratuitously violent extremes to which Zola and other writers pushed fictional realism. But it also reflected a settled preference for ethnic writers who wrote like ethnics: Dunbar's dialect poetry, early Chesnutt, Abraham Cahan. Chesnutt's emphatic rejection of that mask in order to chastise white hegemony seemed a hostile act, as if Janet's retort to Olivia had been directed at him personally. "'Good Lord! How such a negro must hate us,'" Howells wrote a fellow (white) novelist.[49]

Even after the shakeup of the canon of U.S. literature in the 1970s and after began to elevate Chesnutt from minor to major figure and to propose *Marrow* as his "magnum opus,"[50] critics remained ambivalent about the book, as a "badly-plotted melodrama," a "hot-headed performance," overdependent on such threadbare plot devices as the stolen and then fortuitously rediscovered documents.[51] Nor were *Marrow's* fortunes helped by its being so focused on anatomizing whiteness and so much more focused on the fate of the black bourgeois professional Miller and his family than on the fate of his man-of-the-people counterpart, the militants' leader Joe Green. The most strenuous and still the most dexterously penetrating argument for *Marrow's* claims as a masterwork approaches it, significantly, through the conjure tales and attaches special importance to the novel's two blackface scenes, where the most nefarious gentry-class villain impersonates his grandfather's faithful servant, tarnishing his reputation and jeopardizing his life.[52]

Today those early tales still remain Chesnutt's most admired and studied work. But the twenty-first-century tendency to push back against overly normative definitions of African American and other "ethnic" writing—to press Chesnutt's sophistication as sociologist of whiteness, as a pivotal figure within the push for racial uplift crucial to African American literature's cultural politics at that time, and as much of a supporter of black collective resistance as could have been expected given his historical context[53]—is likely to strengthen the case for the Chesnutt of *Marrow* as a GAN contender as legitimate as Cable and Norris if not also Twain.

Meanwhile, *Marrow*'s lukewarm reception in its own time predicted that the most enduring of the nation-defining romances of the North/South and black/white divides would emerge neither from the North nor from escaped southerners, nor from doctrinaire expressions of the "New South" like Dixon, but from the still-newer South that, as the region belatedly modernized, generated the strongest body of regional writing during the first half of the new century. And when it did, that the subject of interracial mingling would be treated even more gingerly than in Twain and Cable, let alone Chesnutt.

9

Faulkner's Absalom, Absalom!, *Mitchell's* Gone with the Wind, *and Literary Interracialism North and South*

> White men: the arbitrary and obstinate men who pursue inflexibly their incomprehensible purposes—beings with weird intonations in the voice, moved by unaccountable feelings, actuated by inscrutable motives.
>
> —JOSEPH CONRAD, "The End of the Tether" (1902)

> It is quite obvious that the ethics of none of us is clearly defined, and we are continually obliged to act in circles of habit, based upon convictions which we no longer hold.
>
> —JANE ADDAMS, *Democracy and Social Ethics* (1902)

W ELL INTO the twentieth century, "American" literature and culture continued to be painted white despite growing evidence to the contrary. "What the powerful and the privileged mean by Americanization," declared W. E. B. Du Bois in 1922, is "but a renewal of the Anglo-Saxon cult, the worship of the Nordic totem, the disenfranchisement of Negro, Jew, Irishman, Italian, Hungarian, Asiatic, and South Sea islander." Under such conditions, he dryly added, the South could be seen as having a special cultural cachet, as "'pure' Anglo-Saxon, despite the fact that it is so widely degraded, reactionary, and without art, literature or humanitarian impulse."[1]

Du Bois's dismissal of the South as wasteland, like H. L. Mencken's better-known "Sahara of the Bozart" (1920), was disconfirmed without being refuted by the sophistication of the southern literary renaissance of the second quarter of the century, which stands as U.S. literary regionalism's high-water mark between the Civil War and World War II. Since the 1940s, William Faulkner has held his place as its towering figure, "literary loner" though he was.[2] But both Faulkner's accomplishment and that of the Southern Renaissance generally also attest to the inertial force of the top-down conception—and self-conception—of the South as distinctively "agrarian" by contrast to the industrial North, and distinctive too, as the southern historian U. B. Phillips wrote in 1928, for the "common resolve indomitably maintained" that it "shall be and remain a white man's country."[3]

The white triumphalism that came into fashion starting with the North's postbellum techno-industrial surge, the "winning of the West," the Spanish-American War, and the rise of the United States as a world power both economically and militarily strengthened these views of southern distinctiveness, reinforcing a heightened sense of essential southernness both outside and within the region. In this, (white) southern regionalism of the 1920s marked an intensification of regional movements generally in the history of a vast republic during which the claims of the federal center relative to the territorial and jurisdictional parts have been debated continually as it has evolved over two centuries from agricultural to metropolitan, with concomitant diversification of the ethnoracial mix. "Region" in this context tends to stand whether positively or negatively, to insiders and outsiders alike, for roots, for heritage, and for the survival of a greater internal cultural coherence than under modernization. Hence Stowe's Poganuc and Jewett's Dunnet Landing, Twain's Mississippi River towns and Garland's rural farming communities in the upper Midwest—and for that matter the urban ethnic neighborhood microregions of Sui Sin Far, Abraham Cahan, Richard Wright, Bernard Malamud, and Sandra Cisneros.

That the imagined South came to seem a kind of successor to the imagined New England of Hawthorne and Emily Dickinson, as such twentieth-century southern intellectuals as Alan Tate and Lewis Simpson proposed, arose from a kindred sense of operating within as well as against a long-embedded place-based tribalism. In both cases, writers often registered cross-currents of allegiance to and entrapment within that heritage by resorting to like strategies of gothicization: warped Calvinistic religiocentrism, skeletons in the ancestral closet, the trope of the haunted house. Faulkner's first working title for *Absalom, Absalom!* was "The Dark House." In this shadow land he achieved the early twentieth century's most original reinvention of the romance of the

North-South divide and established himself as "the avatar and mythic craftsman of so many undead ghosts of our national imaginings."[4]

Burning the House Down: Absalom, Absalom!

In *Uncle Tom's Cabin,* haunting also looms large, but not as an index of regional or ethnic difference. Both its characteristic forms tend to erase those: children's memories of dead mothers or vice versa, and obsession, whether deemed "piety" or "superstition," with the boundary crossings between mundane and spiritual worlds. *Huckleberry Finn* as a reminiscence of antebellum regional grotesque is haunted by implication but keeps the ghosts at bay through its comic plot set in a thoroughly disillusioned nominal present. In *Absalom,* not only is the present time of the plot a quarter century prior to the book's publication, but the novel takes the form of a speculative reconstruction of a story that began a century before. Not only is there no way of telling except by extrapolation that *Absalom* is a work of the Depression years and a point in the history of southern modernization when the South's urban growth was outstripping that of other regions by a large margin albeit from a much lower baseline.[5] *Absalom* even represses the historical context of its nominal 1909–1910 present, soon after the triumph of the counterrevolution against black civil rights, just before the first southerner since Zachary Taylor would become president and go on to approve a back-to-the-future segregation of federal offices. But *Absalom* does hint at what it declines to acknowledge by the obsessiveness with which its present-time characters rehash the remote regional past even when it sickens them. The "very body" of young Quentin Compson has become "an empty hall echoing with sonorous defeated names," "a barracks filled with stubborn back-looking ghosts" like the ancient crone who holds him in unwilling captivity as she rehearses the indignities she suffered a half century before (*AA* 7).

Faulkner could not have written this and the other past-haunted fictions that stand among his greatest works—*The Sound and the Fury* and *Go Down, Moses* chief among them—had he been immune to the lure of what he gothicized and to the continuing market appeal of romances of the North-South divide. That appeal had recently been demonstrated anew by Stephen Vincent Benét's epic poem *John Brown's Body,* which won the Pulitzer Prize in 1928 and remained a best seller throughout the time Faulkner worked on *Absalom. John Brown's Body* dramatizes the bravery, fecklessness, suffering, and confusion on both sides—home fronts as well as battle fronts—by tracing through the war years with almost mathematical evenhandedness the vicissitudes of white counterparts North and South (Abraham Lincoln/Jefferson Davis, Yankee/Confederate generals, representative Billy Yank and Johnny Reb soldiers). Typically for a mainstream northern writer of the day, Benét treats slavery as having catalyzed the spectacle of white strife and reunion without considering the aftereffects the poem unwittingly confesses by romanticizing plantation life and by consigning its typecast black figures to ancillary roles both in slavery and in freedom. Birthright southerners like Faulkner and Margaret Mitchell knew better, although their heterodoxies took the form of unsettling the 1920s theme park version of southern memory from within rather than confronting it head on.

Faulkner scholars have shown that he himself was a southern gentleman of pedigree who acted the part with gusto when he became well-heeled enough to do so. "The squire of Oxford," as James Baldwin snickeringly called him,[6] grew up in a family that depended upon faithful black retainers who knew their place, some of whom became his retainers too, including his mammy, whose funeral elegy he delivered, evidently at her request. When civil rights agitation in the 1950s became too hot for his conservative liberalism to handle, Faulkner went so far as to insist, "My negro boys down on the plantation would fight against the North with me," if he urged them to.[7]

Under the circumstances, it would have been astonishing had the biographical Faulkner been immune from "the South's abiding racist cliché": "blacks as obedient children when enslaved, potential beasts when emancipated."[8] Five years before *Absalom* imagines Quentin telling Shreve what he has heard about the mysterious Sutpen saga and the two of them proceeding to fill in the blanks, the future novelist's first grade teacher had presented him with an inscribed copy of Thomas Dixon's recent novel *The Klansman.* Three years later, an enthusiastically received dramatic adaptation, the basis for *Birth of a Nation,* was staged at the Oxford Mississippi Opera House not long after the local lynching of a black man for allegedly raping a white woman. This too was the year schoolboy William reportedly declared that he wanted to "be a writer like my great-granddaddy," the colorful, hard-driving Confederate officer and prototype of Faulkner's Colonel Sartoris, author of *The White Rose of Memphis,* among other books.[9] In the mid-1930s (and for many years after), lynchings of African Americans still occurred at a disproportionate rate throughout the deep South, albeit a diminishing one. Dixon still lived. *The Klansman* reposed in the library of the antebellum mansion Faulkner had recently acquired; and he himself had begun to favor white linen suits (as had Twain) and to fancy himself a latter-day planter, complete with acreage and black field hands. Like "a slave-era film set," the eminent Martinican writer Édouard Glissant summed up his impression of Faulkner's museumized Rowan Oak after a 1989 visit, noticing the same spatial configuration as "from northeastern Brazil to the Caribbean": "the big House and the slave hut, masters and slaves."[10]

But the side of Faulkner's mind where his best fiction incubated sensed the theatricality of such reenactments: knew that the Old South was yesterday's memory, and largely bogus at that; knew that white dominance and institutionalized racism were indefensible; knew that plantocracy had been based more on power and pretense than civility; knew that African Americans had been given a raw deal, however much he dreaded the prospect of disruptive social change; knew too that "the white man can never really know the Negro because the white man has forced the Negro to be always a Negro rather than another human being in their dealings." Quentin Compson of *The Sound and the Fury* figures as *Absalom*'s most pivotal narrator—so Faulkner told his publisher—precisely to inject a dose of "bitterness" against the South, so as to "keep the hoop skirts and plug hats" of standard historical romance at bay.[11]

Today most Faulknerians agree that *Absalom* was his "most ambitious, detailed, and complex novel" and his most intricately sustained reflection on the romance of the divides of region and race, especially the challenge of trying to think across the racial divide in the knowledge of the systemic barriers in the way of doing so.[12]

The roommates Quentin and Shreve conduct the semitelepathic dialogue that dominates the novel's second half at the historical moment when the memorial reunification of the (white) North and (white) South was about to reach its post-Reconstruction apogee in the semicentennial Blue-Gray commemoration of the Battle of Gettysburg in 1913. Just as *Absalom* elasticizes the South as part of a larger Afro-Caribbean polyglot Creole world when it takes Sutpen to the Caribbean for his induction into the master class, so the novel's present time deploys the Mississippi-Missouri watershed as the geographic matrix within which it reconceives the U.S. North and South as a unitary North American macro-unit by pairing the Mississippian Quentin with the Albertan Shreve: "born half a continent apart yet joined, connected after a fashion in a sort of geographical transubstantiation by that Continental Trough, that River which runs not only through the physical land of which it is the geological umbilical, not only through the spiritual lives of the beings within its scope, but is [*sic*] very Environment itself which laughs at degrees of latitude and temperature" (*AA* 208).[13] What seals their twinship, however, is not the cartographic link per se but their interaction as co-concluders of the story the elders of Jefferson, Mississippi, had begun, in a tense intimacy marked by fascination, rivalry, and disaffection on both sides—Shreve's with southern bizarreness, Quentin's with the burden of having to relive all this stuff yet again and to correct Shreve's mistakes (which are often also shrewd fortuities), like calling "Miss Rosa" "Aunt Rosa," which she literally was but in white southern parlance mustn't be called unless she's black.

Through the mutual fascination with the southern past that arises within and despite these estrangements, *Absalom* underscores that white outlanders were as likely to become swept up by the drama and angst of southern aristocratic memory as scions like Quentin—and Faulkner. *Absalom*'s coup de grace is letting Shreve ultimately take over the narrative—letting him be the one to set in place the last piece of the speculative jigsaw puzzle: the hypothetical scene where Sutpen is imagined telling Henry the real reason why Judith can't marry Bon and Bon retorts to Henry's last plea, *"I'm the nigger that's going to sleep with your sister. Unless you stop me, Henry"* (*AA* 286). Until now, the back-and-forthing of vicarious identification between the roommates and the Sutpen half brothers has tied Quentin more to Henry, Shreve more to Bon. But Shreve's excitement puts his casual racism into high gear as he whirls ahead to Chapter 8's final (pseudo-?)epiphany, that sometime during the return to Sutpen's Hundred "the black son of a bitch" substituted his octoroon mistress's picture for Judith's so that if Henry actually did kill him, Judith would less likely grieve (286). This might be flat wrong. It directly contradicts what Rosa claimed: that she saw the picture with her own eyes, a picture of Judith (114). And the extent to which Shreve is simply recycling what Quentin had previously told him of his own encounter with Clytie, Henry, and Jim Bond during Rosa's and his scary nighttime visit to the decaying house the previous September could be debated forever. What can't be disputed is the novel's readiness to let Shreve hijack the story and be the one to niggerize Bon. This is *Absalom*'s way of harking back to a crucial point made by antebellum southern romances of the divide, acknowledged by Stowe in *Uncle Tom's Cabin*, and reaffirmed many times over by nineteenth-century southern writers, including Dixon: that aversion to intimate contact with African Americans had long since pervaded the North, from at least as early as the abolition of slavery in the first northeastern states' emancipation laws during the Revolutionary era.*

In itself, Shreve's swipe at Bon is a trivial piece of smartass adolescent theatrics compared to the gravity with which the narrators approach Sutpen's disownment of his first wife, his refusal to make any sign of recognition to their grown-up son presuming him to be such, and the fact of Henry's fratricide. But might a further point about the out-of-control toxicity of post-Reconstruction racism be embedded here, given that the novel depends so utterly on these youths to play the race card? As is often pointed out, without the aid of Faulkner's after-the-fact Chronology and such pronouncements as touting *Absalom* to a Hollywood agent as being "about miscegenation,"[14] it's impossible to judge whether there's any basis to Shreve/Quentin's surmise that Bon was Sutpen's discarded near-white son. The narrative overvoice insinuates at several points that their fantasies may have run away with them, and they themselves know that they don't know. *Absalom* is preeminently a book about legend building—and demolition—where nobody's representation of history can be taken at face value. Even to begin to talk about the what and why of the "real" history of the Sutpen clan requires, strictly speaking, that virtually everything you might want to say of importance must be hedged about with caveats and qualifications. But these four things seem clear. One, the two elder narrators, Rosa and Mr. Compson (who retells with his own embellishments what he heard from his father) either don't think or don't allow themselves to think or

---

* Joanne Pope Melish, *Disowning Slavery: Gradual Emancipation and "Race" in New England 1780–1860* (Ithaca, NY: Cornell University Press, 1998), shows that Revolutionary era emancipation of slaves in the northern states led to a white withdrawal from social contact with blacks that aggravated white racism. Elise Lemire confirms this in her intensive case study, *Black Walden: Slavery and Its Aftermath in Concord, Massachusetts* (Philadelphia: University of Pennsylvania Press, 2009).

feel blocked from articulating that miscegenation is at the bottom of the Sutpen family tragedy. Two, Shreve and Quentin do believe it. Three, the Chronology and Genealogy Faulkner appended to the novel sustain the roommates' version, minus such excrescences as the New Orleans shyster that they perhaps invent in order to help solve such puzzles as why Bon wound up at Ole Miss with Henry. And four, the cumulative effect of this unfolding—the elders' version of the story being "corrected" and "completed" by the collegians, their intersubjective consensus then broadly confirmed by the Chronology—adds retrospective cogency to a reading of the novel as a thinking person's mystery story that delivers a solution at the plot level, however conjectural, that comes closer to tying up loose ends than any other.

Why does *Absalom* portray the elders as never even seeming to consider that Bon's putative black blood was what precipitated the civil war among the Sutpens? For though it can't be ruled out that some or all of them do know,[15] none of them come closer to expressing this than Mr. Compson's recycling of the local suspicion that "there was a nigger in the woodpile somewhere" (*AA* 56), which refers rather to Sutpen's shady business dealings. We can't know whether Quentin Compson's grandfather the general, Sutpen's only confidant, was too unimaginative to hazard the guess that race might have been the reason for Sutpen's putting his first wife aside, or for the dilemma he mentions in their last meeting of being forced either to witness his grand design destroyed or destroy it by his own hand. We can't know whether Mr. Compson seriously considered any alternative to his theory that the root cause of Sutpen's stubbornness was rigid opposition to Bon's bigamous marriage to his octoroon mistress, even though the theory didn't satisfy him. Or whether, like Quentin himself in *The Sound and the Fury,* Mr. Compson got so sidetracked by the Composonish fantasy of Henry courting Bon on Judith's behalf as a case of sibling incest that he couldn't think more clearly than the outraged Rosa. Or whether the elders suspected something but didn't say—which admittedly would have been in keeping with their preference for circumlocution over plainness. In any case, the device of the deferred "disclosure" arrestingly synchronizes—almost too well—with certain key currents of nineteenth-century history and memory.

For the novel to have imagined the specter of miscegenation as having been explicitly raised by Sutpen only when the Civil War was almost over is in keeping with the belatedness with which "miscegenation" surfaced in public culture as a neologism (1863) and intensified as a legislative priority. Emancipation made statutory prohibition in the South against racial intermarriage seem more urgent. To imagine Henry as agonizing throughout the war over whether to allow the incest taboo to be violated, then making a kind of peace with his scruples only to go ballistic over the miscegenation prospect, is an eye-popping inversion of views held almost universally worldwide about the relative cogency of taboos against incest and exogamy. It underscores the perversity of orthodox memory of the Civil War both South and North as fratricide with a happy ending via the reunion of the white protagonists. Orthodox memory did this by accentuating the genealogical intimacy between warring parties together with phobic reaction against those of nonqualifying blood. So concludes *The Klansman:* Grand Dragon Ben Cameron and the northerner who has become his most intimate friend, enemies in war but now brothers in allegiance to the doctrine of white triumphalism to which Ben has converted Philip, marry each other's sisters after putting down the intractably bestial and/or menial blacks by lynching and intimidation. Whereas in *Absalom* postbellum southern recuperation fails as spectacularly as secession did when the planter-patriarch's refusal to countenance a black son-in-law rubs off on Henry and the house goes down amid the old man's degradingly bestial attempts to perpetuate a 100 percent pure Caucasian dynasty by coupling with the two last white females within reach.

The extent to which Faulkner intended *Absalom* as demolition of, qualified dissent from, or concession to the afterglow of plantation memory is unknowable. But he surely would have been well aware of the entanglement of incest and miscegenation in southern thought, whether or not he knew about the 1880 statute declaring intermarriage between whites and African Americans "incestuous and void" or the 1854 sociological treatise by fellow Mississippian Henry Hughes claiming that "amalgamation is incest" on the ground that "the same law which forbids consanguineous amalgamation forbids ethnical amalgamation."[16] Even as he was putting the finishing touches on *Absalom* he was mulling the stories of *Go Down, Moses* (1941), which hinges on young Ike McCaslin's horrified discovery that the clan's founding patriarch had forced sex on a female slave and then incest on their daughter, mixing up the family bloodlines irretrievably. This luridly recycled the common charge by nineteenth-century abolitionists and southern matrons alike that the planters had created harems under their own roofs to pleasure themselves and aggrandize their stock of human property. That the ultimate horror for the conventionally filiopietistic Ike is incest rather than miscegenation underscores the anachronism of the roommates' fantasy of race mixing as the ultimate horror. They belong to the next generation, when white purity was even more entrenched.

In late life, Faulkner distanced himself from paranoid purism in venturing the Chesnutt-like prediction that "in the long view, the Negro race will vanish in three hundred years by intermarriage. It has happened to every racial minority everywhere, and it will happen here."[17] Not that he was recommending it happen any time soon. It's hard to imagine him content to see his daughter marry someone with known traces of African ancestry. But *Absalom* overstates the intractability of the barrier posed by "miscegenation as such" for "class transformation" in "the real world of the antebellum south," as critic Walter Benn Michaels points out. The Quentin/Shreve conception of it as "Sutpen's undoing" has been "refigured for Jim Crow."[18] *Go Down, Moses's* tale "Delta Autumn" more directly registers both the impact of the obdurate 1900s segregationism and its coming demise by depicting the octogenarian Ike, circa 1940, recoiling in horror when confronted by the living proof of the amour between his white nephew and a part-black McCaslin cousin *("Maybe in a thousand or two thousand years in America . . . But not now!")*[19] This time around, it's not the consanguinity issue but the interracial sex that panics him.

As for Sutpen's obduracy, that too seems overreactive in its own context. Even a dogmatically racist antebellum planter, Godden points out, could easily have averted the tragedy he brought upon himself. "By letting the community know that 'Bon was part Negro,' he could have legitimized Henry's claim to full inheritance," thus reining in Bon and keeping his grand "design" intact. Faulkner's own great-grandfather the Colonel, whose career also spanned the Civil War, had acknowledged and generously provided for his own biracial daughter, though not as a legitimate heir.[20] So at the very least Sutpen was extremely picky in remaining so standoffish toward Bon. Alternatively, he could have kept silent, let the marriage take place, and no one would have batted an eye since Bon was white enough to pass, and no one else in Jefferson knew anything about Bon's past nor would have been likely to dispute the verdict of the town's richest and most powerful citizen. Throughout the nineteenth century, it seems to have been well known, and up to a point accepted, that planter bloodlines were not 100 percent pure. Hence the chaos of discrepant state laws defining non/whiteness in terms of specified fractional descent. Hence a white South Carolina legislator as late as the 1890s successfully advocated for a minimum one-eighth ancestry as the criterion for defining who was black on the ground that "a one-drop rule would prevent marriage among many white families in South Carolina, since many of them had black ancestry."[21]

Although it can't be ruled out that Faulkner fashioned Sutpen anachronistically in conscious or unconscious accord with the one-drop ideology that was more solidly in place by the 1900s, another explanation seems at least as probable. To depict him as giving no sign that either feasible form of recognition was an option reinforces a point that to very different ends both Chesnutt and Dixon had driven home, that the most rabidly antiblack southerners were uneducated, uncouth, self-made poor whites like *Marrow of Tradition*'s rabble-rousing "Colonel" McBane, the person most responsible for provoking the white mob to violence. As *Absalom* underscores many times over, Sutpen and his poor-white retainer Wash are two peas in a pod. At Sutpen's sufferance, Wash holds his place as a symbolic marker of how far Sutpen's design has carried him. Wash dramatizes both the immense distance between Sutpen's manor house and his shack and the symbolic intimacy between them as his boss's drinking buddy under the "scuppernong" arbor. Sutpen's death under Wash's scythe, an obvious parody of the cliché of death as grim reaper, reduces him to Wash's level at last. Faulkner's 1934 story "Wash," a short-form trial run at this scene, drives home the equation between the two by having the omniscient narrator transmit the realization that impels Wash to cut Sutpen down instead of rendering it as Mr. Compson's conjecture relayed at second hand by Quentin: *"Better if his kind and mine too had never drawn the breath of life on this earth"* (*AA* 233).

So what General Compson (and subsequently his son and grandson) call Sutpen's "innocence" is better understood as a euphemism for the blinkered dogmatism of the uncouth hillbilly parvenu. That the novel never puts it so bluntly follows from wanting to evoke the aura of plantation mythography and bring the house down at the same time: to

dramatize the hold of plantation memory on the national imaginary—
North as well as South, the author included—yet eviscerate it as a
bankrupt hallucination. To magnify Sutpen even more than Fitzgerald
did Gatsby, then chop him back down to Wash's level is only one of
several strategies to that end. Another is to channel the plantation stereotype through Rosa's overheated memories of the halcyon summer
of Judith's and Bon's engagement, even as she demolishes that claptrap
by denouncing Sutpen's monstrousness and her own girlish naïveté.
However much she insists on reliving the past and cherishing her ladylike dignity, Rosa is more cynical about the hogwash of Old South
memory than all the other narrators put together. Another strategy is
to show the roommates oscillating between fascination and contempt
(Shreve) or fascination and despair (Quentin) at the lurid story they
(re)construct. Still another, in some ways the most fundamental, is to
historicize antebellum Mississippi as being, underneath a thin genteel
veneer of Compson decorum and Coldfield respectability, a kind of Wild
West outback.

Significantly, the novel's first, oft-repeated images of Sutpen's arrival read like a dime novel rerun of the man on the horse "who rode
out of nowhere" into an unsuspecting frontier town. Jefferson of the mid-
1830s was a mere "village," Rosa recalls; and even at the height of Sutpen's prewar prosperity, as Mr. Compson dryly notes, a rustic backwater
from the standpoint of a sophisticate from New Orleans like Charles Bon,
by comparison to whom "Henry and Sutpen were troglodytes" (*AA* 74).
He imagines Ellen Coldfield Sutpen hankering for Bon to be "a mentor
and example to correct Henry's provincial manners and speech and
clothing" (59). Mr. Compson goes on to imagine a worshipful Henry
who not only loves Bon but woos Judith for him by proxy thrown for a
loop when his small-town "puritan" proprieties are disarranged by
Bon's guided tour of the New Orleans demimonde to meet his octoroon
mistress—a hypothetical incident that the roommates reinterpret as a
scene of envy on Henry's part rather than consternation. All this comports with the slighting assessment of the state of civilization in hinterland Mississippi by the most articulate northern traveler of the 1850s,
Frederick Law Olmsted, who described all the towns he traveled through
except the state capital, Jackson, as "forlorn, poverty-stricken collections
of shops, groggeries, and lawyer's offices, mingled with unsightly and
usually dilapidated dwelling houses."[22]

In a later stage of the Sutpen saga, after Henry kills Bon, the urbanity versus outback contrast gets repeated in a more melancholy key, when Mr. Compson recalls his father's observation of the surprise visit of Bon's grieving mistress and their young son at his grave. "It must have resembled a garden scene by the Irish poet, Wilde," this "magnolia-faced woman" whom Aubrey Beardsley might have sketched and her delicate son, clad in "expensive Fauntleroy clothing" (*AA* 157, 158). This exoticism partly registers Compson père's fin de siècle aestheticism, still fashionable in 1909 and shared by the young Faulkner himself, a Swinburne enthusiast. But even more it marks the cultural gap between the otherworld of cosmopolitan New Orleans and the threadbare poverty of war-ravaged rural Mississippi, back to which Clytie drags young Charles Etienne de St. Valery Bon after his mother's death. Charles Etienne is traumatized from the start and even more when forced to choose decisively, soon after, between diametrically opposite ethnic options—are you white, or are you black—both of which feel unnatural to him.

Absalom's evocations of Afro-Franco-Caribbean culture and British aestheticism expand the novel's horizons beyond North America per se into what cultural theorist Joseph R. Roach calls a "circum-Atlantic performance" across several stages in time: Thomas Sutpen's story of having "subdued" the slave revolt on the Haitian sugar plantation where he was a young overseer and winning his boss's daughter for his first wife; Sutpen's sudden arrival on the Jefferson scene with his pack of "wild" slaves who speak unintelligible Creole; the complex decorums of Franco-Creole New Orleans personified by the Bon family; the contrast between the nuanced racial codings of that metropole and the stark binary Mississippi imposes first on Bon and then on his son.[23] These transnational expansions of the narrative aperture pursue the double game of reinforcing both the provincial benightedness and the aggressive normativity of backcountry racism and xenophobia, which metamorphose into a synecdoche for white North American one-drop-ism generally when Shreve catches the virus.

Light in August, the novel that precedes *Absalom*, wrestles more overtly with the central formula of conventional North-South divide romance in the form of the amour between the guilt-ridden, tellingly named Joanna Burden and the protagonist, Joe Christmas, whose self-destructive suspicion that he might be part black pathologically activates Joanna's sexual and missionary impulses at the same time. Joanna is a hyped-up rerun of the Reconstruction-era carpetbagger schoolmarm whose conscience impels her to the alien South to help uplift the blacks— treated sympathetically by Tourgée as an embattled idealist and scornfully by Dixon in *The Leopard's Spots* as a self-deluded schemer. *Light in August* leans toward the Dixon side of the ledger, only to expose the far greater pathology of the denouement Dixon would have pictured as a triumph: vigilante justice perpetrated on Christmas (gunning down, castration) for his murder and "rape" of Joanna. In *Light in August's* lynching, the victim of the crime is far less compassionated than the perpetrator.

The terms of *Absalom's* undoing of Old South ideology—likely by happenstance—correspond in at least two ways quite closely to *Uncle Tom's Cabin's*. First, in its ascription of failed master-class marriage (the Shelbys, the St. Clares, Augustine St. Clare's parents) to institutionalized slavery. Second, in its invocation of sisterhood across the color line as a partially countervailing force.

Absalom gives far more airtime to the drama of fathers and sons than to its womenfolk except for Rosa, whose behavior reinforces the narratorial androcentrism. Her hyperboles and Mr. Compson's misogyny make it hard to see (white) women as other than hysterics, figurines, or empty vessels. But over against this, the novel seems seriously invested, up to a point anyhow, in imagining a gynocentric nonpatriarchal Sutpen "counterfamily" that cuts across distinctions of both race and gender that both the patriarch and the book's male narrators impose.[24] The narcissistic Ellen—the caricature rendition of fragile southern womanhood—is counterpointed with the more feisty Sutpen half sisters, Judith and Clytie, who are significantly first pictured as absorbed teenage spectators of their father fighting with his slaves barehanded and half-naked, as Henry cowers and pukes at the fearful sight. Judith learns to plow a furrow as straight as any man. She and Clytie emerge as staunch, steady, stoical, persevering. Although Judith is never pictured as actively reciprocating Bon's overtures, she refuses to give him up regardless of the consequences. Clytie later performs the remarkable feat of fetching Charles Etienne from New Orleans after his mother dies, although she has never left the plantation before and the two of them evidently can't speak each other's language. After war breaks out, the men enlist, and the slaves vamoose, Judith and Clytie keep the farm going—with some help from Wash—joined by Rosa for a time. What stands out especially is the interdependent fortitude of the sisters Sutpen both then and during the long aftermath of Sutpen's demise, which Judith survives by fifteen years and Clytie by forty. Although the novel never depicts a real conversation between Judith and Clytie, clearly they form a stabler bond than do Henry and Bon. This twinning of Clytie and Judith, the critic Thadious Davis observes, "becomes a subtle statement of the oneness of humankind"—womankind especially.[25] In this, *Absalom* offers a more durable exemplification of intimate interdependence across the color line than Twain does with the companionship of Huck and Jim, although in muffled form, in intermittent glimpses through the smoke screen of the narrators' narcissistic androcentricism.

The obverse side of this twinning, Davis also notes, is to isolate Clytie sociologically from visible interaction with other nonwhites outside the Sutpen clan, rather as Bon and his son are insulated from the Negro world by their cosseted New Orleans upbringing. The white family, the white community, and the (im)possibility of maintaining its purity remain *Absalom*'s overriding concerns from start to finish. Hence Édouard Glissant's judgment that "Faulkner's oeuvre" would not be complete until it was "revisited and made vital by African Americans."[26]

Recouping Tara: Gone with the Wind

It would be hard to find a more dramatic example of high culture/ middlebrow culture stratification in U.S. literary history of the past century than the concurrent publication, in 1936, of *Absalom* and Margaret Mitchell's *Gone with the Wind*. These novels still stand as the most monumental sagas of their kinds of the transit from the late plantation era through Civil War and Reconstruction: the modernist masterpiece and the all-time best seller. *Absalom* sold modestly (fewer than 10,000 copies), was reviewed lukewarmly, attained classic status only after the critical establishment had fully embraced experimental modernism, and owes its continued prestige to critically sophisticated readers and to its enshrinement within college and university curricula. *Gone with the Wind*'s hugely greater and no less enduring success must be credited wholly to popular enthusiasm aroused by first the novel and then the Hollywood film starring Vivian Leigh as Scarlett O'Hara and Faulkner's sometime hunting partner Clark Gable as Rhett Butler. It was a top Book-of-the-Month Club selection that broke *Uncle Tom's Cabin*'s old record, with 1.5 million copies sold within a year and thirty million worldwide by 2011. A quarter century into the Faulkner revival, one leading southern literature scholar reckoned that for every reader of *Absalom*, fifty had read *Gone with the Wind*.[27]

The coincidence of two such megascale evocations of the Old South makes a certain historical sense in light of the remarkable outpouring of historical fiction during the American 1930s, as literary historian Gordon Hutner shows in his survey of period novels that have fallen from view: not only of southern history, but also of the Napoleonic wars (Hervey Allen's *Anthony Adverse*), early frontier settlement (Walter Edmonds's *Drums along the Mohawk*), the American Revolution (including Kenneth Roberts's several novels retelling it from a Tory standpoint), and the epic of early twentieth-century U.S. capitalism (Dos Passos's *U.S.A.* trilogy). "No equivalent period of time has produced anything like so much critical and intelligent interpretation of American history in fiction," declared the *New York Times* reviewer Margaret Wallace at decade's end. This "need to stage American history" during the Depression years, Hutner suggests, reflected a broadly perceived "break from the past" that these novels "were enlisted to amend or dispel, not to validate."[28] In a time of economic and political turbulence widely perceived as postapocalyptic, it made sense for works of imagination to renegotiate crises of the near or distant past from the losers' perspective, be they right or left, Tory or Confederate, Dos Passos's requiem to the failure of homegrown IWW (Industrial Workers of the World) socialism in *U.S.A.* or Hemingway's elegy to Spanish Republican resistance in *For Whom the Bell Tolls* (1940). Such projects had international resonance too. The most enthusiastic early readers of Faulkner's autopsies of southern decadence were the French existentialist literati Sartre, Malraux, and Camus. Mitchell was struck that "each nation" where *Gone with the Wind* was translated "applied to its own past history the story of the Confederate rise and fall and reconstruction": "French critics spoke of 1870, Poles of the partitioning of their country, Germans of 1918 and the bitterness which followed,"

Brazilians of their own history of slavery and its aftermath and division into agricultural north and industrial south.*

The telltale differences between the two novels are easy to spot. *Absalom* is less invested in plotline as such than in metafiction and metahistory. Or rather, the challenge of grasping, of articulating, of coming to terms with history is the driving spirit of the plot. *Gone with the Wind* tells you exactly what happened when, and vividly—drawing room decor, period costume, country landscapes, urban bustle—reflecting the author's tireless zest for pinning down such minutiae as "when hoopskirts went out of fashion" in favor of bustles.[29] Genteel party scenes and storied landscapes—urban as well as rural—get painted in racy detail. *Absalom*'s characters are symbolic figments; *Gone with the Wind*'s are earthy and remarkably individuated given the stereotypes on which they rest, like Rhett's Byronism, which draws on Charlotte Brontë's Rochester and Augusta Evans's St. Elmo.[30] *Absalom*'s narrators are forever mulling whether what transpired between Judith and Bon, or Bon and Henry, counts as love. *Gone with the Wind* unfolds the tangled course of the passions of Scarlett O'Hara—"turbulent, willful, lusty with life" (*GW* 5)—complete with soft-porn trimmings. (A heroine-centered work was itself a better fit for middlebrow romance fiction's predominantly female readership.) Both novels monumentalize the sagas of their key characters by correlating individual lifelines with the tide of history; but in *Absalom* all the epochal historic events happen offstage, whereas *Gone with the Wind* thrusts you into the midst of the torching of Atlanta and Scarlett's desperate struggle to escape back to Tara. Although the

---

* Margaret Mitchell, *Margaret Mitchell's "Gone with the Wind" Letters 1936–1949*, ed. Richard Harwell (New York: Macmillan, 1976), 394. *GW* is even more transnationally attuned than *Absalom*, especially through Rhett's role as munitions and consumer goods procurer, shuttling between the Confederacy and the otherworlds of Canada, England, Europe, and the West Indies. Scarlett's dogged provincialism is played off against Rhett's perception of the Confederacy as a fragile affair destined to be overwhelmed by mightier cross-Atlantic force fields. At the end, his plan to recoup his morale by wandering Childe Harold–like through Europe resonates with both Old South Europhilia and neoconservative southern modernist claims of the special affinity between southern high culture and aristocratic Europe, as in poet-critic John Crowe Ransom's lead-off contribution to the 1930 antimodernist manifesto *I'll Take My Stand: The South and the Agrarian Tradition* (New York: Harper, 1962), 3: "The South is unique on this continent for having founded and defended a culture which was according to the European principles of culture," etc. Ransom could not have failed to know that this line of argument had been used for more than a century to euphemize white supremacist claims for the South as the nation's quintessential holistic regional culture.

fall from antebellum glory days to postbellum ruination in both novels potentially played to Depression era anguish, *Gone with the Wind* engages this much more fully by charting the ordeal of Scarlett's transformation from a "girl" with "sachet and dancing slippers" to a "woman" reduced to nothing "except the indestructible red earth on which she stood" (*GW* 482) but refusing to admit defeat ("'As God is my witness . . . I'm never going to be hungry again,'" she vows, in an especially charged moment rendered in lurid Technicolor as the finale to part one of the film [421]). Whereas *Absalom* thrusts master-class racism to the fore, *Gone with the Wind* treats the plantocracy as benignly paternalistic and slaves as devoted, decrying the postbellum threat posed by "half a nation" (Yankeedom) "to force upon the other half the rule of negroes, many of them scarcely one generation out of the African jungles" (*GW* 647).

So it was predictable that Macmillan should have bound the novel "in Confederate gray." And that Mitchell and Thomas Dixon hit it off so well, he lauding her for having written the great American novel, she gratefully responding, "I was practically raised on your books, and love them very much." And that the film's first screening in Atlanta became "a high ritual for the reassertion of the legend of the Old South."[31] Yet these were also co-optations that understate maverick tendencies in some respects as pronounced as Faulkner's.

Scarlett could almost have been a Sutpen daughter, as the offspring of a "hard-headed, blustering" outlander (Irish immigrant) and a southern lady he has snapped up for his bride, far more pedigreed than Ellen Coldfield. Gerald, "self-made" like Sutpen and the majority of other hinterland deep South planters of the King Cotton era of the 1850s, has rebuilt a ruined plantation won at cards in a "rugged section" of north Georgia (*GW* 44, 51, 58). *Gone with the Wind* makes central the self-division Faulkner ascribes to the young Judith, who alternates strangely between out-of-control wildness and genteel acquiescence, goading Sutpen's slaves to make a wild chariot race out of the ride to Sunday service but amenable to Ellen's and Rosa's attempts to micromanage her engagement. Scarlett grows up headstrong and fiery like the father whose favorite child she is, yet anxious to propitiate the model mistress, matron, mother she idealizes. Hence her attraction to such different men, the decorously handsome Ashley whom she fancies must be her destiny and the cynical though no less polished Rhett, who brings out the O'Hara in her, always turning up at the right moment to provoke her to some scandalous act like dancing exuberantly while still in mourning dress for her first husband. Together they become the novel's primary weapon for skewering old order decorums. "Between them" they outrage "every tenet of [the old Confederate] code" (832). The hollowness of that code is reinforced by the disintegration of the maladaptive Ashley, who dutifully marches off to war despite opposing it and clings to the "beauty of the old life" with "a symmetry to it like Grecian art" (519). When he returns exhausted from a northern prison, he cuts a sorry figure first as farmer and then as businessman. Scarlett, meanwhile, through wit, gumption, and trickery saves Tara from foreclosure—at the cost of alienating the family by stealing her sister's prosperous fiancé—then finds as she takes over the enterprise when he falls sick that "a woman could handle business matters as well or better than a man" (610). Despite grievous love disappointments—disillusionment with Ashley, abandonment by Rhett—Scarlett endures, unlike Judith Sutpen, who gets cut down by yellow fever and relegated by the narrators to a bit part in a tale of male angst.

Scarlet's survivalism was well calculated to further "the idea of the New Woman as beleaguered bourgeois American heroine for Depression readers," Hutner observes.[32] Indeed, Mitchell's self-image—"one of those short-haired, short-skirted, hard-boiled young women who preachers said would go to hell or be hanged before they were thirty"—bore a close enough resemblance to make her feel "a little embarrassed" at finding herself "the incarnate spirit of the old South!"[33] Thanking historian Henry Steele Commager for seizing upon Rhett's dismissal of Ashley's anachronistic "breed" as "no use or value in an upside-down world like ours" (*GW* 765), Mitchell claimed that therein lay the remote origins of the whole book—a lesson in living history imbibed from her mother at the age of six. When Margaret balked at having to go to school, her mother drove her down "'the road to Tara,'" showed her "the old ruins of houses where fine and wealthy people had once lived," and warned her, "my own world was going to explode under me, some day, and God help me if I didn't have some weapon to meet the new world."[34] That was just a few years before *Absalom* imagines Quentin's Ashley-esque struggle with the ghosts of the past. Using that event as yardstick, *Gone with the Wind* starts to look like an act of feminist exorcism that *Absalom* can't imagine its male scion being able to rival.

But *Gone with the Wind* also refuses to disown the old order it seems to undo. Scarlett is nagged by pangs of conscience whenever tempted to flout ladylike ideals, and even as the novel sympathizes with her spirited determination, it reproaches her cold-heartedness. Her decision to maximize profit from one of her factories by allowing her manager to exploit convict labor is a prime example. A notoriously corrupt institution to which the postbellum South resorted in lieu of adequate prison systems, convict leasing—through and beyond its official abolition in 1927—was held up as an arch example of egregious abuse by writers across the color line. It prompted one of George Washington Cable's most vehement reform articles. Chesnutt made it the source of the repulsive Colonel McBane's ill-gotten wealth. Fifty years after *Gone with the Wind*, Toni Morrison was to make it the occasion of *Beloved*'s Paul D's most horrific ordeal in Georgia, whose history "shows its practice in its least diluted form."[35] Scarlett's acquiescence to convict labor to gain a competitive edge becomes a key reason why respectable Atlanta comes to see her in cahoots with the Yankee infestation she hates. Although she and Rhett both stand out among their cohort for the freedom with which they move across the North-South cultural divide, the novel treats his unabashed wartime double dealing as daring boldness and her attempts to butter up the Yankees as culpably Machiavellian. Rhett's insistence that he is out to profit from the inevitable Confederate defeat by any means possible is disliked but palliated by his suavity and his spreading the bounty around, while Scarlett's machinations are chastised as self-serving. Whenever she thinks or says, "anything you could get out of the Yankees was fair money, no matter how you got it," either Rhett or the narrator chastises her (*GW* 692). Rhett always knows when to stop, Scarlett never.

This is by no means the only way in which Mitchell deploys Rhett to keep sympathy for Scarlett in check. Another is to show him one-upping her again and again in knowledge, finesse, and scheming. Scarlett progresses a long way from shallow-minded teenage belle, but she is never granted full adulthood; she always remains behind the curve in understanding herself and those around her. Rhett calls her "still a child" to the end (*GW* 1017). But the most decisive recourse for containing her is the sentimentalization of Rhett. After making a fortune from war profiteering, he enlists in a sudden fit of loyalty and valiantly serves the Lost Cause in its last months. After insisting that he'll never marry and that he wants Scarlett only as his mistress, he not only does marry her but becomes a doting father too, as against her own negligent mothering. Above all, Rhett admires—and chides Scarlett for disliking—the woman she sees as her nemesis, Melanie Wilkes. The novel's personification of Old South womanhood in its most high-minded form, Melanie exasperates Scarlett no end as a goody-goody and as Ashley's adored and adoring wife. That Melanie naively cleaves to Scarlett as her soul mate and protector galls her all the more. *Gone with the Wind* makes much more of Scarlett's jealousy and contempt in return for Melanie's trust than of Scarlett's game but grudging perseverance in helping ensure Melanie's survival through childbirth, after their flight from Atlanta to Tara, and Melanie's slow convalescence thereafter. So even as the novel skewers genteel aristocratic ideals through Ashley and Scarlett's fruitless pining for him, it revalidates them through Melanie and the reformed Rhett.

The double game of unleashing and reproaching Scarlett allows *Gone with the Wind* to play both sides of the ideological street. It encourages vicarious identification with bad-boy, bad-girl heretics without trashing the canons of conventional gentility, including the misogynistic stereotype that a smart man can see farther than the smartest woman. It satirizes Old South memory without disowning its moral authority. Herein lies its "miraculous power to disrobe and then re-enshrine the South," as critic Carolyn Porter shrewdly puts it.[36]

Rather the same can be said of *Absalom* too. The old-order mystique mesmerizes the narrators who demolish it. But *Absalom* mainly dramatizes its anachronistic decadence, whereas *Gone with the Wind* caters to the vicarious pleasures of immersion in the exciting past. In *Absalom*, Sutpen's Hundred dwindles to "Sutpen's One" as family fortunes collapse, and Clytie burns the mansion to the ground, leaving the countryside charred and empty except for the howling Jim Bond. In *Gone with the Wind*, Tara also gets reduced to a "'two horse' farm," but the house is spared to remain a spiritual lodestone under Scarlett's control. By symbolically tying her unfinished saga both to Atlanta and to Tara, *Gone with the Wind* pulls off a two-for-one celebration of a New South both urbane and neoagrarian.

The most decisive mark of difference between these novels' admixtures of disaffiliation from and lingering attachment to the Old South is obviously *Absalom*'s intense brooding on the unfinished legacy of slavery as against *Gone with the Wind*'s tenacious adherence to the master-class fantasy that blacks fared better under slavery's benign paternalism than under the anarchy of freedom. That Tara "was built by slave labor" (*GW* 50) is stated as a simple fact, not something to apologize for. Yes, "freedom" was built on "slavery," but so what? That difference alone fixes the imagined world of *Gone with the Wind* within an atavistic conception of human rights. However much *Absalom* itself seems caught in a time warp, its very despair at the impossibility of shaking free from the haunted past at least implies the need to break its hold.

Yet even here, planet Faulkner and planet Mitchell were not so remote from each other as it might seem. *Absalom*'s key device for driving home the family curse—the near-white but still nonwhite son who threatens dynastic impurity—was but a variation on the old "tragic mulatto" theme that had been percolating through American fiction for more than a century from James Fenimore Cooper and Lydia Child through Stowe, Jackson, Cable, and Chesnutt on down. Mitchell herself had developed a more daring variant as the centerpiece of the novella on which she worked before turning to *Gone with the Wind:* a tragic Reconstruction era love affair between a planter's daughter and the mulatto son of one of the family's ex-slaves. She set " 'Ropa Carmagin" aside when her husband disapproved the theme but didn't abandon it until her publisher rejected it as too short to make a book. Eventually the manuscript seems to have been destroyed.[37] Had it survived, almost certainly it would not have strengthened the author's claims to genius; but it might have made the profiles of Mitchell and Faulkner as semi-disaffected insider-interrogators of southern tradition look more similar than they now do.

Both " 'Ropa" and *Absalom* confirm that long before the U.S. Supreme Court ruled Virginia's anti-miscegenation law unconstitutional in 1967, the subject was fair game for national writers both avant-garde and popular. During the 1920s and 1930s, it was in the air as never before. Edna Ferber's popular novel *Showboat* (1926) and the hit musical adaptation by Jerome Kern include a well-known scene in which a Mississippi sheriff, tipped off to a case of miscegenation among the troupe by a jilted admirer of the mulatto wife, is persuaded by the company's oath that her Nordic husband (who has prudently swallowed a bit of her blood) really meets the one-drop test of blackness. The first film version (1929) omitted the scene in deference to white southern sensitivities, but the 1936 remake restored it. In between came George Schuyler's Harlem Renaissance novella *Black No More* (1931), a rompish speculative fiction that imagines a new surgical process for whitening skin, touching off a rush to whiteness by African Americans and paranoid panic among whites, followed by a mass fashion shift to brown is beautiful after an all-white(ned) population starts producing nonwhite babies. Not merely a few "literary loners" like Faulkner, in other words, but a growing number of artists of the era both "serious" and "popular" were building thought experiments around the idea that there was something weird about the fetishization of blood purity.

None of these experiments, though, treats interracial white-black love or sex as a mundane event. When would that happen? The answer seems to be both "very soon" and "not for a long time, if ever." Though it would require a whole book to unpack that paradox, perhaps we can get a workable sense of options and pathways from a final trio of case studies: Lillian Smith's *Strange Fruit* (1944), Ann Petry's *The Narrows* (1953), and Alice Randall's *The Wind Done Gone* (2001). The first two are ambitious postrealist sociological novels of the 1940s and 1950s by writers of high talent, one a southern white and the other a northeastern African American, that imagine the (un)natural and social history of interracial sex in small-town America. The third is a turn-of-the-twenty-first-century satirical reinvention of *Gone with the Wind,* with a nod at *Absalom* along the way, that deserves notice both as artful parody and as literary criticism.

Mirrors of Miscegenation for the Civil Rights Era and Beyond

Faulkner's and Mitchell's exact contemporary, Lillian Smith, truly was the kind of engaged public intellectual the aging Faulkner made sporadic attempts at being. (She dismissed them as contemptible temporizing.) During the early years of the civil rights movement until felled by cancer, she was one of the white South's most outspoken advocates for nonviolent protest against segregation, which she called "spiritual lynching."[38] No significant white writer before her had made so concerted an attempt to assimilate African American literary history from Phillis Wheatley to Frederick Douglass, Paul Laurence Dunbar and the Harlem Renaissance literati, down to Richard Wright.[39]

Strange Fruit's town of Maxwell is an early 1920s variant of the paradigmatic ingrown community of American regionalism, rendered in a sensuous, multiperspectival, expressionist style reminiscent of Jean Toomer's *Cane,* which Smith admired. The frontispiece illustration etches a starkly segregated village of sturdy trim dwellings on one side, shanties on the other, with hints of swamp in the background. The novel lays out with minute precision the everyday routines of the whole range of white and black inhabitants, from the top of the social ladder to the bottom, within and at the edges of the compartmentalized yet interwoven parallel universes of White Town and Colored Town—white and black ministers and doctors, separate hangouts for white and black youth, major black women characters working as maids in the households of the leading white families. *Strange Fruit* portrays the losing struggle between youthful desire for individuation and the inertial forces of family and social norms, with special emphasis on small moments that add up, like a family breakfast scene where a father's insouciant chuckling over the newspaper comics grates against the wife's fussiness about his rumpled coat or a friend tries to soften another's grimness by silly jokes and reminiscences.

Smith hoped this minutely realized virtual world would seem a plausible site for an interracial relation of "special tenderness" yielding a "fable that applies not only to the South but to the white race in its relationships the world over: the ambivalences, the conflicts, the love, the hate, the anger, the frustration, the terrible humiliations of the dark man's spirit . . . the gradual wearing away of the white man's civilized and humane feelings." She had seen white segregationism not only as an "American dilemma" but as a worldwide pathology ever since a brief stint teaching music in China in the 1920s. "The first time I saw a Chinese coolie brutally lashed . . . by a British policeman," she recalled, "my mind tore wide open. It has never closed up since."[40]

Strange Fruit was successful enough to make it to the top of the *New York Times* best-seller list and become the first novel by a white southerner to receive front-page notice in the *New York Times Book Review* by a leading African American intellectual, W. E. B. Du Bois, who shared Smith's commitment to top-down reform through a synergy of cultural leadership and activist politics. He praised *Strange Fruit* as "a magnificently detailed picture of the small-town South lashed by an urge for self-destruction as old as time" that should be "required reading" in "every deanery, every parsonage—and every Legislature, on both sides of the Mason-Dixon Line." As to the fable, however, Du Bois cautioned that its stereotypical character detracted from the main point, that black and white Maxwell "are caught in a skein (economic, ethnic, emotional) that only evolution can untangle or revolution break."[41]

He was right. Smith's effective portrait of weak-willed Tracy Dean, detribalized just enough by his war experience to sympathize with the beautiful near-white object of his desire but not nearly enough to resist ditching her for the girl of his parents' choice, comes at the cost of reducing Nonnie Anderson to the cipher her nickname (Non) implies, as other African American reviewers quickly pointed out. The high bar the novel sets by its nuanced rendering of other Maxwellites striving to coexist with minimal decency in a climate of toxic racism makes the puppyish abjection of this Spelman graduate to the needy college-dropout lover she has adored since age six seem all the more infantilizing and blinkered, not to mention her readiness to bear his child yet remain his mistress and her insistence that race is "not real."[42] That *Strange Fruit* has Nonnie's two pragmatic older siblings tell her so flatly doesn't disguise the formulism that overtakes the novel when it comes to imagining the kind of exceptional figure Smith clearly meant for her to be. The state of emergency to which her pregnancy gives rise seems almost as contrived: Tracy bribing the family retainer who was his boyhood pal to be Nonnie's substitute bridegroom; her enraged brother's murder of Tracy; and the lynching of the substitute on the village idiot's garbled testimony after the brother's last-minute escape.

Smith halfway conceded the failure of these contrivances when she regretted having opted for the same title as the 1939 song about lynching made famous by Billie Holiday. She meant, she claimed, to refer not to the lynched body but to "the 'strange fruit' of our racist culture," to how "all the *people* came out of our twisted way of life."[43] Smith was right that community ethnography was her forte. That's what keeps the long lynching sequence which takes up the last third of the book from degenerating into programmatic spectacle. The white minister's befuddled chagrin at the sudden collapse of his revival on the fateful night; the doomed man's housemaid girlfriend breaking five of her employer's dishes but not daring to tell kind Christian Mrs. Harris why, prompting a weirdly hilarious cross-questioning about whether her bowels are in order; Nonnie forced to endure her boss's hemming and hawing about what flowers should go in Tracy's funeral wreath and then to deliver it to the Deans herself; Miss Sadie the town telephone operator, on record as declaring "that the entire Negro race was a mammoth trick which nature had played on the white race,"[44] nonetheless trying to keep Crazy Carl from bearing false witness against the wrong man, then absurdly having to defend herself with a broom after he turns ugly, until she can turn danger into a game—these constellated bits of negligence, misery, and incongruous microscale heroics give poignancy and substance to what might have come across as gratuitous sensationalism.

In Ann Petry's *The Narrows* (1953) the strong suit is also the ethnography of a segregated town, in the eastern coastal Connecticut region Petry had known from girlhood, not the plot of interracial sex and revenge killing after the relation is broken off. Bearing out the charge of duplicity that southerners had leveled for generations against Yankee judgmentalism, the lines of racial division in Petry's Monmouth seem even more extreme than in Smith's Maxwell. Rarely except in school do whites and blacks interact. Wealthy whites are so sequestered that the protagonist, Link Williams, despite being an Ivy League Phi Beta Kappa with four years of service in naval intelligence, doesn't realize before seeing her image in a newspaper that the woman with whom he's become involved is the heiress of the town's leading family. When they meet by happenstance in the black neighborhood into which she's come trolling for adventure, at first he takes her for a light-skinned Negro.

The Narrows differs markedly from *Strange Fruit* in its obvious aversion to the relationship that drives its plot. Where Smith strains to evoke an incipient tender mutuality sadly quashed by Tracy's inability to get beyond his cultural conditioning, Petry portrays the Camilla-Link affair as abrupt, stormy, and charged with resentment. These are smart, passionate, but incompatible people driven to imagine they love each other by the lack of perceived options on either side: she bored by respectability including a loveless marriage, he with no future in sight beyond tending bar. When he breaks off the affair in disgust at her deceit, she angrily retaliates by charging rape and unleashing the power of the domineering matriarch, who ordains a smear campaign against blacks by the local newspaper and, when the trial is delayed by a conscientious judge, Link's kidnapping and murder. Link has supposedly been "working on a history of slavery in the United States" in his off-hours,[45] but the novel never shows him doing this. Instead he ironically winds up suffering another chapter. These whites know exactly what stereotype cards to play when, even though they don't, it turns out, hold every single one. At the end, the novel lets in a faint ray of hope for a better future by having the police catch Camilla's mother and husband red-handed with Link's body in the back of Mom's Rolls.

Even more than in *Strange Fruit*, interracial romance seems important to Petry chiefly as a means to the end of anatomizing the context of her imagined town. In particular, it enables a next-stage development, beyond her better-known first novel *The Street* (1946), of a vein of reflection Wright and Ellison largely ignored that aligns her work more closely with Chesnutt's: respectability under duress. *The Narrows*'s exfoliation of the dramatis personae of the small black community is its centerpiece: the adopted mother with whom Link lives, Abbie Crunch, a fretful "paragon of aging black middle-class propriety" as critic Lawrence Jackson rightly calls her; Abbie's formidable Wellesley-educated friend who runs the local funeral parlor; the painfully conscientious Treadway family butler Prowther, whose life is made both bearable and miserable by his sensual wife Mamie's affair with the crusty streetwise owner of the Last Chance bar, Bill Hod—who is also Link's boss, former father-figure, and still sometime mentor, feared by Abbie as the embodiment of the raffishness that threatens to drag her and Link down. In this context, the spotty and tangled backstory of Link's upbringing makes sense. That he was adopted by Abbie and her late husband, then taken in and proxy-fathered by Bill during Abbie's tailspin after Major's death, and is now living with one while working for another, makes for the contradictory mix that *The Street*'s protagonist Lutie Johnson becomes only at the very end when her goal-oriented rectitude is finally cracked apart: a high achiever with "permanent ties to the black lower class."[46]

In *The Narrows* as in *The Street*, interracial sex is a white-instigated thing, crucial for Camilla but for Link not more than incidental. Indeed neither *The Narrows* nor *Strange Fruit* treats it as a credible pathway to bridging the racial divide, although the integrationist Smith might have hoped for such a future, so much as a limit case to highlight the obstacles to cross-racial amity of any kind by prejudices on both sides of the color line. That shared diagnosis together with the narrative-of-community genre they also share in common attest to consensus across the regional divide. For both novels present near-identical ethnographies of segre-gated, racist, closed communities South and North. Indeed with regard to interracialism both past and present, the imagined worlds of na-tional fiction seem to have lagged behind the accumulating instances of cross-racial union in practice. Has there ever been a prominent U.S. novel in which black-white interracial sex is unabashedly celebrated— and the taboo wholly discounted as irrelevant? Perhaps you might think of one or two, though likely they would be borderline cases like Octavia Butler's *Kindred*. Meanwhile, however, another way of getting interracialist dreams past the long bad history of white-on-black sex-ploitation presents itself in the form of a revised version of the futurism that Charles Chesnutt treated earnestly in "The Coming American" and George Schuyler satirically in *Black No More*.

Alice Randall's *The Wind Done Gone* (2001) made legal as well as lit-erary history when the Eleventh U.S. Circuit Court of Appeals rejected the Margaret Mitchell estate's suit to block publication on the ground of copyright infringement, a victory for "literary freedom" perhaps as-sisted, literary historian Gene Jarrett notes, by Henry Louis Gates Jr.'s expert testimony that "parody is at the heart of African American ex-pression." As the author of the preeminent work on Afro-diasporic "sig-nifying" practices from slave narrative on down, Gates knew whereof he spoke.[47] Randall's parody does to *Gone with the Wind* what Ishmael Reed's *Flight to Canada* did to *Uncle Tom's Cabin*. Actually, in some ways *The Wind Done Gone* was no more pungent a critique of Mitchell's racism than Frank Yerby's costume romance *The Foxes of Harrow* (1946), the book that ensured his future as African American literature's first million-aire. But whereas Yerby, like Mitchell, kept his bloodlines distinct while recasting the story of his leading black family into a saga of up-from accomplishment during and after slavery, Randall dared to color the O'Haras black.*

---

* By no means are Yerby and Randall the only later twentieth-century African American writers to target *GW*. Margaret Walker's *Jubilee* (1966), the novel that inaugurated con-temporary neo-slave fiction, was avowedly written against *GW*'s white-dominationist version of southern history (Margaret Walker and Kay Bonetti, "An Interview with Margaret Walker," *Missouri Review* 15, no. 1 [1992]: 131). The argument that *Jubilee* pit-ted itself against *GW* (especially its Mammy stereotype) is extended to a number of other historical fictions by African American women writers from Walker through Gloria Naylor by Mary Condé, "Some African-American Fictional Responses to *Gone with the*

The Wind Done Gone pretends to be diary of the Scarlett figure's much smarter and even more beautiful half-sister Cyanara, Mammy's daughter by "Planter." We first see her at age twenty-eight, as "R.'"s once and present mistress. R.'s now-broken relation with "Other" she claims to have orchestrated in the first place: "I wanted someone who loved her to love me more than her."[48] Cyanara detests Other for monopolizing Mammy's love and attention from the wet-nurse stage onward. But then she discovers that everything she had thought true was wrong. Mammy and her husband Garlic (Pork in *Gone with the Wind*) were running the show the whole time. Garlic had drugged the man from whom Planter then won "Tata" at cards. Mammy, who really loved Cyanara all along, reared Other to become an instrument of white gentlemen's undoing. The two of them together saw to it that all the male heirs would be killed in infancy. Soon Other takes sick and dies; R. inherits and, marrying Cyanara, tosses her the keys to the plantation. But the crucial turning point for her turns out to be a cache of old love letters R. gives her, between "Lady" and the long-dead cousin who was her first and only true love, that reveal their knowledge of a black bloodline in their ancestry, a great-grandmother who was part Haitian "negresse." Here the novel plays the same card, but to very different purpose, that *Absalom* had in Africanizing Mrs. Sutpen the first of Haiti.

So Other herself was part black, and the bond between Cyanara and Lady, dating back to the time she encouraged the toddler to suckle when Mammy brushed her aside, ran deeper than self-indulgent pity. These realizations reconcile Cyanara to the white part of her family but also drive her away from Tata and from R. to seek out the charismatic black politician who's attracted her from the time they first met, and vice versa. "Lady loved her black man in the bright light of day," and Cyanara will have her congressman if she can. The fact that he won't marry "the Confederate's concubine" doesn't matter now. They work out a secret arrangement whereby he marries an eminently respectable wife who can't have children and Cyanara secretly bears his son and heir. After all, as she said before about R., "loving him is the only work I'm trained to do."[49]

This bare-bones summary scarcely captures the alternation of tricky allusive banter and ironic melancholy that raises *The Wind Done Gone* above the level of run-of-the-mill parody or remake. Especially relevant here are two related further points about the relevance of Randall's design to American romances of the racial divide.

First is the coexistence of forced interracial sex decried with the assumption of consensual interracial sex, including marriage, as okay to dramatize even with erotic flourishes. Unlike *Strange Fruit* and *The Narrows, The Wind Done Gone* doesn't telegraph the sense of writing amid a climate of public disapproval of the underlying idea. Readerly reactions bear this out. Among Amazon.com reviews that criticize the novel, as many do, the usual complaints are flimsy execution, hit-and-run besmirchment of a beloved original, and gratuitous shock effects like the infanticides—not defiance of proper sexual mores. Clearly the novel-reading public's views of interracialism have greatly changed since the days of Smith and Petry, and the 1960s Hollywood film *Guess Who's Coming to Dinner* (the dad is aghast when the daughter brings home a black fiancé). *The Wind Done Gone* takes that liberalizing trend line a long way further.

Second, however, the fact that interracial commingling feels less radioactive for Randall than for Smith and Petry doesn't in itself imply hugely greater zest for interracialism, sexual or otherwise, much less a desire to move toward a postracial sense of identity and solidarity. The novel's chief instance of interracial intimacy, the R.-Cyanara liaison, is ambiguated from the start. Often Cyanara seems quite at ease, but she never stops feeling at least residually entrapped. Her discovery of just how scrambled the family's genes actually are reinforces her sense of blackness. "It's not in the pigment of my skin that my Negressness lies," but in "the color of my mind," she thinks. Sister Other had the "blood but not the mind."[50] She herself could pass, and R. wants her to: to emigrate to England and live as white. But conscious of being nonwhite inwardly, she ditches him for her black lover. This anti-passing denouement upends Chesnutt's and Faulkner's pronouncements about a unitary future American race, not to mention the white-as-normal world of Margaret Mitchell. To the contrary, implies the novel, the point of deconstructing biological race is not to achieve better understanding across racial lines, though that's good too, but to embolden and justify nonwhite self-identification. As Cyanara discovers first to her disorientation and then to her delight, in this novel's world there seems to be "no white act that doesn't have its origin in African American dreaming," as critic Patricia Yeager puts it.[51] It's a discovery Cyanara has intuited from the start through her management of the R.-Other affair, though it takes the whole narrative for her to realize its possibilities.

Cyanara's epiphany is hardly unique to this one funky fictional world. It's an insight more or less pervasive within neo-slave narrative generally, of which *The Wind Done Gone* is a third-generation instance. Beyond that, it's been accelerating on many fronts during the last half century with the intensification of critical interest worldwide in subaltern agency—although the remote beginnings are of course much more ancient. Nor are the pleasures of discovery confined to subalterns alone. "Mainstream" readers, never more so than today, seem to participate much more enthusiastically than not in the sense of disorienting mind expansion that comes from finding *Huckleberry Finn* retold with "my Jim" as hero or seeing Hester Prynne refigured as black welfare mother by Suzan-Lori Parks or as an Indian princeling's mistress by Bharati Mukherjee. *The Wind Done Gone*'s countervision of Mitchell's Scarlett as Mammy's construct or Pork/Garlic as the brains behind Gerald/Planter's prosperity continues an already established trend line of coloring U.S. Euroclassics nonwhite. To think this way about the dotted line that runs from *Gone with the Wind* to *The Wind Done Gone* helps suggest why it might have been more than just happenstance of genius that Faulkner's most celebrated successor at the end of the twentieth century should have been an African American novelist whose work has been far more invested in exploring black identity and history than in the possibilities of interracialism, and never more so than in the book most likely to continue to seem her closest approximation to the Great American Novel.

10

Morrison's Beloved *as Culmination and Augury*

It is when we think of the world the aesthetic of indifference might bring into being that we recognize the urgency of re-membering the stories we have not written.

—AMITAV GHOSH, "The Ghosts of Mrs. Gandhi" (1995)

Being naturalized as an other in America has always meant moving in its spaces conscious of borders, of places where you cannot or should not venture.

—ROBERT T. HAYASHI, *Haunted by Waters* (2007)

T ONI MORRISON'S *Beloved* (1987) has never lacked for controversy. Initial reviews were mixed despite Morrison's stature both as novelist and power broker in the literary-critical world. *Beloved* won its Pulitzer over Philip Roth's *The Counterlife* only after an unprecedented lobbying effort.[1] Its almost instant canonization continued to be roiled by controversy over whether Morrison's reputation had been inflated by political correctness anxiety, reignited by the 2006 *New York Times* poll that named *Beloved* the best American novel of the previous quarter century. Yet today it seems clear that Morrison was at least as deserving of her Nobel Prize for Literature (1993) as most previous American laureates and the other leading novelists in the unusually gifted cohort of U.S. writers born during the interwar years—Roth, Don DeLillo, Thomas Pynchon, John Updike, Cormac McCarthy, Ishmael Reed, and Joyce Carol Oates. And that *Beloved* is likely to stand for some time to come among all Morrison novels as the likeliest Great American Novel candidate.*

---

* Morrison has suggested that *Beloved* should be considered the first of a trilogy of novels about pivotal chapters in African American history together with *Jazz* (1992: the Harlem

Beloved's primary setting is the African American district of Cincinnati, the largest city on the northern bank of the Ohio River, the dividing line between slave states and free from Pennsylvania's western border to the Mississippi. The main action happens in 1873–1874, a few years before Twain started work on *Huckleberry Finn*. But the novel is haunted from start to finish by traumatic memories of the protagonist Sethe that began eighteen years before when her family and fellow slaves became victims of regime change at their "Sweet Home" Kentucky plantation. After its tough but comparatively liberal master died and his ruthless brother-in-law "Schoolteacher" and two bullying nephews took over at the behest of Garner's kind but timid and sickly widow, they suffered horribly. In an escape attempt that miscarries, the male slaves are recaptured or killed, but the pregnant Sethe's three children make it to the Cincinnati place of their paternal grandmother, Baby Suggs. Sethe barely manages to join them after a harrowing trek during which she gives birth, with the help of a poor white teenage vagrant, Amy Denver, after whom Sethe names the baby. But a month later the slave catchers track them down, prompting the frantic Sethe to try to kill her children rather than have them retaken. Schoolteacher abandons the case as hopeless; Sethe is released after a high-profile trial for the murder of her toddler; and a local white grocer hires her as a cook. But the black community shuns her; Baby Suggs languishes and dies; and the two older kids, both boys, take off for good as the house becomes haunted by the slain Beloved's angry ghost. The novel discloses most of this backstory in flashbacks and conversational bits after the 1873 event that initiates the present-time plot: the unexpected arrival of the lone survivor of the six Sweet Home men, Paul D, from his own eighteen-year ordeal of sufferings, escapes, recaptures, and post-emancipation wanderings that is also replayed as the book unfolds.

In the first and longest of the three sections, Paul D makes love to the lonely Sethe, banishes the poltergeist, and moves in against the wishes of the now-adolescent Denver, who feels excluded. But soon the ghost returns in embodied form, as a young woman in white mysteri-

---

Renaissance) and *Paradise* (1966: the fitful dawn of the civil rights era), and some critics agree, per Justine Tally, "The Morrison Trilogy," in *The Cambridge Companion to Toni Morrison*, ed. Justine Tally (Cambridge: Cambridge University Press, 2007), 75–91. But the interlinkages, such as they are, seem more tenuous than for Roth's American trilogy, let alone Updike's *Rabbit Angstrom* and Dos Passos's *U.S.A.*

ously arisen from the stream behind the house. On the way to reasserting her power over the household of "124," Beloved seduces Paul D, who begins to withdraw from Sethe and abruptly decamps in midwinter, after learning of the infanticide, for the cold sanctuary of the local black church basement.

Part two turns on the hyper-intense intimacy that then envelops the three remaining denizens of 124. Sethe and Denver dote more and more on Beloved, and she in turn fixates upon Sethe with a hungry ferocity that intensifies Denver's need for a sibling as well as Sethe's tangled burden of love, loss, and guilt. Beloved swells into what looks like pregnancy while Sethe wizens as she increasingly dedicates all her waking hours to serving Beloved. Meanwhile, the community, alerted by its informal communications agent, Stamp Paid, who in a fit of officiousness he now regrets had been the one who tipped Paul D off to Sethe's disgrace, senses that something is horribly wrong: that the ostracism has gone so far as to endanger not Sethe and Denver alone but the community as well. In part three, matters come to a head when Denver manages to tear herself away in an effort both to normalize and to keep the three of them from starving. She lands a housemaid's job with their landlords, the Bodwins, an aging white ex-abolitionist brother and sister. Stamp's matriarchal counterpart Ella rallies the community's women to stage a ritual exorcism in front of the house, by coincidence at the very moment that Bodwin arrives to pick up Denver to begin her job. Sethe, standing bewildered at the front door with Beloved, mistakes him for Schoolteacher and attacks with a knife; Ella flattens her with a punch to the head; Beloved disappears, evidently forever; and the bruised Sethe takes despairingly to her bed like Baby Suggs. But the return of a repentant Paul D offers promise of a future. "Me and you," he says, "we got more yesterday than anybody. We need some kind of tomorrow" (*B* 273). A pungently encrypted epilogue follows, of which more below.

Of all the novelists discussed at length in this book, Morrison is the only one with a graduate degree in literature (MA Cornell, with thesis on Faulkner and Virginia Woolf), and together with Bellow and Ellison the closest to an academic professional. At the time of completing *Beloved,* she was also working out a landmark critique, reminiscent of Ellison's but more trenchant, of white American literature as influenced throughout its history by a usually underacknowledged sense of "a constituted Africanism," characteristically "deployed as rawness and savagery." Even "when American texts are not 'about' Africanist presences or characters or narrative or idiom, the shadow hovers in implication."[2] This was the first broad critical formulation of a movement already well underway among creative writers and artists generally to reconceive canonical classics through the lenses of African American and other minority cultural histories, of which the satirical aspects of such neo-slave narratives as Ishmael Reed's, Charles Johnson's, and Alice Randall's (see Chapters 6 and 9) are striking examples. It comes as no surprise, then, to find the narrative pathways of *Beloved* crisscrossing and taking issue with such white-authored romances of the North/South regional and ethnic divides as *Uncle Tom's Cabin, Huckleberry Finn,* and *Absalom,* all the more so given that Morrison the critic has written extensively on the latter two.

Reinventing Tales White and Black

One measure of *Beloved*'s achievement is its brilliantly subtle reinvention of key strategies, even individual scenes, from the novels examined in Chapters 7–9. The Sethe/Amy Denver interlude reruns the Huck-Jim relation in cameo form: another ad hoc two-person same-sex "community of the disempowered" between mature black fugitive and juvenile poor-white hobo. Like Huck, "Amy enacts her ethical care," as critic F. Clifton Spargo observes, "only through the anti-idealistic expression of her bigotry." Morrison desentimentalizes the relation more resolutely, however. Sethe's company is obviously a much more transient distraction from this white runaway's quest after Boston and "velvet" compared to Huck's intensely felt need for a raft buddy.[3] For her part, Sethe, who like Jim really needs her companion's ministrations, is careful even in extremis to keep up her guard, "Miss"-ing Amy and concealing her real name. The house at 124 feels like a downscale postage-stamp reduction-with-a-difference of *Absalom*'s southern gothic haunted manse. It happens to be set on eighty acres, exactly one-eighth of a square-mile section according to the late eighteenth-century survey grid mandated by Thomas Jefferson that parceled out the nation's hinterland for settlement, including both Mississippi and Ohio. The downsizing and the deterioration of the house from the days when it was Bodwin's birthplace recall the postbellum erosion of Sutpen's vast holdings and fortifies *Beloved*'s Jamesian diagnosis of the era as antiheroic aftermath—for old abolitionist warhorses like Bodwin, a time of wistful nostalgia and for African Americans a time of broken promises, a time to feel haunted by the memory of plantation slavery days in far more credibly terrifying ways than the likes of Quentin Compson, Rosa Coldfield, and even Henry Compson ever were. The breakup of Sweet Home intensifies the irony of *Uncle Tom's Cabin*'s opening claim that Kentucky exhibits slavery in its most benign form. Yes, *Beloved* retorts, the Garners may have been better masters than most, but the place was a bubble even for Kentucky; George Harris's predicament was the norm; and the aftermath of the "good" master's death was far more likely to produce outcomes like the St. Clares—a far worse tyranny for which mildly treated slaves were unprepared—than liberation by Master George.

One could pile up other instances of *Beloved*'s resonance as an echo chamber of reinvented motifs from earlier white American writing, such as *The Scarlet Letter*'s rendition of the quasi-masochistic dependence of Hester Prynne on little Pearl, Pearl's uncanny oscillation between little girl and elf-child, the many resemblances between the climactic crowd scenes at the end, and the secret hand-holdings.[4] But as most discerning critics who have unearthed these and other similarities recognize, the point of doing so is not merely to demonstrate Morrison's interpretative genius but better to understand the execution of her particular project of recuperation, of filling in the inevitable blanks of slave narrative—the most important generic tradition informing *Beloved*—so as to reimagine the experience of slavery from diaspora to aftermath. Her "job," as she put it, was "to rip" the "veil" that slave narrative drew over "'proceedings too terrible to relate'"—to "fill in the blanks" through "a kind of literary archaeology."[5]

In this *Beloved* follows the long-standing practice of antislavery writing, black and white, from the early national era onward, of grounding one's narrative on the awful buried truth. One of Morrison's early editorial ventures was to support publication of the remarkable *The Black Book* (1974), a scrapbook-like documentary anthology, both tender and horrific, of textual and pictorial glimpses of history and folk life from African origins to the twentieth century: newspaper articles, photographs, advertisements, posters, film clips. These include a journalistic account of the fugitive slave Margaret Garner, on whose much-publicized 1856

Cincinnati infanticide *Beloved* was loosely based.[6] This was just the kind of horrific incident on which antislavery advocates liked to pounce in order to dramatize slavery's inhumanity, a tactic criticized both then and now as pandering to vicarious interest in the pornography of violence, as sadistic representations of lynching during the Jim Crow era on photographic postcards later did to racist prurience.[7] Given how Stowe herself was accused of such pandering, it is striking that she found maternal infanticide imperative to acknowledge yet too radioactive to confront except glancingly. Her *Key to "Uncle Tom's Cabin"* laconically cites an even more spectacular case than Garner's, of quadruple infanticide; and she injects into *Uncle Tom's Cabin* itself, through Cassy's mournful recollection of killing her infant octoroon son rather than have him sold, the plight of the mother driven to the most antimaternal act conceivable as the less dreadful alternative. But *Uncle Tom's Cabin* relegates to the edges this extreme instance that Morrison puts front and center and pictures Cassy's act in the gentlest possible way, as euthanasia by laudanum as she holds him, Madonna-like, "close to my bosom" (*UTC* 334). Whereas Morrison does not flinch from the image of frantic Sethe with one hand on "blood-soaked" Beloved trying to bash baby Denver against the barn wall, with the two boys bleeding on the sawdust by her feet (*B* 149).

In a powerful combination of tact and irony, the novel refrains from presuming to get inside Sethe's head at this point but instead refracts the violence, shock, and chaos of the scene chiefly through the mind streams of the frustrated predators, Schoolteacher and his nephew. Here *Beloved* stays faithful to the historical fact that Margaret Garner's story found print only through white intermediaries and the author's own sense of awe and mystery. Morrison claimed to see Garner's infanticide as an extreme act done on principle. Unlike the Medea of Greek mythology that killed "her children because of some guy," Garner seemed a "classic example of a person determined to be responsible." As to the rightness of the deed, however, the author refrained from judgment; "The only person I felt had the right to ask [Sethe] that question," she declared, "was Beloved, the child she killed."[8] In developing this insight, the novel swerves from its pre-text in two opposite directions. Sethe is spared the historical Garner's fate of being returned to slavery with her surviving children. But she is denied the veneer of Garner's seeming imperturbability, according to the journalistic reports at least, by the huge price she is shown as paying both socially, as a pariah, and psychologically, haunted by inability to forget the child she killed.

Beloved treats respectable community-think much less sympatheti- cally than it treats the exceptional person who is driven to extremes the community won't tolerate. That will come as no surprise to seasoned Morrison readers. The transgressive high-voltage title figure in *Sula* is made to seem far more compelling than her conventional friend Nel, the disreputable Pilate Dead in *Song of Solomon* far more than her slum- lord brother Macon, the scandalous women of the Convent in *Paradise* far more than the pillars of Ruby, Oklahoma. *Beloved* even blames the local black community for the tragedy itself, by refusing out of "mean- ness" (*B* 157) to warn the family against the approaching slave catchers because of jealousy at Baby Suggs's celebration of the too-perfect escape of Sethe and all her children. As if eighteen years of shunning were not enough, Paul D gets maneuvered into dealing Sethe the ultimate blow in his reaction to the muddled narrative he forces from her after Stamp Paid shows him a clipping of the trial: "You got two feet, Sethe, not four" (165). In effect he throws back in her face her horrified memory of School- teacher instructing his pupils to record her "animal" and "human . . . characteristics" side by side.[9]

The Cincinnati black community plays a secondary role, however, albeit crucial. The same goes to an even greater extent for the whites in *Beloved,* who mostly lurk around the edges of the narrative as alien be- ings among whom the African Americans must pick their way with ex- treme care, whom they prefer not to think about unless forced. Even the benevolent Bodwins, who allow Baby Suggs and then Sethe the use of 124, are tarnished by a comical darky piggy bank by their back door—a nod at the protagonist's Harlem landlady Mary in *Invisible Man?*—that unsettles Denver. And even more so by Bodwin's self-focused rumination (like Henry James's old-guard Bostonian reformer Miss Birdseye), as he rides toward his childhood home in the climactic scene, about the glory days "of letters, petitions, meetings," when his "Society" had the satisfac- tion of turning "infanticide and the cry of savagery around" and building "a further case for abolishing slavery"—using Sethe's case for propaganda, that is (*B* 260). That Bodwin has no idea of the meaning of the fracas he unwittingly precipitates confirms his blinkered smugness.

The saga of Sethe's escape, infanticide, ostracism, haunting, and apparent eventual redemption is not the full measure of the novel's reach, any more than the saga of Thomas Sutpen is in *Absalom*. Rather it's the matrix or nexus of a vision of far larger sweep, in which the ordeals of Sethe and her family (including Paul D and the other Sweet Home men, along with the husband she never sees or hears from after her escape) evoke the memory of the entire Afro-diasporic experience through slavery to "freedom."

Most of those memories are intensely painful and tamped down as much as possible. Whereas Faulkner's white southerners, no less haunted, take mordant pleasure in grandiloquent rehashing of past catastrophes, Sethe "worked hard to remember as close to nothing as was safe," just as Paul D, the book's other main center of consciousness, conditioned himself to keep his own memories and feelings stashed in the "tobacco tin" of his heart (*B* 6, 72). Ironically, even the remembered lushness of Sweet Home tortures Sethe because the "shameless beauty" of her mental images of it "never looked as terrible" as it turned out to be (6). Meeting each other after such long repression unleashes a need to talk, but they can only do so in fits and starts, in anguished indirections and circumlocutions that hold back as much as they express, so firmly in place is their protective reserve. The other black characters scarred by slavery put up similar defenses against remembrance or attachment, like Ella's motto: "Don't love nothing" (92).

This defensiveness recalls the author's professed recalcitrance toward her chosen subject as "something that the characters don't want to remember, I don't want to remember, black people don't want to remember, white people won't want to remember."[10] Coming in the late 1980s, this can't be taken at face value. *The Black Book* had exposed all this and more. Neo-slave fiction was already a familiar, established genre. In 1987 there was nothing new about an African American novel filling in slave narrative's silences and absences. Morrison's pronouncement is better glossed as a reflection on the gradual shift over the course of her own career as fiction writer from the near-home focus of her mid-twentieth-century girlhood in Lorain, Ohio, in *The Bluest Eye* and *Sula* (with back-glancings at the protagonists' family's southern origins), to the fuller engagement with the theme of multigenerational pilgrimage backward in *Song of Solomon* (Milkman's family-history quest from midcentury urban Michigan back to small-town Pennsylvania postbellum antecedents back to their Virginia roots), to *Beloved*'s mid-nineteenth-century evocation of the first major wave of black migration northward. Be that as it may, *Beloved* takes advantage of the belatedness of its engagement with the nineteenth-century past to orient its narrative method more powerfully than any predecessor around the anguish of having to come to terms with the traumatic past that binds and threatens to define you.* After an immersion in Faulkner, it may seem hard to imagine this being done more profoundly. But *Beloved* makes good on Édouard Glissant's dictum that Faulkner's work can only be taken to completion by black writers revisiting the same epoch as Toni Morrison had begun to do.[11]

Beloved's circlings through time and space make it the most panoramically national of all Morrison's novels, even though it shares her usual partiality for concentration on delimited spaces apart: a small town, a neighborhood, an isolated house, a room within that house, a patch of a single object within that room like a square of Baby Suggs's quilt. As much as *Uncle Tom's Cabin*, *Beloved* undertakes a far-reaching geographical scan of the nineteenth-century United States, especially by tracing Paul D's peregrinations South to North and back again during and after the war: incarceration in Alfred, Georgia, refuge among the Cherokees, temporary shelter with the "weaver woman" in Delaware, impressment in a Confederate foundry, reimpressment by the conquering Union army, roaming north to New Jersey and across country to Cincinnati and 124. All this gets unfolded in pinpoint glimpses that create, like one of Whitman's best poetic catalogs, a sense of inexhaustible fecundity—but it cuts oppositely from the usual Whitmanian gusto. The wandering Paul D "could not help being astonished by the beauty of this land that was not his," so "he made himself not love it," he "tried hard not to love it" (*B* 268). The excruciation of the bountiful not-ours, not-mine.

---

* Before *Beloved*, perhaps the closest novelistic approximation was David Bradley's *The Chaneysville Incident* (1981), whose historian-protagonist starts from a position so antipathetic to his late father and his Appalachian hometown that the genealogical quest he eventually undertakes becomes possible only after a long transitional period during which his aversion is slowly overcome. But as the novel unfolds the narrator becomes increasingly purposeful and the plot increasingly takes the form of a detective story whose mysteries finally get resolved.

Refiguring the Divides

This is but one of several ways in which *Beloved* reinforces the interdependence of place and race—more than Stowe, as much as Twain and Faulkner—in constituting personal and social identity. As with Twain's river-rat penchant for Mississippi basin minutiae and Faulkner's for fleshing out the material particularities of Yoknapatawpha's parallel universe, this side of Morrison's genius has a distinctively idiosyncratic stamp. Her staple strategy for conjuring up what the print record has left out "is the recollection that moves from the image to the text."[12] Hence the reliance on visual patches, sometimes repeated several times over, inexpressibly painful even when beautiful: the trees of Sweet Home; Baby Suggs on her deathbed; Halle driven mad by having to witness the nephew's assault on Sethe, slobbering his mouth with "clabber" from the butter churn; Paul D with the bit in his mouth mocked by "Mister" the rooster. Hence the "animated worldliness" of the supernaturalism, as the sociologist Avery Gordon calls it. *Beloved*'s "sparse talk is like a series of picture books."[13] "Rememory," Sethe's term for a remembered figure or incident that haunts the present (Beloved herself being the key example), is always connected to place as well as to mobile body, and it is socially shared. You can bump into somebody else's rememory, Sethe warns Denver.

Less noticed than *Beloved*'s rememory work is the extent to which it gives itself over to a descriptivism that, to appearances at least, goes far beyond what narrative economy would require. Take the scene in part three where Denver breaks free from the overheated intimacy that has enveloped Sethe and Beloved and traverses a route she hasn't taken for a dozen years, to the house of her old teacher Lady Jones. "She was shocked to see how small the big things were: the boulder by the edge of the road she once couldn't see over was a sitting-on rock. Paths leading to houses weren't miles long. Dogs didn't even reach her knees. Letters cut into beeches and oaks by giants were eye level now" (*B* 245). This comes near the end of a barrage of suchlike impressions of this once familiar/now strange route long untaken. The novel didn't require all that minutiae, but this and other passages like it produce a sense of character, family, community existing in guarded but irresistible reciprocity with landscapes this text knows with intimate specificity. In this way *Beloved* offers a subjectified version of traditional realism's thick description ideally tailored to represent anxiety about needing to dodge or hide at a moment's notice, as against the more confident, expansive place-stimulated impressionism of literature's famous *flâneurs* and *flâneuses:* Whitman, Charles Baudelaire, Joyce's Leopold Bloom, Woolf's Clarissa Dalloway. What *Beloved* delivers is the defensive, anxiety-riddled sense of placeness that follows, as Robert Hayashi puts it in this chapter's second epigraph, from having been "naturalized as an other in America."[14]

An equally telling mark of *Beloved*'s tailoring of landscape interaction to dramatize disempowerment is its repeated portrayal of souls in crisis, or near it, latching onto some near-to-hand natural thing in order to stay sane. Like the "fistful of salsify" Sethe brings Mrs. Garner every day in order to take the "ugly" out of her work: "the only way she could feel at home on Sweet Home was if she picked some pretty growing thing and took it with her" (*B* 22). Or the tree there that Paul D calls "Brother" (21). Here the novel anticipates the title concept of Indo-Anglian novelist Arundhati Roy's *The God of Small Things* (1997), whose lovers seize hold of tiny natural things in which they can delight in order to avoid having to think about the mightier forces that threaten to doom them. Denver's secret play place among the symmetrically arranged boxwoods at the rear of the property is another example. Such hyperconcentration on bits of the external world the characters inhabit and respond intensely to without possessing extend the repertoire of what political anthropologist James Scott calls "weapons of the weak"—"petty theft," "foot dragging," "feigned ignorance," "dissimulation," "slander," "gossip," "rumor" are some he takes up, most of them also on display in *Beloved*—seized upon by persons and communities subjugated by repressive regimes worldwide in order to preserve a measure of autonomy, agency, sanity.[15]

Out of its many transactions, microscopic and panoramic, between character or community and their material/environmental surroundings, *Beloved* reinvents the romance of the North/South, black/white divides in directions that Stowe, Twain, and Faulkner intimate but can't quite bring themselves to think. *Uncle Tom's Cabin* makes it clear enough that under slavery fugitive slaves dare not feel safe south of Canada, however kindly their white protectors. *Beloved,* set perhaps coincidentally in the same city where Stowe gathered most of her scanty firsthand knowledge of African American culture, takes this sense of chronic peril much further by stressing the impossibility of any substantive mutual understanding between white do-gooders and their black beneficiaries. The rapport between Eliza and Mrs. Shelby, George Harris and Phineas Fletcher, not to mention Eva and Tom or Topsy, is unthinkable in the world of *Beloved*. The closest approximation is Mrs. Garner's semi-maternal relation with the teenage Sethe, whom she can understand only as a child whose innocence shouldn't be disabused—ironic confirmation of *Uncle Tom's Cabin*'s default view of blacks as virtual children. That Garner himself is shown as cordially acquainted with Bodwin when he delivers Baby Suggs to her doorstep, even though Bodwin asserts the difference between them in a friendly poke at Garner's brand of kindness toward blacks, insinuates the fragility of white benevolence compared to white solidarity.

Beloved confirms the insistence of Stowe and antebellum abolitionists generally across the color line that proslavery advocates were flat wrong in denying that slaves cared greatly about family, seconding findings by modern historians as to the importance slaves attached to solemnizing marriages and to keeping family intact intergenerationally despite forced breedings and dispersals.[16] George Harris's fellow fugitive Jim risks recapture to free his aged mother; *Beloved* makes the same point more grimly when Sethe's husband Halle mortgages his future to release his lame old mother Baby Suggs. *Beloved*'s emotional epicenter is a limit-case version of sentimental abolitionism's great emotional trump card for eliciting white middle-class sympathy, the mother's loss of a child. To be sure, the novel ambiguates this via Beloved's nearly lethal takeover of 124; but the epilogue reinstates the icon by holding out the possibility of something quite like the restoration of normative family unification (around Sethe, Paul D, and Denver) at which *Uncle Tom's Cabin* arrives, with George's and Eliza's known-to-be-surviving relatives together, or Harriet Jacobs's satisfaction of being under a roof of her own with her children. But *Beloved* stops far short of affirming family solidarity as a widely shared ethic or practice on either side of the color line. Such white family life as portrayed here seems to lead nowhere, nor is there even a durable black marriage or family in view—only the hint of that possible future one.

Much more aggressively than *Huckleberry Finn*, *Beloved* casts itself as a postbellum reflection on the slavery issue that submits "emancipation" meant distinction with minimal difference. The Ku Klux Klan, founded in the late 1860s, ranges freely across the Ohio River terrorizing northern blacks as well as southern. In this postabolitionist era, even decent whites give little thought to their black neighbors. Sethe's employer at first cuts her a little slack when tending Beloved makes her a less clockwork-predictable worker, but then summarily fires her. The date 1873 is well timed: the start of Grant's second administration, when Reconstruction began to collapse.

Beloved's choice of setting makes additional sense in this context: a border state in "greater Appalachia," as a recent cartography of U.S. culture regions calls it, with historically shared values whether "in slaveless Indiana or slavery-friendly Tennessee" that included in the Reconstruction era the KKK, in those days "almost entirely an Appalachian phenomenon."[17] Seemingly at cross-purposes but actually in keeping with this conflation of regional cultures that modern memory has tended to see as so distinct from one another during the antebellum era is *Beloved's* handling of stereotypical North/South climate difference. Reminiscent of Stowe's and Faulkner's tropicalizations of the deep South, the climate of *Beloved's* Kentucky is distinguished more sharply from its cross-border Yankee neighbor than the geographical facts warrant by having Sethe and Paul D remember Sweet Home as warm and fecund and by setting much of the plot proper during the cold months, especially the winter sequence when Paul D retreats to the shed and then the church basement. But the anomalous nighttime temperature dip during Sethe's August escape is a tipoff that cultural logic rather than meteorology is what chiefly drives the novelistic weather, as with Eliza's thrilling February escape across the ice floes, by contrast to which the weather on both sides of the Ohio in *Uncle Tom's Cabin* seems amazingly temperate before and after. That Paul D's late summer arrival soon gives way to fickle fall and deep freeze seems to reprise Baby Suggs's tragically abbreviated four weeks of premature rejoicing after Sethe's escape, with Beloved dying and reborn at the same time of year. For the reprise to put such emphasis on the frost-belt aspect of Ohio's southern verge intensifies the fragility of the great regional divide, the failed promise in the long run as well as the short of the crossing of the Jordan for which slaves so yearned in story, song, and dream.

Afro-Atlantic Diasporic Imagination

Morrison is the first indisputably front-rank U.S. novelist to have gone on record as insisting, "I write in order to enlighten black people, not from a need to explain to the others." Never mind that this pronouncement is belied by *Beloved*'s publishing venue—a mass-market trade press—and by its range of actual readership. Never mind that in other interviews Morrison qualified her pronouncement, and that what she said in that particular interview was surely affected by her rapport with the questioner, the Afro-British critic Paul Gilroy. There seems no reason to doubt the sincerity, if not the sufficiency, of her insistence (again to Gilroy, who was soon to write a landmark essay on *Beloved* as a masterpiece of black Atlantic imagination, with *Beloved* as the centerpiece of his final chapter), "I have found more to share with Third World peoples in the diaspora."[18]

Up to a point, such assertions put Morrison in the company of other great American novelists from Hawthorne on down. They too have disaffiliated from the social mainstream more often than not. They too have self-identified as resident aliens. They too have deplored, even when they have also celebrated, that the United States is a culture "where the past is always erased and America is the innocent future," to quote another Morrison pronouncement from the same interview.[19] But her claim about national amnesia is of course more specific than that, more specific although at the same time (even) more sweeping than Ali Behdad's analysis of American immigrant discourse as testifying to a dominant tradition of enforced forgetfulness of one's country and culture of origins as the trade-off for becoming American. In broadest terms, in the spirit of this chapter's opening epigraph from Amitav Ghosh, *Beloved* pits itself furiously against the default "aesthetic of indifference" toward the buried skeletons of the collective past.[20] But Morrison's animus is more pointedly directed against the forgetting of a particular diasporic heritage. Indeed *Beloved* is committed to the uniqueness of Afro-diasporic memory to the point of seeming to put outsiders on notice that they shouldn't expect to understand.[21] Yet the way the novel delivers on that implication of blocked access to the Afro-diasporic past potentially addresses insiders and outsiders both.

Antebellum slave narratives contain occasional Afrocentric traces, but none come close to matching Olaudah Equiano's extended (and possibly fictitious) recollections of his African boyhood and kidnapping in the early section of his *Interesting Narrative* (1789). In linking the title figure's prophetism to his Africanity, Stowe's *Dred* is more Afrocentric than most slave narratives are. That suggests why they aren't: to avoid the taint of primitivism. Fitness for freedom, not African continuity, was the message that slave narrative's abolitionist sponsors wanted to impress on the public at large. Despite the long history of calls for African return by black American intellectuals and activists from Martin Delany and Alexander Crummell onward, with such scattered exceptions as Zora Neale Hurston, major African American novelists through Wright, Petry, Ellison, and Baldwin showed scant interest in tracing the African roots of African American experience. This changed in the 1960s, thanks in large part to Ellison's nemesis, the Black Arts movement, of which the older generation of turn-of-the-twenty-first-century African American creative writers and intellectuals like Morrison are ambivalent successors. Robert Hayden's masterful poem "Middle Passage" (1966), Amiri Baraka's multimedia play *The Slave Ship* (1970), and Alex Haley's middlebrow TV serial *Roots* (1976) are a few of the pre-Morrison examples that show the range of attempts across the spectra of avant-garde to popular, militant to melioristic, to evoke African diasporic memory indelibly marked by the horrors of the Middle Passage from Africa to the Americas.

One reason, possibly the most crucial, why *Beloved* is widely thought to have surpassed these and other precursors is the combined intensity of its commitment to framing slavery and its aftermaths in deep-time Afro-diasporic context and its insistence that latter-day remembrance of that past can only be in quotation marks. As Morrison herself has stressed in essays and interviews, memory of slavery days and the Middle Passage can only be recuperated in the present in the context of acknowledging the blockages that impede access: language barriers, laconic hints of elders hurriedly imparted in secret, erosion of memory over time, forced separations, the haze of nightmare and fear; the need to protect against being crushed by a potentially unbearable burden of pain, humiliation, and outrage. All this her novel concretizes through its uncanny figuration of Beloved, killed in order to protect her against the remembered state of enslavement that has left physical and emotional scars so indelible that Sethe and all the novel's other ex-slaves must strive to try to forget that past simply to survive.

To this end *Beloved* works its way tortuously and obliquely toward disclosure that the case of Beloved is to be understood both as a uniquely personal tragedy of murder, loss, and haunting and as an epitome of all the human losses of the whole dispensation of slavery, the "Sixty Million and more" of *Beloved*'s "notorious" epigraph—controversial for its swipe at Holocaust exceptionalism.[22] Sethe, Denver, and the reader quickly sense that the apparition in white is the lost daughter/sister miraculously returned. But the revelation of Beloved's ulterior significance as carrier of pan-African diasporic memory doesn't emerge until much later, as befits the present-time characters' attenuated, fragmentary, self-defensive engagement with that past. None of Sethe's generation comes directly from Africa except Sweet Home's Sixo. Sethe must struggle, prodded by Denver and Beloved, to recall her own mother through the fog of "something privately shameful" (her mother's gruesome execution for some unnamed offense? her infanticides? suspected connection between the two? [*B* 61]). That in turn precipitates another recollection of "small girl Sethe" being told by her mother's compatriot Nan—a scene "forgotten, along with the language she had told it in"— that Nan and Sethe's "Ma'am" were gang-raped on the Middle Passage and that Sethe, named for her father, was the only baby her Ma'am had let survive because all the others were forced impregnations by whites. For Sethe in 1873, this remembering feels like "picking meaning out of a code she no longer understood" (62)—or preferred not to try to decipher. Either way, these memory scenes dramatize, as critic Madhu Dubey observes, that "unmediated recovery of folk tradition putatively rooted in Africa is impossible."[23]

Yet the recovery process continues, culminating in the remarkable monologue in which Beloved recalls her passage in a series of discontinuous incoherent vignettes from a kind of prenatal position as a forever "crouching" figure among densely packed and dying captives on a slave ship piloted by "men without skin" (*B* 210), to be (re)born as per her apparition from the waters of the creek behind 124, waters both amniotic and transoceanic, then coming together with "the face I found and lost," which is Sethe's (214). In this fantasia of birthing, the passages of Ma'am, Sethe, and Beloved converge. The stacked bodies and the near suffocation of the slave ship may also evoke Paul D's "living burial within the prison camp 'box'"—for just about the same length of time as a slaver's cross-Atlantic voyage.[24]

Beloved's magical passage through deep time offers flickering promise of some decisive epiphany, or at least a nodal point around which the rest of the novel might be seen to gather. But any attempt to grasp it is frustrated by its incoherence, by its positioning as one of a series of equally discontinuous interior monologues by the others cloistered in 124, and above all by Denver's breakout and Beloved's ensuing exorcism. Here the novel pits the ethics and the pragmatics of memory and forgetting against each other. Repression/amnesia and remembrance are made symbiotically problematic. The claims of Beloved to be remembered are not to be denied, but neither is the need to avoid being engulfed by the past if one is to survive. "If Sethe is to live, Beloved must depart," as critic Trudier Harris sums up.[25] The solitude within which repressed memory returns with a vengeance has been aggravated by the community's denial of responsibility for its part in triggering the infanticide. Its exorcism of Beloved is both a defensive act of self-protection against the threat posed by the insurgent ghost and a culmination of its belated atonement for that willed amnesia.

But then the epilogue laconically notes a return to amnesia: the community "forgot her like a bad dream" (*B* 274). Even the central trio of characters—Denver, Sethe, Paul D—might be headed for a future disencumbered from the past, the text hints.

Perhaps there is something fishy about Beloved's permanent-seeming evacuation, perhaps by design. Presumably the novel trusts that the story of Beloved is certain not to be forgotten by the reader. Yet the epilogue reads, as Spargo suggests, a bit like the perfunctory renormalizations in the final lines of Shakespearian tragedies—Fortinbras marching in to oversee Hamlet's funeral arrangements, Albany and Edgar wearily vowing to clean up in the aftermath of *King Lear's* catastrophe.[26] An abrupt pull-down of the lifted curtain onto the deep past also seems faithful, though, to the novel's opacity effects overall. As Sethe's own near-death experience has dramatized, much more has been evoked, both for the characters and even for the secondary witnesses, the readers, than can be borne actively in mind while maintaining the ability to function. And as the strategy of semi-explication of the intractably mysterious title figure has demonstrated, whatever can be saved from the wreckage of the slavery era, some things have been sacrificed that can never be recovered. Meaning in the first instance, of course, the sacrifice of Beloved as intensified by Sethe's and to a lesser extent Denver's unfulfilled longings for reunion. But beyond that, as Dubey points out, also sacrificed is what's represented by "the displacement of Beloved, the orally desirous daughter, by Denver, the literate daughter."[27] Denver, it seems, may now be prepared by Lady Jones and bankrolled by the Bodwins for college at Oberlin. Access to the Beloved era will increasingly come through the more distanced medium of print, just as it did for the author herself when she came across the story and image of Margaret Garner in that ancient newspaper account, however passionately Morrison then conjured it back into something like virtual flesh and blood by novelistic shamanism. The final expulsion of Beloved and the community's alleged forgetting of her reconfirms the felt necessity both of the conjuration and the exorcism. Morrison did not so much contradict as unpack *Beloved*'s cryptic coda ("It was not a story to pass on") when she declared, "the struggle to forget, which was important in order to survive, is fruitless and I wanted to make it fruitless."[28] That these opposite-seeming thrusts fit together as part of a single design is signaled by the work of rememory, which guarantees that even as bodies and spirits seem to disappear for good at the plot level, "nothing ever dies" (*B* 36); that for better or worse haunting can persist down through the generations.

Such is *Beloved*'s Afro-diasporic intensification of U.S. fiction's long-standing critique of the phenomenon of American innocence, meaning for most of the novelists we've been closely examining in this book the lure of the perpetual possibility of starting afresh. Morrison intensifies the critique that Fitzgerald and Faulkner make of the likes of Gatsby and Sutpen, whose hubristic "innocence," destructive though it's shown to be, also gets suffused with romantic wonder. In Morrison-land, innocence is a disenabler if not a curse, more so even than for Ellison's Invisible Man. Philip Weinstein's assertion that Morrison was as "repelled by innocence as Christians are by corruption" scarcely overstates the case.[29] From Pecola Breedlove's longing in *The Bluest Eye* for a blue-eyed doll and blue eyes herself, oblivious to how that desire simply rechannels mass-culture iconography, to *A Mercy*'s Jacob Vaark, who insists on dying in his unfinished mansion when smallpox frustrates his proto-Franklinesque dream of self-transformation from orphan to patron, Morrison characters bonded to their platonic images of themselves get humiliated or destroyed.

The original turn *Beloved* gives its critique of national innocence is nowhere better glimpsed than in one of the most inventive turns it gives to the Sethe-Amy Denver encounter, where black-white rapport gets treated most generously. Before settling in for the night at their rude shelter, probably more to comfort herself than Sethe, Amy sings several stanzas of Eugene Field's "Lady Button Eyes" (*B* 80–81). Why does the novel go to the trouble of interpolating twenty-nine whole lines of this ditty by a popular white late-century journalist-poet for children (better known for his nursery rhymes "Little Boy Blue" and "Wynken, Blynken, and Nod") versus nearly zero in the way of African American lyric and song? One point Amy immediately makes clear is that it's "my mama's song. She taught me it" (81). Whether or not she's literate, for her this is an oral text, a lullaby meant for her. The episode resonates with the luminous moment later on when the ghost's identity is proven conclusively. Sethe is startled to overhear Beloved humming a song she herself made up. "Nobody knows that song but me and my children." "I know it," Beloved replies. Then comes a rush of calm delight, for the time being at least: "No gasp at a miracle that is truly miraculous because the magic lies in the fact that you knew it was there for you all along" (176). Another lullaby. What could be more innocent than a mother's lullaby? But the Field poem gives off a creepy sort of innocence, reminiscent of the European folk culture from which Amy's mother probably came. In its archaized language, Lady Button Eyes "cometh" as a kind of soothing sandman to "smooth the eyelids down"; but she approaches "our quiet cozy home" as a kind of weird swamp sprite "through the muck and mist and gloom." What at first seems a kid-friendly doll-like visage on second thought sounds very creepy. It's hard not to think of the visitant closing "those two eyes of brown" as the seal of death, and all the more so when the novel makes lullaby the pathway to the dead daughter's usurpation of Sethe. Anglo-American "innocence" metamorphoses into Afro-diasporic uncanny.*

Conversely, however, for *Beloved* to incarnate rememory work in a story of guilty haunting by a dead child is to give a uniquely diasporic tragedy an exoteric face of the broadest appeal. A historically knowledgeable student of U.S. literature will be driven back to its first powerful

* That Amy warbles a lyric not composed until forty years after the imagined time of this event may be accidental; but it's in keeping with the preemption of orality by print that "Lady Button Eyes" exemplifies and that lies in wait for Amy's namesake Denver, not to mention *Beloved*'s readership.

novel of the black/white North/South divide. Whether intentionally or not, *Beloved*'s defining event suits its time of genesis, the 1980s, when resurgent interest in nineteenth-century American sentimentalism reached its high point, including the reinstatement of *Uncle Tom's Cabin* as a literary "classic"—although no less controversial this time around than before. As a time-traveling narrative built around the loss of a mourned child, *Beloved* pulls together with as well as against the single most potent trope of the hegemonic sentimental culture of its imagined time and its single most celebrated fictional instance. As critic Karen Sánchez-Eppler writes, "dying is what children do most and do best in the cultural imagination of nineteenth-century America." *Uncle Tom's Cabin* looms large among her cornucopia of literary and photographic snapshots, both the highly charged scene where Eliza moves Mrs. Bird to tears by making her think of the baby she lost and Stowe's insistence that her own loss of a child drove home to her what slave mothers must feel when robbed of theirs. These "repetitive portrayals of a dead or dying child," Sánchez-Eppler points out, "articulate anxieties about growth and loss for a young nation characterized by abundance, geographic expansion, and industrialization but also threatened by economic instability and sectional divisions."[30]

With obvious qualifications for one denied the benefits of national growth and abundance, this holds for Sethe as well. Beloved's death is the traumatic downside of the upside of an escape so miraculous that even after the tragedy her mother-in-law taunts her with the difference between her own case (all eight children taken from her) and Sethe's (three of four kids still at home): "You lucky" (*B* 5). It scarcely exaggerates to see *Beloved* and *Uncle Tom's Cabin* as both pivoting around cases of authorial child murder designed to rivet the attention of frustratingly resistant or passive publics. The emotional repercussions surrounding the two central supremely beloved and mourned-for children's untimely deaths, drastically different though their orchestrations are, drive home the wrongness of the world that let it happen.

This is not to suggest that Morrison designedly adapted Stowe's master motif or self-consciously drew upon the tropes of antebellum sentimentalism. The key point here is the common realization of the enormous rhetorical power of the slaughter of the innocents, of literary infanticide as a remedy against willful innocence, against closing one's eyes. So too infanticide became a defining theme in Scottish border ballads and literary imitations thereof by Wordsworth and others. So *The Diary of Anne Frank* became a talismanic text for the Holocaust imaginary in the wake of her murder. So too, moving closer in time and place to Morrison and her significant literary others, in Leslie Silko's *Almanac of the Dead* (1991) the teenage white ex-druggie's book-long mourning for the loss of the probably murdered infant son kidnapped at a moment of stoned inattentiveness becomes a pathway for accessing the novel's outrage at the genocide of Mesoamerican indigenes by officialdom from the Aztec Empire to the conquistadores to the present-day gringo-Mex military-economic establishments and their underworld cronies.

If, as seems likely, *Beloved* remains for the foreseeable future "one of the most celebrated contemporary novels of the slave experience and one of the most highly acclaimed novels of the twentieth century," one major reason is likely to be its deployment of its transculturally recognizable horrific defining scene combined with its "textual recalcitrance" and the attendant psychological and historical insight that this bespeaks in impeding access of its readers as well as its characters to the past so dimly glimpsed, so fitfully, painfully grasped and understood.[31] Since *Beloved,* other novels have undertaken more detailed frontal portrayal of the Middle Passage ordeal, such as Charles Johnson's fabulistic novel of that title briefly discussed in Chapter 6. Other novels have memorialized African American life under slavery and its aftermaths more densely and with no less equal subtlety, such as Edward D. Jones's remarkable *The Known World* (2003), also a Pulitzer Prize winner, which follows an intergenerational black clan in Virginia who became slaveholders through intrafamilial tensions and transactions with their white patrons and neighbors through the greater part of the nineteenth century. Both before and since Morrison, others have created more multiperspectival cartographies of the memory and history of slavery across the black Atlantic, such as Paule Marshall's *The Chosen Place, The Timeless People* (1969) and Caryl Phillips's *Cambridge* (1991), also deft and relentless in exposing the stark realities of slavery's history through the fog of un-initiated outsidership. Among these other accomplished fictions of slavery and its aftermaths, however, *Beloved* stands out for its rendition of the reflexive aversion, emotional hazard, ethical urgency, and epistemological confusion involved in recuperating the African diasporic past both then and now.

Even if neo-slave narrative falls out of fashion, something like this oblique version of it will surely endure not just on its intrinsic merits, but also because of the fit between *Beloved*'s "postmodern" assumption of history's simultaneous inaccessibility and omnipresence with African American literature's often fervent yet contested assessments of the claims of Afro-diasporic continuity, of African cultural forms as models for African American art and the ethics or desirability of African return. W. E. B. Du Bois's expatriation to Ghana looks less typical of African American literary and cultural history than the expatriations of Richard Wright, James Baldwin, and William Demby, none of whom became more Afrocentric in consequence. Zora Neale Hurston's keen interest in Afro-Caribbean cosmology and folklore is less representative of African American creative writing generally than John Edgar Wideman's more circumscribed and targeted engagements. Melvin Tolson will always be better known for his *Harlem Gallery* than for his "Libretto for the Republic of Liberia" as that nation's poet laureate.

Beloved mediates adroitly between alternatives by conceiving diaspora as both constitutive and attenuated. African American slavery is not framed as an American story pure and simple; yet Africanity inheres as inchoate memory rather than as either the geohistorical "actuality" of Alex Haley's *Roots* expedition or the synthetic virtuality of Charles Johnson's Allmuseri. In this, Morrison's fifth novel built upon her previous two, *Song of Solomon* and *Tar Baby.* There too diasporic memory is powerfully evoked and grasped after, amid and against the sense of having to overcome snapped links, cultural reprogramming, and hesitancy if not aversion to going back there. In *Solomon,* Milkman Dead's quest for family origins culminates with him seemingly either on the verge of trying to replicate his great-grandfather's legendary flight back to Africa, the stuff of local legend ever since, or getting killed by his ex-friend Guitar. In *Tar Baby,* the Franco-Caribbean island sanctuary of a mismatched white rich couple and their proper middle-class black retainers is penetrated by a peripatetic but folk-rooted Hurstonesque seaman from the Florida backwater hamlet of Eloe who temporarily seduces its black Miranda, the house servants' niece who has become the resident Prospero's protégé; but when she ditches "Son" to resume her upscale career, he seems—although here as in *Solomon* the novel breaks off—about to follow an island conjure woman's exhortation to take his place among the mystic cohort of fugitive "horsemen" who haunt the place. Her tales, Trudier Harris observes, "carry the same connotations for spiritual rebirth" for him "as the tales of the flying Solomon carry for Milkman."[32] *Beloved* builds upon these novelistic experiments but also moves beyond them both in the decisiveness with which it seizes hold of diaspora as inescapable, constitutive historical legacy and in the firmness with which it emphasizes the blockages to accessing or reenacting that past—for better as well as for worse—except as imagined construct.

Other Divides, Other Diasporas

In 2000, the novelist Russell Banks issued a call for a new kind of Great American Novel that would dramatize "a single believable story" of "our origins" with which all Americans might be able to identify. Banks worried that the imagined country of American literature was "fast becoming a Balkanized cluster of small colonies"—a concern that recalls J. W. De Forest's back in 1868, except that for Banks the balkanization had to do with race rather than region and it threatened the undoing of a unitary sense of imagined nationness that De Forest thought impossible until quite recently. De Forest would have been astonished, however, by Banks's proposal that "the single defining" story line that dramatized the "essential, and specifically American, political and moral meaning of every American's life"—"north, south, and meso-"—was the story of African diaspora.[33]

This millennial milestone is partly discountable as a white writer's plea for the field of black history to be kept open at a time when white and black literatures seemed to be diverging on separate tracks.[34] But as a wager that a credibly nation-defining narrative must orient itself around the diasporic saga of a non-Euro minority and that this particular saga must be it, the essay testifies to the transnational turn in U.S. literary thought during the last several decades, as well as to the broad acceptance among the nation's creative writers of the line of argument advanced by Ellison and elaborated by Morrison that blackness has been a formative constituent for Euro-American literature whether as a presence or as telling absence. Dave Eggers's *What Is the What* (2006), a collaboratively composed autobiographical novel of a young Dinka refugee orphaned by the long Sudanese civil war who eventually makes his way to the United States, might be seen as one among many possible reaffirmations of

Banks's way of thinking among Euro- as well as African American writers.

But milestones are laid down in order to be got past. African diaspora as "*the* single defining" narrative? Even for 2000, but certainly in the 2010s, that threatens to take a good thing too far and risk foreclosure of another sort. Up to a point, to hold up Afro-Atlantic as a corrective to the traditional Euro-monopoly on the theory of American hemispheric origins seems salutary, timely, and honorable. But having done so, to privilege it or any other particular line of Americo-ethnogenesis at this late date as the touchstone seems arbitrary. Most obviously, it overlooks the renaissance in Native American letters during the past half century and the increasingly distinguished bodies of transpacific literature by Asian American writers from various ancestral homelands and pan-hemispheric literature by Latino/a writers from Mexico, the Caribbean, and elsewhere in the Latino/a world.[35] Although it goes beyond the bounds of this book and my own expertise to do more than gesture in those directions, I want to close this section with some brief reflections on southwestern borderlands imagination, as one sure-fire example of those alternative emergent futures now in the making.

Southwestern borderlands imaginary, or imaginaries, clearly require some ways of thinking about ethnic and regional division quite different from thinking in terms of the axes of North/South and black/white that have been so salient in U.S. divide fiction from the antebellum era through the late twentieth century. For Americans of Mexican ancestry, for instance, territory and ethnos are likely to seem more intimately connected, and in such a way as to call official U.S. official cartography itself more directly into question. The late twentieth-century Chicano movement thought Atzlan, the mythic place of ancestral origin, to be located in the northern half of old Mexico appropriated after the U.S. conquest of 1848 as part of the present-day U.S. Southwest from Texas to California. To Latinos from the south, it's still El Norte. From this standpoint—and the same holds for Native Americans whose homelands stretch across the official U.S.-Mexico national border—the concept of jurisdictional border as marking off different cultural districts looks even more specious than the nominal North-South division in the postbellum era of *Beloved*'s present-time action, let alone the imagined antebellum world of Stowe's *Uncle Tom's Cabin*. What cultural critic José David Saldívar has called "the great discontinuity between the American frontier and *la frontera*"[36]—the elastic zone of U.S.-Mexican borderland that Américo Paredes was the first to call "greater Mexico"—seems all the more sinister in the 2010s given the Berlin Wall–like fortification and policing of the boundary line intensified by resurgent anti-immigrationism and the so-called war on drugs.* That a far higher percentage of Americans of Mexican and other Latin American backgrounds who have migrated to the United States speak Spanish and retain close contact with families and communities in their homelands makes for a more robust sense of diasporic identity than would have been possible for many if not most African American slaves within a generation after the Middle Passage. So images of homeland are less dependent on historical research and speculative conjuration and more likely to connect themselves with landscapes and communities fresher in collective memory and likelier to have been directly experienced.

Add to this the demographic fact that U.S. residents of Latino/a extraction now constitute the nation's largest minority—likely to become a majority in several states before long—and it seems certain that how the national imaginary at large envisages its defining romances of ethnoregional divide will change greatly during the twenty-first century from the era when North-South/white-black seemed the defining polarities, and the era prior to and overlapping with that when they were East-West/white-red. Lines of ethnic division are likely to seem (even) more porous and ethnic identity more complexly hybridized. Ethnicity

---

* "Greater Mexico" has been variously defined, denoting as it does both physical territory and cultural-diasporic experience, with a tendency over time to stretch the boundaries to encompass the entire area of residence of people of Mexican descent with their increase and dispersal northward. As Héctor Calderón remarks, "though linked . . . especially to cultural conflict along the Lower Rio Grande Valley, it is a term that is for me broadly embracive" (Héctor Calderón, *Narratives of Greater Mexico* [Austin: University of Texas Press, 2004], xiii). Américo Paredes's classic study of the *Corrido* seems to favor the former (Américo Paredes, *With His Pistol in His Hand: A Border Ballad and Its Hero* [Austin: University of Texas Press, 1958], 142–143). But Ramón Saldívar's comprehensive biographical study of Paredes's career as scholar and creative writer quotes him as later declaring that "Greater Mexico begins at the border of Guatemala and extends all the way to the Great Lakes, to New York, or wherever there are *mexicanos*" (Ramón Saldívar, *The Borderlands of Culture: Américo Paredes and the Transnational Imaginary* [Durham, NC: Duke University Press, 2006], 141–142). Saldívar elsewhere observes that Paredes envisaged Greater Mexico as a "composite hybrid" of "two Mexicos," one the republic of Mexico per se and the other "composed of all the persons of Mexican origin in the United States" (37).

and physical place may seem more intertwined, perhaps at once more place-centric and more migratory or cosmopolitan.

What then of the future of the Great American Novel under such conditions? If in fact fictions of Latino/gringo divides overtake, even supersede, the prominence over the two centuries of North/South, black/white divide narrative in U.S. writing, the upshot, as critic Kirsten Silva Gruesz proposes, will surely be metamorphic rather than merely additive: "not to integrate Latinos to an existing national tradition" but "to reshape that tradition in a way that recognizes the continuous life of Latinos within and around it."[37]

But how, exactly? Perhaps no one dominant paradigm for U.S. ethnoterritorial border fiction will predominate in this century of multiple diasporic story lines. Perhaps anything resembling such will look like the Los Angeles of Karen Tei Yamashita's *Tropic of Orange* (see Introduction to Part V), whose leading characters constitute an all-minority mix of Asian, Latino, and African migrants and residents. Perhaps Latino/a literature will find its place as one among many such diasporic matrices.

Meanwhile, these points seem clear. First, the archive of consequential Chicano/a border artistry and other novels from elsewhere in the Latino/a world focused on cultural and political negotiation of cross-border issues will continue to gather: Arturo Islas, Sandra Cisneros, Ana Castillo, Helena María Viramontes, Sylvia Sellers-Garcia, Francisco Goldman, Julia Alvarez, Cristina García, Junot Díaz, and the many others already known to the novel-reading public will be joined by many more.

Second, the one work of Anglo/Latino border fiction to rank high in the *New York Times* 2006 poll of best U.S. novels since 1980, one of the five novels named as runners-up to *Beloved*, was a back-to-the-future defamiliarization of an iconic Eurocentric genre: Cormac McCarthy's *Blood Meridian* (1985). An elegantly sculpted apocalyptic novel, *Blood Meridian* follows the picaresque wanderings of a teenage drifter ("the kid") from Tennessee across the southwestern borderlands from Texas to California in the wake of the Mexican War as he joins and parts company with marauding irregulars, many of them more messed-up and violent than he, as they prey on the Mexican villagers they have contracted to protect, hunt Indians for scalp bounty, and get hunted down in turn. McCarthy drastically inverts the triumphalist aura of the traditional literary Western. His rangers are far more barbarous than the darker races to whom they imagine themselves superior—"tattered, stinking, ornamented with human parts like cannibals." The embodiment of human learning and knowledge, the gargantuan "Judge," is a "vast abhorrence" who holds that "war is god" and "moral law is an invention of mankind for the disenfranchisement of the powerful in favor of the weak."[38] After finding favor, the kid ironically runs afoul of him for not being murderous enough. Although he starts out as a sardonic cartoon inversion of Huck Finn lighting out for the territory—touchy, sullen, irascible; quick with fists, knife, gun—immersion in borderland hell conditions him into a kind of defensive stoicism that the Judge deems or pretends to deem an unpardonable betrayal, even though he owes his own life to it when the kid declines to shoot him down in cold blood when he has the chance. In this way the novel disputes the necessity even as it confirms the facticity of the cultural historian Richard Slotkin's post-Vietnam critique of Euro-American male experience in the frontier contact zone as ritual "regeneration through violence."[39]

Blood Meridian tracks speech and behavior rather than thinking. The energy that might have been so directed gets channeled into haunting evocation of landscape with minute precision and baroque extravagance, as with this sunrise at moonset in a flat desert of mesquite and pyracantha: "the sun whitehot and the moon a pale replica, as if they were the ends of a common bore beyond whose terminals burned worlds past all reckoning." This makes for a great work of environmental imagination, not just its ecological literacy but its enlistment of that to render the disorientation of neophytes intruding into "a land of some other order out there whose true geology was not stone but fear."[40] But as a landscape of lunar alterity and devastated camps and villages with a human foreground dominated by gringo riffraff to whom Mexicans and Indians seem subhuman, *Blood Meridian* can't offer more than a negative route for borderlands imagination. Its service is rather as an ultimate dismantling of old-style U.S. Manifest Destiny–think and the aura built up around it by a century and a half of celebratory fiction, film, Texas Ranger hagiography, Buffalo Bill performance art, and so on.

The other monumental Southwestern borderlands fiction of the past several decades that seems to have "Great American Novel" written on it most indelibly—aspiring to an enormously greater geo-historical reach than *Blood Meridian*'s—is Leslie Silko's *Almanac of the Dead* (1991).

Stretching out from the author's home bases of Tucson and Laguna Pueblo of western New Mexico, *Almanac* takes in a half millennium of hemispheric history, with recurring glimpses of Euro- and Afro-Atlantic intertwinements too. Though the novel had been germinating for many years, the finished result has the look of an attempted fulfill-ment of Maxine Hong Kingston's 1989 prediction that "the dream of the great American novel" will be superseded by "the global novel" set "in the United States, destination of journeys from everywhere."[41] *Al-manac* takes a no less apocalyptic view of historical process than does *Blood Meridian*, but resting on a mythico-political vision of deep-time indigeneity antipathetic to McCarthy's cosmic indifferentism. The ho-locaust of Native America must and will be exposed. "There was not, and there never had been, a legal government by Europeans anywhere in the Americas." The land unlawfully seized and abused will be re-deemed. "The world that the whites brought with them would not last," as one character mentally sums up both Native hopes and white fears.[42]

In *Blood Meridian* borders are factitious because uncontrollable. In *Almanac* they are corrupt legal fictions all the worse for the ferocity with which they are patrolled. So *Almanac* sympathizes with, indeed to some extent glorifies, lawbreaking and insurgency as *Blood Meridian* does not. That the mestizo smuggler Calabazas, with family on both sides of the border, considers his profitable cross-border transactions principled civil disobedience is shown as self-interested but not merely so. The "all-tribal" insurgency that gathers momentum throughout, partly modeled on the likewise Chiapas-based Zapatista uprising but here imagined as rolling northward into the U.S. Southwest, is framed as heroic, although carefully presented as a heterogeneous front with armed militants and cultural prophets not of one accord. What is wholly unambiguous is that officialdom on both sides of the border and those in cahoots with it are without exception corrupt, most of them kinky sexual predators to boot. And so it has been for more than five centuries, the novel stresses, ever since the Aztec insurgency. Cortés and Montezuma deserved each other. They were "members of the same secret clan" of Destroyers.[43]

Almanac resists simple white/nonwhite Manichaeism, then, al-though even more than in Silko's previous novel *Ceremony* whiteness is tied to "witchery" and its ultimate disappearance prophesied. One of the most sympathetic characters is the repentant white ex-druggie

Seese who attaches herself to the Yaqui psychic Lecha as secretary in the vain hope of recovering her kidnapped infant son. But no authority structure is given a free pass, including the Laguna, "the first of the Pueblos to realize wealth from something terrible done to the earth," uranium mining for nuclear weaponry, and for banishing the rightly named Sterling on trumped-up charges. The "self-made" Mexican tycoon ashamed of his indigenous roots who casts his fortunes with the police state gets wasted. Doctrinaire Latino Marxists fare little better than capitalists. The insurgents execute their self-appointed Cuban attaché Bartolomeo (to whom nothing in American history before Castro counts as history) for his "crimes against history," that is, for denying the indigenous holocaust.[44]

Committed though it is to an exhaustive secular critique of the complexities of North American political, economic, racial, and sexual fault lines and power structures, *Almanac* accords most moral authority to the charismatic power of a handful of indigenous and indigenous-identified Natives and mestizos, among whom perhaps the most salient are Lecha and the insurgent leader La Escapía, the coming revolution's most forceful voice. Lecha in particular, a retired celebrity medium famous for detective work and daytime TV performances using her psychic powers to identify where dead bodies are buried, personifies the link between the novel's cultural-geographic epicenter of Tucson, *Almanac*'s squalid quotidian secular city, and the nexus of spiritual indigeneity from which the approaching storm of insurgency has arisen. She is the custodian of the surviving fragments of the titular almanac, an ancient scripture now corrupted—yet also enhanced—by multiple eclectic addenda. Interspersed excerpts from it create a palimpsest effect insinuating that the novel itself aspires to serve as something like a carrier of prophetic authority in full awareness of its own secular encrustations.

In degree of difficulty attempted, geographical and historical reach, panoramic cultural anatomy and synthesis, *Almanac of the Dead* ranks with the century's most ambitious hemispheric epics, such as Pablo Neruda's *Canto General* and Derek Walcott's *Omeros*. In a number of ways it too seems to offer itself as a template for hemispheric reimagination: its counterhistory on behalf of the dispossessed, its deconstruction of imposed borders, its mobility across regions and landscapes without sacrifice to local density, its vision of interethnic convergence. To the extent that *Almanac* envisages territorial reconquest of the Americas by insurgent indigeneity with authority grounded in the pre-Aztec primordium, however, it advertises itself as a Native rather than a panhemispheric intervention. Significantly, the novel measures the worth of its Mexican characters in proportion to their acceptance of their Indianness, however vestigial. It pushes to an extreme Gloria Anzaldúa's caveat that "the worst kind of betrayal lies in making us believe that the Indian woman in us is the betrayer."[45]

Relative to *Almanac*, Latino/a hemispheric writing that concerns itself with U.S.-ness—Cuban and Puerto Rican as well as Chicano/a—seems to my nonexpert eye less insistent that ethnic divisions be resolved one way, less apocalyptic than dialogic, more given over to exploring the phenomenon of parallel universes of compatriots that exist on both sides of North-South jurisdictional borders, more oriented toward questioning the legal and epistemological authority of institutionalized nation forms and the scandal of border fortification buildup than toward territorial reclamation per se. But who can say what forms it will take? Only that the twenty-first century may well see a boom in American Latino/a writing that puts the midcentury magical realist heyday in the shade and changes the "American" imaginary beyond all power to forecast now. Almost certainly, the best is still to come.

PART FIVE

SCRIPT FOUR: IMPROBABLE COMMUNITIES

Introduction

Fatalisms of the Multitude

THE UP-FROM NARRATIVES and romances of the divide discussed in Parts III and IV build on preexisting plot prototypes from Western literary history. The scenario the novels featured in this final section loosely share in common has no such readily identifiable ancestors. Part V takes up a series of novels from the antebellum era to the present given over in different degrees to tracking heterogeneous cross-sections of characters, whether closely interacting or widely dispersed, conjoined by a common task, challenge, or threat that dramatizes democracy under siege or duress. Often sprawling performances of encyclopedic scope with multiple agendas from the ethnographic to the metaphysical, these novels offer thought experiments in imagining forms of possible and/or balked "democratic" collectivity in the contexts of their eras. That means confronting characteristic disparities between the "ought" and the "is" resulting from dissension or fecklessness within the mix of characters who populate these imagined worlds and the forms of authoritarian manipulation that become more draconian, opaque, insidious, and pervasive as "civilization" becomes more complex.

Chapters 11–13 center on three meganovels of this kind: Herman Melville's *Moby-Dick* (1851), John Dos Passos's *U.S.A.* trilogy (1929–1938), and Thomas Pynchon's *Gravity's Rainbow* (1973). Taken together, they span the eras of U.S. fiction history on which this book has chiefly focused: the formative years leading up to the birth of the GAN idea after Civil War and reunification; the realist-naturalist era and its early modern deliquescence; and the later twentieth century, when the GAN was discredited in theory but reasserted itself in practice more vigorously than ever in ways that involved both absorption of predecessors and major swerves.

Each of the three novels takes up a watershed moment for national history that is also seen as having world-historical significance. In sequence, they mirror different stages of socioeconomic development from early industrial to high-tech and—relatedly—stages of national advance from gadfly upstart to dominant world power and how those techno-economic and politico-military advances threaten fatally to compromise democratic principles under the guise of furthering them, the promise of egalitarianism in particular. In each work these matters get represented, reflected upon, and given a certain aesthetic and conceptual ordering that is left inchoate and ambiguated through a style of narrative management in which a hyperactive narrative consciousness—or consciousnesses—more instinctively partial to ordinary humanity than the powers that be is hard put to fathom, much less control, the increasingly subtle and depersonalized forms of authority that prevent the characters from congealing into anything like a coherent solidarity of free and equal agents.

The inquests into the hazards of the democratic prospect that Melville, Dos Passos, and Pynchon all pursue tend to turn on two complementary obstacles to the realization of democratic promise that had been identified by political theory of the early national era. Two notable works of the 1830s shed helpful light on those, Alexis de Tocqueville's *Democracy in America* (1835, 1840), justly acclaimed as the most searching assessment of national culture ever made by a foreign observer, and James Fenimore Cooper's sententious *The American Democracy* (1838), of special interest here given Cooper's authorship of the first landmark novel in U.S. literary history of the kind I'm describing.

Cooper's tract mounts a conservative defense of democracy that goes out of its way as his later writing also often did to hammer home unpalatable truths, one of them being that the Declaration of Independence is not to be taken literally. "All men are not 'created equal,' in a physical or even in a moral sense," Cooper insists. "The very existence of government at all" implies inequality—and it's a good thing too, "since the result would be to force all down to the level of the lowest."[1] Cooper not only accepts disenfranchisement of women and slaves but even expresses grave reservations about universal white manhood suffrage, especially given the "painful and humiliating fact" of the undersocialized immigrants crowding into U.S. cities. He favors majority rule nonetheless as the least bad option, as a check against "the unceasing desire of men to turn their advantages to their own particular benefit," but in so doing cautions against "the besetting vice of democracies to substitute publick opinion for law."[2]

Tocqueville also famously worried about "the tyranny of democracy," the catchphrase by which he is known even by those who haven't read him.[3] It's a phrase Cooper himself might have coined. But in reflecting further about the kinds of tyranny to which members of democratic societies seemed subject, Tocqueville gave voice to a related concern that Cooper's anxieties about uppity ignorance kept him from pinpointing: mass acquiescence. "As the conditions of men become equal," individual citizens, Tocqueville thought, tend to get "lost in the crowd," and to concede power to their delegated representatives after having once established the principle that "power ought to emanate from the people."[4] Here he anticipates the shrewd redescription of his "tyranny of the majority" as "the fatalism of the multitude," in James Bryce's magisterial summa *The American Commonwealth* (1888) a half century later. But Tocqueville shrewdly anticipated another line of explanation that Bryce's Gilded Age diagnosis glossed over despite being struck that "the most remarkable economic feature" of U.S. history since the Civil War had been "the growth of great fortunes."[5] The abolition of formal social distinctions under American-style democracy, Tocqueville thought, was accelerating the growth of the manufacturing sector so as to provide luxuries to those who could afford it that would resupply the social gradations the new political order had in principle erased. Already this growth spurt seemed to have created a widening gap between a mercantile oligarchy and a workforce ever "more weak, more narrow-minded, and more dependent" with the increasing specialization of labor as the Industrial Revolution advanced. "If ever a permanent inequality of conditions and aristocracy again penetrates into the world," Tocqueville predicted, this is "the gate by which they will enter."[6] As the social distortions produced by the maritime, managerial, and technocratic power structures charted in *Moby-Dick*, *U.S.A.*, and *Gravity's Rainbow* all attest, restratification has proven to be a much greater danger than the remote contingency Tocqueville believed it to be.*

Overall, Cooper and Tocqueville present themselves much more as critical expositors friendly to the American democratic experiment than as doom criers. Yet neither is under any illusion that the founding pledges of liberty and equality will operate with anything like justice for all. For Cooper, humanity is too fallible for democracy to work without serious flaws, dependent as the system is upon constituencies of informed and morally responsible self-policing stakeholders by no means to be expected even among the elite. For Tocqueville, the democratic system itself, despite the potential advantages he details elsewhere, seems fated to produce suboptimal agents with lowered expectations. Their assessments, taken together, anticipate the general mixture of hope and disillusionment and a number of the specific grounds of critique to be found in U.S. novels that conjure up heterogeneous assemblages of characters as social microcosms of democratic promise under duress.

Over the years, two partially overlapping literary strategies for undertaking this kind of social anatomy have evolved—minor and major, they might be called for short. The "minor," about which this section has little to say for reasons that will soon be obvious, consist of narratives of bounded communities of people juxtaposed by birth or happenstance in combinations of cooperation and apartness that put supposedly shared values and social cohesion to the test: lifeboat situations figurative or literal (the four survivors in Stephen Crane's "The Open Boat"); prairie settlements (the immigrant community of Hanover, Nebraska, in Cather's *O Pioneers!*); villages and towns with a high density of rooted eccentrics (Stowe's Oldtown, Jewett's Dunnet Landing, Anderson's Winesburg, the Morgana of Eudora Welty's *The Golden Apples*). These, however, are defined as more or less hermetic and archaic counter-spaces to society at large, as were earlier narratives of community that foreshadow them, John Galt's *Annals of the Parish* (1821), Mary Russell Mitford's *Our Village* (1824–1832) and Elizabeth Gaskell's miniaturized version, *Cranford* (1851).[7]

---

* That Tocqueville ventures his prediction tentatively, as an unlikely outcome, despite having called attention to the dramatic concentration of mercantile wealth already, is perhaps because in his European frame of reference "aristocracy" was no mere metaphor but a social actuality entrenched by stature and custom.

Such "minor" literature starts to become more consequential for our purposes when the bounded microcosmic community comes, through some disruption from without or within, into continuous interaction with society at large and thereby a more visible marker or barometer of it—that is, when it crosses the line of separation between the quartet in Crane's dinghy and the crew of Melville's *Pequod*. The one example Part V treats at any length is John Steinbeck's *Grapes of Wrath* (see Chapter 12), which forces its tightly knit cohort of dispossessed Okie farmers into a series of traumatic mind expansions when it pries them loose from their provincial embeddedness and sends them west after their farms are dispossessed. But a number of other analogous fictional experiments also deserve mention despite not (yet), like *Grapes of Wrath*, having made it onto the public radar screen as possible Great American Novels. Two instructively different cases in point are Arthur A. Cohen's *In the Days of Simon Stern* (1973), in which an Americanized Jewish tycoon turned charismatic prophet establishes a secret fortified enclave in Manhattan for a multinational collective of Holocaust survivors; and Richard Powers's *Gain* (1998), which intertwines an ordinary downstate Illinois community with the history of the multinational Clare Soap and Chemical Company headquartered there. The microcosmic communities in these novels, one ethnic and the other regional, become flashpoints for registering disarrangement at the national level and different kinds of unacknowledged catastrophe at the global. Whether or not they are ever so recognized, both demonstrate how what I have called the minor strategy for dramatizing socially microcosmic communities can give rise to script-four Great American Novels.

In the "major" approach to narratives of socially symbolic collectives, the path taken by the three novels here most intensively discussed as well as by most others mentioned along the way, the collective in question is framed more robustly as a microcosm of society at large—as it is, as it might be, as it threatens to become in a worst-case scenario, or as a compound of all of those.

A final pair of novels that straddle major and minor approaches, one earlier and one later than the trio of meganovels featured here, will help prepare for what's ahead: the first and in some ways most ambitious of Cooper's Leatherstocking series, *The Pioneers* (1823), and Karen Tei Yamashita's *Tropic of Orange* (1997). The combination of continuity and difference over time is revealing. Both novels anatomize the travails of community making in paradigmatic habitats that they hold up as auguries for the future. In time, style, and location the two could not be more different—which makes their shared premises all the more telling.

The Pioneers is a stylized reminiscence of the early (1790s) years of the settlement of Cooperstown, New York, founded by the author's father. By no means simply backward-looking however, *The Pioneers* is U.S. literary history's quintessential novel about the growing pains of a town newly carved out on the expanding U.S. frontier where law, order, and planning are hard put to keep pace with the booming development instigated by its increasingly heterogeneous and fractious mix of settlers. As such, declares critic David Simpson with pardonable hyperbole, *The Pioneers* is one of those books "without which any model of the development or continuity of American literature simply makes no sense."[8]

Tropic of Orange (1997) unfolds a surrealistic plot around a state of emergency in contemporary Los Angeles, regularly held up by urbanists as the quintessential American city of the future. *Tropic* is a more playfully lighthearted novel with a gritty underside more or less in the tradition of Los Angeles disaster narrative from Nathanael West's *The Day of the Locust* (1939) to such films as *Chinatown* (1974) and *Blade Runner* (1982) and Mike Davis's mordant nonfiction *Ecology of Fear* (2000). Here the crisis of community building centers on the illegal ad hoc community of the homeless who opportunistically move in to populate the hundreds of abandoned vehicles gridlocked for a whole week by a massive freeway crash. The manifestations both of semianarchic communitarianism and of police crackdown thereafter—a massive aerial bombardment ends the occupation—are magnified and spectacularized by the maldistribution of technopower and the egregious disparity between the actual threat of civil disorder and the scale of retaliation.

Both novels imagine their dramatis personae as global mélanges of different kinds. In Cooper's Templeton, Anglo, Dutch, French, German, British, Indian, and African, clashing religious sects, college-educated gentry and unlettered backwoodsmen converge with their distinctive accents and conflicting agendas, by turns cooperative and at odds. The contrast to Crèvecoeur's vision of middle states Eurofusion could not be more dramatic, not to mention the social enclave *American Farmer* treats in most detail, the "nation" of Nantucket, where insular clannish homogeneity is seen as key to its prosperity. Cooper's Templeton is a no less dynamic and far more accurate approximation of the heterogeneity of early national settlements in formation, especially in the middle states. *Tropic of Orange*'s demography is even more global in scope, in keeping with Los Angeles's standing as the premier U.S. megacity located in a border region.

Tropic mimics and satirizes metropolitan compartmentalization by constructing each of its seven chapters (Monday through Sunday) in seven-block sequences featuring each of its seven major characters: a well-educated Chicano reporter; a Chicana housemaid; her Vietnamese Chinese immigrant husband; a self-focused Japanese American female TV executive; an eccentric homeless ex-symphony conductor eventually revealed as her long-lost grandfather; a gigantic but also angelic son of the ghetto who befriends the homeless and helps engineer journalistic coverage; and an ancient-looking Mexican migrant who turns out to have miraculous strength and, in the avatar of El Gran Mojado, fights near the end a wrestling match with the evil SUPERNAFTA in which—or so it seems—they destroy each other.[9] The hyperextended gridspace within which these and the other characters operate means that none of them ever meets all the others although all interact at least casually with some. It also means that no one person, including narrator and reader, ever perceives a sense of territorial and social place with anything like the clarity with which Cooper's Templeton and environs get depicted. "Somebody else must have the big map," one character thinks. "Or maybe just the next map. The one with the new layers you can't even imagine."[10]

In *The Pioneers*, then, a workable democratic community of cooperative and coexisting stakeholders is presumed attainable whereas in *Tropic*, as the structural grid implies, it's ruled out from the get-go with the ironic exception of the homeless occupiers, who inject a carnivalesque ad hoc communitarianism abruptly cut short. Templeton too is an embattled community, however. Its volatility goes to show that "society cannot exist without wholesome restraints," as Judge Temple the town patriarch cautions.[11] Much of the novel is given over to a running debate about the relative claims of liberty and law as the judge's top-down support for instituting such restraints gathers momentum. Temple and Natty Bumppo become the chief spokesmen for the two sides. Critic Sandra Gustafson rightly calls attention to Cooper's fiction, Natty's loquacity in particular, as a theater that dramatizes "deliberative democracy" in action.[12] *The Pioneers* is a prime instance. As the rightness of this or that measure is debated, down to the minutest details of courtroom etiquette, the novel often seems like an elaborate civics lesson or debate. The nub of the contention between the judge and the Leatherstocking, as Cooper scholar John McWilliams points out, turns on the question, "Are there limits to the authority which a just and necessary civil law should have over the individual?" The judge's commitment to instituting law and order, even if it means depending on unworthy minions to carry it out, results in Natty's conviction and imprisonment for killing a deer out of season. But Natty's conviction that "the civil law is an impingement upon the rights of the natural man" is implicitly conceded by the sympathetic treatment of his rescue from prison, by the judge's reaffirmation of his sterling virtues, and by the decampment of this most worthy of all the novel's characters for the further frontier.[13] Even as the novel seems to accept the pragmatic necessity of legal institutions for the settlements, it telegraphs a certain "covert distrust of the social order" to which it seems to subscribe.[14] *Tropic,* however, wastes no time debating the pros and cons of duly constituted legal authority, which manifests itself chiefly in the form of officially sanctioned retaliatory overkill at the end. When Rafaela is attacked by a malevolent drug and organ trafficker, her only recourse is private retaliation. Immigration authority is an institution to be circumvented not just by the villains but by the sympathetic figures too.

Perhaps the contrast just drawn between these two novels that I am using to bracket the chapters to come should be framed differently. Perhaps it would be more accurate to say that the ethos of democratic egalitarianism—of a society of free agents of equal worth interacting consensually with minimal constraints, like Natty and his intimates and the freeway homesteaders—is a utopian ideal that plays through both *The Pioneers* and *Tropic* so as to produce or aggravate the sense of injustice surrounding even relatively benign attempts of the Judge Temple kind to institutionalize, let alone the hyperintensified version in *Tropic.* Be that as it may, both novels, particularly *Tropic,* recognize the two hazards identified in *The American Democrat* and *Democracy in America,* the suboptimality of institutionalized democracy in practice, and the systemic tendency of those institutions to aggravate the inequalities they were supposed to alleviate through the vacuum created by the fatalism of the acquiescent multitude—the crew of Melville's *Pequod*, the disorganized and demoralized laboring and middle classes of Dos Passos's *U.S.A.*, the flummoxed "preterite" of Pynchon's *Gravity's Rainbow*.

11

Moby-Dick

From Oblivion to Great American Novel

This is Americana at its best, print culture at its profoundest
and most believing. . . . Melville lives? Melville *lives*.

—DAVID DOWLING, *Chasing the White Whale: The "Moby-Dick"
Marathon; Or, What Melville Means Today* (2010)

As long as the classic needs to be protected from attack, it can
never prove itself classic.

—J. M. COETZEE, "What Is a Classic?" (1998)

AMONG ALL Great American Novel candidates, perhaps *Moby-Dick*
(1851) best meets Nobel laureate J. M. Coetzee's test.[1] At least for
now, the case for *Moby-Dick* seems to need least defense. By no means
was it always so. Like Ishmael, *Moby-Dick* had to survive the shipwreck
of its author's fall from early fame into half a century of oblivion. In
1920, first editions could be bought for less than a dollar.[2] The Melville
revival in the second quarter of the twentieth century of which *Moby-
Dick* was the centerpiece had to make its way against charges both just
and unjust: that *Moby-Dick* was a messy uneven book (true) and that it
had left no mark on the history of art and literature (increasingly
false). The critical symposium that marked the 1951 *Moby-Dick* centennial did not find a more prestigious publisher than Southern Methodist University Press, although the editors confidently trumpeted what
they sensed was the growing consensus that this was "the one un-
doubted classic of American literature" and the contributors included
some of the leading Americanists of their day.[3]

Sure enough, *Moby-Dick was* gathering what soon came to seem unstoppable momentum among academics and readers at large, as a media metaphor in the realms of politics, industry, and sport, and as an

inspiration for artists in virtually every conceivable genre high and low—painting, sculpture, film, music, poetry, novelistic reprise, cartoons, pop-up books for kids. In 1952, the novel received the most erudite, elaborate job of scholarly editing ever yet accorded a work of American literature.[4] Since then the *Moby-Dick* industry, one scholar waggishly remarked, has come to rival the place of whaling in the antebellum United States. Not only academics but the public at large have signed on. For the past two decades cross-sections of folks from many walks of life have maintained not one but two American Bloomsday celebrations at two historic New England whaling ports—Mystic, Connecticut (summers, since 1985), and New Bedford, Massachusetts (winters, since 1995)—featuring marathon nonstop collective readings of the novel.

Moby-Dick's dissemination as text, and its fertility as object of imitation, as icon, as logo, as metaphor, have no more stopped at the nation's borders than the *Pequod* did. Melville's iconic whale has been "reincarnated as a toothy ferry boat in Berlin and as Japanese origami; it emerges in a Paris bar, an Istanbul restaurant, a Zagreb coffee shop." It has inspired the naming of a Greek yacht supplier as well as at least one *Fortune* 500 company—Starbucks.* On top of that, *Moby-Dick*'s plot has served for more than half a century to allegorize national and world affairs in miniform. A series of national leaders from Adolf Hitler to George W. Bush to Barack Obama have been framed as Captain Ahabs. To those who consider that war a dreadful mistake, the novel "speaks the awful truth of the American intervention in Vietnam."[5]

All this *Moby-Dick*-ering, in itself, says less about the novel than about the cultural capital of the brand. But the very fact that Melville's

---

* Cofounder Gordon Bowker reportedly wanted the name *Pequod* but finally settled for Starbucks when his creative partner objected, "No one's going to drink a cup of Pee-quod!" (Howard Schultz and Dori Jones Yang, *Pour Your Heart into It: How Starbucks Built a Company One Cup at a Time* [New York: Hyperion, 1997], 32–33). Previous quotation from Elizabeth Schultz, "Seeing *Moby-Dick* Globally," in *Melville "Among the Nations,"* ed. Sanford E. Marovitz and A. C. Christodoulou (Kent, OH: Kent State University Press, 2001), 418. For more on *MD* in contemporary popular culture, the arts, and the media, see Cotkin, *Dive Deeper,* which is also very illuminating on *MD* as an inspiration for front-tank modern writers, artists, and philosophers; David Dowling, *Chasing the White Whale: The "Moby-Dick" Marathon; Or, What Melville Means Today* (Iowa City: University of Iowa Press, 2010); Jeffrey Insko, "'All of Us Are Ahabs': *Moby-Dick* in Contemporary Public Discourse," *Journal of the Midwest Modern Language Association* 40 (Fall 2007): 19–37; and Elizabeth Schultz, *Unpainted to the Last: "Moby-Dick" and Twentieth-Century American Art* (Lawrence: University Press of Kansas, 1995).

masterpiece has been so often invoked from the mid-1900s onward as a frame for understanding how we live now is itself a wake-up call to reassess what it is about this vast and sprawling novel, some parts of which test the patience even of its admirers, that seems so compelling after more than a century and a half. The beginnings of an answer lie in its peculiar combination of the linear and the centrifugal—a search-and-destroy mission at the center, but with tantalizing circumlocutions, ponderings, digressions, and enigmas along the way that hold out so many handles for readers of wildly different tastes and persuasions. *Moby-Dick* is all of these and more: an adventure narrative; an anatomy of the workings of an American signature industry during its glory days; a metaphysical quest for the ultimate meaning of the universe; an inquiry into the relative merits of philosophic systems or world religions; a protoecological treatise on interspecies relations; a self-conscious reflection on the work of creative imagination that plays the utilitarian artisanal trade of whaling off against the art of book making; and a sociopolitical allegory of American destiny and/or global humanity in crisis. To the extent the United States can be thought of as a culture of boundless aspiration at core, that in itself for some will clinch the case for *Moby-Dick* as the Great American Novel; for never was there an American novel of greater volcanic gusto. To anchor things down more manageably for present purposes, however, I concentrate especially on the last of the multiple facets listed above: *Moby-Dick* as an inquest into the state and possible fate of democratic society, American style, as it appears in the era of early industrial capitalism.

First Lowering: Some Basic Terms of Engagement

A well-born youth descended on both sides from heroes of the American Revolution, Melville became an author almost by happenstance after the collapse of family fortunes and personal wanderlust sent him off to sea as a green hand on a whaling ship built by the father of future novelist Elizabeth Stoddard (see Chapter 4). When he returned home several years and voyages later after jumping ship in the Marquesas, his yarn-spinning success prompted him to work up a highly colored narrative of his three-week sojourn there—Melville stretched it to three months—*Typee: Or, A Peep at Polynesian Life* (1846). Its lively narrative of "Tommo's" adventures among the friendly seeming cannibals who hosted him (or were they fattening him up for future consumption?) spiced with anti-missionary barbs, hedonistic dallying that jostled Victorian sexual proprieties, and ethnographic portraiture of a remote tribe in the crosshairs of French, British, and American competition for dominance in Polynesia—all this made for a piquant compound that was greeted enthusiastically on both sides of the Atlantic. So Melville's career was launched.

Speaking more generically, *Typee* owed its success to being a slightly more irreverent than average variation on a long-established prototype that still flourishes: narratives of Westerners' experiences among "primitive" cultures at or beyond the verge of Eurocentric influence. Defoe's *Robinson Crusoe* (1719) was the first canonical example in English of an immensely prolific and polyform genre that Euro-American migrants already had been practicing for more than a century—narratives of military and botanical expedition, of the ordeals of New World settlement, of harrowing captivity among hostile Indians. In the hands of Sarah Wentworth Morton, Charles Brockden Brown, Washington Irving, James Fenimore Cooper, Lydia Sigourney, and many others it became a defining subject for early national belles lettres. But Melville was unusual if not unique among his U.S. literary peers for having had some actual experience living beyond the Euro-pale, for being an accidentally popular author with aspirations to make himself into a writer of the first rank, and also as an author who was neither at first nor for most of the last several decades of his career particularly U.S.-identified. He was a self-defined cultural cosmopolitan first and foremost who only gradually and for a limited period of time invested himself deeply in matters of U.S. national destiny. He wrote *Typee* expressly for the British publisher John Murray's Home and Colonial Library of Anglophone travel writing. His next three novels were all maritime narratives intermittently preoccupied with the American scene, though gradually more so. The two masterpieces of his late career, his epic poem *Clarel: A Poem and Pilgrimage to the Holy Land* (1876) and his unfinished novella *Billy Budd, Sailor* focus respectively on a multinational assortment of pilgrims who debate the clash of world religions and the failure of the world revolutions, and on a crisis in British naval history after the French Revolution.[6]

Moby-Dick was the novel in which Melville decisively broke loose from popular fiction, at the cost of baffling much of his original audience;

and it marked an intensification of his concentrated engagement with national themes—although always also, from the standpoint of viewing the United States comparatively, as a nodal point in the interplay of wider political, cultural, environmental, cosmological force fields—that continued through his last three novels (*Pierre*, 1852; *Israel Potter*, 1855; and *The Confidence-Man*, 1857) and the first of his four books of poems, *Battle-Pieces and Aspects of the Civil War* (1866).

The first twenty-odd chapters of this 135-chapter novel, however, look like a slightly morphed version of Melville's earlier tales. All of them also feature literate young men shipping out as ordinary seamen and undergoing a mixture of irksome routine, danger, humiliating contretemps, and strange unexpected encounters. In all of these, pseudo-autobiographical narrative gets augmented by semi-digressive descriptivism and philosophic musing spiced with innuendo, satire, teasing ambiguation. But seldom is the plotline hard for a linear-minded reader to follow except in Melville's third novel, *Mardi*, his one prior experiment with quest romance, where the main narrative gets buried by loquacious politico-metaphysical dialogue and redundant proliferation of the allegorical islands among which Taji and his escort of Polynesian aristocrats venture searching for Taji's lost Yillah. All those earlier novels including *Mardi* favor a loose-hanging structure of short chapters that double as mini-narratives and platforms for reflective side glimpses as they move forward in time.

After a curious opening barrage of "extracts" from the millennia-long archive of whaling punditry (of which more later), *Moby-Dick*'s plot proper initially seems to signal that its central actor will be the first-person narrator who calls himself Ishmael.* A congenial but somewhat moody ex-schoolmaster down on his luck, Ishmael arrives in New England's then-whaling capital of New Bedford determined to ship out from the island of Nantucket, "the Tyre of this Carthage" where American whaling aboriginally began (*MD* 23). After he over-

---

* "Call me Ishmael," one of world fiction's most famous opening sentences, implies all of the following and more: "This might be an alias"; "Don't expect me to tell all"; and "I cast myself as a rootless wanderer." The biblical Ishmael was Abraham's son by the bondwoman Hagar (a name often used, as in *Uncle Tom's Cabin*, for female slaves in antebellum times), whom his wife Sarah insisted on banishing. In *The Prairie*, which Melville knew, Ishmael Bush is the patriarch of the novel's rough-hewn squatter family; popular midcentury novelist E. D. E. N. Southworth later made her Ishmael the hero of an 1876 up-from novel of that title.

comes his fright at getting tricked into sharing a bed with the fearsomely tattooed Maori harpooner Queequeg,* Ishmael and Queequeg
become fast friends. The novel manages to pull off the tricky feat of
dramatizing Queequeg as admirable without reducing him to formulis-
tic noble savagery; of complicating the native sidekick stereotype by
showing Ishmael more dependent on him than vice versa. But soon
after the new friends ship out on the *Pequod,* selected by Ishmael for its
look as "a ship of the old school" (69), the Ishmael-Queequeg story gets
upstaged by monomaniacal Captain Ahab's quest to destroy Moby
Dick, the gigantic albino whale that bit off his leg on his last voyage. To
the dismay of first mate Starbuck and the other officers, in his first public appearance above decks Ahab announces that the real purpose of
this voyage will not be profit but revenge. His impassioned speech rallies the crew, and despite murmurings of revolt by Starbuck and from
the ranks, from then on it's clear that the *Pequod* will circle the globe
across the Atlantic and Indian oceans for its fateful encounter with the
white whale in the western Pacific. There, on the third day of a thrilling chase, the exasperated whale rams and sinks the ship and carries
furious Ahab away in an instant when he gets snagged in the line of
the harpoon forged expressly for his enemy.

During the voyage, the Ishmael-Queequeg comradeship crops up
sporadically. But Queequeg mostly gets folded into his workforce role
as one of a troika of formidable "pagan" harpooners together with the
African Daggoo and Tashtego, an "unmixed" Gay Head Wampanoag,
the novel's living proof of ongoing Native presence in New England,
despite Ishmael's Yankee misconception that the tribe of the Pequod
(Pequot) were "now extinct as the ancient Medes" (*MD* 69). Ahab's agon
drives the plot, with Ishmael relegated to commentator, alternately
grave and farcical: expositor of whale biology and whaling know-how,
ruminator on the symbolism of the voyage and the relation between
human and nonhuman worlds, purveyor of philosophic reflections on

* Geoffrey Sanborn demonstrates convincingly that *Moby-Dick*'s primary real-life model
for Queequeg was the Maori chief Te Pehi Kupe, who became bosom friends with the
English captain of the vessel that took him to England (Geoffrey Sanborn, *Whipscars and
Tattoos: "The Last of the Mohicans," "Moby-Dick," and the Maori* [New York: Oxford University Press, 2011], 73–92). But it's no less crucial that the novel insists—in keeping with
the strategy of seeing the whole crew, Ishmael included, as deterritorialized "isolatoes"—
that Queequeg is said to have come from the imaginary island of Kokovoko ("not down
in any map; true places never are," *MD* 59).

the meaning of history and of comparative analysis of world cultures and religions. Ishmael's fortuitous survival—saved from the vortex of the sinking ship by Queequeg's unused coffin/life preserver—underscores three paths the novel might have taken but didn't. It might have continued its male romance of the divide. It might have unfolded as Ishmael's bildungsroman. Or it might have been framed, as several times hinted but never developed, as a lone survivor's trauma narrative.[7]

The preemption of Ishmael's and Ishmael/Queequeg's stories by Ahab's, combined with fragmentary biographical evidence and a number of puzzling loose ends, suggests that *Moby-Dick* was composed in two if not three stages: first written as a relatively straightforward whaling narrative, then rewritten as an epic of cosmic-encyclopedic proportions under the inspiration of Melville's excited reading of Shakespearean tragedy, particularly *King Lear* and *Macbeth,* and his encounters as reader and then as friend with Nathaniel Hawthorne, to whom he dedicated *Moby-Dick,* "in token of my admiration for his genius" (*MD* 3). The impact of Shakespeare and Hawthorne was surely monumental. The evidence that Melville refashioned his manuscript in immensely more ambitious terms after a first go is on the whole convincing. The plethora of loose ends is unmistakable. (Having the African American cabin boy Pip hail both from Connecticut and Alabama, and introducing the mysterious mariner Bulkington early on as if he were to be a defining figure only to kill him off summarily as the voyage gets underway, are two among scores of examples.) But critical attempts to divine the stages of *Moby-Dick* chiefly on the basis of those loose ends and redundancies together with selected passages from letters by and about Melville tend to dissolve into guesswork;[8] and the novel itself casts doubt on the utility of such speculation by again and again calling attention to the necessary unfinishedness of immense endeavors, such as Ishmael's "God keep me from ever completing anything. This whole book is but a draught—nay, but the draught of a draught" (*MD* 125). *Moby-Dick*'s continual straining toward horizons of possibility that no actual book could hope to encompass becomes one of its marks of distinction not despite but because of such admissions of necessary imperfection. As for the seeming anomaly of having Ishmael's story and the story of his comradeship with Queequeg trumped by Ahab's, that was no random course correction but inherent in the novel's teleology from Chapter

1, from the moment that Ishmael seriocomically affirms that his voyage must have been decreed by the Fates.

Ahab, Ishmael, Melville

Moby-Dick's narrative architecture is an idiosyncratic variant of the bipolar observer/hero narrative structure we have seen before in Fitzgerald's *The Great Gatsby*, Faulkner's *Absalom, Absalom!*, and Roth's *American Pastoral*. Like them, *Moby-Dick* puts those figures in symbiotic opposition. Ishmael is fascinated by Ahab's grand obsession but also tries to resist it by a combination of fearful recoil and standoffish mockery. Ahab and Ishmael become different species of questers played off against each other without ever exchanging words, a telling omission given the ship's close quarters and small crew, the captain's penchant for micromanagerialism when he has a mind for it, and Ishmael's selection as replacement oarsman for Ahab's boat on the last day of the chase. Ahab's quest is to hunt the whale; Ishmael's is to understand what to make of both whale and hunt.

Ahab's mentality seems at first sight anachronistic next to Ishmael's. Ahab thinks in stark Manichean polarities, conceiving the whale as a symbolic embodiment of the demonic forces he is commissioned by Providence or Fate to hunt down. He approaches the material cosmos as an allegorical system to be decoded for its networked symbolic significances, like Hawthorne's Puritan Bostonians in *The Scarlet Letter* reading the A-shaped meteor in the sky as signifying the late Governor Winthrop's metamorphosis into Angel or, better, Dimmesdale's paranoid interpretation of the same meteor as a lesson expressly for him. Of course Ahab is not a religiocentric thinker of the old Puritan school but a montage of mutant Calvinist and quasi-Zoroastrian fire worshipper.[9] A proper Puritan or Quaker would have resigned himself to loss of leg without further ado and would not have considered any natural creature inherently malevolent. By the same token, Ahab is also a figure of nostalgia for lost certainty in that he embodies the prospect of decisive, clear-cut understanding and moral action inaccessible to the kind of relativist Ishmael is. "If man will strike, strike through the mask!" (*MD* 140), he cries from the quarterdeck. What a catharsis that would be, if only we could achieve it! From a certain standpoint, any kind of purposefulness seems preferable to anomie or to stultification by workaday trivialities. From that standpoint anachronistic Ahab is the perfect answer to the hankering after whaling in its most primordial form that attracted Ishmael to Nantucket and the old-fashioned-looking *Pequod.* Ishmael, though, mainly inhabits a post-religious mental world of hypotheses and probabilities. Whereas for Ahab the white whale is an adversary of cosmic proportions to be taken with utmost seriousness, for Ishmael Moby Dick, indeed the whole creation, is a riddle, and what's more a riddle best approached when kept at arm's length and not taken seriously for too long. "Look not too long in the face of the fire, O man!" he warns (328). Laughter proves this subaltern's best defense. Ishmael is capable of mocking everything including Ahab and himself, and a number of his learned explanations are elaborate put-ons, like his pseudo-Linnaean taxonomy of the various species of whales according to size via the metaphor of bibliography (folio whales, octavo whales, etc., *MD* 115–125).

Moby-Dick tempts readers to turn to Ishmael as the author's stand-in. He after all is the book's most ordinary-seeming mortal as well as its chatty docent, who keeps the demented Ahab at a distance. Then too, the strategies of incremental buildup seem to want to keep you in Ishmael-land by deferring Ahab's final unleashing as long as possible even as they lead up to it. As many have noted, the "aesthetic of the entire novel" seems encapsulated in Ishmael's slow, perplexed pondering of what the smoked-up painting in the Spouter Inn is all about— which after a series of wild guesses ("It's the Black Sea in a midnight gale," "It's the unnatural combat of the four primal elements") he takes to be a picture of a "half-foundered" dismasted storm-tossed ship on which "an exasperated whale" is about to impale itself (*MD* 26), an impossible feat of cetacean acrobatics that prefigures Moby Dick's extraordinary feat of boat smashing.[10] Never was there a novel that so compulsively anticipated its closure. Chapter 1 prefigures all that follows in working circuitously around to the final image of "one grand hooded phantom, like a snow hill in the air" (22). This is the first in a series of umpteen rehearsals for the endgame—which for that matter was the thrust of the prefatory "Extracts" too: an incremental series of inadequate approximations, sometimes ludicrously off base, of what eventually gets revealed, sort of.

Three chains of incremental repetition are especially notable. First, the gams—encounters with other vessels. Of the ships that have tangled with Moby Dick, by and large there's an increasingly close analogy to what will happen to the *Pequod*. Second, encounters with whales. These get increasingly momentous. At first lowering, the pursuers barely make contact. The next two calls are false alarms. But each time there's something ominous. After that they make some routine kills. Then comes "The Grand Armada," when the *Pequod* encounters whales en masse at the gateway to the China Sea. Then, after weathering the scariest crisis yet, a typhoon off the coast of Japan, comes the southeastward cruise toward the equator to confront Moby Dick himself in open ocean. Third and most elaborately, the cetology chapters—the parts first-time readers love to hate but dyed-in-the-wool Melvillians come to love. A short review of the method of the novel's cetomania may make it seem more intriguing to readers still averse.

These several dozen chapters start abstractly with whaling history from antiquity on down, the formal classification of whales, and the chart of global migration routes in Ahab's cabin. Then follow digests of second-hand reports of the malice of whales generally and of Moby Dick specifically and commentary on whale illustrations presented (like the Extracts) in more or less increasing order of modernity and accuracy, starting with the oldest and crudest cave drawings and working up to modern etchings, just as the book itself is edging slowly, slowly, slowly toward the real thing.

Ishmael caps this section with an omnibus disquisition "Of Whales in Paint; in Teeth; in Wood; in Sheet-Iron; in Stone; in Mountains; in Stars," a wayward cornucopia from the ultrahumble to the ultrasublime: a London beggar's street picture to the constellation Cetus. Then and only then are living whales described, in the fifty-eighth chapter, "Brit," and even then, not sperm whales like Moby Dick but a pod of right whales. (In *Moby-Dick*, the right whale is the "wrong" one, though any is fair game.) After this sighting, the novel follows a similar circuitousness in scrutinizing sperm whale anatomy. The chapters move, roughly, from outer to inner and from front to rear. Ishmael starts with the skin, then the blubber, then the head and its components, working from tough exterior to nut-sized brain. He then moves down the body to the spout, the tail, the intestines, to the most private part of all, the penis, and finally to the skeleton. The disquisition on cetology ends by drawing a kind of circle back to the start in two chapters that chart the whale's development as a species and assert its immortality for all time.

Individual chapters tend to follow certain ground rules: accumulation of data; speculation about the meaning of the data, both utilitarian and symbolic; skepticism about those inferences, often humorous, that grant the difficulties of grasping the subject fully; insistence, nonetheless, on the wisdom of accrued savvy and expertise; reinforcement despite whatever joshing along the way of the sense of sperm whales generally and Moby Dick particularly as beasts of mythic proportions to whose giganticism and uncanniness all seafaring cultures of the world bear witness in legend, image, and deed. Meandering, talky, and minutiae laden as these chapters are, they're crucial to the multiplex agenda of anatomizing this paleoindustrial signature industry—the first enterprise of global scope where Yankees constituted the leading edge—and to achieving a "mythic investiture," as Robert D. Richardson Jr. terms it, of the hunt for the most formidable of living creatures in a way that does justice to the reach of its audacity, its intelligence, and its danger, and to the multiethnic composition of the participants in the transnational oceanic interspace where the main plot unfolds.[11]

To dwell on such incremental repetition risks reinforcing the impression that Ishmael controls the narrative even if Ahab drives the plot, that the novel "sides" with his mental agility over Ahabian monomania. It's hardly that simple. True, the denouement seemingly bears out the wisdom, or at least the prudence, of friendly Ishmael's vacillating pragmatism over Ahab's obsessive linearity. Ishmael at least survives. Yet the two figures also converge. Ishmael is drawn by Ahab's spell however much he resists; indeed his voice is even more responsible than Ahab's for conjuring up that spell to begin with. Ahab too follows a circle-the-planet strategy in pursuit of Moby Dick, going through most of the motions of a regular whaling voyage even after having announced from the start (as Ishmael did in "Loomings") that the crucial quarry is Moby Dick. Ahab too confesses at different points to the mysterious unreadability of the natural world however tenaciously he sticks by his own reading of it. At times their voices blur to the point that Melvillians argue over who speaks.[12] In their bedrock feelings toward nature in particular, they are strangely alike. Despite several romanticizing sallies, Ishmael shares Ahab's seasoned seafarer's distrust of physical nature as a hostile presence, however tranquil it may seem. Although Ahab mystifies nature's hostility as purposeful malignancy whereas Ishmael sees a blank "heartless immensity" (*MD* 321), the second is little more than a secularization of the first. For both the traditional belief that the universe is run by a benevolently purposeful God seems incredible, and for both that prospect is horrifying and uncanny. In the pivotal juxtaposed chapters "Moby Dick" and "The Whiteness of the Whale," Ishmael makes a show of differentiating himself from Ahab but winds up seconding, Milder points out, "how fluidly naturalism can pass into paranoid supernaturalism" when mind gets trumped by emotion.[13]

The telltale mark of Ishmael's inextricability from Ahab is his loss of control over the narrative voice. This happens in two ways, first through the interposition, starting at the point when Ahab is first introduced, of a number of chapters orchestrated as drama, without a narrator figure at all; and later, during the last fifth of the main narrative after entry into the Pacific Ocean (chapters 112–135), when Ishmael as a named character disappears entirely until he pops back in the epilogue. What to make of these aberrancies from the observer-hero narrative method? Most readers tend to grasp for some theory that preserves Ishmael's status as the book's presiding consciousness, in the spirit of Walter Bezanson's much-reprinted centennial lecture-essay, "*Moby-Dick:* Work of Art," which commonsensically distinguishes between "forecastle Ishmael," the rookie whale man, and "narrator Ishmael"—"young Ishmael grown older," insisting that despite whatever appearances to the contrary "the Ishmael voice is there every moment from the genesis . . . to the final revelation," setting "the terms of discourse."[14]

More often than not *Moby-Dick* criticism has followed some version of this line of thinking. During the years of the Melville revival and well beyond, this Ishmael consciousness tended to be seen as a counter to or containment of Ahab's madness by humanness, circumspection, laughter. Some recent critics have taken issue with traditional Ishmael-centrism, whether by dismissing his "corporatist" appeal as "the scholar's antecedent doctor to society,"[15] or by rehabilitating "Ishmael's centerless and errant 'narrative'" as a contrarian critique of artistic business as usual by breaking down "the distinction between the privileged author and the first-person narrator."[16] But these readings rarely if ever confront the question of why *Moby-Dick* should have invented such a brainy, engaging dramatized narrator figure in the first place only to suppress him.

Perhaps there is no logic. Maybe the point is that the novel's greatness, as Leo Bersani suggests in one of the most penetrating essays on

Moby-Dick ever written, lies in its ceaseless proliferation of abortive and self-undermining initiatives, its staged "chaos of interpretative modes."[17] Certainly this is a book that overspills its bounds, a book whose author wasn't sure how he'd bring it to closure even when it was nearly done. "I'm going to take him by his jaw . . . and finish him up in some fashion or other," Melville writes Hawthorne the month before *Moby-Dick* went to press (quoted in *MD* 539). Maybe the best answer lies more in Melville's overall career trajectory than in the logic of this one book; for *Moby-Dick* marks a transition after which Melville's longer fiction switches permanently from first person to third, as Hemingway's did in the 1930s. Melville was clearly becoming restive with pseudo-autobiographicalism— the ordinary seaman ploy at any rate. (When he turned to first-personness again, in shorter tales of which "Bartleby the Scrivener" is best-known, he switched to a middle-aged gentleman's mask.) At any rate, Ishmael's effacement seems the logical upshot of Ahab's totalizing sway.

From first to last, Melville's fiction is acutely conscious of the anomaly of shipboard authoritarianism in a supposedly egalitarian society. That's Tommo's excuse for jumping ship in *Typee*, and Omoo's for joining the mutinous refuseniks in its sequel. *White Jacket*, the novel immediately before *Moby-Dick*, decries brutal and arbitrary punishment on an American naval vessel, including a scene where the narrator comes within a whisker of being flogged unjustly. And Melville's valedictory work, *Billy Budd*, turns on a commander's rigged trial and hanging of a young man he knows does not deserve to die. Like *Moby-Dick*, these other novels show a keen eye for top-down perversion of institutions in societies that supposedly uphold rule of law and how such discipline hardens and mechanizes those who enforce and comply. No less for Melville than for Michel Foucault, "the ship is the heterotopia par excellence": a microcosmic other-space for reimagining social actuality at its utopian or nightmarish extremes.[18]

Abuse of power was a charge often leveled by sailors against whaling captains in Melville's day. The *Pequod* is an extreme instance of a captain aggrandizing his position into something like dictatorship, such that even the ranking officer feels hamstrung. Even before the ship gets underway, the possibility is foreshadowed in captains Peleg and Bildad's high-handed treatment of Ishmael and their frank expectations as to how seamen should kowtow. This makes it impossible to type Ahab simply as a uniquely pathological figure who goes haywire only after the whale zaps him. His madness is rather an extreme toward which decades of internalized arrogance conditions commanders.

Every reader notices how *Moby-Dick* paradoxically acts out its aspiration to make whaling the stuff of democratic epic by draping Ahab and the officers as a group in feudal garb.[19] The relationship between mates and harpooners is like that of knights and squires; Ahab is the "Sultan," the "Mogul," the king, as his biblical name implies, even though the narrative goes to equally great lengths at other points to shrink him down again to a "grey-headed, ungodly old man, chasing with curses a Job's whale round the world" with a crew of riffraff (*MD* 158). Such vacillations bespeak both a have-your-cake-and-eat-it strategy on the author's part of aspiring to make heroic literature out of an extraordinary but also grueling and bloody business without euphemizing overmuch, and Ishmael's subaltern admixture of resentment and awe. Most telling in this latter regard, however, is his willing abjection. From Chapter 1, he's prepared for effacement ("Who aint a slave? Tell me that" [21]). As the ship prepares to launch, he feels "horror" but not outrage at his "first kick," from Peleg for slacking off (94). He's as much excited as upset by Ahab's usurpation. Starbuck's behavior shows that Ahab has the capacity to drive even mild-mannered subordinates to the brink of mutiny. But Ishmael shows no signs of wanting to mutiny himself despite being a far more outside-the-box thinker than the first mate, for all his loose talk about being "a savage" at heart, "owing no allegiance but to the King of the Cannibals, and ready at any moment to rebel against him" (222). This isn't just a matter of literary convention, of not wanting to violate Ishmael's role as observer, because even as observer he tends not to criticize Ahab for abusing the crew or for deviating from the proper business of whaling into romantic questing.

All this adds up to a figure whose agency is vulnerable from the start, who despite knowing that Ahab is deranged is quite disposed to acquiesce as the price of admission to an adventure. Far from evincing the sense of grievance about the captain that Melville's earlier narrators do in *Typee, Omoo, Redburn*, and *White-Jacket*, Ishmael is more excited by Ahab's hubris than intimidated. The eclipse of "forecastle Ishmael" confirms that prior submission of self, an acquiescence not merely personal but conditioned by the shipboard regime, which in turn stands in by implication for the fatalism of society's multitudes. The chapter that makes the point most explicitly comes right before the *Pequod*'s first shot at a whale, "The Mat-Maker." It opens with Ishmael idly musing about free will, fate, and necessity as he and Queequeg while away their time at the ship's loom. He fancies for the moment that he is a free agent. "Here, thought I, with my own hand I play my own shuttle and weave my own destiny into these unalterable threads." But then comes the "there she blows!" cry and "the ball of free will dropped from my hand" (*MD* 179), after which forecastle Ishmael disappears from the chapter, as if the focalization has completely changed from inner to outer, from dramatized to omniscient narration. That is precisely what will happen in the later stages of the book. Significantly, when Ishmael next returns to center stage after "The Mat-Maker," it's to stress, "I must resign my life into the hands of him who steered the boat" (189). He's learned a lesson about the necessity of total effacement in this microcosmic society.

The point can be pressed still further. *Moby-Dick* doesn't limit itself to dramatizing subjection of personhood as grudging necessity, as with Starbuck's first shuddering realization of his "miserable office—to obey, rebelling" (*MD* 144). An almost masochistic pleasure often seems to derive from the act of submission. Pip delights in being adopted by gruff old Ahab. Ahab and Starbuck develop a queer sentimental bond that climaxes at the last departure when "Their hands met; their eyes fastened; Starbuck's tears the glue." "Oh my captain," moans Starbuck, "my captain—noble heart—go not—go not!—see, it's a brave man that weeps" (421). That may seem like protest, but it's a lot closer to unconditional surrender than Starbuck's early recoil. Then there's that strange dream of Stubb's in the "Queen Mab" chapter, in which he's kicked by an Ahab figure then counseled by a mysterious old merman out of outrage into submission. It's not just Ishmael who practices self-effacement.

Here and elsewhere *Moby-Dick* dramatizes the effects of a warping shipboard culture Ishmael expresses but doesn't wholly face up to. When Ishmael puts Ahab's "Sultanism" in question, it's not so much to unmask it as to remystify it. No sooner does he self-critique the extravagance of likening Ahab to princes and czars and confess that such "majestic trappings and housings" don't fit "a poor old whale-hunter like him" than he strains to recoup them: "Oh, Ahab! What shall be grand in thee, it must needs be plucked at from the skies, and dived for in the deep, and featured in the unbodied air!" (*MD* 122). It's as if Ishmael is casting about for a way to hypnotize himself as Ahab proceeds to recast what ought to be a business enterprise in the grand manner. That's also where the Shakespearean analogies come in: Ahab as King Lear (with Pip as fool); Ahab as Macbeth (with Fedallah as the three witches rolled into one). These are ways of shoring up the heroic stature of captain and quest despite knowing that Ahab's only a "shaggy" old salt from Nantucket.

Ishmael's effacement, then, works oppositely from Nathan Zuckerman's disappearance into the "realistic chronicle" of Seymour Levov in Philip Roth's *American Pastoral*. Whereas Zuckerman's disappearing act gives him greater latitude for narratorial manipulation, Ishmael's signifies the suppression of the novel's primary countervoice. Yet that suppression doesn't authorize the usurping hero who now comes even more completely to the fore. To be sure, the process of slow incremental buildup through all that navigational and discursive tacking around the world, a slog for many first-time readers, finally delivers a thrilling catharsis in the action-packed chase in which Ahab emerges from hundreds of pages of simmering discontent and Ishmaelian sophistry with guns blazing. But the long-awaited encounter with Moby Dick, at the end of which Ahab is dispatched in one short sentence, undercuts if not destroys his pretensions to being a new-style democratic-era hero, an Andrew Jackson of the high seas risen from cabin boy to star commander. The kind of heroism to which this book subscribes, such as it is, attaches more to whaling than to the whaler in chief. Ishmael's hundreds of pages of dithering have prepared the reader to surmise more clearly than he what Bersani shrewdly calls "the oxymoronic impasse of democracy": that "the democratic dream of equality" should be embodied in a "great man's despotism."[20] This isn't to say that Ahab is just another Coriolanus, a haughty neofeudal strongman. Starbuck shoots wide of the mark in complaining that he's "a democrat to all above" who "lords it over all below" (*MD* 144). Ahab is not a despot in principle. He's as ready—under certain conditions—to consort with lowly Pip as with Starbuck, in a quasi-parallel to Ishmael-Queequeg.[21] He's not a replay of Coriolanus so much as an updated reinvention of how hard-driving hubris plays through in the age of democratic individualism. He personifies "the oligarchical consequences" of democratic society, in which "individual personality counts, indeed is determinant, in the distribution of power," yet "it is the very assertion of the rights of self which risks destroying those conditions in the first place."[22] The catastrophic results of his ability to foist his will on the *Pequod* foreshadows, as C. L. R. James writes in a strikingly heterodox reading of the novel (1953) on which more anon, "how the society of free individualism would give birth to totalitarianism and be unable to defend itself against it." As veteran Melville critic John Bryant sums up, "Ahab is democracy's worst nightmare."*

To showcase the democratic dilemma of individualism gone awry through the instance of Ahab's abuse of power was not only a predictable upshot of Melville's experience, and of seafaring misadventure generally. It also reflected the status of whaling itself as an early industrial-era enterprise that required an exceptional degree of risk. Although hardly the only fruitful way of reading *Moby-Dick*, certainly of great importance is its politico-economic allegory of the *Pequod* as an image of the new factory system and the appalling working conditions and multiple hazards to which the work force was subjected; of the aggrandizement of the Anglo-overseer class at the expense of the heteroglot subalterns on whose labor they depended; and of the insouciance with which the owners and captains of Yankee whalers strove to harvest the wonders of the oceanic world.[23] Not Ahab's final comeuppance so much as his vain attempt throughout the voyage to harden himself into the kind of soulless machine that his prosthetic leg already is becomes the novel's chief mark of the system's warping effects.

In this *Moby-Dick* slyly alludes to the first great postmonarchical treatise, Thomas Hobbes's *Leviathan* (1651), written during the English

---

* Bryant, *"Moby-Dick* as Revolution," in *The Cambridge Companion to Herman Melville*, ed. Robert S. Levine (Cambridge: Cambridge University Press, 1998), 78; C. L. R. James, *Mariners, Renegades and Castaways: The Story of Herman Melville and the World We Live In* (orig. 1953), ed. Donald E. Pease (Hanover, NH: University Press of New England, 2001), 54. James draws a straight line from Ahab to Hitler and Stalin, with highly inventive— although sometimes also highly erratic, idiosyncratic—results. The extra whaleboat Ahab secretly bankrolls under Fedallah's charge James shrewdly compares, for instance, to the "special force, loyal to themselves alone" and "entirely dependent" on them for life that modern dictators create to supplement "the normal protection of power" by army and police (54). Delbanco, in the most cogent critical interpretation to date of Ahab in relation to the mid-nineteenth-century U.S. political scene, connects Ahab with both the stony, divisive proslavery senator John C. Calhoun and the northern abolitionist zealot William Lloyd Garrison, but also wisely cautions that Ahab is best understood as "a brilliant personification of the very essence of fanaticism" who cannot be "confined to any one exemplar of it" (Delbanco, *Melville*, 166).

civil wars when king was temporarily ousted by commonwealth. "Leviathan" is Hobbes's master metaphor for the authoritarian state, personified as a gigantic artificial man, that he deems necessary to maintain order in civil society. *Moby-Dick* cleverly insinuates the vulnerability of this political model by throwing back in Hobbes's face his desperation to protect humankind against the anarchic state of nature. Even the *Pequod*'s rigorous authority structure doesn't meet the Hobbesian test, for "the new Leviathan" can "hardly become incarnate in Ahab's disintegrating body"; and at all events human force of whatever kind is impotent before the mightiest natural forces, here incarnated by the novel's leviathan, Moby Dick.[24]

It was a stroke of genius to have seized on an industry then at its peak that was destined to go under within a decade owing to the disruption of the American whaling fleet in the Civil War and the displacement of sperm oil by fossil fuel, not to mention the increasing length of voyages required by the retreating whale population. In retrospect, the sinking of the *Pequod* seems a prescient allegory of capitalist obsolescence. Although Melville had no way of foreseeing this turn of events, *Moby-Dick* displays throughout, as Cesare Casarino and Jamie L. Jones argue, a keen sense of rapid changes in the industry and an intuitive grasp of Karl Marx's view of capitalism as inherently self-destructive. Ishmael's antiquarian hankering to seek out and embark from American whaling's historic inception point prepares the way for more pervasive intimations throughout the novel that whaling itself is "a relic of an ancient artisanal world that is to be swept away by the forces of progress."[25]

The Crew as Global Village and/or "Democratic" Microcosm

If neither captain nor narrator can be trusted as a credible exemplar of democratic aspiration, what about the rest of the crew? Some such intimation surfaces repeatedly throughout *Moby-Dick*, as in Ishmael's hyperbolic apostrophe to the "great democratic God" to vindicate his ascription of "high qualities" to "meanest mariners" (*MD* 103–104). Despite, apart from, interwoven with its cautionary somber plot of demonic overreaching and Ishmael's vacillating mind games, *Moby-Dick* crackles with exuberant and even upbeat, utopian energy. Geoffrey Sanborn rightly calls attention to "the narrative's inspirational quality to suspend the uncertainties . . . long enough for our fantasies of greatness to fill with energy and begin to rise."[26] As Melville was well aware, nineteenth-century whalers were not simply heterotopias of incarceration but also venues of opportunity for bottom dogs on the social ladder.

Not despite but because of the risks involved—one in three New Bedford whaling ships was eventually lost at sea[27]—the enterprise of whaling provided a somewhat more level playing field than did shore-side occupations for able-bodied men of color who sought to rise in the world. Racial antagonism continued to smolder, as *Moby-Dick* makes clear. But nonwhite officers were common; Polynesian and Native har-pooners were prized; and black captains and even all-black crews were not unknown, even though upward mobility for nonwhite whalers di-minished as the Civil War approached. The "lays" or fraction of future profits for which all hands contracted were assigned according to per-ceived skill and experience. Stingy Captain Bildad lied when he told Queequeg that a 1/90 lay was "more than ever was given a harpooner yet out of Nantucket" (*MD* 85); but as Melville knew from personal ex-perience, it was standard practice for white green hands like Ishmael to be paid considerably less than experienced nonwhite seamen, let alone skilled nonwhite harpooners like Queequeq. Although the multiethnic composition of the *Pequod*'s crew is overstated—there may never have been an actual whaling ship staffed with harpooners of four different non-European ethnicities—the crews of nineteenth-century New En-gland whalers were an exceptionally diverse and multinational lot compared to the average shoreside American community, and they were treated in a more egalitarian fashion. it was no fluke that the son of fugitive slave Harriet Jacobs turned to whaling to avoid his cowork-ers' harassment when they discovered he was black.*

One of *Moby-Dick*'s most memorable images for encapsulating this aspect of the *Pequod*'s crew is its allusion to an incident from the French Revolution Melville read about while writing the novel that seems to

---

* On whaling as a space of opportunity, especially for nonwhites, see W. Jeffrey Bolster, *Black Jacks: African American Seamen in the Age of Sail* (Cambridge, MA: Harvard Univer-sity Press, 1997); Briton Cooper Busch, *"Whaling Will Never Do for Me": The American Whaleman in the Nineteenth Century* (Lexington: University Press of Kentucky, 1994), 32–50; and Jia-rui Chong's outstanding 1999 Harvard AB honors thesis, *"'Federated along One Keel,'"* whose archival research calibrates the published accounts by specific refer-ence to *Moby-Dick,* including the discovery of Bildad's lie (25 n.22).

have haunted him ever after. This was the spectacle of the thirty-some delegation—the same size as the *Pequod*'s crew—purporting to represent "the 'oppressed nations of the universe'" that was paraded in 1790 before the French Assembly in their national costumes by the Prussian Jacobin Jean-Baptiste (aka "Anacharsis") Cloots (1755–1794), the self-styled "orator of the human race." Cloots congratulated that body for having "'restored primitive equality among men,'" and he prophesied that "'encouraged by the glorious example of the French, all the peoples of the universe . . . would soon break the yoke of the tyrants who oppress them.'"[28] Melville resorted to this image of omnicivilizational collective not only in *Moby-Dick* but also in his last full-length novel, *The Confidence-Man* (1857), and again in *Billy Budd*. Other Melville works feature similar social panoramas, such as *Clarel*'s assortment of Palestine pilgrims and its spectacle of the "intersympathy of creeds" witnessed by the disoriented American student-protagonist on the streets of Jerusalem. Here are the three passages from his fiction that focus specifically on Cloots's symbolic pageant.[29]

> They were nearly all Islanders in the Pequod. *Isolatoes* too, I call such, not acknowledging the common continent of men, but each *Isolato* living on a separate continent of his own. Yet now, federated along one keel, what a set these Isolatoes were! An Anacharsis Clootz deputation from all the isles of the sea, and all the ends of the earth, accompanying Old Ahab in the Pequod, to lay the world's grievances before that bar from which not very many of them came back.

> As among Chaucer's Canterbury pilgrims, or those oriental ones crossing the Red Sea towards Mecca in the festival month, there was no lack of variety. Natives of all sorts, and foreigners; men of business and men of pleasure; parlor men and backwoodsmen. . . .Northern speculators and Eastern philosophers; English, Irish, German, Scotch, Danes; Santa Fé traders in striped blankets, and Broadway bucks in cravats of cloth of gold; fine-looking Kentucky boatmen, and Japanese-looking Mississippi cotton-planters; Quakers in full drab, and United States soldiers in full regimentals; slaves, black, mulatto, quadroon; modish young Spanish Creoles, and old-fashioned French Jews; Mormons and Papists; Dives and Lazarus; jesters and mourners, teetotalers and convivialists; deacons and blacklegs; hard-shell Baptists and clay-eaters; grinning negroes, and Sioux chiefs solemn as high-priests. In short, a piebald parliament, an Anacharsis Cloots congress of all kinds of that multiform pilgrim species, man.

In jovial sallies right and left, his white teeth flashing into view, he [the handsome black sailor the narrator remembers having once seen in Liverpool] rollicked along, the center of a company of his shipmates. These were made up of such an assortment of tribes and complexions as would have well fitted them to be marched up by Anacharsis Cloots before the bar of the first French Assembly as Representatives of the Human Race. At each spontaneous tribute rendered by the wayfarers to this black pagod of a fellow—the tribute of a pause and stare, and less frequently an exclamation—the motley retinue showed that they took that sort of pride in the evoker of it which the Assyrian priests doubtless showed for their grand sculptured Bull when the faithful prostrated themselves.

The first of these passages gives a snapshot of the *Pequod*'s crew; the second of passengers on the ironically named Mississippi River steamboat *Fidèle;* the third a Liverpool street scene of shipmates surrounding a black sailor whose charisma reminds the narrator of the story's own handsome sailor protagonist.

The immediate source of this cameo was Thomas Carlyle's *History of the French Revolution* (1837), which scoffingly treats the incident as a sideshow of absurd "whiskered Polacks, long-flowing turbaned Ishmaelites [sic], astrological Chaldeans" rounded up by a loony utopian and hypocrite to boot, a bon vivant patrician masquerading as a man of the people. In the leading modern historical account, Simon Schama follows suit, lumping Cloots with the "lunatics and thugs on the left."[30] Some of this sarcasm rubbed off onto Melville in the form of Ishmael's bemusement at what still seems to him at this stage of the voyage an astonishing spectacle. Yet it's striking that Melville returned again and again to this and other such images of a global village of wildly heterogeneous types; that he wound up idealizing it in *Billy Budd;* and that taken together in their contexts the three Cloots passages also shimmer and wobble in several provocative ways: not just in their sympathy versus irony ratio but also in the nature or lack of social solidarity that they see, the extent to which a staged ritual is happening as against a happenstance event, the hierarchy if any to which the ensemble seems subject, and the sense in which they suggest a sort of national microcosm as against a snapshot of planetary humanity.

Whether or not Melville knew it, he seems to have sensed that Cloots was an unstable overreacher destined to join the ringleaders of the Terror only to be purged as an extremist by Robespierre just before his own fall, yet also an advocate of the first-ever statutory declaration of human rights—the 1789 Declaration of the Rights of Man and Citizen. Indeed, Cloots stood out from his fellow revolutionaries for his insistence on the extension of equal rights to all peoples of the world.

From the short but dramatic career of his older brother Gansevoort, a forceful orator and Democratic Party operative, Melville would have recognized "Anarcharsis Cloots" as a byword in conservative circles of the 1840s for political demagoguery.[31] That in itself would probably not have repelled him, especially given Gansevoort's proactive efforts at the time to land a publisher for *Typee*. Thomas Paine's *Age of Reason* would have alerted Melville to the fraternity between Cloots and the most outspokenly egalitarian among the nation's founders. Paine warmed to Cloots as a fellow anticlerical, as the only other non-French member of the Revolutionary Convention, as a conscious disseminator of the idea of human rights transnationally, and as a prison mate after both were arrested in 1793 when the Terror intensified.[32]

To view *Moby-Dick*'s social microcosms through a Clootsian lens is to highlight the instability of Melville's investment in the United States as the site of the providentially designated concourse of global humanity. *The Confidence-Man*'s passenger list embeds what at first looks like a collage of national types within a universalizing vision of all humanity on pilgrimage, as if frontier America were just one site of a more far-reaching ritual process or agenda of social possibility. Its detached bemusement sits at the opposite end of a continuum from the open-eyed wonder of Malcolm X beholding the unimaginably diverse multiracial concourse of the Hajj. The handsome black sailor vignette has much more to do with comradeship than nationness. It functions in the novella as one of several wishfully idealistic side glimpses that deepen the irony of the ensuing plot of Billy's impressment and eventual execution on trumped-up mutiny charges aboard a British warship that seizes him from a smaller vessel symbolically named *The Rights of Man*, after Paine's famous pamphlet. The *Moby-Dick* passage conceives the *Pequod*'s federation of isolatoes at least as much as a funky League of Nations as of capitalism Yankee style headed for destruction, though it's that too. It too underscores how Melville's microcosmic settings, like Cooper's Templeton, are an age-of-revolution legacy extended across widening spatial scales.

Even more elastic and more complex than the symbolic geography of Melville's versions of Cloots is the conception of social coherence and order that informs them. *The Confidence-Man* nonjudgmentally pictures a leaderless assemblage wandering at will, little more than a gaggle of disparate etceteras. *Billy Budd* imagines a natural aristocracy spontaneously unified by the handsome sailor's charisma. The *Moby-Dick* passage imagines an otherwise inassimilable group of men marshaled into ad hoc order by a leader purporting to rectify the world's grievances. The pivotal verbs "federated" and "accompanying" equivocate as to the degree of compulsion required, and the metaphor of petition also equivocates as to the nature and validity of the "grievances." Comprehensive inclusiveness and purposeful orderliness imply both worth and danger.

Moby-Dick's version of the Cloots cameo confirms that Melville was under no illusion that whaling ships generally and the *Pequod* specifically resembled the revolutionary counter-sites described by Peter Linebaugh and Marcus Rediker in their enticing account of the beyond-the-law "hydrarchy" that multiethnic bands of pirates, runaway sailors, and fugitive slaves sometimes formed on the high seas.[33] Nor, despite some gestures of the kind in earlier novels, was he particularly drawn by the fervor of Crèvecoeur's homogenizing melting-pot fantasy of "the American" as a "new man" in whom all the European races are synthesized. He was too hardheadedly aware of the obduracy of ethnic and cultural difference, too suspicious of reducing civilization to Eurocentrism, and too sensitive to the actual maldistribution of power to rest for very long in such facile lumping images. Ishmael's quickie summation of the industry's power structure right before he trots out the Cloots pageant is decisive: "not one in two of the many thousand men before the mast employed in the American whale fishery are Americans born, though pretty nearly all the officers are." That Ishmael then stretches this generalization to apply to the American military, the merchant marine, and the construction of canals and railroads, offhandedly concluding that "the native American liberally provides the brains" with "the rest of the world as generously supplying the muscles," suggests that the author saw matters more coolly than his narrator (*MD* 107).[34]

The one important Melville critic to take the Cloots allusion seriously, C. L. R. James, also strives mightily to distance the two. "Whereas Clootz thought of uniting all men in a Universal Republic, based on liberty, equality, fraternity, brotherhood, human rights, etc.," Melville "had not the faintest trace of these windy abstractions. . . . His candidates for the Universal Republic are bound together" by their world of work. James's anxiety to immunize Melville against Cloots comports with his distaste for Ishmael as an impotent narcissistic intellectual type ("the man without will"), vastly inferior to the veteran seafarer Ahab's mastery of the planetary movements of whales, as well as with James's resolve to strip all pretext of legitimacy from Ahab's victimization of the crew, by contrast to whom he's a mad despot.[35] James goes so far as to claim that Melville "intends to make the crew the real heroes of his book, but is afraid of criticism." Hence James distinguishes even more sharply between the fantast Cloots and the "meanest mariners, renegades and castaways," who "remain sane and human."[36]

James's conception of the crew as would-be heroes was colored by the "future anterior" mode of his reading, as his editor and interpreter Donald Pease astutely terms it.[37] James composed *Mariners, Renegades and Castaways* (1953) while interned on Ellis Island and petitioning to be allowed to remain in the United States. Indeed the book itself was a crucial part of that petition.[38] In his preface and again near the close, James characterizes "the Island, like the *Pequod*," as "a miniature of all the nations of the world and all sections of society": "Germans, Italians, Latvians, Swedes, Filipinos, Malays, Chinese, Hindus, Pakistanis, West Indians [James himself was Trinidadian], Englishmen, Australians, Danes, Yugoslavs, Greeks, Canadians, representatives of every Latin American country. As I write each word, I see someone whom I knew." In such circumstances it was understandable that he should have seized upon *Moby-Dick*'s vision of "the harpooners and the crew" as a rendition of "the ordinary people of the world." And that he should have delighted in the novel's many demonstrations of the crew's competence as skilled workmen—the "heroism" of "their everyday doing of their work."[39] And been thrilled by the wonderful passage in the chase sequence that portrays these isolatoes under extreme duress working in perfect coordination as "one man, not thirty," with "all the individualities of the crew, this man's valor, that man's fear, guilt, and guiltiness, all varieties . . . welded into oneness" like the ship itself, "put together of all contrasting things—oak and maple, and pine wood; iron, and pitch, and hemp" (*MD* 415).

As petitioner-critic, James cast himself in effect as a wiser Cloots, an advocate made wise by *Moby-Dick* itself, "the first comprehensive statement in literature of the conditions and perspectives for the survival of

Western Civilization." The prescience of its dignification of the crew seemed confirmed by James's fellow inmates, to whom he warmed as his wearisome incarceration in the Ellis Island *Pequod* wore on.[40]

It wasn't anachronistic, however, for James to claim Melvillian support for the idea of the heteroglot crew as a distant augury of a multinational cosmopolitanism that deserved to flourish under American auspices. Twice he quotes from Redburn's outburst: "We are not a nation, so much as a world. . . . On this Western Hemisphere all tribes and peoples are forming into one federated whole."[41] He could have cited much more suchlike testimony, of praise for common sailors of different lands throughout Melville's work, or for that matter his assertion in the famous review of Hawthorne that presages the scope of his own intent: that "Shakespeares are this day being born on the banks of the Ohio" (repr. in *MD* 524). Melville's writing repeatedly pushes against the limits of the decorums it acknowledges as the ways of the world. Perhaps this helps explain why so many notable works of Melville criticism, like *Mariners*, are also idiosyncratic sorties of highly personal stamp, different though their aesthetic and ideological proclivities are: Charles Olson's *Call Me Ishmael* (1947), Lawrance Thompson's *Melville's Quarrel with God* (1952), James Baird's *Ishmael* (1956), William Spanos's *The Errant Art of "Moby-Dick"* (1992), Clare Spark's *Hunting Captain Ahab* (2001), and Peter Szendy's *Les prophéties de texte-Léviathan* (Prophecies of Leviathan, 2004) to name a handful. James outdoes all the others, however, in his enlistment of *Moby-Dick* as witness to his *personal* ordeal, right down to detailing such medical woes as his duodenal ulcer. But even here he follows Melville. For critics to "make themselves characters in a Melvillian story of authorial affliction," critic Andrew DuBois points out, follows from "Melville's having done so"—follows from the repeated eruptions into the text of the titanic struggle: "Give me a condor's quill! Give me Vesuvius' crater for an inkstand! Friends, hold my arms!" (*MD* 349).[42]

Despite viewing Melville's mariners a tad wishfully, James was on the same page with David Dowling's no-nonsense bottom-line assessment: Melville "had compassion for the sea dogs, for indeed he was but one, yet he could not put his faith in them as a revolutionary force." *Mariners* goes to great pains to explain why no mutiny took place even though it was entirely justified by Ahab's countermanding of owner's orders. This becomes the centerpiece of James's brief for *Moby-Dick's* prophetic modernity, to which the vindication of the crew is corollary: the book's demonstration of the capacity of a Hitlerish, Stalinesque personality, forged by American capitalism and backed by a formidable expertise in his profession second to none, to enforce compliance; and, reciprocally, the readiness of subordinates to rationalize "subservience to tyranny."[43]

This seems on the whole quite faithful to *Moby-Dick*'s framing of the mismatch between ideology and utopia. *Moby-Dick*'s device of subjecting its shipboard microcosm of human types—a symbolic global village akin to the omni-national patchwork Redburn wishfully sees in U.S. society—points to a conundrum at the heart of the democratic ethos: can a diverse public of independent agents ("isolatoes") chart its course absent the discipline of some form of top-down management? *Moby-Dick* makes it impossible to say no and rest content by imagining a type of floating society whose neofeudal regime is intrinsically undemocratic and fatal to free-spirited camaraderie as well as independent agency and then immediately worsening the scandalous disparity by dramatizing the ease with which an authority figure can bend the rules of an already one-sided covenant to his own ends. But this being the only imagined society shown at any length, we're left to wonder, like poor James in his confinement, whether the machinations of hierarchs, understrappers, and demagogues, and the unevenness of the playing fields on which all real-world action takes place, mean that the "ought" will remain forever trumped by some grotesque regime of "is." *Moby-Dick*'s modern percolations through the capillaries of public culture confirm both the liberating energies of its creative gusto and the unhopefulness of its prognostic.

Moby-Dick *as Cultural Icon*

Since *Moby-Dick* achieved perennial Great American Novel candidate status in the 1950s and started to become a frequent recourse for journalists, cartoonists, and bloggers as well as for artistic imitation and academic dissection, there's been a notable disconnect between the scholarly industry and the consensus of public culture at large as to where the novel's center of gravity lies. The history of *Moby-Dick* criticism shows an investment in Ishmael's angle and narrative (mis)management that public culture does not.[44] Jeffrey Insko's 2007 analysis of the plethora of references in contemporary U.S. media to *Moby-Dick à propos* politics, business, and sport found no "Ishmaelean turn." "Nearly everything else in the novel" seemed to be filtered out except for the "epitome" of "Ahab's quest for the whale."[45] This largely accords with my own research. Modern *Moby-Dick* cartoons are nearly all about Ahab and the whale, like my own personal favorite, Rene Baur's courtroom scene with Ahab in the dock being cross-examined by an attorney, harpoon in hand, on behalf of the white whale, who sulks in the background: "So, Captain Ahab, I put it to you that you were deliberately stalking my client." Critic Randy Laist rightly notes "the perpetual Ahabism characteristic of Hollywood Movies."[46] The 1926 silent film *The Sea Beast* and its 1930 sound-era remake *Moby-Dick* have John Barrymore as Ahab triumphantly returning to Nantucket at the end to claim his sweetheart. Filmgoers of the 1950s are less likely to remember Richard Baseheart's Ishmael than Gregory Peck's Ahab. Orson Welles was inspired by his cameo role as preacher Father Mapple in that John Huston film to devise his own Ahab-centric dramatic adaptation, *Rehearsed,* revived successfully in a 2007 off-Broadway production. Other recent creations that sustain this tilt toward Ahab-beast centripetalism, and in the process testify to the ongoing cultural capital of this Great American Novel to this day, include Wes Anderson's film *The Life Aquatic with Steve Zissou* (2004), whose title figure montages Ahab and Jacques Cousteau; the futuristic 2010 film *Moby-Dick* starring Barry Bostwick, in which the *Pequod* disaster is conflated with its chief real-life prototype, the sinking of the whale ship *Essex,* and the golden age of whaling with Cold War surveillance and pursuit; the 2011 TV miniseries *Moby-Dick;* and Jake Heggie's comic opera *Moby-Dick* (2010). Taken together such works confirm what seems almost an iron rule for popularization of classic texts—*Gulliver's Travels, Robinson Crusoe,* and countless others[47]—that their plots tend to get boiled down to lowest terms: meaning for *Moby-Dick* the face-off between Ahab and the white whale.

The evidence doesn't point all one way. Some popular reinventions complicate the prototype by embroidering or superimposing other formulas, such as teasing out the figure of the lover/wife for Captain Ahab whom the original novel mentions only in passing, as with the first two Hollywood films; the TV miniseries; the first two novels in Louise Gouge's 2004 trilogy, *Ahab's Bride* and *Hannah Rose;* and Sena Jeter Naslund's feminist pastiche *Ahab's Wife* (1999), a Book-of-the-Month

Club main selection that charts the odyssey of "Una Spenser" in relation to a copious array of antebellum literati and leaves her contentedly
paired off at the end with a seasoned Ishmael.[48] Similarly, *Moby-Dick*
adaptations for youth may play up the Ishmael bildungsroman angle, as
in Roy Thomas's 2007–2008 adaptation for Marvel Comics and the Michael Lehrman film *Heathers* (1988), in which Ishmael/Ahab are reinvented in an Ohio high school relationship in which a female teenage
Ishmael is almost fatally drawn into the orbit of an incendiary Ahabish
peer, who ultimately destroys himself.

A work like *Heathers* also suggests, as Melville himself did when he
transposed *Macbeth* and *King Lear* into his own literary universe, the
inventiveness of which latter-day adaptations are capable when artists
of superior creativity push back against the reductive stereotypes that
have been handed down to them.[49] Indeed during the past half century
Moby-Dick's impact as inspirational force for top-flight art in different
media has been greater and more polyform even than that of *The Scarlet
Letter* or *Huckleberry Finn*. Other intricate creative reinventions within
their chosen media include Nobel laureate Patrick White's novel *Voss*
(1957), a perennial candidate for Great Australian Novel for those to
whom it matters; Frank Stella's 138 artistic renderings in different media titled after every chapter of *Moby-Dick;* the metal band Mastodon's
2004 *Leviathan;*[50] and the Spymonkey comedy troupe's 2010 *Moby-Dick*,
a Monty Pythonish staging of an attempted performance of the novel
in which Ahab and Ishmael fight over who gets to narrate.

Still, these variations do not seriously disrupt three general patterns.
First, the "Ishmael trope," as Insko calls it, survives most vigorously in
the antiheroes of "serious" twentieth-century U.S. literature, chief
among them Tyrone Slothrop of Thomas Pynchon's *Gravity's Rainbow*
(1973; see Chapter 13), and in such miniform gestures as the opening
gambits of Kurt Vonnegut's *Cat's Cradle* ("Call me Jonah") and Philip
Roth's *The Great American Novel* ("Call me Smitty"). Second, the more
cursory the allusion, and the less the presumption that the listener recalls the book itself, the more likely *Moby-Dick* will get reduced to the
bare-bones formula of Ahab versus whale. Third and most striking, in
such cases the ethical and political valences vary wildly. "In American
public discourse," Insko reports, "Ahabs appear both as reckless au-
thoritarians and as heroic strivers . . . either to praise or to condemn."[51]
They aren't monopolized either by the left or the right; nor do they

always give Ahabian presumption a "totalitarian" spin. As a negative image of vengeful monomania, Ahab may stand not only for the American military-industrial establishment's obsession with Vietnam or communist China, or Reagan's with the Sandinistas in Nicaragua, or Kenneth Starr's prosecution of Clinton, but also for the liberal media's alleged conspiracy against Nixon, for Nixon's fraught relation to Eisenhower ("awe and fascination soured with fear and a desire to supplant"), for anticorporate harassment of Microsoft's monopolism, for Rudolph Giuliani's prosecution of Drexel Burnham Lambert as district attorney of New York City, for Canadian fishery officials' voting for selective lifting of the international ban on whaling, and so on. Ahabism has also been palliated into a synonym for appealing quixoticism of various kinds, like British Prime Minister John Major trying to control a "whale of a depression," Adlai Stevenson III trying to form a third party in Illinois to stand against Governor Jim ("The Whale") Thompson, or New York Yankee slugger Roger Maris, the first to break Babe Ruth's home run record in 1961, not quite managing to do it within the span of the old-time 154-game season. In which case, as then-prominent columnist James Reston wrote of the baseball story, Ahab starts to seem one of the great legendary "gallant failures of life."[52] Or as a Quixote who eventually succeeded, like that "Ahab of a quarterback" Peyton Manning of the Indiana Colts, when the team wrested the American Football Conference championship away from the New England Patriots.[53]

Rerun that diagnosis at the level of cultural politics among the intelligentsia, and you find the sympathetic rendition of Ahabian "madness" that launched contemporary Americanist whiteness studies, Toni Morrison's "Unspeakable Things Unspoken" (1988), which rehabilitates Ahab as the indispensable adversary of hegemonic whiteness: "the only white male American heroic enough to slay the monster that was devouring the world as he knew it." In this Morrison unconsciously updated what seems to have been the very first African American commentary on *Moby-Dick*, by the antebellum physician and polymath James McCune Smith, in Frederick Douglass's *Paper* (1856), who enlisted *Moby-Dick* for support in his argument for the necessity of firm antislavery leadership. That Morrison's primary scholarly source for her biographical narrative read Ahab oppositely as a would-be usurper of "the power he attributes to Moby Dick" simply testifies once again, if further testimony be needed, to the multivalent durability of the Ahab-versus-white whale configuration as the book's defining takeaway.[54]

No act of creative or critical repossession of *Moby-Dick* can prove beyond refutation that it does or does not validate Ahabian force against Ishmaelian hedging or the virtues of multiethnic democratic egalitarianism notwithstanding their potential corruptibility. No less self-evidently, however, extra-academic, middlebrow, and even lowbrow-hipshooting takes and retakes on supposed master plots—what Pierre Bourdieu calls "naive citatology"—must be factored into any serious analysis of what counts as great American novelism in order to be faithful to the legacy of this or any culturally influential narrative, all the more so given than the GAN idea itself is and has always been more a demotic than an academic enthusiasm. Books that accrue GAN charisma inevitably get appropriated in discrepant ways uncontrollable beyond a point by the original authorizing "institutions which conserve the capital of symbolic goods," in this case critical and pedagogical establishments.[55] *Moby-Dick* is conspicuous although not unique in provoking such mutiny, readerly hijackings that are orthogonal, even antithetical, to "established" interpretations. Individually, they're often laughable; collectively they're worth noting, sometimes even instructively eye-opening.

For our purposes, one significant revelation to be gleaned from the unofficial discourse generated by *Moby-Dick* in modern times is the reminder that the novel's dominant presence is for better or for worse Ahab, not the crew, nor the Ishmael of Cold War liberal critics who followed Matthiessen's lead, nor the recuperated Ishmael of later critics who break from that earlier model. All this follows from *Moby-Dick*'s casting of the Clootsian microcosm relative to its later cameo appearances in *The Confidence-Man* and *Billy Budd*—*Moby-Dick*'s "Clootz" as the impresario of the otherwise anonymous delegation of heteroglot multinationals. That encapsulation is also in keeping with *Moby-Dick*'s Ishmael-eclipsing swerves from the standard observer-hero framework, first toward drama and then toward narrative omniscience, swerves that themselves helped ensure that when boiled down to the bare bones the face-off between Ahab and white whale would become *Moby-Dick*'s most durable schema.

Meanwhile, the metamorphic reinvention of the Cloots vignette in Melville's later work bears out the experimental cast of his own thinking, registered obliquely by the drollery of a number of the latter-day popular appropriations, the Spymonkey version for instance—far more common than what one finds in the history of (say) *The Scarlet Letter*'s reception. Melville invests Cloots, and much else in *Moby-Dick* besides, with an over-the-top grotesquerie that leaves it to the reader to surmise at every point whether what's being ventured is prophecy or parody or both. *Moby-Dick* stands somewhere in between taking the prospect of some future completion of democratic-style heroism seriously and spoofing it as doomed from the get-go owing to whatever combination of leaderly hubris and subaltern fecklessness. This problematic is more or less shared by the other novels mentioned in this section, from Cooper onward, that employ the heteroglot assemblage device. The admixture of hopeful and sardonic tonalities in *Moby-Dick*'s treatment of the pageant of human rights' rightful but unfulfilled universality fortifies one's sense of the unkillability of the GAN aspiration itself, to the extent that it connects hankering for the GAN with continuing desire for vicarious participation in a process of social envisionment conceived as still and maybe forever incomplete. Whether after another 150 years this process will seem to have worked more toward the end of realizing more robust images of social inclusion than toward reinscribing discredited ideologies or the cynicism of ideals repeatedly betrayed, remains a question to which the next two chapters do not, to say the least, supply very reassuring answers. But nonresolution will help ensure that the GAN lives on as dream if not as achieved result.

12

The Great American Novel of Twentieth-Century Breakdown

Dos Passos's *U.S.A.*—or Steinbeck's *Grapes of Wrath?*

> Hell yes, need advice bad. Any man who writes a trilogy needs
> advice (and a good physician).
>
> —JOHN DOS PASSOS to Ernest Hemingway (1932)

> Yesterday, and ever since history began, men were related to
> one another as individuals. . . . To-day, the everyday relation-
> ships of men are largely with great impersonal concerns, with
> organizations, not with other individual men.
>
> —WOODROW WILSON, *The New Freedom* (1913)

JOHN DOS PASSOS'S PANORAMIC anatomy of "the role of the United States in the western world" during the first three decades of the twentieth century in his *U.S.A.* trilogy (1930–1938) makes a macrocosmic complement to Melville's world-circling shipboard microcosm under Yankee control. In size, scale, and profusion of actors and events stretching over 1,200 small-print pages in the Library of America edition, *U.S.A.* was the most ambitious assault on the Great American Novel yet attempted. Dos Passos's aw-shucks plea for his then-friend Hemingway's assistance belied the prophecy of the nation's premier literary critic, Edmund Wilson, in his review of volume one just quoted, that the trilogy might well become "the most important" American novel "of Dos Passos' generation."[1]

U.S.A. suffers as well as gains from being national fiction's Texas or Alaska. As with Whitman's *Leaves of Grass,* which next to Thackeray's *Vanity Fair* seems to have been the key inspiration for its "satirical chronicle" approach, monumental accomplishment came at the cost of proliferation of semi-interchangeable scenes.[2] The trilogy's early critics largely forgave that because of the timeliness of *U.S.A.*'s stringent Depression-era critique of the promise of industrial democracy derailed— *U.S.A.* is the most overtly politicized of all serious GAN contenders, *Uncle Tom's Cabin* included—and its au courant fusion of modernist and realist styles. In 1936, it was Dos Passos and not the authors of *Absalom, Absalom!* and *Gone with the Wind* who made the cover of *Time* magazine with the appearance of *The Big Money,* installment number three, and when it was published together with its predecessors *The 42nd Parallel* (1930) and *1919* (1932), *U.S.A.* was widely touted by journalists and academic critics alike as the closest approximation yet to the mythical Great American Novel. Jean-Paul Sartre proclaimed Dos Passos "the greatest writer of our time." But well before George Steiner named him "the principal American literary influence of the twentieth century" in 1964, his luster had faded.[3] A deluxe illustrated edition of 1947 sold better than the first editions, but not for long.* The U.S. literary left was in retreat (Dos Passos himself had begun to turn conservative a decade earlier), and what yesterday seemed cutting edge was starting to look suspiciously like pastiche. Even Michael Denning, the foremost champion of *U.S.A.*'s importance in its day as the "ur-text" of the radical/progressive Popular Front, treats it as time bound and bygone: "no longer a contemporary novel, no longer important to readers and critics." By and large, today *U.S.A.* is known today on the literary-critical street as "the Great American Novel that wasn't."[4]

But not so fast. Even as Denning wrote (1997), historico-political meganovels were making a comeback (Madison Smartt Bell's trilogy on Toussaint L'Ouverture; Don DeLillo's *Underworld;* three volumes of William Vollmann's projected *Seven Dreams* about the messy history of Euro-Native encounters from the Vikings on down). In the 2010s, the explosion of communications technologies and the scandalously rewidened gap between haves and have-nots—social problems pivotal to *U.S.A.* as well—again seem the crucial fault lines dividing wired from

---

* Dos Passos often complained that the three volumes weren't big sellers, a judgment seconded by the editor of the 1947 Houghton Mifflin reprint (note added to Dos Passos, 19 June 1944 ms. letter to Paul Brooks, in which Dos Passos cites the 6,000 sales of a 1937 Modern Library reprint of *42nd Parallel* as his best success, Houghton Library, Harvard University). On disappointing sales of *1919* and the challenges faced by Harcourt Brace in deciding how to market it and *The Big Money* to a broad reading public, see Catherine Turner, *Marketing Modernism: Between the Two World Wars* (Amherst: University of Massachusetts Press, 2003), 126–143.

unwired, rich America from its disprivileged underclasses, global north from global south. Journalist George Packer may be right that *U.S.A* is "overdue for a revival," as his own panoramic documentary nonfiction *The Unwinding* (2013) seeks to demonstrate by adapting the trilogy's structure to the subjects of turn-of-the-twenty-first-century corporate greed, high-octane political lobbying, outsized personal ambition, and their impacts on Americans from top to bottom of the social ladder.[5] Simply taken on its own terms, moreover, as a literary "tombstone" for "the decline and fall of the Lincoln republic,"[6] *U.S.A.* stands as a remarkable achievement both in comprehensiveness of scope and ironic bite in its "collective" aesthetic, which envisages "the group as a phenomenon greater than—and different from—the sum of the individuals who constitute it," envisaging personhood not autonomously but sociologically and disrupting the illusion of transparent realism by experimental devices that reinforce the sense of experience orchestrated by mass media and other forms of industrial-era standardization. Historical forces and events play through the trilogy in barrages of biographical cameos and recycled mass media tidbits that dramatize the perplexity and confusion of contemporary life experienced at the ground level.*

This collective aesthetic was a distinctive product of the 1930s, foreshadowed by the deterministic naturalism of works like Frank Norris's unfinished trilogy of wheat production—in which scores of dispersed characters are bent, defined, aligned, fused by their participation in production, marketing, and speculation in this commodity crop—and by the caricature-inflected satire of Sinclair Lewis, but without attaching anything like the priority they do to rendering their characters' autonomous consciousness, as if personal lives could be conceived as

---

* Here I adapt Barbara Foley's definition of the collective novel in *Radical Representations: Politics and Form in U.S. Proletarian Fiction, 1929–1941* (Durham, NC: Duke University Press, 1993), 398–402. Because Foley understands "collective fiction" as specifically "proletarian" and as Marxist in ideological thrust, although she claims Dos Passos as "the single most important pioneer in the form of the collective novel" in U.S. history (425), she also finds fault with his lapses from Marxism, particularly in *U.S.A.*'s third volume, concluding that these go to show that "the decision to use and develop" the collective novel genre does not "free the proletarian writer from the snares of bourgeois ideology" (440). For Dos Passos, however, neither "proletarian" nor the ethics of collective fiction seemingly stood in absolute contrast with "bourgeois," as when in 1932 he declared that the U.S. had a robust but non-revolutionary tradition of proletarian writing descending from Whitman to Dreiser (*JDPP* 150).

happening in spaces even partially immune from the social forces that shape them. After the 1930s, as we'll see in Chapter 13, collective fiction did not vanish so much as transmute into the form of the still-more-post-realistic late twentieth-century "historiographic metafiction" of such novelists as E. L. Doctorow, Thomas Pynchon, and Karen Tei Yamashita, in which the issues of what counts as "history" and what counts as "political" are themselves put under question.

Novelistic Architecture: Collective Fiction in the Machine Age

Dos Passos called himself a "frustrated architect," and during the 1920s and 1930s he often likened writers to "technicians," both to affirm solidarity between physical labor and intellectual work and to recognize that novelistic form should reflect the reengineering of social and inner life by contemporary technologies of mass media and mass production. The most obvious mark of this in *U.S.A.* is its modular construction from four components or tracks: narrative episodes centered on "the more or less entangled lives" of twelve fictive characters, twenty-seven biographical portraits mostly of historical notables, fifty-one impressionistic stream-of-consciousness glimpses of the author growing up from early childhood in tandem and tension with the century, and sixty-eight short "Newsreel" collages of newspaper headlines, advertising come-ons, snatches of popular lyric, conversational bits, and the like.[7] These strands were sketched out independently, then spliced and interwoven to produce an effect of the flux of history and experience subjected to forms of manipulation at once arbitrarily imposed and resistant to executive control.[8] Walt Whitman's catalog rhetoric, Hemingway's clipped prose, the interplay in Joyce's *Ulysses* between mental wandering through the urban buzz and such hyperstructuring devices as tabloid headlines and terse question-answer dialog, cubist and abstract expressionist painting, the geometric turn in modern architecture, cinematic experiments in montage, the then-new genre of documentary film, Fordist assembly lines—these were the aesthetic prototypes for the unique concoction piloted in *Manhattan Transfer* (1925), the novel that won Dos Passos wide critical notice, then brought to culmination in *U.S.A.*

As a means of rendering "the basic tragedy" of "man's struggle for life against the strangling institutions he himself creates," this aesthetic was a high-risk strategy. Pursued nonstop over three volumes, modular construction risked becoming a strangling institution of its own, a redundant gimmick. Then too the calculated flatness of tone with which the misadventures of the twelve semi-intersecting protagonists and their milieux are narrated—the track given far the most airtime—threatens to seem deadening by contrast to the pungent capsule biographies of Eugene Debs, Woodrow Wilson, Henry Ford, and Thorstein Veblen and the lyrical Camera Eye sequence, which the author tellingly described as "a way of draining off the subjective by getting in little bits of my own experience."[9] Structural gimmickry and tonal flatness produce a kind of mental sound barrier that readers must break through, rather as the compulsive proliferation of cetological minutiae and omni-allusiveness in *Moby-Dick* must be got past, in order to appreciate the trilogy's achievement both as art and as social intervention.

A helpful first step is to clear up the misconception, as one otherwise admiring reviewer put it, that *U.S.A.*'s "rigorous behaviorism" reduces its characters to robots, "automatons" with "no emotions of any kind."[10] True, *U.S.A.* never displays even toward its more sympathetic figures anything like the kind of affection that Dickens, say, shows for many of his most venial. Rarely do Dos Passos's characters think coherently or feel deeply for very long, on top of which the narrative voice tilts toward telegraphing interiority through social surface viewed from a satirical distance: "a softvoiced man with a large smooth pinkish face and large smooth white deadlooking hands" (*USA* 191), "a fraillooking woman with very transparent alabaster skin and a sharp chirpy voice" (662). But not only are these surfaces at best finely nuanced, as here, the featured characters themselves are hardly flat in the Dickensian sense of invariant syndromes like a Carker, a Krook, an Inspector Bucket, a Tiny Tim, a Mark Tapley. To the extent they seem so, it's because conditioning and/or purposefulness have made them so, as with J. Ward Moorehouse's tenaciously dutiful secretary Janey Williams, determined never again to fall below the poverty line, or his stylish soul mate the quasi-lesbianic Eleanor Stoddard, she of the alabaster skin and chirpy voice. Even Moorehouse himself, the most chameleonlike, a stereotypical poor boy on the make who rises to the top of the emerging public relations industry through his affable glibness at recycling promotional cliché language, will drop the mask. After holding forth "about the gigantic era of expansion that would dawn for America after the war" as if "rehearsing a speech," he charms his companion by adding, "with a funny deprecatory smile," "And the joke of it is, it's true" (551). Other characters struggle more visibly with the malforming roles into which they are drawn, like Mac the off-and-on radical trying to decide between loyalty to the Industrial Workers of the World (IWW) versus bourgeois marriage or Mexican mistress versus Mexican revolution. Others, like the socialist organizers Ben Compton and Mary French, must contend against potential derailments, internal as well as from without, that compromise the committed idealism that many of those with whom they interact see as reducing them to stereotypes.

So the work of stereotype in *U.S.A.* is far from stereotypical in the usual sense, and by no means always dismissive. Stereotype may present itself as a necessary reduction to which characters, and narrator too, resort in order to navigate an unassimilably proliferate and shifting social world. It may come as a predictable by-product of social interaction, as when the aspiring shopgirl Eleanor Stoddard and artsy/aimless Eveline Hutchins first meet in the Art Institute of Chicago and bond around the misperception of each other's defensive wariness as refinement incarnate—one of many cases where mimetic desire "levers up the mutual confidence necessary for a friendship," which may then unravel upon closer contact, as this one does.[11] Relatedly, stereotype may betoken strategic adaptation for the sake of survival, as when Janey and Joe Williams grow apart in their roles as secretary and seaman to the point they can no longer communicate although they continue to care about each other. Deindividuation may also present itself as a brake on full personhood in the name of some higher cause whether worthy or suspect, as when IWW agitator Fred Hoff tells Mac that a good Wobbly shouldn't have "wife or children, not till after the revolution" (*USA* 96) and at least two characters in *1919* are admonished that it's "criminal to allow yourself the luxury of private opinions" during wartime (537).

All that said, the work of stereotype in *U.S.A.* is more sociological than psychological, above all a mark of societal condition that follows from the division of labor in the Fordist epoch of standardized production. As Ralph Waldo Emerson presciently remarked at the dawn of the industrial era, "the priest becomes a form; the attorney a statute-book; the mechanic, a machine; the sailor, a rope of a ship."[12] That's especially why the inner lives of the twelve major fictive characters seem so flattened, envisaged more through their behavior than their mindwork relative to traditional realism. But the genius of *U.S.A.*'s collective aesthetic is that it dramatizes not just the results of standardization but also the psychic and moral messiness of the adaptational process.

Character stereotype and the rhetorics that inform it—in-group codes and cliché language, the popular hits and fashions of the day that provide the impetus and social glue for chitchat—bind the four tracks together. This holds most obviously for the newsreels, "a scrolling wallpaper of [collective] desire to which the vast, fictional *U.S.A.* itself is an imitative and rivalrous kind of response."[13] But much the same could be said of the biographies, and even of the more subjectified Camera Eye. The biographies profile exceptional individuals who stand out from the herd, but they too are homogeneously wrapped in pungent, staccato, usually ironized chronological item-list profiles of similar length that usually show the subject defeated or contained or neutralized in the long run by forces outside his or (in the one case of Isadora Duncan) her control. Teddy Roosevelt and Woodrow Wilson overreach themselves and fall into eclipse. Reform journalists John Reed and Paxton Hibben meet with ostracism and premature death and burial in Russia. Eugene Debs and Robert La Follete campaign vainly against entry into World War I, the one jailed for sedition and the other frustrated from delivering his speech in Congress. Charles Proteus Steinmetz the inventor may express dissent only at the price of dedicating his brain to General Electric. Even Henry Ford, who outsmarts the big bankers to become the richest man in the world, lives to see his automotive empire lose its competitive edge and dwindles into antiquarian nostalgia for horse-and-buggy days. Only a few figures escape satire unscathed if not unscarred— Thorstein Veblen, the Wright brothers, and Frank Lloyd Wright—original geniuses who somehow managed not to compromise or get taken down. So the difference between how the defining personages of the early twentieth century and their quotidian fictional counterparts struggle within and against their social context is more of degree than of kind. Significantly, the most durably successful biographee is not an individual but an institution, the House of Morgan, the chief bankroller and beneficiary of the Allies during World War I—a satirical thrust toward the end of *1919* (644) that cost Dos Passos *U.S.A.*'s initial publisher, Harper, which J. P. Morgan had once saved from bankruptcy.[14]

The Camera Eye, the lyric persona Dos Passos described as an auto-biographical implant, seems a voice of finer sensitivity than those of the other tracks from the very first installment, which registers the small child's confusion as he is dragged by his panicky mother to a place of refuge in some Dutch city from a crowd incensed by the Boer War that mistakes them for English:

> Easier if you hold Mother's hand and hang on it that way you can kick up your toes but walking fast you have to tread on too many grass-blades the poor hurt green tongues shrink under your feet maybe thats why those people are so angry and follow us shaking their fists they're throwing stones grownup people throwing stones She's walking fast and we're running her pointed toes sticking out sharp among the poor trodden grassblades under the shaking folds of the brown cloth dress Englander. (*USA* 13)

The pathos of the child as the innocent, frightened target; the mystifying anger of the protestors; the aversion to crowdthink and offstage war-mongering alike—all this gets transmitted through the subjective tonality that makes this and the other Camera Eye passages seem, at first sight, a reproach to the blinkered, unreflective dream machine state in which most of the fictional characters and biographees seem to operate.

But the Camera Eye is also tied to what it seems to, and partly does, oppose. As Eye, this witness has no agency beyond the capacity to register the feel of where he happens to be. As Camera, he is only another technological medium, albeit a more sensitive recording instrument than newsreels or newspapers. Nor can cameras, any more than news-reels, avoid offering back images that are framed and cropped. In the passage above, a telltale sign is the child stomping on the grass blades ("the poor hurt green tongues shrink under your feet"). Even casual readers of *Leaves of Grass* will notice the rerun of Whitman's master metaphor for democratic-egalitarian solidarity, the "many uttering tongues" that sprout "alike in broad zones and narrow zones."[15] But here the "poor hurt green tongues" are being "hurt" ironically by the person who sympathizes with their pain. He doesn't hurt them on purpose, of course, but he can't avoid trampling them as his mother flees the pursuing crowd who sees them as a symbol of the English oppressor. The disconnect between the boy's hypersensitivity to the fate of the plants that don't actually feel injured and his incomprehension of the humans who do shows the buffered state of the child of privilege within and against which the persona must struggle throughout the book. The sequence as a whole unfolds as a lyricized bildungsroman of the Eye that oscillates between classist recoil against ugliness, vulgarity, bloodshed, and danger and self-disgusted resistance to the constraints of juvenile dependence, Harvard pseudo-aestheticism, adolescent self-indulgence, and inability to do more than decry the injustices of the world to which he is awakened. This is the paradigmatic participant-observer's dilemma, of felt disjunction from the reified material world of which the bourgeois observer is inevitably part, that critic Carolyn Porter has identified as a defining motif in classic American narrative and autobiographical consciousness: the consciousness that ranges beyond without being able to break from his middle-class reference group.[16]

The Camera Eye's eloquent impotence is also the measure of *U.S.A.*'s achievement, however, as the most significant carrier of Whitmanian aesthetics in the early twentieth century together with the poetry of Ferdinand Pessoa and Hart Crane. Allen Ginsberg's conflation of dissident nostalgia and parodized media talk in "America" ("America when will we end the human war?" "Are you going to let your emotional life be run by Time Magazine?" "America Sacco & Vanzetti must not die") is closer to Dos Passos's Camera Eye than to Whitman himself,[17] especially the passages leading up to *U.S.A.*'s climactic historical event, the framing and 1927 execution on trumped-up murder charges of the Italo-American immigrant anarchist workmen Nicola Sacco and Bartolomeo Vanzetti:

> Don't let them scare you how make them feel who are your oppressors America (*USA* 1135)

> America our nation has been beaten by strangers who have turned our language inside out who have taken the clean words our fathers spoke and made them slimy and foul (*USA* 1157)

> we stand defeated America (*USA* 1158)

The strength of these lines, as of Ginsberg's next-generation rhetoric, lies not in the voice of the persona alone but in their revision of the bond between speaker and social macrocosm established during the course of *Leaves of Grass*.

On the one hand, the Camera Eye is a pathetic comedown from the expansive persona of Whitman's strongest poems. Dos Passos's frightened little boy is a far cry from the infinitely curious lad of Whitman's

"There Was a Child Went Forth" who ranges from home base to far-thest horizon, as is the fretfully bookish pupil of later episodes in *U.S.A.* from the Whitmanian persona who grandly dismisses the learned as-tronomer's lecture upon sallying forth to behold the stars: "I go home after a drink and a hot meal and read (with some difficulty in the Loeb Library trot) the epigrams of Martial and ponder the course of history and what leverage might pry the owners loose from power and bring back (I too Whitman) our storybook democracy" (*USA* 893).

Yet to embed the Camera Eye within the damaged society it yearns to expose and see healed is also wholly in keeping with Whitman's stated aspiration for *Leaves of Grass:* "to articulate and faithfully express in literary or poetic form, and uncompromisingly, my own physical, emotional, moral, intellectual, and aesthetic Personality, in the midst of, and tallying, the momentous spirit and facts of its immediate days, and of current America."[18] How *U.S.A.* builds on this premise recalls the evo-lution of the Whitman persona from the assertively demiurgic force of the early editions of *Leaves of Grass* to a more vulnerable entanglement, forced to "sit and look out upon all the sorrows of the world" without power to remedy.[19]

The later poems' anticipation of the self-effacing Camera Eye belies the extent to which from start to finish Whitman's reconnaissance of the social landscape in motion unsettles business-as-usual perception even when it affirms nothing more than the is-ness of what comes under view.

> Through me many long dumb voices,
> Voices of the interminable generations of prisons and slaves,
> Voices of the diseas'd and despairing and of thieves and dwarfs,
> Voices of cycles of preparation and accretion,
>
> And of the rights of them the others are down upon,
> Of the deform'd, trivial, flat, foolish, despised,
> Fog in the air, beetles rolling balls of dung.[20]

Merely to insist that these "long dumb voices" get expressed is to thrust forth a democratizing reform initiative even though no action is shown as taken other than to itemize and to utter, even though the speaker confesses himself overwhelmed by the force of his vision. The same holds to a still greater degree for *U.S.A.*'s more aversive social panora-mas. In neither case does the social energy of the magnum opus stand or fall on the efficacy of the autobiographical persona as an embodied actor, but on the imaginative reach of the panorama within which the Whitmanian speaker and the Camera Eye are shown as entangled.

Democracy Derailed: The Fate of the Working Classes

U.S.A. unfolds as a three-stage chronicle of the betrayed promise of industrial democracy, from the top down and from the bottom up. *The 42nd Parallel* sweeps through the early years of the twentieth century; *1919* centers on the last stages of World War I and its aftermath; *The Big Money* follows the 1920s from postwar return through the stock market crash and looming Depression. The series gathers linear momentum through the Camera Eye's odyssey and the individual lifelines of the twelve featured characters but also palimpsestically through scores of flashbacks, reclocking back to prewar years as each new major character gets introduced no matter when; through the sometimes anachronistic placement of the biographies; through the redundant newsreel motifs; and above all through the prevailing sense of being inside the whale of historical process, enveloped in clouds of unknowing.

Newsreel one of *The 42nd Parallel* juxtaposes mordant sound bites of British defeat in South Africa and the cost of American conquest of the Philippines with triumphalist politicians' pronouncements that "the twentieth century will be American"; that thanks to America's abundant mineral and agricultural surpluses and "invention and economy in production" we are "now leading by the nose the original and the greatest of the colonizing nations" (*USA* 12). Whether or not by design this ironically reprises the opening gambit of John Dos Passos Sr.'s *The Anglo-Saxon Century* (1903), a manifesto reminiscent of Rudyard Kipling's iconic poem "The White Man's Burden" (1899), which called upon the United States to assume its proper place among the family of empires. The Spanish-American War together with America's late nineteenth-century transformation, Dos Passos senior declares, must "force her, *nolens volens,* to assume all the new burdens and responsibilities which the new rank demands . . . to second the interests of her people, who are now spreading out in all directions in search of greater wealth and wider business relations."[21] He proceeds to sketch out his vision of a grand Anglo-Saxon alliance, with the United States as the dominant partner, that would—peacefully, he stresses—guide the world to greater heights of prosperity.

At the turn of the twentieth century, such racialist globalism seemed more plausible than in the 1930s, with Western capitalism on the ropes, rather as early 1990s upbeat visions like Francis Fukuyama's *The End of History and the Last Man* (1992) seemed more plausible in the wake of the Soviet Union's collapse than they do in the shadow of the "Great Recession" of 2008 and challenges to American dominance from China and the Islamic world. The consolidation of Yankee power that Union victory in the Civil War made possible triggered what sociologist Barrington Moore (prematurely) called "the last capitalist revolution."[22] It enabled transcontinental settlement across the Great Plains to the Pacific networked by railway infrastructure of epic scale. Gilded Age America became the late nineteenth-century equivalent of turn-of-the-twenty-first-century China. "From a commercially peripheral, agriculturally based, capital- and good-importing nation," historian Daniel Rodgers sums up, "the United States vaulted almost overnight into the role of the world's engine of capitalist social and economic production." By 1900, the country was producing one-third of the world's industrial output, "more than Great Britain, France, and Germany combined."[23] Although the Spanish-American War was almost as divisive as the Mexican War, few disputed that the ten-day conquest showed the nation could acquire an empire if it so chose.

In *U.S.A.*, however, questions of imperial hubris become ancillary to the issues of social inequality and human rights at home under industrial capitalism. The trilogy's vista remains expansively international but concentrates on Euro-America, with brief side glimpses south to Mexico and the Caribbean, rather than the global periphery. All three novels accordingly lead off their sequences of chapters on the featured dramatis personae with extended treatment of the misadventures of an embattled young working-class white male who eventually gets balked and/or destroyed. In *The 42nd Parallel* he is Mac, an orphaned youth who drifts from Chicago to the Pacific down to Mexico in a hand-to-mouth, freight-hopping existence that leaves him too unskilled, unglued, and indecisive to make either a satisfactory petit bourgeois or a disciplined revolutionary. In *1919* he is Joe Williams, Janey's brother, who we know from *42nd Parallel* has escaped to sea from a stifling lower-middle-class home only to get bounced around the Atlantic in a series of jolting, coarsening misadventures made worse by his chip-on-the-shoulder pugnacity first in the navy (which he deserts after slugging an officer) and then the merchant marine. His big break, promotion to third officer, comes to nothing when his ship is wrecked, his captain-patron dies, his wife betrays him, and he's killed in a barroom brawl. In *The Big Money* he is Charley Anderson, first seen at the end of *42nd Parallel* as an auto mechanic of half-digested socialist views drifting toward Europe, but now shown as a lieutenant returning home after the war with a reputation as an ace pilot and an idea for an airplane engine starter that turns a tidy profit when he and his partners take it public. But restless undisciplined Charley isn't equipped to become the high-rolling capitalist he hankers to be. Before long he's undone by greed, stock speculation, alcoholism, and bad choices of business and love partners. A plane crash in a test flight of his new design, possibly sabotage by his overworked and bullied underlings, cripples him, and not long after he dies in a drunken driving bender—a sardonic encapsulation of his role in the two key early twentieth-century breakthroughs in high-speed transportation technology. Charley is great with gadgets but hopeless when put in charge.

Taken together, these portraits might seem to bear out hard-headed Pittsburgh union activist Gus Moscowski's assertion to his idealistic coworker Mary French that the working class is its own worst enemy (*USA* 884): self-divided, undisciplined, seducible by management. Capping the hapless but somewhat appealing Mac and Joe with Charley, the ablest but also the most corrupt, drives the point home. Partially offsetting this, though, is the counter-momentum built around the featured labor activists, Ben Compton, introduced toward the end of *1919*, and Mary French, a major figure in *The Big Money*. Both are smart, well-educated people who might have become successful bourgeoisie but instead opt for downwardly mobile solidarity with the working class despite privations, life-endangering risks to their personal safety, multiple arrests, police brutality, and in Ben's case traumatic expulsion from the Communist Party as a Trotskyite schismatic. In particular *U.S.A.* ennobles Mary—far the most admirable of the twelve—for her part in the final, failed protest on behalf of Sacco and Vanzetti, the emotional and political climax of *The Big Money* and the trilogy as a whole.[24]

Sacco and Vanzetti exist on an altogether different plane within *U.S.A.* from the other historical personages. They are the book's Christ figures, martyrs of a broken system. No taint of veniality or confusion or indecisiveness attaches to them. In keeping, the trilogy never depicts them directly except through one pungent quotation apiece: Sacco's last letter to his son ("Much I thought of you when I was lying in the death house") and Vanzetti's public statement ("If it had not been for these things, I might have lived out my life talking at streetcorners to scorning men") (*USA* 1156, 1158). This constrained epitaphic rechanneling of their voices as if already from the grave confirms and reinforces their fame as a progressive cause célèbre. So too the Camera Eye's laconic bottom-line outcry: "all right we are two nations" (1157). By 1936, Sacco and Vanzetti were already canonized. Dos Passos himself had helped to ensure this, in a documentary pamphlet calling for "justice, not clemency" when the last appeals were still pending, and in other journalistic writings of the 1920s. "America must not be allowed to forget," he admonished shortly after the execution, fearful the "idiot lack of memory" that plagued "industrial society of the present day" might efface memory of the scandal.[25] *U.S.A.* accomplished the *literary* canonization of Sacco and Vanzetti as working-class saints, as the most exhaustive scholarly analysis of the legal history of the case confirms by taking "all right we are two nations" as the epigraph for a major section.[26]

U.S.A.'s rendition of the last days of Sacco and Vanzetti brings to culmination a series of other martyrdoms of workers and labor activists interspersed throughout the trilogy, most notably in the biography sections—Eugene Debs and Big Bill Haywood in *42nd Parallel*, broken by imprisonment; the execution of Joe Hill; the horrific lynching of Wesley Everett in *1919*—plus dozens of ancillary characters like Charley Anderson's loyal foreman Bill Cernak, who loses his life vainly trying to persuade his self-absorbed boss to take his workers' grievances seriously. Vis-à-vis this accumulating series, the Sacco-Vanzetti sequence recalls both Whitman's tribute to the slain Abraham Lincoln in "When Lilacs Last in the Dooryard Bloom'd" as the singular loss that also personifies all of the Civil War dead, and the chase that ends *Moby-Dick*, where the rhetorics of cetology, anticipation, speculation, and episodic tales give way to a sustained action narrative with the appearance at last of the spectacular creature whose supercharge of imputed significances and uncanny shrewdness seem to put it on a higher plane of being altogether. The Sacco and Vanzetti sequence looms up as the preeminent example of "all the terrible perversions of justice after the last war that made American democracy a mockery to a whole generation of young men," as Dos Passos put it in 1941, propelling the rhetoric of protest to a pitch of rhapsodic apotheosis unmatched by anything before.[27] By contrast, Ben Compton and Mary French, even Big Bill Haywood and Gene Debs and Joe Hill, seem like trench fighters struggling in the coils of *U.S.A.*'s gray world of vested interests and institutional juggernauts.

Opinion Management

But that is presumably just what the author wanted: a satirical "novel without a hero," to quote the subtitle of Thackeray's *Vanity Fair* that he loved to recall. Chiefly the trilogy registers the downside of industrial modernity evoked by Woodrow Wilson at the start of *The New Freedom* (1913), a depersonalization of social relations whereby person-to-person suddenly no longer seemed the defining model. *U.S.A.* rendered aesthetically the alienating effects of that socioeconomic shift far more cogently than did *The New Freedom*, a conspectus of Wilson's presidential agenda hastily cobbled together after the election. Wilson falls back on the archaic mantra that what the nation needs in order to realize its balked promise is to remove the roadblocks imposed by vaguely defined big interests to the unleashing of the autonomous energies of smaller entrepreneurs, "the men who are on the make rather than the men who are already made."[28] *U.S.A.*'s counterthrust becomes clear when seen against the background of novelistic precursors that also deploy the template of the sociocultural cross-section as national microcosm or heterotopia: Cooper's *The Pioneers*, Melville's *Moby-Dick*, William Dean Howells's *A Hazard of New Fortunes*, and Frank Norris's *The Octopus*. All dramatize chapters of national development by gathering an assemblage of figures, more or less heterogeneous in background and interest, interacting within a bounded space as players in a socially symptomatic enterprise or struggle. In Cooper, the project is a frontier town in the making where people of very different ethnoracial and class backgrounds rub shoulders. In Melville, it is a signature industry of the national economy in its paleotechnic phase that puts the social microcosm represented by the literal confinement of the *Pequod*'s crew in the same interdependent boat. In Howells, it is a magazine venture that draws upon and almost founders as the result of the dissonant class, ethnic, regional, aesthetic, and ideological agendas that the various players bring with them to the nation's cultural metropolis at a moment of acute labor unrest. In Norris, it is the clash of city-based railroad and finance versus land-based ranching interests, themselves complexly fissured, as to who will have what degree of control over real estate and agricultural production. In each case the principal contending parties epitomizing the history-defining moment are embodied actors who, sooner or later, confront each other face to face.

Not so in *U.S.A.* Here the social interaction becomes much more diffuse, fleeting, happenstance, compartmentalized, abstract, mediated. The biographied figures occupy spaces apart from each other and from the fictive characters, who almost never catch sight of them and who think of them, if they do at all, in stock images and catchphrases. The Camera Eye drifts about in its own sphere disjunct from the others. The newsreels register both groupthink and nobodythink. In the narrative episodes, bosses interact sparingly with employees even in the workplace, let alone socially, and when they do the relation feels strained, as when Charley foists himself on the Cernaks one Christmas.

Orthogonal to but joined at the hip with the political reform thrust that culminates in the apotheosis of Sacco and Vanzetti is the sociological narrative that binds the Camera Eye also to the circle of the public relations mogul J. Ward Moorehouse and through it to the historical personage who stands at the center of the biographies, Woodrow Wilson.

Among *U.S.A.*'s twelve characters, Moorehouse connects directly or indirectly with the greatest number of the others, partly because he comes closest to achieving public figure status.* He too is the character whose life gets most fully traced from early childhood in *The 42nd Parallel*, where we're told that Johnny was born on the fourth of July around 1880, to the brink of premature old age in the late 1920s, when an attack of angina confirms his irreversible decline if not imminent death.

Two notable episodes from near the trilogy's start and close help anchor down Moorehouse's significance. The first involves the reappearances of Doc Bingham, who crops up at the end of *The Big Money*

---

* Like Mac, J. W. logs time in youth as an itinerant bookseller—far more successfully— and the two briefly cross paths in Mexico City. Eleanor Stoddard becomes J. W.'s semi-confidante, through whom he meets and has a semifarcical fling with her sometime friend and partner Eveline Hutchins. Dick Savage becomes one of the chief understrappers in his PR firm as well as Eleanor's protégé; and their joint blandishments induce him to end his affair with pregnant "Daughter" (Anne Elizabeth Trent). Janey Williams is J. W.'s long-term secretary, from whom her brother Joe picks up scraps of rumor about the course of the war.

transformed from the scruffy womanizing peddler who briefly enlisted Mac as sidekick into the septuagenarian king of the patent medicine trade who retains J. W. to lobby against an FDA-sponsored regulatory bill. The other involves the two players in Johnny's first bold venture after re-branding himself at age thirty-two as the Fifth Avenue "Public Relations Counsel" J. Ward Moorehouse (*USA* 233). J. W. brokers a genial meeting, lubricated by whiskey and soda, between the corrupt labor lobbyist George Barrow and the even more corrupt judge and mineral speculator Bowie Planet at which he holds forth on the power of "properly distrib-uted information" to ameliorate tensions between labor and management (236), following this up with a speech at Planet's Rotary Club that makes clear his first priority is to sell big business on the need to "take advantage of the possibilities of modern publicity" in order to avoid "the grave dan-gers of socialism and demagoguery and worse" (238). At the end of *The Big Money* Planet, now a U.S. senator, reappears in the penultimate epi-sode as the key politician who must be bribed after Dick Savage has clev-erly landed the Bingham account in order for the lobbying campaign to succeed, while Barrow, who has popped up a number of times along the way as the workingman's false friend and a sexual predator to boot, gets rebuffed by Mary French, whom he had earlier seduced.

Some implications of these circlings can be ticked off briskly. Bing-ham's return confirms that high-rolling 1920s capitalists are old-style hucksters writ large, lofty in talk but lewd and self-serving underneath. Planet's and Barrow's shenanigans underscore that fat cats will always try to make themselves fatter, that the lobbying game stays pretty much the same as it had been in the Gilded Age even as the issues change, and that labor is perpetually at risk of getting sold out by its self-styled spokesmen. Dick Savage's machinations as J. W.'s cynical but compliant minion, too convoluted to detail here except for the delicious clincher of winning over the pious old hypocrite Bingham by regaling him with a burlesque show, underscores the idealism of Mary's rejection of what Barrow and Planet jointly stand for. All this is obvious enough. But the stakes of J. W.'s transit need more explaining. For one thing, although he's a rank opportunist and social climber, he's also an aesthete of sorts who aspires to write popular song lyrics, loves opera, and hates the messiness of bribery. It's the combination of drive to become a picture-perfect success story hero and the traces of a residual person more com-plex than the persona with the charisma that clinches Janey's loyalty and attracts the likes of Eleanor, Eveline, and Dick, all fastidiously aesthetic types who would be beautiful as well as rich. In a provocative moment during a marathon session to work out the Bingham pitch, first the weary J. W. and then Dick seem to drop the mask. "To think once upon a time I was planning to be a songwriter," J. W. wryly confesses, to which Dick responds, "Shake hands, J. W., with the ruins of a minor poet" (*USA* 1181). Dick is also buttering up the boss here—he's been jockeying all along to one-up his colleagues—but the self-disgust is genuine; it's dogged him since adolescence, as emphasized for the *n*th time at this chapter's start: "he felt sour and gone in the middle like a rotten pear" (1169).

So the prospect of the big coup satisfies neither man. The prematurely aged J. W. wants out; and Dick proceeds almost to kill himself in a drunken binge as Charley Anderson did before. But what makes their hollowness consequential is not the shopworn story of worldly "success" experienced as empty but the historic significance of the profession in question: public relations. To have J. W. set himself up as a PR executive circa 1912 is to imagine not just a new departure for this one individual but the birth of a profession. "A new phrase has come into the language," wrote Edward Bernays a decade later, "counsel on public relations." He was well equipped to judge. Already a key player in the field, the long-lived Bernays (1891–1996) "dominates the history of propaganda and public relations, appearing like Zelig in the shadows at major world events," publishing one of the first histories of the profession in 1952.[29] A more imposing early twentieth-century figure in the field, and a likelier prototype for J. W., was Ivy Ledbetter Lee (1877–1934), whose dates more precisely coincide.* Of chief importance for

---

* Joshua L. Miller, *Accented America: The Cultural Politics of Multilingual Modernism* (New York: Oxford University Press, 2011), 173–175. Lee, who attracted Dos Passos's interest when they met in Russia, started his career in the early 1900s; see Alan Raucher, *Public Relations and Business 1900–1929* (Baltimore, MD: Johns Hopkins University Press, 1968), 17–31. Like J. W., Lee directed PR for the American Red Cross in World War I and, analogous to J. W.'s postwar employment by Standard Oil, was known as an agent/advisor for Rockefeller interests, starting with a damage control campaign after the "Ludlow Massacre" (1916) in reprisal against striking Colorado mine workers, for which Lee was derisively nicknamed "Poison Ivy" by pro-labor activists; see Upton Sinclair, *The Brass Check: A Study of American Journalism* (Pasadena, CA: author, 1919), 311–313. Miller's *Accented America* is particularly insightful in the connections it draws between *U.S.A.*'s emphasis on the rise of PR and its concern for the debasement of language in the context of an increasingly polylingual scene.

our purposes, however, is the status of public relations as a defining "field" and species of discourse for the era of *U.S.A.*

The first American PR startups date from the early 1900s, but they received a crucial boost with President Wilson's Committee on Public Information (1917–1919), organized to promote the war effort, on which both Lee and Bernays served.[30] This was "the first time that government policy" was "systematically promoted through commercial techniques of mass persuasion." The rise of the "new profession" of public relations, Bernays thought, occurred "from the end of World War I to the stock market crash."[31] This history was largely a story of well-connected media-savvy communications entrepreneurs lobbying on behalf of moneyed clients, either to broader publics or, as with the Doc Bingham commission, governmental bodies. Though PR professionals described themselves as value-neutral specialists offering mediatorial expertise to any clients in need, in practice they didn't shrink from the more Machiavellian view, as Bernays put it, that "the conscious and intelligent manipulation of the organized habits and opinions of the masses is an important element in democratic society" and from celebrating "those who manipulate this unseen mechanism" as "an invisible government which is the true ruling power of our country." From this followed in short order the systematization of "public opinion" as a specialized field of academic inquiry in the 1930s with Bernays a contributor to the inaugural issue of *The Journal of Public Opinion* concurrently with the German chemical cartel IG Farben's retention of Ivy Lee at the dawn of the Nazi era to promote German-American relations and Joseph Goebbels's use of Bernays's books in planning the Nazi propaganda against Jews.[32] Public relations, then, became as much a signature industry of the American 1920s as the Prohibition-era bootlegging operation that bankrolled Gatsby; and the stature of its leading operators made it a signature export to boot.

Considering the trilogy's indictment of the hijacking of industrial democracy by moneyed interests, *U.S.A.* might have chosen to demonize a figure like Moorehouse, and all the more so because of the contrast Dos Passos repeatedly draws between straight-talking "westerners" like radical journalist John Reed for whom "words meant what they said" (*USA* 373) and self-serving manipulation of verbal smokescreens. Yet *U.S.A.* opts for the subtler approach of picturing Moorehouse as brittle and insecure behind his facade, anxiously improvising amid a fog of uncertainty. In the Rotary Club speech that impresses Judge Planet, "he hardly knew what he was saying" (238). During his startup phase especially he relies on winging it through the clichés of the new PR-speak, discountenancing "the night of old individualistic methods" for the mantra of "coordination" of "inventor's brain," "capital," "labor, the prosperous contented American working man," that promises "prosperity unequaled before or since in the tragic procession of recorded history or in the known regions of the habitable globe" (234). This snake oil he dispenses with enough suavity and panache to impress even skeptics like Mac ("that's a smooth bastard," 277) and to perplex his closest associates. Dick Savage confides to Eveline in *The Big Money*, "I've been working for him for years now and I don't know whether he's a genius or a stuffed shirt" (1177).

The reader knows, however, that J. W. doesn't feel himself to be the big shot outsiders to his circle take him to be. Serving as a high-profile "dollar a year" man (*USA* 693) for Wilson's war effort, a shrewdly timed move whose seeming patriotism induces his alienated wife to drop divorce proceedings, J. W. is thought to be "the key to the key men" (617): to have the ear of the president or at least that of his chief advisor Colonel Edward House (662). But he himself feels rebuffed by the "Chinese wall" around the president and frets that the president "doesn't realize the power of a modern campaign of scientific publicity" that would clinch European public support for American democracy and American business after the Treaty of Versailles (624, 625). So *U.S.A.* makes J. W.'s "word-mongering empire" a "cohering center around which many of the characters move" only to expose its inability to "furnish a hegemonic principle of structural unity." In this way, *U.S.A.* conjures up the image of World War I as having ushered in what became seen as a "'golden age' of democratic social engineering" that was both stultifyingly oppressive and inefficiently bumbling.[33]

The significance of *U.S.A.*'s portrait of J. W. as befuddled PR mogul is underscored by analogy to "schoolmaster" Wilson himself, whose biography occurs exactly in the center of the series of twenty-seven. Wilson is the key political figure in *1919*—"the most powerful man in the world" at war's end (*USA* 568)—and perhaps in the trilogy as a whole. But he too is defined chiefly as a speechifier whose talk is better than his follow through, who harangues Congress "like a college president addressing the faculty and students" (567), who presides over a victory that advances vested interests abroad ("oil was trumps") while it crushes dissent at home (the Wobblies "shot down like dogs"). Wilson's idealistic defense of the treaty and the League of Nations rings hollow ("talking to save his faith in words"), and his frenetic barnstorming tour "to sober public opinion" (570)—"the most extensive effort any president has ever made to try to educate the public about foreign policy," Wilson's most authoritative biographer calls it—utterly fails and shatters his health.[34]

Wilson's rise-and-fall trajectory doesn't differ greatly from that of most other public men of the word in the biographies: politicos, labor agitators, reform journalists. William Jennings Bryan, Big Bill Haywood, Eugene Debs, fighting Bob La Follette, Jack Reed, Teddy Roosevelt, Randolph Bourne, Joe Hill, Paxton Hibben—all enjoy moments of triumphant eloquence only to end with a whimper forgotten, disdained, disillusioned, broken, or all of the above. Taken together, this collage of foiled channelers, framers, redirectors of public opinion reinforce culture critic Walter Lippmann's influential analysis of public opinion at this time (1922) as itself an incoherent muddle under the conditions of modern democratic society. How a person thinks and acts is "based not on direct and certain knowledge, but on pictures made by himself or given to him." Except in our few areas of expertise, "we cannot choose between true and false accounts"; what we call the news "is not a mirror of social conditions, but the report of an aspect that has obtruded itself" through a series of behind-the-scenes decisions by journalists, editors, advertisers, wire services, and so forth. Like the chained prisoners in Plato's allegory of the cave, the public relates not to actual environments but to "a pseudo-environment."[35] Taking fictions for truth because we need some compass points, "our addled minds" are perpetually "caught up and tossed about in a kind of tarantella by headlines and catchwords." All this might have served as a playbook for *U.S.A.* Lippmann's barrage of "headlines and catch-words" is the premise of the newsreels. His postulate that "great men" usually become "known to the public only through a fictitious personality" is the premise of the trenchantly stylized biographies. His understanding of stereotypes as reductive but necessary "defenses" that help us "order" our world becomes fundamental to *U.S.A.*'s conception of character as well as to the newsreels and biographies. The perception that "under modern industrialism thought goes on in a bath of noise" also stands behind the wayward associationism and voyeuristic alienation of the Camera Eye sequence.[36]

That Lippmann's *Public Opinion* seems not to have impressed Dos Passos one way or another makes it all the more striking that *U.S.A.* did what it did with its fictional PR executive. Edward Bernays's *Crystallizing Public Opinion* (1923) seizes upon Lippmann's diagnosis of a hopelessly confused public sphere as scripture and cites his proposed remedy—a "specialized class" of independent expert information gatherers—as justification for the new profession of opinion management.[37] *U.S.A.*'s casting of Moorehouse in relation to the rest of the characters and to President Wilson replays this aspiration ironically, confirming the professionalization of public relations as a hallmark of the era but exposing its quixoticism and mendacity. Here Dos Passos was on the same page as the philosopher John Dewey, who broadly concurred with Lippmann's view of the problem but warned that no polity "in which the masses do not have the chance to inform the experts as to their needs can be anything but an oligarchy managed in the interests of the few." But Dewey's counterproposal, a strengthening of "local communal life" and its propagation nationwide,[38] would have struck Dos Passos as wishful nostalgia, on a par with the idealized evocation of bygone New England village life in Thornton Wilder's popular play *Our Town*, published the same year *U.S.A.* was issued as a trilogy. Even if Dos Passos was not so "resolutely anti-agrarian" in principle as Denning holds, *U.S.A.* takes for granted—as *Our Town* also does in its own way—that like it or not contemporary Euro-American culture is being defined by its cities, not its hinterlands. Whereas Dewey posits that "the local is the ultimate universal, and as near an absolute as exists," the early twentieth-century world of *U.S.A.* is a metropolitan milieu where the commonest form of sociality is casual interaction among strangers and conversation is driven by the gossip, rumor, fashion of the moment.[39] Even though this leaves the characters dissatisfied, they favor it over small-town or country life. Most grow up in eastern or midwestern cities; those that don't gravitate there; and they prefer to shuttle about among the cities of the United States and western Europe: New York, Chicago, Los Angeles, Paris, Rome. As an ensemble, they constitute the fissured suboptimal public-as-it-is described by both Lippmann and Dewey, for whom what is "known" is known at second or third hand, a public whose representative figures are its echelons of mediators, even the most socially prestigious of whom—Moorehouse—is more a cog or a conduit than a man in charge, a peripheral actor in an endless game of catch-up.

That is also why the style of *U.S.A.* is *not* "mostly," as the preface misleadingly announces, "the speech of the people" (*USA* 3)—not, at least, in the customary senses of regional or ethnic folk speech or identifiable urban twang, but rather in the sense of a generic, prefabricated cohort lingo like Daughter's "when I tell Dad and the boys about it they'll see red" (595)—a far cry from a Texas drawl—or Joe Williams's "What the hell do they want to be fartin' around here for" (380), which might be any raunchy guy talking trash. Slanguage of this kind forms the lower rungs in a hierarchy of prefabricated grouptalk that extends upward on the social scale through newsreel argot and the platitudes of professional wordsmiths, to the dumbed-down flatness of the narrator's packaging of the characters' mental substrate ("It was too crowded and Margie would be scared of getting something on her pretty dress," 908), to the more finely ironized cliché dropping of the magisterial biographies ("His mother had told him not to drink, smoke, gamble, or go into debt, and he never did," 808). Such banalities are the linguistic infrastructure of *U.S.A.*'s satirical rendition of an urban soundscape increasingly subjected to "institutional regulation of particular information" from the top down, too inchoate, too confused, and too happenstance to allow itself to be disciplined into uniformity beyond a point but too insouciant not to be influenced far beyond one's conscious realization.[40]

U.S.A.'s foregrounding of the texture of urban life under democratic-industrial modernity somewhat muffles the thrust of the tragic and indignant all-right-we-are-two-nations narrative that culminates with the executions of Sacco and Vanzetti, the narrative of an increasingly decadent elite ruthlessly suppressing the working class. Given Dos Passos's anti-capitalism, *U.S.A.* might have been more firmly conceived as a clash between the failed promise of industrial democracy and a potentially socialist alternative. But although Dos Passos continued to value Communist "agitators" as latter-day counterparts of the antebellum abolitionists, by the mid-1930s such was his disillusionment with Stalinism that he went so far as to declare to his Russia-bound friend Edmund Wilson that "the despotism of Henry Ford, the United Fruit

[Company] and Standard Oil" seemed preferable to that of the American Communist Party's apparatchiks and to urge protection of "any latent spores of democracy that there may still be in the local American soil," such as "the almost obliterated traditions of trial by jury common law etc."[41] These pronouncements sit ironically at odds with the perversion of democratic-style due process showcased in the book he was then completing, not to mention the bleak cameo of the homeless "Vag" later added as a coda to the trilogy. To the extent they can be reconciled, the key lies in Dos Passos's metaphor of comparative despotisms, reminiscent of Marlow's "choice of nightmares" (between Kurtz and the colonial bureaucracy as usual) in Conrad's *Heart of Darkness*. From this it followed that *U.S.A.* would give more play and sympathy to the spontaneous, from-the-heart Marxist insurgencies of native Wobblies than to programmatic communism emanating from Russia, and that its immigrant martyrs would be anarchists rather than socialists.

For such reasons as these *U.S.A.* was and continues to be criticized by some on the left for not being Marxist enough—the key defect, opined one reviewer, that kept it from being truly the Great American Novel.[42] *U.S.A.* stacks its deck in other ways too, in addition to its regional and urban biases. For the most part it stigmatizes homosexuals; it relegates ethnics and racial immigrants to the periphery (including the two martyrs); it tilts strongly toward white and mostly bourgeois dramatis personae. All the biographees are white; and the twelve featured characters (six white men and women) include just one Catholic, one Jew, and two men of bona fide working-class origins. Racial slurs are recycled continually by narrator as well as characters. Blacks, Hispanics, and Asians play little part except as subalterns, disposable lovers, and denizens of ghettoes and dives, frequented for easy drinks and sex. To some readers, *U.S.A.* therefore looks in some ways suspiciously like a reprise of his father's Anglo-Saxonism, a comparison Dos Passos himself invited in some offhand remarks at the time and, even more, in his rightward turn thereafter.[43] Small wonder Ralph Ellison didn't exempt him from the charge that white American writers after Mark Twain except for Faulkner had been blind to African American experience. For all its proliferation of scene and character, *U.S.A.* delivers a less heterogeneous social panorama than *Moby-Dick*'s *Pequod* or even the frontier-era Cooperstown of James Fenimore Cooper's *The Pioneers*.

The justification of this restrictedness, to the extent it can be, lies in *U.S.A.*'s commitment to anatomize the pathologies of the nation's hegemonic imagined culture, which Dos Passos rightly saw as strongly coded white and Protestant through the 1920s, with particular emphasis on the role of agents of communication across the sociopolitical spectrum—journalists and political figures of differing stripes, artistic performers, publicists for hire like Moorehouse and Barrow, activist agitators—whose collective babel of competing (mis)representations comprises the muddled public sphere that they compete to define but that defines them as more its ventriloquizers than its orchestrators. This donnée required demographic overemphasis on literate, educated, more or less socially networked actors more or less attuned to the media. In short, *U.S.A.* cannot be tidily categorized either as "proletarian" fiction, except insofar as it subjects bourgeois industrial democracy to stringent critique, or as an ethnonational manifesto like his father's, except aversively. It made sense, then, both for Dos Passos to drop his original plan for ending *The Big Money* by reintroducing Mac's sometime traveling buddy Ike Hall in *42nd Parallel* and to strip Anglo-Saxon triumphalism down to Vag at last.[44]

Another telling index of what this way of framing the American early twentieth century delivers is the counterpoint between the Camera Eye and J. W.'s understrapper, Richard Ellsworth Savage. Just as the Camera Eye's unfolding subjectivity roughly tracks that of the author, Savage seems to have been more or less based on Dos Passos's college friend Robert Hillyer. At least Hillyer himself thought so, reacting "with shocked indignation" to *1919*.[45] And understandably so: *U.S.A.* contrasts Savage's two-faced sellout to the Camera Eye's fragile integrity. Yet that states the relation too simply. The many parallels between the two figures break down the illusion that the Camera Eye stands apart from the shoddier world of the fictive characters. Both Savage and the Camera Eye are from genteel backgrounds but with little or no home life who grow up emotionally distanced from parents, without close friends. Both are messily initiated into sex by older women. Both are fastidious literati, sensitive precocious disaffects with a taste for Whitman and Swinburne (whose aestheticized protest against Napoleon II's Second Brumaire, "Song in Time of Order," cycles through both their heads during the war, *USA* 447, 538). Both are boarding school products haphazardly processed by Harvard at the same time ("four years under the etherdome" thinks the Camera Eye, 262). Both volunteer for ambulance service duty before the United States enters the war, following itineraries that at first match up pretty closely: Bordeaux landing, Parisian loitering, traumatic duty under fire on the French front followed by redeployment to Italy, where both (and Joe Williams too) witness the burning of a Standard Oil tanker off the coast of Genoa (487, 525).

Dismissed for insubordination, Dick betrays his professed pacifism by accepting a lieutenancy brokered by the patron who had bankrolled his college education. Then, having impressed both Moorehouse and Eleanor with his air of detached sophistication, he happily resigns to work for J. W., fancying, "it's the type of work that will allow me to continue my real work on the side," writing presumably (*USA* 693). Actually, inner rot is well underway, and becoming a PR executive clinches it. From now on, the big money will call his tune. Meanwhile, the Camera Eye, also now in the U.S. military but as an enlisted man, extricates himself from military service more laboriously, but with integrity more intact, having avoided the binges of drunkenness and sexual entanglements that embroil Dick. After returning home, because he doesn't let himself grow callous, doesn't view others instrumentally, and struggles to make ends meet, Camera Eye develops a sense of solidarity with the downtrodden that lays the groundwork for his protest on behalf of Sacco and Vanzetti.

Still, the two figures remain secret sharers as increasingly desperate ironists, prone to ennui and self-flagellation, frustrated by the gap between acuity of perception and inability to make a mark on the world of any felt significance. Dick the bright still-young-but-getting-older climber long since disillusioned about the gold rings he keeps feeling impelled to snatch after is antipode but also counterpart to the Camera Eye, in his final appearance in the next scene, transported to Harlan County, Kentucky, after the tragedy in Dedham to relive the role of outraged onlooker to still another case of justice miscarried, a group of blatantly abused striking miners hauled up before a kangaroo court, "the judge an owner himself" (*USA* 1209).

Years later, Dos Passos recalled a joint venture he and Hillyer started during their wartime days in the French ambulance service, "what we called the Great Novel, or more simply the GN." They worked "in a cement tank that protected [them] from the shelling."[46] The collaborative GN went nowhere, nor did the posthumously published manuscript novel Dos Passos cobbled together from this starting point, "Seven Times around the Walls of Jericho." But if one takes Savage as an oblique reminiscence of Hillyer and the Camera Eye as a self-critical assessment of the limits of the author's own political activism, it becomes hard not to think of Dos Passos's serious shot at the Great American Novel as somehow connected with that aborted project of yore. Perhaps especially by dint of its abandonment. As Denning remarks with some justice, Dos Passos's fictional United States "has no future."[47] The trilogy can't imagine a next generation. The characters grow up, but not their children—of the few who have kids still alive at book's end. The one real fighter who fights on, Mary French, has no time for love, in the spirit of *The 42nd Parallel*'s Fred Hoff of the *Nevada Workman*, who admonishes Mac that Wobblies shouldn't have families till after the revolution. That's hard doctrine. Social revolution may be pie in the sky, partly because, as Mac protests in self-defense, most people feel themselves to be "made of flesh and blood like everybody else" (*USA* 96). This is the double-sided dilemma that yoking Camera Eye to Dick Savage drives home: social justice idealism that finds no traction, rudderless hyperactivity that can't congeal. But it would be a mistake to equate dilemma with resignation. The Camera Eye/Dick Savage diptych nominally reads like the end of the road, but the intensity of their aversion, from their opposite sides of the ideological divide, to the way we seem forced to live now converges with the unfinished saga of Mary French, with the "vindication" of the megascale defrauder Samuel Insell (the last of the biographees) in another grotesque court case, and with the pathetic image of Vag to produce an aesthetics of disgust that ensures the trilogy will instill restlessness, not closure. In this sense *U.S.A.* does envisage a future. Its refusal to outline a future is a challenge to find one.

The Steinbeck Alternative

Vag's isolation, the nonconvergence of Savage and Camera Eye despite their parallel lifelines, and the dispersion of the twelve leading characters across the *U.S.A.*'s vast geographical and textual spaces make even such quasi-intimacies as the rapport between Eleanor and J. W. and the sibling loyalty of Janey and brother Joe seem all the more tenuous, reinforcing the effect of a collective more nominal than substantive. Up to a point, the same holds for the other great American collective novel of the Depression era, John Steinbeck's *The Grapes of Wrath* (1938), which tracks the disintegration of a family of dispossessed tenant farmers from Sallislaw, Oklahoma, through their marathon drive to California and their desperate, disillusioning, demoralizing attempts to survive as migrant workers there. The Joads start as a close-knit extended clan, but this starts to change once they hit the road in their overloaded jalopy, especially after they reach California. Grampa—who never wanted to leave in the first place—soon dies of heatstroke, then Granma during the drive through the Mojave Desert. All but one of the younger men eventually decamp, culminating in the decision by Tom, the strongest brother and the novel's chief protagonist, to become a labor militant after killing a factory farm thug makes him a risk to the family. With winter approaching and the family's meager savings long gone after months of catch-can piecework at piddling wages, the increasingly desperate matriarch Ma Joad, "the citadel of the family" (*GOW* 74), is left with a depressed husband and brother-in-law, a self-focused pregnant daughter about to give birth, an irascible teenage son, and two feckless youngsters. No sooner does Rose of Sharon bear her stillborn child than the Joads must flee their flood-threatened trailer for a ramshackle barn, whereupon the book abruptly ends, with the family's fate unresolved, in the image of Rose offering her breast to a decrepit stranger they find there. Like *U.S.A.*, *Grapes of Wrath* refuses to imagine a future for its have-nots beyond immiseration.

Here and throughout, however, the Joads' ordeal is made uniquely poignant as well as representative of the larger cohort of the several hundred thousand "Okies" who had flocked to California since the early 1930s from the southern plains after losing their farms in the double-whammy of Dust Bowl drought, the worst "natural" disaster in U.S. history, and the consolidation of property resulting from the bankruptcy of small holders and the industrialization of agriculture. Ironically, the Okies undertook their hazardous odysseys only to find a more ruthless agribusiness establishment than the one that dispossessed them. *Grapes of Wrath*'s closing image grimly updates the front cover photograph of a pretty but set-jawed young white mother in a raggedy dress breast-feeding a frightened infant on Steinbeck's 1938 pamphlet *"Their Blood Is Strong,"* a collection of his earlier investigative newspaper reports on the dire condition of the migrants, whose preface warns that conditions are "worse than they ever were due to the constant flow of people into the state and the increasing mechanization of agriculture."[48]

To dramatize the collective plight, *Grapes of Wrath* intersperses a score of "interchapters" that Steinbeck allowed might have been "influenced by Dos Passos to some extent."[49] In these an anonymous narrator channels bits of group experience, groupthink, grouptalk:

> In the towns, on the edges of the towns, in fields, in vacant lots, the used-car yards, the wreckers' yards, the garages with blazoned signs— Used Cars, Good Used Cars. Cheap transportation, three trailers, '27 Ford, clean. Checked cars, guaranteed cars, Free radio. Car with 100 gallons of gas free. Come in and look. Used Cars. No overhead. (*GOW* 61)

> Harness, carts, seeders, little bundles of hoes. Bring 'em out. Pile 'em up. Load 'em in the wagon. Take 'em to town. Sell 'em for what you can get. Sell the team and the wagon, too. No more use for anything. (86)

> The people in flight streamed out on 66, sometimes a single car, sometimes a little caravan. . . . How far between towns? It is a terror between towns. If something breaks—well, if something breaks we camp right here while Jim walks to town and gets a part and walks back and—how much food we got? (119)

> In the camps the word would come whispering. There's work at Shafter. And the cars would be loaded in the night, the highways crowded—a gold rush for work. (235)

> Hunch along now, fill up the bag 'fore dark. Wise fingers seeking in the bolls. Hips hunching along, dragging the bag. Kids are tired, now in the evening. They trip over their feet in the cultivated earth. And the sun is going down. (408)

But *Grapes of Wrath*'s brand of collective reform fiction, as these snippets suggest, differs markedly from *U.S.A.*'s, in ways that ensured that Steinbeck's novel rather than any of Dos Passos's trilogy would top the best-seller list, would become one of American fiction's most durable sellers (fifteen million by the early 2000s, *GOW* xi), and would one day inspire the creation of an international author society, a Center for Steinbeck Studies in San Jose, California, and a succession of scholarly journals devoted to Steinbeck that have run almost continuously since 1969. The critical reputations of both authors suffered declines after World War II from which they may never recover, due partly to the inferiority of their later work but mostly to the swerve in novelistic fashion away from politicized documentary. But today, Steinbeck scholarship out-paces Dos Passos scholarship by a factor of three, and *Grapes of Wrath* garners twenty times the number of Amazon.com reviews as *U.S.A.*

Grapes of Wrath was guaranteed broader appeal from the get-go as a saga with a firm plotline that transfused indignation with empathetic pathos. *Grapes of Wrath* displays an intense and urgent sense of caring for the immiserated that *U.S.A.* matches only in the Sacco-Vanzetti sequence. Steinbeck's searching case study of a single imperiled family contrasts with *U.S.A.*'s ironic colloidal suspension of its dispersed characters in a limbolike state. Whether or not by design, *Grapes of Wrath* much more closely follows the example of the two protest novels that had made the greatest public impact in U.S. history, Stowe's *Uncle Tom's Cabin* (1852) and especially Upton Sinclair's *The Jungle* (1906), which dramatizes the plight of immigrant stockyard workers through the destruction of an originally hopeful and close-knit Lithuanian family.[50]

Grapes of Wrath also draws adeptly on other key ingredients of traditional mainstream imagination that *U.S.A.* largely disregards: the lure of westwarding; the Jeffersonian vision of hinterland small-farm agrarianism as the iconic national experience; and the just-like-us whiteness of the pitiable collective. In Dos Passos, the failed promise of the California dream is little more than sideshow, relegated to *42nd Parallel's* snapshots of Mac on the road and in his L.A. bungalow and *The Big Money's* episodes on Margo Dowling's Hollywood years. *Grapes of Wrath* updates—and upends—for the automotive age the mythic odysseys of covered wagons and the gold rush, becoming among its other firsts the first major road novel in U.S. literary history. Related to this is Steinbeck's attentiveness to the reciprocity between people and place. Dos Passos's characters never engage more than fleetingly with their physical environments, urban or rural. Real estate in *U.S.A.* is just that: asset, not affect. In *Grapes of Wrath*, much more the naturalist novel in this respect, the symbiosis between personhood and physical place is crucial; at-homeness or the lack thereof matters intensely. Sociocultural landscapes are always also ecological.[51] Finally, although as we've seen *U.S.A.* stacks the racial deck by foregrounding native-born white characters, next to *Grapes of Wrath* it looks almost multicultural. The Mexicans and Asians who comprised a substantial percentage of the 1930s California migrant labor force are invisible in *Grapes of Wrath*, which dismisses them as bygone (*GOW* 231–232) and presents the Okies as the sole victims of big-grower exploitation. Steinbeck's protest journalism was still more pointed. Whereas "the earlier foreign migrants invariably" came "from a peon class," the new ones are "resourceful and intelligent Americans." With them "the old methods of repression and starvation are not going to work; these are American people"—of "English, German and Scandinavian descent," proud American farmers for generations, and so on.[52]

Steinbeck was right that the Dust Bowl–driven influx had changed the face of the California migrant workforce. His contemporary Carey McWilliams, a far more informed and dedicated pro-migrant activist acutely mindful of the shameful exploitation of Mexican, Japanese, Chinese, and Filipino farm workers, went so far as to contend the same year that *Grapes of Wrath* was published that the shifting demography of the "labor-camp population," 50 percent of it "native white American" as early as 1934, meant that "the race problem" had "largely been eliminated," leaving no pretext for equivocation about whether to remediate the appalling conditions of the past half century, especially given the unanimous testimony of "field investigators" that the "dust-bowl refugees are orderly, neighborly—a patient and kindly folk" who quickly assimilate.[53] Historical accuracy aside, however, playing the race card as forcibly as it did clearly helped bring *The Grapes of Wrath* to the fore, among tastemakers as well as general audiences. In his *New Yorker* review, for instance, Clifton Fadiman prophesied that *Grapes of Wrath* might become a contemporary *Les Miserables* or *Uncle Tom's Cabin* or *The Jungle* for its exposé of "the slow murder" of "a people of old American stock, not Reds or rebels of any kind." Indeed, he continued, "if ever The Great American Novel is written, it may very possibly be composed along the lines here laid out by Steinbeck."[54]

Today this pronouncement seems so tunneled—it's hard to think of a plausible candidate for a Great American Novel since 1940 except for John Updike's *Rabbit Angstrom* so exclusively focused on the phenomenon of white Protestant culture under duress—that it takes a large effort to realize how self-evident it would have seemed to the U.S. critical establishment and to mainstream reading audiences of 1940. Ellison's master metaphor of invisibility a dozen years later spoke all too trenchantly to the gap between the demographic realities on the ground and the inertial force of mainstream national memory.

Not that the power of Steinbeck's novel, either then or now, can be equated with its populist appeal to white agrarian nostalgia, as if *The Grapes of Wrath* were nothing more than a southwestern *Gone with the Wind*. For one thing, like McWilliams Steinbeck deployed the Okies' like-usness strategically, to gain a hearing for amelioration of migrant worker conditions generally from a predominantly white readership. By no coincidence was *Grapes of Wrath*—its plotline, its structure, its human drama—an inspirational text for Isabel Wilkerson's much-acclaimed documentary narrative of the African American Great Migration, *The Warmth of Other Suns* (2010), which similarly interweaves panoramic social history with the sagas of several representative families who dared to make the risky venture.[55] This is only one example of how the reach of what Don DeLillo has called Steinbeck's "geography of conscience" has proven to stretch across ethnoracial boundaries to include "the joys and tribulations of common people, farmers, the uprooted" generally, as Chicano novelist Rudolfo Anaya attests. Native American writer-critic Louis Owens wryly recalls his "slightly disparaging" remarks about Steinbeck's stereotyping of Mexican Americans being challenged by two "middle-aged Latinos" in the audience at a Steinbeck festival, both self-identified farm workers who affirmed that Steinbeck's fiction spoke to them.[56] In fact *The Grapes of Wrath* delivers a more flexible and pluriform conception of what counts as a human community of worth arising from its faith in the instinctive neighborliness that can prompt bottom-dog strangers to help one another. Community can be identified with kin, with neighborhood, with occupational group or work unit, with strangers helping each other on the road or in a camp like the federally run sanctuary that harbors the Joads for a time,[57] and ultimately with the neo-transcendental sense of human totality that helps draw Tom into labor activism: "maybe . . . a fella ain't got a soul of his own, but on'y a piece of a big one" (*GOW* 419). At every stage, like appearance and folkways promote solidarity, to be sure. But that hardly defines the limit of the mystery of human solidarity as *Grapes of Wrath* understands it. Hence the calculated strangeness of the closing image, which swerves from character probability in order to dare the reader to look away from the uncanny scene of Rose of Sharon smiling "mysteriously" as she breast-feeds the emaciated, maybe dying stranger (*GOW* 455), a "selfless gesture" that as Barbara Foley notes "makes little sense in terms of individual character development" yet "works well as an indicator that Ma Joad's collective outlook has won out."[58]

Between *U.S.A.* and *The Grapes of Wrath*, however, Dos Passos's less broadly popular trilogy would better anticipate the later monumental American novelistic evocations of social collectives during the Cold War era and beyond—Pynchon's *Gravity's Rainbow*, DeLillo's *Underworld*, Wallace's *Infinite Jest*. These too are self-consciously metafictional constructs in which human subjectivity is under threat of manipulation by powerful and increasingly ubiquitous technologies manifesting themselves by turns chaotically and hypersystemically, often in the form of media info-barrages echoed and mocked by garrulous, more-or-less ironic narrators.

Any such resemblances almost certainly have little or nothing to do with direct influence. Although the narratorial irony in Sartre's fictional tetralogy on World War II starting with *The Age of Reason* (1945) has a certain *U.S.A.*-like panoramic tinge and although Dos Passos helped inspire some of Alexander Solzhenitsyn's documentary and montage techniques in *August 1914* (1971), the only significant younger-generation American novelist to claim him as a formative inspiration was Norman Mailer, who was never so close an emulator as Edith Wharton was of Henry James, Richard Wright of Theodore Dreiser, or William Styron of William Faulkner. Mailer's *The Naked and the Dead* (1948), for instance, adapts *U.S.A.*'s biography genre for its "Time Machine" portraits of its heteroglot collective, the reconnaissance platoon charged with an ill-fated mission in the jungle of the Japanese-held Pacific island of Anopopei.[59] But the mission itself more closely resembles the voyage of the *Pequod* and the figure of General Cummings seems a latter-day Captain Ahab. So *The Naked and the Dead* is better conceived as one of the first novelistic fruits of the modern Melville revival than as a laying-on of hands from Dos Passos to the late twentieth century. That doesn't in itself refute the possibility of *U.S.A.*'s persistence as a kind of subterranean force, as cultural critic Alfred Kazin surmised in the 1980s: that "Dos Passos was a writer whom other writers will always imitate without knowing it." Without Dos Passos's invention of a "cinematic machine to record the momentum carrying an industrial mass society headlong into moral chaos," Kazin maintains, "a good deal of our present sophistication in fiction, in the classy new journalism, even in the formal writing of American history, would not exist."[60] Maybe so. But even if so, *U.S.A.*'s chief significance for U.S. literary history, unlike *Moby-Dick*'s, will probably continue to seem more like precedent than prototype for the later assaults on the GAN by the sociohistorical megafictions of the late twentieth century and beyond to which we now turn.

13

Late Twentieth-Century Maximalism

Pynchon's *Gravity's Rainbow*—and Its Rainbow

Except for that succession of the criminally insane who have enjoyed power since 1945, including the power to do something about it, most of the rest of us poor sheep have always been stuck with simple, standard fear. I think we all have tried to deal with this slow escalation of our helplessness and terror in the few ways open to us, from not thinking about it to going crazy from it. Somewhere on this spectrum of impotence is writing fiction about it.

—THOMAS PYNCHON, *Slow Learner* (1984)

No one at all is in the executive suite. What looks like a man is only a representation of a man who does what the organization requires. He (or it) does not run the machine; he *tends* it.

—CHARLES REICH, *The Greening of America* (1970)

EVEN AS "THE DREAM of the Great American Novel disintegrated," writes a leading literary historian of the 1960s, "the novels that continued to be written were some of the most staggeringly ambitious that America had produced."[1] He refers specifically to the contradictory aftereffects of what had seemed the demise of the "mystique of fiction" with the midcentury ascendancy of cinema and the collapse of the distinction between high and popular culture. The point applies with still greater force to the more extravagant "historiographic metafiction" of the 1970s and after,[2] in which the documentary and the fabulistic, apocalypse and parody, collide and congeal around intricately scene-shifting, sprawling plots with scores of dispersed actors and events that often turn on the decoding or exposure of cabals and conspiracies with world-historical stakes. Notable cases in point—they hardly exhaust the list—include Ishmael Reed's *Mumbo Jumbo* (1972), Thomas Pynchon's *Gravity's Rainbow* (1973), E. L. Doctorow's *Ragtime* (1975), William

Vollmann's in-progress *Seven Dreams* septet on Euro-dispossession of indigenous North America (1990–); Leslie Silko's *Almanac of the Dead* (1991), David Foster Wallace's *Infinite Jest* (1996), Don DeLillo's *Underworld* (1997), and Karen Tei Yamashita's *I Hotel* (2010).

Often a fetishized text or other material object and the challenge of "reading" it becomes a central focus: the secreted scriptures in Reed and Silko; the V-2 rocket and its fateful Schwarzgerät (black box) variation in Pynchon; the 1951 game-winning home-run baseball in *Underworld* (precisely the size of the nucleus of the atomic bomb detonated by the Soviets on the same day as the Giants-Dodgers playoff); the missing master copy of the last video made by Wallace's James Incandenza, also considered a weapon of mass destruction for its capacity to reduce viewers to addicts impelled to watch it repeatedly forever.

Several mutually reinforcing social anxieties converged in the 1960s to incentivize such projects, three perhaps especially: the sense of private lives as increasingly subject to powerful technologies of corporate and governmental manipulation; the Cold War, including the space race; and the fracturing of what in hindsight was perceived as a speciously harmonious era of postwar incremental prosperity and social liberalization by increased militancy on behalf of minority and women's rights, urban violence, the rise of the counterculture, and the divisive Vietnam War.

The resurgence of postrealist investment in maximalist conjuration of social textures and networks after the subjective turn of the 1940s and 1950s discussed in Chapter 6 can't be explained wholly in terms of social megatrends. It was predictable that the sheer accumulation of plots turning on the psyches of disaffected "outsiders," self-conceived if not socially defined—Salinger's *Catcher in the Rye*, Flannery O'Connor's *Wise Blood*, Ellison's *Invisible Man*, Wright's *The Outsider*, Bellow's *Henderson the Rain King*, Kerouac's coterie of dharma bums, Nabokov's *Lolita*, Kenneth Kesey's *One Flew over the Cuckoo's Nest*, Roth's *Portnoy's Complaint*—should produce a countermovement toward thicker contexting of such aberrancies. Then too the border between "fiction" and "history" became increasingly blurred during the 1960s and after with the rise of such research-based genres as neo–slave fiction and "nonfiction" novels like Capote's reconstruction of a gruesome Nebraska murder case in *In Cold Blood* (1966) and with the "new journalism" of Norman

Mailer's *Armies of the Night* (1968) and Tom Wolfe's *The Electric Kool-Aid Acid Test* (1968). It was only a matter of time before novelists would start claiming—or taking for granted—that "there is no fiction or non-fiction as we commonly understand the distinction: there is only narrative."[3] This line of thinking also resonated with the turn in critical theory toward reconceiving scholarly analysis as discourse. Clifford Geertz influentially defined the work of ethnography as close reading and "thick description" of cultural practice. Hayden White and other "metahistorians" argued that historical writing was structured less by listening to one's data than by characteristic narrative strategies and tropes. Paul de Man, the most influential agent of the poststructuralist revolution in U.S. literary theory at the time, went so far as to insist (1971) that "what they call anthropology, linguistics, psychoanalysis is nothing but literature reappearing, like the Hydra's head, in the very spot where it had supposedly been suppressed."[4]

The symbiosis between academic and creative projects was reinforced by the rise of creative writing programs within college and university curricula after World War II, such that during the late twentieth century an increasing number of U.S. writers were drawn in as students, faculty, visitors, or occasional performers—including all seven of the novelists mentioned at the outset.[5] Reed, Wallace, and Yamashita have, or had, long careers as academics. Doctorow, DeLillo, and Silko have done extensive stints as writers in residence. Creative writing workshops taken as a Cornell undergraduate helped Pynchon transition from engineering physics to fiction.

One consequence of this symbiosis was to give serious late-century fiction an unprecedentedly academic tinge. There is a world of difference between Willa Cather's *The Professor's House* (1925), in which the protagonist's life as teacher-scholar is largely relegated to backstory, and such late-century campus-centric novels as John Barth's *Giles Goat-Boy* (1966), whose protagonist is the birth child of the university computer, and DeLillo's *White Noise* (1985), which foregrounds a non-German-speaking professor's fraudulent expertise in "Hitler Studies." These are only the most obvious symptom of a more pervasive tendency. Reed's *Mumbo Jumbo* was clearly enabled by the rise of Afro-American studies, especially the rediscovery of the Harlem Renaissance and intensification of claims earlier African American intellectuals like Ellison had made for the power of black music as a force in American culture at large (here hilariously instanced by the "Jes' Grew" "epidemic" that induces exuberant hyperactivity deemed subversive by the straight-laced white authority figures who try to stamp it out). The reception of Silko's *Almanac of the Dead*'s scene of indigenous resistance to corrupt, repressive regimes both capitalist and Marxist was pre-prepared by the hemispheric turn in American studies quickened by late twentieth-century Native and Chicano activism, as the civil rights movement of the 1950s and 1960s had helped catalyze Afro-American studies. Yamashita's *I Hotel* focuses on the history and consequences of Yellow Power militancy on and around California campuses in the 1960s.

The scene collectively showcased by the latter three brainy, inventive, and ambitious novels has troubled readers skittish about the consequences of "multiculturalism," insofar as they seem to define a literary marketplace with trend lines defined by a fissiparous patchwork of imagined ethnic identitarianisms that the so-called culture wars within academia have been blamed for provoking. Using Silko's *Almanac* as a case in point, critic Walter Benn Michaels goes so far as to accuse fictional critiques of racial injustice of functioning as a distracting cover-up of economic injustice under capitalism.[6] But as we've seen in earlier chapters, contemporary academia didn't invent subnational identitarianism. In U.S. literary history, the ethnic and regional versions of it date back to colonial times. Nor is it a uniquely U.S.-national practice to fictionalize nationness from the ethnogeographical margins. More or less the same now holds throughout the English-speaking world, as in the fiction of Amitav Ghosh, Zakes Mda, Alexis Wright, Thea Astley, Keri Hulme, and Albert Wendt, to name a few of the many distinguished practitioners.

A more serious charge against the academicization of creative writing is its alleged propensity to cater to "the mediated satisfaction of classroom exegesis." The aging Leslie Fiedler grumbled in 1980 that this held not only for writers like John Barth and William Gass who had "made their permanent homes in the university" but even for many sometime denizens like Nabokov and Donald Barthelme and those "who spurn it utterly, like Thomas Pynchon." All, Fiedler lamented, "end up by addressing merely themselves and their post-modernist critics, who, in turn, address only each other."[7] Yet here too allegation overstates its case. The careers of Wallace Stegner (Stanford), Joyce Carol Oates (Wayne State, Princeton), and Marilynne Robinson (Iowa Writers Workshop), among many others, are proof positive that novelists can spend entire working lifetimes closely attached to creative writing programs without sacrificing accessibility to broader audiences. Nor are most of the books I ticked off at the outset inaccessible reads. At least one, *Ragtime,* was a best seller. But what about the novel on which this chapter centers, Pynchon's *Gravity's Rainbow?* It was by far the most formidably "researched" and polymorphically allusive novel yet published by a U.S. writer, compared to which even Joyce's *Ulysses* seems like "play for a child-detective," as a penetrating reader of both novels wryly puts it.[8] Fiedler's ghost would take it as confirmation of the perversely cloistral drift he saw in contemporary U.S. fiction to single out *Gravity's Rainbow* as a late twentieth-century equivalent of *Moby-Dick.*

Yet the choice makes sense. *Gravity's Rainbow*'s status as a benchmark for later achievement can't be denied. Wallace's *Infinite Jest* acknowledges that in scene one, when the intimidated narrator stares "into the Kekuléan knot of the middle Dean's necktie," a winking nod to the nineteenth-century German scientist's dream of the shape of the benzene ring *Gravity's Rainbow* holds up as the epiphany that led to the invention of chemical synthetics, and with it the crucial breakdown of the distinction between the realms of animate and inanimate.[9] A number of the signature ingredients of *Gravity's Rainbow*'s landscape— transnational gamesmanship among elites in which subalterns figure as disposable pawns and take precarious refuge in squalid undergrounds; the equation of technology with scatology and waste, both material and symbolic; addiction conceived simultaneously as escape and as instrument of social control—get replayed in Wallace's and DeLillo's fin de siècle blockbusters, and not just there alone. But the main reason for singling out *Gravity's Rainbow* is the work itself—the scope of its knowledge base, its geographical and historical reach, its nuanced and multilayered subtlety of implication, the epochal significance of its narrative backbone, and finally but not least—for now at least—its staying power as a landmark achievement still "widely recognized" after almost half a century "as the most important American novel published since World War II."[10]

Melville, Dos Passos, Pynchon

Moby-Dick had to wait the better part of a century to get its due, but since the 1940s its status as the most imposing premodern U.S. novel has seemed secure, whereas *U.S.A.* was recognized at once as the most masterful fictive encapsulation of the first third of the "American century," only to fade from view. Of the novelists named above only Doctorow seems to have read Dos Passos at all attentively.[11] *Gravity's Rainbow* makes a striking commentary on those different outcomes. As an encyclopedic metafiction of big metaphysical and geohistorical stakes built around hubristic/quixotic questing after an ultimate symbol of phallic power, it comes so close to seeming a twentieth-century reinvention of *Moby-Dick* that the rest of this chapter could easily be given over to the ways the one book reprises the other, many of them surely not coincidental even when *Gravity's Rainbow*'s text gives no overt sign. What else, for instance, is the erotically hypersensitive Impolex G polymer suit forced upon Greta, and then Gottfried, but a reinvention of the mincer's "cassock" in chapter 99 of *Moby-Dick*—the whale's penis turned inside out, which equips him for the work of his "archbishoprick" of blubber cutter for the hellish furnace of the try-pots (*MD* 324–325)? As for Dos Passos, Pynchon's representation of advanced industrial modernization as a bewilderingly bureaucratized social order that entraps even its power figures in "we-they" systems seemingly owes nothing to *U.S.A.*'s account of the perversion of industrial democracy, even though *Gravity's Rainbow* is on the same page with *U.S.A.*'s diagnosis that world war was promoted by and in turn quickened the ascendancy of self-serving modern techno-economic systems hierarchical and bureaucratized to the point of impenetrability, and therefore disruptive, destructive, and chaotic in their effects. The same goes for Pynchon's later *Against the Day* (2006), which covers a good deal of the same historical ground that Dos Passos had.

But even if Melville had not been hypercanonized, even if Dos Passos's brand of quasi-experimental chronicle fiction had not fallen off the critical radar screen, it would have made sense for *Gravity's Rainbow* to be less reminiscent of *U.S.A.* than of *Moby-Dick*. For one thing, the human conquest of nature was for Dos Passos a fait accompli of marginal interest by contrast to the gap thereby opened up between human haves and have-nots, whereas in the fictional worlds of Melville and

Pynchon the historic significance and romantic/demonic hubris of that attempted conquest are of utmost urgency. *Moby-Dick* and *Gravity's Rainbow* both have strongly ecological thrusts: *Moby-Dick*'s book-long meditation on cross-species links (and antipathies) between human and cetacean, human and nonhuman generally; *Gravity's Rainbow*'s anatomy of the doleful upshot of the synthetics revolution.[12] Relatedly, *U.S.A.* lacks Melville's and Pynchon's fascination with technodetail, with the arcana of whaling or ballistics as the case may be, with the minutiae of whaling vessels or rocket design. Here both *Moby-Dick* and *Gravity's Rainbow* build on the long penchant in U.S. fiction for infusing utilitarian data with a sense of larger stakes. Richard Henry Dana's *Two Years before the Mast*, the slaughterhouse scenes in Sinclair's *The Jungle*, Dreiser's anatomy of the Griffiths shirt collar factory in *American Tragedy*, Wallace's *Infinite Jest* on tennis and recreational drugs are a few other cases in point.[13]

Then too, *Gravity's Rainbow* resembles *Moby-Dick* more closely than *U.S.A.* in its emphasis on regimes of surveillance as a definer of its imagined world. Although *U.S.A.* anticipated what historians of national security now consider axiomatic, that the initial groundwork for modern state propaganda and espionage apparatuses was set in place during World War I,[14] Dos Passos does little with this insight except for cursory reminders in *1919* like the signs in European public places warning that the enemy is listening. For Dos Passos, infiltrators and secret services are chiefly not governmental but private outfits like Pinkerton detectives and corporate goon squads employed reactively to quell labor agitation. In the worlds of *Moby-Dick* and *Gravity's Rainbow*, more proactive and pervasive manipulation is seen as needed to keep the pawns in place.

In keeping with the rigid shipboard discipline enforced on whalers' notoriously raggle-taggle crews, little happens on the *Pequod* that is not both ordered and intensely watched. Ishmael's mental meanderings belie his own role as a vigilant auxiliary monitor, rendered all the more hyperactive for the awareness that Ahab and Starbuck, Ahab and crew, eye each other warily throughout the voyage after the captain announces his resolve to hijack the voyage for his vendetta. In *Gravity's Rainbow* surveillance is intensified by wartime emergency, by state-of-the-art technology, and by the multiplicity of (internally rivalrous) governmental and corporate actors, and reintensified by the climate of

paranoid apprehensiveness all that induces. Just as *Moby-Dick* lends itself to allegorization as a paranoid fable of the ship of state turned authoritarian in reaction to the threats posed by the failed European
revolutions of 1848 and ideological conflict at home, so *Gravity's Rainbow* lends itself to allegorization as a fable of Cold War conspiracy fears
intensified by the concurrence of the Vietnam War with the space race,
for which World War II was the launching pad.

Far more even than Melville, Pynchon clearly "swam through libraries" (*MD* 116) in order to write *Gravity's Rainbow*—a massively intensified research effort by contrast to his earlier fiction. The copious
archive on Germany's interwar industrial and military resurgence; the
history of collusion of Allied business interests in that buildup; the development of early rocket science from inception to co-optation by the
military; the competition between Allied powers to take possession of
German land and its military-technological secrets; the links between
militarism, racism, and genocide in German history dating back to the
conquest of South-West Africa (now Namibia) at the turn of the twentieth century—all this *Gravity's Rainbow* has assimilated and much
more.[15] The way for *Gravity's Rainbow* was further prepared by the increasing World War II–inspired archive of Euro-American film and
fiction that showcased military-industrial bureaucratization, gamesmanship, and corruption from Thomas Heggen's *Mister Roberts* (1946,
later a popular play, film, and TV series), Mailer's *The Naked and the
Dead* (1948), James Jones's *From Here to Eternity* (1951), Faulkner's *A
Fable* (1954, nominally set during World War I), Joseph Heller's *Catch-
22* (1961), and Kurt Vonnegut's *Slaughterhouse-Five* (1969). We may
never know what notice Pynchon took of these precursors, though it is
hard to imagine that Heller's cartoonlike ethnography of military culture and the paranoid Yossarian's alienation and eventual desertion
would have failed to interest him. However that may be, Pynchon's
early fame on the basis of *V.* and *The Crying of Lot 49*, both tricksy and
intricate novels but with more accessible detective plots also turning on
inconclusive attempts to penetrate seeming conspiracies of global scope,
would also have made readers more receptive to the whopper of *Gravity's Rainbow* and helped sustain his fame despite his disappearance
from public view and the dearth of substantial new work for nearly two
decades, until *Vineland* (1990). That *V.* and *Crying of Lot 49* both became
avant-garde and popular sellers—topping three million copies apiece

by century's end—helps explain how the immensely more difficult *Gravity's Rainbow* sold as many as 300,000 copies within a decade.*

Plotlines

Gravity's Rainbow's labyrinthine plot focuses on the last months of World War II and their aftermath, November 1944 to autumn 1945. Its historical nexus is Germany's development of the V-2 rocket (A-4 in German coding), the prototype for Cold War intercontinental ballistic missile systems; the damage to Britain and panic caused after the rocket finally became operational in September 1944; and attempts by the Allies to defend against it and get their hands on rockets, blueprints, and key enemy scientists and engineers as the Reich collapsed. The novel is bookended by surrealistic scenes: 1944 London under siege as hallucinated in the predawn nightmare of British intelligence agent "Pirate" Prentice, and a glimpse of a 1970s Los Angeles theater managed by a parody version of then-President Nixon seemingly on the verge of being struck by an ICBM (recalling an actual early V-2 bombing of a crowded cinema in Belgium). The arc from one missile phantasmagoria to another a quarter century later is one of many ways in which *Gravity's Rainbow* insinuates the present-time aftereffects of 1944–1945.[16]

To the extent a 760-page novel ranging across five continents that deploys several hundred named characters spanning more than a century of modern history but with retrospects that stretch back to the dawn of Eurocolonization can be said to have a protagonist, he is Lieutenant Tyrone Slothrop. Slothrop is a New England WASP from a small

---

* For these statistics and more, see publisher Gerald Howard, "Pynchon from A to V," *Bookforum* (Summer 2005), http://bookforum.com/archive/sum_05/pynchon.html, a lively, informative memoir that recalls the author's first excited reading of the novel together with a friend as "metafiction therapy in the outer boroughs" when he was a newly minted, still unemployed Cornell graduate ("No overmarketed-to baby boomer could fail to identify with the suggestion that Slothrop has been from birth the subject of a secret experiment in behavioral modification"). The novel was "admittedly a slog" yet compelling to the end. Howard confesses that rereading it in 2004 on top of a full-time job was even harder work but affirms that *GR* "impressed me even more" the second time around, that "there is simply no work in all of American literature that approaches its staggering reach and erudition." Alongside the essay are sidebar tributes by such major contemporary novelists as Don DeLillo, Richard Powers, and Jeffrey Eugenides attesting to Pynchon's importance to them.

town in the Berkshires, a Harvard product a couple of classes behind John F. Kennedy. We first see him as a London-based Allied intelligence analyst—or, rather, we see the star-decorated map of London at his messy workstation being photographed by Pirate's roommate Teddy Bloat, because of what seems an uncanny correspondence between the location of Slothrop's sexual conquests and the sites of the supersonic V-2 blasts soon after. His erections interest Bloat's vaguely defined "Firm"—which includes the Foreign Office's political intelligence wing but with numberless tentacles extending across enemy lines interconnecting all major military-industrial establishments.[17] For the Firm knows (as Slothrop later discovers) that circa 1920 "infant Tyrone" was the subject of a penis-conditioning experiment by one Laslo Jamf, a Pavlovian psychologist and also research chemist who later developed for the German drug cartel IG Farben the sexually stimulating polymer Impolex G somehow connected with the V-2 program. The question of whether Slothrop's sex drives really do reflect some kind of conditioned anticipatory response to the rocket blasts is hotly debated, never resolved, and dwindles into a joke compared to the significance of his having been manipulated instrumentally by the powers that be almost from the cradle onward—in which respect Slothrop's singularity broadens into an exemplum of the human fallout of advanced scientific-industrial military modernism. As Tölölyan sums up, "readers begin by wanting to decipher the mystery of Slothrop's erections; by the end, it is the suspended Rocket and the ever-imminent war it symbolizes that become the dominating facts of the book."[18]

Although it's obvious from the start that *Gravity's Rainbow* will be more than a protagonist-centered affair, for the first three of the four unequal parts Slothrop's accident-ridden picaresque supplies the main thread. After interrogating him under sodium amytol ("truth serum"), for reasons not fully explained the Firm consigns him to a closely watched Monacan casino.[19] There his identity papers are stolen, presumably to keep him under wraps, and he is set to work mastering technical German and the caches of documents about the V-2 program sent in batches from London. Increasingly wary and fearful as familiar faces disappear and as he senses a sinister interlinkage between the rocket and an international conspiracy involving his own past, Slothrop escapes to Switzerland, then to Germany just as the war ends. In part 3, by far the longest, aided by a series of disguises he hopscotches around the devastated "Zone" that the Allied powers are racing to occupy. Strongly at first and intermittently thereafter, he's drawn toward the mysterious Schwarzgerät (black box) named in his top-secret documents as referring to a unique rocket design coded 00000 that is seemingly bound up with Jamf, Impolex G, and his own childhood. But he repeatedly gets sidetracked by sex and dope (including the IG product Oneirine, chemically close to Impolex); by having to evade the obese and scabrous American Major Marvy, who mistakes him for a spy; by run-ins with the Russian agent Tchitcherine, who's seen the Soviet dossier on his history; and by near-death from bullets and drowning. When he finally meets up with the underworld kingpin who can steer him to the S-gerät for a price, Slothrop is more eager to bargain for his identity and discharge papers and vamoose.

He succeeds at neither. He never tracks down the quintuple zero, though he hears about its firing and zips through the underground Nordhausen Mittlewerk factory where V-2s were assembled as well as what's left of Peenemünde, the bombed-over Baltic island site where much of the research and testing had been conducted. Nor does he get his papers at the rendezvous place on the German coast, narrowly missing capture and castration by the Firm's frustrated Pavlovian Pointsman, British intelligence's point man for monitoring Slothrop's sex life, now bent on terminating it.

In part 4 Slothrop pulls off his last escape—back into the Zone itself. Until now the novel has held up hope that he might find a way out. Even maybe within the Zone, "while all the fences are down," with "the Zone cleared, depolarized," Slothrop muses, "somewhere inside the waste of it a single set of coordinates from which to proceed, without elect, without preterite, without even nationality to fuck it up" (*GR* 556). No dice, it seems. Nations are already rushing in to take over. Institutions will reconsolidate. Slothrop's zigzaggings throughout part 3—whimsical to the reader, exasperating to those assigned to keep track—have mostly been reactive; and it's hinted, although only hinted, that they may have been even more "determined" than his London sexcapades, concerning which Pointsman's conditioned reflex theory seems less plausible than statistician Roger Mexico's countertheory of random "Poisson distribution" of sites of both rocket bombings and sex acts. In Monaco, the Firm had redeployed Dutch double agent Katje Borgesius from her assignment as sex slave to the novel's Nazi arch villain to seduce Slothrop, and assigned others to observe whether immersing himself in the stash of V-2 documents would make him hornier. In Berlin, ex-actress Greta Erdman coerces Slothrop, equipped now with the false ID of the liquidated Jewish actor who she's certain begot her daughter in a gang-rape SM film, to beat and fuck her repeatedly—her urgency intensified by the orgy that had been forced on her by German officers during the launch of the 00000. When Slothrop couples explosively with daughter Bianca soon after, their "singular detonation of touch" is likened to "the kingly voice of the Aggregat itself" (470). And Slothrop's final sexcapade, unbeknownst to himself, just happens to be with the estranged wife of Franz Pökler, the apparatchik chemist who designed the quintuple zero's special Impolex G encasement, whom Slothrop had met a few days before, disconsolately waiting for their daughter Ilse, conceived like Bianca by Franz's arousal over (watching) that selfsame SM film. This series of accidental-seeming encounters winds up reinforcing the links between Slothrop, rocket, and the multinational "preterite" subjugated to it.

So it makes a certain sociopsychological sense that when the long-manipulated Slothrop finds himself left alone, instead of recouping he seems to deliquesce. His identity, which had long since begun "to thin, to scatter" (*GR* 509)—we're told from the start that "a lot of stuff prior to 1944 is getting blurry" (21)—seems to disintegrate altogether. Soon Slothrop recedes from foregrounded to briefly spotted figure to overheard or rumored phantom.

For a time the goal of rescuing him or at least holding him in memory serves as a rallying point for the loosely defined "Counterforce." Most are disgruntled subalterns on the Allied side. The group includes Prentice, whose libido the Firm also commandeered for espionage; Katje, who repents gulling him; Roger Mexico, enraged at his lover's desertion; and the raunchy Seaman Bodine, a carryover from *V.* who's helped Slothrop out while enlisting him in his own cross-national drug deals. But the Counterforce, to appearances at least (more on this later on), amounts to nothing better than a bunch of loose cannons that can perpetrate carnivalesque disruptions of a board meeting or an evening party but not congeal into anything like a united front. Even who counts as Counterforce never gets defined with the specificity of the *Pequod*'s crew or *U.S.A.*'s dozen featured characters. Obviously, *Gravity's Rainbow* wants to suggest the *possibility* of some counterpublic insurgency of troublemakers that might also include even Tchitcherine and Enzian, the Zone-Herero leader, both of whom like Slothrop are on private V-2 missions at odds with their prescribed scripts, although neither seems closely linked to the Counterforce so-called. So the novel plays on readerly desire for a collective of the disempowered only to suggest almost at once the impossibility of a robust "We-system" emerging to oppose the dominant "They-system," as Pirate laconically sums up the best-case scenario to a flummoxed Roger (*GR* 638). In synchrony, the narrative consciousness itself fragments, insinuating that ever to have taken Slothrop's fate as the novel's central interest to begin with, and ever to have supposed that a Counterforce could take form, was wishful thinking.

After seeming to dispose of Slothrop and Counterforce, *Gravity's Rainbow* moves erratically but relentlessly toward its closing intimations of the Cold War era that will take shape from the ruins of World War II, capped by an apparently imminent rocket strike on the Los Angeles theater. Slothrop's disappearance is counterpointed by the escape to the United States of the horrific Captain Weissmann, aka Blicero, who has overseen the creation and launch of the *Schwarzgerät,* the unique quintuple zero rocket Slothrop has fitfully searched for. One scene near the end parses their discrepant fates through their tarot card readings, which "confirm" Slothrop's lowly status as Fool and Blicero's as a future master of the world.

Dominus Blicero (Weissmann's military code name, thus symbolically both lord of death and whiteness incarnate: Ahab and the whale rolled into one as it were) is a gothicized recasting of the twenty-something lieutenant who appears in the South-West Africa chapter of *V.* as the urbane escort of one of the avatars of the title figure, an adventuress with a taste for espionage who pops up throughout the early twentieth century in unstable regions of the earth. Weissmann/Blicero is a demented fetishist of rockets, sexually enticing young men, and quasi-mystical lust for transcendence that both forms of phallic power symbolize. Ignited in youth by the rhapsodic angelology of Rilke's *Duino Elegies* (1923), then by rapturous sex with his Herero protégé Enzian,[20] Weissmann rises to administrative chief of V-2 operations. But his ruling passions become his catamite Gottfried—a picture-perfect Aryan teenager who replaces an increasingly standoffish Enzian—and the quintuple-zero he fires off just before war's end, a V-2 uniquely tailored to contain the ritually bound and Impolex-wrapped Gottfried as payload and haplessly willing sacrifice. The rocket is fired due north, a direction militarily useless but symbolically fraught as the abode of death and the gods in Norse mythology—also the origin-place of Herero cosmology. Its preparation has been mentioned many times over and the story of its firing twice told by two imperfect witnesses, Greta and her husband Thanatz. But detailed narration is deferred till the very end, and by juxtaposing the 00000's 1945 ascent with the descent of the 1970s rocket on the L.A. theater, as if the two missiles must be one and the same. As, symbolically, they are.

American Genesis of the Modern Rocket State

By making its Yankee GI-protagonist disappear, *Gravity's Rainbow* provides a more extreme counterpart to Ishmael's suppression during the latter stages of *Moby-Dick* and Dos Passos's confinement of his autobiographical Camera Eye to intermittent recording device. Ishmael's defensive outburst in Chapter 1 predicts all three outcomes: "'Who aint a slave?'" (*MD* 21). Even as these focal figures command readerly interest as exemplars of relatively alert, sane, empathetic, fallible humanness, they get contained, contorted, eclipsed by mightier force fields. Hence too *Gravity's Rainbow*'s reprise of *Moby-Dick*'s spoofing its ostensible protagonist as a greenhorn bumpkin. The novel oscillates between framing Slothrop as plausible flesh-and-blood virtual person and as caricature. Sometimes he sounds like a possible Harvard man but more often talks in the "jeepers," "golly," "uh, but" babble of a dimwit middle schooler. Again and again his fantasy life and "real-time" action morph into the stuff of adventure comics, as when he eludes aerial pursuit of his balloon escape from Nordhausen by Marvy's foul-mouthed "Mothers" by splattering the crew with black-market pies. Slothrop's repertoire of disguises makes slapstick out of part 3's zigzag quest-flight-and-pursuit plot. In his next, decked out in a comic book–hero Rocketman suit, he conducts a sortie as absurd as he looks at the behest of the nutty Berlin host from whom he gets it to find a packet of hash buried on the grounds of the ad hoc "White House" at 2 Kaiserstrasse where Harry Truman, Joseph Stalin, and Clement Attlee are sealing the agreement to carve up Germany into zones of Allied control.

Poking fun at Slothrop/Rocketman's waywardness as a caricature of a bona fide sleuth threatens to undermine any lingering expectation that he (or anyone else in view) might pose a serious threat to the "Rocket-cartel" in the making, of which the trilateral Potsdam Agreement is to usher in the next stage. As his Soviet counterpart Tchitcherine later imagines the situation: "a State begins to take form in the stateless German night, a State that spans oceans and surface politics, sovereign as the International or the Church of Rome, and the Rocket is its soul. IG Racketen" (*GR* 566).* This intimation sums up the futuristic thrust of *Gravity's Rainbow*'s historical fable. The launching pad for this mega-state-in-the-making has been Germany's remilitarization, thanks especially to the formation of the giant IG Farben cartel, which developed a score of products from synthetic fuel and rubber to (never-utilized) poison gas for the massive Nazi war effort—a spectacular achievement enabled by a combination of R&D genius and shrewd deals with Western multinationals—more than 2,000 by 1939 including Standard Oil, DuPont, and Dow Chemical—from which IG benefited twice over by deploying their executives as lobbyists and buffers while maintaining strict control over IG's secret formulas. So, for instance, the United States remained rubber-strapped throughout the war despite Standard Oil's business relationship, which at the same time helped shield IG from military attack and serious postwar retribution.[21]

Pynchon might have chosen to spotlight other military-industrial collusions no less egregious, such as IBM's hugely profitable deals with its German subsidiary to supply state-of-the-art computation technology for swift, efficient census-taking and identity cards for Jews within the expanding Reich, even the planning of train schedules that incorporated concentration camps into the national railway system.[22] Perhaps he should have. *Gravity's Rainbow* might be questioned for confronting the Holocaust no more than obliquely, as in its treatment of the bygone German genocide of the Herero in its African colony, the fairy-tale framing of Blicero as wicked witch tending the oven for which Gottfried-Katje/Hansel-Gretel may be destined, and the skein of

---

* Also deployed to find the S-gerät but also on a mission of his own, Tchitcherine has a grudge against his black half-brother Enzian (conceived during their sailor-father's 1904 layover in an African port), whose existence he blames—wrongly it's suggested—for compromising his record so that his career ambitions were derailed by banishment to central Asia. So if any Allied agent is a logical candidate to "destroy the blacks" it would be Tchitcherine, although in the end the confrontation with Enzian proves a nonevent. Thanks to the spell cast by his witch-lover, they meet without recognizing each other.

references to Camp Dora, originally part of Buchenwald, that supplied the slave labor—virtually all non-Jewish—for the excruciatingly difficult construction of the underground Nordhausen Mittlewerk production site. Engaging IBM informatics would have had the additional advantage of bringing up to date *Gravity's Rainbow*'s depiction of human thought and behavior regulated by regimes of what Michel Foucault was to call "biopower"; for by century's end the info-tech revolution would be held up as the culminating factor in effecting the "control revolution" that enabled the unprecedented invasiveness of private lives by techno-bureaucratic regimes today.[23] However one judges *Gravity's Rainbow*'s tactics here, Pynchon's commitment to reconstruct the Rocket State's origins and possible future makes it understandable that he should have opted to build centrally on the man-as-mechanical-system model of early stage cybernetics and to conceive holocaust as part of a long-term planetary-scale process of regime oppression begun under colonialism but vastly accelerated by the techno-modernity of the Third Reich war machine and the clandestine networks of international politico-economic-military collusion of which it was a part, as were the Allies also.

The novel's inception point for this process, anchoring *Gravity's Rainbow*'s claim as a landmark of U.S. fiction despite an imagined geography much more Euroglobal than U.S.-national, is the career of Slothrop's first colonial ancestor, pictured as a member of the first band of Puritan settlers who sailed on the *Arabella* (1630) under John Winthrop. This fictive William Slothrop, a ship's cook–turned–pig farmer, puckishly recalls the author's forebear William Pynchon, first settler and governor of present-day Springfield, Massachusetts, a Puritan grandee made prosperous by the fur trade. Pynchon's rendition of the heresy that drove the historical Pynchon back to England in 1652 is more serious, though also drolly rendered. *The Meritorious Price of Our Redemption* (1650) and *The Jewes Synagogue* (1652) challenged orthodox Puritan Calvinism's dogma that Jesus died only for the elect and its efforts to limit church membership to the ranks of the (seemingly) elect alone, provoking further offense among the latter by appealing to the inclusiveness of ancient synagogues as a model for Protestantism.[24] *Gravity's Rainbow*'s version of this is William Slothrop's treatise *On Preterition*, which lodges a claim on behalf of the "holiness" of the unwashed "without whom there'd be no elect" (*GR* 555). The novel imagines him dreaming up the idea out of sympathy for the pigs he drives overland from Berkshire to Boston for market.

Long before this flashback, "preterite" has been the novel's conjuring term for disposable populations of whatever time, place, and ethnicity manipulated and destroyed at will by the powers that be. This stretchable category potentially seems to include everyone not in positions of high authority as well as many who fancy they are.* To trace its antecedence back to Puritan Calvinism's stark binary of elect versus damned confirms that the imagined future Rocket State originated not in modern colonial conquests like Germany's in Africa or the Soviets' of central Asia but the Reformation theology that propelled the Puritan sortie and the founding of Harvard. So there's a direct line of descent from seventeenth-century Puritanism to German industrial modernism. It makes perfect cultural-historical sense that Laslo Jamf should pop up as a Cambridge-based experimenter in between stints as instructor in Munich's institute of technology and IG Farben research chemist; that Tyrone's high-rolling "Uncle" Lyle Bland—whose later mysterious rapture into a Masonic otherworld sardonically confirms his status among the Elect—should have cooked deals with the shady German financier Hugo Stinnes to print the Deutschmarks that fueled Weimar hyperinflation at the "Slothrop Paper Company" on whose board he then sat; and that an IG Farben agent working for the Berkshire branch of General Electric (itself in cahoots with Siemens) to which Bland's "Institute" has subcontracted part of an "electronic-surveillance" design program for the "then-fledgling FBI" should be assigned the long-term monitoring of young Slothrop (*GR* 285, 583).[25]

Mad Captains and Whale Rockets

The future of the Euro-American continuum that links post-Puritan America to Third Reich Germany is augured by Weissmann/Blicero's prophesied escape to high places in the boardrooms of the United States.

---

* Pynchon reinforces the idea of ruthless, fruitless Eurosettler targeting of disposable creatures on the colonial periphery from the seventeenth century onward and also extends the concept of "preterite" to nonhumans by flashbacks to Katje's seventeenth-century ancestor Franz Van der Groov (*GR* 108–111), another pig farmer whose inexplicable hatred of dodos is shown as hastening their extinction on Mauritius.

440 Script Four: Improbable Communities

In no way is this character an even halfway plausible mimesis of a human being. He's the least so of any in *Gravity's Rainbow*'s bestiary— and that is really saying something. He's the example par excellence of people metamorphosing into monsters by indulging will to power, or subjection, to the uttermost. Captain Ahab hardening himself into the image of the thing he hates, hyperintensified by modern technopower, which enables far greater excesses than Melville ever dreamed of. Gottfried's abjection, Katje's compliance when under Blicero's (and others') control, and to a lesser extent the attenuated but lingering loyalty of Enzian to his old mentor/lover ("Weissmann's Monster," Peenemünde colleagues call Enzian, *GR* 404) threaten to derealize them too into grotesques. Blicero's oft-quoted prophecy to Gottfried shortly before sending him off into space, of the imminent *translatio imperii* from European to U.S. dominance, sums up the world-historical stakes of his hubris: "In Africa, Asia, Amerindia, Oceania, Europe came and established its order of Analysis and Death. . . . In time the death-colonies grew strong enough to break away. But the impulse to empire, the mission to propagate death, the structure of it, kept on. Now we are in the last phase. American Death has come to occupy Europe. It has learned empire from its old metropolis" (*GR* 722).

But this is also the rant of a delusional madman haranguing his captive pupil. It's no more to be taken literally than the *"personal* hatred for the covalent bond" Franz Pökler remembers Laslo Jamf spewing out to his chemistry class (577). The passage suggests what might portend if the Bliceros of the world are allowed to have their way. In the wartime world of *Gravity's Rainbow,* this happens. The most spectacular manifestation is Blicero's sexual power games, which connect up with the novel's other explosive pornographic scenes of sadomasochism, polymorphous group orgy, coprophagia, and more conventional one-on-one couplings throughout the book. This produces a frisson that doubtless helps explain *Gravity's Rainbow*'s appeal as a cult classic for self-identified anti-mainstreamers (maybe even today some readers flip the pages for the juicy parts). But like the kinky Jacobean tragedy parodied in Pynchon's *The Crying of Lot 49,* the gratuitousness is also to the end of dramatizing a world gone mad.

Weissmann/Blicero's exploitation of the Nazi rocket program to subserve his own fixations obviously stands for Third Reich megalomania, and his escape for the impossibility of rebottling the genie given that the key players who stand to profit from warmongering can't be—and weren't—held to account. More historically significant, though, is the underlying story of the V-2's past and future. This story gives even the wildest fantasy elements in *Gravity's Rainbow* a certain probabilistic ground.

Military and political historians, war memoirists, and Pynchon critics all stress that the V-2 was a fearsome but hugely complex and expensive missile that took an inordinately long time to develop and proved less destructive than its predecessor, the V-1 "buzz bomb," which had almost as large a payload and was far cheaper. Dogged by mechanical failures, by vacillating support from the top brass (Hitler was warned in a dream that the V-2 would fail), by turf battles between the army and the SS, the V-2 finally "captured the imagination" of Nazi leaders. Awed by the film of a test launch, Joseph Goebbels proclaimed in the summer of 1944, "this missile will force England to her knees."[26] But prioritizing the V-2 required so great a deviation of human and material resources that it hastened the Reich's collapse. So the upshot was remembered by the general in charge, Walter Dornberger, as a case of backing come "too late" thanks to "the errors and neglect of high authority"; but more decisively, it was a wasteful preference of "the spectacular to the strategic."[27]

Gravity's Rainbow hyperintensifies this misdirection. If the V-2 was a dubious venture, the 00000 is totally useless. Weissmann/Blicero's fetishisms—cross-dressing, wicked-witch-tormenting-Hansel-and-Gretel games with Gottfried and Katje in their cages or forced into bizarre group sex, the erotic polymer, the arcane tailoring of the 00000's design—all these underscore the weird superfluity of Nazi phallocentrism. So too the baroque system of parallel tunnels of the underground Nordhausen Mittlewerk through which Marvy chases Slothrop. Their construction extracted an immense human cost, here accentuated by picturing their rough SS-like shape as a piece of elaborate political (and mathematical) symbolism designed by a fictitious underling of the Reich's chief architect, Albert Speer, a key V-2 backer.[28] So too the imaginary "Toiletship," which spoofs German fussiness about matters of hygiene and compartmentalization and "stands for all the absurd ideas that the war spawned and the laboratory proved useless, such as the Wehrmacht's work on sonic pulses, wind-generating weapons, and guns that shot around corners."[29]

Not that the Germans had a monopoly on gratuitous excrescence. The gaggle of operatives on the British side that populate the White Visitation, a converted abbey near the coastal town drolly named Ick Regis—Pavlovians, mediums, mystics, propaganda filmmakers, keyhole gazers, spies spying on each other—reflects the chaos of nutty reports Allied intelligence actually generated: "the Germans were going to fire huge tanks of poison gas to annihilate every inhabitant of Great Britain; they were going to bombard London with gigantic containers filled with a 'Red Death'; the curious structures on the French coast were really refrigerating apparatuses, designed to stop R.A.F. bombing by dropping ice clouds over England."[30] But the centerpiece remains the V-2, as feat of human engineering, as obsession, as charismatic symbol. On Pynchon's intricate/erudite/satirical phantasmagoria of its combined absurdity and epochal significance for the weaponization of rocketry *Gravity's Rainbow*'s stature as historiographic metafiction hinges.

The story of the events of 1944–1945 starts with the co-optation of the band of wonky theorists and experimenters ignited by the visions of space travel in Hermann Oberth's 1923 pamphlet *Die Rackete zu den Planetenraümen* by a resurgent military establishment looking for a way around prohibitions against German rearmament in the Treaty of Versailles—one way in which *Gravity's Rainbow* recalls *U.S.A.* on industrial modernization. The treaty left out rockets because they hadn't yet been invented. The VfR, as the fledgling German rocket society (Verein für Raumschiffahrt) was called for short, seems to have had no interest in military applications. But its eagerness for funding and legitimation made it all too willing to oblige the emerging war machine.

General Dornberger's right-hand man Wernher von Braun (1912–1977) was a precocious VfR enthusiast from his late teens who masterminded the Nazi missile program of which the V-2 became the top priority and went on to become the key figure in U.S. development of long-range ballistic missiles in the 1950s who also later oversaw the NASA space program culminating in the 1969 Apollo 11 moon shot. In 1951 he offered this self-serving though not altogether mendacious reminiscence of the VfR's acquiescence to military takeover: "we needed money, and the Army seemed willing to help us. . . . The idea of war seemed to us an absurdity. The Nazis weren't yet in power. We felt no moral scruples about the possible future use of our brainchild. We were interested solely in exploring outer space. It was simply a question with us of how the golden cow could be milked most successfully." Just six years out from his defection to the United States as a prize catch, von Braun was already well on his way to becoming, as his biographer Michael J. Neufeld puts it, a "bona fide American hero, the Western world's most prominent gladiator in a celestial contest with the Soviets."[31] With the launching of the first satellite to compete with Sputnik, von Braun made the cover of *Time* (1958); and his personal magnetism, his persuasiveness as spokesperson, and his track record as a superintelligent hard-driving engineer-manager made him a celebrity scientist and frequent guest at state affairs. When *Gravity's Rainbow* appeared in 1973, he was at the peak of his prestige.

Yet his ascent to the helm of NASA and the gratification of his primary passion as a scientist, space travel, had come only after devoting many years to developing ballistic missile technology for the U.S. military, as he had for the Nazis. However much he tried to distance himself from it, he continued to be dogged by his Nazi past, which included SS membership and oversight of slave labor both at Peenemünde and at Nordhausen Mittlewerk, which he always minimized and sometimes lied about. A euphemistic 1960 Hollywood film of his life starring Curt Jürgens was lukewarmly received; a succession of U.S. presidents from Eisenhower through Nixon were put off by his pushiness; and approval of a long-coveted presidential Medal of Science was extracted for the dying von Braun from a reluctant President Ford only after the 1976 election had been decided. As Neufeld sums up, he was memorable both "as one of the seminal engineers and scientists" of the century and as "a twentieth-century Faust," a symbol of "the temptation to work on weapons of mass destruction with an evil regime in return for the resources to carry out the research closest to one's heart."[32] His impeccable pedigree and physiognomy, his elite cosmopolitan education and social standing, combined with his managerial and engineering genius made it all too easy for him to adapt to and rise within the power structure both in Nazi Germany and Cold War America.

The specter of von Braun haunts *Gravity's Rainbow* from page 1 (part 1's epigraph mischievously quotes one of his later-life professions of faith after self-identifying as a Protestant believer),[33] as pervasively as the more embodied presence of Napoleon in Tolstoy's *War and Peace*. Indeed von Braun is as diffused throughout *Gravity's Rainbow* as the figure of Slothrop is "scattered all over the Zone" (*GR* 712). The novel's accomplishment as a work of historical imagination in this regard lies not in its sprinkling of allusions to the biographical figure, direct or indirect, but in the uncanny percolation through the capillaries of the novel of the contradictory ingredients of the "Rocketman" story of which von Braun was the real-life embodiment.* Almost no episode, scene, incident, personage is without pertinence. For present purposes, though, some broad brushstrokes should suffice.

Pökler's absorption into rocket development registers at different points the naive excitement of early VfR days; its Faustian bargain with the military with the choice "between building what the Army wanted" or "pushing on in chronic poverty" (*GR* 400–401); and the team spirit of intensive research when "no one could really claim credit 100% for any idea" and "specialization hardly mattered, class lines even less" across the spectrum "from von Braun the Prussian aristocrat, down to the likes of Pökler, who would eat an apple on the street" (402). Pökler's increasing self-abjection to this new "monastic order" becomes significant both plotwise and historically. That he became "an extension of the Rocket, long before it was ever built" makes him an ideal tool for manipulation by Weissmann, who later assigns him the secret mission of designing the 00000's special "plastic fairing" that will encase Gottfried (431), and ensures that even after he gets relocated from Peenemünde to Nordhausen and learns his wife and daughter are imprisoned at Dora a few yards from his workroom he will repress, as von Braun also seems to have done, the thought that there might be anything seriously amiss.

On Weissmann's orders, Pökler dutifully acquiesces to an act of extreme obedience actually performed by von Braun at Dornberger's urging: the risky business of standing on ground zero of a Polish test site in

* Direct references include the photograph of broken-armed von Braun on the eve of his thirty-third birthday (and imminent defection) (*GR* 237); Blicero/Weissmann's rejection ("not my department") of understrapper Pökler's plea for a budgetary increase (417), alluding to MIT mathematician/cabaret musician Tom Lehrer's satirical lyric on von Braun as a compartmentalizer; and the anticipatory reflection on the near-coincidence of von Braun's March 23 birthday and what we later find was the April 1 date of the 00000 firing with the impromptu "Rocket-raising" festival Slothrop stumbles on outside Berlin: "Soon it will come to the folk-attention how close Wernher von Braun's birthday is to the Spring Equinox, and the same German impulse that once rolled flower-boats through the towns and staged mock battles between young Spring and deathwhite old Winter will be erecting strange floral towers out in the clearings, and the young scientist-surrogate will be going round and round with old Gravity or some other such buffoon, and the children will be tickled and laugh" (361).

1944 in order to get a better view of possible rocket malfunction during flight.[34] Both in the novel and in history, this episode comes as part of the frenetic speed-up of work activity leading to the September 1944 rollout of the V-2, roiled by chaotic nonresolution of funding and top-down chain of command crises as well as the need to relocate operations from the bomb-vulnerable Peenemünde to the frenetically constructed Nordhausen Mittelwerk. Weissmann/Blicero's aberrant state is a gothicized intensification of von Braun's hyperactivity as he "rushed from factories to launch sites to construction projects,"[35] and the agitated distress of this section of Dornberger's memoir, Pynchon's chief inside source for the V-2 buildup.

Gottfried is the ultimate embodiment of what's said to be Pökler's typical "German" male compulsion to submit to authority as well as the perversity of the historical fact that the VfR cohort recruited for the military so readily acquiesced to the sacrifice of human lives for the sake of reaching the stars, even to the point of celebrating the human carnage wrought by the V-2s. Gottfried also recalls the epicene beauty of the teenage von Braun that led some VfRs to nickname him "Sonny Boy." "Physically," his older VfR colleague and memoirist Willy Ley remembered, "he happened to be a perfect example of the type labeled 'Aryan Nordic' by the Nazis during the years to come. He had bright blue eyes and light blond hair and one of my female relatives compared him to the famous photograph of Lord Douglas of Oscar Wilde fame."[36] Gottfried's abjectness—obedient to the demon unto death—reflects the historical von Braun's fixation on space travel from adolescence onward, whatever the cost.[37] Whether intentionally or not, Weissmann/Blicero's predatory exploitation of the smitten Gottfried also mockingly resonates with von Braun's reputation as (hetero)sexual idol as well as spare-time womanizer, not to mention his reputation for driving subordinates very hard.

Weissmann's Gottfried fetish and before him Enzian (whom Pökler and his colleagues then saw as "closest to the zero among them all, perhaps" [GR 404]), is only one of many ways in which the sexual charisma of rockets is dramatized throughout the text, most directly by the erotic polymer. So too Thanatz's uncontrollable erection at the launch of the S-gerät and the gang rape of the equally excited Greta. And Enzian and his band of (male) Zone Hereros seizing upon the rocket as symbol and their 00001 launch project as a path to recovery of lost manhood.

And Tchitcherine's lover Geli Tripping posing for a rocket insignia ("a pretty young witch straddling an A_4" she tells Slothrop [293]). And of course Slothrop's putatively conditioned erections.

Apocalypse When?

Given *Gravity's Rainbow*'s phantasmagoria of lethally misdirected rocket play and the conclusion toward which it seems to drive, nothing might seem more logical than to read the novel as an even grimmer account of victimization of ordinary humanity by those in power than the tragedy of the *Pequod*'s crew sacrificed for its commander's vengeance and the plutocracy's usurpation of the Lincoln republic in *U.S.A.* At the plot level, the bright line between "elite" and "preterite" seems reinforced by the fates of their main exemplars. Blicero/Weissmann escapes to future glory; Slothrop falls into oblivion. By labeling Weissmann "the father you will never quite manage to kill" (*GR* 747), the narrator backglances at earlier glimpses of Slothrop's father and "Uncle" Lyle Bland as part of the "They-system" that reduces even scions of the patriarchs to its tools.

In Wimpe's announcement to Tchitcherine of IG Farben as "the model for the very structure of nations" (*GR* 349) and Weissmann/Blicero's prophecy about the *translatio imperii* of the regime of death to contemporary America, *Gravity's Rainbow* invites a reading of world conspiracy, as critic Thomas Schaub puts it, that is not "fully psychotic" but rather "an 'operational paranoia' which discovers connections that have an actual basis in economic and political reality."[38] Read this way, *Gravity's Rainbow* seems a historical allegory of the inexorable upshot of Eurocolonization—England's of America, Holland's of Mauritius, Germany's of South-West Africa, Russia's of central Asia—the upshot of which is the late twentieth-century "colonization of Europe" by the coming Rocket State recentered in the United States thanks to the military-industrial cartel modeled by Germany and the advanced industrial technologies that have increasingly cyberneticized human life and displaced "natural" environments by transmuting them into engineered simulacra. From this standpoint, the Counterforce and the VfR are mirror images, collectivities that either can't achieve or can't maintain integrity against the "They-system."

The regime of instrumentalization potentially includes everybody, high as well as low. "To be a person in *Gravity's Rainbow*," writes critic Timothy Melley, "means to recognize . . . that your 'personality' might not be yours, that it constitutes and is constituted by global control structures." "Agency panic" kicks in with special force for lower-rung folk upon sensing their disposable pawnship.[39] As with Slothrop's spiraling dread as his assigned reading on the rocket program at the creepy casino pulls him backward toward forgotten early childhood and the realization that "all in his life of what has looked free or random" might turn out to have "been under some Control, all the time, the same as a fixed roulette wheel" (*GR* 209). But those in power aren't totally free agents either. Weissmann is as captive to the rocket as Pökler or Gottfried, and much more so than Slothrop. As Charles Reich tellingly declared in his classic 1960s indictment of corporate America, so too for *Gravity's Rainbow:* substantively, if not literally, "No one at all is in the executive suite."[40]

This scary prospect, not to mention the rocket's descent at the end, might seem to make for a(n even) more decisively apocalyptic closure than the sinking of the *Pequod* (for at least Ishmael survives) and *U.S.A.*'s vision of industrial democracy betrayed (for at least Mary and Vag remain to soldier on). For some readers, that intensified somberness will be what clinches the case for *Gravity's Rainbow* as the Great American Novel of the Cold War era—the ultimate fictive retort to the publishing mogul Henry Luce's proclamation that the twentieth was to be "The American Century," in a 1941 manifesto that made the phase a mantra.[41] Such a reading would also be in line with the overwhelming tendency of most GAN contenders to stress the failed promise of national destiny, with the additional advantage of situating *Gravity's Rainbow* as a prophetic anticipation of what might be called the revisionist grand counternarrative of American settlement culture history that has tended to define the anti-exceptionalist, postnational cast of thinking that has dominated turn-of-the-twenty-first-century American literature studies: From genocidal conquest to manifest destiny to new imperium. Yet hostile as the novel obviously is to American Century–style swagger, it delivers a less desperate retort than the author himself does in this chapter's first epigraph. It also resorts to a combination of strategic self-contradiction and farce to question its own seeming premise that the forces of "Control" have actually seized total control.

As to self-contradiction, critic Ursula Heise notes four dissonant assumptions at the macro level about temporality interwoven throughout
the text.* A reading of *Gravity's Rainbow* that presses the apocalyptic
closure thesis effectively privileges the first, cause and effect, over the rest
despite the discreditation of its leading theorist, Pointsman. The "catastrophic" finale, Heise stresses, is never shown. Extinction by rocket looms,
but it doesn't happen (yet). By contrast, Pynchon's next novel, *Vineland*
(1990), delivers much tidier closure—of a traditionally melodramatic sort
in fact. But *Gravity's Rainbow* ends more like novels one and two, which
break off with the mysteries of V. and the Tristero unresolved.

This leaves the door open a crack as to whether the dystopian Rocket
State death trip is inevitable. So too does placing the crucial prophecy in
a lunatic's mouth. Equally suggestive is *Gravity's Rainbow*'s depolarization of conventional images of U.S. versus USSR Cold War struggle as a
Manichaean battle between good and evil ideologies. This it does partly
by feathering in scattered instances of generally polite exchange within
the Zone, but especially in the sympatico that develops between Tchitcherine and Slothrop.

Both are on personal quests shadowed by paranoid fear of manipulation by IG Farben/military intelligence combines. Each gets doped
with Oneirine and sodium amatol; each is a reengineered cyborg,
counting Slothrop's penis as well as Tchitcherine's metallic prostheses.
The sex lives of both have long been monitored. Both are headed for
obscurity if not extinction far from home. Tchitcherine's empathy at
Potsdam for the Slothrop whom he's just nabbed and drugged ("in any
normal period of history they could easily be friends") (*GR* 390) is replayed in their curiously non-rancorous encounter at Peenemünde. As
Slothrop makes them switch uniforms—symbolic in itself—after getting
the drop on the Russians, Tchitcherine banters about the "Schwarzphän-
omenon" hang-ups that torque both their foraging around the Zone
into identitarian quests (513)—Tchitcherine's for his black half-brother,
Slothrop's for the link between his Schwarzknabe past and the S-gerät
(286).[42] That Tchitcherine knows before they meet that Slothrop has

---

* Namely, cause and effect, statistical probabalism, concurrence, and what Heise calls
ontological pluralism: e.g., the imagination of a parallel spirit realm of "the other side"
existing alongside chronological time (Ursula Heise, *Cronoschisms: Time, Narrative, and
Postmodernism* [Cambridge: Cambridge University Press, 1997], 179–218).

bedded down with his mistress Geli seemingly matters not at all. Their intertwinement runs counter to the closing intimation of apocalypse. That seems precisely the point: to suggest a counterpoise to the Cold War paranoia—even though both Slothrop and Tchitcherine are themselves paranoid—upon which the closing image of an apparent 1970s missile attack on Los Angeles seems to play.

The kinship between Slothrop and Tchitcherine, if that's not too strong a word for it, anticipates the kind of conciliatory hands-across-the-divide gesture found in such Vietnam-era dissent literature as Wendell Berry's "To a Siberian Woodsman" (1968), which imagines his counterpart on the other side of the world enjoying a similar moment of bucolic peace: "In the thought of you I imagine myself free of the weapons and the official hates that I have borne on my back like a hump."[43] In *Gravity's Rainbow* the depolarization gesture is less sentimentalized for being embodied in tense confrontations and for being timed prior to the schism between governments so as to hint, though only hint, that the official narrative of Cold War polarization might never have held at the grass roots.

But parodistic farce is the novel's chief reliance for questioning its ostensible diagnosis of the impending order of Rocket State total control and the Manichaean ideology undergirding it. Here Slothrop's deliquescence works against as well as for the "operational paranoia" thesis. His absurd impersonation of Rocketman zigzagging around the Zone and generating funky/fabulous legends in his wake parodies the juggernaut that seems about to crush him and underscores the farcical element of the rocket-launching folk festival he stumbles across near the time of von Braun's birthday. Rocketman's comic hijinks makes Blicero's high passion silly. Picturing Blicero bewigged in high drag—Slothrop too, later on—is another form of silliness, however creepy. By no means is it clear that he disintegrates by becoming preempted by or "identified with the social order."[44] Even as the Counterforce scatters, and Slothrop too, a Slothrop effect persists as a pesky disruptive element, like the offstage "mouth harp" blues (*GR* 642) overheard by Pfc. Eddie Penseroso as he prepares to give the major from Kenosha a perhaps lethal haircut. From start to finish the protean narrator's own shifty multi-tonalism is inseparable from this Slothrop effect.

True, the novel's last long glimpse of him wandering about naked and hirsute with his miraculously rediscovered harmonica as his sense of purpose trickles away, playfully hippyish and redolent with hints of symbolic rebirth, turns somber as he metamorphoses into a symbolic "crossroad," reminiscent of how executed witches were buried in olden times (*GR* 626). His fragmentation can't be decoupled from the legend of Orpheus torn apart by the Maenads. Yet the comic tweaking of Orphean lyre into Yankee mouth organ, reducing Slothrop's folk-hero pretensions to the "singing nincompoop" Tannhäuser (364), sends a snicker through the seeming high seriousness of the contrast between his tarot and Weissmann's. The same holds for how the closing scenes toggle between the rapt fury of Weissmann/Blicero launching Gottfried into space and the 1970s "catastrophe" sequence, whose first frame (titled "Orpheus Puts Down Harp") opens with a farcical rendition of Richard Zhlubb/Nixon as Orpheus Theater manager fulminating against the "irresponsible use of the harmonica" (754) only to be serenaded by a "caravan of harmonica players" (Slothrop's final toot, as it were) on the Hollywood Freeway, as Zhlubb fantasizes death by random garbage bag blown in through car window ("A plastic shroud, smothering me") (756). This absurdity pulls against the seeming superseriousness of the snapshot soon after of space-bound Gottfried wrapped in Impolex G.

So there seems to be something substantive after all to that farcical bit about "a spokesman for the Counterforce" pontificating to the *Wall Street Journal* that "we were never that concerned with Slothrop *qua* Slothrop" (*GR* 738). Slothrop qua distinctive character with whom we might identify is far less significant than the Slothrop effect that inflects the narrative voice from start to finish, driving it to mock its own seemingly fixed coordinates. Although it may be "doubtful if [Slothrop] can ever be 'found' again" (712), he's never caught.

Likewise, the elect/preterite distinction itself starts to crumble— just as William Slothrop's *On Preterition* intended. At least one antithetical definition gets offered, when Enzian and other Zone Hereros think of themselves as "preterite" not in the sense of being doomed but, to the contrary, of having been "passed over" during the 1904 genocide (*GR* 362, 563). True, the destiny to which they feel called seems little better: the assemblage and launching of the 00001, a copycat rival to the great European death wish of Blicero, "a dear albatross I cannot let go" as Enzian calls him (661). Yet at the least *Gravity's Rainbow* confirms critic David Cowart's assessment of a "deepening commitment to the preterite in history" in Pynchon's fiction.[45] This may take the straightforward form of compassion for the unfairly screwed. Or the more complex form of remorse at having instrumentalized another while being manipulated oneself, like Katje's for having diddled Slothrop, or Pökler's at his willful blindness to the plight of his wife and daughter at Dora. More surprising survivals, rescues, and evasions also happen. Leni Pökler, thought dead, survives, as does her daughter Ilse, dead Bianca's counterpart. But the most decisive insinuation that the nominally monolithic category of preterite is a porous container is the injection of farce.

Take Slothrop's last and most ludicrous disguise: a pig suit that he puts on for a seacoast village folk festival at the behest of local children in order to reenact the role of the legendary "Pig-Hero" Plechazunga, who had "routed a Viking invasion" a thousand years before (*GR* 567). After this minor triumph, the disguise helps him make friends with a real pig, which leads him to Pökler, and after that it serves him and poetic justice too when his cover gets blown and he must flee Pointsman's surgical team, who neuter the piglike Marvy instead. So pigness, the defining image of preterition, is a mixed bag. It can doom you; but it can also make you a hero; and it can help you fly below the radar. Also, there are pigs and pigs. The mighty Plechazunga versus the pigs William Slothrop drives pityingly to slaughter. Good-guy Seaman Bodine— called "Pig" in *V.*, as Pynchon knew his fans would know, though not so identified here—versus Marvy, who looks like a pig, acts like a pig, and gets what's coming to him in the end. So the T-shirt with the Porky Pig icon sported by the members of the inchoate Counterforce gestures both ways.

All this is in keeping with the novel's oscillation between and crunching together ludic and grave, high canonical icons (Wagner, Rilke) and mass-culture kitch (*King Kong, Rocketman* comics, the [film version of] *The Wizard of Oz*). Lyle Bland's rapture confirms his status as scarily demonic while also parodying Masonic mumbo jumbo as Ishmael Reed did. The Rocket fearsomely symbolizes the thrust of post-Enlightenment technomodern (ir)rationalism to secularize the sacred and bend the order of nature to human will. But unassimilated macrocosmic effects persist: the Kirghiz light, the "other side" evoked in the séance scenes, the primordial specters of the Brocken and the Titans. The controllers of the earth appear themselves to be enmeshed, in some measure anyhow, within the telluric or supernatural powers they would control. As by his own confession was Wernher von Braun, and not just as the dutiful servant of the most convenient rocket state.

After Pynchon: DeLillo, Wallace, Vollmann

All that happened long ago. It's now forty years since *Gravity's Rainbow*'s launch and von Braun's exit from the world. Since then: Watergate, the Carter and Reagan years, Soviet collapse, Bush I, Clinton, NAFTA, Bush II, 9/11, Iraq, Afghanistan, Obama. Since then: the Internet and cell phone revolutions, predator drones, four big economic downturns. Since then: the "great divergence" in incomes between ultra-affluent and the less well off, few cases more dramatic than the United States. Since then: energy crisis, global warming anxiety, world population uptick by 80 percent and extinction of nonhuman species at no less alarming a rate—no one knows the full count.

These years have been good for Pynchon. He emerged from his long seclusion in Mexico, and after the seventeen-year pause following *Gravity's Rainbow* completed five more novels as of the early 2010s. His work has been monumentalized by an author society, a scholarly journal devoted to his work, and one of the classiest of author websites (thomaspynchon.com), complete with wikis for all novels, links to the proliferating worldwide industry of Pynchon studies, and an intermittent blog with subhead "everything connects." Since 1987 if not before, marathon readings of *Gravity's Rainbow* have been staged at Princeton, Brown, UCLA, and elsewhere. In 2006 it became the first U.S. meganovel, so far as I know, to be treated to a start-to-finish series of visuals, Zak Smith's *Pictures Showing What Happens on Each Page of Thomas Pynchon's "Gravity's Rainbow,"* which prompted Matt Kish to do the same for *Moby-Dick* in 2011.

Pynchon scholar David Cowart names several dozen turn-of-the-twenty-first-century writers whom he might be understood to have mentored, influenced, or otherwise enabled. It's a deep, diverse, and talented group.[46] It includes cyberpunk/science fiction writers William Gibson and Neal Stephenson; historical fabulists Kathryn Kramer and Emily Barton; intricately allusive metafictional postrealists David Foster Wallace and William Vollmann; and novelists practicing more distilled but no less brainy, intricate, and variegated forms of experimentalism, notably the polymathic Richard Powers. But by the same token their accomplishments, and others'—not to mention history itself—had made it clear by the 1990s if not before that *Gravity's Rainbow* wouldn't stand forever as the closest approximation in recent times to definitive embodiment of the script of focalizing the transnational stakes of a defining epoch in U.S. history via the state and fate of a heterogeneous cohort of representative semi-intertwined characters. As the years go on, the novel, monumental though it was and is, begins to look more like an anticipatory benchmark.

The introduction to Part V took note of one such alternative, Yamashita's *Tropic of Orange,* that seemingly owes nothing to Pynchon stylistically and focuses on crises of hemispheric and transpacific immigration and cross-border trafficking not on *Gravity's Rainbow*'s radar screen. But even if you stick with Cowart's dramatis personae, the two post-Pynchonian blockbuster novels of the 1990s most often held up as GAN aspirants or nominees suggest the same conclusion: David Foster Wallace's *Infinite Jest* (1996) and Don DeLillo's *Underworld* (1997). Up to a point, both novels do fit Timothy L. Parrish's assessment of DeLillo's whole career "as an attempt to make sense of the implications of Pynchon's seminal work":[47] of a world that technological systems have made irreversibly interdependent, in which humans can no longer be separated from machines, in which extremes of order produce extremes of chaos and vice versa, in which the world of preterite souls that seems about to collapse somehow keeps turning. Yet despite these parallels and many more, from the standpoint of both DeLillo's Cold War retrospect and Wallace's postmillennial futurism, *Gravity's Rainbow* seems a long time gone.

Underworld differs most strikingly from *Gravity's Rainbow* in its vein of reminiscence. Of course *Gravity's Rainbow* also centers on the generation before the time of writing, often scrolling back much further; but it ensnares you much more in its 1944–1945 time present, so that the few prophetic anticipations of the next-stage Rocket State seem hallucinatory cartoons. In *Underworld* it's the opposite. Instead of hyperactive young Slothrop zipping from one peril to the next, the focal figure is the middle-aged executive Nick Shay revisiting parts of his checkered past from the aftermath of stabilized banality. It wouldn't be forcing things too much to think of 1990s Nick as a warier, wearier update of Sinclair Lewis's George Babbitt once he puts midlife crisis behind him. "I long for the days of disorder," Nick muses near the end, for "the days when I was alive on the earth."[48] *Underworld* is shot through with such nostalgia, however ironized by DeLillo's typically flattish impersonal style of narration. Nostalgia for the big game so long ago, which young Dodger fan Nick heard by rooftop radio and grieved about ever after; his quest for the fetishized ball; artist Klara Sax's fetishistic project of fashioning installation art out of mothballed bombers; Nick going out of his way to reconnect with her decades after their brief affair during his teen years; Nick recollecting the Cuban Missile Crisis of 1962 and the great power outage of 1965; the evocations of the doppelgänger namesakes J. Edgar Hoover and Sister Edgar of the Shay brothers' parochial school, creepy symbolic policemen of the true-believing regimes that defined the Cold War era who fade into confusion and death as it does.

Nick and his brother Matt both work in occupations that Pynchon's work had helped make signature operations for later fiction. Matt's part of a research team sequestered in the New Mexico desert ("one of those nice tight societies that replaces the world" speaking a language "inaccessible to others"). Nick's with the transnational WhizCo, a waste containment firm, which among other ventures oversees the nation's largest landfill; a Flying Dutchman–type ship laden with toxics that it seems not even third world countries want to take; and a deal with Russian counterparts to dispose of nuclear waste in Kazakhstan. Weapons and waste, muses Nick's Russian partner, "maybe one is the mystical twin of the other."[49] But both seem lower-stakes concerns compared to *Gravity's Rainbow*, the sense of emergency defused into foggy gray. Matt's research has no seeming outcome. The most explosive moment of Nick's disorienting whirlwind trip to central Asia, which includes a tour of a museum of deformed fetuses, turns out, bathetically, to be his assault on his WhizCo partner Brian for sleeping with his wife. After which follows the descent into normalcy. To *Gravity's Rainbow*'s warning, "Look out for tomorrow," *Underworld* answers, "That was yesterday."[50]

Not so Wallace's *Infinite Jest*. Here a new state of trans/national emergency looms, this time hemispheric. In the new "experialist" order, North America in the 2000s has become a single U.S.-dominated "Interdependence" with upper New England and the Adirondacks forced upon Canada as a massive dump into which toxic waste is catapulted to feed the complex fusion/fission process that can't succeed in keeping the rest of the continent clean any more than the authorities can succeed in keeping enraged Quebecois separatists from plotting to undermine the United States, especially the ultramilitant Wheelchair Assassins. If all this sounds strangely improbable, chalk it up to the combination of my nutshell encapsulation and Wallace's panache. *Infinite Jest's* over-the-top narrative and intellectual exuberance easily rivals that of *Gravity's Rainbow,* which it outdoes in length and comes close to equaling in erudite arcana.

Of special importance for our purposes are two features of *Infinite Jest* that recall *Gravity's Rainbow* yet mark it as an intervention distinctively its own. One is its byzantine ethnography of the two starkly different, yet interlinked, closed communities that coexist as near neighbors in the fictitious near-Boston town of Enfield: an elite tennis-intensive prep school on the high ground, and a halfway house for recovering alcohol and drug addicts in a building once part of a medical complex. The two are made to seem almost equally gender inclusive (strong-minded women preside over both) and multiethnic (the tennis camp includes kids and staffers of many races and countries; the halfway house is also a rainbow collage of local folks reduced to street people). Each set of inmates is at once regimented, fractious, volatile. Living in both habitats, especially the Enfield Tennis Academy, means subjection to the discipline of complicated protocols of training, testing, physical examination, and curricular indoctrination opaque to the uninitiated and described in almost unassimilably profuse and technical detail, as are the motions and mood swings of the individual inmates.

This matched pair of ethnographies looks like a sharp contrast between privileged and downscale, elect and preterite, and in a way it is. Poor and rich kids alike at E.T.A. are groomed by a phalanx of vigilant staffers; the key thing is how good you are. You need talent to get in. The residents of Ennet House weren't all originally down and outers, but they've all hit bottom before arrival. The matron, challenged herself, runs as tight a ship as she can but has to rely more on self-discipline to keep the place in line partly because it's so under resourced compared to the E.T.A. All this powerfully dramatizes the stratification of contemporary North American "peacetime" society into mutually alien niches however proximate, with caregiving distributed in blatantly unequal ways. But *Infinite Jest* then proceeds to collapse the binary by showing hyperintensive E.T.A. students like the founder's son Hal Incandenza coming undone by addiction to the recreational drugs from which the Ennet House inmates are trying to recover. The gigantic messed-up ex-con Don Gately, Hal's counterpart as Ennet's most salient figure, seems at least partly on the road to patching himself back together as Hal implodes.

Key to this difference is the "recreational" itself: as technology, as addiction, as defining social ideology. In *Gravity's Rainbow* drugs and virtual reality simulation (cinema especially) figure alternately as avenues of escape and instruments of top-down manipulation. In *Infinite Jest*, the institutions of recreation themselves, both individual and mass scale, have become more formidable threats than bombs or rockets or other military hardware. The substance abuse that's wasted both the E.T.A. kids and the Ennet House folks is one form. Another is sports. The totalizing tennis world that Coach Schtitt would implant into the brains of his protégés ("this second world that is always the same") is mirrored by Eschaton, an esoterically ritualized war-of-the-worlds game where each of the 400 tennis balls stands for five-megaton warheads, with which the student body commemorates Interdependence Day.[51] But media technology is the crucial example.

The new order of Interdependence runs on "revenue-enhancing subsidized time" so that even the names of years are branded ("Year of the Depend Adult Undergarment," etc.). At the grass roots, mass entertainment has become "inherently pro-active, consumer driven."[52] The defining entertainment genre is the self-produced video, and the defining product is the last made by the E.T.A.'s late founder James Incandenza, *Infinite Jest* (aka "The Entertainment"), which no one can watch without becoming addicted. The Wheelchair Assassins hunt for a master copy to use as a weapon of mass destruction that would reduce Americans to zombies while the U.S. "Department of Unspecified Services" tries to balk them. One surrealistic sequence interwoven throughout much of the novel features a mountaintop debate between a U.S. agent and a Quebecois assassin who will eventually defect as to why "The Entertainment" should not be made publicly available when "America" supposedly stands, as the former agrees, for free choice and pursuit of happiness. This running debate becomes a voice-over for the book-long inquiry into how if at all the denizens of its "elite" and "preterite" communities can keep from getting self-destructively hooked to the hedonic society's pleasure machines. No closure is reached, though it's insinuated that old-fashioned AA therapy, which requires that the individual confess and accept the blame for his or her wrongdoings, is more likely to put people back together than the E.T.A. regime is to keep them from falling apart. Clearly *Infinite Jest* means at some level to suggest what the first-incredulous Gately discovers, that old-fashioned moral bootstrapping and social solidarity might make the best counterforce to abuse of the pursuits of happiness even in the hyperwired, narco-saturated society of the twenty-first century now.

At all events, *Infinite Jest*'s concentration on hedonic institutions and ideology as the root of social rot marks it as a post–Cold War but pre–"War on Terror" diagnosis. Far be it from me to deny that it and *Underworld* too are possible GAN material. But because both are so visibly post-Pynchonian and also so postapocalyptic, despite *Gravity's Rainbow*'s growingly anachronistic feel as technologies and cultural-political agendas evolve, its proleptic cast may guarantee it greater staying power as an augury of nation-bending disarrangements to come, including but not limited to the attacks of 11 September 2001.

What, then, of William Vollmann, also of Wallace's rather than De-Lillo's generation, also an explosively productive writer emerging in the later 1980s, also classified by Cowart as post-Pynchonian although he himself—with justice, I think—disclaims consanguinity and influence? Vollmann's *Seven Dreams* project, a septet of novels on the (dis)arrangement of North America over the thousand-year period of Eurosettler-Native contact from the Vikings to the ancient past, surely qualifies as the hands-down boldest attempt ever launched at fictionally historicizing the whole trajectory of modern American "civilization" from first contact to the near-present. The four installments published so far (1, 2, 6, and 3 respectively)—*The Ice-Shirt* (1990: Norse versus "Skrellings" during the short-lived Vineland sortie to Newfoundland); *Fathers and Crows* (1992: secular colonizers, Jesuit missionaries, Natives competing for power in seventeenth-century Quebec and the Maritimes); *The Rifles* (1994: British explorer James Franklin's four explorations of the Canadian Arctic); and *Argall* (2001: early Jamestown, featuring John Smith and Pocahontas revisited) are, taken together, unequalled by any post-1950 megafiction in heft as well as time span (2,500 pages, and counting). All, especially the latter three, are at best bravura performances of historical imagination and narrative reflexiveness. Each is minutely researched, complete with maps, notes, chronologies, bibliographies, and glossaries.[53] The panache with which each novel interbraids minute facticity of event including the twang of original sources (saga pastiche, Jesuit Relations-speak, Elizabethan English, the complete works of John Smith, the material and print trails of Victorian polar expeditioners, and much more), with the ruminations of "William the Blind" (just one of the many names the shape-shifting author-narrator gives himself) during his peregrinations in body or mind through the territories in question, make for as daring and out-there a realist/fabulist hybrid as you'll find anywhere.

The autobiographical cameos do get self-indulgent (the tale of Vollmann trying to survive for two wintry weeks at the North magnetic pole), prompting one critic to conclude that although "his topic is history his subject is himself";[54] and the mock-period rhetoric gets stagey and overstrained, as in "Howbeit (for which we must thank OUR RE-DEEMER), some converted Salvages of good accompt did turn tattletale, out of pity for their Masters, or Machiavellian *Politick.*"[55] Such histrionics as these, however, are the perhaps inevitable downside of the attempt at something like full-disclosure rendition of the theatrical, agenda-and-impulse-driven character of Euro-Native encounters (including the author's own) and the self-interested opacity of the sources from which he must cobble these tales together.

Seven Dreams as published so far is remarkable for its sly unpacking of colonial history's most stalwart actors, perhaps especially Samuel de Champlain in *Fathers and Crows,* and John Smith in *Argall,* as they get balked by a combination of shifting transatlantic power structures they can't control and inner devils of their own. And even more so for its taxonomy of the forms of Euro-obsessiveness with (conquering) New World autochthony such as Père Brebeuf's religio-erotic fixation on the biracial seeress Born Underwater in *Fathers and Crows,* Freydis's and Franklin's romances with the Arctic in *The Ice-Shirt* and *Rifles,* John Rolfe's semi-aversive yet also loyally possessive marriage to Pocahontas in *Argall.* Most worth stressing, however, is the mordant teleology of the triumph of "civilization" by degrees when Native culture and the magical order of shamanism increasingly crumble before technopower as the colonizers' tools become more potent and more coveted. In *Ice-Shirt*, the Micmacs expel the Greenlanders by force of numbers, with help from bow-and-arrow weaponry, and spurn their axes. Even at that, the New World Eden is spoiled: the most aggressive invader is shown as bestowing the underworld-begotten gift of ice on the New World, then (self-destructively) taking it back to her own—symbolically anticipating the little ice age that eliminated the Norse from Greenland. But in *Fathers and Crows* and even more in *Argall* and *Rifles,* techno magic outcompetes indigenous ritual magic. Nails, guns, and bullets quickly surpass beads and other trinkets as objects of native desire, which together with overharvesting of beaver and other game for trade spells eventual demise for the traditional native hunting economy and reduction of Inuit and other First Peoples to pathetic remnants.

The four novels resist this fatalism as best they can—stressing Norse implosion, refusing to pursue the narrative of seventeenth-century Quebec or Jamestown beyond their struggling startup stages other than for hasty after-glimpses of later Native collapse, taking grim satisfaction in the starvation of Franklin's band precisely because its dependence on technology (including rifles) that doesn't deliver keeps them from making contact with already gun-shy natives close by. This raises the question of whether Vollmann, after evidently having blocked out the whole septet in his mind two decades ago, will be able to bring himself to complete it. At times, he confessed in 2001, "the whole project just seemed so sickeningly depressing that I felt like I didn't want to do anything more with it. That's one of the reasons I've deliberately interrupted [the series] rather than trying to finish them up all at once, consecutively."[56] After more than a decade since *Argall,* one can't help but wonder about the report by Vollmann's editor that the next volume, *The Dying Grass* (number 5), "will most likely not see print until summer of 2015."[57] How long can the dream of the Great American Novel hold out against the Vollmannish apprehension that "most of this continent's transformation is over with"; that whatever of significance happens to it in future will involve some "global balance of power" shift or other threat that will take the United States downhill?[58] Not that Vollmann or his admirers have ever, so far as I know, proposed the Seven Dreams project as a GAN. Still, the

question's a fair one, all the more so because of how strongly anxieties about U.S. national futures run through all the meganovels this
chapter has discussed, not to mention America-watching cultural criticism of the 1990s and 2000s, both at home and abroad. I'll address it in
the epilogue.

Epilogue

I've always hated writing "conclusions." Far better to open things up than strain after definitiveness. Literary historians are always better at reframing pasts than at predicting futures. But it doesn't take a prophet to foresee sharply different possible futures for the dream of the Great American Novel.

The truth of the matter will almost certainly lie somewhere between these extremes.

On the one hand, the dream of the Great American Novel may at long last be headed for permanent eclipse. History is propelling us farther and farther away from "the American century." Indeed it looks increasingly possible that "the central event of the last century for the majority of this world's population" may come to be seen as "the intellectual and political awakening of Asia and its emergence from the ruins of both Asiatic and European empires."[1] Insofar as the GAN's original takeoff in the late 1800s and its recovery of traction in the mid-1900s benefited from the sense of the United States rising to assume a preeminent place among the nations—not the whole story, we've seen, but surely a part—such a shift in perception would seem to be bad news for the GAN. The prospect of national decline might discourage more writers than William Vollmann (see Chapter 13) from pressing forward with megafictional epics about the course of North American settlement.

So conceivably the dream of the Great American Novel really might be a "residual formation" on its last legs,[2] destined to wind down with the decline of U.S. clout in the world combined with the forms of domestic gridlock that come from being an increasingly "mature" country with a mounting weight of bureaucratic complexity, legal precedent, and other historical baggage. Perhaps at this late date, as a Don DeLillo character muses in *Falling Man* (2007), one of the first major post-9/11 novels, "Nothing is next. There is no next"—no better future to be hoped for.[3] That GAN talk from the very start was so suffused by bemusement and/or sheepish quixoticism reinforces one's sense of its vulnerability. So too, perhaps, the obstinate tendency even into the 2010s—however at cross-purposes with the discrepant stylistic experimentalisms of most GAN candidates since Ellison and Bellow—to yoke it to "retro-realist" fiction. As critic Kevin J. Hayes cautions in a thoughtful short reconnaissance of the GAN idea, for so traditional a practitioner of fictional realism as Jonathan Franzen to be widely proposed as a great American novelist "may indicate the reactionary quality of the label" today.[4] Besides, during the past several decades, novelists and critics alike, Franzen included, are increasingly defining their creative projects less in terms of nationality and more in terms of cross-cutting affiliations or "scales of aggregation," in critic Wai Chee Dimock's phrase.[5]

On the other hand, we've also seen that the dream of the GAN has a history of refusing to disappear after being pronounced dead. Resistance to the idea of American nationness as a securely durable force also has a very long history. It's been wired into aspiring or thought-to-be Great American Novels from the start. From the mid-nineteenth century onward the most likely suspects have not been briefs for national aspiration, preeminence, and pride so much as diagnoses of its fragilities that question the legitimacy of the aspiration again and again. To imagine *The Scarlet Letter, Moby-Dick, Uncle Tom's Cabin,* and *Huckleberry Finn* as defining works of U.S. imagination is to reinforce images of the United States as smothered in its cradle, driven to shipwreck by hubris, torn apart by racial and sectional division, shrinking into a caricature of itself. From that standpoint, nothing would seem more probable than for U.S. novelists to (continue to) seize with gusto upon the prospect of future relative decline of national power and prestige worldwide, and the fissurings within national culture, as an opportunity to outdo their predecessors—as Roth, Morrison, Pynchon, and others have done.

As we've also seen, the fractious heterogeneity that has made the United States look to many critics and creative writers less like a solid object than an unstable patchwork or centrifuge has not spelled terminus but continuous revisitation and updating of the master tropes of GAN practice: enshrinement by reinvention, the ethnic turn in Americanized bildungsroman plotlines, reinvention of the formulas of divide romance, reconception of the geocultural and demographic composition of the imperiled social collective. Even if the GAN mantra itself should get cast aside, the strands of discursive DNA that animate the shifting corpus of fiction named by those who have kept the mantra in circulation will likely remain very much alive.

An important if not the sole cultural driver here has surely been the long-embedded assumption of the United States as a project in the making, forever grasping after—and fighting about—the elusive promise of freedom, equal rights, equal respect for all.[6] At this moment of writing, midway through the presidency of Barack Obama, the United States displays levels of economic stratification not seen since the 1920s, rates of incarceration alarmingly greater than most of the developed world, and a grotesquely outsized ecological footprint—but also an unprecedented openness to alternative sexualities, of professional opportunity for women in an increasing number of fields, and of nonwhite representation at the highest levels of leadership. All this is a sure-fire recipe both for can-do optimism and stony-eyed skepticism about the prospect of future national metamorphosis that promises to keep novelists attuned to the sense of something portentous about U.S.-ness worth writing about if only to put down.

Between the either and the or just described, at least three futures seem more certain. First, so long as the United States remains a desirable place of immigration for non-Americans broadly and for literary emigrants specifically, and so long as New York remains the most formidable publishing center in the Anglophone world, "America" and "the American experience" will continue to be a subject and/or target for creative writers—especially although perhaps diminishingly novels based in the United States.

Second, prose fiction will continue to be produced and read by Americans—and throughout the world—in quantity and with gusto, whatever the "anxiety of obsolescence" about the novel as a form— Kathleen Fitzpatrick's resonant phrase for fear of competition from TV and newer media. As Fitzpatrick points out, the novel "has always been a nervous genre" on this account, at least as far back as its early history in English, when Samuel Richardson worried in the mid-1700s that novels might be a fad about to fade.[7] Chances are that digitization will prove as much a boon as a detriment for fiction, and the study of fiction too, even if readers turn more to talking books and e-editions and critics come to spend more and more time online than in libraries. In any case, the novel in the United States is without doubt far more solidly "institutionalized" than a century ago, taken for granted to be a legitimate art form as it most definitely was not in 1850, whatever questions continue to be raised about its future.

Third, and by the same token, novelistic fashions are bound to look quite different thirty years from now, and in ways no critical analysis published in the 2010s can anticipate. The distance between Dreiser and Bellow, between Dos Passos and Pynchon, between the mid-1900s canonizers and the late 1900s canon-busters, is proof positive. The significance of many of the authors and novels of 1850–2010 will be evaluated differently, in some cases drastically so. Some of the books given top billing in these pages will fall off the radar screen. Others I haven't mentioned may come to seem pivotal. My fourfold map of "recipes" or templates for generating Great American Novels will need to be updated and augmented.

To let one hypothetical case stand for all, it should come as no surprise if speculative fiction—science fiction—came to seem a much more important carrier of the DNA of the national imaginary than the pop-fringe pursuit it's still often taken to be. After all, even traditional ways of conceiving the United States have, as we've seen, been strongly future oriented. What better means than "the multiple mock-futures" of science fiction to reimagine presents or pasts as anticipations "of something yet to come"?[8] What genre better showcases the shift in U.S. fiction toward planetary levels of thinking? What better way to dramatize the weirdness of "normal" life as lived now?[9] Most important, the array of serious American practitioners since the mid-1900s is loaded with talent, and across gender and ethnic lines too—Ray Bradbury, Philip K. Dick ("The Shakespeare of Science Fiction," Fredric Jameson calls him),[10] Ursula Le Guin, Octavia Butler, Samuel L. Delany, Gerald Vizenor, Junot Díaz, and many others. With a bit more oomph from the critical community, the mounting collective accomplishment of these latter-day writers might be linked back to earlier classics this book has either mentioned only in passing or left out entirely: Edgar Allan Poe's *The Narrative of Arthur Gordon Pym* and *Eureka,* Edward Bellamy's *Looking Backward* (Chapter 8), William Dean Howells's trilogy of socialist romances, Mark Twain's late experimental fiction and Sutton Griggs's

Imperium in Imperio, Henry James's *The Sense of the Past,* Charlotte Perkins Gilman's *Herland,* George S. Schuyler's *Black No More.* Is the 4–11 June 2012 *New Yorker* special issue on science fiction a straw in the wind? I don't know, nor can anyone else know for sure absent a seismic-scale reinvention of the American "field-imaginary" that persuades enough people. But it might happen. The sheer possibility is just one of many evidences this book has tried to offer that the Great American Novel remains a field of dreams.

Notes

Introduction

1. Henry James to William Dean Howells, 5 December 1880, in Michael Anesko, *Letters, Fictions, Lives: Henry James and William Dean Howells* (New York: Oxford University Press, 1997), 157.

2. Alan Williams, "Whatever Happened to the Great American Novel? (Part Deux)," *Simon Magazine*, 10 May 2007, http://thesimon.com/magazine /articles.

3. George Knox, "In Search of the Great American Novel," *Western Review* 5 (Summer 1968): 64.

4. James L. Allen, "The Great American Novel," *Independent* 24 (July 1991): 1403.

5. Raymond Williams, *The Country and the City* (New York: Oxford University Press, 1973), 9–12.

6. William Van O'Connor, "The Idea of an American Novel: An Introduction," in *The Idea of an American Novel*, ed. Louis D. Rubin Jr. and John Reed More (New York: Crowell, 1961), vii; Maxine Hong Kingston, "Cultural Mis-readings by American Reviewers," in *Asian and Western Writers in Dialogue: New Cultural Identities*, ed. Guy Amirthanayagam (London: Macmillan, 1982), 57–58.

7. Peter Baker and Michael A. Fletcher, "Rove to Leave White House Post," *Washington Post*, 14 August 2007, A1.

8. Henry David Thoreau, *Walden*, ed. J. Lyndon Shanley (Princeton, NJ: Princeton University Press, 1971), 29.

9. Upton Sinclair, "What Life Means to Me," *Cosmopolitan Magazine* 41 (October 1906): 592, 593; Mark Schorer, *Sinclair Lewis: An American Life* (New York: McGraw-Hill, 1961), 302; *The Letters of Edith Wharton*, ed. R. W. B. Lewis and Nancy Lewis (New York: Scribner's, 1988), 146. The novel Wharton singled out for praise (see Chapter 5) was Anita Loos's *Gentlemen Prefer Blondes* (1925).

10. Martin Amis, "A Chicago of a Novel," *Atlantic Monthly* 276 (October 1995): 114–127; Gillian Reagan, "Elegy for the Great American Novel," *Observer,* 14 November 2007, http://observer.com/2007/11/a-elegy-for-the-great-american-novel/; Mailer, in *The Odyssey of John Dos Passos,* produced by Stephen Talbot (Annandale, VA: Educational Film Center, 1994).

11. Georgio Agamben, *Homo Sacer: Sovereign Power and Bare Life,* trans. Daniel Heller-Roazen (Stanford, CA: Stanford University Press, 1998), 80.

12. Pierre Bourdieu, *The Field of Cultural Production,* ed. Randal Johnson (New York: Columbia University Press, 1993), 257.

13. Janice Radway, *A Feeling for Books: The Book-of-the-Month Club: Literary Taste and Middle-Class Desire* (Chapel Hill: University of North Carolina Press, 1997), 166.

14. Christopher Castiglia, *Interior States: Institutional Consciousness and the Inner Life of Democracy in the Antebellum United States* (Durham, NC: Duke University Press, 2008), 13; Kundera quoted in Philip Roth, *Shop Talk: A Writer and His Colleagues and Their Work* (Boston: Houghton Mifflin, 2001), 100.

15. See for example Andrew Levy, *The Culture and Commerce of the American Short Story* (Cambridge: Cambridge University Press, 1993), 27–57.

16. Not that "canon" means permanence either. Unlike the canons of scripture, literary canons also evolve over time as fashions and attitudes change. Melville's *Moby-Dick* (1851) is now as canonical as any work of national literature, but it didn't become securely so until the mid-1900s. The poet Longfellow seemed securely canonical in the 1800s but was then decanonized. Furthermore, the nearer in time and (as today) the more heterogeneous and nonunitary the literary scene, the more question-begging it becomes to stipulate "a" canon. For two important short discussions of these matters, see Wendell V. Harris, "Canonicity," *PMLA: Publications of the Modern Language Association* 106 (January 1991): 110–121 (on literary canons in general); and David Palumbo-Liu, "Introduction," in *The Ethnic Canon: Histories, Institutions, Interventions,* ed. David Palumbo-Liu (Minneapolis: University of Minnesota Press, 1995), 1–27 (on ethnic canons as distinct from traditional canons).

17. By "national imaginary" I mean the ongoing activity, partly conscious but mostly unconscious, of collective imagination about nation and nationness by those who feel themselves connected to that collective, whether citizens or not—a fluid and shifting process rather than a fixed state that encompasses a sense of national heritage as well as anticipated future. "National imaginary" in the singular admittedly risks giving a false impression of stable holism—a defect in the work of the social philosopher most influential in generating the concept (Cornelius Castoriadis, *The Imaginary Institution of Society,* trans. Kathleen Blamey [Cambridge, MA: MIT Press, 1987], 131, 148). British cultural critic Graham Dawson's rough-and-ready definition of "cultural imaginaries" as "those vast networks of interlinking discursive themes, images, motifs and narrative forms that are publicly available

within a culture at any one time, and articulate its psychic and social dimensions" is more flexible (*Soldier Heroes: British Adventure, Empire and the Imagining of Masculinities* [London: Routledge, 1994], 48). Flexibly understood, "national imaginary" can be a useful lumping term for ongoing collective processes unfolding over time at a mostly unselfconscious level. Not that creative works, including possible GANs, are generated by national imaginaries alone, but in interaction with an array of other aesthetic and conceptual factors, as demonstrated by Winfried Fluck, *Das culturelle Imaginäre: ein Funktionsgeschishte des Amerikanishen Romans, 1790–1900* (Frankfurt: Suhrkamp, 1997), 7–29.

18. Sommer, *Foundational Fictions: The National Romances of Latin America* (Berkeley: University of California Press, 1991). See Jonathan Culler, "The Novel and the Nation," in *The Literary in Theory* (Stanford, CA: Stanford University Press, 2007), 43–72, for an astute comparative assessment of this book's claims vis-à-vis those of anthropologist Benedict Anderson's *Imagined Communities*, rev. ed. (London: Verso, 1991), the most seminal disquisition on nation making as a work of collective imagination, which also discusses the work of selected novels to that end.

19. Carlos Fuentes, "A Despot, Now and Forever," *New York Times Book Review*, 6 April 1986.

20. Susan F. Ferlito, *Topographies of Desire: Manzoni, Cultural Practice, and Colonial Scars* (New York: Lang, 2000), 9–10; Simon Edwards, "The Geography of Violence: Historical Fiction and the National Question," *Novel: A Forum on Fiction* 34 (Spring 2001): 303–308.

21. For a helpful overview, see Ken Stewart, "Life and Death of the Bunyip: History and 'the Great Australian Novel,'" *Westerly* 28 (June 1983): 39–44, which names three proposed novels (Marcus Clarke, *His Natural Life;* H. H. Richardson (pseud.), *The Fortunes of Richard Mahony;* and Patrick White, *Voss*) and eight defining motifs (an analysis that the author told me in 2010 he would today revise in some respects). Robert Dixon's multidimensional account of the basis of the celebrity of a single recent novel, Tim Winton's *Cloudstreet* (1991), includes perceptive discussion of ways its "style and concerns could be read back into the tradition of the Great Australian Novel" (Dixon, "Tim Winton, *Cloudstreet* and the Field of Australian Literature," *Westerly* 50 [November 2005]: 254). Murray Gray's *The Great Australian Novel* (1987) is an intermittently amusing parody.

22. Édouard Glissant, *Caribbean Discourse: Selected Essays*, trans. J. Michael Dash (Charlottesville: University Press of Virginia, 1989), 104.

23. John Sutherland, *Fiction and the Fiction Industry* (London: Athlone, 1978), 64.

24. Amanda Claybaugh, "The Great [National] Novel," *Public Culture*, 17 July 2012, www.publicbooks.org/fiction/the-great-national-novel, identifies the prominent critic James Wood as the first to call attention to this anxiety uptick in 1992. Also notable for his outspokenness on the subject of the quixotic hubris of the GAN, as in his 2001 review of Jonathan Franzen's

The Corrections (James Wood, *The Irresponsible Self: On Laughter and the Novel*
[New York: Farrar, Straus and Giroux, 2004], 195–209), Wood occupies
the unprecedented position of preeminent voice among Anglo-American
critics of fascinated skepticism toward great national novel aspirations on
both sides of the water in this seemingly new era of mutual Anglo-
American attraction to the idea. For more by Wood on the subject of contemporary British apprehension of the United States as an outsized literary
power, see his "Prize of the Yankees," *New York Magazine,* 21 May 2005.

25. Paul Giles, *The Global Remapping of American Literature* (Princeton, NJ: Princeton University Press, 2011), 1–25.

26. Caroline F. Levander, *Where Is American Literature?* (Oxford: Wiley-
Blackwell, 2013), 39 and passim. In addition to works cited above and below, formative studies bearing especially on the nineteenth century and
beyond include all the following, and more. For the theory of transnational cultural hybridization, Homi K. Bhabha, *The Location of Culture* (New
York: Routledge, 1994); and Arjun Appadurai, *Modernity at Large: The Cul-
tural Dimensions of Globalization* (Minneapolis: University of Minnesota
Press, 1996). For Atlantic world transnationalism both Afro- and Euro-,
Henry Louis Gates Jr., *The Signifying Monkey: A Theory of Afro-American Liter-
ary Criticism* (New York: Oxford University Press, 1988); Paul Gilroy, *The
Black Atlantic: Modernity and Double Consciousness* (Cambridge, MA: Harvard
University Press, 1993); Joseph Roach, *Cities of the Dead: Circum-Atlantic
Performance* (New York: Columbia University Press, 1996); Brent Hayes Ed-
wards, *The Practice of Diaspora: Literature, Translation, and the Rise of Black Inter-
nationalism* (Cambridge, MA: Harvard University Press, 2003); Robert
Weisbuch, *Atlantic Double-Cross: American Literature and British Influence in the
Age of Emerson* (Chicago: University of Chicago Press, 1986); and Amanda
Claybaugh, *The Novel of Purpose: Literature and Social Reform in the Anglo-
American World* (Ithaca, NY: Cornell University Press, 2007). For hemi-
spheric studies, José David Saldívar, *The Dialectics of Our America: Genealogy,
Cultural Critique, and Literary History* (Durham, NC: Duke University Press,
1991), and later books; Kirsten Silva Gruesz, *Ambassadors of Culture: The
Transamerican Origins of Latino Writing* (Princeton, NJ: Princeton University
Press, 2002); Anna Brickhouse, *Transamerican Literary Relations and the
Nineteenth-Century Public Sphere* (Cambridge: Cambridge University Press,
2004); and Ramón Saldívar, *The Borderlands of Culture: Américo Paredes and
the Transnational Imaginary* (Durham, NC: Duke University Press, 2006). For
transpacific studies, Lisa Lowe, *Immigrant Acts: On Asian American Cultural
Politics* (Durham, NC: Duke University Press, 1996); and David Palumbo-Liu,
Asian/American: Historical Crossings of a Racial Frontier (Stanford, CA: Stanford
University Press, 1999). Among more general studies, Wai Chee Dimock,
Through Other Continents: American Literature across Deep Time (Princeton, NJ:
Princeton University Press, 2006). Brickhouse, *Transamerican Literary Rela-
tions,* R. Saldívar, *Borderlands of Culture,* and Anita Haya Patterson, *Race,*

American Literature and Transnational Modernisms (Cambridge: Cambridge University Press, 2008), offer particularly arresting testimony as to the impossibility of prying "hemispheric," "Atlantic," and "transpacific" fields apart from one another.

27. Caroline F. Levander and Robert S. Levine, "Introduction: Essays beyond the Nation," in *Hemispheric American Studies,* ed. Caroline Levander and Robert S. Levine (New Brunswick, NJ: Rutgers University Press, 2008), 7.

28. The term "field imaginary" was coined by American literature scholar Donald E. Pease to refer to the "tacit assumptions, convictions," language and structure underlying a scholarly field's dominant critical practice, with specific attention in fact to the "crisis" then overtaking older "consensus" approaches to defining American culture's supposed distinctiveness that he and other "new Americanists" saw as justifying anti-Soviet Cold War–era claims for the United States as "a realm of pure possibility" (Pease, "New Americanists: Revisionist Interventions into the Canon," *boundary 2* [Spring 1990]: 11–12). Perhaps the most influential embodiment of New Americanist critical thinking, which continues strongly to influence American studies today, has been Amy Kaplan and Donald E. Pease, eds., *Cultures of United States Imperialism* (Durham, NC: Duke University Press, 1993).

29. Winfried Fluck, *Romance with America? Essays on Culture, Literature, and American Studies,* ed. Laura Bieger and Johannes Voelz (Heidelberg: Winter, 2009), 81.

30. Partha Chatterjee, *The Nation and Its Fragments* (Princeton, NJ: Princeton University Press, 1993), 3–4.

31. Thomas Bender, *A Nation among Nations: America's Place in World History* (New York: Hill and Wang, 2006), 296–297.

32. K. Anthony Appiah, "The Limits of Pluralism," in *Multiculturalism and American Democracy,* ed. Arthur M. Melzer, Jerry Weinberger, and M. Richard Zinman (Lawrence: University Press of Kansas, 1998), 37–38.

33. Pascale Casanova, *The World Republic of Letters,* trans. M. B. De Bevoise (Cambridge, MA: Harvard University Press, 2004), 77–81, 189.

34. Mark McGurl, *The Program Era: Postwar Fiction and the Rise of Creative Writing* (Cambridge, MA: Harvard University Press, 2008), 330.

35. Ibid., 334.

1. Birth, Heyday, and Seeming Decline

1. "New Publications: 'Waiting for the Verdict'" [advertisement], *Philadelphia Inquirer,* 5 November 1867; P. T. Barnum, *Humbugs of the World* (New York: Carleton, 1866), 13.

2. John W. De Forest, "The Great American Novel," *Nation* 6 (9 January 1868): 27, 28.

3. Trish Loughran, *The Republic in Print: Print Culture in the Age of U.S. Nation-Building, 1770–1870* (New York: Columbia University Press, 2007), 303–344.

4. John Jay Chapman, *Emerson and Other Essays* (London: Nutt, 1898), 96.

5. Nina Silber, *The Romance of Reunion: Northerners and the South, 1865–1900* (Chapel Hill: University of North Carolina Press, 1993); David W. Blight, *Race and Reunion: The Civil War in American Memory* (Cambridge, MA: Harvard University Press, 2001).

6. John Austin, "United States, 1780–1850," in *The Novel*, vol. 1, ed. Franco Moretti (Princeton, NJ: Princeton University Press, 2006), 455.

7. Nina Baym, *Novels, Readers, and Reviewers: Responses to Fiction in Antebellum America* (Ithaca, NY: Cornell University Press, 1984), 44; and Nina Baym, letter to author, 14 July 1994.

8. Mary Elizabeth Wormeley, "A Sectional Appeal," *National Era*, 11 August 1853, 128.

9. See especially Michael Winship, "'The Greatest Book of Its Kind': A Publishing History of *Uncle Tom's Cabin*," *Proceedings of the American Antiquarian Society* 109 (Part 2, 1999): 309–332. The "greatest of American tales" was a much-recycled phrase lifted from a notice in the *Barre Patriot* for an end-of-book advertisement during the first edition (1852) print run. Early editions of *Uncle Tom's Cabin*, such as those in the excellent collection at the Stowe-Day Foundation, Hartford, Connecticut, often append pages of advertisements that use these and other commonly circulated phrases for marketing the book at home and abroad.

10. Forrest Wilson, *Crusader in Crinoline: The Life of Harriet Beecher Stowe* (Philadelphia: Lippincott, 1941), 260.

11. William Dean Howells, *Selected Literary Criticism*, vol. 3: *1898–1920*, ed. Ronald Gottesman et al. (Bloomington: Indiana University Press, 1993), 227; Frank Norris, *The Literary Criticism of Frank Norris*, ed. Donald Pizer (Austin: University of Texas Press, 1964), 95.

12. Brad Evans, *Before Cultures: The Ethnographic Imagination in American Literature 1865–1920* (Chicago: University of Chicago Press, 2005), 12–13, 92.

13. Ernest Renan, "What Is a Nation?" repr. in *Nation and Narration*, ed. Homi K. Bhabha (London: Routledge, 1990), 19; Benedict Anderson, *Imagined Communities: Reflections on the Origin and Spread of Nationalism*, rev. ed. (London: Verso, 1991), 15.

14. Timothy Brennan, "The National Longing for Form," in Bhabha, *Nation and Narration*, 49.

15. Thomas Sargent Perry, "American Novels," *North American Review* 115 (October 1872): 368; "Democracy," *Literary News* 1 (May 1880): 97.

16. Sergio Perosa, *American Theories of the Novel: 1793–1903* (New York: New York University Press, 1983), 79.

17. Colson Whitehead, *Apex Hides the Hurt* (New York: Anchor, 2007), 208.

18. James, "The Art of Fiction," 44.

19. "Literature and Nationality," *Every Saturday: A Journal of Choice Reading* 2 (8 August 1874): 163.

20. James Huneker, *Unicorns* (New York: Scribner's, 1917), 83.

21. James L. Allen, "The Great American Novel," *Independent* 24 (July 1891): 1403; Norris, *Literary Criticism of Frank Norris*, 123; Edward Eggleston, *The Hoosier Schoolmaster: A Story of Backwoods Life in Indiana*, rev. ed. (New York: Grosset and Dunlap, 1899), 7; M. G. Van Rensselaer, "American Fiction," *Lippincott's Monthly Magazine* 23 (June 1879): 757; "The Great American Novel," *Nation* 54 (24 March 1892): 224; Perry, "American Novels," 378.

22. H. H. Boyeson, "Why We Have No Great Novelists," *Forum* 2 (February 1887): 619.

23. The contemporary critical practice of coding regional realism female and placing some positive or negative judgment on the self-restrictedness of the chosen imagined country that follows from the gendering of the genre starts with Ann Douglas Wood, "The Literature of Impoverishment: The Women Local Colorists of America, 1865–1914," *Women's Studies* 1 (1972): 3–46 (negative); and Josephine Donovan, *New England Local Color Literature: A Woman's Tradition* (New York: Ungar, 1983) (positive). The judgments and the grounds thereof have since become much more complex, but the gender-coding tendency still persists—to the comparative neglect of such male practitioners as Eggleston, George Washington Cable, Rowland Robinson, and Hamlin Garland.

24. Especially influential in this regard have been Amy Kaplan, "Nation, Region, and Empire," in *Columbia History of the American Novel*, ed. Emory Elliott (New York: Columbia University Press, 1991), 250–256; Richard Brodhead, *Cultures of Letters: Scenes of Reading and Writing in Nineteenth-Century America* (Chicago: University of Chicago Press, 1993), 142–176; and (scanning back to antebellum antecedents) Amy Kaplan, "Manifest Domesticity" (1998), revised for Kaplan's *Anarchy of Empire in the Making of U.S. Culture* (Cambridge, MA: Harvard University Press, 2002), 23–50.

25. Paul Lauter, *Canons and Contexts* (New York: Oxford University Press, 1991), 22–47.

26. Hamlin Garland, "The Future of Fiction," *Arena* 7 (April 1891): 520–521; "Our Monthly Gossip," *Lippincott's Magazine* 37 (April 1886): 440.

27. Annie Steger Winston, "America as a Field for Fiction," *Arena* 23 (June 1900): 658–659.

28. Michael Lind, *The Next American Nation: The New Nationalism and the Fourth American Revolution* (New York: Free Press, 1995), 55–96.

29. Robert Herrick, "The American Novel," *Yale Review* 3 (April 1914): 434.

30. Julian Hawthorne, "The American Element in Fiction," *North American Review* 139 (August 1884): 168.

31. Edith Wharton, "The Great American Novel," in *Uncollected Critical Writings*, ed. Frederick Wegener (Princeton, NJ: Princeton University Press, 1996), 157, 151–152.

32. Mark Schorer, *Sinclair Lewis: An American Life* (New York: McGraw-Hill, 1961), 275.

33. James Herbert Morse, "The Native Element in American Fiction," *Century* 26 (July 1883): 374; Frank Norris, ["He Thinks It's 'Ben-Hur'"], *San Francisco Examiner*, 17 January 1897.

34. James F. Muirhead, "Howells and Trollope," *The Living Age* 308 (1921): 309; W. L. B., "A Scheme for a Novel," *Literary World: A Monthly Review of Current Literature*, 4 February 1888, 19.

35. Perry, "American Novels," 378.

36. Wharton, "Great American Novel," 154.

37. Theodore Dreiser, "The Great American Novel," in *American Spectator Yearbook*, ed. George Jean Nathan et al. (New York: Frederick A. Stokes, 1934), 24; G. W. Benjamin, "The American Novel," *Independent* 41 (21 November 1889): 3; De Forest, "The Great American Novel," 28; Henry James to W. D. Howells, 31 January 1880, in Michael Anesko, *Letters, Fictions, Lives: Henry James and William Dean Howells* (New York: Oxford University Press, 1987), 147.

38. Michael Denning, *The Cultural Front: The Laboring of American Culture in the Twentieth Century* (London: Verso, 1997), 167.

39. John Dos Passos, "Contemporary Chronicles," *Carleton Miscellany* 2 (Spring 1961): 26; Malcolm Cowley, "Dos Passos and His Predecessors," *New York Times Book Review*, 19 January 1947, 1.

40. Fred Lewis Pattee, *The New American Literature 1890–1930* (New York: Century, 1930), 180.

41. Norris, *Literary Criticism of Frank Norris*, 344; Sinclair Lewis, Nobel Prize Address (1931), repr. in *The Theory of the American Novel*, ed. George Perkins (New York: Holt, 1970), 307.

42. See especially Amy Kaplan, *The Social Construction of American Realism* (Chicago: University of Chicago Press, 1989); and Michael Davitt Bell, *The Problem of American Realism: Studies in the Cultural History of a Literary Idea* (Chicago: University of Chicago Press, 1993).

43. Sherwood Anderson, "A Writer's Conception of Realism" (1939), repr. in Perkins, *The Theory of the American Novel*, 296, 299; Mary Austin, "The American Form of the Novel," in *Beyond Borders: The Selected Essays of Mary Austin*, ed. Reuben J. Ellis (Carbondale: University of Southern Illinois Press, 1996), 87, 84, 86.

44. Catherine Turner, *Marketing Modernism between the Two World Wars* (Amherst: University of Massachusetts Press, 2003), 116–127.

45. Steven Meyer, editorial introduction, in Gertrude Stein, *The Making of Americans: Being a History of a Family's Progress* (London: Dalkey Archive, 1995), xiv.

46. Gertrude Stein, *Fernhurst, Q. E. D., and Other Early Writings* (New York: Liveright, 1971), 144–145.

47. Stein, *Making of Americans*, 290, 289, 47.

48. Stein recalled that during the course of writing *Making* it "changed from being a history of a family to being a history of everybody the family knew and then it became the history of every kind and of every individual hu-

man being. But in spite of this there was a hero and he was to die" (*The Autobiography of Alice B. Toklas* [1933], in *Selected Writings of Gertrude Stein,* ed. Carl Van Vechten [New York: Modern Library, 1947], 106).

49. Stein, *Making of Americans,* 291.

50. Sianne Ngai, *Ugly Feelings* (Cambridge, MA: Harvard University Press, 2005), 271; Lisa Ruddick, *Reading Gertrude Stein: Body, Text, Gnosis* (Ithaca, NY: Cornell University Press, 1990), 125.

51. Gertrude Stein, *Lectures in America* (1935), ed. Wendy Steiner (Boston: Beacon, 1985), 160–161.

52. George Knox, "The Great American Novel: Final Chapter," *American Quarterly* 21 (Winter 1969): 681; Susan Mizruchi, "Fiction and the Science of Society," in Elliott, *Columbia History of the American Novel,* 213.

53. "Magazine Data File," Galactic Central, http://www.philsp.com/data /data181.html.

54. Joseph Csicsila, *Canons by Consensus: Critical Trends and American Literature Anthologies* (Tuscaloosa: University of Alabama Press, 2004), 134–144.

55. Benjamin Spencer, *The Quest for Nationality: An American Literary Campaign* (Syracuse, NY: Syracuse University Press, 1957), 331, 328; Charles A. Campbell Jr., "'The Great American Novel': A Study in Literary Nationalism, 1870–1900," PhD diss., University of Minnesota, 1951.

56. Charles F. Richardson, *American Literature, 1607–1885,* vol. 2 (New York: Putnam, 1888), 450; Herbert R. Brown, "The Great American Novel," *American Literature* 7 (March 1935): 2.

57. Herbert R. Brown, *The Sentimental Novel in America, 1789–1860* (Durham, NC: Duke University Press, 1940).

58. L. Lockridge, *Shade of the Raintree,* 340; "Six Reasons Why *Raintree County* by Ross Lockridge, Jr., will be the most important book of the new year," flyer in Houghton Mifflin archives, Houghton Library, Harvard University, quoted L. Buell, "The Rise and 'Fall' of the Great American Novel," *Proceedings of the American Antiquarian Society* 104 (Part 2, 1994): 277. In a statement sent to the publisher for PR purposes, Lockridge declared that he had hoped from the time he began working on the novel in 1934 that it might be the GAN. Significantly, the publisher's advertisements ignored Lockridge's comparisons to European masterpieces, exclusively touting *Raintree*'s Americanness, and reviewers followed suit by comparing Lockridge solely to other American authors.

2. Reborn from the Critical Ashes

1. Quotation from D. H. Lawrence, *The Symbolic Meaning: The Uncollected Versions of Studies in Classic American Literature,* ed. Armin Arnold (London: Centaur, 1962), 17.

2. Pascale Casanova, *The World Republic of Letters,* trans. M. B. De Bevoise (Cambridge, MA: Harvard University Press, 2004), 336.

3. See for example Thomas Bender, *New York Intellect: A History of Intellectual Life in New York City from 1750 to the Beginnings of Our Own Time* (New York: Random House, 1987), 334–335; Laura Fermi, *Illustrious Immigrants*, 2nd ed. (Chicago: University of Chicago Press, 1971); and John R. Thelin, *A History of American Higher Education* (Baltimore, MD: Johns Hopkins University Press, 2004), 224–225. As Thelin notes, however, the impact on student bodies was "at best uneven"; the dislocations experienced by the refugee intellectuals were often severe (Donald Peterson Kent, *The Refugee Intellectual: The Americanization of the Immigrants of 1933–1941* [New York: Columbia University Press, 1953], 111–187); and some leading institutions were resistant because of ties to German academe, outright anti-Semitism, or both, as at Harvard (Morton Keller and Phyllis Keller, *Making Harvard Modern: The Rise of America's University*, rev. ed. [New York: Oxford University Press, 2001], 152–169).

4. George Knox, "'The Great American Novel': Final Chapter," *American Quarterly* 21 (Winter 1969): 682.

5. Vernon L. Parrington, *The Beginnings of Critical Realism in America 1860–1920* (New York: Harcourt, 1930), xxviii; George Snell, *The Shapers of American Fiction 1798–1947* (New York: Dutton, 1947), 198.

6. Arthur Hobson Quinn, *American Fiction: An Historical and Critical Survey* (New York: Appleton, 1936), 722–723; Harlan Hatcher, *Creating the Modern American Novel* (New York: Farrar and Rinehart, 1935), 34, 53; Snell, *Shapers*, 256.

7. Philip Rahv, *Image and Idea: Twenty Essays on Literary Themes*, rev. ed. (Norfolk, CT: New Directions, 1957), 150.

8. Leslie Fiedler, *An End to Innocence: Essays on Culture and Politics* (Boston: Beacon, 1955), 175, 196.

9. Rahv, *Image and Idea*, 142.

10. T. S. Eliot, "Ulysses, Order, and Myth," in *Selected Prose*, ed. Frank Kermode (London: Faber, 1975), 175–178.

11. Wanda Corn, *The Great American Thing: Modern Art and National Identity 1913–1935* (Berkeley: University of California Press, 1999), 43–90.

12. Nina Baym, "Melodramas of Beset Manhood: How Theories of American Fiction Exclude Women Writers" (1981), repr. in Baym, *Feminism in American Literary History* (New Brunswick, NJ: Rutgers University Press, 1992), 3–18; John P. McWilliams Jr., "The Rationale for American Romance," *boundary 2* 17 (Spring 1990): 71–82.

13. Critical theorist John Guillory's magisterial *Cultural Capital: The Problem of Literary Canon Formation* (Chicago: University of Chicago Press, 1993) is especially pointed and pungent in its assessment of the aftereffects of New Criticism generally, not solely its Americanist face: it nurtured "a kind of recusant literary culture, at once faithful to the quasi-sacred authority of literature but paying tribute at the same time to the secular authority of a derogated mass culture" from which it had fled (175).

14. David S. Shumway, *Creating American Civilization: A Genealogy of American Literature as a Discipline* (Minneapolis: University of Minnesota Press, 1994), 337.

15. Some well-known cases in point: Matthiessen was a socialist who authored the first important critical book on Dreiser as well as the first notable extended study of Henry James's late fiction, the revisionists' touchstone for consummate Anglophone narrative art; Robert Penn Warren's political views became significantly more progressive over time; and Fiedler "the guardian of maturity was himself invested in immaturity" (Ross Posnock, "Innocents at Home," *Book Forum* [Summer 2003], www.bookforum .com/archive.sum03/posnock.html). For late twentieth-century acknowledgment of the internal complexities of the two main semi-interlocking groups of midcentury critical revisionists—the Yale-centered New Critics and the "New York" intellectuals (including Trilling, Fiedler, and Rahv) associated with the *Partisan Review's* retreat from the left-wing politics of the 1930s—see for example Harvey M. Teres, *Renewing the Left: Politics, Imagination, and the New York Intellectuals* (New York: Oxford University Press, 1996); and Geraldine Murphy, "Romancing the Center: Cold War Politics and Classic American Literature," *Poetics Today* 9 (Winter 1988): 737–747. Two helpful studies of the constraints of Cold War ideology on U.S. novelistic imagination are Thomas H. Schaub, *American Fiction of the Cold War* (Madison: University of Wisconsin Press, 1991); and Alan Nadel, *Containment Culture: American Narrative, Postmodernism, and the Atomic Age* (Durham, NC: Duke University Press, 1995).

16. W. T. Lhamon, *Deliberate Speed: The Origins of an American Cultural Style in the 1950s* (Cambridge, MA: Harvard University Press, 2002), 99.

17. G. R. Thompson and Eric Carl Link, *Neutral Ground: New Traditionalism and the American Romance Controversy* (Baton Rouge: Louisiana State University Press, 1999), 2; Lionel Trilling, *The Liberal Imagination: Essays on Literature and Society* (New York: Viking, 1950), 278; Fiedler, *An End to Innocence,* 207.

18. Tom Wolfe, "Why They Aren't Writing the Great American Novel Anymore," *Esquire* 78 (December 1972): 157.

19. Tom Wolfe, "Stalking the Billion-Footed Beast: A Literary Manifesto for the New Social Novel," *Harper's* 279 (November 1989): 45–56.

20. Malcolm Cowley, *The Literary Situation* (New York: Viking, 1954), 14–15.

21. Leslie Fiedler, *Love and Death in the American Novel* (New York: Criterion, 1960), 485–591; Jay P. Hubbell, *Who Are the Major American Writers? A Study of the Changing Literary Canon* (Durham, NC: Duke University Press, 1972), 289–291, which summarizes the results of a 1926 *Golden Book Magazine* poll to which 400 teachers responded. *The Scarlet Letter, Huckleberry Finn,* and *Moby-Dick* were ranked 2, 3, and 6, with the other top spots accorded Poe's *Tales* (1), Cooper's *The Last of the Mohicans* (4), and Joel Chandler Harris's *Uncle Remus* (5). From a twenty-first-century standpoint, the testimony to Harris's durability and to Melville's early acclaim in 1926 are equally arresting.

22. PBS, "The American Novel: Top Novel Lists" (2007), www.pbs.org/wnet /americannovel/topnovel/index; Christopher Schmitz, "Contenders for Great American Novel" (2003), www.amazon.com/Contenders-for-Great -American-Novel/Im/33H3DJF07GCDY.

23. Fiedler, *Love and Death*, 260, 175, 173.

24. Leslie Fiedler, *The Inadvertent Epic: From "Uncle Tom's Cabin" to "Roots"* (Toronto: CBC, 1979), 19. Fiedler's equivocal title is a clear misnomer, reflecting his value judgment and not the project's original intent. With the possible exception of the self-consciously rookie author Margaret Mitchell in *Gone with the Wind,* all five of the figures Fiedler discusses—the others being Stowe, Thomas Dixon (his Reconstruction trilogy), Griffith, and Haley— set out to make a big splash. See Chapters 6–9 for discussion of them all.

25. Schmitz, "Contenders for Great American Novel."

26. Alfred Kazin, "The Great American Bore," *Reporter* 19 (11 December 1958): 31.

27. Marc McGurl, *The Novel Art: Elevations of American Fiction after Henry James* (Princeton, NJ: Princeton University Press, 2001), 57–77.

28. "Modern Library 100 Best Novels," Wikipedia, http://en.wikipedia.org /wiki/Modern Library_100_Best_Novels.

29. Tyler Cowen, "Attack of the Great American Novel," *Arcane Gazebo,* 12 February 2006, www.arcanegazebo.net/2006/02/.

30. Shumway, *Creating American Civilization*, 358.

31. The James chapter was omitted in 2006 but restored the next year; a Poe chapter was added in 1971, then dropped in 1997; a Wharton-Cather chapter was added in 1997; Hemingway-Fitzgerald was changed to Fitzgerald-Hemingway in 1971. More striking have been the expansion of omnibus chapters covering other novelists (e.g., "Fiction: 1930s to the 1960s") and the increasing attention to "International Scholarship."

32. For "never," see for example Jonathan Wallace, "Edith Wharton's *House of Mirth,*" www.spectacle.org/0401/wharton.html; for never again, see Roger Kimball, "The Great American Novel: Will There Ever Be Another?," *Weekly Standard,* 27 February 2012 (which maintains that the novel has declined as a cultural force); and Jonathan Yardley, "State of the Art," *Washington Post,* 14 July 2002, http://www.washingtonpost.com/ac2/wp-dyn?pagename=article &contentld=A57244-2002J (which deems the contemporary novel too fixated on "the inner lives and private experiences of the author-surrogates who are its central characters"). For the claim that the GAN is not a myth but has yet to be realized, see Lawrence Buentello, "The Writing of the Great American Novel," http://www.lawrencebuentello.com/id12.html. For nomination of Chabon, Williams, and Díaz, see Jeremiah Schmidt, "Ten Great American Novels since 1980," *Bookstove,* 8 September 2011, http://bookstove.com /book-talk/ten-great-american-novels-since-1980/. For Verghese, see Dick Cummins's reply to Eric Olson, "The Great American Novel—What Is It, and Who Cares?," *Portland Book Review,* 4 February 2012, http://portlandbookre

view.com/2-4-12-the-great-american-novel/. For *Gatsby* versus Salinger and/or Lockridge, see "Great Gatsby—Great American Novel?," www .goodreads.com/topic/show/1054749-great-gatsby---great-american-novel, and David Brent Johnson, "The Riddle of Raintree County," indianapublic media.org/nightlights/the-riddle-of-raintree-county. For Kasia Boddy on Tillman, see her "Lynne Tillman and the Great American Novel," *Electronic Book Review,* 17 April 2011, 9, http://www.electronicbookreview.com/thread /fictionspresent/american.

33. John Updike, *Howells as Anti-novelist* (Kittery Point, ME: William Dean Howells Committee, 1987), 42.

34. Toni Morrison, *Conversations with Toni Morrison,* ed. Danielle Taylor-Guthrie (Jackson: University Press of Mississippi, 1981), 124.

35. Ibid., 124; and Larry Schwartz, "Toni Morrison and William Faulkner," *Cultural Logic* 5 (2002), http://clogic.eserver.org/2002/schwartz.html.

36. Updike later returned to Rabbit in his novella *Rabbit Remembered* (2001), but as a coda to rather than as an integral part of the tetralogy.

37. Ian McEwan, "On John Updike," *New York Review of Books,* 12 March 2009, 4. For other memorial tributes associating Updike with the GAN, see Geeta Sharma Jensen, "Updike Pioneered Suburban Novel," *Milwaukee Sentinel,* 27 January 2009, http://www.jsonline.com/news/obituaries/38514459.html; and Louis Proyect, "John Updike," 28 January 2009, http://louisproyect .wordpress.com/2009/01/28/john-updike.

38. James English, *The Economy of Prestige: Prizes, Awards, and the Circulation of Cultural Value* (Cambridge, MA: Harvard University Press, 2005), 245.

39. A. O. Scott, "In Search of the Best," *New York Times Book Review,* 21 May 2006, 16–19.

40. Moreover, the contrast narrows greatly if one goes by the ratings for the four Rabbit novels individually: 4.06 for a total of 358 reviews. It would seem that those who read through the tetralogy are a small, self-selected group predisposed to admire and less likely to criticize the Rabbit saga as white men's fiction.

41. John Updike, "Introduction," in *Rabbit Angstrom: A Tetralogy: "Rabbit Run," "Rabbit Redux," "Rabbit Is Rich," "Rabbit at Rest"* (New York: Knopf, 1995), x, vii–viii.

42. Susan Goodman, *Civil Wars: American Novelists and Manners, 1880–1940* (Baltimore, MD: Johns Hopkins University Press, 2003), 17; Updike, *Rabbit Angstrom,* 713, 876–878.

43. Updike, "Introduction," vii.

44. Eric Kauffman, *The Rise and Fall of Anglo-America* (Cambridge, MA: Harvard University Press, 2004), 207–282.

45. Updike, *Rabbit Angstrom,* 512.

46. Morrison, *Conversations with Toni Morrison,* 257.

3. The Reluctant Master Text

1. Richard Brodhead, *The School of Hawthorne* (New York: Oxford University Press, 1986), 51, 11. All this is not to say that Hawthorne's reputation has been wholly stable. He has always also had his detractors, from some early reviewers who thought *The Scarlet Letter* immoral to complaints by some twentieth-century feminist critics that *The Scarlet Letter* stacks its deck against Hester and that his literary reputation has been systematically inflated by male critical establishments operating from specious aesthetic premises. See for example David Leverenz, "Mrs. Hawthorne's Headache: Reading *The Scarlet Letter,*" *Nineteenth-Century Literature* 37 (March 1983): 552–575; and Jane Tompkins, *Sensational Designs: The Cultural Work of American Fiction, 1790–1860* (New York: Oxford University Press, 1984), 3–40. The question of whether Hawthorne leaned more toward urbane irony (as Henry James thought) or toward somber probing of the mysteries of human iniquity (as Melville thought) has been debated over and over. As we'll see further below, so have the questions of whether his sympathies as to politics, morality, and religion were predominantly conservative or liberal, and whether he was deeply invested in historical research or merely used history as a venue for fables directed at contemporary issues.

2. Henry James, "Hawthorne" (1879), in *Literary Criticism,* vol. 1: *Essays on Literature: American Writers, English Writers,* ed. Leon Edel (New York: Library of America, 1984), 403.

3. As of June 2013, about one-quarter of Amazon.com reviewers—an unusually high percentage compared to reviews of other GAN candidates discussed in this book—volunteered that they had first read *The Scarlet Letter* as an assigned text. A disproportionate number of the reviewers who gave the book low ratings (one or two stars) were from this group.

4. Michael T. Gilmore, *Surface and Depth: The Quest for Legibility in American Literature* (Chicago: University of Chicago Press, 2003), 84; Michael Davitt Bell, *Hawthorne and the Historical Romance of New England* (Princeton, NJ: Princeton University Press, 1971).

5. Lauren Berlant, "Fancy-Work and Fancy Foot-Work: Motives for Silence in *Washington Square,*" *Criticism* 29 (Fall 1987): 447; and Brodhead, *School of Hawthorne,* 189 and passim.

6. Other titles than those just mentioned include Christopher Bigsby, *Hester* (1994), and Paula Reed, *Hester: The Missing Years of "The Scarlet Letter"* (2011) (novels); Phyllis Nagy, *The Scarlet Letter* (1994), and Carol Gilligan, *The Scarlet Letter* (2002) (plays); Mark Governor, *shAme* (1994), Terry Quinne and Stephen Paulus, *Hester Prynne at Death* (2004), and Lori Laitman, *The Scarlet Letter* (2008) (operas); *The Scarlet Letter,* dir. Roland Jaffe (1995), *The Scarlet Letter,* dir. Byun Hyuk (2004), and *Easy A,* dir. Will Gluck (2010) (films); Michael Barr, *The Scarlet Letter* (2002), and Melissa Hart, *The Scarlet Letter*

(2011) (musicals); "I'm a Frayed Knot" (1990), choreo. Byron Suber, and "The Scarlet Letter," choreo. Dianna Cuatto (dance).

7. Jonathan Arac, "The Politics of *The Scarlet Letter*," in *Ideology and Classic American Literature*, ed. Sacvan Bercovitch and Myra Jehlen (Cambridge, MA: Harvard University Press, 1986), 247–268; Bharati Mukherjee, *"The Scarlet Letter,"* in *A New Literary History of America*, ed. Griel Marcus and Werner Sollors (Cambridge, MA: Harvard University Press, 2009), 268–273.

8. Suzan-Lori Parks, "Tradition and the Individual Talent," *Theater* 29.2 (Fall 1999): 30.

9. Nathaniel Hawthorne, *Letters, 1857–1864*, ed. Thomas Woodson et al. (Columbus: Ohio State University Press, 1987), 8–9, 543; Brenda Wineapple, *Hawthorne: A Life* (New York: Knopf, 2003), 187.

10. J. W. De Forest, "The Great American Novel," *Nation* 6 (9 January 1868): 27–29.

11. Hawthorne consistently represented himself as a political innocent wrongfully victimized by regime change from a Democratic to Whig administration, pleading his even-handed restraint as an indulgent boss presiding over a largely incompetent, superannuated staff. True up to a point, these claims belie his lobbying effort to keep the job, and omit a key reason why it failed: the revelation of his role as "Democratic party enforcer" of a scheme of higher pay for Democratic employees than Whig on condition of return of a percentage of the extra to party coffers (Stephen Nissenbaum, "The Firing of Nathaniel Hawthorne," *Essex Institute Historical Collections* 114 [April 1978]: 70). As Nissenbaum evenhandedly sums up: Hawthorne wasn't "the practicing machine politician" he was accused of being, but "neither was he the political innocent pictured by his friends"—and by himself (80).

12. And perhaps not even then? Critic Denis Foster accuses Dimmesdale of "confessional evasion," in the book-long generalized sermonic protestations of sinfulness that his parishioners mishear as confirmation of his saintliness and even in the last scaffold scene, when he silences Hester, avoids facing that "the source of his eloquence" has been "the desire that arises from Hester," and "is careful never to confess any specific act which might interfere with his role as signifier of the divine" (Foster, "The Embroidered Sin: Confessional Evasion in *The Scarlet Letter*," *Criticism* 25 [Spring 1983]: 150).

13. Larry Reynolds, *European Revolutions and the American Renaissance* (New Haven, CT: Yale University Press, 1988), 79–96; Laura Doyle, *Freedom's Empire: Race and the Rise of the Novel in Atlantic Modernity, 1640–1940* (Durham, NC: Duke University Press, 2008), 310.

14. I say "protagonists," plural, to grant that Hester and Dimmesdale are given equal time. But although some (male) critics contest the point, Hester dominates. She is the focal figure at start and close; the two halves of the plot lead off with her; and the narrator identifies the fictitious "original"

tale as Hester's story. Small wonder, then, that the overwhelming majority of readers have found her the more commanding and sympathetic figure.

15. Hawthorne professed disinterest in historical precision, but his homework was exceedingly careful. That every Bostonian in *The Scarlet Letter* has a historical antecedent except the elfin Pearl and the demoniacal Chillingworth is demonstrated by Charles Ryskamp, "The New England Sources of *The Scarlet Letter,"* *American Literature* 31 (November 1959): 257–272; and Michael Colacurcio, "'Footsteps of Anne Hutchinson': The Context of *The Scarlet Letter,"* *ELH: English Literary History* 39 (September 1972): 459–492. At the same time, typically for his day, Hawthorne viewed Puritanism through contemporary debates over (for example) child rearing practices, women's rights, and the threat/allure of Catholicism as seen through mainstream Protestant eyes. Hester's parenting, for instance, looks indulgently un-Puritan; to call Dimmesdale a "priest" is to Catholicize him; under Puritanism adultery would have called for jury trial, here avoided partly to accentuate the magistrates' power (Laura Hanft Korobkin, "The Scarlet Letter of the Law: Hawthorne and Criminal Justice," *Novel* 30 [Winter 1997]: 206). Other attempts to adjudicate between the novel's nineteenth- and seventeenth-century frames of reference include L. Buell, *New England Literary Culture* (Cambridge: Cambridge University Press, 1986), 261–280; Lauren Berlant, *The Anatomy of National Fantasy: Hawthorne, Utopia, and Everyday Life* (Chicago: University of Chicago Press, 1991); and Doyle, *Freedom's Empire*, 301–330.

16. T. Walter Herbert, *Dearest Beloved: The Hawthornes and the Making of the Middle-Class Family* (Berkeley: University of California Press, 1993), 125. On critiques of the institution of marriage during this era generally, see Nancy Cott, *Public Vows: A History of Marriage and the Nation* (Cambridge, MA: Harvard University Press, 2000), 56–78.

17. Michael Colacurcio, *Doctrine and Difference: Essays in the Literature of New England* (New York: Routledge, 1997), 188.

18. Note that Dimmesdale is subjected to even harsher narratorial criticism. Hester's impulsiveness he partly extenuates: she has been driven beyond the pale into isolation and moral wilderness, and as a woman (here he sounds misogynistic but actually makes pretty much the same claim as Mary Wollstonecraft's landmark *Vindication of the Rights of Woman*, 1792) she has not been disciplined in rational analysis. But for a pillar of the community like Dimmesdale no such excuses can be made.

19. Edwin Percy Whipple, Review of *SL*, *Graham's Magazine* 36 (May 1850): 346.

20. Larry Reynolds, *Devils and Rebels: The Making of Hawthorne's Damned Politics* (Ann Arbor: University of Michigan Press, 2008); Sacvan Bercovitch, *The Office of "The Scarlet Letter"* (Baltimore, MD: Johns Hopkins University Press, 1991), quotation p. 30. Reynolds's and Bercovitch's respect for the integrity and complex consistency of Hawthorne's position do not typify

turn-of-the-twenty-first-century diagnoses of Hawthorne as a political moderate or conservative, particularly on the subject of race and slavery. Following more in the line of Arac's influential critique of *The Scarlet Letter*'s evasion of the slavery issue as synchronous with Hawthorne's temporizing presidential campaign biography of his southern-sympathizing friend Franklin Pierce (n. 7 above), the present critical "consensus on Hawthorne and politics," as Michael T. Gilmore tartly sums up, would rather seem to be he was "an *inactivist* who fetishized deferral" (Gilmore, *The War on Words: Slavery, Race, and Free Speech in American Literature* [Chicago: University of Chicago Press, 2010], 87, 299 n. 1). For strong defenses of Hawthorne as neither so racist nor so anti-antislavery as he has often been taken to be, see Reynolds, *Devils and Rebels;* and Robert S. Levine, *Dislocating Race and Nation: Episodes in Nineteenth Century American Literary Nationalism* (Chapel Hill: University of North Carolina Press, 2008), 119–178. For rebuttal of *The Scarlet Letter*'s political insouciance, see Bercovitch, *Office,* 73–112.

21. Robert S. Levine, "Antebellum Feminists on Hawthorne: Reconsidering the Reception of *The Scarlet Letter,*" in Leland S. Person, ed., *"The Scarlet Letter" and Other Writings* (New York: Norton, 2005), 274–290.

22. Critical quotations above from, respectively, Colacurcio, "'Footsteps,'" 495, 481; Nina Baym, *"The Scarlet Letter": A Reading* (Boston: Twayne, 1986), 29; Myra Jehlen, *American Incarnation: The Individual, the Nation, and the Continent* (Cambridge, MA: Harvard University Press, 1986), 138; and Berlant, *Anatomy of National Fantasy,* 34, 137.

23. Christopher Castiglia reads them optimistically as creating a space over against the authorities for "a new sociality"; see Castiglia, *Interior States: Institutional Consciousness and the Inner Life of Democracy in the Antebellum United States* (Durham, NC: Duke University Press, 2008), 296. Richard Millington suspects that they bespeak lingering dissent: Hester's reported modesty at these gatherings (acknowledging that she herself is not to be the destined prophetess of a new order) "may indicate less her new quietism than an estimate of her audience's sympathy." See Millington, *Practicing Romance: Narrative Form and Cultural Engagement in Hawthorne's Fiction* (Princeton, NJ: Princeton University Press, 1992), 101. Berlant, more warily, describes these exchanges as "the only remaining places where [dissenting] historical narrative and social fantasy might be transmitted" (*Anatomy of National Fantasy,* 156).

24. Robert Darnton, *The Great Cat Massacre and Other Episodes in French Cultural History* (New York: Basic Books, 1984), 242.

25. Nathaniel Hawthorne, *French and Italian Notebooks,* ed. Thomas Woodson (Columbus: Ohio State University Press, 1980), 556; Leslie Fiedler, *Love and Death in the American Novel* (New York: Criterion, 1960), 496.

26. Critical quotations, respectively, from Frederick Newberry, *Hawthorne's Divided Loyalties: England and America in His Works* (Rutherford, NJ: Associated University Presses, 1987), 168; Paul Giles, *Transatlantic Insurrections:*

British Culture and the Formation of American Literature, 1730–1860 (Philadelphia: University of Pennsylvania Press, 2001), 178; and Doyle, *Freedom's Empire*, 329.

27. Foster, "The Embroidered Sin," 161.

28. In an earlier scene, however, Pearl is glimpsed skipping among the tombstones of the same burying ground, stopping to dance on "the broad, flat, armorial tombstone of a departed worthy,—perhaps of Isaac Johnson himself"—the lot's first owner (*SL* 89).

29. It also violates one of heraldry's few taboos—"*Never* place a colour on a colour"—according to Stefan Oliver, *An Introduction to Heraldry* (New York: Gallery, 1987), 22. Although there's no evidence either way, it's hard not to suspect that the emblem-literate Hawthorne would have known that his gules-on-sable configuration was transgressive.

30. For previous critical discussion, see Patricia Crain, *The Story of A: The Alphabetization of America from "The New England Primer" to "The Scarlet Letter"* (Stanford, CA: Stanford University Press, 2000), 201–202; and John Stubbs, "A Note on the Source of Hawthorne's Heraldic Device in '*The Scarlet Letter*,'" *Notes and Queries* 15 (May 1968): 175–176.

31. Andrew Marvell, *The Poems and Letters of Andrew Marvell*, ed. H. M. Margoliouth (Oxford: Clarendon, 2007), 1:29.

32. Walter Scott, *Waverley* (Edinburgh: Constable, 1901), 13–14.

33. George Dekker, *The American Historical Romance* (Cambridge: Cambridge University Press, 1987), 131. Hawthorne wrote his sister Elizabeth in 1820 that he had read all of Scott's books to date except *The Abbot* (Nathaniel Hawthorne, *Letters 1813–1843*, ed. Thomas Woodson et al. [Columbus: Ohio State University Press, 1984], 132). His son Julian remembered his father reading aloud to the family "the whole of Walter Scott's Novels" a few years before his death (Julian Hawthorne, *Nathaniel Hawthorne and His Wife* [Boston: Houghton, 1884], 2:9).

34. For Hawthorne's nineteenth-century readers, the closing scene would have been made more resonant by the tradition of soulful graveyard pondering as both a literary device and a religious/recreational practice. Most would have known Thomas Gray's "Elegy Written in a Country Churchyard" and the frame narrative of Scott's *Old Mortality*, as well as the burgeoning homiletic and popular meditational literature about the new "rural" cemeteries like Mount Auburn in Cambridge, Massachusetts.

35. Rufus Choate, *The Works of Rufus Choate*, ed. Samuel Gilman Brown (Boston: Little, 1852), 1:319–346.

36. Dekker, *American Historical Romance*, 170; Robert Milder, *Hawthorne's Habitations* (New York: Oxford University Press, 2013), 117.

37. Berlant, *Anatomy of National Fantasy*, 202; Wai Chee Dimock, *Through Other Continents: American Literature across Deep Time* (Princeton, NJ: Princeton University Press, 2006), 7. Dimock's observation is made not apropos *The Scarlet Letter* but at the start of her exploratory analysis of Thoreauvian and

Emersonian imagination as rooted in ancient Asian texts, scriptural and literary, one of a series of mind-expanding experiments in elasticizing the spatiotemporality of "American" literature that have influenced my thinking here, from which I have greatly profited.

38. Brodhead, *School of Hawthorne*, 200.

39. Ralph Waldo Emerson, *Essays, Second Series*, ed. Joseph Slater et al. (Cambridge, MA: Harvard University Press, 1983), 127.

40. Doyle, *Freedom's Empire*, 319.

41. Frederic I. Carpenter, "Scarlet A Minus," *College English* 5 (January 1944): 173–180.

42. Bharati Mukherjee, *The Holder of the World* (New York: Knopf, 1993), 284, 285, 283. Judie Newman's thoughtful summation is also pertinent here: "Mukherjee's strategy is to guard against the danger of overhistoricizing"; "the problems of handling [historical] data" that culminate with the defects of the time-travel software "are a thread which runs through the whole novel" (Newman, *Fictions of America: Narratives of Global Empire* [London: Routledge, 2007], 26).

43. Mukherjee, *Holder of the World*, 285, 286.

44. Bharati Mukherjee, "A Four Hundred-Year-Old Woman," in *The Writer on Her Work*, vol. 2: *New Essays in New Territory*, ed. Janet Sternberg (New York: Norton, 1991), 34. Perhaps instead of insisting that Hawthorne got his story wrong, *Holder* might have given *The Scarlet Letter* more credit for triggering her own revisionism through those fleeting glances that break the illusion of a monolithic self-contained community. On the other hand, a number of transnationally oriented Hawthorne critics might think Mukherjee not severe enough: for example, John Carlos Rowe's verdict that "Hawthorne's romantic regionalism is a trick that serves expansionist political and cultural purposes" and Doyle's that through Hester the novel fashioned "an individualist race-fantasy of freedom through Anglo-American women" that "borrows the figure of the Indian as a model for Hester's freedom" while largely banishing literal Natives from the text. See Doyle, *Freedom's Empire*, 329, 321; Rowe, "Nathaniel Hawthorne and Transnationality," in *Hawthorne and the Real: Bicentennial Essays*, ed. Millicent Bell (Columbus: Ohio State University Press, 2005), 91.

45. For much more on Howells's and James's absorption of Hawthorne, see Brodhead, *School of Hawthorne*, 81–200.

46. Christopher Bigsby, *Hester: A Novel* (New York: Viking, 1994), 185; John Updike, *Roger's Version* (New York: Ballantine, 1986), 51.

47. David S. Reynolds, *Beneath the American Renaissance: The Subversive Imagination in the Age of Emerson and Melville* (New York: Knopf, 1988), 267. Philip F. Gura, *Truth's Ragged Edge: The Rise of the American Novel* (New York: Farrar, Straus, 2013), 223–228, rightly characterizes *Hagar: A Story of To-Day* as a rendition of key parts of *The Scarlet Letter* even more somber—and far more sensational—than the original.

48. Nina Baym, "Passion and Authority in *The Scarlet Letter*," *New England Quarterly* 43 (June 1970): 222.
49. Carrie Tirado Bramen, "The Americanization of Theron Ware," *Novel: A Forum on Fiction* 31 (Fall 1997): 65.
50. Bramen points out that the Irish "represented a comparatively safe alien in the late nineteenth century" (ibid., 68), being by this time well on their way to social acceptance in the United States. The novel broadly confirms this by representing the Irish of Octavius, New York, as upstanding citizens, and by contrast to Dr. Ledsmar's opium-addicted Chinese servant, who remains intractably alien not only to Theron but also to the reader. Yet even though the novel evinces a far more cosmopolitan acceptance of religious and cultural variety than (say) the phobic anti-Catholicism of antebellum evangelist Lyman Beecher's *A Plea for the West* (1835), it plays upon as well as satirizes ancient anxieties about the combined menace and exoticism of Catholic/Celtic others by viewing Catholicism through ignorant Protestant eyes.
51. Harold Frederic, *The Damnation of Theron Ware, or Illumination*, ed. Carlyne Dodge and Stanton Garner (Lincoln: University of Nebraska Press, 1985), 243.
52. Bercovitch, *Office*, 66–69, and *The Rites of Assent* (New York: Routledge, 1993), 168–193; Wineapple, *Hawthorne*, 128–129.
53. Jonathan Arac, *The Emergence of American Literary Narrative: 1820–1860* (Cambridge, MA: Harvard University Press, 2005), 146–165.
54. Kai Erikson, *Wayward Puritans: A Study in the Sociology of Deviance* (New York: Wiley, 1966).

III. Introduction. American Dreamers in Context

1. M. M. Bakhtin, "The *Bildungsroman* and Its Significance in the History of Realism," in *Speech Genres and Other Essays*, trans. Vern W. McGee, ed. Caryl Emerson and Michael Holquist (Austin: University of Texas Press, 1986), 25; Jed Esty, *Unseasonable Youth: Modernism, Colonialism, and the Fictions of Development* (New York: Oxford University Press, 2012), 44.
2. Franco Moretti, *The Way of the World: The Bildungsroman in European Culture*, new ed., trans. Albert Sbragia (London: Verso, 2000), 15, 233, 228.
3. Joseph Slaughter, *Human Rights, Inc.: The World Novel, Narrative Form, and International Law* (New York: Fordham University Press, 2007), 115; Pheng Cheah, *Spectral Nationality: Passages of Freedom from Kant to Postcolonial Literatures of Liberation* (New York: Columbia University Press, 2003). Cheah's key Europhone example is José Rizal's *Noli Me Tangere* (1887), then as now considered the great Filipino novel, in which the naively idealistic young Ibarra's development "parallels and symbolizes that of the emergent nation" (239): his belated political awakening upon returning home to find his compatriots suffering under the corrupt colonial establishment that includes some of his own relatives.

4. Leela Gandhi, "'Learning Me Your Language': England in the Postcolonial *Bildungsroman*," in *England through Colonial Eyes in Twentieth-Century Fiction,* ed. Anne Blake, Leela Gandhi, and Eve Thomas (New York: Palgrave-Macmillan, 2001), 56.
5. Esty, *Unseasonable Youth,* 13.

4. "Success" Stories from Franklin to the Dawn of Modernism

1. Frederick Douglass, *The Narrative of Frederick Douglass,* ed. Benjamin Quarles (Cambridge, MA: Harvard University Press, 1960), 104–105.
2. The history of "sentimental" both as adjective and as genre designation is complex. During the eighteenth century, the primary connotation of sentiment shifted from the cognitive (sentiment as opinion) to the affective (sentiment as feeling). In Americanist criticism, fictional "sentimentalism" was at first slightingly associated with the allegedly unrestrained emotionalism of early national and antebellum Richardsonian novels by women, then extended both pejoratively (as in Ann Douglas, *The Feminization of American Culture* [New York: Knopf, 1977]) and honorifically (as in Jane Tompkins, *Sensational Designs* [New York: Oxford University Press, 1984]) to denote more broadly a cultural valuation of affective bonding that came to be seen as shared by men as well as women (as by Douglas, *Feminization;* Julie Ellison, *Cato's Tears* [Chicago: University of Chicago Press, 1999]; Mary Louise Kete, *Sentimental Collaborations* [Durham, NC: Duke University Press, 2000]; Glenn Hendler, *Public Sentiments* [Chapel Hill: University of North Carolina Press, 2001]). Concurrently, the potentially subversive side of sentimental feminism was both asserted (as by Tompkins, *Sensational Designs;* Caroll Smith-Rosenberg, *Disorderly Conduct* [New York: Knopf, 1985]; Cathy N. Davidson, *Revolution and the Word* [New York: Oxford University Press, 1986]) and countered as complicit with white middle-class domination and/or U.S. expansionism and imperialism (as by Lori Merish, *Sentimental Materialism* [Durham, NC: Duke University Press, 2000] and Amy Kaplan, *The Anarchy of Empire* [Cambridge, MA: Harvard University Press, 2005], 23–50). Relatedly, sentimentalism was decoupled from impulsiveness and reconceived as part of more complex strategies of self-fashioning and social negotiation. Shirley Samuels, ed., *The Culture of Sentiment* (New York: Oxford University Press, 1992), remains an indispensable collection of critical perspectives; June Howard, "What Is Sentimentality?," *American Literary History* 11 (Spring 1999): 63–81, provides a valuable essay-length definition; Lauren Berlant, *The Female Complaint* (Durham, NC: Duke University Press, 2008), is a marvelously incisive, sophisticated—and disillusioned—argument for sentimentalism's persistence to this day as a force within popular culture. Stowe's *Uncle Tom's Cabin,* the Great American Novel featured in Chapter 7, was U.S. sentimentalism's high-water mark, although its political vehemence and swerve from protagonist-centrism and marriage plot are atypical of the genre.

3. Robert Wuthnow, *American Mythos: Why Our Best Efforts to Be a Better Nation Fall Short* (Princeton, NJ: Princeton University Press, 2006), 108.

4. Timothy Noah, *The Great Divergence: America's Growing Inequality Crisis and What We Can Do about It* (New York: Bloomsbury, 2012), 144–163. Citing a 2007 study by the Organisation for Economic Co-operation and Development of relative income heritability across various developed countries, Noah stresses the irony that a far larger percentage of polled Americans today believe in the chance of upward mobility from the bottom quintile to the top than do Canadians, for whom the statistical chances are far better.

5. J. Hector St. John de Crèvecoeur, *Letters from an American Farmer* (New York: Dutton, 1957), 39.

6. James Truslow Adams, *The Epic of America* (Boston: Little, Brown, 1932), 404. Perhaps unbeknownst to Adams, some years before the cultural critic Walter Lippmann had tossed out the phrase in passing, with a rather different spin—that "the undisciplined man is the salt of the earth" (*Drift and Mastery: An Attempt to Diagnose the Current Unrest* [New York: Kennerley, 1914], 178). The common denominator with Adams is the dignity that U.S. public culture accords, on principle anyhow, to the ordinary person. For insightful discussion of Adams's *Epic* in relation to popular literary and historical fiction of the 1930s, see Gordon Hutner, *What America Read: Taste, Class, and the Novel, 1920–1960* (Chapel Hill: University of North Carolina Press, 2009), 108–110.

7. See especially Franco Moretti, *The Way of the World: The Bildungsroman in European Culture*, new ed., trans. Albert Sbragia (London: Verso, 2000), 229–245; Gregory Castle, *Reading the Modernist Bildungsroman* (Gainesville: University of Florida Press, 2006); and Jed Esty, *Unseasonable Youth: Modernism, Colonialism, and the Fictions of Development* (New York: Oxford University Press, 2011).

8. Walter Scott, *Sir Walter Scott on Novelists and Fiction,* ed. Ioan Williams (New York: Barnes and Noble, 1968), 240.

9. For an excellent summary of the genre's plot conventions and rationale, see Nina Baym, *Woman's Fiction* (Ithaca, NY: Cornell University Press, 1978), 22–50.

10. Philip Fisher, *Still the New World: American Literature in a Culture of Creative Destruction* (Cambridge, MA: Harvard University Press, 1999), 275.

11. Esty, *Unseasonable Youth,* 121.

12. Nina Baym, "Melodramas of Beset Manhood: How Theories of American Fiction Exclude Women Authors" (1981), repr. in Nina Baym, *Feminism and American Literary History* (New Brunswick, NJ: Rutgers University Press, 1992), 3–18.

13. Nina Baym, *Women Writers of the American West, 1833–1927* (Urbana: University of Illinois Press, 2011), 1, 265–309.

14. Esty, *Unseasonable Youth,* 92, 57.

15. Moretti, *Way of the World*, 189.

16. Joseph Slaughter, *Human Rights, Inc.: The World Novel, Narrative Form, and International Law* (New York: Fordham University Press, 2007), 40, 29.

17. Marianne Hirsch, "The Novel of Formation as Genre: Between Great Expectations and Lost Illusions," *Genre* 12 (Fall 1979): 300; Slaughter, *Human Rights, Inc.*, 133, 19.

18. Bruce Robbins, *Upward Mobility and the Common Good: Toward a Literary History of the Welfare State* (Princeton, NJ: Princeton University Press, 2007); Nancy Armstrong, *How Novels Think: The Limits of British Individualism from 1719–1900* (New York: Columbia University Press, 2005), 56, 63.

19. Jay Parini, *Promised Land: Thirteen Books That Changed America* (New York: Doubleday, 2008), 61.

20. John Stauffer, *Giants: The Parallel Lives of Frederick Douglass and Abraham Lincoln* (New York: Twelve, 2008), 72; Frederick Douglass, "Self-Made Men: An Address Delivered in Carlisle, Pennsylvania, in March 1893," in *Frederick Douglass Papers, Series One: Speeches, Debates, and Interviews*, vol. 5, ed. John W. Blassingame and John R. McKivigan (New Haven, CT: Yale University Press, 1992), 569.

21. Douglass, "Self-Made Men," 556, 545, 566. From Douglass's standpoint, Lincoln especially deserved pride of place, however, as "the man who rose highest and will be remembered longest as the most popular and beloved President since Washington" (566), and the man most responsible for Emancipation—albeit only after a delay that seemed maddeningly slow to Douglass and other progressives at the time. As historian John Stauffer points out, "the crux of self-making" for Douglass "was to remake your world as well" (*Giants*, 166).

22. Alexis de Tocqueville, *Democracy in America,* trans. and ed. Phillips Bradley (New York: Vintage, 1945), 1:269–271.

23. John Cawelti, *Apostles of the Self-Made Man* (Chicago: University of Chicago Press, 1965), 39–75.

24. William Dean Howells, "A Tale of Love and Politics: Adventures of a Printer Boy," *Ashtabula Sentinel,* 1 September 1853.

25. Daniel Walker Howe, *Making the American Self: Jonathan Edwards to Abraham Lincoln* (Cambridge, MA: Harvard University Press, 1997), 137.

26. Robbins, *Upward Mobility and the Common Good*, 70, 72.

27. Thomas Augst, *The Clerk's Tale: Young Men and Moral Life in Nineteenth Century America* (Chicago: University of Chicago Press, 2003), 270; William Dean Howells, *The Rise of Silas Lapham*, ed. David Nordloh (Bloomington: Indiana University Press, 1971), 5.

28. Robert Herrick, "The American Novel," *Yale Review* 3 (April 1914): 430, 431.

29. Frank Luther Mott, *Golden Multitudes: The Story of Best Sellers in the United States* (New York: Macmillan, 1947), 261—unless we count Charles Sheldon's tractarian *In His Steps* (1899), the high-water mark of social gospel–era "religious

realism," as the literary historian Gregory Jackson terms it, for which the author claimed sales of 22 million by the mid-1920s (Mott, 195) and which continued through the second half of the twentieth century to sell 100,000 copies annually (Gregory Jackson, *The Word and Its Witness: The Spiritualization of American Realism* [Chicago: University of Chicago Press, 2009], 349–350).

30. For differing assessments, see Myra Jehlen, *American Incarnation: The Individual, The Nation, and the Continent* (Cambridge, MA: Harvard University Press, 1986), 76–122; John Carlos Rowe, *At Emerson's Tomb: The Politics of Classic American Literature* (New York: Columbia University Press, 1997), 17–41; and L. Buell, "Manifest Destiny and the Question of the Moral Absolute," in *The Oxford Handbook of American Transcendentalism*, ed. Joel Myerson, Sandra Petrulionis, and Laura Dassow Walls (New York: Oxford University Press, 2010), 180–197.

31. Nicholas Bromell, *By the Sweat of the Brow: Literature and Labor in Antebellum America* (Chicago: University of Chicago Press, 1993), 213–239.

32. George Lorimer, *Letters from a Self-Made Merchant to His Son* (Boston: Small, Maynard, 1903), 143.

33. On the impact of social Darwinism upon U.S. literary history, still indispensable is Ronald E. Martin, *American Literature and the Universe of Force* (Durham, NC: Duke University Press, 1981), whose analysis of Jack London (184–214) has influenced mine below. On the relation between aestheticism and naturalism, see especially Mao's keen analysis of "the material basis" of Walter Pater's aestheticism (Douglas Mao, *Fateful Beauty: Aesthetic Environments, Juvenile Development, and Literature 1860–1960* [Princeton, NJ: Princeton University Press, 2008], 78) and of Theodore Dreiser, whom I discuss in Chapter 5, as a latter-day exemplar of Paterian "aesthetics of acuteness" (66–81, 109–176). On neither count was actual naturalistic practice entirely self-consistent, however, as Mao shows in Dreiser's case.

34. Christopher P. Wilson, *The Labor of Words: Literary Professionalism in the Progressive Era* (Athens: University of Georgia Press, 1985), 93.

35. For *Lamplighter* as great American romance, see the New York City bookseller H. Lang's broadside advertisement (New York Historical Society broadside SY1854 no. 85); for the second hype, and others, see Susan Williams, *Reclaiming Authorship: Literary Woman in America, 1850–1900* (Philadelphia: University of Pennsylvania Press, 2006), 78. Both presumably would have been encouraged if not written by Jewett. My analysis below is influenced by Williams's subtle argument that despite any appearances to the contrary, *The Lamplighter* should be understood as "a generically and thematically open text" with multiple incipient trajectories (ibid., 92).

36. Richard Brodhead, *Cultures of Letters: Scenes of Reading and Writing in Nineteenth-Century America* (Chicago: University of Chicago Press, 1993), 17–18.

37. Castle, *Reading the Modernist Bildungsroman*, 200–212.

38. Maria Cummins, *The Lamplighter*, ed. Nina Baym (New Brunswick, NJ: Rutgers University Press, 1988), 202.

39. Ibid., 144. Editor Nina Baym tellingly calls this "the obligatory moment in the female Bildungsroman" when "the heroine defies unjust patriarchal authority" (ibid., xxiii).

40. Ibid., 63.

41. Cindy Weinstein, "'A Sort of Adopted Daughter': Family Relations in '*The Lamplighter*,'" *ELH: English Literary History* 68 (Winter 2001): 1044; Berlant, *Female Complaint*, 65.

42. Elizabeth Stoddard, *The Morgesons and Other Writings*, ed. L. Buell and Sandra Zagarell (Philadelphia: University of Pennsylvania Press, 1984), 253; Moretti, *Way of the World*, 188.

43. Stoddard to John Bowen, publisher of *The Independent*, 9 October 1889, quoted in L. Buell, *New England Literary Culture* (Cambridge: Cambridge University Press, 1986), 363.

44. Susan Fraiman, *Unbecoming Women: British Women Writers and the Novel of Development* (New York: Columbia University Press, 1993), 59–87.

45. Willa Cather, *Song of the Lark, Early Novels and Stories*, ed. Sharon O'Brien (New York: Library of America, 1987), 410.

46. See Michael Gorra, *Portrait of a Novel: Henry James and the Making of an American Masterpiece* (New York: Liveright, 2012), 234–237 (chapter 42 marks the effective beginning of modernist representation of consciousness and James's stature as a master of international literary modernism) and 114–115 (its "account of the limits of self-sufficiency is what, above all, makes *Portrait of a Lady* stand as a great American novel").

47. Cather, *Song of the Lark*, 687.

48. Wharton's one direct reference to *Custom* as a would-be GAN was almost certainly tongue in cheek, in a 1908 remark to her friend Sara Norton that she had "taken up again [her] sadly neglected great American novel" (*Letters of Edith Wharton*, ed. R. W. B. Lewis and Nancy Lewis [New York: Scribner's, 1988], 146). But her later enthusiasm for Anita Loos's *Gentlemen Prefer Blondes* (1925), which Wharton in fact acclaimed as the Great American Novel (see Chapter 5), shows the value she set on *Custom*. *Blondes*, especially its on-the-make heroine, "seemed to her like a latter-day *Custom*," observes Wharton's best biographer, Hermione Lee, in *Edith Wharton* (New York: Knopf, 2007), 620.

49. Peter Brooks, *Henry James Goes to Paris* (Princeton, NJ: Princeton University Press, 2007), 44–52; Christine de Maupeou, "Henry James and the French Aristocracy under the Napoleonic Code: Madame de Vionnet and a Contextual Reading of *The Ambassadors*," master's thesis, Harvard University, 2005.

50. Wharton, *A Backward Glance* (New York: Appleton-Century, 1934), 182–183.

51. Lee, *Edith Wharton*, 436.

52. Jennifer Fleissner, *Women, Compulsion, Modernity: The Moment of American Naturalism* (Chicago: University of Chicago Press, 2004), 197.

5. Belated Ascendancy

1. Gordon Hutner, *What America Read: Taste, Class, and the Novel, 1920–1960* (Chapel Hill: University of North Carolina Press, 2009), 55.
2. Susan Hegeman, "Taking Blondes Seriously," *American Literary History* 7 (Autumn 1995): 535.
3. Paul Kennedy, *The Rise and Fall of the Great Powers: Economic Change and Military Conflict from 1500 to 2000* (New York: Random House, 1987), 277, 327; Ann Douglas, *Terrible Honesty: Mongrel Manhattan in the 1920s* (New York: Farrar, Straus and Giroux, 1995), 185.
4. Gregory Castle, *Reading the Modernist Bildungsroman* (Gainesville: University Press of Florida, 2006), 71.
5. Jerome Loving, *The Last Titan: A Life of Theodore Dreiser* (Berkeley: University of California Press, 2005), 302.
6. H. L. Mencken, "Theodore Dreiser," in *A Book of Prefaces* (New York: Knopf, 1917), 83.
7. F. Scott Fitzgerald, *The Crack-Up*, ed. Edmund Wilson (New York: New Directions, 1945), 271.
8. H. L. Mencken, "Dreiser in 840 Pages," *American Mercury* 7 (March 1926): 381; Joseph Wood Krutch, "Crime and Punishment," *Nation* 122 (10 February 1926), 152.
9. F. Scott Fitzgerald, "Introduction" to 1934 Modern Library rpt. of *Gatsby*, in *F. Scott Fitzgerald in His Own Time*, ed. Matthew J. Bruccoli and Jackson R. Bryer (New York: Popular Library, 1971), 156.
10. Thomas P. Riggio, "Dreiser, Fitzgerald, and the Question of Influence," in *Theodore Dreiser and American Culture*, ed. Yoshinobu Hakutani (Newark: University of Delaware Press, 2000), 235; F. Scott Fitzgerald, *Conversations with F. Scott Fitzgerald*, ed. Matthew J. Bruccoli and Judith S. Baughman (Jackson: University Press of Mississippi, 2004), 83.
11. Martha Banta, *Taylored Lives: Narrative Productions in the Age of Taylor, Veblen, and Ford* (Chicago: University of Chicago Press, 1993), 298, 299.
12. Noted in Walter Benn Michaels, "An American Tragedy, or the Promise of American Life," *Representations* 25 (Winter 1989): 91. On *AT*'s use of the Aladdin story, see Ellen Moers, *Two Dreisers: The Man and the Novelist as Revealed in His Two Most Important Works, "Sister Carrie" and "An American Tragedy"* (New York: Viking, 1969), 271–285.
13. Joseph Karganis, "Naturalism's Nation: Toward *An American Tragedy*," *American Literature* 72 (March 2000): 154. Of Clyde's comeuppance and the storm of publicity that his arrest and trial provoke, Karganis astutely remarks that "infamy emerges as a horrible express lane to the spectacularity" he's dreamed of: to become part of the fast set of newspaper gossip columns (165).
14. Robert Herrick, "The American Novel," *Yale Review* 3 (April 1914): 311.
15. This insight is elegantly developed in Joseph O'Neill's reinvention of *Gatsby* as a multiethnic transnational fable in his post-9/11 novel *Netherland*

(2008). O'Neill recasts Nick (with a nod to the end of *GG* and to his own Dutch-Irish background) as a Dutch expatriate investment banker who develops a close rapport around a common passion for cricket with a West Indian immigrant Gatsby-figure who similarly combines idealism—here exemplified especially by the code of sportsmanship on the playing field—and an underground empire of numbers-running racketeering that leads to his murder. On *GG* in relation to 1920s xenophobic racism, see Walter Benn Michaels, *Our America: Nativism, Modernism, and Pluralism* (Durham, NC: Duke University Press, 1995), 23–28, for a perceptively disgruntled analysis.

16. Stephen S. Visher, "A Study of the Type of the Place of Birth and of the Occupation of Fathers of Subjects of Sketches in '*Who's Who in America*,'" *American Journal of Sociology* 30 (March 1925): 551–557; Irvin G. Wyllie, *The Self-Made Man in America: The Myth of Rags to Riches* (New York: Free Press, 1954), 24.

17. Pitrim Sorokin, "American Millionaires and Multi-Millionaires: A Comparative Statistical Study," *Journal of Social Forces* 3 (May 1925): 635. Income inequality had been growing since 1915 (the first year of reliable record keeping, as the year the federal income tax was first levied). From the mid-1930s through the early 1970s, the United States saw what economists Claudia Goldin and Robert Margo dubbed "the Great Compression" in an influential article of that title (*Quarterly Journal of Economics* 107 [February 1992]: 1–34). Since then, however, what economist Paul Krugman no less influentially has called the "Great Divergence" has widened the gap again such that the top 1 percent of U.S. earners again garners nearly 25 percent of all income, as in 1928 (Timothy Noah, *The Great Divergence: America's Growing Inequality Crisis and What We Can Do about It* [New York: Bloomsbury, 2012]).

18. Robert Penn Warren, *Homage to Theodore Dreiser* (New York: Random House, 1971), 138; Thomas Strychacz, *Modernism, Mass Culture, and Professionalism* (Cambridge: Cambridge University Press, 1993), 96.

19. Theodore Dreiser, *Theodore Dreiser: Interviews,* ed. Donald Pizer and Frederick E. Rusch (Chicago: University of Illinois Press, 2004), 157; Theodore Dreiser, "I Find the Real American Tragedy" (1935), ed. Jack Salzman, *Resources for American Literary Study* 2 (Spring 1972): 6.

20. For details, see Craig Brandon, *Murder in the Adirondacks: "An American Tragedy" Revisited* (Utica, NY: North Country Books, 1986). Kathryn M. Plank, "Dreiser's Real American Tragedy," *Papers on Language and Literature* 27 (Spring 1991): 268–287, contends that Dreiser overstated the importance of a single case, that *AT* is rather "a portrayal of a sociological phenomenon" (269) based on a number of incidents that had caught Dreiser's eye by his own admission. Her carefully documented essay probably takes a good point too far. Yes, Clyde's story did attempt to typify a broader phenomenon, but the novel draws much more on the Gillette case than any other.

21. Theodore Dreiser, *A Selection of Uncollected Prose*, ed. Donald Pizer (Detroit: Wayne State University Press, 1977), 267; F. O. Matthiessen, *Theodore Dreiser* (New York: Sloane, 1951), 203–208.

22. Raymond Williams, *Modern Tragedy* (Stanford, CA: Stanford University Press, 1966), 14, 26, 48–49.

23. Arthur Miller, "Tragedy and the Common Man," in *The Theater Essays of Arthur Miller* (New York: Viking, 1977), 3; Williams, *Modern Tragedy*, 104; Dreiser, *Uncollected Prose*, 297.

24. Dreiser, *Uncollected Prose*, 209.

25. Jennifer Fleissner, *Women, Compulsion, Modernity: The Moment of American Naturalism* (Chicago: University of Chicago Press, 2004), 9, 67, 211–217.

26. Douglas Mao, *Fateful Beauty: Aesthetic Environments, Juvenile Development, and Literature 1860–1960* (Princeton, NJ: Princeton University Press, 2008), 172. Mao rightly characterizes Dreiser as a self-conflicted materialist "captivated by the Spenserian grand narrative" yet sometimes "repelled by the thought of a cosmos built on the constant subjugation of weak by strong" and thus self-divided in his aesthetics too: "he could accept neither a privileging of the desire that seemed to drive organisms endlessly through brutal trials nor a clear dismissal of desire so understood" (175). Fitzgerald was never so smitten by social Darwinist reductionism, although to a considerable extent he shared Dreiser's ambivalent fascination with self-destructive desire, intensifying it with a non-Dreiserian *amor fati*.

27. A truly omniscient narrator would either be the impersonal detached god of D. A. Miller's conception of Jane Austen (D. A. Miller, *Jane Austen, or, The Secret of Style* [Princeton, NJ: Princeton University Press, 2003]) or a madman like Faulkner's Darl (in *As I Lay Dying*), whose seeming transparency and gift of second sight come at the cost of an emotional repression that drives him haywire.

28. Donald Pizer, "Dreiser and the Naturalistic Drama of Consciousness," *Journal of Narrative Technique* 21 (Spring 1991): 208–211. In the subtlest examination of the novel's handling of Roberta's death, Jason Puskar argues that *AT*'s nonadjudication of the degree to which it was accidental or intentional marks a crisis of authorial confidence in realism's commitment to verisimilitude itself, confirmed by the fact that Dreiser never completed another novel (Jason Puskar, *Accident Society: Fiction, Collectivity, and the Production of Chance* [Stanford, CA: Stanford University Press, 2012], 195–202).

29. Leonard Cassuto, *Hard-Boiled Sentimentality: The Secret History of American Crime Stories* (New York: Columbia University Press, 2009), 26–27.

30. Bruccoli and Bryer, *F. Scott Fitzgerald in His Own Time*, 168–169.

31. Robert Emmet Long, *The Achieving of "The Great Gatsby": F. Scott Fitzgerald, 1920–1925* (Lewisburg, PA: Bucknell University Press, 1979), 97; Kenneth A. Bruffee, *Elegiac Romance: Cultural Change and Loss of the Hero in Modern Fiction* (Ithaca, NY: Cornell University Press, 1983), 97.

32. Mallios, *Our Conrad*, 235.

33. Joseph Conrad, *Heart of Darkness*, 3rd ed., ed. Robert Kimbrough (New York: Norton, 1988), 50.

34. Geoffrey Harpham, *One of Us: The Mastery of Joseph Conrad* (Chicago: University of Chicago Press, 1996), 42–44.

35. Harold Bloom, "The Internalization of Quest-Romance," in *Romanticism and Consciousness*, ed. Harold Bloom (New York: Norton, 1970), 3–24.

36. For a fuller account, see Lawrence Buell, "Observer-Hero Narrative," *Texas Studies in Literature and Language* 21 (Spring 1979): 93–111, although it now strikes me as overemphasizing the epistemological relative to the ideological and failing to distinguish sufficiently among variants. By no means can all the copious observer-hero fictions in U.S. literary history be allegorized in the metasocial terms discussed here: Poe's "The Fall of the House of Usher" and "Ligeia," to name just two examples. For critical accounts that discuss examples of the observer-hero form to the end of stressing the preeminence of one or the other of the two intertwined figures, see for example Bruffee, *Elegiac Romance* (the observer); and Walter L. Reed, *Meditations on the Hero* (New Haven, CT: Yale University Press, 1974).

37. To all the cases of split-focused observer-hero fiction discussed here and below, critic Philip Fisher's diagnosis of the characteristic imprint of the U.S. culture of capitalist "creative destruction" more or less applies: "What does not exist, but might someday, takes on a half-real, half-unreal quality long before it exists. But all that now exists is equally half-real, half-unreal because it exists under the threat that it might soon become obsolete or be discarded" (Philip Fisher, *Still the New World: American Literature in a Culture of Creative Destruction* [Cambridge, MA: Harvard University Press, 1999], 13).

38. Joseph Conrad, "To My Readers in America," in *The Nigger of the Narcissus* (New York: Doubleday and Page, 1914), ix.

39. That Joe Christmas gets portrayed from the inside as well as out may be because the text leaves it unresolved, even to him, whether he actually has the trace of black blood that he's been told he has and that the community believes. To grant him the interiority of a white character is to underscore the absurdity of peremptorily branding him black.

40. William Faulkner, *Faulkner's MGM Screenplays*, ed. Bruce F. Kawin (Knoxville: University of Tennessee Press, 1982), 429–543.

41. Joseph Blotner, *Faulkner: A Biography* (New York: Random House, 1974), 1: 892; Frederick L. Gwynn and Joseph Blotner, eds., *Faulkner in the University: Class Conferences at the University of Virginia, 1957–1958* (New York: Vintage, 1965), 73.

42. Eric J. Sundquist, *Faulkner: The House Divided* (Baltimore, MD: Johns Hopkins University Press, 1983), 102.

43. William Faulkner, *Requiem for a Nun* (New York: Vintage, 1975), 80.

44. Simon Karlinsky, ed., *Dear Bunny, Dear Volodya: The Nabokov-Wilson Letters* (Berkeley: University of California Press, 2001), 212.

45. Leslie Fiedler, *Love and Death in the American Novel* (New York: Criterion, 1960), 327; Susan Mizruchi, "*Lolita* in History," *American Literature* 75 (September 2003): 629–652; Jeffrey Meyers, "Lewis Carroll and Lolita: A New Reading," *Salmagundi* 172–173 (Fall 2011–Winter 2012): 88–93.

46. Irving Howe, "Afterword," in Theodore Dreiser, *An American Tragedy* (New York: Signet, 1964), 815, 817.

47. Richard Anderson, "Gatsby's Long Shadow: Influence and Endurance," in *New Essays on "The Great Gatsby,"* ed. Matthew J. Bruccoli (Cambridge: Cambridge University Press, 1985), 26.

48. Tony Tanner, *The American Mystery: American Literature from Emerson to DeLillo* (Cambridge: Cambridge University Press, 2000), 199.

49. Werner Sollors, *Ethnic Modernism* (Cambridge, MA: Harvard University Press, 2008).

50. See Yoshinobu Hakutani, *Richard Wright and Racial Discourse* (Columbia: University of Missouri Press, 1996), 84–100, for a more detailed account somewhat less fully persuaded of the closeness between the two novels than I am.

51. Richard Wright, *Native Son*, in *Richard Wright: Early Works*, ed. Arnold Rampersad (New York: Library of America, 1991), 671, 849.

52. Richard Wright, *Black Boy*, in *Later Works*, ed. Arnold Rampersad (New York: Library of America, 1991), 239.

53. Quoted in Hazel Rowley, *Richard Wright: The Life and Times* (New York: Holt, 2001), 163.

54. Richard Wright, "How Bigger Was Born," in Rampersad, *Early Works*, 870; W. E. B. Du Bois, *The Souls of Black Folk*, ed. Henry Louis Gates Jr. and Terri Hume Oliver (New York: Norton, 1999), 11.

55. Marcus Klein, *Foreigners: The Making of American Literature, 1900–1940* (Chicago: University of Chicago Press, 1981), 37.

56. Wright, "How Bigger Was Born," 863.

57. Dreiser, *Uncollected Prose*, 234; Wright quoted in Rowley, *Richard Wright*, 239, 289.

58. Quoted in Rowley, *Richard Wright*, 335.

59. J. T. Adams, *The Epic of America* (Boston: Little, 1932), 416.

60. Unbeknownst to Adams, as her editor Werner Sollors shows, Antin had long since disavowed her youthful optimism, disillusioned by a combination of marital unhappiness and—especially—resurgent American nativism and anti-Semitism after World War I (Werner Sollors, "Introduction," in Mary Antin, *Promised Land* [New York: Penguin, 1997], xxxix–l).

61. Adams, *Epic of America*, 417.

62. Barack Obama, for instance, reports as a young man feeling uniformly depressed reading the giants of African American literature from Du Bois to Baldwin (all seemed to have ended up "exhausted, bitter men, the devil at their heels")—except for Malcolm, whose "repeated acts of self-creation spoke to me" and so too his "vision of a new and uncompromising order,"

while "all the other stuff, the talk of blue-eyed devils and apocalypse, was incidental to that program, I decided, religious baggage that Malcolm himself seemed to have safely abandoned toward the end of his life" (Barack Obama, *Dreams from My Father* [New York: Three Rivers, 2004], 86).

63. Martin Japtok wisely observes in his study of selected African American and Jewish bildungsromans that "not all ethnic novels agree with the notion of ethnic solidarity or see the communal good as unequivocally more important than the individual good" (Martin Japtok, *Growing Up Ethnic: Nationalism and the Bildungsroman in African American and Jewish American Fiction* [Iowa City: University of Iowa Press, 2005], 20).

64. Henry Seidel Canby, review of *Native Son* (1940), repr. in *The Critical Response to Richard Wright,* ed. Robert J. Butler (Westport, CT: Greenwood, 1995), 23–24; Margaret Wallace, "A Powerful Novel about a Boy from Chicago's Black Belt" (1940), repr. in ibid., 29.

65. James Baldwin, *Notes of a Native Son* (Boston: Beacon, 1955), 36; Ralph Ellison, *Conversations with Ralph Ellison,* ed. Maryemma Graham and Amritjit Singh (Jackson: University Press of Mississippi, 1995), 139; Ralph Ellison and Albert Murray, *Trading Twelves: The Selected Letters of Ralph Ellison and Albert Murray,* ed. John Callahan (New York: Modern Library, 2000), 29.

66. James Baldwin, *Nobody Knows My Name: More Notes of a Native Son* (New York: Dial, 1961), 152; Rowley, *Richard Wright,* 262; Ellison, *Conversations with Ralph Ellison,* 211.

67. George Garrett, "Fire and Freshness: A Matter of Style in *The Great Gatsby,*" in Bruccoli, *New Essays on "The Great Gatsby,"* 101.

68. Saul Bellow, *Conversations with Saul Bellow,* ed. Gloria L. Cronin and Ben Siegel (Jackson: University Press of Mississippi, 1994), 61.

69. Fitzgerald, *The Crack-Up,* 310.

70. Saul Bellow, "Dreiser and the Triumph of Art," *Commentary* 11 (May 1951): 502, 503.

71. Bellow, *Conversations with Saul Bellow,* 210.

72. Leslie Fiedler, "Saul Bellow" (1957), repr. in *Saul Bellow and the Critics,* ed. Irving Malin (New York: New York University Press, 1967), 3.

73. On the trend line overall, see for example Carrie Tirado Bramen, *The Uses of Variety: Modern Americanism and the Quest for National Distinctiveness* (Cambridge, MA: Harvard University Press, 2000), 67–198; Susan Mizruchi, *Multicultural America: Economy and Print Culture, 1865–1915* (Chapel Hill: University of North Carolina Press, 2008).

74. Maxwell Geismar, "Saul Bellow: Novelist of the Intellectuals" (1958), in Malin, *Saul Bellow and the Critics,* 17; Bellow, *Conversations with Saul Bellow,* 34, 63.

75. Bellow, *Conversations with Saul Bellow,* 162, 209, 217.

76. Ibid., 282.

77. Ralph Freedman, "Saul Bellow: The Illusion of Environment," in Malin, *Saul Bellow and the Critics,* 60.

Notes to Pages 176–180

6. Up-From Narrative in Hyphenated America

1. Richard Wright, "Blueprint for Negro Writing," *New Challenge* 2 (Fall 1939): 53–65; Arnold Rampersad, *Ralph Ellison: A Biography* (New York: Knopf, 2007), 205.
2. Ralph Ellison, *Conversations with Ralph Ellison,* ed. Maryemma Graham and Amritjit Singh (Jackson: University Press of Mississippi, 1995), 122.
3. Kenneth W. Warren, *So Black and Blue: Ralph Ellison and the Occasion of Criticism* (Chicago: University of Chicago Press, 2003), 1–3.
4. Harold Bloom, *The Anxiety of Influence: A Theory of Poetry,* 2nd ed. (New York: Oxford University Press, 1997), 68.
5. Ralph Ellison, *The Collected Essays of Ralph Ellison,* ed. John F. Callahan (New York: Modern Library, 1995), 670, 94; Ellison, *Conversations with Ralph Ellison,* 334.
6. Quoted in Adam Bradley, *Ralph Ellison in Progress* (New Haven, CT: Yale University Press, 2010), 170–171.
7. Ellison, *Conversations with Ralph Ellison,* 72, 261–262, 233.
8. The two novels are often compared, most helpfully for our purposes in Kasia Boddy's comparison of them as GAN attempts. She identifies both as "anti-Horatio Alger" bildungsromans whose creation and afterlives both show the authors struggling with and against "a perception of themselves (internal and external) as writers of the ghetto," but with *IM* facing the harder challenge because its youthful protagonist is both more smitten by the American dream and, as African American, more socially stigmatized (Kasia Boddy, "The White Boy Looks at the Black Boy, the Black Boy Looks at the White Boy: Saul Bellow, Ralph Ellison, and the Great Omni-American Novel," *Saul Bellow Journal* 16–17 [2000–2001]: 55, 58).
9. Ellison, *Conversations with Ralph Ellison,* 18.
10. Ibid., 12.
11. Though such gestures of homage to Eliot were not without basis, as Barbara Foley shows in her detailed study of the composition of *IM,* they understate both Ellison's initial aversiveness to Eliot and his prior investment in a more politicized and specifically Marxist literary realism, much of which he edited out in the final version. See Barbara Foley, *Wrestling with the Left: The Making of Ralph Ellison's "Invisible Man"* (Durham, NC: Duke University Press, 2010), 71, 107, 170–171, and passim. The politics of Ellison's self-revisions during and after *IM* were not simply a matter of backpedaling from Marxism, either. For instance, he also tended to play down his early debt to Hemingway; see Brian Hochman, "Ellison's Hemingways," *African American Review* 42 (Fall–Winter 2008): 513–532.
12. On the cross-pollination between Euro- and Afro-vernacular voices in U.S. writing of the first half of the twentieth century, see especially Michael North, *The Dialect of Modernism: Race, Language, and Twentieth-Century Literature* (New York: Oxford University Press, 1994); and Joshua L. Miller,

Accented America: The Cultural Politics of Multilingual Modernism (New York: Oxford University Press, 2011).

13. Thomas Schaub, *American Fiction in the Cold War* (Madison: University of Wisconsin Press, 1991), 69.

14. Ellison's evolution from and underacknowledged degree of indebtedness to politically radical social realism generally and to Richard Wright particularly has been well explored. On the former, see especially Foley, *Wrestling with the Left*. On Ellison's personal and literary ties to Wright, see Lawrence Jackson, "The Birth of the Critic: The Literary Friendship of Ralph Ellison and Richard Wright," *American Literature* 72 (June 2000): 321–355; and Timothy Parrish, *Ralph Ellison and the Genius of America* (Amherst: University of Massachusetts Press, 2012), who rightly declares that "without Wright, there would be no *Invisible Man*" (98). Ellisonians will doubtless continue to differ in their judgments of his ingratitude toward Wright and African American literary elders generally, and as to the degree to which his shift from protest realism toward a less politicized modernism was strategic or principled. As to the latter, Ellison never seems to have experienced the external pressure to alter his aesthetic for political reasons that pushed Wright to redact *American Hunger,* and the rift between Ellison and more politically oppositional African American literati during the 1960s took so great a toll on him that it seems unlikely to have been driven mainly by desire to fulfill critical mainstream expectations.

15. Bradley, *Ralph Ellison in Progress,* 214.

16. Toni Morrison, "Unspeakable Things Unspoken: The Afro-American Presence in American Literature," in *The Tanner Lectures XI 1988* (Salt Lake City: University of Utah Press, 1990), 121–163; Morrison, *Playing in the Dark: Whiteness and the Literary Imagination* (Cambridge, MA: Harvard University Press, 1992).

17. Jonathan Arac, *"Huckleberry Finn" as Idol and as Target: The Functions of Criticism in Our Time* (Madison: University of Wisconsin Press, 1997), 93.

18. Ibid., 135.

19. Ellison, *Conversations with Ralph Ellison,* 372.

20. Ernest Hemingway, *The Green Hills of Africa* (New York: Scribner's, 1935), 123.

21. Neil Schmitz, *Of Huck and Alice: Humorous Writing in American Literature* (Minneapolis: University of Minnesota Press, 1983), 123, 117 (first and third quote); Neil Schmitz, "Twain, *Huckleberry Finn,* and the Reconstruction," *American Studies* 12 (Spring 1971): 60 (second quote).

22. James Cox, *Mark Twain: The Fate of Humor* (Princeton, NJ: Princeton University Press, 1966), 175–176.

23. Ellison, *Conversations with Ralph Ellison,* 17.

24. Ralph Ellison and Albert Murray, *Trading Twelves: The Selected Letters of Ralph Ellison and Albert Murray,* ed. John Callahan (New York: Modern Library, 2000), 170.

25. Henry James, *Hawthorne* (1879), in *Henry James: Literary Criticism: Essays on Literature, American Writers, English Writers,* ed. Leon Edel (New York: Library of America, 1984), 212.

26. Leslie Stephen, "American Humor," *Cornhill Magazine* 13 (January 1866): 28–43.

27. Louis D. Rubin Jr., "Introduction: 'The Great American Joke," in *The Comic Imagination in American Literature* (New Brunswick, NJ: Rutgers University Press, 1973), 12.

28. Larry Neal, "An Afterword," in *Black Fire: An Anthology of Afro-American Writing,* ed. LeRoi Jones and Larry Neal (New York: Morrow, 1968), 652.

29. Larry Neal, "Ellison's Zoot Suit," in *Speaking for You: The Vision of Ralph Ellison,* ed. Kimberly W. Benston (Washington, DC: Howard University Press, 1987), 117.

30. Alan Nadel, *Invisible Criticism: Ralph Ellison and the American Canon* (Iowa City: University of Iowa Press, 1988), 85–103.

31. Leslie Fiedler, "Come Back to the Raft Ag'in, Huck Honey!," *Partisan Review* 25 (June 1948): 664–671.

32. Brook Thomas, *Civic Myths: A Law-and-Literature Approach to Citizenship* (Chapel Hill: University of North Carolina Press, 2007), 125.

33. Bradley, *Ralph Ellison in Progress,* 190.

34. Robert O'Meally, *The Craft of Ralph Ellison* (Cambridge, MA: Harvard University Press, 1980), 103.

35. Bradley, *Ralph Ellison in Progress,* 202, 203.

36. Jonathan Arac, "Toward a Critical Genealogy of the U.S. Discourse of Identity: *Invisible Man* after Fifty Years," *boundary 2* 30 (Summer 2003): 200.

37. Kenneth Burke, "Ralph Ellison's Trueblooded *Bildungsroman,*" in Benston, *Speaking for You,* 351.

38. O'Meally, *The Craft of Ralph Ellison,* 82.

39. Lawrence Jackson, *Ralph Ellison: Emergence of Genius* (New York: Wiley, 2002), 440.

40. Michael D. Hill and Lena M. Hill, *Ralph Ellison's "Invisible Man": A Reference Guide* (Westport, CT: Greenwood, 2008), 142.

41. Ernest Kaiser, "A Critical Look at Ellison's Fiction and at Social and Literary Criticism by and about the Author," *Black World* 20 (December 1970): 95.

42. Eric P. Kaufmann, *The Rise and Fall of Anglo-America* (Cambridge, MA: Harvard University Press, 2004), 239.

43. Ann Fabian, *The Unvarnished Truth: Personal Narratives in Nineteenth-Century America* (Berkeley: University of California Press, 2000), 4–5, 161, and passim.

44. Shelley Fisher Fishkin, *Was Huck Black? Mark Twain and African American Voices* (New York: Oxford University Press, 1993); Eric Lott, *Love and Theft: Blackface Minstrelsy and the American Working Class* (New York: Oxford University Press, 1993), 33–36; and Eric Lott, "Mr. Clemens and Jim Crow: Twain, Race, and Blackface," in *Cambridge Companion to Mark*

Twain, ed. Forrest G. Robinson (Cambridge: Cambridge University Press, 1995), 129–152; Anthony J. Berrett, "*Huckleberry Finn* and the Minstrel Show," *American Studies* 27 (Fall 1986): 37–49.

45. See for example D. L. Smith, "Huck, Jim, and American Racial Discourse," *Mark Twain Journal* 22 (Fall 1984): 4–12; and D. L. Smith, "Black Critics and Mark Twain," in Robinson, *Cambridge Companion to Mark Twain*, 116–129; and Elaine Mensh and Harry Mensh, *Black, White and "Huckleberry Finn"* (Tuscaloosa: University of Alabama Press, 2000).

46. Nancy Rawles, *My Jim: A Novel* (New York: Crown, 2005), 180.

47. William L. Andrews, "Mark Twain and James W. C. Pennington: Huckleberry Finn's Smallpox Lie," *Studies in American Fiction* 9 (Spring 1981): 103–112; Lucinda MacKethan, "Huck Finn and the Slave Narratives: Lighting Out as Design," *Southern Review* 20 (Spring 1984): 247–264; Carl L. Wieck, *Refiguring "Huckleberry Finn"* (Athens: University of Georgia Press, 2000), 20–39.

48. "Neo-slave narrative" was coined by novelist Ishmael Reed, who went on to make an important contribution to the genre; but it was first defined and put in circulation as a critical term by Bernard W. Bell, who characterized it as "a residually oral, modern narrative of escape from bondage to freedom" (Bernard W. Bell, *The Afro-American Novel and Its Tradition* [Amherst: University of Massachusetts Press, 1987], 289), although critical understanding of the genre has since ramified and expanded to encompass texts stretching forward in time long after slavery's abolition and many stylistic registers from research-based documentary to surrealism (Valerie Smith, "Neo-slave Narratives," in *Cambridge Companion to the African American Slave Narratives*, ed. Audrey Fisch [Cambridge: Cambridge University Press, 2007], 168). Nor is neo-slave narrative U.S.- or Anglophone-specific; like slavery and slave narrative itself, it links African American literature to the larger Afro-diasporic world and indirectly to analogous kidnapping-captivity narratives from other languages and cultures.

49. Ellison, *Conversations with Ralph Ellison*, 372; "Introduction: The Language of Slavery," in *The Slave's Narrative*, ed. Charles T. Davis and Henry Louis Gates Jr. (New York: Oxford University Press, 1985), xxiii.

50. Lawrence Jackson, *The Indignant Generation: A Narrative History of African American Writers and Critics, 1934–1960* (Princeton, NJ: Princeton University Press, 2011), 298–299.

51. Hortense Spillers, *Black, White, and in Color: Essays on American Literature and Culture* (Chicago: University of Chicago Press, 2003), 179; Randall Kenan, "An Interview with Octavia Butler," *Callaloo* 14 (Spring 1991): 498.

52. Charles Johnson, "The Singular Vision of Ralph Ellison," in Ralph Ellison, *Invisible Man: The Commemorative Edition* (New York: Modern Library, 1994), xii.

53. Charles Johnson, *Oxherding Tale* (Bloomington: Indiana University Press, 1982), 147.

54. *Middle Passage* and especially *Oxherding Tale* display an allusiveness much more dense than Ellison's. *Oxherding Tale*, for instance, features a metaphysical interchapter given over to an Afrogenetic exegesis of Augustine's *Confessions*, here invoked *as* the fountainhead of slave narrative. Both novels turn on pivotal encounters with an imaginary African people who personify an Afrocentrically inflected kind of East Asian nonindividualism that approximates the author's own brand of Zen.

55. Colson Whitehead, *The Intuitionist: A Novel* (New York: Random House, 1999), 6.

56. Ibid., 151, 240, 254–255.

57. Charles McGrath, "Interview: Zuckerman's Alter Brain," *New York Times Book Review*, 7 May 2000, www.nytimes.com.

58. Alison Flood, "Philip Roth Wins Man Booker International Prize," *Guardian*, 18 May 2011, www.guardian.co.uk.

59. Philip Roth, *I Married a Communist* (New York: Vintage, 1998), 71.

60. Ibid., 189.

61. Catherine Morley, *The Quest for Epic in Contemporary American Fiction: John Updike, Philip Roth, and Don DeLillo* (New York: Routledge, 2009), 110.

62. Eric J. Sundquist, *Strangers in the Land: Blacks, Jews, Post-Holocaust America* (Cambridge, MA: Harvard University Press, 2005), 515.

63. Ross Posnock, *Philip Roth's Rude Truth: The Art of Immaturity* (Princeton, NJ: Princeton University Press, 2006), 194–195; Parrish, *Ralph Ellison and the Genius of America*, 42–84.

64. Posnock, *Philip Roth's Rude Truth*, 21.

65. Ibid., 109.

66. Debra B. Shostak, *Philip Roth: Countertexts, Counterlives* (Columbia: University of South Carolina Press, 2004), 241–242.

67. Aimee Pozorski, *Roth and Trauma: The Problem of History in the Later Works (1995–2010)* (New York: Continuum, 2011), 42–53.

68. Philip Roth, *The Facts: A Novelist's Autobiography* (1988) (New York: Vintage, 1997), 32.

69. Philip Roth, *Reading Myself and Others* (New York: Vintage, 2001), 78.

70. Ibid., 79, 80.

71. Timothy Noah, *The Great Divergence: America's Growing Inequality Crisis and What We Can Do about It* (New York: Bloomsbury, 2012), 27.

72. Ha Jin, *A Free Life* (New York: Pantheon, 2007), 619.

73. Ali Bedhad, *A Forgetful Nation: On Immigration and Cultural Identity in the United States* (Durham, NC: Duke University Press, 2005), 7, 9, 36.

74. Hector St. Jean de Crèvecoeur, *Letters from an American Farmer* (New York: Dutton, 1957), 37; Behdad, *Forgetful Nation*, 37.

75. Hector St. Jean de Crèvecoeur, *More Letters from the American Farmer*, ed. Dennis D. Moore (Athens: University of Georgia Press, 1995).

76. Christine Holbo, "Imagination, Commerce, and the Politics of Association in Crevecoeur's *Letters from an American Farmer*," *Early American Literature*

32 (January 1997): 57; Christopher Iannini, *Fatal Revolutions: Natural History, West Indian Slavery, and the Routes of Early American Literature* (Chapel Hill: University of North Carolina Press, 2012), 134–136, 141–144, 158–168.

77. In American literature studies, the most forceful spokesperson for the extreme position is Walter Benn Michaels, most recently in "Real Toads," in *The Imaginary and Its Worlds: American Studies after the Transnational Turn*, ed. Laura Bieger, Ramón Saldívar, and Johannes Voelz (Hanover, NH: Dartmouth College Press, 2013), 177–191. But the broader conviction that "economic inequality now trumps racial inequality" (David Brooks, "Speed of Ascent," *New York Times*, 25 June 2013, A21) is gaining ground in public culture, and with it the dubious assumption that barriers of class or wealth have historically been more formidable problems in U.S. history than barriers of race or ethnicity.

IV. Introduction. Shifting Ratios, Dangerous Proximities

1. Anne Goldman, *Continental Divides: Reinvisioning American Literature* (New York: Palgrave, 2000), 44.

2. Philip Mead, "Nation, Literature, Location," in *The Cambridge History of Australian Literature*, ed. Peter Pierce (Cambridge: Cambridge University Press, 2010), 549–551.

3. Hsuan L. Hsu, *Geography and the Production of Space in Nineteenth-Century American Literature* (Cambridge: Cambridge University Press, 2010), 195.

4. Ibid., 166.

5. Harriet Beecher Stowe, *The Minister's Wooing* (Boston: Houghton Mifflin, 1996), 1–11.

6. Nina Silber, *The Romance of Reunion: Northerners and the South, 1865–1900* (Chapel Hill: University of North Carolina Press, 1992), 145–151; Robert L. Dorman, *Revolt of the Provinces: The Regionalist Movement in America, 1920–1945* (Chapel Hill: University of North Carolina Press, 1993), 163–165.

7. Bramen, *Uses of Variety*, 127.

8. Dorman, *Revolt of the Provinces*, 167–181.

9. Bramen, *Uses of Variety*, 119.

10. Neil Evernden, *The Natural Alien: Humankind and Environment* (Toronto: University of Toronto Press, 1985), 103–124.

11. Jeff Karem, *The Romance of Authenticity: The Cultural Politics of Regional and Ethnic Literatures* (Charlottesville: University Press of Virginia, 2004), 70–90.

12. Edward L. Ayers and Peter S. Onuf, "Introduction," in *All Over the Map: Rethinking American Regions*, ed. Edward L. Ayers, Peter S. Onuf, Patricia Nelson Limerick, and Stephen Nissenbaum (Baltimore, MD: Johns Hopkins University Press, 1996), 4.

13. Philip J. Fisher, *Still the New World: American Literature in a Culture of Creative Destruction* (Cambridge, MA: Harvard University Press, 1999), 171–188.

14. William Nelson Parker, *Europe, America and the Wider World: Essays on the Economic History of Western Capitalism* (Cambridge: Cambridge University Press, 1984), 2:88.

15. Ezra Tawil, *The Making of Racial Sentiment: Slavery and the Birth of the Frontier Romance* (Cambridge: Cambridge University Press, 2006), 1–18.

7. Uncle Tom's Cabin *and Its Aftermaths*

1. Lauren Berlant, *The Queen of America Goes to Washington City: Essays on Sex and Citizenship* (Durham, NC: Duke University Press, 1997), 24–53. Berlant's touchstones are the title figures of the films *Mr. Smith Goes to Washington* (1939) and *Forrest Gump* (1994). For a strong case on the opposite side for the progressive power of spontaneous sympathetic identification in antislavery writing and other media, see legal historian Elizabeth Clark, "'The Sacred Rights of the Weak': Pain, Sympathy, and the Culture of Individual Rights in Antebellum America," *Journal of American History* 82 (September 1995): 463–493. In a scrupulous analysis centering on the percolation effects of *Uncle Tom's Cabin* in U.S. culture, cultural historian Robin Bernstein demonstrates that "the invocation of imagined children" as icons could subserve "directly opposing racial arguments," either "to justify granting or withholding the rights of living adults and children" (Robin Bernstein, *Racial Innocence: Performing American Childhood from Slavery to Civil Rights* [New York: New York University Press, 2012], 3).

2. Henry James, *A Small Boy and Others* (New York: Scribner's, 1913), 159; Joy Jordan-Lake, *Whitewashing "Uncle Tom's Cabin": Nineteenth-Century Women Novelists Respond to Stowe* (Nashville, TN: Vanderbilt University Press, 2005), 162.

3. Gregg Crane, *Race, Citizenship and Law in American Literature* (Cambridge: Cambridge University Press, 2002), 79. For further evidence of politicians' testimony to the novel's catalytic impact, see David Reynolds, *Mightier Than the Sword: "Uncle Tom's Cabin" and the Battle for America* (New York: Norton, 2011), 150–151, 117–167. On the plausibility of Stowe family legend, see Joan Hedrick, *Harriet Beecher Stowe: A Life* (New York: Oxford University Press, 1994), 306.

4. Reynolds, *Mightier Than the Sword*, 175; Shu Lin, "Translator's Notes to *Uncle Tom's Cabin*," in *Land without Ghosts: Chinese Impressions of America from the Mid-Nineteenth Century to the Present*, ed. R. David Arkush and Leo O. Lee (Berkeley: University of California Press, 1989), 79.

5. John W. De Forest, "The Great American Novel," *Nation* 6 (9 January 1868): 28; Harry Stone, "Charles Dickens and Harriet Beecher Stowe," *Nineteenth-Century Fiction* 12 (December 1957): 193.

6. Jack London, "'The Jungle,'" in *Novels and Social Writings*, ed. Donald Pizer (New York: Library of America, 1982), 1145.

7. On this aspect of marketing *UTC*, see especially Michael Winship, "'The Greatest Book of Its Kind': A Publishing History of *Uncle Tom's Cabin*," *Pro-*

ceedings of the American Antiquarian Society 109 (Part 2 1999): 309–332. Stowe probably thought of herself as a kind of lay preacher. On *UTC* as an alternative form of preaching, see Dawn Coleman, "The Unsentimental Woman Preacher of *Uncle Tom's Cabin*," *American Literature* 80 (June 2008): 265–292.

8. Barbara Hochman, *"Uncle Tom's Cabin" and the Reading Revolution: Race, Literacy, Childhood, and Fiction, 1851–1911* (Amherst: University of Massachusetts Press, 2011), 81.

9. Harriet Beecher Stowe, *A Key to "Uncle Tom's Cabin"* (Boston: Jewett, 1853), 1.

10. Trish Loughran, *The Republic in Print: Print Culture in the Age of U.S. Nation Building, 1770–1870* (New York: Columbia University Press, 2007), 384–385, 364–365.

11. Ann Douglas, "Introduction," in Stowe, *Uncle Tom's Cabin* (New York: Penguin, 1981), 23.

12. Jennifer Rae Greeson arrestingly argues that *UTC*'s plot nadir in the New Orleans slave market and Legree's plantation should be understood as a Blakean allegory of the "perfect modernization" of a factory-style regime (Jennifer Rae Greeson, *Our South: Geographic Fantasy and the Rise of National Literature* [Cambridge, MA: Harvard University Press, 2010], 190). Even if so, however, the novel draws more explicitly in ways that would have been familiar to literate readers on the tradition of descent into medieval horror and entrapment popularized by Ann Radcliffe's *The Mysteries of Udolpho* and other gothic fiction and revived in such mid-nineteenth-century provincial gothic fiction as Charlotte Brontë's *Jane Eyre* and Hannah Crafts's recently recovered *The Bondwoman's Narrative*.

13. William E. Huntzicker, "'This Inherited Misfortune': Gender, Race, and Slavery in *Uncle Tom's Cabin* and *Gone with the Wind*," in *Memory and Myth: The Civil War in Fiction and Film from "Uncle Tom's Cabin" to "Cold Mountain*," ed. David B. Sachsman, S. Kittrell Rushing, and Roy Morris Jr. (West Lafayette, IN: Purdue University Press, 2007), 16.

14. George Frederickson, *The Black Image in the White Mind: The Debate on Afro-American Character and Destiny, 1817–1914* (Middletown, CT: Wesleyan University Press, 1987), 97–129.

15. Jason Richards, "Imitation Nation: Blackface Minstrelsy and the Making of African American Selfhood in *Uncle Tom's Cabin*," *Novel* 39 (Spring 2006): 204.

16. Quotations from Claire Parfait, *The Publishing History of "Uncle Tom's Cabin," 1852–1902* (Aldershot, UK: Ashgate, 2007), 126, 137. Werner Sollors, "Was Roxy Black: Race as Stereotype in Mark Twain, Edward Windsor Kemble, and Paul Laurence Dunbar," in *Mixed Race Literature*, ed. Jonathan Brennan (Stanford, CA: Stanford University Press, 2002), 70–87, plausibly contends that cultural historians' traditional dismissal of Kemble as a rac(ial)ist oversimplifies the actual variegation of his illustrations in tone and nuance. Still, Kemble's forte seems to have been comic renditions of blacks, and

Robin Bernstein argues convincingly that Kemble's art helped perpetuate the demeaning pickaninny stereotype (*Racial Innocence,* 34–35, 74–80).

17. Marcus Wood, *Blind Memory: Visual Representations of Slavery in England and America, 1780–1865* (New York: Routledge, 2000), 186; Richard Yarborough, "Strategies of Black Characterization in *Uncle Tom's Cabin* and the Early Afro-American Novel," in *New Essays on "Uncle Tom's Cabin,"* ed. Eric J. Sundquist (Cambridge: Cambridge University Press, 1986), 72.

18. Edmund Wilson, *Patriotic Gore: Studies in the Literature of the American Civil War* (New York: Oxford University Press, 1962), 4–5.

19. Philip Fisher, *Hard Facts: Setting and Form in the American Novel* (New York: Oxford University Press, 1985), 97–114.

20. Michael J. Meyer, "Toward a Rhetoric of Equality: Reflective and Refractive Images in Stowe's Language," in *The Stowe Debate: Rhetorical Strategies in "Uncle Tom's Cabin,"* ed. Mason I. Lowance Jr. et al. (Amherst: University of Massachusetts Press, 1994), 241.

21. Frederickson, *Black Image in the White Mind,* 104–106; Thomas F. Gossett, *"Uncle Tom's Cabin" and American Culture* (Dallas: Southern Methodist University Press, 1985), 83–85.

22. Harriet Beecher Stowe, *The Minister's Wooing* (Boston: Houghton, 1896), 248.

23. Michael T. Gilmore, *The War on Words: Slavery, Race, and Free Speech in American Literature* (Chicago: University of Chicago Press, 2010), 15–42.

24. Harriet Beecher Stowe, *Uncle Tom's Cabin* (Boston: Houghton, 1879), xxi.

25. Marianne Noble, "The Ecstasies of Sentimental Wounding in *Uncle Tom's Cabin,"* *Yale Journal of Criticism* 10 (Fall 1997): 296–297; Hortense Spillers, *Black, White, and in Color: Essays on American Literature and Culture* (Chicago: University of Chicago Press, 2003), 191–194.

26. Stowe, *A Key to "Uncle Tom's Cabin,"* 200; James Baldwin, "Everybody's Protest Novel," in *Notes of a Native Son* (Boston: Beacon, 1955), 18.

27. Lynn Wardley, "Relic, Fetish, Femmage: The Aesthetics of Sentiment in the Work of Stowe," in *The Culture of Sentiment,* ed. Shirley Samuels (New York: Oxford University Press, 1992), 208.

28. Robert Stepto, "Sharing the Thunder: The Literary Exchanges of Harriet Beecher Stowe, Henry Bibb, and Frederick Douglass," in Sundquist, *New Essays on "Uncle Tom's Cabin,"* 149.

29. Lori Merish, *Sentimental Materialism: Gender, Commodity Culture, and Nineteenth-Century American Literature* (Durham, NC: Duke University Press, 2000), 163.

30. Amy Kaplan, *The Anarchy of Empire in the Making of U.S. Culture* (Cambridge, MA: Harvard University Press, 2002), 23–50.

31. Quoted in Gossett, *"Uncle Tom's Cabin" and American Culture,* 172.

32. Stowe, *A Key to "Uncle Tom's Cabin,"* 495.

33. Quoted in Hedrick, *Harriet Beecher Stowe,* 258.

34. John Carlos Rowe, "Stowe's Rainbow Sign: Violence and Community in *Dred,"* *Arizona Quarterly* 58 (Spring 2002): 40.

35. Harriet Beecher Stowe, *Dred: A Tale of the Great Dismal Swamp* (Boston: Houghton, 1896), 567.

36. Elaine Showalter, *A Jury of Her Peers: American Women Writers from Anne Bradstreet to Annie Proulx* (New York: Knopf, 2009), 116.

37. Significant critical discussions start with Eric J. Sundquist, *Faulkner: The House Divided* (Baltimore, MD: Johns Hopkins University Press, 1983), 96–100, and include Robert S. Levine, "The African-American Presence in *Dred*," in *Criticism and the Color Line: Desegregating American Literary Studies,* ed. Henry B. Wonham (New Brunswick, NJ: Rutgers University Press, 1996), 171–190; Rowe, "Stowe's Rainbow Sign"; Crane, *Race, Citizenship, and Law,* 73–76; Laura Hanft Korobkin, "Appropriating Law in Harriet Beecher Stowe's *Dred*," *Nineteenth-Century Literature* 62 (December 2007): 380–406; Elizabeth Duquette, "The Republican Mammy? Imagining Civic Engagement in *Dred*," *American Literature* 80 (March 2008): 1–28; Gilmore, *The War on Words,* 110–118; and Caleb Smith, *The Oracle and the Curse: A Poetics of Justice from the Revolution to the Civil War* (Cambridge, MA: Harvard University Press, 2013), 151–156. In its own day, *Dred* was received more enthusiastically in Britain, where one successful stage adaptation of *Uncle Tom's Cabin* employed the scenario of future stateside slave revolt, whereas in the United States from the start the adaptations hyperaccentuated the pious and the droll, Eva's death and Topsy's hijinks. See Judie Newman, "Staging Black Insurrection: *Dred* on Stage," in *The Cambridge Companion to Harriet Beecher Stowe,* ed. Cindy Weinstein (Cambridge: Cambridge University Press, 2004), 114–116; and Sarah Meer, *"Uncle Tom" Mania: Slavery, Minstrelsy, and Transatlantic Culture in the 1850s* (Athens: University of Georgia Press, 2005), 131–160.

38. De Forest, "Great American Novel," 28; see also James M. Cox, "Harriet Beecher Stowe: From Sectionalism to Regionalism," *Nineteenth-Century Fiction* 38 (March 1984): 444–466.

39. Sarah Josepha Hale, *Northwood, or, Life North and South, Showing the True Character of Both* (New York: H. Long, 1852), 394, 393, 399, iv, 408.

40. Greeson, *Our South,* 74.

41. Caroline Lee Hentz, *The Planter's Northern Bride* (Chapel Hill: University of North Carolina Press, 1970), 136.

42. Ibid., 212.

43. The association of the South with violence, a staple in fiction about the South by writers from both regions, has historical basis. Summing up the statistical evidence from 1915 to 1964, historian Sheldon Hackney found "a distinctly Southern pattern" of high murder rates (also low suicide rates), "one that must rank with the caste system and ahead of mint juleps in importance as a key to the meaning of being Southern" (Sheldon Hackney, "Southern Violence," in *Violence in America: Historical and Comparative Perspectives,* rev. ed., ed. Hugh Davis Graham et al. [Beverly Hills, CA: Sage, 1979], 394–395). Hackney's findings, originally published in 1969, helped

motivate Raymond D. Gastil's *Culture Regions of the United States* (Seattle: University of Washington Press, 1975), which arrives at similar conclusions (97–116). Even today, although the North-South gap has narrowed, the former slave states bear disproportionate responsibility for the U.S. homicide rate being higher than that of most other nations in the developed world. In 2009, all but Delaware and Virginia had homicide rates above 5 per 100,000 (Louisiana leading with 12.3), whereas no New England state reported higher than 2.7.

44. Henry Louis Gates Jr. and Hollis Robbins, "Introduction," in *The Annotated "Uncle Tom's Cabin"* (New York: Norton, 2006), xi.

45. Amanda Claybaugh, *The Novel of Purpose: Literature and Social Reform in the Anglo-American World* (Ithaca, NY: Cornell University Press, 2007), 36, 34.

46. Quoted in Nancy Glazener, "The Novel in Postbellum Print Culture," in *The Cambridge History of the American Novel*, ed. Leonard Cassuto, Clare Virginia Eby, and Benjamin Reiss (Cambridge: Cambridge University Press, 2011), 349.

47. Helen Hunt Jackson, *Ramona* (Boston: Roberts, 1884), 17; David Luis-Brown, *Waves of Decolonization: Discourses of Race and Hemispheric Citizenship in Cuba, Mexico, and the United States* (Durham, NC: Duke University Press, 2008), 36–37.

48. Jackson, *Ramona,* 119.

49. Critic Laura Lomas observes that Martí tended to endorse "the most conventional of gender roles for 'his' women," and certainly *Ramona*'s ultimate disposal of its heroine is wholly in keeping (Laura Lomas, *Translating Empire: Jose Martí, Migrant Latino Subjects, and American Modernities* [Durham, NC: Duke University Press, 2008], 247).

50. Nina Baym, *Women Writers of the American West, 1833–1927* (Urbana: University of Illinois Press, 2011), 192.

51. J. W. De Forest, *A Volunteer's Adventures: A Union Captain's Record of the Civil War,* ed. James H. Croushore (New Haven, CT: Yale University Press, 1946), 131.

52. Alfred Habegger, *Gender, Fantasy, and Realism in American Literature* (New York: Columbia University Press, 1992), 42.

53. Kenneth W. Warren, *Black and White Strangers: Race and American Literary Realism* (Chicago: University of Chicago Press, 1993), 86.

54. Albion W. Tourgée, *A Fool's Errand,* ed. John Hope Franklin (Cambridge, MA: Harvard University Press, 1961), 339.

55. Henry James, *The Complete Notebooks*, ed. Leon Edel and Lyall H. Powers (New York: Oxford University Press, 1987), 19; William James, *The Correspondence of William James,* ed. Ignas K. Skrupskelis and Elizabeth M. Berkeley (Charlottesville: University Press of Virginia, 1993), 2:9.

56. Claybaugh, *Novel of Purpose,* 138.

57. James, *The Complete Notebooks*, 20. A third trend-line that caught James's interest, no less important to *The Bostonians* (see note 59 below), was "the decline in the sentiment of sex," presumably meaning heterosexuality.

58. Henry James, *The Bostonians*, ed. Charles Anderson (New York: Penguin, 1986), 189, 138, 62.

59. In a subtle, erudite analysis that argues for *The Bostonians* as an intricately allusive refiguration through Olive, Verena, and Ransom of the featured triangle of characters in Zola's *Nana*, Terry Castle claims James as "the first major modern writer . . . to open a space for a sympathetic reading of a lesbian character" (Terry Castle, *The Apparitional Lesbian: Female Homosexuality and Modern Culture* [New York: Columbia University Press, 1993], 177), despite the guarded skittishness with which *The Bostonians* intimates the subject and despite the standoffish fastidiousness of James's critical analyses of prior nineteenth-century French novels that engaged lesbianism much more directly. To the extent that *The Bostonians* edges toward being a novel with a purpose in anything like a robust sense, this is it.

60. James, *Bostonians*, 49, 202, 327, 46, 384.

61. Warren, *Black and White Strangers*, 101; Gilmore, *War on Words*, 221.

8. The Adventures of Huckleberry Finn *and Its Others*

1. Jonathan Arac, *"Huckleberry Finn" as Idol and Target: The Functions of Criticism in Our Time* (Madison: University of Wisconsin Press, 1997), 6; "Mark Twain's Huckleberry Finn," America's Story, Library of Congress, http://www .americaslibrary.gov/aa/twain/aa_twain_huckfinn_1.html.

2. Leland Krauth, *Mark Twain and Company: Six Literary Relations* (Athens: University of Georgia Press, 2003), 87–125; Joan Hedrick, *Harriet Beecher Stowe: A Life* (New York: Oxford University Press, 1994), 392.

3. H. L. Mencken, *H. L. Mencken on American Literature*, ed. S. T. Joshi (Athens: Ohio University Press, 2002), 33; Ernest Hemingway, *The Green Hills of Africa* (New York: Scribner, 1935), 22.

4. Mark Twain, *Autobiography of Mark Twain*, ed. Charles Neider (New York: Harper, 1959), 59.

5. Ibid., 273.

6. Albert Bigelow Paine, *Mark Twain: A Biography* (New York: Harper, 1912): 2, 1034.

7. Andrew Lang, "The Art of Mark Twain," *Illustrated London News*, 14 February 1891, 222; Kenzaburo Oe, "Japan, the Ambiguous, and Myself: Nobel Lecture 1994," *World Literature Today* 69 (Winter 1995): 5.

8. William Van O'Connor, "Why *Huckleberry Finn* Is Not the Great American Novel," *College English* 17 (October 1955): 7; E. L. Doctorow, [On *Huckleberry Finn*,] *New Yorker* 75 (26 June–3 July 1995): 132.

9. T. S. Eliot, "Introduction," in *HF* (1950), repr. in *The Critical Response to Mark Twain's "Huckleberry Finn,"* ed. Laurie Champion (New York: Greenwood, 1991), 45.

10. Lionel Trilling, *The Liberal Imagination: Essays on Literature* (New York: Viking, 1950), 110.

11. Guy A. Cardwell, *Twins of Genius* (East Lansing: Michigan State College Press, 1953), 58.

12. Nancy Glazener, "The Novel in Postbellum Print Culture," in *Cambridge History of the American Novel,* ed. Leonard Cassuto, Clare Virginia Eby, and Benjamin Reiss (Cambridge: Cambridge University Press, 2011), 347.

13. D. L. Smith, "Huck, Jim, and American Racial Discourse," *Mark Twain Journal* 22 (Fall 1984): 9.

14. Stacey Margolis, "*Huckleberry Finn,* or, Consequences," *PMLA* 116 (March 2001): 340.

15. Leslie Fiedler, "Come Back to the Raft Ag'in, Huck Honey!," *Partisan Review* 25 (June 1948): 664–671; later absorbed as part of Fiedler's more extended discussions of *HF* in *Love and Death in the American Novel* (New York: Criterion, 1960), esp. 268–272, 584–591, a book that stresses the presence of white-dark homoerotic bonding throughout U.S. masculinist wilderness romance from Cooper to Faulkner. Controversial from the start, the Fiedler thesis has been bashed by critics both black and white, especially for its emphasis on eroticization, which for Ellison (see Chapter 6) trivialized the seriousness with which *HF* takes the issue of black-white relations and which some gay studies critics have seen as homophobic; see Christopher Looby, "'Innocent Homosexuality': The Fiedler Thesis in Retrospect," in *"Adventures of Huckleberry Finn": A Case Study in Critical Controversy,* ed. Gerald Graff and James Phelan (Boston: Bedford, 1995), 535–550. Although both criticisms have basis, nonetheless the general line of argument—that white male wilderness romance exoticizes to the point of eroticizing its dark double figures—also has basis; and it stands as one of the most striking cases on record of U.S. literary criticism affecting novelistic thinking and behavior, starting with Hemingway, who was unnerved by it. At least two neo-wilderness romances, Norman Mailer's *Why Are We in Vietnam?* (1967) and James Dickey's *Deliverance* (1970), clearly seem Fiedler-inflected, and perhaps also the Weissman-Enzian relation in Pynchon's *Gravity's Rainbow* (see Chapter 13). So Fiedler really seems to have been onto something significant about the (male) national imaginary, however much he may have overshot the mark.

16. Toni Morrison, "Introduction" to *The Adventures of Huckleberry Finn,* ed. Shelley Fisher Fishkin (New York: Oxford University Press, 1996), 155–156.

17. Neil Schmitz, *Of Huck and Alice: Humorous Writing in American Literature* (Minneapolis: University of Minnesota Press, 1983), 104.

18. Critical theorist Roland Barthes coins this term to describe what he takes to be the gratuitously prolix descriptivism of traditional realist fiction (Roland Barthes, *The Rustle of Language,* trans. Richard Howard [New York: Hill and Wang, 1986], 141–148). Yet such cases as *HF* and the forest romances of James Fenimore Cooper show that "superfluity" can serve important ends that Barthes fails to consider.

19. Josephine Donovan, *European Local-Color Literature: National Tales, Dorfgeschichten, Romans Champêtres* (New York: Continuum, 2010), 22.

20. Jennifer Rae Greeson, *Our South: Geographic Fantasy and the Rise of National Literature* (Cambridge, MA: Harvard University Press, 2010), 237–251. Historian James C. Cobb reports that "as northern wealth grew by 50 percent during the 1860s, southern wealth had declined by 60 percent" (James C. Cobb, *Away Down South: A History of Southern Identity* [New York: Oxford University Press, 2005], 67). As late as the 1890s, we find José Martí insisting that "the clean and concerned people of the North are worlds apart from the choleric, poverty-stricken, broken, bitter, lackluster, loafing Southern shopkeepers sitting on their cracker barrels" (José Martí, *José Martí Reader: Writings on the Americas*, ed. Deborah Shnookal and Mirta Muñiz [New York: Ocean Press, 2007], 186).

21. The second, third, and fourth readings of *Yankee* are proposed, successively, in the *Cambridge History of American Literature* (1917–1921, by Stuart Sherman), *The Literary History of the United States* (1948, by Dixon Wecter), and *The Columbia History of the American Novel* (1988, by Philip J. Fisher)—a palimpsest suggestive of the changing national self-image during the twentieth century. For more on this, see L. Buell, "Literary History as a Hybrid Genre," in *New Historical Literary Study*, ed. Jeffrey N. Cox and Larry J. Reynolds (Princeton, NJ: Princeton University Press, 1993), 216–229.

22. Stephanie LeMenager, *Manifest and Other Destinies: Territorial Fictions of the Nineteenth-Century United States* (Lincoln: University of Nebraska Press, 2004), 201.

23. Tom Lutz, *Doing Nothing: A History of Loafers, Loungers, Slackers, and Bums in America* (New York: Farrar, Straus, and Giroux, 2006), 47.

24. Amanda Claybaugh, *The Novel of Purpose: Literature and Social Reform in the Anglo-American World* (Ithaca, NY: Cornell University Press, 2007), 162.

25. Michael T. Gilmore, *The War on Words: Slavery, Race, and Free Speech in American Literature* (Chicago: University of Chicago Press, 2010), 231; Claybaugh, *Novel of Purpose*, 162.

26. David Blight, *Race and Reunion: The Civil War in American Memory* (Cambridge, MA: Harvard University Press, 2001), 194.

27. Tour manager Enoch Pond thought that Cable "assumed Mark's drawl in his readings and it became almost a second nature to him to the extent that he was imitating Mark even in his conversation" (quoted in Stephen Railton, "Pond on Twins Tour," http://etext.virginia.edu/railton/huckfinn/pond1.html). Cable took issue with this, but unquestionably he was awed by the charisma of his more celebrated co-performer (who also garnered the lion's share of the profits). Offstage it was somewhat different: Cable's upright propriety and piety, which spilled over into attempts to evangelize Twain, provoked his friend to ribald exasperation. Still, throughout his life Cable expressed for Twain "admiration unblurred by vanity and untinctured by envy" (Cardwell, *Twins of Genius*, 24).

28. Arlin Turner, *George W. Cable: A Biography* (Baton Rouge: Louisiana State University Press, 1966), 156–157.

29. Brian Hochman, "Hearing Lost, Hearing Found: George Washington Cable and the Photo-Ethnographic Ear," *American Literature* 83 (September 2010): 519–551.

30. George Washington Cable, *The Grandissimes*, ed. Michael Kreyling (New York: Penguin, 1988), 1.

31. *The Grandissimes* may be the first significant work of British American literature to call attention to the specious pride Euro-American whites have often taken in alleged traces of Indian lineage, as against Natty Bumppo's insistence on being a white foster child of the Delawares.

32. Cable, *The Grandissimes*, 196, 156.

33. George Washington Cable, *The Silent South* (New York: Scribner, 1885), 54, 100–101.

34. Ben Railton, *Contesting the Past, Reconstructing the Nation: American Literature and Culture in the Gilded Age* (Tuscaloosa: University of Alabama Press, 2007), 223. Cable did achieve a qualified triumph for the history of progressive racial representation in resisting, at least partway, his press readers' misjudgment that the pivotal Bras-Coupé episode, which had been twice rejected as a magazine story, was disruptive to the nationalist reading of postwar reunification (Cable, *The Grandissimes*, ix; Railton, *Contesting the Past*, 218–223).

35. Turner, *George W. Cable*, 99–104.

36. Charles W. Chesnutt, "'To Be an Author'": Letters of Charles W. Chesnutt 1889–1905, ed. Joseph R. McElrath Jr. and Robert C. Leitz III (Princeton, NJ: Princeton University Press, 1997), 159, 160.

37. Eric J. Sundquist, *To Wake the Nations: Race in the Making of American Literature* (Cambridge, MA: Harvard University Press, 1993), 414; Gilmore, *War on Words*, 258. *Marrow* was not the only novelization of this episode, then or now. African American polemicist David Bryant Fulton had already published *Hanover, or the Persecution of the Lowly* (1900). Thomas Dixon's *The Leopard's Spots* (1902, see below) includes a short-form white triumphalist version. The Wilmington massacre figures pivotally in filmmaker-novelist John Sayles's recent *A Moment in the Sun* (2010), which stresses the cultural logic of its concurrence with the American conquest of Cuba, the signature triumph of the 1898 Spanish-American War.

38. Chesnutt, "'To Be an Author,'" 118; Charles W. Chesnutt, *Stories, Novels, and Essays*, ed. Werner Sollors (New York: Library of America, 2002), 873.

39. Charles W. Chesnutt, *The Marrow of Tradition*, in *Stories, Novels, and Essays*, 718.

40. Chesnutt, *Stories, Novels, and Essays*, 873; Chesnutt, "'To Be an Author,'" 182.

41. Elizabeth Duquette points to *Marrow*'s demolition of postbellum white society's icon of the ex-slave childishly loyal to the former master by having both such characters callously murdered by the white mob (Elizabeth Duquette, *Loyal Subjects: Bonds of Nation, Race, and Allegiance in Nineteenth-Century America* [New Brunswick, NJ: Rutgers University Press, 2010], 161–164). Chesnutt's pairing of the tended-to white child and the slain black child may be a bleak rendition of turn-of-the-twentieth-century evolutionary-

pragmatist thinking about childhood as the sociobiological seedbed of adulthood (Jane Thrailkill, "Pragmatism and the Evolutionary Child," *American Literary History* 24 [Summer 2012]: 275). Wellington whiteness in this novel has a guaranteed future that blackness does not. Not that *Marrow* rejects the legitimacy of sentimentalism altogether. As Brook Thomas observes, the legally sophisticated Chesnutt—a trained attorney—"uses sentimental bonds ideally present in any marriage" to supplement and to expose the inadequacy of the contractual and economic spheres, starting with the complicated mixture of love and moral accountability that prompts the half-sisters' grandfather to legalize his union with his former slave (Brook Thomas, "The Legal Argument of Charles W. Chesnutt's Novels," *Yearbook of Research in English and American Literature* 18 [2002]: 324).

42. Chesnutt, *Stories, Novels, and Essays*, 847, 862.
43. Chesnutt, "'To Be an Author,'" 171.
44. Thomas Dixon, *The Leopard's Spots* (New York: Doubleday, Page, 1902), 440, 459, 412.
45. John Milton Cooper Jr., *Walter Hines Page: The Southerner as American, 1855–1918* (Chapel Hill: University of North Carolina Press, 1977), 169.
46. Blight, *Race and Reunion*, 138.
47. Sydney Bufkin, "Reviewers, Race, and Charles Chesnutt's *The Marrow of Tradition*," presented at American Literature Association Conference, 26 May 2011, Boston MA.
48. Chesnutt, "'To Be an Author,'" 156.
49. Quoted in Joseph McElrath Jr., "W. D. Howells and Race: Charles W. Chesnutt's Disappointment of the Dean," *Nineteenth-Century Literature* 51 (March 1997): 485.
50. William L. Andrews, *The Literary Career of Charles W. Chesnutt* (Baton Rouge: Louisiana State University Press, 1980), 175.
51. Robert Bone, *The Negro Novel in America* (New Haven, CT: Yale University Press, 1958), 37; McElrath, "W. D. Howells and Race," 475; Andrews, *Literary Career of Charles W. Chesnutt*, 201.
52. Sundquist, *To Wake the Nations*, 406–454.
53. See, respectively, Matthew Wilson, *Whiteness in the Novels of Charles W. Chesnutt* (Jackson: University Press of Mississippi, 2004), 99–147; Gene Andrew Jarrett, *Representing the Race: A New Political History of African American Literature* (New York: New York University Press, 2012), 82–91; and Jae H. Roe, "Keeping an 'Old Wound' Alive: *The Marrow of Tradition* and the Legacy of Wilmington," *African American Review* 33 (Summer 1999): 231–242.

9. Faulkner's Absalom, Absalom!, Mitchell's Gone with the Wind, and Literary Interracialism North and South

1. W. E. B. Du Bois, "Americanization," in *The Oxford W. E. B. Du Bois Reader*, ed. Eric J. Sundquist (New York: Oxford University Press, 1996), 384. Du

Bois's implied distinction between unimpeachably respectable whites and whites not (yet) accepted as bona fide American becomes, we'll see below, a ground both of affinity and difference between Faulkner's *Absalom* and Mitchell's *Gone with the Wind*.

2. Cleanth Brooks, "Faulkner and the Fugitive Agrarians," in *Faulkner and the Southern Renaissance*, ed. Doreen Fowler and Ann J. Abadie (Jackson: University Press of Mississippi, 1981), 32.

3. U. B. Phillips, "The Central Theme of Southern History," *American Historical Review* 34 (October 1928): 30–43.

4. William Faulkner, *Selected Letters*, ed. Joseph Blotner (New York: Random House, 1977), 78; Houston A. Baker, *I Don't Hate the South: Reflections on Faulkner, Family, and the South* (New York: Oxford University Press, 2007), 117.

5. John C. McKinney and Linda Brookover Bourque, "The Changing South: National Incorporation of a Region," *American Sociological Review* 36 (June 1971): 399–412.

6. James Baldwin, *Nobody Knows My Name: More Notes of a Native Son* (New York: Dial, 1961), 101.

7. William Faulkner, *Lion in the Garden: Interviews with William Faulkner, 1926–1962*, ed. James B. Meriwether and Michael Millgate (New York: Random House, 1968), 262.

8. Philip M. Weinstein, *Becoming Faulkner: The Art and Life of William Faulkner* (New York: Oxford University Press, 2010), 119.

9. Joseph Blotner, *Faulkner: A Biography* (New York: Random House, 1974), 1:105.

10. Édouard Glissant, *Faulkner, Mississippi*, trans. Barbara Lewis and Thomas C. Spear (New York: Farrar, Straus and Giroux, 1999), 13, 10.

11. Faulkner, *Lion in the Garden*, 157; Faulkner, *Selected Letters*, 79.

12. Eric J. Sundquist, *Faulkner: The House Divided* (Baltimore, MD: Johns Hopkins University Press, 1983), 123.

13. For more on Faulkner's ongoing interest in mapping U.S. environment and culture in terms of the Mississippi watershed, see Susan Scott Parrish, "Faulkner and the Outer Weather of 1927," *American Literary History* 24 (March 2012): 34–58.

14. Blotner, *Faulkner*, 1:946–947.

15. Richard Godden, *Fictions of Labor: William Faulkner and the South's Long Revolution* (Cambridge: Cambridge University Press, 1997), 134.

16. Quoted in Werner Sollors, *Neither White nor Black Yet Both: Thematic Explorations of Interracial Literature* (New York: Oxford University Press, 1997), 315, 298.

17. Faulkner, *Lion in the Garden*, 258.

18. Walter Benn Michaels, "*Absalom, Absalom!* The Difference between White Men and White Men," in *Faulkner in the Twenty-First Century*, ed. Robert W. Hamblin and Ann J. Abadie (Jackson: University Press of Mississippi, 2003), 145.

19. William Faulkner, *Go Down, Moses* (New York: Vintage, 1990), 344.

20. Godden, *Fictions of Labor,* 76; Joel Williamson, *William Faulkner and Southern History* (New York: Oxford University Press, 1993), 64–71.

21. F. James Davis, *Who Is Black? One Nation's Definition* (University Park: Pennsylvania State University Press, 1991), 45. See also Daniel J. Sharfstein, "The Secret History of Race in the United States," *Yale Law Journal* 112 (April 2003): 1473–1509.

22. Frederick Law Olmsted, *A Journey in the Back Country* (New York: Mason, 1861), 159.

23. Joseph R. Roach, *Cities of the Dead: Circum-Atlantic Performance* (New York: Columbia University Press, 1996).

24. Andrea Dimino, "Fathers and Strangers: From Patriarchy to Counterfamily in Faulkner's *Absalom, Absalom!,*" in *Critical Essays on William Faulkner: The Sutpen Family,* ed. Arthur F. Kinney (Boston: Hall, 1996), 143.

25. Thadious Davis, *Faulkner's "Negro": Art and Southern Context* (Baton Rouge: Louisiana State University Press, 1983), 201.

26. Glissant, *Faulkner, Mississippi,* 66.

27. Louis D. Rubin Jr., "Scarlett O'Hara and the Two Quentin Compsons," in *Recasting: "Gone with the Wind" in American Culture,* ed. Darden Asbury Pyron (Miami: University Presses of Florida, 1983), 81.

28. Gordon Hutner, *What America Read: Taste, Class, and the Novel, 1920–1960* (Chapel Hill: University of North Carolina Press, 2009), 164. Wallace quotation in ibid., 166.

29. Ellen Firsching Brown and John Wiley, *Margaret Mitchell's "Gone with the Wind": A Bestseller's Odyssey from Atlanta to Hollywood* (Lanham, MD: Taylor Trade, 2011), 30.

30. Mitchell, *Margaret Mitchell's "Gone with the Wind" Letters,* 36.

31. Brown and Wiley, *Margaret Mitchell's "Gone with the Wind,"* 59; Mitchell, *Margaret Mitchell's "Gone with the Wind" Letters,* 52; W. J. Cash, *The Mind of the South* (New York: Knopf, 1941), 430.

32. Hutner, *What America Read,* 173.

33. Mitchell, *Margaret Mitchell's "Gone with the Wind" Letters,* 24.

34. Ibid., 38.

35. George Washington Cable, *The Silent South* (New York: Scribner, 1885), 113–182; Matthew J. Mancini, *One Dies, Get Another: Convict Leasing in the American South 1866–1928* (Columbia: University of South Carolina Press, 1996), 82.

36. Carolyn Porter, "Margaret Mitchell and William Faulkner," in *A New Literary History of America,* ed. Greil Marcus and Werner Sollors (Cambridge, MA: Harvard University Press, 2009), 708.

37. Brown and Wiley, *Margaret Mitchell's "Gone with the Wind,"* 27; Anne Edwards, *Road to Tara: The Life of Margaret Mitchell* (New Haven, CT: Ticknor and Fields, 1983), 129–131, 173–174.

38. Lillian Smith, *How Am I to Be Heard? Letters of Lillian Smith,* ed. Margaret Rose Gladney (Chapel Hill: University of North Carolina Press, 1993), 87.

39. The progressive little magazine Smith and her lifetime partner Paula Snelling issued and largely wrote for a decade (1935–1945) under several titles (eventually *South Today*) favorably reviewed Claude McKay's *A Long Way from Home*, Wright's *Native Son*, and Du Bois's *Dusk of Dawn*, as well as Steinbeck's *Grapes of Wrath*, Carson McCullers's *The Heart Is a Lonely Hunter*, and James Agee and Walker Evans's *Let Us Now Praise Famous Men*. It also reviewed a number of Faulkner novels (equivocally, recognizing for example *Absalom*'s greatness but preferring some of Faulkner's pithier stories) and dismissed *Gone with the Wind* as a "puffball compounded of printer's ink and bated breath" (Smith and Snelling, "One More Sigh for the Old South" [1936], repr. in *From the Mountain: Selections from Pseudopodia (1936), The North Georgia Review (1937–1941), and South Today (1942–1945)*, ed. Helen White and Redding S. Sugg Jr. [Memphis, TN: Memphis State University Press, 1972], 30). The magazine enlisted an impressive array of contributors across the color line: Du Bois, James Weldon Johnson, Sterling Brown, Pauli Murray, W. J. Cash, and others. *From the Mountain* gives a sense of the range of contributions.

40. Ibid., 72; Lillian Smith, *The Winner Names the Age*, ed. Michelle Cliff (New York: Norton, 1978), 135.

41. W. E. B. Du Bois, "Searing Novel of the South," *New York Times Book Review*, 5 March 1944, 1, 20.

42. Lillian Smith, *Strange Fruit* (New York: Riley and Hitchcock, 1944), 95.

43. Quoted in Anne C. Loveland, *Lillian Smith: A Southerner Confronting the South* (Baton Rouge: Louisiana State University Press, 1986), 67.

44. Smith, *Strange Fruit*, 271.

45. Ann Petry, *The Narrows* (Boston: Beacon, 1988), 329.

46. Lawrence Jackson, *The Indignant Generation: A Narrative History of African American Writers and Critics, 1934–1960* (Princeton, NJ: Princeton University Press, 2011), 394—one of the few critical discussions to do justice to Petry's powerful but neglected second novel.

47. Gene Andrew Jarrett, *Representing the Race: A New Political History of African American Literature* (New York: New York University Press, 2011), 130, 133; Henry Louis Gates Jr., *The Signifying Monkey: A Theory of Afro-American Literary Criticism* (New York: Oxford University Press, 1988).

48. Alice Randall, *The Wind Done Gone* (Boston: Houghton Mifflin, 2001), 47. "Cyanara" is, fittingly, named for the mistress addressed in the world-weary neo-Horatian poem by British aesthete Lionel Johnson from which Mitchell took the phrase "gone with the wind." By giving this figure voice and agency, *The Wind Done Gone* talks back not just to Mitchell but to the whole male lyric tradition of framing women as disposable objects of play.

49. Ibid., 196, 191, 96.

50. Ibid., 162.

51. Patricia Yeager, "Circum-Atlantic Superabundance: Milk as World-Making in Alice Randall and Kara Walker," *American Literature* 78 (December 2006): 797.

10. Morrison's Beloved *as Culmination and Augury*

1. James English, *The Economy of Prestige: Prizes, Awards, and the Circulation of Cultural Value* (Cambridge, MA: Harvard University Press, 2005), 237–245.
2. Toni Morrison, *Playing in the Dark: Whiteness and the Literary Imagination* (Cambridge, MA: Harvard University Press, 1992), 44, 46–47.
3. F. Clifton Spargo, "Trauma and the Specters of Enslavement in Morrison's *Beloved*," *Mosaic* 35 (March 2002): 129. Richard Moreland thoughtfully likens the "two altogether different kinds of stories" that circulate through both *Huck* and *Beloved:* e.g., "the magically or heroically safe" story of Denver's birth as she fancies it to have been versus "the defenselessly unprepared" event that Sethe herself experiences (Richard Moreland, "'He Wants to Put His Story Next to Hers': Putting Twain's Story Next to Hers in *Beloved*," in *Toni Morrison: Critical and Theoretical Approaches*, ed. Nancy J. Peterson [Baltimore, MD: Johns Hopkins University Press, 1997], 163).
4. Carla Namwali Serpell, "The Ethics of Uncertainty: Reading Twentieth Century American Literature," PhD diss., Harvard University, 2008, 239, 259, 299–314.
5. Toni Morrison, *What Moves at the Margin: Selected Nonfiction*, ed. Carolyn C. Denard (Jackson: University Press of Mississippi, 2008), 70, 71.
6. Middleton A. Harris et al., *The Black Book: 35th Anniversary Edition* (New York: Random House, 2009), 10–11.
7. Saidiya V. Hartman, *Scenes of Subjection: Terror, Slavery, and Self-Making in Nineteenth-Century America* (New York: Oxford University Press, 1997), 21–23; Russ Castronovo, *Beautiful Democracy: Aesthetics and Anarchy in a Global Era* (Chicago: University of Chicago Press, 2007), 106–135.
8. Paul Gilroy, "Living Memory: A Meeting with Toni Morrison," in Gilroy, *Small Acts: Thoughts on the Politics of Black Cultures* (London: Serpent's Tail, 1993), 177; Toni Morrison, *Conversations with Toni Morrison*, ed. Danielle Taylor-Guthrie (Jackson: University Press of Mississippi, 1994), 272.
9. Sethe's outraged sense of violation at the out-of-control nephews stealing "[her] milk" that drove her to tell on them to her protector Mrs. Garner, only to result in the savage whipping that left a horrific tree-shaped scar on her back and catalyzed her decision to escape, may have been provoked as much by the humiliation of being reduced to animality—a humiliation parallel to Paul D's later punishment of being tied and bridled—as from the violation of maternity, crucial though that violation obviously was to Morrison and other neo-slave novelists and artists like Kara Walker and Alice Randall (see Chapter 9).

10. Morrison, *Conversations with Toni Morrison*, 257.

11. Édouard Glissant, *Faulkner, Mississippi*, trans. Barbara Lewis and Thomas C. Spear (New York: Farrar, Straus and Giroux, 1999), 55.

12. Morrison, *What Moves at the Margin*, 72.

13. Avery Gordon, *Ghostly Matters: Haunting and the Sociological Imagination*, rev. ed. (Minneapolis: University of Minnesota Press, 2008), 165, 167.

14. Robert Hayashi, *Haunted by Waters: A Journey Through Race and Place in America* (Iowa City: University of Iowa Press, 2007), 152.

15. James Scott, *Weapons of the Weak: Everyday Forms of Peasant Resistance* (New Haven, CT: Yale University Press, 1985), 29, 248–273; James Scott, *Domination and the Arts of Resistance* (New Haven, CT: Yale University Press, 1990), 142–147.

16. Herbert G. Gutman, *The Black Family in Slavery and in Freedom, 1750–1925* (New York: Pantheon, 1976), 30–60.

17. Colin Woodard, *American Nations: A History of the Eleven Rival Regional Cultures of North America* (New York: Viking, 2011), 197, 266.

18. Gilroy, "Living Memory," 176–177, 180.

19. Ibid., 179.

20. Ali Behdad, *A Forgetful Nation: On Immigration and Cultural Identity in the United States* (Durham, NC: Duke University Press, 2005); Amitav Ghosh, *Incendiary Circumstances: A Chronicle of the Turmoil of Our Times* (Boston: Houghton Mifflin, 2005), 203.

21. In her arresting discussion of *Beloved* as one of a series of American hemispheric narratives designed to evade the pertinacious outsider-interlocutor, critic Doris Sommer asks, "Could the epilogue be telling us that while we already know what is being concealed, what we [ethnic outsiders] know is empty, because the meaning or the affect of the story is reserved and not transferable?" (Doris Sommer, *Proceed with Caution, When Engaged by Minority Writing in the Americas* [Cambridge, MA: Harvard University Press, 1999], 264).

22. Eric J. Sundquist, *Strangers in the Land: Blacks, Jews, Post-Holocaust America* (Cambridge, MA: Harvard University Press, 2005), 459.

23. Madhu Dubey, "The Politics of Genre in *Beloved*," *Novel* 32 (Spring 1999): 197.

24. Dennis Childs, "'You Ain't Seen Nothin' Yet'; *Beloved*, the American Chain Gang, and the Middle Passage Remix," *American Quarterly* 61 (June 2009): 281.

25. Trudier Harris, *Fiction and Folklore: The Novels of Toni Morrison* (Knoxville: University of Tennessee Press, 1991), 163.

26. Spargo, "Trauma and the Specters of Enslavement," 126.

27. Dubey, "Politics of Genre," 198.

28. Gilroy, "Living Memory," 178.

29. Philip Weinstein, *What Else but Love? The Ordeal of Race in Faulkner and Morrison* (New York: Columbia University Press, 1996), 115.

30. Karen Sánchez-Eppler, *Dependent States: The Child's Part in Nineteenth-Century American Culture* (Chicago: University of Chicago Press, 2005), 101, 102.

31. Valerie Smith, "Neo-slave Narratives," in *The Cambridge Companion to the African American Slave Narrative,* ed. Audrey Fisch (Cambridge: Cambridge University Press, 2007), 174; James Phelan, "Toward a Rhetorical Reader-Response Criticism: The Difficult, the Stubborn, and the Ending of *Beloved,*" in Peterson, *Toni Morrison,* 229.

32. Harris, *Fiction and Folklore,* 147.

33. Russell Banks, "Who Will Tell the People? On Waiting, Still, for the Great Creole-American Novel," *Harper's Magazine* 300 (June 2000): 83, 88, 86.

34. Morrison is the one African American novelist Banks cites, a bit oddly given his reliance on her critical authority. Her post-*Beloved* novels *Jazz* and *Paradise,* he claims, "have higher walls around them than did the more inclusive *Beloved* and *Song of Solomon*" (ibid., 88). Banks's own best-known book at this time, incidentally, was probably *Continental Drift* (1985), an American-dream-gone-wrong novel that turns on the encounter between a white New England man and Haitian immigrants in Florida.

35. Another recent trend line, internal to contemporary African American studies, that Banks's essay overlooks is increased concern about limitation of engagement with the full range of African American artistic practice as a result of overconcentration on race issues per se and/or unduly restrictive conceptions of blackness, as for example Kenneth W. Warren, *What Was African American Literature?* (Cambridge, MA: Harvard University Press, 2011); and Touré, *Who's Afraid of Post-Blackness? What It Means to Be Black Now* (New York: Free Press, 2011). The likeliest upshot, however, as Gene Jarrett foresees in his *Representing the Race: A New Political History of African American Literature* (New York: New York University Press, 2011), will be to make the field of African American studies more expansive and complex, not to terminate it.

36. José David Saldívar, *Border Matters: Ramapping American Cultural Studies* (Berkeley: University of California Press, 1997), xiv.

37. Kirsten Silva Gruesz, *Ambassadors of Culture: The Transamerican Origins of Latino Writing* (Princeton, NJ: Princeton University Press, 2002), 211.

38. Cormac McCarthy, *Blood Meridian: Or the Evening Redness in the West* (New York: Vintage, 1985), 189, 249, 250.

39. Richard Slotkin, *Regeneration through Violence: The Mythology of the American Frontier 1600–1860* (Middletown, CT: Wesleyan University Press, 1973).

40. McCarthy, *Blood Meridian,* 86, 47.

41. Maxine Hong Kingston, "The Novel's Next Step," *Mother Jones* 14 (December 1989): 39. See Introduction above, second footnote, for more on Kingston's pronouncement.

42. Leslie Silko, *Almanac of the Dead: A Novel* (New York: Simon and Schuster, 1991), 133, 235. In a possible echo of *Beloved*'s epigraph, *Almanac* sets the genocidal death toll at sixty-two million (531, 723). The scores of notable

characters include Clinton "the first black Indian" (404), an Afro-indigene descended from Cherokee slaveholders who sees Africans and (indigenous) Americans as culturally akin: "Africans in the Americas had always been 'home' because 'home' is where the ancestor spirits are" (742).

43. Silko, *Almanac,* 760.

44. Ibid., 34, 531.

45. Gloria Anzaldúa, *Borderlands/La Frontera: The New Mestiza* (San Francisco: Aunt Lute Books, 1987), 22. *Almanac* also counterbalances its ethnocentric tendencies somewhat, however, by making its own sympathetic La Malinche/La Llorona figure—Anzaldúa's point of reference here—the neglectful grieving white mother Seese.

V. Introduction. Fatalisms of the Multitude

1. James Fenimore Cooper, *The American Democracy; or Hints on the Social Relations of the United States of America,* ed. Robert E. Spiller (New York: Vintage, 1956), 45, 46, 47.

2. Ibid., 141, 51, 69.

3. Alexis de Tocqueville, *Democracy in America,* trans. and ed. Phillips Bradley (New York: Vintage, 1945), 1:269–272.

4. Ibid., 2:307.

5. James Bryce, *The American Commonwealth* (London: Macmillan, 1888), 2:297–306, 711. A respected liberal jurist and academic, Bryce later served as British ambassador to the United States.

6. Tocqueville, *Democracy in America,* 2:169, 171.

7. For an important analysis of such narratives in the nineteenth century that has influenced my own, see Sandra Zagarell, "Narrative of Community: The Identification of a Genre," *Signs* 13 (Spring 1988): 498–527, although I do not see the genre as so closely tied to women's writing or gynocentric communities as she does.

8. David Simpson, *The Politics of American English, 1776–1850* (New York: Oxford University Press, 1986), 156.

9. Yamashita based this figure on Mexican performance artist Guillermo Gómez-Peña, in some ways following quite closely the moves of his *Border Brujo* (1988–1989) and other essays and scripts in *Warrior for Gringostroika* (1993). See Alvina E. Quintana, "Performing Tricksters: Karen Tei Yamashita and Guillermo Gómez-Peña," *Amerasia Journal* 28 (Summer 2002): 217–225. The battle itself ironically allegorizes both the inequalities of the North American Free Trade Agreement (NAFTA) of 1994 and the futility of trying to put a brake on Mexican immigration into what has long since irreversibly become a world city.

10. Karen Tei Yamashita, *Tropic of Orange* (Minneapolis: Coffee House Press, 1997), 82.

11. James Fenimore Cooper, *The Pioneers, or the Sources of the Susquehanna: A Descriptive Tale*, ed. James Franklin Beard et al. (Albany: State University of New York Press, 1980), 382.

12. Sandra Gustafson, *Imagining Deliberative Democracy in the Early American Republic* (Chicago: University of Chicago Press, 2011), 167–179.

13. John McWilliams, *Political Justice in a Republic: James Fenimore Cooper's America* (Berkeley: University of California Press, 1972), 108, 110.

14. Alan Taylor, *William Cooper's Town: Power and Persuasion on the Frontier of the Early American Republic* (New York: Knopf, 1995), 423.

11. Moby-Dick

1. J. M. Coetzee, *Stranger Shores: Essays 1986–1999* (New York: Viking, 2001), 16.

2. George Cotkin, *Dive Deeper: Journeys with "Moby-Dick"* (New York: Oxford, 2012), 175.

3. Tyrus Hillway and Luther S. Mansfield, eds., *"Moby-Dick": Centennial Essays* (Dallas: Southern Methodist University Press, 1953), viii.

4. Herman Melville, *Moby-Dick; or, The Whale*, ed. Luther S. Mansfield and Howard P. Vincent (New York: Hendricks House, 1952).

5. William Spanos, *The Errant Art of "Moby-Dick": The Canon, the Cold War, and the Struggle for American Studies* (Durham, NC: Duke University Press, 1995), 183.

6. For more on Melville's disaffiliation from U.S.-ness, see L. Buell, "Melville and the Question of American Decolonization," *American Literature* 64 (June 1992): 215–237; Paul Giles, *Virtual Americas: Transnational Fictions and the Transatlantic Imaginary* (Durham, NC: Duke University Press, 2002), 47–87; Cyrus R. K. Patell, "Cosmopolitanism and Zoroastrianism in *Moby-Dick*," in *The Turn around Religion in America: Literature, Culture, and the Work of Sacvan Bercovitch*, ed. Nan Goodman and Michael P. Kramer (Burlington, VT: Ashgate, 2011), 19–36; and Robert Milder, *Exiled Royalties: Melville and the Life We Imagine* (New York: Oxford University Press, 2006), which tellingly remarks that just twice in his career (in the run-up to *Moby-Dick* and to *Battle-Pieces*) Melville "was impelled by a belief that American writers might exercise a formative influence upon their culture," but both times his "optimism did not survive the reception of the book" (256).

7. Chapter 1's opening lines intimate what later chapters confirm: that Ishmael is a seasoned sailor recalling his rookie experience from the perspective of both extensive later reading in whaling lore and roaming that has taken him to Lima ("The Town-Ho Story"), the Solomon Islands ("A Bower in the Arsacides"), and again to the *Samuel Enderby*, a British whaler with which the *Pequod* gams ("The Decanter"). But *MD* refuses to draw anything like a direct line backward from the denouement to Ishmael's sardonic opening shot that seagoing is an extreme act of suicidal desperation, "my substitute for pistol and ball" (*MD* 18).

8. Robert Milder cuts to the heart of the matter: How far should we "be willing to impoverish our reading of *Moby-Dick* to accommodate compositional
speculation founded upon insufficient evidence and doubtful methodol-
ogy?" (Robert Milder, "The Composition of *Moby-Dick:* A Review and a
Prospect," *ESQ: A Journal of the American Renaissance* 23 [4th Quarter 1977]:
215). Textual scholar John Bryant goes further: "there is little concrete evidence, and nothing at all conclusive, to show that Melville radically altered
the structure or conception of the book" (John Bryant, "*Moby-Dick* as Revolution," in *The Cambridge Companion to Melville,* ed. Robert S. Levine [Cam-
bridge: Cambridge University Press, 1998], 67). That said, the best of this
speculation repays examination. In addition to work that Milder cites, see
especially Harrison Hayford, "Unnecessary Duplicates: A Key to the Writing
of *Moby-Dick,*" in *New Perspectives on Melville,* ed. Faith Pullin (Edinburgh:
Edinburgh University Press, 1978), 128–161; Harrison Hayford, Hershel
Parker, and G. Thomas Tanselle, eds., "Historical Note," in Herman Melville,
Moby-Dick, ed. Harrison Hayford, Hershel Parker, and G. Thomas Tanselle
(Evanston, IL: Northwestern University Press, 1988), 635–659; and Robert
Sattelmeyer, "'Shanties and Chapters and Essays': Rewriting *Moby-Dick,*"
ESQ: A Journal of the American Renaissance 49 (4th Quarter 2007): 213–247.

9. Patell, "Cosmopolitanism and Zoroastrianism," demonstrates the parochialism of typing Ahab solely as some species of heretical Christian, stressing
the importance of his tie to Fedallah, the privately hired Parsee harpooner
whose *Macbeth*-like prophecy of three seemingly impossible events that
must come to pass before the quest will fail (as indeed they do) emboldens
Ahab. Patell may go too far in claiming Fedallah as "the orthodox follower
of an orthodox faith" (34), but he is right that the shuddering aversion to
him as a Mephistopheles by both narrator and crew is a way of marking
the "limits to Ishmael's cosmopolitanism" by contrast to Melville's—and
Ahab's too (35).

10. Robert Wallace, *Melville and Turner: Spheres of Love and Fright* (Athens: University of Georgia Press, 1992), 325. Wallace demonstrates that Melville's
inspiration was likely a magazine description by the novelist Thackeray
(writing under the pseudonym of Michael Angelo Titmarsh) of Turner's
painting *The Whale Ship,* which Melville had almost certainly never seen, although he admired Turner's work; *v.* ibid., 325–330; and Robert Wallace,
"The Sultry Creator of Captain Ahab? Herman Melville and J. M. W. Turner,"
Turner Studies 5 (Winter 1985): 2–19. That explanation perfectly fits the sense
of the necessarily mediated character of human knowledge that animates
Melville's and Turner's art.

11. Robert D. Richardson Jr., *Myth and Literature in the American Renaissance*
(Bloomington: Indiana University Press, 1978), 210–225.

12. The coeditors of the authorized modern scholarly edition (1988), despite
lack of evidence from the first American and British editions, elected to
attribute a long world-weary monologue toward the end of "The Gilder"

(*MD* 373) to Ahab rather than to Ishmael, a decision that proved quite controversial. See Melville, *Moby-Dick*, ed. Hayford, Parker, and Tanselle, 901 (n. to p. 492 of main text) for the editors' thoughtful if not airtight rationale—which, however, rests on an assumption this chapter questions below, that Ishmael must be thought of as the speaker if Ahab is not. For a perceptive essay by a senior Melvillian who assesses that decision as one among various ways in which *Moby-Dick* has proven a "fluid text" reinvented over time, see John Bryant, "Rewriting *Moby-Dick:* Politics, Textual Identity, and the Revision Narrative," *PMLA* 125 (October 2010): 1043–1060. For critical analysis of Ahab-Ishmael convergence, see John Wenke, "Ahab and 'the Larger, Darker, Deeper Part,'" in *MD*, 702–711.

13. Milder, *Exiled Royalties*, 81.

14. Walter Bezanson, "*Moby-Dick:* Work of Art," in Hillway and Mansfield, "*Moby-Dick*," 36–37, 41.

15. Clare Spark, *Hunting Captain Ahab: Psychological Warfare and the Melville Revival* (Kent, OH: Kent State University Press, 2001), 238, 15.

16. Spanos, *Errant Art of "Moby-Dick*," 38, 75, in friendly dispute with Donald E. Pease's critique of F. O. Matthiessen's defense of Ishmael as liberal free-thinker in his monumental *American Renaissance* (London: Oxford University Press, 1941), 396–446; Donald E. Pease, *Visionary Compacts* (Madison: University of Wisconsin Press, 1987), 235–275. For other attempts to imagine the Ishmael figure holistically, see for example Henry Golemba, "The Shape of *Moby-Dick*," *Studies in the Novel* 5 (Summer 1973): 209: "Ishmael grows from initiate to erring acolyte to novitiate to meditative Magian, and finally to anonymous monk"; Julian Markels, *Melville and the Politics of Identity: From "King Lear" to "Moby-Dick"* (Urbana: University of Illinois Press, 1993), 114: Ishmael "submits the blank tablet of his mind to nature's power of inscription before embarking on his reflections"; and Bryant, "*Moby-Dick* as Revolution," 71: "Ahab's tragic drama is a projection out of Ishmael's comic sensibility." Among important twenty-first-century critical books on Melville, Andrew Delbanco, *Melville: His World and Work* (New York: Knopf, 2005), 149–175; and Milder, *Exiled Royalties*, 50–117, stand out for resisting the lure of Ishmael-centrism and recognizing that *Moby-Dick* is more decisively Ahab's story, for better or for worse, than Ishmael's.

17. Leo Bersani, *The Culture of Redemption* (Cambridge, MA: Harvard University Press, 1990), 151.

18. Michel Foucault, "Of Other Spaces" (1967), Heterotopias, Foucault.info, http://foucault.info/documents/heteroTopia/foucault.heteroTopia.en.html.

19. Not for the first time, either: Melville uses the same ploy in his previous novel, *White-Jacket* (1850), for example, and the metaphor of shipboard hierarchy as feudal or aristocratic system was not original with Melville either. Conceivably it might have been suggested to him by earlier U.S. literature's foremost maritime classic, Richard Henry Dana Jr.'s *Two Years before the Mast* (1840), an autobiographical narrative Melville greatly admired.

20. Bersani, *Culture of Redemption*, 149.

21. Christopher Freeberg, *Melville and the Idea of Blackness* (Cambridge: Cambridge University Press, 2012), 49–53.

22. Bersani, *Culture of Redemption*, 143.

23. For the seminal analysis of the *Pequod* as early industrial U.S. factory, see Leo Marx, *The Machine in the Garden: Technology and the Pastoral Ideal in America* (New York: Oxford University Press, 1964), 305–308. For *Moby-Dick*'s correlation between harvesting of cetaceans and labor exploitation, see L. Buell, *Writing for an Endangered World: Literature, Culture, and Environment in the United States and Beyond* (Cambridge, MA: Harvard University Press, 2001), 205–223.

24. Agnès Derail, "Melville's Leviathan: *Moby-Dick; or, The Whale* and the Body Politic," in *L'Imaginaire-Melville: A French Point of View*, ed. Viola Sachs (St. Denis, France: Presses Universitaires de Vincennes, 1992), 27. In a brilliant but problematic assessment, Peter Szendy identifies *Moby-Dick*'s counter-Leviathan with Ishmael's "Leviathan-text" itself, in *Prophecies of Leviathan: Reading Past Melville*, trans. Gil Anidjar (New York: Fordham University Press, 2010), 77, 89–93. Szendy is right insofar as *Moby-Dick* is indeed an aspiration of Leviathanic proportions that calls attention throughout (as in "Cetology") to the analogy between whales and books, but mistaken in identifying Ishmael as the author of the aspirant Leviathan-text. The political philosopher who makes the strongest case for the seriousness with which Melville took Hobbes's treatise, Leon Harold Craig, concurs with Derail that Ahab stands exposed as "not quite up to the task" of embodying Leviathan but dubiously claims that Ishmael "approximates" the true Leviathan perspective as Hobbes framed it: "the calm, balanced, and measured overview of the whole" (Leon Harold Craig, *The Platonian Leviathan* [Toronto: University of Toronto Press, 2010], 519).

25. Cesare Casarino, *Modernity at Sea: Melville, Marx, Conrad in Crisis* (Minneapolis: University of Minnesota Press, 2002), 74; Jamie Lynn Jones, "American Whaling in Culture and Memory, 1820–1930," PhD diss., Harvard University, 2011, 43–78.

26. Sanborn, *Whipscars and Tattoos*, 117.

27. Briton Cooper Busch, *"Whaling will Never Do for Me": The American Whaleman in the Nineteenth Century* (Lexington: University Press of Kentucky, 1994), 5.

28. Simon Schama, *Citizens: A Chronicle of the French Revolution* (New York: Knopf, 1989), 474; François Labbe, *Anacharsis Cloots: Le Prussian Francophile* (Paris: L'Harmattan, 1999), 305.

29. The three Melvillian passages are from *MD* 107; Herman Melville, *The Confidence-Man*, ed. Harrison Hayford et al. (Evanston, IL: Northwestern University Press, 1984), 9; and the unfinished, posthumously published *Billy Budd, Sailor*, in *The Norton Anthology of American Literature, 1820–1865*, 8th ed., ed. Nina Baym and Robert S. Levine (New York: Norton, 2012), 1588.

30. Thomas Carlyle, *The French Revolution: A History* (New York: Modern Library, 1934), 269–270; Schama, *Citizens,* 808.

31. Michael Rogin, *Subversive Genealogy: The Politics and Art of Herman Melville* (New York: Knopf, 1983), 61.

32. Thomas Paine, *Collected Writings,* ed. Eric Foner (New York: Library of America, 1995), 731. Cloots was executed; Paine narrowly escaped. In prison, Paine reported, he would visit Cloots daily to talk through the ideas for *The Age of Reason.* Cloots, who admired Paine's revolutionary writings before the two met, also criticized his friend strongly for being hamstrung by "so many religious and political prejudices" (John Keane, *Tom Paine: A Political Life* [Boston: Little, Brown, 1995], 403).

33. Peter Linebaugh and Marcus Rediker, *The Many-Headed Hydra: Sailors, Slaves, and Commoners, and the Hidden History of the Revolutionary Atlantic* (Boston: Beacon, 2000).

34. "The pertinence of the democratic invocation wanes" as "the stature of Ahab grows ever more central," remarks critic John P. McWilliams Jr. in his penetrating study of the cross-currents between *Moby-Dick*'s epic thrust and mock-epic ironies (McWilliams, *The American Epic: Transforming a Genre, 1770–1860* [Cambridge: Cambridge University Press, 1989], 212).

35. C. L. R. James, *Mariners, Renegades and Castaways: The Story of Herman Melville and the World We Live In* (orig. 1953), ed. Donald E. Pease (Hanover, NH: University Press of New England, 2001), 19–20; C. L. R. James, *American Civilization,* ed. Anna Grimshaw and Keith Hart (Cambridge, MA: Blackwell, 1993), 84.

36. James, *Mariners,* 18, 48.

37. Donald E. Pease, "The Extraterritoriality of the Literature for Our Planet," *ESQ: A Journal of the American Renaissance* 50 (1st–3rd Quarters 2004): 216.

38. James saw it as substantiating his claim of rightful belonging. He sent copies to every member of the U.S. Senate and ended the book with a plea to the public to buy copies to support his legal defense.

39. James, *Mariners,* 3, 151, 19, 28.

40. Ibid., 89, 153–154.

41. Ibid., 4, 78.

42. Andrew DuBois, "Melvillian Provocation and the Critical Art of Devotion," in *Melville and Aesthetics,* ed. Samuel Otter and Geoffrey Sanborn (New York: Palgrave-Macmillan, 2011), 61. Elizabeth Renker, *Strike through the Mask: Herman Melville and the Scene of Writing* (Baltimore, MD: Johns Hopkins University Press, 1996), 49–68, provocatively correlates Ahab's frustrated determination to strike through "the pasteboard mask" with the extreme effort, physical as well as mental, involved in Melville's "relentless striking through and crossing out and rewriting" of "his own white page" (67), detailing also the physical maladies and psychic derangement from which he suffered during his binges of day-after-day nonstop desk work as well as the possible relation between those and the spotty but disturbing

evidence of his abuse of his wife and other women relatives in the home who worked as his scribes.

43. Dowling, *Chasing the White Whale,* 104; James, *Mariners,* 53.

44. The first half century of *Moby-Dick* criticism especially, with conspicuous exceptions like C. L. R. James and Lawrance Thompson, saw Ishmael as the key to the narrative—for most its center of sanity too—while accepting Ahab as the plot driver. Matthiessen (*American Renaissance,* 396–466) and Bezanson ("*Moby-Dick:* Work of Art") were perhaps especially influential. The sharp critique of their valorization of Ishmael's temporizing liberalism as "'Cold War' criticism," starting with Pease (*Visionary Compacts,* 235–275), did not put a stop to Ishmael-centrism, as attested by the work of Spanos, Markels, Bryant ("*Moby-Dick* as Revolution"), and Szendy, among many others. That the intensity of academic attention to the novel's most intellectual figure is predictable does not lessen the interest of the divergence from public culture.

45. Insko, "'All of Us Are Ahabs,'" 29, 22.

46. Randy Laist, "Profiles in Ontological Rebellion: The Presence of *Moby-Dick* in *Heathers,*" *Leviathan* 11 (October 2009): 77. For the Baur cartoon, see www .cartoonstock.com/directory/r/rene.asp. A noteworthy exception among cartoonists is Gary Larson's 1982 rearview shot of a frustrated scribbler straining for the right first sentence after five discards: "Call me Bill," etc. (Gary Larson, *The Complete Far Side* [Kansas City, MO: Andrews McMeel, 2003], 1:190). Larson's several other cartoon allusions to *Moby-Dick* follow the norm (*Complete Far Side,* 1:26, 200, 383).

47. Michael J. Preston, "Rethinking Folklore, Rethinking Literature: Looking at *Robinson Crusoe* and *Gulliver's Travels* as Folktales, a Chapbook-Inspired Inquiry," in *The Other Print Tradition: Essays on Chapbooks, Broadsides, and Related Ephemera,* ed. Cathy Lynn Preston and Michael J. Preston (New York: Garland, 1995), 32–33.

48. Gouge's third novel, *Son of Perdition,* centers on the alienation and Christian conversion of Ahab's troubled son, an intergenerational add-on that halfway predicts the 2011 futuristic film *Age of the Dragons,* in which the Ishmael figure forces the daughter of Ahab/Danny Glover to choose between them, and she chooses Ishmael.

49. Laist, "Profiles in Ontological Rebellion," 72–78.

50. Craig Bernardini, "Heavy Melville: Mastodon's *Leviathan* and the Popular Image of *Moby-Dick,*" *Leviathan* 11 (October 2009): 27–44.

51. Insko, "'All of Us Are Ahabs,'" 28.

52. James Reston, "Ahab and the China Whale" (quoting the Sinophile journalist Edgar Snow), *The Nation,* 17 May 1965, 519; Anthony Lewis, "By Hate Possessed: Reagan's Nicaragua Obsession," *New York Times,* 24 March 1986, A19; Arthur Schlesinger Jr., "So Much for the Imperial Presidency," *New York Times,* 3 August 1998, A23; Morrie Ryskind, "What Really Defeated Nixon," *Los Angeles Times,* 14 November 1962; John Leonard, "Mr. Nixon as

the Last Liberal," *New York Times*, 15 October 1970, 45; Lee Gomes, "The Microsoft Ruling: Rivals Rejoice but Await a Remedy Just as Tough," *Wall Street Journal*, 8 November 1999, A30; "Captain Ahab Prosecutors," *Wall Street Journal*, 29 December 1988, 1; John Gray, "Grits Unable to Satisfy Critics Despite Exit from Whale Group," *Globe and Mail* (Toronto), 30 June 1981, P11; Gillian Bennett, Roy Hanania, Mary Gillespie, and Alf Siewers, "Name His Party!," *Chicago Sun Times*, 30 May 1986, 10; James Reston, "The Asterisk That Shook the Baseball World," *New York Times*, 1 October 1961, E8.

53. Insko, "'All of Us Are Ahabs,'" 19.

54. Toni Morrison, "Unspeakable Things Unspoken: The Afro-American Presence in American Literature," in *Tanner Lectures on Human Values XI 1988* (Salt Lake City: University of Utah Press, 1990), 143; James McCune Smith, *The Works of James McCune Smith: Black Intellectual and Abolitionist*, ed. John Stauffer (New York: Oxford University Press, 2006), 146; Rogin, *Subversive Genealogy*, 128.

55. Pierre Bourdieu, *The Field of Cultural Production: Essays on Art and Literature*, ed. Randal Johnson (Cambridge: Polity, 1983), 121.

12. The Great American Novel of Twentieth-Century Breakdown

1. Edmund Wilson, "Dahlberg, Dos Passos and Wilder," *New Republic* 62 (25 March 1930): 157, 158.

2. John Dos Passos, *The Major Nonfictional Prose*, ed. Donald Pizer (Detroit: Wayne State University Press, 1988), 239. Abbreviated below as *JDPP*. For Dos Passos's early and enduring attachment to *Vanity Fair* as model of chronicle fiction (and secondarily Stendahl's *Charterhouse of Parma* and Tolstoy's *War and Peace*), see *JDPP* 238, 272. For his admiration of Whitman, see Kenneth Price, "Whitman, Dos Passos, and 'Our Storybook Democracy,'" in *Walt Whitman: Centennial Essays*, ed. Ed Folsom (Iowa City: University of Iowa Press, 1994), 217–225.

3. Jean-Paul Sartre, "John Dos Passos and *1919*" (1938), trans. Annette Michaelson, in *Dos Passos: The Critical Heritage*, ed. Barry Maine (New York: Routledge, 1988), 175; George Steiner, *Language and Silence: Essays on Language, Literature, and the Inhuman* (New Haven, CT: Yale University Press, 1998), 116.

4. Michael Denning, *The Cultural Front: The Laboring of American Culture in the Twentieth Century* (London: Verso, 1997), 166, 199; Ted Goia, "The Great American Novel That Wasn't" (review of Library of America repr. of *U.S.A.*), *Los Angeles Review of Books*, 20 January 2013.

5. George Packer, *The Unwinding: An Inner History of the New America* (New York: Farrar, Straus and Giroux, 2013), 431. Although Packer's shorter-form rendition is predictably less stylistically innovative than *U.S.A.*, his best celebrity mini-biographies—Newt Gingrich, Oprah Winfrey, Sam

Walton, Colin Powell, Robert Rubin, Elizabeth Warren, and others—are nearly as pungent as *U.S.A.*'s; and the three lifelines of un-famous (actual) citizens *The Unwinding* tracks throughout are more finely tuned than most of *U.S.A.*'s fictional dozen.

6. Denning, *Cultural Front,* 167.

7. *JDPP* 243, 179.

8. Donald Pizer, *Dos Passos' "U.S.A.": A Critical Study* (Charlottesville: University Press of Virginia, 1988), 87.

9. *JDPP* 237, 289.

10. Bernard De Voto, "John Dos Passos: Anatomist of Our Time," *Saturday Review of Literature* 14 (8 August 1936): 12.

11. Matthew J. Packer, "Mimetic Desire in John Dos Passos' *U.S.A.* Trilogy," *Papers on Language and Literature* 41 (Spring 2005): 222.

12. Ralph Waldo Emerson, *Nature, Addresses, Lectures,* ed. Robert E. Spiller and Alfred R. Ferguson (Cambridge, MA: Harvard University Press, 1971), 53.

13. Packer, "Mimetic Desire," 227.

14. Turner, *Marketing Modernism,* 126–127.

15. Walt Whitman, *Leaves of Grass: Comprehensive Reader's Edition,* ed. Harold W. Blodgett and Sculley Bradley (New York: New York University Press, 1965), 34.

16. Carolyn Porter, *Seeing and Being: The Plight of the Participant Observer in Emerson, James, Adams, and Faulkner* (Middletown, CT: Wesleyan University Press, 1981).

17. Allen Ginsberg, "America," in *Howl and Other Poems* (San Francisco: City Lights, 1956), 31, 32, 33. The last phrase reverses *U.S.A.*'s Newsreel headline: "SACCO AND VANZETTI MUST DIE" (*USA* 1156).

18. Whitman, "A Backward Glance O'er Travel'd Roads," in *Leaves of Grass,* 563.

19. Whitman, *Leaves of Grass,* 272–273.

20. Ibid., 52.

21. John R. Dos Passos, *The Anglo-Saxon Century and the Unification of the English-Speaking People* (New York: Putnam's, 1903), 3–4.

22. Barrington Moore Jr., *Social Origins of Dictatorship and Democracy: Lord and Peasant in the Making of the Modern World* (Boston: Beacon, 1966), 111–165.

23. Daniel Rodgers, *Atlantic Crossings: Social Politics in a Progressive Age* (Cambridge, MA: Harvard University Press, 1998), 253; D. W. Meinig, *The Shaping of America: A Geographical Perspective on 500 Years of History,* vol. 3: *Transcontinental America, 1850–1915* (New Haven, CT: Yale University Press, 1998), 240.

24. To a greater extent than any of the other eleven, French was based on a historical figure Dos Passos knew, labor activist Mary Heaton Vorse (1874–1966), who was just as irritated by *U.S.A.*'s portrait of her as was Robert Hillyer by Dos Passos's much more unflattering portrait of Dick Savage (see below.)

25. John Dos Passos, *Facing the Chair: Story of the Americanization of Two Foreign Born Workmen* (Boston: Sacco-Vanzetti Defense Committee, 1927), 23; *JDPP* 99.

26. G. Louis Joughin and Edmund M. Morgan, *The Legacy of Sacco and Vanzetti* (New York: Harcourt, 1948), 221.

27. *JDPP* 200.

28. Woodrow Wilson, *The New Freedom: A Call for the Emancipation of the Generous Energies of a People* (New York: Doubleday and Page, 1913), 17.

29. Edward Bernays, *Crystallizing Public Opinion* (New York: Boni and Liveright, 1923), 11; David Miller and William Dinan, *A Century of Spin: How Public Relations Became the Cutting Edge of Corporate Power* (London: Pluto, 2008), 15.

30. Roland Marchand, *Creating the Corporate Soul: The Rise of Public Relations and Corporate Imagery in American Big Business* (Berkeley: University of California Press, 1998), 90.

31. T. J. Jackson Lears, *Fables of Abundance: A Cultural History of Advertising in America* (New York: Basic, 1994), 219; Edward Bernays, *Public Relations* (Norman: University of Oklahoma Press, 1952), 77.

32. Edward Bernays, *Propaganda* (New York: Liveright, 1928), 9; Miller and Dinan, *A Century of Spin,* 18–19.

33. Barbara Foley, *Telling the Truth: The Theory and Practice of Documentary Fiction* (Ithaca, NY: Cornell University Press, 1986), 204; William Graebner, *The Engineering of Consent: Democracy and Authority in Twentieth-Century America* (Madison: University of Wisconsin Press, 1987), 5.

34. John Milton Cooper Jr., *Woodrow Wilson: A Biography* (New York: Knopf, 2009), 531–532.

35. Walter Lippmann, *Public Opinion* (New York: Harcourt, 1922), 25, 223, 341, 15.

36. Ibid., 74, 7, 95, 73.

37. Lippmann, *Public Opinion,* 310; Bernays, *Crystallizing Public Opinion,* 55 and passim.

38. John Dewey, *The Public and Its Problems* (New York: Holt, 1927), 208, 216.

39. Denning, *Cultural Front,* 177; Dewey, *Public and Its Problems,* 215.

40. Matthew Stratton, "Start Spreading the New: Irony, Public Opinion, and the Aesthetic Politics of *U.S.A.,*" *Twentieth-Century Literature* 34 (Winter 2008): 426 and 419–447 passim,

41. John Dos Passos, *The Fourteenth Chronicle: Letters and Diaries of John Dos Passos,* ed. Townsend Ludington (Boston: Gambit, 1973), 465, 461, 459, 461.

42. T. K. Whipple, "Dos Passos and the U.S.A.," *Nation* 146 (19 February 1938): 211–212. On Dos Passos's politics, Denning's encapsulation of the critical controversy is helpful (*Cultural Front,* 172 n.16) and his assessment on the whole persuasive: Dos Passos should not be identified with any one doctrinal position but with the "mixture of Marx and Veblen, Whitman and Beard, anarchism and populism, that made up American radicalism at this time" (172).

43. Denning, *Cultural Front,* 197; Jon Smith, "John Dos Passos: Anglo-Saxon," *Modern Fiction Studies* 44 (Summer 1998): 282–305. Smith further contends

(293–296) that the novelistic trilogy itself would have been understood as a genre coded ethnic, from the "biological notion of nationhood" that courses through Henryk Sienkiewicz's Polish trilogy of the nineteenth century down through Norwegian-American O. E. Rolvåg's immigration trilogy, which Sienkiewicz influenced (trans. 1927–1931) and James Farrell's *Studs Lonigan* trilogy of the 1930s. This claims too much. Dutch ethnicity, for example, diminishes to a subsidiary element in Cooper's Littlepage trilogy; and it would be perverse to identify Amitav Ghosh's cosmopolitan South Asian–focused Ibis trilogy-in-progress (including *Sea of Poppies* and *River of Smoke*) with a single ethnic strand. But the argument does hold to some extent, especially if one grants the capacity of a trilogy to represent residual ethnonationalism self-critically, as in Roth's American trilogy (see Chapter 6).

44. See Denning, *Cultural Front,* 187–188, for more on the abandoned scenario of Ike's return.

45. Pizer, *Dos Passos' "U.S.A.,"* 143.

46. *JDPP* 243.

47. Denning, *Cultural Front,* 184.

48. John Steinbeck, *"Their Blood Is Strong"* (San Francisco: Simon Lubin Society, 1938), n.p.

49. Robert J. DeMott, *Steinbeck's Reading: A Catalogue of Books Owned and Borrowed* (New York: Garland, 1984), 142.

50. Steinbeck cleverly introduces a renegade outlaw motif in order to trump it with the icon of domesticity. Ma Joad, who knew the mother of Oklahoma bank robber Pretty Boy Floyd (1904–1934), remembers him as a decent lad driven desperate and worries repeatedly that Tom might also have been scarred by his prison experience (for a murder committed in self-defense) and worries too that she herself is "gittin' mean" (*GOW* 403). But in the long run *GOW* conjured up such fears of rampant lawlessness only to underscore the strength with which the Joads and the Okies cling to family and neighborly values by contrast to those who exploit them.

51. If *U.S.A.* can be seen as the brainchild of a would-be architect, *GOW* bears the marks of the serious amateur biologist soon to write *The Sea of Cortez: A Leisurely Journal of Travel and Research* (1941).

52. Steinbeck, *"Their Blood Is Strong,"* 3.

53. Carey McWilliams, *Factories in the Field: The Story of Migratory Farm Labor in California* (Boston: Little, Brown, 1939), 305, 324.

54. Clifton Fadiman, "Highway 66," *New Yorker* 15 (15 April 1939): 81.

55. Isabel Wilkerson, *The Warmth of Other Suns: The Epic Story of America's Great Migration* (New York: Random House, 2010). For Wilkerson's reflections on *GOW*'s influence, see for example Andrea Pitzer's interview, "Isabel Wilkerson on the Great Migration," *Nieman Storyboard,* 4 April 2011 (www.niemanstoryboard.org/2011/04/04/).

56. Quoted in Susan Shillinglaw, ed., *John Steinbeck: Centennial Reflections by American Writers* (San Jose, CA: Center for Steinbeck Studies, 2002), 34, 3, 72.

57. The oasis supplied by this camp, to the historical prototype of whose manager Steinbeck codedicated *GOW,* and the stark contrast between benign but underfunded federal outreach and the hostility of the big growers toward the Okies is a conspicuous mark of the "New Deal Modernism" that marks *GOW* as a more typical 1930s product in this respect than *U.S.A.,* which displays no trust or even interest at all in federal solutions to public economic distress (Michael Szalay, *New Deal Modernism: American Literature and the Invention of the Welfare State* [Durham, NC: Duke University Press, 2000], 174).

58. Foley, *Radical Representations,* 408.

59. Perhaps by coincidence, *The Naked and the Dead* follows Steinbeck in part by giving its main characters more individuation and interiority than does *U.S.A.* It also reflects both wartime conditions and the flow of sociocultural change reinforced in no small measure by them in making its soldiers an ethnic collage of Puerto Rican, Italian, Irish, and Jewish, as well as WASP.

60. Alfred Kazin, *An American Procession* (New York: Knopf, 1984), 382.

13. Late Twentieth-Century Maximalism

1. Morris Dickstein, *Gates of Eden: American Culture in the Sixties* (Cambridge, MA: Harvard University Press, 1997), 92.

2. The term was coined by Linda Hutcheon, *A Poetics of Postmodernism: History, Theory, Fiction* (New York: Routledge, 1988), 106–123, in the course of arguing for the significance of the historical in "postmodern" fiction. For Hutcheon, the postmodern persuasion involves "two simultaneous moves. It reinstalls historical contexts as significant and even determining, but in so doing, it problematizes the entire notion of historical knowledge" (ibid., 89). She wisely leaves open the extent to which the individual work of "historical" imagination may verge toward the empirical, as in so-called nonfiction novels like Truman Capote's *In Cold Blood* (1966) versus toward the fantastic, as in Philip Dick's counterfactual science fiction *The Man in the High Castle* (1962), which presupposes that World War II was won by the Axis powers of Germany, Italy, and Japan. See also Amy J. Elias's proposed coda/revision of Hutcheon, that post-1960s historical fiction à la Pynchon is "metahistorical romance," which she sees as more continuous with traditional historical romance: Amy J. Elias, *Sublime Desire: History and Post-1960s Fiction* (Baltimore, MD: Johns Hopkins University Press, 2001); and Elias, "History," in *The Cambridge Companion to Thomas Pynchon,* ed. Inger H. Dalsgaard, Luc Herman, and Brian McHale (Cambridge: Cambridge University Press, 2012), 129.

3. E. L. Doctorow, "False Documents," in *E. L. Doctorow: Essays and Conversations*, ed. Richard Trenner (Princeton, NJ: Ontario Review Press, 1983), 26.

4. Paul de Man, *Blindness and Insight: Essays in the Rhetoric of Contemporary Criticism*, 2nd ed. (Minneapolis: University of Minnesota Press, 1983), 18.

5. Mark McGurl, *The Program Era: Postwar Fiction and the Rise of Creative Writing* (Cambridge, MA: Harvard University Press, 2008).

6. Walter Benn Michaels, *The Shape of the Signifier* (Princeton, NJ: Princeton University Press, 2004), 23–25, 132–134.

7. Leslie Fiedler, "Literature as an Institution: The View from 1980," in *English Literature: Opening up the Canon*, ed. Leslie Fiedler and Houston Baker (Baltimore, MD: Johns Hopkins University Press, 1981), 89.

8. Leo Bersani, *The Culture of Redemption* (Cambridge, MA: Harvard University Press, 1990), 187.

9. David Foster Wallace, *Infinite Jest* (Boston: Little, Brown, 1996), 5.

10. David Cowart, *Thomas Pynchon and the Dark Passages of History* (Athens: University of Georgia Press, 2012), 111.

11. E. L. Doctorow, *Conversations with E. L. Doctorow*, ed. Christopher Morris (Jackson: University Press of Mississippi, 1999), 38.

12. On this aspect of *GR*, see Thomas Hill Schaub, "Environmental Pynchon: *Gravity's Rainbow* and the Ecological Context," *Pynchon Notes* 42–43 (Spring–Fall 1998): 59–72; and Chris Coughran, "Green Scripts in *Gravity's Rainbow*: Pynchon, Pastoral Ideology and the Performance of Ecological Self," *ISLE: Interdisciplinary Studies in Literature and Environment* 16 (Spring 2009): 265–269.

13. Although U.S. art and culture are often and rightly thought to have a distinctively utilitarian/pragmatic cast, self-evidently its fiction has no monopoly on thick description of work regimes, whether manual or clerical. One immediately thinks of (say) Defoe on desert-island homesteading in *Robinson Crusoe*; Dickens, Gogol, and Naipaul on clerks; Dickens, Dostoyevsky, Levi, and Solzhenitsyn on prison life; factory work in Gaskell; harvesting in Tolstoy's *Anna Karenina*; herding in Joseph Furphy's *Such Is Life*; mining in Zola's *Germinal*; subsistence fishing in Ghosh's *Hungry Tide*.

14. Simon Chesterman, *One Nation under Surveillance: A New Social Contract to Defend Freedom without Sacrificing Liberty* (New York: Oxford University Press, 2011), 18—referring especially, however, to the United Kingdom. The counterpart U.S. institutions, the CIA and NSA, took form just after World War II, as Pynchon would have been well aware.

15. Steven C. Weisenburger's meticulous *A "Gravity's Rainbow" Companion*, 2nd ed. (Athens: University of Georgia Press, 2008) is an indispensable although perforce not exhaustive guide to these matters, as are many of the articles in the journal *Pynchon Notes* (1979–). For a valuable overview of *GR*'s representation of the war, see Khachig Tölölyan, "War as Background in *Gravity's Rainbow*," in *Approaches to "Gravity's Rainbow*," ed. Charles Clerc (Columbus: Ohio State University Press, 1983), 31–68.

16. Another is by having the voice of a maddened Vietnam vet pop up from between brackets on page 739 claiming to have spread a subversive "virus" throughout the text. Some critics take this sequence as a belated revelation of the novel's "true" narrator, although *GR*'s voices—ranging from baby talk to lyricality to various kinds of argot to profspeak—are far too heterogeneous to warrant insisting on a single definitive over- (or under-)voice.

17. Chiefly, however, Germany, the United States, and the USSR as well as Britain. The other Axis and Allied powers—Italy, Japan, France, their colonies and other nations beyond Euro-America—figure scarcely if at all.

18. Tölölyan, "War as Background," 52.

19. In the conversation that ends part 3, a British spymaster remarks, "We sent him out to destroy the blacks, and it's obvious now he won't do the job" (*GR* 615), presumably meaning some reprisal against the Schwarzkommando, Herero tribesmen seeking to assemble the ultimate rocket as a totemic replacement for their religioculture, which the German genocide in South-West Africa (now Namibia) had largely destroyed. (The British had disseminated a propaganda film about an imaginary such group in order to terrify German racists, only to find that it was "real"—in the novel's world, that is. Ironically, Slothrop winds up making friends with the leader, Enzian.) The notion of using Slothrop as weapon might have been suggested by his bizarre drug-induced "memory" of near-rape by black men in a Roxbury, Massachusetts, dance hall lavatory in which the future Malcolm X figures. But to buy into a specific explanation is to belie the mystification and fractiousness of the masterminds themselves and to forget that the interest Slothrop takes from the get-go "in investigating V-bomb 'incidents'" is postulated rather than explained (24).

20. Weissmann names Enzian ("gentian") after a passage in Rainer Maria Rilke's "Ninth Elegy."

21. Antony C. Sutton, *Wall Street and the Rise of Hitler* (Sudbury, UK: Bloomfield, 1976), 33–48; Richard Sasuly, *IG Farben* (New York: Boni and Gaer, 1947), 141–160.

22. Edwin Black, *IBM and the Holocaust* (New York: Crown, 2001), 75–104, 165–166.

23. Michel Foucault, *The History of Sexuality*, vol. 1: *An Introduction*, trans. Robert Hurley (New York: Vintage, 1978), 140–144; James R. Beniger, *The Control Revolution: Technological and Economic Origins of the Information Society* (Cambridge, MA: Harvard University Press, 1986), 390–425.

24. Philip F. Gura, *A Glimpse of Sion's Glory: Puritan Radicalism in New England, 1620–1660* (Middletown, CT: Wesleyan University Press, 1984), 304–322; Michael P. Winship, "William Pynchon's *The Jewes Synagogue*," *New England Quarterly* 71 (June 1998): 290–297.

25. Although *Gravity's Rainbow* makes no mention, the historical prototype for Broderick Slothrop's Berkshire paper manufactory would almost certainly be the Berkshire-based firm of Crane and Co., which since the early nineteenth

century has printed U.S. currency and today has similar contracts abroad with Sweden and Saudi Arabia, among others, as well as a German subsidiary.

26. David Irving, *The Mare's Nest* (Boston: Little, Brown, 1965), 279, 259.

27. Walter Dornberger, *V-2*, trans. James Cleugh and Geoffrey Halliday (New York: Viking, 1954), 260–261; Irving, *Mare's Nest*, 313.

28. *GR* 298–300. For a map of the tunnel system as it was, see Weisenburger, *"Gravity's Rainbow" Companion*, 4th map after p. 173.

29. Tölölyan, "War as Background," 51–52.

30. James McGovern, *Crossbow and Overcast* (London: Hutchison, 1965), 40.

31. Michael J. Neufeld, *Von Braun: Dreamer of Space, Engineer of War* (New York: Knopf, 2007), 4, 312.

32. Ibid., 477.

33. "Nature does not know extinction; all it knows is transformation. Everything science has taught me, and continues to teach me, strengthens my belief in the continuity of our spiritual existence after death" (*GR* 1)—from a short credo published in a 1962 anthology of "Words to Live By" (Weisenberger, *"Gravity's Rainbow" Companion*, 15–16, provides the full text). As always in Pynchon, this is multiply suggestive, e.g., as the self-satisfaction of a wily survivor; as the pious post-Puritan affirmation of one convinced he's a member of the spiritual elect; as (unwitting?) corroboration that nature cannot be subjugated however much scientists may "transform" it through biochemical alchemy or nuclear fission or the like; as prognostication of the polyform spiritual resonances—Kabbalistic, Gnostic, Herero, Norse, New Age—that percolate through the text.

34. *GR* 426; Neufeld, *Von Braun*, 181–182.

35. Neufeld, *Von Braun*, 181.

36. Quoted in ibid., 43.

37. The Hollywood film of von Braun's life was fittingly titled *I Aim at the Stars*. Not long after the 1951 statement quoted above, von Braun went so far as to compose a laboriously detailed sci-fi novel, *Das Marsprojekt*, translated into English (1953) as *The Mars Project: A Technical Tale*.

38. Thomas H. Schaub, *Pynchon: The Voice of Ambiguity* (Urbana: University of Illinois Press, 1981), 88.

39. Timothy Melley, *Empire of Conspiracy: The Culture of Paranoia in Postwar America* (Ithaca, NY: Cornell University Press, 2000), 106, 83–85.

40. Charles Reich, *The Greening of America* (New York: Random House, 1970), 107.

41. Published ten months before Pearl Harbor and U.S. entry into World War II, Luce's essay was actually a defensive attack on what he took to be the retrograde isolationism of both political parties. He blamed the "virus of isolationist sterility" (Henry Luce, "The American Century," *Life*, 17 February 1941, 63) for perversely constraining the nation from assuming its proper place of world dominance notwithstanding the German and Japa-

nese menace. Luce's indignation was intensified by his conviction that the U.S. had bungled its opportunity "to lead the world" after World War I. Now, he warned, "Roosevelt must succeed where Wilson failed" (64). This missionary child's vision of the promise of an American century was philanthropic as well as militaristic, stressing the importance of propagating not only democratic values but also foreign aid ("for every dollar we spend on armaments, we should spend at least a dime in a gigantic effort to feed the world"). But Pynchon, had he read the essay, wouldn't have failed to spot the realpolitik behind the 10:1 ratio and the essay's muscle-flexing rhetoric as well as in Luce's view of the degree to which American commodity culture already penetrated worldwide: "American jazz, Hollywood movies, American slang, American machines and patented products, are in fact the only thing that every community in the world, from Zanzibar to Hamburg, recognizes in common" (65). *GR's* emphasis throughout on Germany as the standard setter for modern techno-scientific, economic, intellectual, and cultural accomplishment undercuts the provincialism of this mentality without refuting Luce's bottom-line assessment (Cowart, *Thomas Pynchon,* 57–81).

42. Given Slothrop's casual racism (his drug-induced dream of assault by Roxbury blacks being an eye-popping early example), it's striking that he makes friends with Enzian and later tries to shield the Schwarzkommando against a raid by Marvy's gang and the Russians, whereas Tchitcherine's hatred for his half-brother is intensified by Enzian's blackness.

43. Wendell Berry, *Collected Poems: 1957–1982* (San Francisco: North Point, 1985), 97.

44. Melley, *Empire of Conspiracy,* 106.

45. Cowart, *Thomas Pynchon,* 165.

46. Ibid., 204–206.

47. Timothy L. Parrish, "Pynchon and DeLillo," in *UnderWorlds: Perspectives on Don DeLillo's Underworld,* ed. Joseph Dewey, Steven G. Kellman, and Irving Malin (Newark: University of Delaware Press, 2002), 80.

48. Don DeLillo, *Underworld* (New York: Scribner, 1997), 810.

49. Ibid., 412, 791.

50. As Phillip E. Wegner points out, the macabre museum that showcases malforming downwind radiation effects eerily echoes another character's earlier reaction to a scene from the rediscovered Sergei Eisenstein film (DeLillo's invention), *Unterwelt* (Underworld), which seemed to anticipate nuclear-era wastage of human bodies (*Life between Two Deaths, 1989–2001: U.S. Culture in the Long Nineties* [Durham, NC: Duke University Press, 2009], 55–56). This echo effect itself is another instance of Pynchonian afterglow—a variation on *GR's* deployment of films that anticipate or produce "real life."

51. Wallace, *Infinite Jest,* 459.

52. Ibid., 223, 417.

53. Vollmann told one interviewer, for example, that he wanted "readers to feel confident that if they picked up, say, *Fathers and Crows,* they could be pretty sure that every detail about the Micmac Indians" was as correct as possible (Michael Hemmingson, "Native American Myths and Legends in William T. Vollmann's *Seven Dreams,*" in *The Intersection of Fantasy and Native America: From H. P. Lovecraft to Leslie Marmon Silko,* ed. David R. Oberhelman and Amy H. Sturgis [Altadena, CA: Mythopoeic, 2009], 80).

54. Carlton Smith, "Arctic Revelations: Vollmann's *Rifles* and the Frozen Landscape of the Self," *Review of Contemporary Fiction* 13 (Summer 1993): 55. "Self-indulgent" does not mean self-aggrandizing, however. "If he is the god of his own texts," his fellow novelist Madison Smartt Bell rightly declares, "he offers himself up for crucifixion every time" (Madison Smartt Bell, "Where an Author Might Be Standing," *Review of Contemporary Fiction* 13 [Summer 1993]: 44).

55. William Vollmann, *Argall* (New York: Penguin, 2002), 615.

56. Interview in 2001 with Larry McCaffery, "Pattern Recognitions," repr. in Michael Hemmingson, *William T. Vollmann: A Critical Study and Seven Interviews* (Jefferson, NC: McFarland, 2009), 137.

57. "Most Anticipated: The Great 2013 Book Review," The Millions, www.themillions.com/2013/01/most-anticipated-the-great-2013-book-preview.html.

58. Larry McCaffery, "An Interview with William T. Vollmann," *Review of Contemporary Fiction* 13 (Summer 1993): 13.

Epilogue

1. Pankaj Mishra, *From the Ruins of Empire: The Intellectuals Who Remade Asia* (New York: Farrar, Straus and Giroux, 2012), 8.

2. For more on "residual" formations, see Raymond Williams, *Marxism and Literature* (New York: Oxford University Press, 1978), 121–127.

3. Don DeLillo, *Falling Man: A Novel* (New York: Simon and Schuster, 2007), 10.

4. Kevin J. Hayes, "The Great American Novel," in *A Journey through American Literature* (New York: Oxford University Press, 2012), 157. The "retro-realist" rubric is from Joseph Tabbi, *Cognitive Fictions* (Minneapolis: University of Minnesota Press, 2001), 79.

5. Wai Chee Dimock, "Scales of Aggregation: Prenational, Subnational, Transnational," *American Literary History* 18 (Summer 2006): 219–228.

6. Eric Foner, *The Story of American Freedom* (New York: Knopf, 1998), provides to my mind a particularly eloquent and well-informed concise account of U.S. history as driven by the ongoing pursuit to realize that ideal, controversial at every stage, insofar as it can be.

7. Kathleen Fitzpatrick, *The Anxiety of Obsolescence: The American Novel in the Age of Television* (Nashville, TN: Vanderbilt University Press, 2006), 13–14.

Although Fitzpatrick argues for this anxiety as a self-protective neurosis specific to "serious" male novelists today (Pynchon, DeLillo, Wallace, Franzen, et al.), I'm inclined to see it as a more pervasive malaise.

8. Fredric Jameson, *Archaeologies of the Future: The Desire Called Utopia and Other Science Fiction* (London: Verso, 2005), 288.

9. Thus Junot Díaz, when interviewed about his in-progress *Monstro,* excerpted in the *New Yorker* issue noted below: "I just loved the idea of these over-privileged doofuses pursuing what we would call a 'mainstream' or 'literary fiction' narrative, while in the background, just out of their range—though they could see it if they wished to see it—there's a much more extreme, terrifying narrative unfolding" in the Dominican Republic and Haiti ("Junot Díaz Aims to Fulfill His Dream of Publishing Sci-Fi Novel with *Monstro*," *Wired* [3 October 2010], www.wired.com/underwire /2012/10/geeks-guide-junot-diaz/).

10. Jameson, *Archaeologies of the Future,* 345.

Acknowledgments

This book could not have been written without a great deal of support over a long period of time from scores of individuals and from a number of organizations.

To the American Antiquarian Society, I owe the invitation that led to the first version of this project, delivered as an annual James Russell Wiggins Lecture and published in the *Proceedings of the Antiquarian Society* (1994) as well as in pamphlet form; and I thank the society for permission to publish revised portions of that essay in Chapters 1 and 2. Research fellowships from the National Endowment for the Humanities and the Mellon Foundation were indispensable in enabling me to complete this book, as were sabbatical and research leaves granted me by Harvard University. The opportunity to inaugurate the annual lecture series of the Oberlin College English Department, my former academic home base, provided a welcome first run at expanding my thinking to book-length proportions as well as a partial subvention of the expenses of publication.

I am also grateful to a number of other institutions for the chance to try out portions of my work in progress and receive valuable feedback from diverse constituencies: the University of Texas–Austin, Georgia State University, Indiana University, Peking University, the Dartmouth Institute, the Kennedy Institute for North American Studies of the Free University of Berlin, the International Association of University Professors of English, and the Nathaniel Hawthorne Society.

Portions of Chapter 3 were previously published in *Hawthorne and the Real: Bicentennial Essays*, ed. Millicent Bell (Columbus: Ohio State University Press, 2005); portions of Chapter 7 in *The Cambridge Companion to Harriet Beecher Stowe*, ed. Cindy Weinstein (Cambridge: Cambridge University Press, 2004); and portions of the Introduction and Chapter 11 in *American Literary History* (Spring/Summer 2008, Oxford University Press). I am grateful to all three publishers for permission to reprint as well as for the opportunity to publish in the first place.

At many points the collections and the librarians of the American Antiquarian Society, the Houghton and Widener libraries of Harvard University, and the Stowe-Day Foundation at Hartford, Connecticut, helped greatly to further my research.

Colleagues at Harvard and elsewhere have been unfailingly generous with critical feedback all the way down the line as the project slowly congealed. Special thanks to Amanda Claybaugh, David D. Hall, Gordon Hutner, Robert Milder, and John Stauffer for their frank and penetrating readings of at least one draft chapter. Michael T. Gilmore and a second (anonymous) reader who evaluated the manuscript for Harvard University Press provided a combination of nuanced enthusiasm for the project and constructively pointed recommendations for its improvement that every author hopes to receive but seldom does. Along the way, I also received valuable help—whether or not they remember giving it—from Daniel Aaron, Michael Anesko, James Baughman, Nina Baym, Lauren Berlant, Homi Bhabha, Carrie Tirado Bramen, Denise Buell, Frederick Buell, Sydney Bufkin, Russ Castronovo, John Cooper, David Brion Davis, Nicholas Delbanco, Wai Chee Dimock, Robert Dixon, Robert Ferguson, Philip Fisher, Christopher Freeburg, Janet Gabler-Hover, Henry Louis Gates Jr., Paul Giles, Maryemma Graham, Jeff Groves, Philip Gura, Yunte Huang, Gene Jarrett, Nicholas Jose, Ju Yon Kim, Emily Kopley, Richard Kopley, John McWilliams, Louis Menand, Leslie Morris, Leonard von Morze, Elisa New, Donald Pease, Leah Price, Eliza Richards, Judith Ryan, James Simpson, Werner Sollors, Doris Sommer, Ken Stewart, Roger Stoddard, Gordon Teskey, Brook Thomas, Marianne Thormahlen, Michael Winship, and James Wood.

Nor could this book have been completed without the active participation, criticism, and support of many present and former students, a number of them now or soon to become distinguished scholars in their own right, who contributed crucial research assistance or other suggestions along the way, including Kimberly August, Adam Bradley, Beth Braiterman, Sally Castillo, Jia-rui Chong Cook, Francesca Delbanco, Brian Distelberg, Margaret Doherty, Nick Donofrio, Erin Drake, Beth Ford, Margaret Gram, Jared Hickman, Michael Hill, Steven Pavlos Holmes, Gretchen Hults, Mark Jerng, Jamie Jones, Tian Kisch, Christopher Le Coney, Camille Owens, William Pannapacker, Jesse Raber, Kathryn Roberts, Daniel Sharfstein, Annie Sloniker, Caroline Vernick, and Kaye Wierzbicki.

Indeed, the remote origins of this book date back to my earliest teaching of U.S. fiction history a half century ago; and it has long since become so impossible for me to separate whatever is original in my own critical thinking from my experiences of working with the students with whom I have been blessed throughout my career, and from the symbiotic enduring intellectual ties formed with many of them, that I dedicate this book to them in gratitude. The only other debt that begins to rival that one is to my wife, Kim, without whose sympathetic but candid responses as she patiently scrutinized my drafts at every stage, it might never have been finished.

Index

Adams, James Truslow, 111, 165–166, 488n6

African American literature and culture: Afro-diasporic/Black Atlantic imagination, 189, 195–196, 236fn, 330–341, 344, 390, 502n54, 519–520n42; belated mainstream recognition of literary achievement, 48, 50, 171; coloring master-class texts black, 73, 193–194, 195, 196, 313–316; early GAN criticism marginalizes, 24, 32; and ethnic turn in up-from narrative, 165–198; Harlem Renaissance, 140, 146, 149, 152, 168, 171, 308, 425–426; historic importance of slave narrative, 109–110, 181, 193–194, 251fn, 330; neo-slave fiction, 194–198, 251fn, 313–339, 501n48; parody traditions in, 186–187, 190, 195–196, 313–316; South/slavery/racism in divide fiction of, 279–285, 311–339; twentieth-century great migration and, 178, 194–195, 420; and twentieth-century protest tradition, 168–169, 191, 331; twenty-first-century "post-blackness," 519n35; and underfulfillment of democratic promise, 164–165, 182, 186, 280–285, 328–329. *See also* Anglo/Euro-Protestant strand in U.S. culture; Divide fiction; Ellison, Ralph; Ethnicity/ethnoracial(ism) in the United States; Faulkner, William; Morrison, Toni; Petry, Ann; Randall, Alice; Stowe, Harriet Beecher; Twain, Mark; Up-from narrative; Wright, Richard

Alcott, Louisa May, 262

Alger, Horatio, 123–124, 127

Alvarez, Julia: *How the Garcia Girls Lost Their Accents*, 209; mentioned, 342

Amazon.com, reviews of American novels, 55, 61, 191, 192, 315, 418, 480n3

American dream: definition and naming, 106, 110–112; differential appeal by social class, 121–123; Franklin/Franklin legend and, 7, 120–129, 141, 143; immigrant experience and, 110–112, 123, 208–214; literary evocations/dismissals of, 141–151, 158–159, 165–166, 203–207, 208–212; material gratification vs. worthier aspiration as goals, 111, 120–129, 136, 143–144, 189–190, 212; odds against fulfilling, 107, 111, 141, 145–146, 208; persistence notwithstanding, 109, 110–111, 208; self-made man stereotype advanced/complicated/questioned, 110–111, 121–132, 141–151, 158–159; WASP-only assumption broadens slowly, 110–112, 122, 159, 165–166. *See also* Bildungsroman; Capitalism; Up-from narrative

American exceptionalism: "America" = equal opportunity myth, 110–112; critical/public suspicion of, 15–17, 208; GAN as instance, 10–19; futurological cast of, 13–14, 154–155, 463; ideology of individual aspiration, 13, 108, 110–112, 167, 213; national innocence assumption,

Field, Eugene, "Lady Button Eyes," 335
Field imaginary. *See* Imaginary, field
Fisher, Philip J., 114, 495n37, 503n13, 506n19, 511n21
Fishkin, Shelley Fisher, 500n44
Fitzgerald, F. Scott: admiration of Conrad, 151–153; admiration of Dreiser, 143; admiration of Lewis, 14; reputation history, 57, 142, 155, 162, 169; mentioned, 48, 180
  The Great Gatsby: plot, 141–150; Conrad's influence on, 151–153; Dreiser's *An American Tragedy* and, 139, 141–150, 494n24; elusiveness of hero-figure, 142; ethnoracialist implications of, 146, 177; "innocence"/regressiveness of hero-figure, 143–144, 145, 148–150, 159, 190, 334; moral judgmentalism in, 149–150; 1920s contexts of, 142, 145–147, 407; observer-hero narrative in, 149–150, 152–155, 365; reception/reputation of, 48, 57, 58, 142, 162, 169, 191; shortest GAN candidate, 29; social stratification in, 145–147; stylistic modernism of, 142, 169; as tragedy, 147–149; mentioned, 44, 60, 183. *See also* Dreiser, Theo-dore; Faulkner, William; Observer-hero narrative; Up-from narrative
  Other works: The Beautiful and Damned, 143; *Crack-Up,* 139; *Tender Is the Night,* 143
Fitzpatrick, Kathleen, 463, 537n7
Flaubert, Gustave, *Sentimental Education,* 107, 141
Fleissner, Jennifer, 138, 149
Fluck, Winfried, 469n17; quoted, 16
Foley, Barbara, 189, 420–421, 498n11, 499n14; on "collective novel," 391fn; quoted, 408
Foner, Eric, 536n6
Foote, Stephanie, 220fn
Forster, E. M., *Passage to India,* 224, 225
Foster, Denis, 481n12; quoted, 84
Foster, Hannah, *The Coquette,* 82
Foucault, Michel: on biopower, 438; on heterotopia, 370. *See also* Heterotopia
Fox, John, Jr., *Little Shepherd of Kingdom Come,* 159
Fraiman, Susan, 133
Franklin, Benjamin: Americanization of bildungsroman as up-from narrative

and, 7, 122–129, 218; as icon of self-made man myth, 7, 120–123, 198, 334
  Works: Autobiography, 7, 120, 149; *Poor Richard's Almanac,* 109, 121
Franzen, Jonathan, 53, 462, 537n7; *Freedom,* 3–4
Frederic, Harold: and *The Scarlet Letter,* 72, 97, 99–100; *Theron Ware,* 29
Frederickson, George, 506n21; quoted, 233
Freeberg, Christopher, 524n21
Freedman, Ralph, quoted, 174
Fukuyama, Francis, 400
Furphy, Joseph, 270, 532n13

Gandhi, Leela, quoted, 107
Garland, Hamlin, 32, 220, 287, 473n23
Garrett, George, 169
Gaskell, Elizabeth, 523n13; *Cranford,* 352; *North and South* and post-Stowe divide romance, 248–249
Gass, William, 426
Gates, Henry Louis, Jr., 194, 246, 313, 470n26
Geertz, Clifford, 425
Gender: divide fiction and, 218fn; in early GAN theory, 31–32; narrative of community and, 520n7; regionalist authors and, 31–32, 473n23; and "sentimental" fiction, 109–110, 129–132; up-from narrative and, 112–139; among writers on the U.S. west, 116–117. *See also* Child, as cultural symbol; Divide fiction; Region/alism; Sex/sexuality/sexual preference in U.S. literature
Ghosh, Amitav, 317, 330, 426, 530n43, 532n13
Gibson, William, 452
Giles, Paul, 470n25; quoted, 83
Gilman, Charlotte Perkins, 149, 465
Gilmore, Michael T., 274, 483n20, 506n23, 507n37, 509n61, 512n37; quoted, 72
Gilroy, Paul, 330, 470n26
Ginsberg, Alan, "America," 397, 528n17
Glazener, Nancy, 265
Glissant, Édouard: on Faulkner, 290, 300; on Faulkner and Morrison, 325; on postcolonial literary emergence, 12
Godden, Richard, 295, 514n15